F-4 PHANTOM II
PILOT'S FLIGHT OPERATING
INSTRUCTIONS

MCDONNELL AIRCRAFT
NOw60–0134–1
N00019–72–A–0001

Each transmittal of this document outside the Department of Defense must have prior approval of the issuing service.

THIS MANUAL IS INCOMPLETE WITHOUT NAVAIR 01-245FDB-1A.

ISSUED BY AUTHORITY OF THE CHIEF OF NAVAL OPERATIONS AND UNDER DIRECTION OF THE COMMANDER, NAVAL AIR SYSTEMS COMMAND

I	AIRCRAFT
II	INDOCTRINATION
III	NORMAL PROCEDURES
IV	FLIGHT PROCEDURES
V	EMERGENCY PROCEDURES
VI	ALL-WEATHER OPERATION
VII	COMMUNICATIONS PROCEDURES
VIII	WEAPONS SYSTEMS
IX	FLIGHT CREW COORDINATION
X	NATOPS EVALUATION
XI	PERFORMANCE DATA
APPENDIX A	FOLDOUT ILLUSTRATIONS
	ALPHABETICAL INDEX

15 DECEMBER 1971
CHANGE 2 – 15 AUGUST 1972

F-4 PHANTOM
PILOT'S FLIGHT OPERATING MANUAL

©2007-2010 PERISCOPE FILM LLC

WWW.PERISCOPEFILM.COM
ISBN: 978-1-935700-41-8

Reproduction for nonmilitary use of the information or illustrations contained in this publication is not permitted. The policy for military use reproduction is established for the Army in AR 380-5, for the Navy and Marine Corps in OPNAVINST 5510.1B, and for the Air Force in Air Force Regulation 205-1.

LIST OF EFFECTIVE PAGES

Insert latest changed pages; dispose of superseded pages in accordance with applicable regulations.

NOTE: On a changed page, the portion of the text affected by the latest change is indicated by a vertical line, or other change symbol, in the outer margin of the page.

Dates of issue for original and changed pages:

Original .. 0 .. 15 Dec 71
Change .. 1 .. 1 Mar 72
Change .. 2 .. 15 Aug 72

Total number of pages in this manual is .592. consisting of the following:

Page No.	# Change No.
Title	2
A	2
Flyleaf 1	1
Flyleaf 2	0
i - viii	0
1-1 - 1-6	0
1-7	1
1-8	2
1-9 - 1-53	0
1-54 - 1-54A	1
1-54B Blank	1
1-55	0
1-56	2
1-57	0
1-58 Blank	0
1-59 - 1-60	0
1-61	1
1-62 - 1-64	0
1-64A	1
1-64B Blank	1
1-65	1
1-66 - 1-77	0
1-78	1
1-79	0
1-80 - 1-80A	2
1-80B Blank	2
1-81 - 1-84	0
1-85 - 1-86A	1
1-86B Blank	1
1-87 - 1-98	0
1-99	1
1-100 - 1-105	0
1-106	1
1-107 - 1-112	0
1-112A	1
1-112B Blank	1
1-113	1
1-114 - 1-129	0
1-130 - 1-130A	1
1-130B Blank	1

Page No.	# Change No.
1-131 - 1-146	0
2-1 - 2-4	0
3-1 - 3-8	0
3-9 - 3-10A	1
3-10B Blank	1
3-11	0
3-12 - 3-13	1
3-14	2
3-15 - 3-36	0
3-37	2
3-38 - 3-49	0
3-50 Blank	0
4-1 - 4-28	0
4-29	2
4-30 - 4-38	0
5-1 - 5-7	0
5-8	2
5-9	0
5-10 - 5-11	2
5-12 - 5-27	0
5-28	1
5-29 - 5-38	0
5-39 - 5-43	1
5-44 - 5-57	0
5-58 Blank	0
6-1 - 6-6	0
7-1 - 7-8	0
8-1 - 8-2	2
8-3 - 8-7	0
8-8 Blank	0
9-1 - 9-4	0
10-1 - 10-20	0
11-1 - 11-196	0
A-1	0
A-2 Blank	0
A-3	2
A-4 Blank	0
A-5	2
A-6 Blank	0
A-7	0

Page No.	# Change No.
A-8 Blank	0
A-9	2
A-10 Blank	0
A-11	1
A-12 Blank	0
A-13	1
A-14 Blank	0
A-15	0
A-16 Blank	0
A-17	1
A-18 Blank	0
A-19	1
A-20 Blank	0
Index 1	1
Index 2	0
Index 3	1
Index 4 - Index 7	0
Index 8 Blank	0

Zero in this column indicates an original page.

DEPARTMENT OF THE NAVY
OFFICE OF THE CHIEF OF NAVAL OPERATIONS
WASHINGTON, D.C. -20350

1 July 1968

LETTER OF PROMULGATION

1. The Naval Air Training and Operating Procedures Standardization Program (NATOPS) is a positive approach towards improving combat readiness and achieving a substantial reduction in the aircraft accident rate. Standardization, based on professional knowledge and experience, provides the basis for development of an efficient and sound operational procedure. The standardization program is not planned to stifle individual initiative but rather, to aid the Commanding Officer in increasing his unit's combat potential without reducing his command prestige or responsibility.

2. This manual standardizes ground and flight procedures but does not include tactical doctrine. Compliance with the stipulated manual procedure is mandatory except as authorized herein. In order to remain effective, NATOPS must be dynamic and stimulate rather than suppress individual thinking. Since aviation is a continuing progressive profession, it is both desirable and necessary that new ideas and new techniques be expeditiously evaluated and incorporated if proven to be sound. To this end Type/Fleet/Air Group/Air Wing/Squadron Commanders and subordinates are obligated and authorized to modify procedures contained herein, in accordance with the waiver provisions established by OPNAVINST 3510.9 series, for the purpose of assessing new ideas prior to initiating recommendations for permanent changes. This manual is prepared and kept current by the users in order to achieve maximum readiness and safety in the most efficient and economical manner. Should conflict exist between the training and operating procedures found in this manual and those found in other publications, this manual will govern.

3. Checklists and other pertinent extracts from this publication necessary to normal operations and training should be made and may be carried in Naval Aircraft for use therein. It is forbidden to make copies of this entire publication or major portions thereof without specific authority of the Chief of Naval Operations.

THOMAS F. CONNOLLY
Vice Admiral, USN
Deputy Chief of Naval Operations (Air)

INTERIM CHANGE SUMMARY (continued)

Interim Changes Outstanding - To be maintained by the custodian of this manual:

INTERIM CHANGE NUMBER	ORIGINATOR/DATE (or DATE/TIME GROUP)	PAGES AFFECTED	REMARKS/PURPOSE

TABLE OF CONTENTS

FDB-1-(277)

FOREWORD

SCOPE

The NATOPS Flight Manual is issued by the authority of the Chief of Naval Operations and under the direction of Commander, Naval Air Systems Command in conjunction with the Naval Air Training and Operating Procedures Standardization (NATOPS) Program. This manual contains information on all aircraft systems, performance data, and operating procedures required for safe and effective operations. However, it is not a substitute for sound judgement. Compound emergencies, available facilities, adverse weather, or terrain may require modification of the procedures contained herein. Read this manual from cover to cover. It's your responsibility to have a complete knowledge of its contents.

APPLICABLE PUBLICATIONS

The following applicable publications complement this manual:

NAVAIR 01-245FDB-1A (supplement)
NAVAIR 01-245FDB-1B (checklist)
NAVAIR 01-245FDB-1C
NAVAIR 01-245FDB-1T (tactical manual)
NAVAIR 01-245FDB-1T(A) (tactical manual supplement)
NAVAIR 01-245FDB-1T(B) (tactical manual pocket guide)

HOW TO GET COPIES

AUTOMATIC DISTRIBUTION

To receive future changes and revisions to this manual automatically, a unit must be established on the automatic distribution list maintained by the Naval Air Technical Services Facility (NATSF). To become established on the list or to change distribution requirements, a unit must submit NAVWEPS Form 5605/2 to NATSF, 700 Robbins Ave., Philadelphia, Pa. 19111, listing this manual and all other NAVAIR publications required. For additional instructions refer to BUWEPSINST 5605.4 series and NAVSUP Publication 2002.

ADDITIONAL COPIES

Additional copies of this manual and changes thereto may be procured by submitting Form DD 1348 to NPFC Philadelphia in accordance with NAVSUP Publication 2002, Section VIII, Part C.

UPDATING THE MANUAL

To ensure that the manual contains the latest procedures and information, NATOPS review conferences are held in accordance with OPNAVINST 3510.11 series.

CHANGE RECOMMENDATIONS

Recommended changes to this manual or other NATOPS publications may be submitted by anyone in accordance with OPNAVINST 3510.9 series.

Routine change recommendations are submitted directly to the Model Manager on OPNAV Form 3500-22 shown on the next page. The address of the Model Manager of this aircraft is:

Commanding Officer
Fighter Squadron 121
U.S. Naval Air Station
Miramar, California 92145
Attn: F-4B Model Manager

Change recommendations of an URGENT nature (safety of flight, etc.,) should be submitted directly to the NATOPS Advisory Group Member in the chain of command by priority message.

YOUR RESPONSIBILITY

NATOPS Flight Manuals are kept current through an active manual change program. Any corrections, additions, or constructive suggestions for improvement of its content should be submitted by routine or urgent change recommendation, as appropriate, at once.

NATOPS FLIGHT MANUAL INTERIM CHANGES

Flight Manual Interim Changes are changes or corrections to the NATOPS Flight Manuals promulgated by CNO or NAVAIRSYSCOM. Interim Changes are issued either as printed pages, or as a naval message. The Interim Change Summary page is provided as a record of all interim changes. Upon receipt of a change or revision, the custodian of the manual should check the updated Interim Change Summary to ascertain that all outstanding interim changes have been either incorporated or canceled; those not incorporated shall be recorded as outstanding in the section provided.

NATOPS/TACTICAL CHANGE RECOMMENDATION
OPNAV FORM 3500/22 (5-69) 0107-722-2002

DATE

TO BE FILLED IN BY ORIGINATOR AND FORWARDED TO MODEL MANAGER

FROM (originator) | Unit

TO (Model Manager) | Unit

Complete Name of Manual/Checklist	Revision Date	Change Date	Section/Chapter	Page	Paragraph

Recommendation (be specific)

☐ CHECK IF CONTINUED ON BACK

Justification

Signature	Rank	Title

Address of Unit or Command

TO BE FILLED IN BY MODEL MANAGER *(Return to Originator)*

FROM | DATE

TO

REFERENCE
(a) Your Change Recommendation Dated _____

☐ Your change recommendation dated _____ is acknowledged. It will be held for action of the review conference planned for _____ to be held at _____

☐ Your change recommendation is reclassified URGENT and forwarded for approval to _____ by my DTG _____

/S/ _____ MODEL MANAGER. _____ AIRCRAFT

CHANGE SYMBOLS

Revised text is indicated by a black vertical line in either margin of the page, adjacent to the affected text, like the one printed next to this paragraph. The change symbol identifies the addition of either new information, a changed procedure, the correction of an error, or a rephrasing of the previous material.

WARNINGS, CAUTIONS, AND NOTES

The following definitions apply to "WARNINGS", "CAUTIONS", and "NOTES" found through the manual.

WARNING

An operating procedure, practice, or condition, etc., which may result in injury or death, if not carefully observed or followed.

CAUTION

An operating procedure, practice, or condition, etc., which, if not strictly observed, may damage equipment.

Note

An operating procedure, practice, or condition, etc., which is essential to emphasize.

WORDING

The concept of word usage and intended meaning which has been adhered to in preparing this Manual is as follows:

"Shall" has been used only when application of a procedure is mandatory.

"Should" has been used only when application of a procedure is recommended.

"May" and "need not" have been used only when application of a procedure is optional.

"Will" has been used only to indicate futurity, never to indicate any degree of requirement for application of a procedure.

NATOPS FLIGHT MANUAL GLOSSARY

AAA	Airborne, invisible light, heat radiation, auxiliary assembly
ac	Alternating current
ACM	Air Combat Maneuvering
ACP	Aircraft Communications Procedures
ADC	Air Data Computer
ADCS	Air Data Computer Set
ADI	Attitude Director Indicator
ADIZ	Air Defense Identification Zone
AFC	Automatic Frequency Control
AFCS	Automatic Flight Control System
agc	Automatic gain control
AI	Airborne Intercept
AJB	Airborne, -mechanical, bombing
AMCS	Airborne Missile Control System
AOA	Angle of Attack
AOJ	Acquisition On Jam
APA	Airborne, radar, auxiliary assembly
APN	Airborne, radar, navigational aid
APQ	Airborne, radar, special purpose
ARI	Aileron Rudder Interconnect
ARTC	Air Route Traffic Control
ARC	Airborne, radio, control
ASA	Airborne, special type, auxiliary assembly
ASE	Allowable Steering Error
ASN	Airborne, special type, navigational aid
ASQ	Airborne, special type, combination of purposes
ATC	Air Traffic Control
AWW	Airborne, armament, control
AR	Air Refueling
BACSEB	BuWeps Aviation Clothing and Survival Equipment Bulletin
BDHI	Bearing Distance Heading Indicator
BINGO	Return to this channel (radio). Return fuel state
BIT	Built-In-Test
BLC	Boundary Layer Control
Bolter	Hook down, unintentional touch and go (missed wire)
BST	Boresight
Buster	Full military power
CAT	Catapult
CAT	Clear Air Turbulence
CATCC	Carrier Air Traffic Control Center
CAP	Combat Air Patrol
CARQUAL	Carrier Qualifications
CAS	Calibrated Air Speed
CCA	Carrier Control Approach
CG	Center of Gravity
Charlie Time	Expected time over ramp
CIC	Combat Information Center
CIT	Compressor Inlet Temperature
CNI	Communication Navigation Identification
COT	Cockpit Orientation Trainer
cps	Cycles per second
CVA	Aircraft Carrier (Attack)
CV	Aircraft Carrier
cw	Continuous Wave
dc	Direct current
DCU	Douglas Control Unit
Dead Beat	Causing the object, when disturbed to return to its original position without oscillation.

DME	Distance Measuring Equipment
DOG RADIAL	An assigned radial on which to set up a holding pattern
DR	Dead Reckoning
EAC	Estimated Arrival Carrier
EAS	Equivalent Airspeed
EAT	Estimated Approach Time
ECCM	Electronic Counter-Countermeasure(s)
ECM	Electronic Countermeasure(s)
EGT	Exhaust Gas Temperature
FAM	Familiarization
FL	Flight Level
FMLP	Field Mirror Landing Practice
Foxtrot Corpen	Fleet Course
FOJ	Fuse on Jam
G's	Gravity
Gate	Maximum Power
GCA	Ground Control Approach
GCI	Ground Control Intercept
gpm	Gallon per minute
Hangfire	A delay or failure of an article of ordinance after being triggered
Hang Start	A start that results in a stagnated rpm and temperature
Hertz (Hz)	Same as cycles per second.
HOJ	Home On Jam
Hot Start	A start that exceeds normal starting temperatures
HSI	Horizontal Situation Indicator
IP	Identification Point
IAS	Indicated Airspeed
IFF	Identification Friend or Foe
IFR	Instrument Flight Rules or In Flight Refueling
ILS	Instrument Landing System
IR	Infrared
I/P	Identification of Position
JANAP	Joint Army Navy Airforce Publication
JP	Jet Propulsion
Judy	Radar contact with target, taking over intercept
KTS	Knots
LABS	Low Altitude Bombing System
LE	Leading Edge
LID	Limited Instrument Departure
LOX	Liquid Oxygen
lpm	Liters per minute
LSO	Landing Signal Officer (Paddles)
MAC	Mean Aerodynamic Chord
Meatball	Glide slope image of mirror landing system
MIL	Military
MIM	Maintenance Instruction Manual
Misfire	A permanent failure of an article of ordinance being triggered.
MLP	Mirror Landing Practice
MSL	Mean Sea Level
NAMT	Naval Air Maintenance Training
NATOPS	Naval Air Training and Operating Procedures Standardization
NMPP	Nautical Miles Per Pound
NTDS	Naval Tactical Data System
NWIP	Naval Warfare Intercept Procedures
NWP	Naval Warfare Publications

OAT	Outside Air Temperature
OMNI	Omni Directional Range
Paddles	Landing signal officer
PC	Power Control
Pigeons	Bearing and distance
Platform	20 miles, 5000 ft. commence descent at 2,000 ft/min. level off at 1,000 ft.
PMBR	Practice Multiple Bomb Rack
PPS	Pulses per seconds
prf	Pulse repetition frequency
psi	Pounds per square inch
Punch	Target detected, aircraft still under ground control
Q	Dynamic Pressure, psf
radar	Radio Detection and Ranging
RCR	Runway Condition Reading
RCVG	Replacement Carrier Air Group
rf	Radio Frequency
RF	Reconnaissance - Fighter
RIO	Radar Intercept Officer
SAR	Sea Air Rescue
SID	Standard Instrument Departure
SIF	Selective Identification Feature
tacan	Tactical Air Navigation
TAS	True Airspeed
TE	Trailing Edge
TMN	True Mach Number
Trap	Arrested Landing
UHF	Ultra High Frequency
VFR	Visual Flight Rules
VHF	Very High Frequency
Vn	Velocity Acceleration Relationship
VORTAC	Very high frequency - omni range and tactical air navigation
WST	Weapons System Trainer
WSTH	Weapon System Tactical Handbook
10 MILE GATE	10 mi; transition to landing configuration; maintain 1,000 ft.
6 MILE GATE	6 mi; descent to 600 ft.

F-4B
PHANTOM II

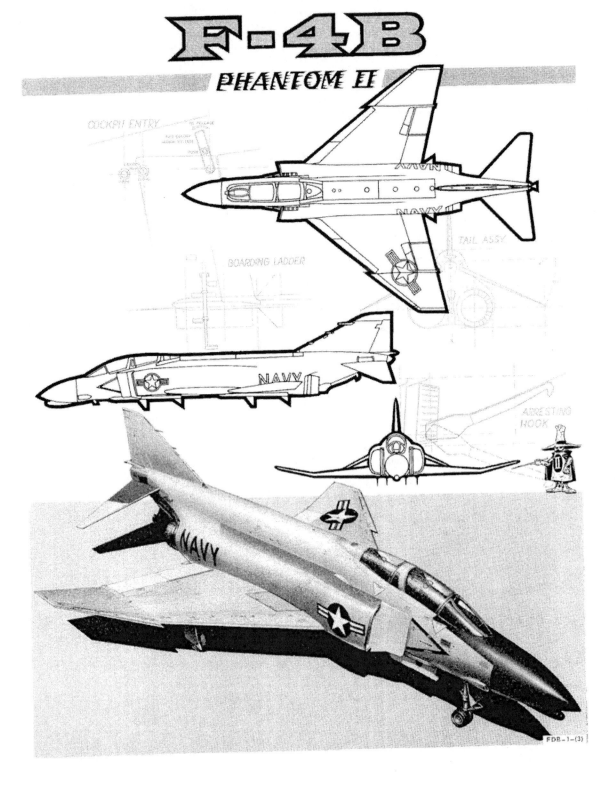

FDB-1-(4)

TABLE OF CONTENTS

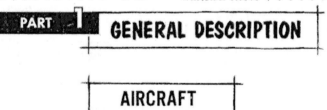

PART 1 GENERAL DESCRIPTION

AIRCRAFT

---- NOTICE ----
Some illustrations referred to within this system writeup may be located in appendix A.
These illustrations are referred to, within the text, as (figure A-, appendix A).

GENERAL ARRANGEMENT

TYPICAL

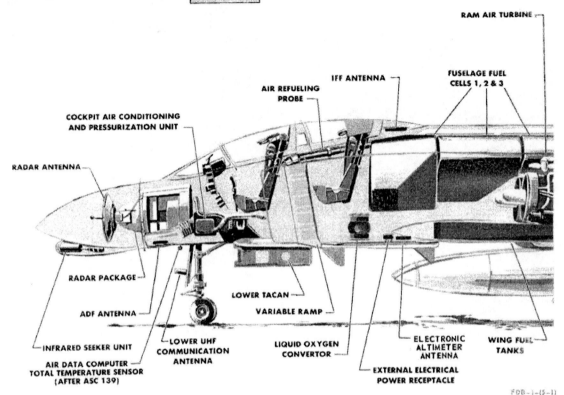

RAM AIR TURBINE

IFF ANTENNA

FUSELAGE FUEL
CELLS 1, 2 & 3

AIR REFUELING
PROBE

COCKPIT AIR CONDITIONING
AND PRESSURIZATION UNIT

RADAR ANTENNA

RADAR PACKAGE

ADF ANTENNA

LOWER TACAN

VARIABLE RAMP

INFRARED SEEKER UNIT

LOWER UHF
COMMUNICATION
ANTENNA

LIQUID OXYGEN
CONVERTOR

ELECTRONIC
ALTIMETER
ANTENNA

WING FUEL
TANKS

AIR DATA COMPUTER
TOTAL TEMPERATURE SENSOR
(AFTER ASC 139)

EXTERNAL ELECTRICAL
POWER RECEPTACLE

FDB-1-(5-1)

Figure 1-1 (Sheet 1of 2

DESCRIPTION

The F-4B aircraft (figure 1-1) is a supersonic, two place, twin engine, jet-propelled all-weather fighter built by McDonnell-Douglas. The aircraft is designed for intermediate and long range high altitude interceptions using missiles as the principal armament, and for intermediate or long range attack missions to deliver special or conventional weapons. A retractable air refueling probe and added electronic equipment such as an infrared detection unit, air data computer, and ground position indicator increases the overall effectiveness of the aircraft as a weapons system. The airplane is powered by two axial flow General Electric J79-GE-8 engines. This power plant is a high pressure ratio, single rotor, turbojet engine with a 17 stage, variable stator compressor and an afterburner with a variable area exhaust nozzle. The aircraft features a low mounted swept-back wing with trailing edge flaps, ailerons, spoilers and speed

brakes. All the control surfaces are positioned by irreversible hydraulic power cylinders to provide desired control effectiveness throughout the entire speed range. A self-charging pneumatic system provides normal and emergency canopy operation, as well as emergency operation for the landing gear, wing flaps and inflight refueling probe. The pressurized cockpit is enclosed by two clamshell canopies. A drag chute, in the aft end of the fuselage, reduces landing roll distances.

AIRCRAFT DIMENSIONS

The approximate dimensions of the aircraft are as follows:

Wing Span (Wings Spread)	38 feet 5 inches
(Wings Folded)	27 feet 7 inches
Length	58 feet 3 inches
Height (To Top of Fin)	16 feet 4 inches

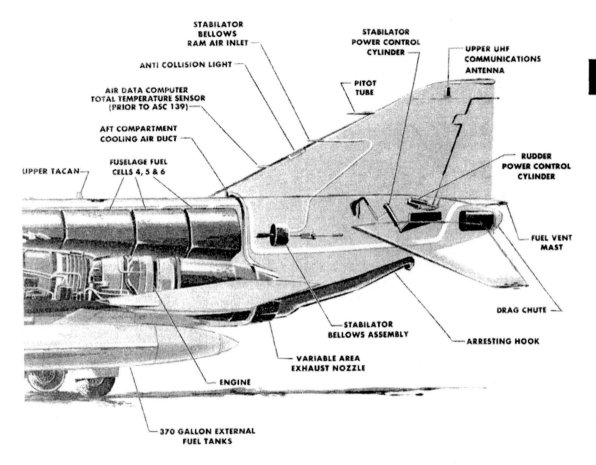

Figure 1-1 (Sheet 2 of 2)

FDB-1-(5-2)

MAIN DIFFERENCES

For technical directive incorporation, and main difference between F-4B aircraft, refer to Main Difference Table, figure 1-2.

BLOCK NUMBERS

Refer to Block Numbers illustration, figure 1-3 for F-4B block production with corresponding assigned aircraft serial numbers.

ARMOR PLATING

On aircraft after AFC 472, provisions for attaching armor plating to doors 15, 16, 22, 23, 28 right and 28 left are provided. This armor, when installed, provides protection for the oxygen bay and hydraulic/engine fuel feed compartment. The armor adds approximately 109 pounds to the weight of the aircraft and shifts the CG forward by approximately 0.1% MAC.

ARMAMENT

The aircraft is equipped to carry and deliver an assortment of conventional and special stores. Radar missiles can be carried on four semi-flush fuselage stations, and two wing stations. Infrared missiles can be carried on two wing stations (two per station). Low drag bombs can be carried in clusters on four wing stations and a centerline fuselage station. Provisions are included for the delivery of a special store from the centerline fuselage station. A 20mm gun pod can also be mounted on the centerline fuselage station. Refer to Airborne Missile Control System, section VIII, and Bombing Equipment, section VIII, for additional information on armament.

AIRPLANE SECURITY REQUIREMENTS

The occasion may arise when it will be necessary to land at a civilian field that does not have a military installation associated with it, or when the airplane is to be presented in a static display. In order to prevent the compromise of classified information, accidental damage to the aircraft, or injury to observers, the following guide lines are provided.

Static Displays

1. Special stores may not be carried or displayed.
2. Dummy missiles may be carried or displayed.
3. Dummy conventional stores may be carried on the aircraft in any combination.
4. External tanks may be carried.
5. The radome must be secured.
6. The front canopy must be secured.
7. The rear canopy, with blackout curtain in place, must be secured.
8. The pneumatic system must be bled to prevent the canopies from being opened.

9. No smoking rules must be enforced.

RON at Civilian Fields

1. Make necessary security guard arrangements.
2. Secure radome.
3. Secure front canopy.
4. Secure aft canopy with blackout curtain in place.
5. Bleed off pneumatic systems to prevent opening of the canopies.

— NOTICE —
Some illustrations referred to within this system writeup may be located in appendix A. These illustrations are referred to, within the text, as (figure A-, appendix A).

DESCRIPTION

Although the cockpits are separately enclosed, the cockpit pressure-oxygen environment is the same. Each cockpit incorporates an ejection seat that is adjustable in the vertical plane for comfort. The forward cockpit instrument panel contains the flight and engine instruments. Engine controls, autopilot and fuel management panels are on the left console. Communication, navigation, heating and lighting controls are on the right console. Left and right vertical panels forward of the consoles contain the flight control trim position indicators and the telelight panels. The aft cockpit instrument panel contains the necessary instruments for navigation, plus miscellaneous switches and indicator lights. Radar equipment is below the instrument panel. The right side of the cockpit contains the circuit breaker panels and the left side contains the communication, oxygen and suit pressurization controls. Refer to figures A-1 and A-2, appendix A for the instrument panels and consoles.

DUAL CONTROL COMPATIBILITY

A dual control kit is available for installation in the aircraft. These kits enable the aircraft to be converted into a dual controlled aircraft for pilot training purposes. The kit is installed in the aft cockpit and can be easily removed to return the aircraft to its primary configuration. The dual flight control kit provides the pilot in the converted RIO's cockpit with a control stick, rudder pedals, throttle control for each engine, and an instrument panel which contains additional instruments needed by the aft cockpit pilot.

MAIN DIFFERENCE TABLE

In accordance with BUWEPS Instruction 5215.8, Technical Directive concerning modification, inspection, maintenance or operating procedures and limits of all Naval aircraft and related equipment are titled as follows:

Airframe Change (AFC) or Airframe Bulletin (AFB)
Power Plant Change (PPC) or Bulletin (PPB)
Aviation Armament Change (AAC) or Bulletin (AAB)
Avionics Change (AVC) or Bulletin (AVB)
Accessory Change (AYC) or Bulletin (AYB)
Support Equipment Change (SEC) or Bulletin (SEB)
Photographic Change (PHC) or Bulletin (PHB)
Air Crew System Change (ACC) or Bulletin (ACB)

Air Launched Missile Change (AMC) or Bulletin (AMB)
Target Control System Change (TCC) or Bulletin (TCB)
Clothing and Survival Equipment Change (CSEC) or Bulletin (CSEB)
Aircraft Service Change (ASC)
Air Crew Survival Equipment Bulletin (ACSEB)

SYSTEM	DIFFERENCE	AIRCRAFT PRODUCTION INCORPORATION	BLK NO.	RETROFIT INCORPORATION
Structural	Increased acceleration envelope	148387g	7	AFC 86
Air Refueling	Air refueling probe light for night refueling	148411h	8	ASC 42
Ejection Seat	Ground level, 130-knot ejection capability	148403i	9	ACSEB 22-61
Flaps	Flaps in transient will be indicated by a barber pole	149403i	9	NONE
Fuel	External fuel transfers to fuselage cells 1, 3 and 5	149403i	9	AFC 84
Navigation	Navigation computer (AN/ASN-39)	149403i	9	ASC 76
Fuel	Master caution light will not illuminate with ext tank fuel lights	150406L	12	ASC 97
Speedbrakes	Retract position of emerg speedbrake sw. hyd closes speedbrakes	150406L	12	NONE
Speedbrakes	No speedbrake override safety switch	150406L	12	NONE
Structural	Increase airspeed envelope when carrying 600-gal ₵ tank	150406L	12	ASC 17 ASC 78 AFC 160
Weapons	Multiple Weapons system	150406L	12	ASC 78
Angle of Attack	Indexer lights intensity control	150436m	13	ASC 133
Arresting Hook	Control handle warning light illuminates while hook retracts	150436m	13	ASC 92
Oil	Oil pressure transmitter (decreased oil pressure readings)	150436m	13	ASC 115
ARI	ARI engages only when flaps are down	150642n	14	ASC 125
Anti-Ice	Engine anti-ice lights	150652o	15	ASC 69
ARI	ARI actuation with half flaps	150652o	15	AFC 305
Structural	Increases acceleration envelope	150652o	15	ASC 151
ADC	Total temp sensor located on left air conditioning inlet duct	151399p	16	ASC 139
Flight Controls	Stabilator actuator functional check not required	151448r	18	AFC 203 or AFB 37
Flight Controls	Reduced stick free longitudinal oscillations with aft c.g. condition	151448r	18	AFC 190
Stabilator Control	Heaters installed in bellows ram air inlet probe and venturi	151448r	18	ASC 153
Structural	Launching of fwd station fuselage missiles	151448r	18	AFC 158 ASC 138
CNI	Individual upper and lower TACAN antennas	151473s	19	ASC 186
Starting	Start switch uses ess 28 vdc (no remote start cable req'd)	151473s	19	AFC 176
Arresting Hook	Arresting hook cable fairlead; fabrication and installation of	151473s	19	AFC 216
Air Cond & Press	Hi-Low switchover (footheat-defog) at 50% of handle travel	151498t	20	AFC 217
Air Cond & Press	No rain removal on windshield left side panel	151498t	20	AFC 178

Figure 1-2 (Sheet 1 of 4)

SYSTEM	DIFFERENCE	AIRCRAFT PRODUCTION INCORPORATION	BLK NO.	RETROFIT INCORPORATION
Weapons	MK 43 and MK 57 capability	151498t	20	AFC 162
Electrical	Fire/overheat lights and PC2 indicators on essential 28 volt ac bus.	152216u	21	AFC 262
AMCS	Pilots radar scope, secondary restraining device	152249v	22	AFC 193
Structural	Increased maximum weight for arrested landing	152258v	22	AFC 173 or AYC 104 AFC 174 and 206
Emer. Equip.	Eject light	152266v	22	AFC 165
Navigation	AN/AJB-3 ground test switch	152273w	23	AFC 202
Weapon	20 mm gun pod	152278w	23	AFC 241
Canopy	Canopy alignment tape	152292w	23	AFC 267
Air Refueling	Refuel ready light	152303w	23	AFC 213
AFCS	3-axis stab aug, no AFCS mach hold	152331x	24	AFC 203
APCS	Reverse position of APCS engage and air temperature switch	152965g	25	AFC 317
Approach Power Compensator	Approach power compensator	152965y	25	AFC 172
Electrical	60 KVA generator system	152965y	25	NONE
Fuel	Hyd driven trans pumps operate only in A/B or when "Fuel Level Low" light illuminates	152965y	25	AFC 273
Hydraulic	No emerg hyd pump. Emerg gen operates down to approx 90 knots	152965y	25	AFC 220
Flight Control	Drooped ailerons, slotted stabilator, "on speed" 19.0 units, stall warning 21.3 units	152995z	26	AFC 218
Electrical	No auto paralleling feature (split bus operation) Removes radar test switch	152995z	26	AFC 227
Ejection Seat	Lumbar pad	153005z	26	AFC 274
Survival Kit	Universal upper block assembly	153005z	26	ACC 69
Survival Kit	RSSK-1A survival kit (no suit controller or exhaust hose)	153005z	26	NONE
BLC	BLC malfunction light with 1/2 flaps	153030aa	27	AFC 263
Fuel	Automatic fuel transfer. "Fuel Level Low" light in aft cockpit	153030aa	27	AFC 249
Oil	Oil quantity indicator lights	153030aa	27	AFC 252 PPC 62
CNI	No mark X IFF operation, all mode squawk emergency	153912ab	28	NONE
Ejection Seat	Top Latch plunger (locking indicator)			ACC 19
Ejection Seat	Koch parachute riser, shoulder harness release fittings			ACC 41
Ejection Seat	Drogue gun cocking indicator			ACC 56
Ejection Seat	Personnel parachute deploys at 11,500 + 3,000 ft.			ACC 94
Landing Gear	Gear beef-up for increased landing gross weight			AFC 230
Warning Lights	Adds dimming capability for "TK" light			AFC 287
ECM	Provisions for AN/APR-27 receiver			AFC 296
Ejection Seat	H-7 Rocket Ejection Seat			AFC 307
Flight Controls	Stabilator downsprings removed			AFC 308
CNI	KY-28 Speech Security Unit			AFC 331
ECM	Provisions for AN/APR-30 radar homing and warning set, AN/ALQ-51/00 countermeasures set and AN/ALE-29 chaff dispenser			AFC 333
ECM	Provisions for AN/APR-27 or AN/ALQ-91 countermeasures set			AFC 334 or AFC 339
Warning Lights	Improved Fire/Overheat Warning light caps			AFC 335
Radar Beacon	Provisions for AN/APN-154 radar beacon			AFC 363
ECM	Provisions for AN/APR-25 radar homing and warning set			AFC 375
ECM	Forward cockpit audio control for AN/APR-27 receiver			AFC 383
ECM	Impact box destruct switch for countermeasures sets			AFC 386
ECM	Arm-safe switch for AN/ALQ-91 countermeasures set			AFC 390
CNI	Mode 3, Code 77 automatically squawks upon seat ejection			AVC 170
AMCS	IR Lock-out capability			AVC 192

Figure 1-2 (Sheet 2 of 4)

COCKPIT AIR-CONDITIONING AND PRESSURIZING SYSTEM

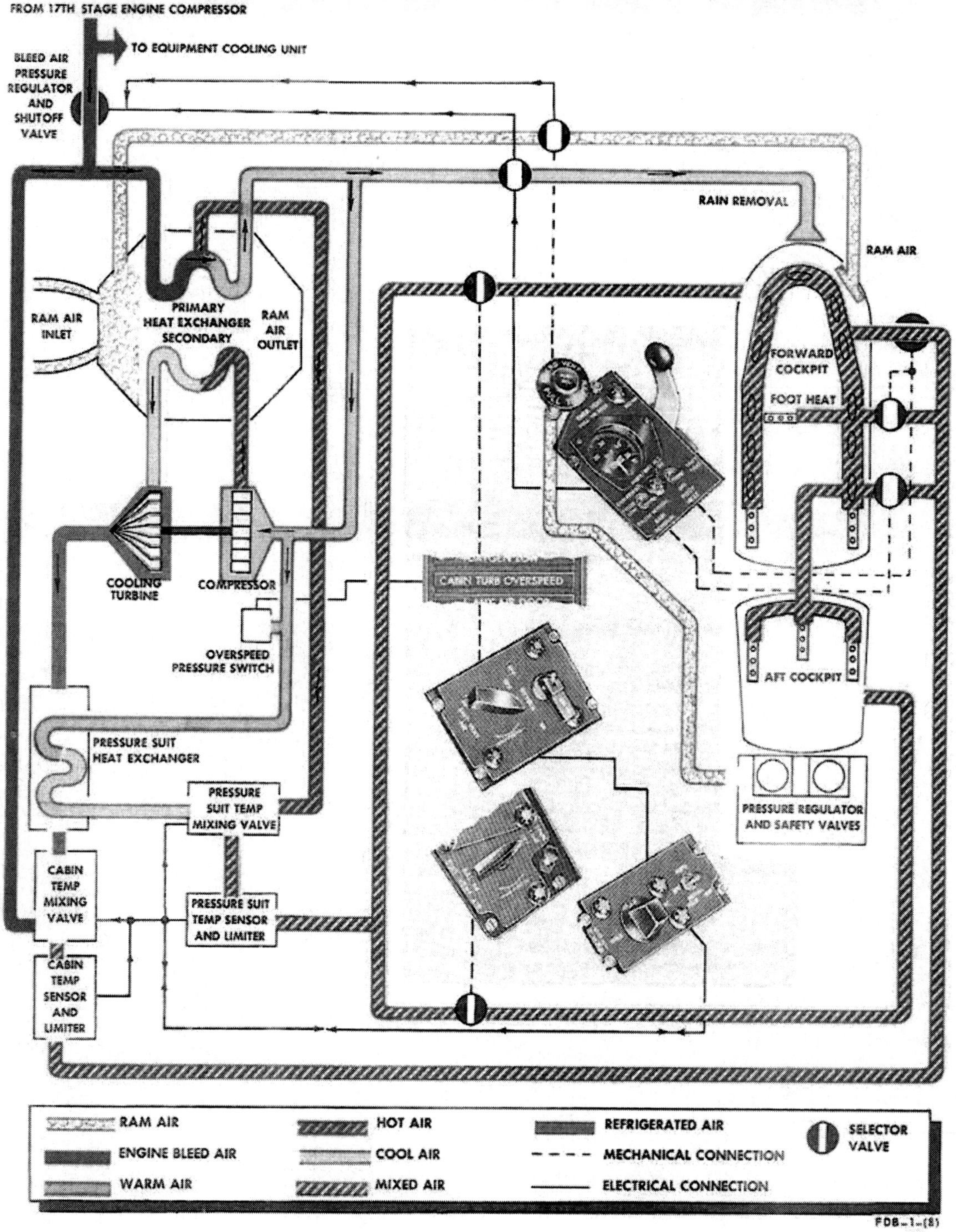

FROM 17TH STAGE ENGINE COMPRESSOR

TO EQUIPMENT COOLING UNIT

BLEED AIR PRESSURE REGULATOR AND SHUTOFF VALVE

RAIN REMOVAL

RAM AIR

RAM AIR INLET

PRIMARY HEAT EXCHANGER SECONDARY

RAM AIR OUTLET

FORWARD COCKPIT

FOOT HEAT

COOLING TURBINE

COMPRESSOR

CABIN TURB OVERSPEED

AFT COCKPIT

OVERSPEED PRESSURE SWITCH

PRESSURE SUIT HEAT EXCHANGER

PRESSURE SUIT TEMP MIXING VALVE

PRESSURE REGULATOR AND SAFETY VALVES

CABIN TEMP MIXING VALVE

PRESSURE SUIT TEMP SENSOR AND LIMITER

CABIN TEMP SENSOR AND LIMITER

RAM AIR	HOT AIR	REFRIGERATED AIR	SELECTOR VALVE
ENGINE BLEED AIR	COOL AIR	MECHANICAL CONNECTION	
WARM AIR	MIXED AIR	ELECTRICAL CONNECTION	

FDB–1–(8)
RB

Figure 1-4

COCKPIT/PRESSURE SUIT TEMPERATURE SCHEDULE

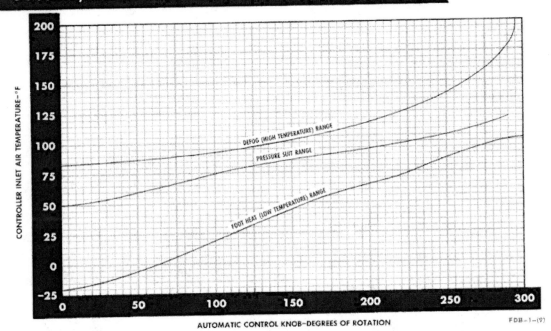

Figure 1-5

Manual Override-Cockpit Temperature Mixing Valve

If the automatic temperature control malfunctions, the manual position of the temp control auto-manual switch can be used to select a full range of temperatures up to 230°F. The HI/LOW switch on the defog-foot heat lever is bypassed. Thus the entire temperature range for both foot heat and defog air is scheduled directly by the mixing valve position, which in turn is moved only when the temperature control switch is held to either HOT or COLD. The switch is spring-loaded to OFF and in the OFF position the mixing valve is held stationary.

Cockpit Ambient Fog

It is possible, through selection of cold temperature settings, particularly on humid days, for the air conditioning system to deliver air at temperatures well below the dew point, with resultant cockpit fogging. This fog can be rapidly dissipated by selecting a slightly warmer temperature. When operating in high humidity conditions, it is recommended that warmer than normal temperatures be selected prior to starting the takeoff run, to prevent cockpit fogging as thrust is increased.

Manual Override-Pressure Suit Temperature Mixing Valve

Manual override operation complicates the picture a bit when the pressure suit is involved, in that only the pressure suit mixing valve is actuated when the override switch is moved to HOT or COLD. The cockpit air mixing valve remains in its last automatic selected position. The relative volumes of defog and foot heat air can be changed by defog-foot heat lever action, but the temperature is fixed when manual override is selected. This characteristic can cause an undesirable situation if the automatic temperature control becomes inoperative during the cruise portion of a flight. Cockpit air temperature normally will not be at a high setting with the pressure suit on, so when manual override is selected, the cockpit air mixing valve remains at a fixed, moderate temperature position. Therefore, when higher temperature defog air is desired for letdown, it is not available since manual override only controls suit vent air. However, when the suit vent air lever is turned off, the suit mixing valve becomes stationary at the cold position and the cockpit mixing valve again is operative. Since suit vent air would not be absolutely necessary during letdown into fog producing altitudes, this method to control cockpit air temperatures is plausible. However, when operating in manual override, the suit vent air must be off, if manual control of cockpit temperatures is desired. Suit vent air can be turned on again after increasing defog air temperature. It also must be remembered that the RIO has no control over pressure suit air temperature. He can control flow, but must accept the pilot selected temperature. So if the pilot turns vent air off, driving the mixing valve to cold, the RIO will be receiving full cold air, unless he elects to turn it off.

| CAUTION |

The manual override should be used only if an automatic temperature control system malfunction occurs. To increase the temperature in this mode, the manual control switch should be held toward the HOT position for no more than 1/2 second at a time between pauses of at least 3 seconds until the desired temperature is reached. Actuating the switch for more extended periods does not allow the temperature limiter adequate time to function, and may result in an overheat condition. Detection of smoke to the cockpit after use of manual control is evidence of improper use of the switch and requires the selection of a colder valve position to avoid overheating of the cockpit distribution ducting.

| WARNING |

The full hot manual position can momentarily produce temperatures in excess of 300°C (572°F) at military power settings.

Emergency Vent Knob

The cockpits may be cleared of undesired smoke or fumes and the cabin/pressure suit air conditioning unit may be shut off by pulling up on the emergency ventilating handle (figure A-1, appendix A). Push button on top of knob and then pull up on the knob. The handle may be placed in an intermediate position to obtain desired amount of emergency ventilation. When pulled up, three actions occur simultaneously:

a. All air conditioning and pressurization air from the cabin/pressure suit air conditioning unit to the cockpits, rain removal system, and pressure suit is shut off.
b. The cabin/pressure regulator and safety (dump) valve is opened and the cockpit becomes completely depressurized.
c. A ram air shutoff valve is opened and the atmospheric air is allowed to enter the cockpit through a port just forward of the pilot's feet.

WINDSHIELD DEFOGGING

Fogging of the windshield is prevented by heating the inside surface with incoming cabin air that is diverted into the defogging manifolds located along the lower surfaces of the side and center panels. The defog lever (figure A-1, appendix A) on the pilot's right console, outboard of the right utility panel, is provided to select windshield defogging. The lever proportions the cabin air flow between the foot heaters and windshield defogging tubes such that in the full aft (FOOT HEAT) position approximately 90% of the total cockpit airflow is delivered to the pilot's and RIO's air distribution manifolds and 10% through the windshield defog manifold. At the full forward (DEFOG) position approximately 20% of the total airflow is delivered through the foot heat manifold and 80% through the windshield defog manifold. Ob-

taining adequate defog air is achieved only after the defog-foot heat lever has been moved to the HI range. The pilot should attempt to anticipate fogging conditions and preheat the windshield.

Note

If the windshield starts to fog over and it is imperative that the pilot maintain visual contact outside the cockpit, the temperature rheostat should be turned full cold and windshield defog air applied. In the HOT position the warm air picks up moisture in the air conditioning system, and when it encounters the relatively cold windshield, condensation (fogging) invariably occurs. Generally, applying hot air to a partially fogged windshield will completely fog it over in a matter of seconds.

WINDSHIELD RAIN REMOVAL

Windshield rain removal is controlled by a rain removal switch (figure A-1, appendix A) on the right utility panel, front cockpit. Placing the switch ON opens a valve causing warm air to flow through nozzles directed up the outer surface of the windshield center and left side panels. On airplanes 151498t and up, and all others after AFC 178, the rain removal nozzle for the left side panel has been removed. On these airplanes, the temperature and pressure of the rain removal air has been increased also. This air breaks up the rain drops into small particles and diverts the majority of them over the windshield. A W SHIELD TEMP HI light over the telelight panel illuminates if the windshield material approaches a temperature which causes optical deterioration. If the light illuminates, the system should be turned off immediately. If the windshield rain removal system cannot be shut down, pull up on the cockpit emergency vent knob. Engine bleed air is shut off before entering the rain removal ducts. Before flight, a rain repellent should be applied to the windshield. If the windshield temperature sensors have not been calibrated properly, the light may illuminate as a result of aerodynamic heating (occurs only near level flight maximum speed with maximum afterburning). In this event, the overheat signal may be disregarded. On airplanes after AFC 328, the rain removal switch is changed to a three position switch with positions RAIN REM-ON, PRESS LOW, and PRESS NORMAL. To activate the rain removal system, place the switch to RAIN REM-ON.

| CAUTION |

- For a static ground check, the system is limited to operation with leading edge flaps in the down position and engines running at or below 88 percent rpm.

- Do not operate the rain removal system in flight with a dry windshield or at airspeeds above Mach 1.0.

- Unless visibility is seriously restricted the rain removal system should not be used in conjunction with afterburner.

COCKPIT PRESSURE SCHEDULE

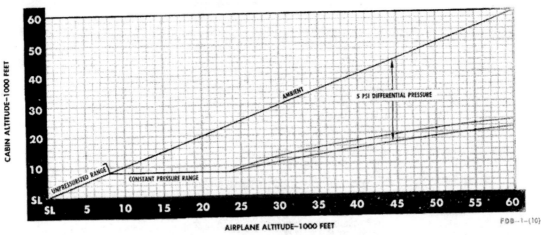

Figure 1-6

COCKPIT PRESSURIZATION

With the canopy closed and the cockpit refrigeration system in operation, the cockpit automatically becomes pressurized at an altitude of 8000 feet and above (figure 1-6). The pressure in the cockpit is maintained by the cockpit pressure regulator (on the cockpit floor aft of the RIO's seat), which controls the outflow of air from the cockpit. Below 8000 feet, the regulator relieves cockpit air at a rate to keep the cockpit unpressurized. Above 8000 feet, the regulator relieves cockpit air as necessary to follow a definite cockpit pressure schedule. Operation of the pressure regulator is completely automatic. The cockpit safety (and dump) valve prevents the cockpit pressure differential from exceeding the limit positive or negative differential pressure in case of malfunctioning of the cockpit pressure regulator, and to provide an emergency means of dumping the cockpit air. The dump feature of the safety valve is pneumatically connected to a dump feature on the cockpit pressure regulator. Both valves, operated pneumatically, from a single control have sufficient capacity to permit the cockpit differential pressure to be reduced from 5.5 psi to 0.05 psi within 5 seconds.

CAUTION

Opening the canopy when the cockpit is overpressurized may result in canopy hinge damage, or a canopy separation. Therefore, when the cockpit is overpressurized, dump cockpit pressurization prior to operating the canopies.

Cockpit Pressure Altimeters

The pressure altitude of the cockpit is indicated on a pressure altimeter. The pilot's cabin altimeter (figure A-1, appendix A) is on the right console. The RIO cabin altimeter (figure A-2, appendix A), is in a panel on the left side of the aft cockpit. The cabin altimeters are vented directly to cockpit pressure.

Cabin Turbine Overspeed Indicator Light

The cabin turbine overspeed indicator light (figure A-1, appendix A), is on the pilot's telelight panel. The indicator light illuminates when the cooling turbine in the cockpit pressure suit refrigeration unit is being subjected to pressures and temperatures in excess of normal operation, and is subject to premature failure. If possible, the airplane speed and engine power should be reduced until the light goes out. If the light fails to go out, the pilot should then select ram air by pulling up on the emergency vent knob, which diverts ram air into the cockpit and at the same time shuts off bleed air to the refrigeration unit, stopping the cooling turbine. The cooling turbine may also be shut down by pulling the cockpit heat and vent circuit breakers (L7, M7, No. 2 panel).

PRESSURE SUIT PRESSURIZATION SYSTEM

The cockpit air conditioning system delivers up to 10 cfm of air per suit at any temperature selected by the pilot. This air is provided at a pressure of 3.0 ± 0.2 psi above cockpit pressure to insure proper flow of ventilating air through the suit. For operation when the cockpit altitude exceeds 35,000 feet, the air is provided at a pressure of 6.5 ± 0.2 psi. If the pilot selects ram air for the cockpit, shutting off the flow of conditioned air, the flow of air from the refrigeration unit to the pressure suit is also stopped. If the pilot selects ram air above 35,000 feet, suit pressurization automatically and instantly is provided by the airplane oxygen system. The RIO can control flow through his pressure suit by a manual flow control and shutoff valve on the left side of the cockpit. The RIO has no control over cockpit or pressure suit temperatures.

MK IV PRESSURE SUIT

The full pressure suit (figure 1-7) consists of a two-layer garment. The inner garment is an air-tight, ozone resistant, neoprene rubber layer, the only interruption being at the entrance which is sealed by a pressure sealing entrance slide fastener. The outer restraining garment is of nylon and is equipped with the necessary straps, tie-down, slide fasteners and adjustments to enable donning and fitting of the suit. The neck ring on the suit is the attachment point for the helmet and is also a pivot for the head and neck. On the left side of the suit are two ports, one for ventilating air attachment, and one for the G suit attachment. On the right side of the suit is an exhaust port. The helmet incorporates the breathing regulator and communication equipment. Suit ventilating air is supplied from the aircraft conditioned and regulated supply via the composite disconnect to the ventilating air hose and suit inlet port. From the suit inlet port, air flows through ventilation tubes built into the pressure suit body and exits at the wrists, ankles, and the back of the neck. It then flows into the body of the suit, out through the exhaust port and through a hose to the suit controller which is in the survival kit. In normal flight, air is allowed to pass through the suit controller and is expelled through its exhaust port underneath the right forward corner of the survival kit. After CSEC 14, the suit controller is in the pressure suit exhaust port. After this modification and CSEC 15, the pressure suit exhaust hose need no longer be plugged into the survival kit. There is no need for the suit to be pressurized when safe cockpit pressure prevails. Any slight pressurization that occurs is due to some suit resistance to ventilation airflow. However, the pressure suit system is devised so that the suit is instantly pressurized if the ambient (cockpit pressure) falls to a value causing the pressure altitude to raise above 35,000 feet. The full pressure suit system responds to and functions under several distinct conditions that might be encountered in flight, namely:

a. In normal flight with adequate cabin pressurization, the suit is pressurized only to a very slight extent due to the suit resistance to airflow.

b. When cockpit pressure falls below 3.4 psi, the suit becomes pressurized by the ventilating air.

c. If ventilation air supply is lost, the airplane oxygen supply pressurizes the suit as well as supplies breathing oxygen. After CSEC 14 and 15, the air present in the suit at ventilation pressure loss becomes trapped (with cockpit pressure above 35,000 feet) to maintain 3.4 psi in the pressure suit. In the event of minor suit leakage for this condition, the suit pressure loss is made up by exhaled air and the oxygen supply system.

d. If the airplane oxygen supply fails, or in the event of bailout, the bailout oxygen should be used to pressurize the suit as well as supply breathing oxygen.

Helmet

The helmet is equipped with an oxygen regulator (Model GR90) face visor, visor seal, face seal, helmet liner adjusting mechanism, sun visor and a dynamic (AIC-10) lip mike and headset. The oxygen regulator controls the flow of oxygen to the facial area. The regulator is divided into two compartments separated by a diaphragm. One compartment has an opening leading directly to the facial area, while the other compartment has an opening directly to the area behind the face seal. The second opening senses the suit pressure, and keeps the oxygen to the facial area at slightly higher pressure than that of the suit, so that the suit air never flows into the facial area. When the demand valve is opened by the negative pressure of inhalation, oxygen is emitted to the facial area via the perforated visor defogging tube. During exhalation, a positive pressure of 0.072 psi forces the exhaled gases to pass from the facial area of the pressure suit body via exhalation valves below the chin. These valves permit flow in one direction only and prevent gases from the suit area from flowing into the facial area. The face visor is sealed when closed by means of a tube which is inflated by oxygen when the supply switch on the regulator is switched ON. On current issue helmets equipped with GR 90 oxygen regulators, the face visor seal is deflated by merely turning the supply switch OFF and inhaling. If the oxygen is turned on when the visor is up, oxygen flows freely to atmosphere from the visor defogging tube. Oxygen is prevented from flowing directly into the rear of the helmet and into the body section of the suit by a face seal. The face seal forms the closure that separates the 100% oxygen in the face compartment from the gases of the suit. CSEC 15 installs an aneroid make-up valve in the oxygen regulator which allows oxygen to make up pressure losses due to minor suit leakages. The seal is shaped to form a continuous line over the occupant's forehead, down along his cheeks and across his chin. To gain this seal, contact with the subject's face should be as complete as possible. This requires that the seal be properly fitted and shaped when donning the helmet. A badly fitted face seal is easily noted by a continuous flow of oxygen from the regulator. The helmet liner adjusting mechanism consists of an external knob and internal straps wrapped around a tightening mechanism. Turning the knob in either direction tightens the helmet liner on the head and also forces the head forward into the face seal. The face seal, when formed properly, provides the occupant with the best possible degree of comfort while wearing the helmet. The crash protection provided by the full pressure suit helmet is equivalent to that provided by the standard Navy helmet. However, due to the nature of its attachment to the suit body, the pressure suit helmet has superior retention qualities.

Suit Controller

The suit controller, in the survival kit, is the heart of the pressure suit system. After CSEC 14, the suit controller is in the pressure suit exhaust port. It is completely automatic and requires no adjustment or control by the suit occupant. All exhaust air must pass through the suit controller before being exhausted. Through restriction of the exhaust flow of vent air, the controller prevents the suit pressure from dropping below a pressure equal to 35,000 feet.

PRESSURE SUIT

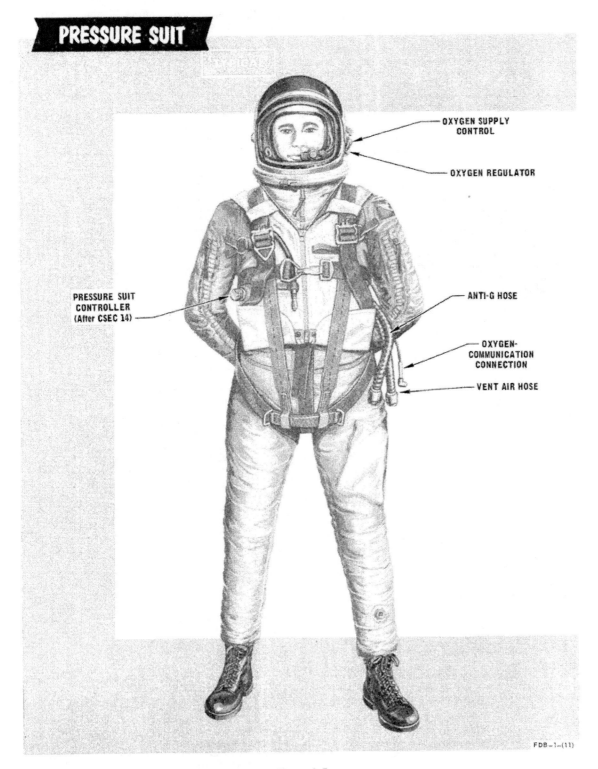

OXYGEN SUPPLY CONTROL

OXYGEN REGULATOR

PRESSURE SUIT CONTROLLER (After CSEC 14)

ANTI-G HOSE

OXYGEN-COMMUNICATION CONNECTION

VENT AIR HOSE

FDB-1-(11)

Figure 1-7

As the cockpit altitude rises above 35,000 feet, the controller begins to restrict the exhaust flow causing a pressure build-up in the suit. This pressure is maintained at an absolute pressure equal to 35,000 feet pressure altitude. The differential suit pressure is the difference between 35,000 feet equivalent and the cockpit pressure. The suit controller operates on a balance pressure being kept between the suit and the internal altitude reference chamber of the controller. The internal altitude reference chamber of the controller is continuously fed with a metered flow of the airplane oxygen at approximately 100 to 150 cc/min. The outlet flow of this oxygen from the reference chamber is controlled by an aneroid operated valve which senses cockpit pressure and regulates the outlet flow to maintain a pressure equal to 35,000 feet within the suit controller. In the event of ventilation air loss to the pressure suit, the pressure in the suit controller drops, causing the suit controller exhaust valve to close. A tilt valve also opens allowing oxygen to flow through the suit controller and exhaust hose to the suit. After CSEC 14 and 15, the functions of the internal reference chamber and tilt valve are taken over by the helmet oxygen regulator. The suit is then pressurized by oxygen. The suit controller continues to maintain suit pressures in the same way as it did when the suit was using ventilation air for pressurization. A check valve in the ventilation inlet line prevents any oxygen in the suit from escaping. There is no ventilation air flow when the suit is being pressurized by oxygen. Upon ejection above 35,000 feet, the suit controller maintains a 35,000 feet pressure altitude in the suit. The only difference is that the oxygen supply for controller operation and suit pressurization comes from the occupant's bailout oxygen supply which is triggered upon ejection.

EQUIPMENT AIR CONDITIONING SYSTEM

The equipment air conditioning system consists of an air-to-air heat exchanger, pressure regulating and shutoff valve, expansion turbine, mixing valve and temperature controls. The unit provides conditioned air for cooling the nose radar equipment and the communication navigation identification equipment under the RIO's cockpit floor. It also provides high pressure air (auxiliary air) for fuselage fuel tank pressurization, wing fuel tank pressurization and transfer, anti-G suits, electronic equipment pressurization, high pressure pneumatic system air source, ADC, and canopy seal pressure. Operation of the system is entirely automatic with airflow initiated on engine start. Engine bleed air, after flowing through the heat exchanger and pressure regulating valve, is expanded through the cooling turbine and then mixed with warm bleed air as necessary to provide a delivery temperature of 85°F from sea level to 25,000 feet, and 40°F above 25,000 feet. The air is then ducted directly to the electronic equipment. In the event of a system failure such that air temperature exceeds 150 ±10°F, the air conditioning unit is automatically shut off and emergency ram air cooling is provided. A warning light labeled RADAR CNI COOL OFF illuminates on the radar intercept officer's instrument panel and the pilot's right vertical

panel whenever ram air is being utilized for cooling. A reset button labeled COOLING RESET is on the RIO's main instrument panel, and on the console below the pilot's right vertical panel. If the RADAR CNI COOL OFF light illuminates, attempt to restart the refrigeration unit by reducing speed below that at which the light illuminated, waiting at least 15 seconds and then pressing the COOLING RESET button. If the refrigeration unit fails to restart, no further restart attempt should be made. Illumination of the RADAR CNI COOL OFF light shall be logged on the yellow sheet (OPNAV Form 3760-2).

CAUTION

- When operating with emergency ram air cooling avoid high speed flight if possible. Maximum allowable cooling temperatures may be exceeded during high speed flight and the life and/or reliability of the AIM-7 missile four channel tuning drive, radar package, tacan, IFF/SIF, and UHF communication, and receiver-transmitter may be affected.

- If the RADAR CNI COOL OFF light does not go out when the reset button is pressed, place the UHF comm, the TACAN, IFF/SIF, and radar to STBY and operate only when necessary.

- Malfunction of equipment cooling turbine may be indicated by high pitch whine and/or vibration in nose of aircraft. Turbine may be shut-off by pulling equipment cooling circuit breaker, No. 2 circuit breaker panel, zone L-6. This shuts off equipment air conditioning and turns on emergency ram air cooling. Auxiliary air is not affected.

EQUIPMENT AUXILIARY AIR SYSTEM

The equipment auxiliary air system utilizes partially cooled 17th stage engine bleed air after it has passed through the equipment air conditioning air-to-air heat exchanger. This partially cooled air is distributed to the anti-G suits, canopy seals, air data computer, fuel system pressurization, pneumatic system air compressor, radio receiver-transmitters (TACAN), radar wave guide, and radar antenna.

Anti G Suit System

The aircraft is equipped to accomodate an anti-G suit system. The anti-G system delivers low pressure equipment auxiliary air to the anti-G suit control valve and then to the suit. The suit remains deflated below 1.5 G. As the force of 1.5 G is reached, a weight inside the valve forces a demand valve open and allows air to flow into the suit in proportion to the G forces experienced. The suit pressure remains constant as long as the G forces do not change. When the G force becomes less than 1.5 G, the diminishing force on the weight opens an exhaust valve and allows the suit to de-pressurize. A manual inflation button in the anti-G suit control valve allows the crewman to manually inflate his suit for checking the system and for fatigue relief. A pressure relief valve incorporated within the system is set to relieve at approximately 11 psi and is used as a safety back-up in the event of a malfunction. The system is automatic and operates any time an engine is running.

RADAR COMPARTMENT PRESSURIZATION

The airplane nose section is automatically pressurized to nominal 1.6 psi above ambient pressure by an outflow type pressure regulator mounted on the forward wall of the nose gear compartment. Pressurization is initiated when the landing gear is raised, and is relieved when the gear is lowered or equipment package shutoff occurs.

NORMAL OPERATION

Optimum cockpit environment can be achieved by placing the override selector switch on the temperature control panel in AUTO, and adjusting the temperature control knob for the desired cockpit temperature. Adjust the defog control lever on the right utility panel for personal comfort and effective windshield defogging. If the automatic temperature control system fails, or if a cooler or hotter temperature is desired within the pressure suit, a temporary adjustment may be obtained by bumping the override selector switch to HOT or COLD. To prevent windshield defogging during letdown into hot humid atmosphere, place the override selector switch in AUTO and have the defog lever positioned about 3/4 of the way forward. Five minutes before letdown select the full defog position and adjust the temperature control knob to the 2 o'clock (200 degrees clockwise rotation) position, and maintain these settings throughout the letdown. If fogging persists, and does not clear up, retract flaps if extended, or increase power (use speed brakes as necessary) to maintain airspeed to provide more engine bleed air to the mixing valves. If cockpit and pressure suit temperatures become too high at low altitudes and cannot be lowered, some degree of comfort can be achieved by opening the face plate, removing the gloves, and unzipping the pressure suit.

PRESSURE SUIT OPERATION

After donning the suit, vent air should be applied if it is available, especially if any delay is anticipated before going out to the aircraft. It doesn't take long to become dehydrated in warm weather. To avoid visor fogging, coat the visor with recommended antifog compound. On the way to the airplane, a portable pressure suit ventilating unit should be used. After arriving at the airplane, vent air is available from the auxiliary power unit (RCPP-105) either in the cockpit or standing outside the airplane. Before entering the cockpit, the vent air hose, anti-G hose, and exhaust hose connections to the suit should be checked. After climbing in the cockpit, connect the composite disconnect to the upper block and connect the exhaust hose. On aircraft 153005z and up, and all others after ASC 69, the pressure suit leads are connected to the universal upper block assembly by means of in-line connections. There is no requirement to connect the pressure suit exhaust hose on suits after CSEC 14. The exhaust hose cannot be connected until the composite disconnect is locked. After these two connections are made the vent air may be turned on before finishing the job of getting strapped in. (If the exhaust hose is not connected, greater than normal suit ballooning will occur and ballooning will be slow to dissipate even after vent air has been turned off.) After the helmet and gloves have been donned and the assistant has plugged in the communications and oxygen line to the helment, the oxygen system should be checked by closing the visor, turning on the oxygen and checking the visor seal. If the system checks out satisfactorily, remain on oxygen. Normal flight procedures are then followed until takeoff position is reached where the vent air should be turned down to prevent suit ballooning as power is advanced on the takeoff roll. As soon as the airplane is cleaned up after take-off the vent air should be adjusted to a comfortable level. Vent air temperature is adjustable by use of the cockpit temperature control. To monitor suit altitude, a suit altimeter is installed on the left leg of the suit. Pressure suit operation can be checked during flight by pulling the emergency vent knob between 12 and 20,000 feet climbing 40,000 feet and checking that suit inflates, and holds an absolute pressure equal to 35,000 feet. The anti-exposure suit uses the same air conditioning system as the pressure suit, except, exhaust air is vented from the suit through the neck, wrist and ankle outlets.

WARNING

Do not turn pressure suit vent air more than 1/4 ON when the BLC is operating. When the flaps are raised, the additional engine bleed air to the air conditioning and pressurization system can cause the pressure suit to balloon. If the pressure suit controller should malfunction, the increased suit pressure could become high enough to cause immobilization.

CAUTION

Before making an inflight pressure suit check, turn radar equipment off to prevent possible arcing of the pilot's radar scope.

EMERGENCY OPERATION

Although there are no provisions made for emergency operation of the cockpit/pressure suit air conditioning system, emergency ventilating air is available. The cockpits may be cleared of undesired smoke or fumes and the cockpit/pressure suit air conditioning unit may be shut off by pressing the button and pulling up on the emergency ventilating knob. The handle may be placed in an intermediate position to obtain the desired amount of emergency ventilation.

LIMITATIONS

There are no specific limitations pertaining to the operation of the air conditioning and pressurization system.

AIR DATA COMPUTER SYSTEM (ADC)

NOTICE

Some illustrations referred to within this system writeup may be located in appendix A. These illustrations are referred to, within the text, as (figure A-, apprndix A).

DESCRIPTION

The air data computer system (figure 1-9) receives inputs of static pressure, pitot pressure, total temperature and angle of attack. The inputs are supplied by two static ports, one on each side of the aft part of the radome; a total temperature sensor, on the vertical fin (aircraft prior to 151399p before ASC 139, or on the left air conditioning inlet duct aircraft 151399p and up and all others after ASC 139), a pitot tube on the vertical fin, and an angle of attack probe, on the left forward side of the fuselage. These inputs are corrected in the ADC to compensate for errors in the sensing equipment installation. The corrected inputs are converted to usable outputs by the ADC and are displayed on the airspeed Mach indicator, altimeter, and vertical velocity indicator; Corrected signals are also used by: the induction air system to position the variable ramps; the flight control group for gain signals and for operation of the flight control group in altitude and Mach hold modes, the navigation computer to compute present position and range information; and by the airborne missile control system for use in computing missile guidance signals and altitude compensation.

ADC SYSTEM FAILURE

The instruments and/or systems utilizing the outputs from the ADC are inoperative or in error if a failure or an interruption occurs in the essential ac power supply, essential dc power supply, or engine bleed air system. An interruption or failure in any of the above systems illuminates the STATIC CORR OFF indicator light.

STATIC PRESSURE COMPENSATOR INDICATOR LIGHT

One of the functions of the ADC is to supply all systems requiring static pressure inputs with a static pressure which has been corrected for static source position error. This correction is accomplished through the static pressure compensator. When operating normally, the compensator utilizes static air pressure as a balancing force only. The corrected static pressure output is actually auxiliary equipment air, corrected for the static source error as dictated by the instantaneous flight situation. If a malfunction occurs in the compensator, a fail safe solenoid is deenergized allowing static pressure from the static source to be routed directly to all systems requiring static pressure inputs. With a malfunction, overall accuracy suffers, but no system dependent on static pressure becomes inoperative. The pilot is alerted to a compensator malfunction by illumination of the STATIC CORR OFF indicator light, on the telelight panel (figure A-1, appendix A). Light illumination may be accompanied by a rapid change in the altimeter reading. A static pressure compensator switch on the inboard engine control panel (figure A-1, appendix A), with positions of RESET CORR, NORM and OFF, is used to reset or turn off the compensator. With the STATIC CORR OFF indicator light illuminated, moving the compensator switch to RESET returns the compensator to normal operation and extinguishes the indicator light. The switch may then be released and it returns to NORM. If the compensator cannot be reset, as evidenced by the indicator light again illuminating when the switch returns to NORM, move the switch OFF. The pressure instruments are in error any time the light is illuminated or the switch is OFF. Refer to the Airspeed and Altimeter Position Error Correction charts in section XI and the NATOPS Pocket Checklist.

ALTITUDE ENCODER UNIT

Aircraft with AFC 353 have an altitude encoder unit installed. The altitude encoder is a dual purpose electronic unit in the left side of the nose that receives static pressure signals from the air data computer. The altitude encoder in turn provides a digital output of altitude in 100-foot increments to the IFF coder-receiver-transmitter, and a synchro output to two servoed altimeters. When mode C is selected on the IFF control panel, automatic altitude reporting, in a coded form, is provided to the air traffic control system, eliminating a need for voice communications.

ADC PREFLIGHT CHECK

The static pressure compensator must be reset before each flight, by momentarily placing the spring

ALTITUDE REPORTING FAILURE INDICATIONS

AFTER AFC 353

TYPE OF FAILURE	ALTIMETER (AAU-19/A)	ALT ENCODER OUT LIGHT	STATIC CORR OFF LIGHT	MASTER CAUTION LIGHT	RESULTING SYSTEM OPERATION
ALTIMETER SERVO FAILURE OR MANUAL STBY SELECTION	STBY	OFF	OFF	OFF	ALTIMETER REVERTS TO PNEUMATIC OPERATION ON CORRECTED STATIC PRESSURE.
ALTITUDE ENCODER UNIT FAILURE OR AIR DATA COMPUTER LPC MODULE FAILURE	STBY	ON	OFF	ON	ALTIMETER REVERTS TO PNEUMATIC OPERATION ON CORRECTED STATIC PRESSURE, AND NO ALTITUDE INFORMATION SUPPLIED TO ALTITUDE REPORTING TRANSPONDER.
AIR DATA COMPUTER SPC FAILURE OR MANUAL OFF SELECTION	STBY	ON	ON	ON	ALTIMETER REVERTS TO PNEUMATIC OPERATION ON UNCORRECTED STATIC PRESSURE, AND NO ALTITUDE INFO SUPPLIED TO ALTITUDE REPORTING TRANSPONDER.

FDB-1-(12)

Figure 1-8

loaded CADC switch to reset, after starting the engine. The altimeter readings before and after reset must not vary over ± 40 feet. This variation is an indication of the accuracy of the compensator and its effect on other instruments. It is possible to experience large errors in both altitude and airspeed if the altimeter variations exceed ± 40 feet.

NORMAL OPERATION

Normal operation of the static pressure compensator commences by momentarily placing the CADC switch in the spring loaded RESET CORR. position after starting engines. The static pressure compensator then provides a static source position error correction to all systems requiring static pressure inputs. When this occurs, the STATIC CORR OFF light extinguishes. If the STATIC CORR OFF light illuminates in flight and cannot be reset, the navigation computer, AMCS, and most flight instruments are in error. On aircraft in which the total temperature sensor is mounted on the left air conditioning duct (151399p and up and all others after ASC 139), the variable area inlet ramps may extend while taxiing close behind operating jet aircraft engines.

Note

Ensure that the variable area inlet ramps are fully retracted before takeoff.

EMERGENCY OPERATION

There are no emergency operations pertaining to the air data computer system.

LIMITATIONS

After initial altimeter jump, the altimeter variation should not exceed plus or minus 40 feet when the SPC is reset. Refer to section XI for SPC off airspeed and altimeter position error corrections.

AIR DATA COMPUTER

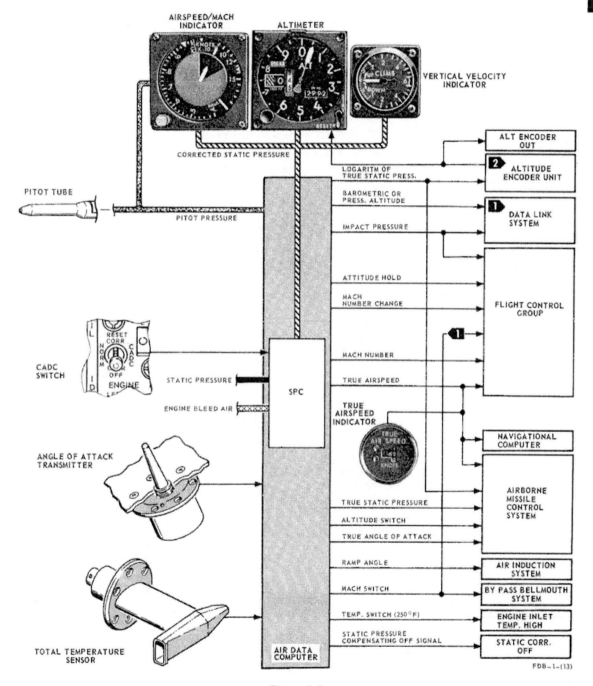

Figure 1-9

FDB-1-(13)

AIR REFUELING STORE

── NOTICE ──
Some illustrations referred to within this system writeup may be located in appendix A.
These illustrations are referred to, within the text, as (figure A-, appendix A).

DESCRIPTION

The airplane can be used as a probe-and-drogue type air refueling tanker upon the installation of an air refueling store (referred to as buddy tank). The tank (figure 1-10) is divided into three major sections: power supply, fuel cell, and hose-reel mechanism. The power supply section contains an electrically feathered and governed ram air turbine, a hydraulic pump, a hydraulic fluid radiator and a hydraulic reservoir. The fuel cell contains a hydraulically driven fuel transfer pump, gravity and pressure fueling receptacles, emergency fuel dump and manual drain valves, float actuated fuel shutoff and vent valves, and electrical, fuel and air connections. The hose-reel mechanism section, contains a spool with 50 feet of hose, a drogue refueling receptacle, a level wind mechanism, a hydraulic motor, and a cartridge actuated guillotine for emergency hose and drogue jettisoning. The ram air turbine drives the hydraulic pump which, in turn, drives the fuel transfer pump and hydraulic motor. The fuel transfer pump is capable of pumping 200 gallons per minute at 55 psi. The hydraulic motor is used to snub the hose and drogue during extension, and to rewind the hose and drogue during retraction. The buddy tank contains 300 gallons of fuel, which can be transferred to the tanker airplane for its own use, or to a receiver airplane. The tanker airplane can transfer its internal and external fuel load to the buddy tank, and subsequently to a receiver airplane.

BUDDY TANK CONTROL PANEL

The buddy tank control panel (figure A-2, appendix A) is on the left side of the rear cockpit instrument panel. The panel is normally installed upon installation of the buddy tank and removed when the buddy tank is removed. The panel contains six switches and two indicators: a power switch, a hose control switch, a fuel transfer switch, a hose jettison switch, a tank light switch, a ship-tanker transfer switch, a drogue position indicator and a gallons delivered indicator.

Buddy Tank Power Switch

The buddy tank power switch is a guarded toggle lock switch with positions of ON, OFF and DUMP. Placing the switch ON energizes the buddy tank electrical system which electrically unfeathers the tank's ram air turbine. Placing the switch OFF feathers the ram air turbine. The DUMP position is guarded. When in DUMP, a solenoid operated dump valve is opened for emergency fuel jettison. In the event of electrical failure while jettisoning buddy tank fuel, the dump valve automatically closes and any fuel remaining in the tank is trapped.

Note

Before dumping buddy tank fuel, ensure that the pilot's buddy fill switch is in STOP FILL to preclude complete depletion of aircraft fuel supply.

Hose Control Switch

The buddy tank hose control switch, marked EXT and RET, is used for normal extension and retraction of the hose and drogue.

Transfer Switch

A solenoid operated transfer switch has positions of OFF and TRANS. Selecting TRANS allows automatic fuel transfer to a receiver airplane upon proper drogue engagement. Selecting OFF discontinues fuel transfer. If an electrical failure occurs while transferring fuel to a receiver airplane, the buddy tank transfer switch reverts to OFF.

Hose Jettison Switch

The buddy tank hose jettison switch, marked OFF and CUT, is a guarded toggle lock switch. Placing the switch to CUT electrically fires a cartridge that actuates the hose guillotine mechanism. Also, all electrical power, except power to operate the dump valve, is shut off.

Buddy Tank Light Switch

The buddy tank light switch, marked BRT (bright) and DIM, controls the brilliance of the two indicator lights on the tail cone of the tank. Normally BRT is selected during daylight hours, and DIM at night.

Ship-Tank Transfer Switch

This switch is not wired into the airplane electrical system and is inoperative. Fuel is transferred to the buddy tank by placing the buddy fill switch on the fuel control panel (figure A-1, appendix A) to FILL. Buddy tank fuel may be transferred to the airplane fuselage cells by placing the external transfer switch on the fuel control panel to CENTER.

Drogue Position Indicator

The buddy tank drogue position indicator has readouts of RET (retract), EXT (extend), and TRA (transfer). The position of the drogue is indicated by a drum dial viewed through a cutout in the panel. The indicator shows RET when the hose and drogue are completely retracted, EXT when the hose and drogue

AIR REFUELING STORE (BUDDY TANK)

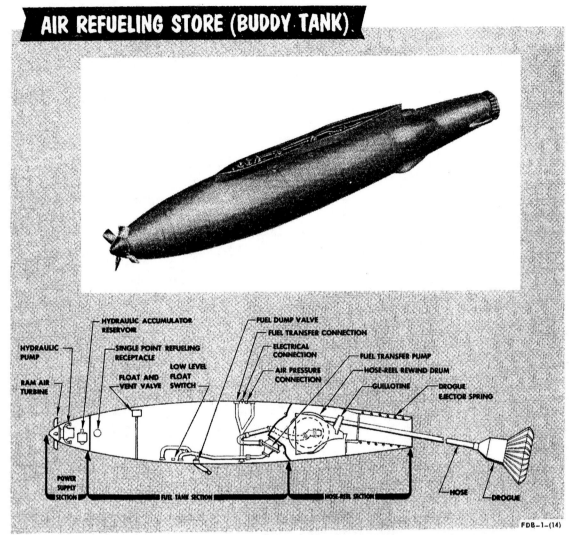

Figure 1-10

are extended and ready for engagement, and TRA when the receiver aircraft has completed engagement and retracted hose and drogue a minimum of 2 feet.

Note

The drogue position indicator does not show TRA unless the hose and drogue have completely extended prior to its 2-foot rewind.

Gallons Delivered Indicator

A gallons delivered indicator presents a direct reading of total gallons delivered, in two gallon increments. A reset knob, immediately adjacent to the indicator windows, permits resetting the gallons delivered indicator to zero.

NORMAL OPERATION

When the buddy tank power switch is placed ON, 28 vdc, and 115/200 vac power energize the buddy tank electrical system. Once the electrical system is energized, the ram air turbine unfeathers and drives the hydraulic pump. When the hydraulic pressure builds to approximately 1600 psi, the hose-reel lock mechanism unlocks to allow action of the hose-reel mechanism. When the hose control switch is then placed to EXT, hydraulic pressure to the rewind motor is decreased from 3000 psi to approximately 1000 psi and the drogue ejector spring ejects the drogue out of its receptacle in the tail cone of the tank. Upon ejection, the drogue blossoms to its full target diameter of 24 inches. Air drag on the drogue then completes the hose extension. The hydraulic rewind motor maintains heavy hose and drogue snubbing during the initial drogue ejection and the last few feet of hose extension. The snubbing reduces shock loading on the hose, drogue, and tank. When the hose and drogue are fully extended, the amber READY light on the tail cone illuminates, and the drogue position indicator displays EXT. For dry receiver hook-ups, the transfer switch must remain OFF. For wet hook-ups, the transfer switch must be placed in TRANS. After engagement of the drogue, the hose must be retracted a minimum of 2 feet before fuel transfers. When the hose and drogue are retracted 2 feet, the drogue position indicator reads TRA. When fuel is being transferred to the receiver aircraft, the green TRANSFER light on the tail cone illuminates and the amber READY light goes out. If the buddy fill switch is in STOP FILL, only buddy tank fuel (300 gallons) is transferred.

Note

If the buddy fill switch is held in FILL, the tanker airplane can transfer its entire fuel supply.

The amount of fuel transferred is indicated on the gallons delivered indicator. Buddy tank fuel transfer may be terminated by three means: by placing the fuel transfer switch OFF; by emergency disengagement of the receiver; and by low level float switch actuation when the buddy tank empties. A major surge or reduction in fuel pressure also terminates buddy tank fuel transfer. After probe separation, the hose control switch should be placed in RET. The hydraulic rewind motor retracts the hose and drogue. When the drogue position indicator reads RET, the buddy tank power switch may be placed OFF. With the power switch OFF, the buddy tank electrical system is deenergized and the ram air turbine feathers, terminating hydraulic pump operation. As the hydraulic pressure decays, the hose-reel lock mechanism mechanically locks the hose and drogue in its retracted position. Also, the buddy tank indicator light goes out.

EMERGENCY OPERATION

Since an empty buddy tank with its hose and drogue retracted produces the same aerodynamic and/or cushioning effect as an empty external fuel tank, no special emergency procedures are required. Fire, structural damage, uncontrollable fuel loss, etc., may require that the tank be jettisoned. Normally the buddy tank may be safetied by placing the buddy tank power switch OFF. Placing the power switch OFF terminates all electrical power to the tank, except for the fuel dump valve, stops hydraulic pump operation, and as a result, mechanically locks the hose and drogue. Buddy tank fuel may be jettisoned at any time by placing the buddy tank power switch to DUMP. Inflight emergencies that do not allow sufficient time for hose and drogue retraction may require hose jettisoning. Placing the hose jettison switch in CUT electrically fires a cartridge which actuates the guillotine cutting blade. The inside segment of the hose is crimped fuel tight by the guillotine blades. Fuel may be dumped after hose and drogue jettison if required.

| CAUTION |

If the buddy tank hose and drogue are lost unintentionally, the buddy tank electrical system is not deenergized by placing the power switch OFF. In this case, the ram air turbine continues to turn and the hydraulic fluid temperature increases causing damage to the O-rings. To deenergize the system and feather the ram air turbine, place the buddy tank power switch OFF, and pull the buddy tank hyd pump circuit breaker (C4, No. 2 panel). Once the buddy tank holding relay is broken, the buddy tank hyd pump circuit breaker may be reset.

HOSE AND DROGUE JETTISONING

A violently whipping hose and drogue, or the inability to retract the hose for any reason, may require hose and drogue jettisoning. Placing the hose jettison switch to CUT, deenergizes the buddy tank electrical system, feathers the ram air turbine, mechanically locks the hose reel mechanism, and electrically fires a cartridge which actuates the guillotine cutting blades. A holding relay delays (5 to 20 seconds) the firing of the guillotine hose cutter until the hose-reel mechanism has locked; thus preventing the hose-reel from rotating and the hose from whipping around the spraying fuel inside the tail cone. Fuel may be dumped after hose and drogue jettisoning if required. To jettison the hose and drogue proceed as follows:

1. Hose jettison switch - CUT

| CAUTION |

Do not change the position of the hose jettison switch after being placed to CUT. If the switch is positioned to NORMAL after jettisoning, the buddy tank electrical system becomes energized.

BUDDY TANK JETTISONING

The buddy tank may be jettisoned individually from the centerline station, or it may be jettisoned along with all external stores. Refer to External Stores Jettison chart, section V.

LIMITATIONS

The following limitations apply for carriage and operation of the buddy tank.

1. With hose retracted and turbine feathered, the maximum airspeed for carriage is 500 knots CAS or 1.1 Mach, whichever is less. The maximum acceleration for carriage is 0 G to +4.0 G.
2. With hose extended, the maximum airspeed is 300 knots CAS or 0.8 Mach, whichever is less.
3. The recommended envelope during refueling is 200 knots CAS to 300 knots CAS or 0.8 Mach and from sea level to 35,000 feet. Maximum acceleration is +2.0 G and no abrupt maneuvers are permitted.

4. The maximum airspeed for hose retraction is 250 knots CAS.

Note

If the hose fails to retract fully at 250 knots, a reduction in airspeed to 230 knots CAS should allow complete retraction.

5. The maximum airspeed for dumping fuel from the buddy tank is 250 knots CAS.

CAUTION

Afterburners should not be used while dumping fuel from the buddy tank due to a fire hazard created by the dumped fuel passing through the engine exhaust close to the aft fuselage.

6. The maximum airspeed for jettisoning the buddy tank is 300 knots CAS or 0.9 Mach, whichever is less.

ANGLE OF ATTACK SYSTEM

NOTICE
Some illustrations referred to within this system writeup may be located in appendix A. These illustrations are referred to, within the text, as (figure A-, appendix A).

DESCRIPTION

An angle of attack system in the airplane presents a visual indication of optimum airplane flight conditions, i.e., stall, landing approach, cruise, etc. Optimum angles of attack are not affected by gross weight, bank angle, load factor, airspeed, density altitude, or flap position. For example, the optimum angle of attack for landing approach is always the same regardless of gross weight. The approach airspeed automatically varies to compensate for the change in weight. The system consists of an angle of attack probe and transmitter, an angle of attack indicator, indexer lights, approach lights, and a stall warning vibrator (rudder pedal shaker). Two electrical heaters, one in the angle of attack probe, and one in the case (adjacent to the fuselage skin), prevent the formation of ice while flying through precipitation. The case heater element is energized when the static pressure compensator switch is placed to RESET CORR. and the probe heater element is automatically energized when weight is off the landing gear. The probe heater receives power from the right main 115 volt ac bus through the angle of attack probe heater circuit breaker, No. 1 circuit breaker panel in the rear cockpit. The case heater is powered from the right main 115 volt ac bus through the angle of attack transmitter heater circuit breaker, B-11 No. 1 circuit breaker panel in the rear cockpit. Refer to figure 1-11 for angle of attack conversions and displays.

WARNING

With gear up and flaps down (bolter configuration) aircraft angle of attack will be 3 units greater than indicated angle of attack due to a difference in the airflow about the AOA probe with the nose gear door closed vice open. Thus the aircraft will stall at about 21 units indicated angle of attack with gear up and flaps down as compared to 24 units indicated angle of attack with both gear and flaps down.

ANGLE OF ATTACK INDICATOR

This indicator (figure 1-11) measures the angle of attack of the airplane by reflecting the direction of airflow relative to the fuselage. This is accomplished by means of a probe protruding through the fuselage skin. Airstream direction is sensed by means of a pair of parallel slots in the probe. When the airplane changes its angle of attack, pressure becomes greater in one slot than the other, and the probe rotates to align the probe slots with the airstream. Probe rotation moves potentiometer wiper arms, producing resistance variations which are sent to the angle of attack indicator. The angle of attack indicator is powered by the essential 28 volt dc bus and is operative with ram air turbine power. The circuit breaker is on No. 1 circuit breaker panel, zone E6. The angle of attack indicator is calibrated from 0 to 30 in arbitrary units, equivalent to a range of -10 to +40 angular degrees of rotation of the probe. A reference bug is provided for approach (ON SPEED) angle of attack which is set at 19.2 units (non-drooped ailerons), and at 19.0 units (drooped ailerons). Approach angle of attack values are only valid with the landing gear down. Gear up angle of attack values are 3 to 4 units lower because of a local flow difference caused by the nose gear door. Additional bugs are provided and can be set at any desired angle of attack. The suggested values for the bug settings are as follows:

Climb (400 KCAS) - 5.5 units
Max Endurance - 8.5 units
Stall Warning - 22.3 units (non-drooped ailerons)
            21.3 units (drooped ailerons)

The angle of attack indicator also contains a switch that actuates the stall warning vibrator. When the indicator is inoperative, the word OFF shows in a small window on the face of the dial. Refer to Airspeed Indicator Failure illustration, section V to obtain angle of attack ranges for various drag indices and flight conditions.

ANGLE OF ATTACK INDEXER

An angle of attack indexer is on the left side of the windshield in the front cockpit. On some airplanes

ANGLE OF ATTACK CONVERSION AND DISPLAYS

AIRCRAFT THRU 152994y BEFORE AFC 218

STALL WARNING
(22.3 UNITS)

APPROACH
(19.2 UNITS)

400 KCAS CLIMB
(5.5 UNITS)

MAX ENDURANCE
(8.5 UNITS)

ALL CONFIGURATIONS-FLAPS AS NOTED, GEAR DOWN

1 G LEVEL FLIGHT

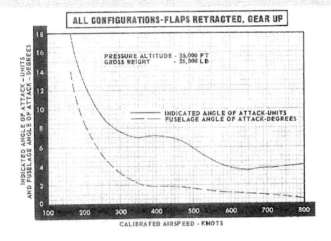

APPROACH LIGHT	INDICATOR	INDEXER	ANGLE OF ATTACK UNIT	AIRSPEED
			20.3-30	VERY SLOW
			19.7-20.3	SLIGHTLY SLOW
			18.7-19.7	ON SPEED
			18.1-18.7	SLIGHTLY FAST
			0-18.1	VERY FAST

HALF FLAPS, GEAR DOWN

GROSS WEIGHT
45,000 LB
40,000 LB
35,000 LB

INDICATED ANGLE OF ATTACK-UNITS

CALIBRATED AIRSPEED - KNOTS

FULL FLAPS, GEAR DOWN

GROSS WEIGHT
45,000 LB
40,000 LB
35,000 LB

INDICATED ANGLE OF ATTACK - UNITS

CALIBRATED AIRSPEED - KNOTS

ALL CONFIGURATIONS-FLAPS RETRACTED, GEAR UP

PRESSURE ALTITUDE - 35,000 FT
GROSS WEIGHT   - 36,000 LB

INDICATED ANGLE OF ATTACK-UNITS
FUSELAGE ANGLE OF ATTACK-DEGREES

INDICATED ANGLE OF ATTACK - UNITS
AND FUSELAGE ANGLE OF ATTACK - DEGREES

CALIBRATED AIRSPEED - KNOTS

FDB-1-(15-1)

FYG

Figure 1-11 (Sheet 1 of 2)

ANGLE OF ATTACK CONVERSION AND DISPLAYS

AIRCRAFT 152995z AND UP, AND ALL OTHERS AFTER AFC 218

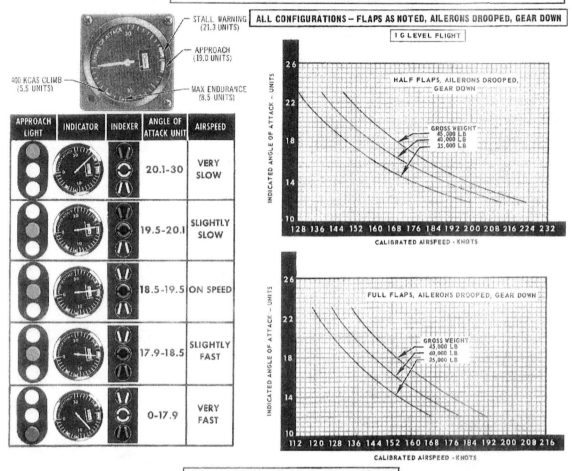

ALL CONFIGURATIONS – FLAPS AS NOTED, AILERONS DROOPED, GEAR DOWN

1 G LEVEL FLIGHT

APPROACH LIGHT	INDICATOR	INDEXER	ANGLE OF ATTACK UNIT	AIRSPEED
			20.1-30	VERY SLOW
			19.5-20.1	SLIGHTLY SLOW
			18.5-19.5	ON SPEED
			17.9-18.5	SLIGHTLY FAST
			0-17.9	VERY FAST

STALL WARNING (21.3 UNITS)
APPROACH (19.0 UNITS)
400 KCAS CLIMB (5.5 UNITS)
MAX ENDURANCE (8.5 UNITS)

HALF FLAPS, AILERONS DROOPED, GEAR DOWN
GROSS WEIGHT
45,000 LB
40,000 LB
35,000 LB

FULL FLAPS, AILERONS DROOPED, GEAR DOWN
GROSS WEIGHT
45,000 LB
40,000 LB
35,000 LB

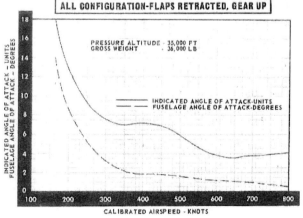

ALL CONFIGURATION-FLAPS RETRACTED, GEAR UP

PRESSURE ALTITUDE - 35,000 FT
GROSS WEIGHT - 36,000 LB

INDICATED ANGLE OF ATTACK-UNITS
FUSELAGE ANGLE OF ATTACK-DEGREES

FDB-1-(15-2)
RYG

Figure 1-11 (Sheet 2 of 2)

there are two angle of attack indexers, one on each side of the windshield. The indexer presents landing approach angle of attack information by illuminating symbols. The symbols are energized through switches in the angle of attack indicator when the landing gear is down. At fast airspeeds (low angle of attack) the lower symbol (an inverted V) is illuminated; at slightly fast airspeeds, the lower symbol and circular symbol is illuminated. At optimum approach speeds only the center circular symbol illuminates. For slightly slow airspeeds, the center symbol and upper symbol illuminates. For slow airspeeds (high angle of attack), only the upper symbol (a V) is illuminated.

Indexer Lights Control Knob

An indexer lights control knob, on airplanes 150436m and up, and all other after ASC 133, is on the front cockpit right console (figure A-1, appendix A). The lights are automatically illuminated when the landing gear is lowered, however, the intensity is increased or decreased by the indexer lights control knob.

STALL WARNING VIBRATOR

Refer to Flight Controls, this section.

APPROACH LIGHTS

An approach light system, with red, amber, and green indicator lights, is used to show symbolic airplane angle of attack during landing approaches. Four switches within the angle of attack indicator determine which of the three lights is illuminated. The lights are energized through switches in the landing gear, wing flaps and arresting gear systems. A hook by-pass switch, on the exterior lights control panel, is used to by-pass the wing flap and arresting gear switches. When the hook by-pass switch is in NORMAL, the landing gear down, the wing flaps 1/2 or full down and the arresting gear up, the approach light flashes. When the hook by-pass switch is in BY-PASS and the landing gear is down, the approach light glows steady regardless of the position of the arresting gear and wing flaps. A green approach light indicates a high angle of attack, low airspeed; an amber light indicates optimum angles of attack; and a red approach light indicates a low angle of attack, high airspeed.

NORMAL OPERATION

There are no controls pertaining to the angle of attack system other than the indexer lights control knob.

EMERGENCY OPERATION

There are no alternate or emergency provisions pertaining to the angle of attack system. However, in the event the indexer lights do not illuminate following a catapult launch, the nose gear catapult extension chamber has failed to deflate. Refer to Nose Gear Strut Extension, this section.

LIMITATIONS

There are no limitations pertaining to the angle of attack system.

APPROACH POWER COMPENSATOR SYSTEM

NOTICE

Some illustrations referred to within this system writeup may be located in appendix A. These illustrations are referred to, within the text, as (figure A-, appendix A).

DESCRIPTION

Note

On aircraft 148363f thru 152304w the APCS is inoperative until after AFC 172.

The approach power compensator system (APCS) maintains the aircraft at optimum approach angle of attack by automatically positioning engine throttles. The system consists of the approach power control set, angle of attack transmitter, integrated torque boosters, control switches, and the warning light. The approach power compensator, when engaged, automatically sets the throttles at the calculated thrust, regardless of previous setting, needed to maintain the aircraft at the proper angle of attack. If the pitch attitude is being changed by the pilot to place the aircraft on the desired glide path, the engine speed automatically stabilizes at the thrust level needed to correct for this change in aircraft attitude. However, engine speed does not increase above 99 percent rpm or decrease below 73 percent. Manual throttle operation is available with the system turned off, and an emergency override feature allows the pilot to manually position the throttles any time the system is engaged by applying a force of 20 to 40 pounds per throttle. The system may be disengaged by moving the speed brake switch to IN or by moving the APCS system switch to OFF or STBY. After AFC 392 the APCS system may be disengaged by moving the speed brake switch to IN regardless of the position of the emergency speed brake switch or the speed brake circuit breaker.

APPROACH POWER CONTROL SET (AN/ASN-54(V)

The approach power control set AN/ASN-54 (V) is connected in parallel with the throttles to provide manual or automatic power control. The set consists of the aircraft accelerometer, throttle control computer, and electronic control amplifier. After AFC 364 the set includes the stabilator position transducer. The APCS compensates for outside air temperature and is capable of controlling one or both engines. The set utilizes normal acceleration and angle of attack error inputs and after AFC 364 includes stabilator position change input to position the throttles of the selected engine, thus commanding thrust changes to maintain an optimum angle of attack.

Aircraft Accelerometer

The aircraft accelerometer measures acceleration perpendicular to the glide path and pitch axis. If the aircraft oscillates about the glide path prior to arriving at the proper airspeed, an electrical signal is generated by the accelerometer. The signal is sent to the throttle computer to dampen these oscillations by positioning the throttles for the proper thrust level.

Stabilator Position Transducer

After AFC 364, a stabilator position transducer is installed to measure the rate of displacement of the stabilator. Stabilator movement from a present position is sensed by the transducer and sent as an electrical signal to the throttles control computer. The transducer signal allows the computer to anticipate an angle of attack change, thus reducing the time required by the APCS to react to pilot and vertical gust induced attitude changes. This function is not operative until the APC computer (CP-911) is modified to the CP-973 configuration which will accept stick input signals.

Throttle Control Computer

The throttle control computer, computes the throttle position required to maintain an optimum angle of attack. The computer utilizes an error input from the angle of attack transmitter and the accelerometer and after AFC 364 a stabilator position change input from the stabilator position transducer. The computer computes the throttle position required for one or both engines as selected by the temperature switch. The throttle control computer delivers the throttle position signal to the electronic control amplifier.

Electronic Control Amplifier

The electronic control amplifier commands throttle movement necessary to maintain the optimum angle of attack. The amplifier receives a desired throttle position signal from the throttle control computer and the actual throttle position from the torque booster feedback. These two signals are compared by the amplifier and a command signal is applied to the torque boosters.

INTEGRATED TORQUE BOOSTER

The torque boosters (one per engine) amplify the input signal from the amplifier and position the throttle linkage as required to satisfy the amplifier signal. The torque boosters are hydro-mechanical servo motors which use engine fuel as the controlling medium. Power to the boosters is controlled by the engine selector switch and the APCS power switch. After AFC 392 power is not available to the torque boosters unless both the throttle control computer and the electronic control amplifier are installed in the aircraft, and modified in accordance with AVC 924.

APCS POWER SWITCH

The APCS power switch is a three-position toggle switch with positions of OFF, STBY, and ENGAGE. In OFF, all power to the system is removed and the throttles must be manually positioned. In STBY, power is supplied to the throttle computer so that the computer may synchronize with the prevailing flight conditions. However, the control amplifier is not active and the throttles must be manually positioned. In ENGAGE, the system automatically controls the engine thrust by varying throttle position. The power switch is held in ENGAGE by a holding coil. Should the pilot disengage the system by placing the speed brake switch to IN, or should disengagement occur due to a malfunction, the power switch automatically moves to STBY and the APCS OFF light illuminates. After AFC 392, the APCS power switch does not remain in ENGAGE unless both the throttle control computer and the electronic control amplifier are installed in the aircraft, and modified in accordance with AVC 924.

ENGINE SELECTOR SWITCH

An engine selector switch, with positions of L (Left), R (Right), and BOTH, allows the pilot to select automatic operation of either or both engines. If a single engine is selected, the manually controlled engine throttle should be positioned so that rpm is between 77 and 82 percent. The engine selector switch can be positioned at any time; however, it is effective only when the APCS power switch is in ENGAGE. This switch will be deactivated upon incorporation of AFC-513. If AVC-743 is incorporated prior to AFC-513, operate engine selector switch in BOTH position only.

AIR TEMPERATURE SWITCH

An air temperature switch, with positions of COLD, NORM, and HOT, allows the pilot to select a temperature input which is representative of the ambient conditions. Since thrust developed for any given throttle setting varies with outside air temperature, the pilot should select the correct temperature before engaging the APCS. COLD is used when temperature is below 40°F and HOT when the temperature is above 80°F. When the temperature is between 40°F and 80°F, NORM is utilized. If the incorrect temperature is selected the APCS throttle command signal is incorrect, but the computer compensates and produces the correct throttle movement. However, less correction time is required if the correct temperature is selected.

APCS OFF LIGHT

The APCS OFF light, on the telelight panel, and the MASTER CAUTION light illuminate whenever the system becomes disengaged or is in STBY, regardless of the cause. On aircraft after AFC 508, an identical APCS OFF light is added on the left side of the glare shield, near the AOA indicator. The APCS OFF light and the MASTER CAUTION light, when illuminated, can be extinguished by pressing the master caution reset button, by engaging the system, or by turning the system off.

NORMAL OPERATION

It is possible to engage the approach power compensator system any time the aircraft is in flight. However, it operates properly only in the 73 to 99 percent rpm throttle range. It is recommended that engagement be made while downwind so that the system operation can be observed before commencing the landing approach. Before engagement, ensure that the speed brake switch is in STOP and the throttle friction lever is full aft. To engage the system, momentarily place the APCS power switch to STBY and then to ENGAGE. The system remains engaged until disengagement is accomplished by the pilot, a malfunction, or immediately after touchdown through the landing gear scissors switch. The pilot must assume manual throttle control after disengagement occurs.

Note

Do not engage approach power compensator unless all components are installed in system. When components are removed, engagement of system causes throttles to assume any setting from 73 to 99 percent. After AFC 392, the APCS does not engage when the throttle control computer and/or the electronic control amplifier is not installed in the aircraft, or the computer and amplifier are not modified in accordance with the AVC 924. Absence of a complete system is indicated to the pilot by the APCS power switch failing to remain in the ENGAGE position.

WARNING

- In drooped aileron aircraft, do not engage APCS with gear up and flaps one-half or full down. Gear up airspeeds at 19 units angle of attack correspond to gear down airspeed at 22 to 23 units (10 to 12 knots slower). This is especially critical because landing configuration stalls occur at 24 units angle of attack.

- If AFC-513 is not incorporated concurrent with AVC-743, operate engine selector switch in BOTH positions only. If L (left) or R (right) is selected on engine selector switch, the APCS computer will continue to schedule for two-engine operation; consequently, power response will be severely jeopardized.

EMERGENCY OPERATION

There are no provisions for emergency operation of the Approach Power Compensator System.

Note

- The pilot can manually override the throttles by exerting a 20 to 40 pound force per throttle. In this case the throttles must be held in the desired position.

- When manually retarding the throttles with the approach power compensator engaged, the throttles can be pulled against the APCS minimum-speed stop. The throttles cannot be retarded below this point unless the force against the minimum speed stop is relieved and the APCS is disengaged.

LIMITATIONS

The approach power compensator system is limited to operation within the 73 to 99 percent throttle range. The APCS should not be utilized for carrier landings until AVC 752 is incorporated.

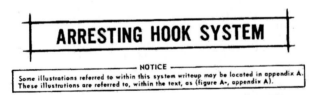

ARRESTING HOOK SYSTEM

— NOTICE —
Some illustrations referred to within this system writeup may be located in appendix A. These illustrations are referred to, within the text, as (figure A-, appendix A).

DESCRIPTION

The arresting hook system consists of an arresting hook, a combination hydraulic actuator and dashpot, a mechanical uplatch, and a control handle. The forward end of the arresting hook is pivoted in a manner which not only permits up and down movement, but left and right motion as well. Coil springs keep the hook centered for retraction. It is retracted up and aft by a hydraulic actuating cylinder, and is caught and held there by a mechanical uplatch. It is extended by the pneumatic action of the dashpot and its own weight. The arresting hook is controlled by a handle on the right side of the front cockpit instrument panel. The handle and the uplatch mechanism

are joined by a control cable. In the event of a cable failure, the arresting hook extends.

ARRESTING HOOK CONTROL HANDLE

The arresting hook is controlled by an arresting hook shaped handle (figure A-1, appendix A) on the right side of the front cockpit instrument panel. When the handle is placed down, the uplatch is released and the arresting hook is extended. Placing the handle up energizes a solenoid valve which directs utility hydraulic pressure to the cylinder. A red warning light inside the control handle illuminates when the control handle is placed down and remains on until the arresting hook is fully extended. The warning light will remain on if the hook is in contact with the ground or deck and prevented from reaching the down limit. On

Note

The pilot shall not use the manual trim button when in AFCS mode except under the conditions specified in the paragraph entitled Auto-Pitch Trim Light.

AUTO-PITCH TRIM LIGHT

An A/P PITCH TRIM light (figure A-1, appendix A) is on the telelight panel. This light illuminates during AFCS operation if the automatic pitch trim is inoperative or lagging sufficiently behind airplane maneuvering to cause an out of trim condition in the basic airplane. Since: (1) auto-pitch trim rate is only 40% of normal trim rate, (2) auto-pitch trim is inoperative anytime the stick grip transducer switches are made (i.e., during CSS maneuvering) and, (3) on airplanes before AFC 203, auto-pitch trim is inoperative outside of the trim cutout acceleration limits (0 to +3 G), it is possible to develop an out of trim condition while maneuvering in the AFCS mode. However, this out of trim condition must exist for approximately 10 seconds before the A/P PITCH TRIM indicator light illuminates, thus eliminating constant light flickering. Momentary illumination of the light does not necessarily indicate a malfunction; however, if the light remains on and it is apparent from the pitch trim indication that the trim is not working, the pilot should realize that a pitch transient may be experienced when the AFCS mode is disengaged. Airspeed pitch trim indicator relationship should provide an indication of the severity of the transient. If an out of trim condition is realized by the steady illumination of the A/P PITCH TRIM light, grasp the stick firmly before disengaging the AFCS mode in anticipation of a pitch bump. However, before disengaging the AFCS following an automatic pitch trim malfunction, the pilot may elect to alleviate the out of trim condition by operating the manual trim button and observing the pitch trim indicator. If the out of trim condition is thus reduced to within 5 pounds of trim, the A/P PITCH TRIM light is extinguished. Illumination of the A/P PITCH TRIM light also illuminates the MASTER CAUTION light. Pressing the master caution reset button only extinguishes the MASTER CAUTION light, leaving the A/P PITCH TRIM light illuminated.

AUTOPILOT DISENGAGED INDICATOR LIGHT

The A/P DISENGAGED light (figure A-1, appendix A) is on the telelight panel. After initial engagement of the AFCS mode of operation, the A/P DISENGAGED light and MASTER CAUTION light illuminates when the AFCS mode is disengaged by any means. Both lights are extinguished by pressing the master caution reset button. The lights remain extinguished until the AFCS is again disengaged.

Note

If PC-1 hydraulic pressure is lost or drops below 500 psi, the pitch axis in stab aug and AFCS is inoperative. If utility hydraulic pressure is lost or drops below 500 psi, the roll axis and yaw axis in stab aug and AFCS are inoperative. In either case, the A/P DIS-

ENGAGED light and the STAB AUG OFF or PITCH AUG OFF light do not illuminate. The CHECK HYD GAGES light and the MASTER CAUTION light illuminate at approximately 1500 psi.

STAB AUG OFF INDICATOR LIGHT - PRIOR TO 153049aa BEFORE AFC 203

A STAB AUG OFF indicator light (figure A-1, appendix A) is on the telelight panel. The STAB AUG OFF light and MASTER CAUTION light illuminate any time power is on the airplane and the stab aug switch is disengaged. Pressing the master caution reset button clears the MASTER CAUTION light, however, the STAB AUG OFF light remains illuminated until the stab aug switch is engaged.

PITCH AUG OFF INDICATOR LIGHT - 153049aa AND UP; ALL OTHERS AFTER AFC 203

The PITCH AUG OFF indicator light is on the telelight panel and remains illuminated unless pitch stab aug is engaged. After pitch stab aug engagement, disengagement also illuminates the MASTER CAUTION light.

NORMAL OPERATION

WARNING

Airplanes 152331x thru 153048aa contain the three axis stab aug controller, but do not contain the modified control amplifier. In these airplanes the AFCS pitch channel is not energized if a malfunction or out of synchronization condition occurs in the pitch channel, even though the AFCS switch can be engaged. This feature can cause a hazardous flight condition if the proper engagement sequence is not followed. If a malfunction exists in the pitch AFCS channel which precludes pitch attitude or stabilator followup synchronization, the pitch channel of the AFCS is unreliable and hazardous. Selecting full AFCS mode of operation (pitch, roll, and yaw) results in an apparently satisfactory AFCS. However, the pitch channel of the AFCS does not engage until the aircraft attitude matches the pitch attitude synchronizer. When this occurs, the AFCS is locked in this pitch attitude. Pitch control stick steering is inoperative and if aircraft pitch attitude is changed by overpowering the AFCS, the aircraft returns to the pitch engagement attitude when stick force is released. This potentially hazardous control condition can be identified by attempting to engage the altitude hold mode immediately after engagement of the AFCS. If the altitude hold switch does not hold in the ENGAGE position, do not use the AFCS. This malfunction in no way affects the stab aug modes. Airplanes 153049aa and up, and airplanes prior to 152331x after AFC 203 do not have this hazardous condition.

Before engaging the AFCS, the following conditions must exist: in airplanes prior to 153049aa before AFC 203, the stab aug switch must be engaged, in all other airplanes, the stability augmentation mode can be selected individually or in any combination for pitch, roll, or yaw axis; however, all three switches must be engaged for complete AFCS operation; the airplane should be in trim, and an attitude within the AFCS limits must be established. AFCS operation can then be achieved by engaging the AFCS switch. On airplanes 153049aa and up and all others after AFC 203, engage the altitude hold switch immediately after inflight engagement of the AFCS. If the altitude hold switch does not remain engaged, a malfunction or out of synchronization condition exists in the pitch channel of the AFCS. If a pitch AFCS malfunction is indicated, do not use the AFCS. This malfunction does not affect stability augmentation operation. In airplanes prior to 153049aa before AFC 203, when altitude or Mach hold is desired, establish a Mach number or altitude and engage the desired mode. It should be remembered that Mach or altitude hold can only be selected after the AFCS is engaged and the desired Mach number or altitude has been established. Fore and aft stick movement disengages the Mach or altitude hold modes. On airplanes 153049aa and up and all others after AFC 203, the Mach hold mode is removed. Manual trim during AFCS operation should not be used unless roll reversal is encountered, and then only a small amount of trim should be used to counteract the roll. On airplanes 148363f thru 149474k, there is a possibility of encountering pronounced vibrations during AFCS operation at very low airspeeds. This is caused by the pitch rate gyros sensing structural vibrations of the airframe, and amplifying these vibrations by generating commands through the autopilot to the stabilator. There should be no cause for alarm if this phenomenon occurs. The vibration or chatter can be eliminated by reverting to the stab aug mode or by increasing airspeed above approximately 190 to 220 knots CAS. Autopilot disengagement can be accomplished by placing the AFCS switch off; the airplane is still in the stab aug mode. In airplanes prior to 153049aa before AFC 203, the AFCS and stab aug modes can both be disengaged by depressing the emergency disengage lever on the control stick. In airplanes 153049aa and up and all others after AFC 203, the AFCS is disengaged when the emergency disengage lever is depressed. The stab aug is disengaged as long as the lever is held depressed but returns to normal operation when the lever is released. To permanently disengage stab aug, the pitch, roll, and yaw stab aug switches must be turned off.

OPERATIONAL PRECAUTIONS

Generator Switching

Power to the autopilot, ADC and AN/AJB-3A may be momentarily interrupted during the starting and stopping of airplane engines or generators. When the right engine or generator is started with the left generator already on the line, the connection between the right and left main buses is momentarily opened to allow the right generator to come on the line. This momentary interruption allows the solenoid held switches to disengage. This necessitates re-engaging the autopilot to bring back autopilot operation. The autopilot, ADC, and AN/AJB-3A are not affected by starting or stopping the left engine or generator with the right generator on the line. If failure of the right generator occurs, place the right generator switch OFF and disengage the stab aug, by depressing the emergency disengage switch, prior to cycling the right generator switch back ON. This prevents the possible occurrence of control surface transients. Stab aug may be engaged by releasing the emergency disengage switch after the right generator has been cycled ON, or may be engaged with the right generator switch retained OFF.

Note

With yaw roll stability augmentation engaged, small transients in yaw and roll are experienced when switching the second generator back on the line after single generator operation.

Roll Reversal

There is a possibility of a condition called roll reversal occurring when operating the AFCS in the autopilot mode. This condition occurs infrequently and is apparent only when attempting small changes in bank angle. Roll reversal is associated with a small out of trim condition in the lateral control system, and is apparent as a slow rolling of the aircraft in the opposite direction of the low lateral force. If, for instance, the airplane is out of trim laterally to the left when the autopilot mode is engaged, roll reversal may occur when low right stick forces are applied. A roll reversal situation may also be caused by operating the lateral trim button while in the autopilot mode, followed by low lateral stick forces being applied opposite to the direction of the trim. There is also a possibility of roll reversal occurring even if the airplane has been trimmed, before engaging the autopilot mode and the manual trim button has not been touched. This condition is brought about by changes in aircraft trim accompanying changed flight conditions.

AFCS Operation With Static Correction OFF

The autopilot operates satisfactorily with the static pressure compensator out, however, the Mach and altitude hold modes may be affected. If the Mach or altitude modes are affected, the reference altitude or Mach number changes when the static pressure compensator fails.

Pitch Oscillations (Altitude Hold Mode)

When using the AFCS altitude hold mode, the aircraft may experience pitch oscillations in the transonic regions and below due to fluctuations in the ADC airspeed system. The nature of these oscillations vary from stick pumping to divergent pitch oscillations. It is recommended that if pitch oscillations occur at subsonic speeds the following corrective steps

steps be attempted: disengage the AFCS; place the CADC switch OFF; re-engage the AFCS; and engage altitude hold. If the oscillations persist after taking corrective action, or if they are encountered at supersonic speeds, disengage the altitude hold mode. In any event, divergent pitch oscillations should not be allowed to develop. If any divergent pitch activity is noted, corrective action should be taken immediately.

Note

When using AFCS/CSS or altitude hold, there are no automatic AFCS cut-out features to prevent the aircraft from flying into a stall. Therefore, it is possible for the aircraft to enter uncontrolled flight with AFCS/CSS or altitude hold engaged if airspeed is allowed to dissipate.

Pitch Oscillations-Mach Hold Mode; - PRIOR TO 153049aa BEFORE AFC 203

When using the AFCS with Mach hold mode engaged, a divergent oscillation may result if thrust is added

and light forward stick force is applied as the nose rises to correct the Mach error caused by the thrust change. At 300 knots CAS the G forces can reach +0.5 to +2.0 G with 2 to 3 inches of stick travel. Mach hold may disengage. The oscillation can be stopped by disengaging the AFCS. Pitch oscillations may become severe if thrust is added while in Mach hold at high airspeeds. Generally, thrust should not be added with Mach hold engaged.

EMERGENCY OPERATION

There are no provisions for emergency operation of the Automatic Flight Control System.

LIMITATIONS

Autopilot operation is interrupted when ± 70° pitch or bank is exceeded. However, the AFCS engage switch remains engaged and the autopilot resumes normal operation when the airplane is returned to within the ± 70° limits. If a load factor of +4 G or -1 G is sensed by the G-limit accelerometer, the autopilot reverts to the stab aug mode and the AFCS engage switch must be re-engaged for AFCS operation.

BRAKE SYSTEM

─── NOTICE ───
Some illustrations referred to within this system writeup may be located in appendix A.
These illustrations are referred to, within the text, as (figure A-, appendix A).

DESCRIPTION

The main landing gear wheels are equipped with power operated brakes. Two power brake valves are in the nose wheel well and each is operated in a conventional manner from linkage attached to the rudder pedals. The brake control valves are power operated rather than a power boost type. Excessive pedal travel and pumping of the brakes to obtain a firm pedal is eliminated since the fluid supply to the wheel cylinders is virtually unlimited. This brake system provides differential wheel brake pressures. With no utility hydraulic pressure available, a 25 cubic inch hydraulic accumulator provides pressure to actuate the normal brake system. In addition, the brake control valves act as master cylinders in a conventional non-power system as long as integrity has been maintained between the control valves and the wheel brakes. Pilot effort in manual operation is capable of securing the airplane in deck rolls up to 8 degrees. Although it has not been determined by test flight, pilot assumption is that the manual brake system should be capable of stopping the airplane on a typical jet runway provided the drag chute is also used. The manual braking feature is selective and may be used for differential brake steering, while the emergency pneumatic brake system is employed in stopping the airplane. Each main landing wheel contains three fuse plugs to protect against tire explosion. If the brakes are used excessively, causing overheating of the wheels and tires, the fuse plugs

should melt and let the tire go flat before a tire explosion can occur.

Note

Only three maximum effort brake applications from the accumulator should be anticipated when utility hydraulic pressure is lost.

EMERGENCY BRAKE SYSTEM

If hydraulic pressure fails, an emergency air system is provided to accomplish maximum braking. Emergency pressure is provided by a 100 cubic inch air bottle charged to 3000 psi. Up to ten maximum effort applications may be made by means of the emergency brake handle (figure A-1, appendix A) just inboard of the right console. It is hand operated, and is spring-loaded to the off or brake released position. It is a power brake valve of conventional design and meters air pressure to completely independent pneumatic brake cylinders, in proportion to applied effort. The emergency pneumatic brake system does not provide differential wheel brake pressure; however, by applying the manual portion of the hydraulic brakes in conjunction with the emergency air brakes, differential braking can be accomplished. Hydraulic and pneumatic systems are entirely separate. Actuation of the emergency pneumatic system does not introduce air into the hydraulic system.

NORMAL OPERATION

The brakes are conventionally operated by toe action on the rudder pedals. This action meters utility hydraulic pressure to force the brake disks together. Pedal pressure felt by the pilot is proportionate to braking force applied. The pilot is capable of locking the brakes by both normal and emergency braking systems. Caution must be exercised in overbraking, since a fully locked wheel offers less retardation than very light normal braking. If one wheel is locked during application of the brakes, there is a very definite tendency for the airplane to turn away from that wheel and further application of brake pressure offers no corrective action. This produces a rapidly decreasing coefficient of friction between the skidding tire and the runway, while the coefficient of friction between the other tire and the runway remains near optimum for braking effectiveness. It is, therefore, apparent that a wheel once locked never frees itself until brake pressure to that wheel is reduced sufficiently to permit the wheel to rotate. It has been found that optimum braking occurs when the wheel is in a slight skid. The wheel continues to rotate, but at a speed of approximately 80 to 85 percent of its normal free rolling rotational speed. Increasing the rolling skid above approximately 15 to 20 percent only decreases the braking effectiveness. Since no anti-skid system is fitted, recognition of maximum braking force is strictly a matter of pilot sensitivity As with other examples of operating "on the limit", the only sure way of determining maximum braking effort is to exceed it. Since this is seldom a desirable technique, the pilot should attempt to mentally catalogue his body response to normal braking, to more readily recognize the maximum, if an emergency should require it. For all conditions normal and emergency, the most desirable braking technique is a single, smooth application of the brakes with a constantly increasing pedal pressure (to just below the skid point) as the airplane decelerates. In the event of a reduction in retardation being felt while exercising maximum braking, pedal force must be fully released to allow the skidding wheels to regain full rolling speed before further application of brakes.

Note

Rough runways tend to emphasize the skip or bounce characteristics of the airplane which are caused by relatively stiff struts. To preclude the possibility of locking a wheel while momentarily off the ground, use light braking until the airplane is solidly on the ground and all skipping has ceased.

WARNING

If it is suspected that the brakes have been used excessively, and are in a heated condition, the airplane should not be taxied into a crowded parking area. Peak temperatures occur in the wheel brake assembly from 5 to 15 minutes after maximum braking.

CAUTION

If it is suspected that the brakes have been used excessively, and are in a heated condition, the airplane should not be taxied into a crowded parking area. Peak temperatures occur in the wheel brake assembly from 5 to 15 minutes after maximum braking. To prevent brake fire and possible tire explosion, the specified procedures for cooling brakes should be followed. It is recommended that a minimum of 15 minutes elapse between landings where the landing gear remains extended in the airstream, and a minimum of 30 minutes between landings where the landing gear has been retracted to allow sufficient time for cooling. Additional time should be allowed for cooling if brakes are used for steering, crosswind taxiing operation, or a series of landings. To minimize brake fuzing when brake-stored energy is known to be high, do not come to a full stop and hold brakes hard on; instead, allow aircraft to roll freely as much as possible.

EMERGENCY OPERATION

If utility hydraulic system fails, the airplane can still be stopped by utilizing accumulator brake pressure. This can be accomplished by depressing the brakes and applying a constantly increasing brake pressure. Do not pump the brakes as this rapidly depletes the accumulator pressure. If accumulator brake pressure fails to stop the airplane, utilize the emergency air brake system. The system meters air in proportion to pilot effort and does not provide differential braking. In most cases asymmetrical braking is prevalent when utilizing the air brakes due to runway crown, crosswinds, and unequal brake torque; however, the manual hydraulic brakes (because of fluid trapped between the brake valves and brakes) are still capable of furnishing flow and pressure to accomplish differential braking.

WARNING

Do not use emergency air brakes when a known hot brake condition exists. Some combustible substance such as oil, grease, hydraulic fluid etc, may be present in the wheel assembly. The combination of heat and the introduction of 3000 psi compressed air sets up a highly explosive combustible situation.

CAUTION

There is a noticeable time lag between pulling the emergency brake handle and braking action. Failure to take the system delay into consideration often results in blown tires.

LIMITATIONS

There are no specific limitations pertaining to the brake system.

position may also be employed for intercockpit communication if the pilot's switch is set at COLD MIC. RADIO OVERRIDE is a momentary switch position. If the RIO has selected either EMER ICS or EMERG RAD and then selects RADIO OVERRIDE, a one-way conversation results. The RIO can talk to the pilot, but the pilot cannot talk to the RIO until the RIO releases his function selector switch and allows it to return to the NORMAL position.

Intercom Foot Switch (RIO)

A foot operated switch is on the left foot ramp in the RIO's cockpit. This switch is wired in parallel with the pilot's intercom switch. By depressing the foot switch, the RIO may override any of the positions selected on the radio override switch, allowing intercom transmission without the necessity of releasing other manual controls.

Emergency Amplifier Selector Knobs

The emergency amplifier selector knobs are three-position rotary type switches and are in the center of both intercom control panels. The operator uses these controls to bypass an amplifier if it should go dead. Both operators may have occasion to switch to one of the emergency settings at the same time. In certain instances of amplifier failure, this arrangement is necessary to maintain intercockpit communication. There are three possible settings for each control. NOR is used when both amplifying stages in the respective control boxes are functioning properly. The other two positions for each control are EMER RAD and EMER ICS, which are used when it is desired to bypass a faulty or dead amplifier. On aircraft after AFC 433 (Part II) the emergency amplifier selector knobs have positions of B/U, NORM, and EMER. If the headset amplifier in either ICS station fails, place the switch to the B/U (back-up) position in the cockpit with the defective station. This switches from the normal headset amplifier to the back-up amplifier and restores normal operation. If selecting B/U does not restore ICS operation, select EMER (emergency). Audio from the operative station is then connected directly to the back-up headset amplifier in the defective station. The volume control on the station with EMER selected has no effect on the audio level. The switch is left in NORM (normal) if the amplifiers in both ICS stations are operating normally.

Note

If both amplifier selector knobs are in an emergency position (EMER RAD and/or EMER ICS), and both intercom volume control knobs are above 75% of their volume range, a loud squeal is heard in both headsets. To eliminate the squeal, turn either volume control knob to a position below 75% of its volume range.

Microphone Button

The microphone buttons are used to connect microphone outputs to the UHF transmitter. The pilot's

microphone button is on the inboard throttle grip, the RIO's microphone button is a foot-operated switch on the right foot ramp. When either crewmember wishes to transmit, he depresses the microphone button, and the output from the microphone is fed into the transmitter. The positioning of other controls in no way affects the transmitting operation from either cockpit.

MAIN RECEIVER-TRANSMITTER

The main receiver-transmitter is designed to broadcast and receive UHF frequencies in a range of 225.0 to 399.9 MHz for air-to-air or air-to-ground communications. Complete control over the operation of the main radio receiver-transmitter can be maintained by either the pilot or the RIO through the comm-nav group control panels (figures A-1 and A-2, appendix A), in each cockpit. The pilot's comm-nav group control panel is on the right console; the RIO's panel is on the left console. The comm-nav group control panel provides controls for the operation of the main receiver-transmitter on any of 1750 manually selected frequencies, on any of 18 preset channels plus a guard channel, and for ADF operation with associated direction finder equipment.

Note

On aircraft after AFC 331, provisions for the installation of the speech security system (KY-28) are provided. This system can have a direct effect on UHF transmission and reception. Refer to NAVAIR 01-245FDB-1T(A) for detailed description of the system and its operational application.

MAIN RECEIVER-TRANSMITTER CONTROLS

The controls for the operation of the main receiver-transmitter are in the middle of each comm-nav group control panel (figures A-1 and A-2, appendix A). The controls consist of manual communication frequency controls, communication channel selector knob, function switch and volume control knob.

Communication Frequency Controls (Comm Freq MC)

Three control knobs at the top of the comm-nav group control panel are used to manually adjust the operating frequency of the radio receiver-transmitter when the communication channel control knob is in the M position. When the communication channel control knob is not in the M position, the communication frequency control knobs do not affect the operating frequency.

Communication Channel Control (Comm Chan)

The communication channel control knob is at the upper left on the comm-nav group control panel. This knob when rotated selects 18 preset channels of operation that are shown in the UHF remote channel indicator window. There is also an M position which permits the operator to select manually the operating frequency and a G position, which permits operation on the guard frequency of 243.0 MHz.

UHF Remote Channel Indicator

A remote channel indicator is on each instrument panel (figures A-1 and A-2, appendix A). This enables the crewmember to dial a channel with the communication channel control knob without shifting his vision from the instrument panel.

Function Switch

The function switch is in the right center of the comm-nav group control panel. The switch is labeled UHF COMM and AUX REC. Only the UHF COMM portion of the switch is discussed at this time. The switch consists of five positions described below.

STBY	- Only filament power is applied to the radio receiver-transmitter to warmup the set.
T/R	- Radio receiver-transmitter is activated for transmitting and receiving operations. The set is normally on receive until the microphone button is depressed.
T/R+G	- Radio receiver-transmitter operates on transmit or receive within the 225.0 to 399.9 MHz range; in addition, the guard receiver is turned on.
ADF+G	- Radio receiver-transmitter operates with the receiver-ADF-power supply unit and the antenna unit in an automatic direction finder system. This position also furnishes guard channel reception.
ADF	- Radio receiver-transmitter operates with the receiver-ADF-power supply unit and the antenna unit in an automatic direction finder system.

AUXILIARY RECEIVER

An auxiliary receiver operates in conjunction with the main radio receiver-transmitter under normal conditions, and operates an emergency receiver if a power failure occurs in the main radio receiver-transmitter. The auxiliary receiver can be used as a conventional radio receiver for reception of AM radio signals in the frequency range of 265.0 to 284.9 MHz or as an ADF receiver, for reception of radio signals in the same frequency range. A guard receiver preset to 243.0 MHz is contained within the auxiliary receiver. Guard channel can be monitored when the AUX REC portion of the function switch is placed to GRD. The auxiliary receiver can be placed in either function by operation of the controls on either comm-nav group control panel. The auxiliary receiver contains 20 channels preset to frequencies within the receiver's range. Channel selection is also accomplished by operation of the aux chan control on one of the comm-nav group control panels. The function switch controls the functions of the auxiliary receiver equipment and provides for either the auxiliary receiver or the main radio receiver-transmitter to be operating as an ADF receiver while the other equipment is operating as a voice receiver. Audio can be heard on the auxiliary receiver when in ADF. The

direction finder group of the auxiliary receiver provides the pilot with continuous indication of the direction of radio frequency signals intercepted by either the radio receiver-transmitter or the auxiliary receiver which is used in conjunction with the ADF system. These receivers function to intercept amplitude modulated and unmodulated signals in the frequency range of 225 through 400 MHz and 265 through 284.9 MHz depending on which receiver is used. The bearing pointer on the horizontal situation indicator, with ADF selected, points to the station selected and the bearing is relative to the aircraft heading. Necessary primary power, 115 vac, is applied to the auxiliary receiver when the electrical system is energized.

AUXILIARY RECEIVER CONTROLS

The controls for the operation of the auxiliary receiver are in the middle of each comm-nav group control panel. The controls consist of a channel control knob, volume control and function switch.

Channel Controls

The operating channels for the auxiliary receiver are selected by operation of the auxiliary channel control knob on the left side of each comm-nav group control panel. The channel, selected by rotating the control, is shown in the window directly to the left of the auxiliary channel control knob.

Volume Control

The auxiliary receiver volume control knob is directly below the auxiliary channel window on the comm-nav group controls. Operating this control varies the audio input level to the intercom loop.

Function Switch

The function switch labeled UHF COMM-AUX REC is at the right side of the group controls. This control provides facilities for selection of the various modes of operation of the auxiliary receiver and the main radio receiver-transmitter. As the control is rotated, different modes of operation are selected for the radio receivers. There are five possible control settings for each receiver. One control position for one receiver corresponds to a control position for the other. The auxiliary receiver functions are selected from the positions at the bottom of the dial. These positions are GRD, CMD, ADF, ADF and STBY.

GRD	- When the function switch is positioned so that the auxiliary receiver setting is at GRD, the main receiver is in ADF. This allows the operator to monitor the guard channel frequency and maintain ADF operation at the same time.
CMD	- When the auxiliary receiver is set at CMD, a command antenna is connected to the auxiliary receiver. The main receiver is positioned in ADF+G.

ADF — The auxiliary receiver is placed in ADF operation at either of two positions. At one of these switch settings, the ADF antenna is connected to the auxiliary receiver and the radio receiver-transmitter is set at T/R+G for receiving, transmitting and monitoring the guard channel frequency. When the auxiliary receiver function switch is placed in the other ADF position, the main receiver is positioned to T/R. This setting connects the ADF antenna to the auxiliary receiver and at the same time the main receiver is set for receiving and transmitting operations.

STBY — When the auxiliary receiver is set for standby the main receiver is also positioned at standby.

COMM COMMAND CONTROL

A communication command push button control marked COMM CMD is in the lower left corner of each comm-nav group control panel. Operation of this push button allows the operator to take or relinquish command of the communication system. A green light in the center of the push button lights when the operator has control of the radio receiver-transmitter, the auxiliary receiver and the ADF functions. When one of the operators has command of the communication functions, pressing the communication command button on the comm-nav group control panel transfers the communication functions to the other operator. If one of the operators does not have control of the communication functions, pressing the communication command button takes control away from the other operator. The volume controls on each comm-nav group control panel are independent and are not affected by the take command functions.

Note

To prevent an inadvertent change of channels on the user's set, do not switch UHF channel when other operator is utilizing the UHF communications transmitter.

ANTENNA SELECTOR SWITCH

A two-position antenna selection switch is in each cockpit. The pilot's antenna switch is on the left console outboard of the throttles; the antenna switch for the RIO is on the RIO's instrument panel. The switch positions are UPR and LWR and are used to select one of two communication antennas to be used with the command communications set. The circuitry of the anntenna selection switch is wired through the take command relay. Therefore, whoever has command of the comm-nav group control panel has command of the antenna selection switch. All aircraft after AFC 288 have the data link system installed. In these aircraft, the antenna selection switch is on the cockpit lights/data link control panel in the rear cockpit on the left side. When the antenna selection switch is placed to UPR, the upper communications antenna is selected for UHF communica-

tions, and the lower antenna is selected for the data link system. Placing the antenna switch to LWR selects the lower communications antenna for UHF communications and the upper antenna for the data link system.

TACAN (TACTICAL AIR NAVIGATION) SYSTEM

The tacan system gives bearing and distance information at ranges up to approximately 196 miles (depending on aircraft altitude) from an associated ground or shipboard radio beacon. It determines the identity of the beacon and indicates the dependability of the beacon signal. It also provides deviation indication from a selected course. The tacan system employs UHF radio frequencies, the propagation of which is virtually limited to line of sight distances. The maximum distances from the beacon at which reliable tacan signals can be obtained depend on the altitude of the aircraft and the height of the beacon antenna. Tacan information is presented on the horizontal situation indicator and the attitude director indicator in the pilot's cockpit (refer to Navigation Equipment, this section) and on the No. 2 needle of the bearing-distance-heading indicator in the RIO's cockpit. The BDHI is a conventional RMI display with the additional feature of displaying distance to a tacan station. The No. 2 bearing pointer is the tacan needle and indicates magnetic heading to the tacan station. The No. 1 pointer provides a magnetic heading to the selected UHF station when the compass is properly aligned. The BDHI indicator is also capable of displaying distance information to a tacan station. When the received signal is unreliable, the red warning flag partly obscures the distance indicators from view and the word OFF in black letters appears in the window. The units digit indicator dial is divided into 1/2 mile increments. The BDHI is controlled strictly from the aft cockpit by a CNI-NAV COMP switch on the aft instrument panel. Switch positions selected on the mode-bearing distance selector panel in the pilot's cockpit have no effect on BDHI operation.

TACAN CONTROLS

All operating controls for the tacan system are on the lower third of the comm-nav group control panels. The controls and their functions are as follows:

Function Switch

The function switch is a three-position rotary switch whose positions are marked STBY, REC and T/R.

STBY — Only filament and blower power are being supplied to the system receiver and transmitter.

REC — The receiver portion of the system is in operation and only bearing information is furnished to the BDHI.

T/R — The airborne transmitter sends a signal to the beacon and receives a signal which is used to determine the aircraft distance from the beacon.

Navigation Channel Controls

Two control knobs, one to the right and one to the left of the navigation channel window, permit channel selection. The left knob selects the tens and hundreds figures of the operating channel. The right knob selects the units figures of the operating channel. The dial system is numbered from 0 to 129, each number from 1 to 126 represents a specific pair (transmitting and receiving) of frequencies. Numbers 0, 127, 128 and 129 on the channel dial are not usable.

Volume Control Knob

The volume control knob is used to adjust the volume of the audio identification signal received from the beacon. The identification signal, audible in the pilot's headphones when they are connected into the intercom system, consists of a two or three letter tone signal in International Morse Code. The identification signal is normally transmitted by the beacon every 30 seconds.

Nav Take Command Control

The navigation command push button transfers control of UHF navigation (tacan) functions from one cockpit to the other. When the green light in the center of the navigation command button in one cockpit illuminates, command of the tacan functions has been obtained in that cockpit. Specifically, the navigation channel control and function switch in that cockpit are effective. The navigation volume control is effective in both cockpits regardless of the take command situation.

IFF/SIF INTEGRATED RADAR IDENTIFICATION SYSTEM - AIRPLANES 148363f THRU 153070ab

The radar identification system provides automatic identifications of the airplane in which it is installed when challenged by surface or airborne radar sets. Supplementary purposes are to provide momentary identification of position upon request, and to transmit a coded response to indicate an emergency. In operation, the radar identification system receives coded interrogation signals and transmits coded response signals to the source of the challenge. Proper reply indicates the target is friendly. Three modes of operation are provided for interrogation or response to interrogation signals. They are mode 1, mode 2 and mode 3, which are used for security identification, personal identification and traffic identification, respectively.

Note

- There are three possible configurations of IFF/SIF in the aircraft. Since all three configurations use identical cockpit controls, it is not possible to determine which configuration is installed from the inside of the cockpit. The three configurations are: an IFF/SIF unit with a basic KY-311/ASQ-19 Coder-Receiver-Transmitter installed, and IFF/SIF unit with a modified KY-311/ASQ-19 Coder-Receiver-Transmitter installed and an IFF/SIF unit with a KY-532/ASQ-19

Coder-Receiver-Transmitter installed. The modified KY-311 provides the additional SIF capability of responding to mode 3 interrogations when using the I/P switch. It also provides for automatic mode 3 code 77 emergency replies when the master switch is placed to the EMERGENCY position or when either or both crewmembers eject. All KY-311 with AVC 170 installed posses this additional SIF capability. The KY-532, which eliminates the IFF feature, provides the additional SIF capabilities of responding to mode 1, 2 and 3 interrogations when using the I/P switch, and provides emergency replies on modes 1, 2 and 3 when the master switch is placed to EMERGENCY.

- On aircraft with KY-311 the radar identification system can be preset for Mark X operation. In Mark X operations the SIF (Selective Identification Feature) is eliminated rendering the SIF code selector switches inoperative. However, the set still operates in all three IFF modes of operation providing limited preset interrogation and response signals.

Radar Identification Controls

Two control panels marked IFF and SIF are on the pilot's right console. No SIF or IFF control panels are in the aft cockpit. The control panels contain the system master switch, two mode switches, two code selector switches and an I/P switch. The five-position master switch is marked OFF, STBY, LOW, NORM and EMERGENCY. In STBY, the system is inoperative but ready for instant use. In LOW, the system operates with reduced sensitivity and replies only in the presence of strong interrogations. In NORM, the system operates in full sensitivity which provides maximum performance. In EMERGENCY, a special coded signal is transmitted to indicate an emergency. The emergency IFF (and mode 3, code 77 after AVC 170) is tripped automatically upon ejection of either or both seats (regardless of any switch position-no warm up required). The mode 2 switch placarded MODE 2 and OUT, is used by the pilot for personal identification. The mode 3 switch, placarded MODE 3 and OUT, is used for traffic identification. The identification of position (I/P) switch, placarded I/P, OUT and MIC, is utilized by the pilot upon request, to provide momentary identification of position when held in the spring-loaded I/P position. When placed in MIC, the identification of position signals are transmitted while the microphone button is held pressed. Two rotary code selector switches are used to select the specified code signals to be used in mode 1 and mode 3 operation. The specified coded signals to be used in mode 2 are preset on the ground and cannot be changed in flight.

IDENTIFICATION SYSTEM-IFF-AIRPLANES 153912ab AND UP

The identification system provides automatic identifications of the airplane in which it is installed when challenged by surface or airborne radar sets. Supplementary purposes are to provide momentary identification of position upon request, and to transmit a coded response to indicate an emergency. In operation, the identification system receives coded interrogation signals and transmits coded response signals to the source of the challenge. Proper reply indicates the target is friendly. Three modes of operation are provided for interrogation or response to interrogation signals. They are mode 1, mode 2, and mode 3/A, which are used for security identification, personal identification and traffic identification, respectively. Controls are provided on the IFF control panel for a fourth mode, mode 4. The codes for mode 1 and 3/A can be set in the cockpit, but the code for mode 2 must be set on the ground. Mode 2 can be set from code 0000 to code 7777.

IFF CONTROLS AND INDICATORS

The controls and indicators for operation of the IFF are on the IFF control panel (figure A-1, appendix A). The controls consist of the MASTER switch, the mode 1, mode 2, mode 3/A and mode 4 selector switches, the mode 1 and mode 3/A code selectors, the identification of position switch, the mode 4 indication switch (with positions AUDIO, OUT, LIGHT), the mode 4 function switch (with positions ZERO, B, A, HOLD), the monitor-radiation test enable switch, and the mode C selector switch (labeled MC-ON-OUT). On aircraft after AFC 353, the IFF system contains mode C and mode 4 operating capabilities. The IFF indicators are on the IFF control panel (figure A-1, appendix A). They consist of the self test reply indicator light (labeled TEST), and the mode 4 reply indicator light (labeled REPLY). The TEST light is operative on aircraft after AFC 353. There is also an IFF and an ALT ENCODER OUT light on the telelight panel on the front cockpit right vertical panel. The IFF light is inoperative until mode 4 is made operative; however, it illuminates with the warning light test switch. The ALT ENCODER OUT light illuminates if the altitude reporting signal from the altitude encoder unit is unreliable.

Master Switch

The master switch is a five position rotary switch which controls the operation of the entire system as indicated below:

OFF	Identification system deenergized.
STBY	Full power supplied to the system, but with interrogations blocked.
LOW	Causes identification system to operate with reduced sensitivity.
NORM	Allows system to operate at full sensitivity.
EMER	Allows the system to respond to interrogations in modes 1, 2 and 3/A. The reply for modes 1 and 2 is the mode selected on the applicable dials, while mode 3/A transmits code 7700. Upon ejection from either cockpit emergency operation automatically becomes active.

Mode 1 Selector Switch

The three position mode 1 selector switch controls the operation of mode 1 as follows:

M-1	Self test position.
ON	Enables mode 1 for operation.
OUT	Disables mode 1.

The above functions are inoperative on aircraft before AFC 353. In these aircraft mode 1 is made operative when the master switch is in an operating mode. On aircraft after AFC 353, the ON and OUT positions are operative.

Mode 2 Selector Switch

The three position mode 2 selector switch controls operation of mode 2 as follows:

M-2	Self test position. On aircraft before AFC 353, the self test position is inoperative. On aircraft after AFC 353 the self test position illuminates the TEST light if mode 2 is operating properly.
ON	Enables mode 2 for operation.
OUT	Disables mode 2.

Mode 3/A Selector Switch

The three position mode 3/A selector switch controls operation of mode 3/A as follows:

M-3/A	Self test position. On aircraft before AFC 353 the self test position is inoperative. On aircraft after AFC 353 the self test position illuminates the TEST light if mode 3/A is operating properly.
ON	Enables mode 3/A for operation.
OUT	Disables mode 3/A.

Mode 4 Selector Switch

The two position selector switch controls the operation of mode 4 as follows:

ON	Enables mode 4 for operation.
OUT	Disables mode 4.

Mode C Selector Switch

The three position mode C selector switch controls operation of mode C as follows:

M-C	Self test position (Inoperative)
ON	Enables mode C for operation.
OUT	Disables mode C.

Mode 4 Indication Switch

This switch has positions of AUDIO, OUT, and LIGHT. In AUDIO, an audio signal indicates that mode 4 interrogations are being received, and illuminations of the mode 4 REPLY light indicate when replies are transmitted. In LIGHT, the mode 4 REPLY light illuminates when mode 4 replies are transmitted and no audio is present. In OUT, both light and audio indications are inoperative.

Mode 4 Function Switch

This switch has positions of ZERO, B, A, and HOLD. In the A position, the system's transponder responds to mode 4 interrogations from an interrogator using the same setting as set into the A position. In the B position, interrogations from an interrogator using the same code setting as that set into the B position are answered. The code settings for the A and B positions are inserted before flight. Both code settings can be zeroized at any time by placing the mode 4 function switch to ZERO. The HOLD position on the mode 4 function switch is not used in flight.

Monitor-Radiation Test Switch

This switch has positions of RAD TEST, MON, and OUT. The switch is placed to the OUT position and is not used during flight.

Mode 1 and Mode 3/A Code Selectors

The mode 1 code selector is used to select mode 1 codes from 00 to 73. The mode 3/A code selector is used to select mode 3/A codes from 0000 to 7777.

Self Test

To self test mode 2 or mode 3/A, hold the respective switch to the upper position with the other mode switches in OUT. If the receiver and transmitter are operating properly, the green TEST light illuminates. Mode 1 and mode C cannot be self tested.

Identification of Position Switch

The identification switch is a three position toggle switch utilized by the pilot upon request to provide momentary identification of position. The three positions are as follows:

IDENT	Allows the system to respond with identification of position replies in all modes that are being used. The response is continued for a 15 to 30 second duration after the switch is released.
OUT	Disables identification of position capability.
MIC	Same as positioning the switch to IDENT, except that the UHF microphone button must be keyed.

AIR-TO-AIR INTERROGATOR SET AN/APX-76(XN-1)

For aircraft having air-to-air interrogator set AN/APX-76 (XN-1) installed, refer to NAVAIR 01-245FDB-1T(A).

AIR-TO-AIR INTERROGATION SYSTEM (GAINTIME)

The air-to-air interrogation system is installed in aircraft with AFC 290. For description and operation of the system refer to NAVAIR 16-45-1181.

NORMAL OPERATION

INTERCOM SYSTEM

The intercom system is placed in operation without additional switching as soon as the aircraft receives electrical power. The controls should be set in the following manner to check the equipment before take-off:

```
Pilot's Controls
  Switch                            Position
  Function Selector Switch . . HOT MIC
  Emergency Amplifier
    Selector Switch . . . . . . NOR
  Volume . . . . . . . . . . Rotate Clockwise

Radar Intercept Officer's Controls
  Switch                            Position
  Function Select Switch . . . NORMAL
  Emergency Amplifier
    Selector Switch . . . . . . NOR
  Volume . . . . . . . . . . Rotate Clockwise
```

With controls positioned as stated, check the duplex operation of the equipment by talking into the microphones. Rotate the VOL controls to insure that they are operating properly. Switch to EMER ICS, NOR, EMER RAD to ensure that they are mechanically sound. The radio override functions of the interphone should be checked by each operator. To check the equipment properly, the operators should not switch to RADIO OVERRIDE at the same time, since reduction in the volume for the radio receivers is accomplished in both headsets when only one of the operators selects RADIO OVERRIDE. Therefore, each control must be positioned at different times to check the radio override circuitry in each unit. With all four of the amplifying stages working and the intercom system functioning normally, the pilot and RIO should place their function selector switches in HOT MIC and NORMAL respectively. Both the pilot's and RIO's emergency amplifier switches should be placed in NOR and the volume controls on each panel should be set as desired. No further switching is necessary to operate in duplex. The system is turned off when aircraft electrical power is removed.

COMMUNICATIONS TRANSMITTER AND RECEIVERS

With aircraft power activated, the main UHF radio receiver-transmitter and the auxiliary UHF receiver are placed into operation by moving the function selector switch out of STBY. The desired frequencies for the functions selected can be obtained by utilizing the aux chan, comm chan and comm freq controls. A quick check to prove the main UHF equipment is operating at an adequate power level should be made by performing a receiver-transmitter check with the base control tower on several frequencies. The auxiliary receiver should be checked by selecting the CMD position and rotating the auxiliary volume control fully clockwise. A live sound should be heard on the headsets. A further check may be made by receiving from the control tower, if deemed necessary. The ADF loop should be preflight checked with each of the two receivers utilized in the system, the main radio receiver-transmitter, and the auxiliary receiver. Place the function switch on either comm-nav group control panel to the main receiver ADF or the main receiver ADF +G. Tune the main radio receiver transmitter to the frequency of a station of known geographical location by use of the main channel frequency selector control knobs, and adjust the main volume control knob to obtain a comfortable listening level in the headset. Select ADF of the BRG/DIST switch on the mode selector control in the front cockpit, and select CNI of the cni-nav-comp switch in the rear cockpit. Observe the bearing pointer on the HSI and the No. 1 needle on the BDHI, and note that they indicate the approximate direction of the signal relative to the airplane heading. Place the function switch in the auxiliary receiver ADF position and tune the auxiliary receiver to a station of known geographical location by use of the auxiliary channel control knob. Note that the needle on the indicator indicates the approximate direction of the signal relative to the airplane heading. Adjust the auxiliary volume control to obtain a comfortable listening level. (A 100 Hertz buzz should be heard in the headset while the antenna is searching.) A preflight check may also be accomplished by utilizing the transmitting facilities in the control tower if the aircraft is taxied to a remote point of the airstrip.

Note

- When in the gear down configuration, the ADF antenna pattern is distorted because of the close proximity of the nose landing gear door to the antenna. Therefore, the ADF system should not be relied upon as a primary navigational aid while in the gear down configuration.

- When used on the ground, bearing error in the system will likely exceed 30° and therefore no accuracy tolerances are established for this condition.

Because of ADF pattern distortion at the higher frequencies of the UHF band, sizable bearing inaccuracies can be expected at frequencies above 310 MHz. Precise navigational operation should be limited to assigned ADF frequencies (265 to 284.9 MHz) when using the auxiliary receiver, and to frequencies lower than 310 MHz when using the main receiver.

TACAN

Starting and stopping of the tacan system is controlled by the function switch. When this switch is in STBY, only the equipment filament and blower are on. When the switch is in either REC or T/R, the equipment is ready to operate. To operate the tacan receiver and transmitter, set the function switch to REC if only bearing information is desired, or to T/R if both bearing and distance information is desired. Allow a warm-up period of approximately 90 seconds. Turn the navigation selector dials to the channels of a tacan station within operating range. Place the bearing/distance selector switch on the pilot's instrument panel in TACAN, and the cni-nav-comp switch in the aft cockpit in TACAN. Bearing and distance to the tacan station are displayed on the HSI and BDHI. The identification signal for the selected tacan station should be heard in the headphones. Should the tacan information be unreliable, the vertical director warning flag, and the vertical displacement warning flag will come into view on the ADI.

Note

The tacan system may occasionally be subject to a false lock-on, which results in an erroneous bearing indication. Due to an inherent characteristic of the system, the error occurs in multiples of 40°. Therefore, when using the tacan cross check for false lock-on with ground radar, airborne radar, dead reckoning, or other available means. These cross checks are especially important when switching channels. If a false lock-on is suspected, switch to another channel, check it for correct bearing and then switch back to the desired channel. If a false lock-on still persists, utilize other equipment or aids available.

RADAR IDENTIFICATION SYSTEM - AIRPLANES 148363f THRU 153070ab

To operate the system rotate the master switch to the norm position and set the mode 2 and mode 3 switches IN unless otherwise directed. Mode 1 (security identification feature) is automatically operated when the master switch is in NORM. Set the mode 1 and mode 3 code selector switches as directed. The system is now ready for interrogation or response signals. In the event of an emergency, press master switch dial, rotate switch to EMERGENCY, and set mode 3 in operation on code 77. The set automatically transmits a special coded distress signal in response to interrogation.

Note

When placing the master switch of an IFF/SIF unit containing an unmodified KY-311 to EMERGENCY, the unit responds to mode 1 interrogations only. Normally, only GCI sites search on mode 1 and traffic control radars normally search on mode 3 only. Therefore, in aircraft which do not have AVC 170, you must squawk EMERGENCY mode 3 code 77 for maximum radar coverage. IFF/SIF units with modified KY-311 and KY-532 installed automatically give emergency replies to mode 3 interrogations when the master switch is in EMERGENCY.

The OFF position removes all power except filament voltage which is supplied any time the aircraft bus system is energized. Therefore, the unit operates immediately upon selecting LOW or NORMAL.

IDENTIFICATION SYSTEM-IFF-AIRPLANES 153912ab AND UP

To operate the system, rotate the master switch to NORM and set the mode 1, mode 2, and mode 3/A switches OUT unless otherwise directed. On aircraft before AFC 353, mode 1 (security identification feature) is automatically made operative when the master switch is in an operating mode. On aircraft after AFC 353, the ON and OUT positions are operative. Set the mode 1 and mode 3/A code selector dials as directed. The system is now ready for interrogation and response signals. In the event of an emergency, rotate the master switch to EMER. The reply for modes 1 and 2 are special emergency signals of the codes selected on the applicable dials, while mode 3/A reply is special emergency signal of code 7700. The same special emergency signals are replied when either or both crewmembers eject. For I/P switch operation, place the I/P switch in IDENT, or place it in MIC and key the UHF microphone. The IFF system responds with special I/P signals.

EMERGENCY OPERATION

| CAUTION |

Operation of the CNI while utilizing ram air with the RADAR CNI COOL OFF light illuminated, could affect equipment life and/or reliability. If the RADAR CNI COOL OFF light does not go out when the reset button is pressed, place the communication transmitter and receiver, the tacan and the IFF/SIF to STBY and operate only when necessary.

INTERCOM SYSTEM

Each cockpit's ICS unit is equipped with two amplifiers, both of which are used during normal duplex (hot mic) operation. An emergency switch with EMER ICS, EMER RAD and NOR positions is provided on the ICS panels. These selections enable an operator to bypass a faulty or dead amplifier in his unit. Assuming the pilot has selected HOT MIC, the operation during the various emergency selections is as follows:

Pilot's Switch Position	RIO's Switch Position	Resulting ICS Operation
NOR	NOR	Normal hot microphone
EMER ICS	NOR	Normal hot microphone
NOR	EMER ICS	Pilot's microphone is hot. RIO must actuate radio override switch to transmit on ICS. Foot button inoperative.

NOR	EMER RAD	Pilot's microphone is hot. RIO must actuate radio override switch to transmit on ICS. Foot button inoperative.

If both pilot's and RIO's intercom systems are in NOR operation, and the pilot then selects COLD MIC on the function switch, actuation of either front or rear seat radio override switches or front or rear seat ICS mic switches opens the system to HOT MIC operation from both cockpits. If it is necessary for both front and rear seat operators to select an emergency position, rear seat emergency conditions prevail. In addition, under NOR operation, both front and rear cockpit ICS microphone switches perform the same function as the radio override switches, reducing UHF volume.

Note

Even though the pilot's function selector switch is set at COLD MIC, the RIO may talk and listen to the pilot if he switches to RADIO OVERRIDE, or depresses the foot operated ICS switch. This is the only instance where duplex operation may be maintained when the pilot is not at HOT MIC. This switching arrangement normally is not used for intercockpit communication, since the pilot is usually at HOT MIC regardless of the settings of the other controls and the RADIO OVERRIDE settings are momentary switch positions.

On aircraft after AFC 433 (Part II), the emergency amplifier selector knobs have positions of B/U, NORM, and EMER. If the headset amplifier in either ICS station fails, place the switch to B/U (back-up) in the cockpit with the defective station. This switches from the normal headset amplifier to the back-up amplifier and restores normal operation. If selecting B/U does not restore ICS operation, select EMER (emergency). Audio from the operative station is then connected directly to the back-up headset amplifier in the defective station. The volume control on the station with EMER selected has no effect on the audio level. The switch is left in NORM (normal) if the amplifiers in both ICS stations are operating normally.

COMMUNICATIONS TRANSMITTER AND RECEIVERS

A warning light labeled EMER POWER is at the bottom of each comm nav group control panel. This light only informs the crewmember that a failure has occurred, but does not identify the type of failure. If the light illuminates, the crewmember by observation and operation should determine what equipment is still available. Transition from normal to emergency operation is automatic and is caused by a malfunction in one of the major power sources, except for the case when the ram air turbine is extended manually. The following is a list of affected equipment for a given failure:

a. A malfunction occurs in one or both of the +430 volt and +130 volt dc rectifiers in the integrated electronic central power supply.

The EMER POWER light illuminates and the tacan is inoperative. The intercom, main UHF receiver, auxiliary UHF receiver, ADF, and IFF/SIF operate normally. The main UHF transmitter operates at reduced power.

b. A malfunction occurs in the +275 volt dc rectifier.

The EMER POWER light does not illuminate; however, the tacan is inoperative. All other systems continue to operate normally.

c. A malfunction occurs in the electrical system and the ram air turbine is extended.

The EMER POWER light does not illuminate. The tacan, auxiliary UHF receiver, and ADF are inoperative. The intercom, main UHF receiver, and the IFF/SIF operate normally. The main UHF transmitter operates on reduced power.

LIMITATIONS

When the radios are operating on external power without cooling air, they are limited to 10 minutes of accumulated operation in a 1-hour span. This limitation applies to all CNI equipment except the intercom. The maximum permissible altitude with CNI equipment ON is 70,000 feet. Flight above 70,000 feet with CNI equipment ON may result in damage to equipment due to arcing.

DRAG CHUTE SYSTEM

— NOTICE —
Some illustrations referred to within this system writeup may be located in appendix A.
These illustrations are referred to, within the text, as (figure A-, appendix A).

DESCRIPTION

The airplane is equipped with a 16-foot, ring slot type parachute which is deployed after touchdown to aid in reducing landing roll distances. The drag chute may also be utilized for out of control/spin recovery. The chute is carried in a compartment within the empennage at the base of the vertical stabilizer, and is pulled into the airstream by a pilot chute when the spring-loaded compartment door is opened. The design of the attaching mechanism is such that if the compartment door opens, without operating the cockpit control handle, the chute is released and falls free of the airplane. The drag chute is retained to the airplane structure upon normal deployment. There is no breakaway fitting within the attaching mechanism.

DRAG CHUTE HANDLE

The drag chute is deployed by means of a control handle (figure A-1, appendix A) beside the left console. A cable joins the handle, the release and jettison mechanism, and the door latch mechanism. Rotating the handle aft without depressing the button on the handle, releases the door latch mechanism. The spring-loaded actuator then opens the drag chute door, and at the same time the hook lock is positioned over the drag chute attach ring. The spring-loaded pilot chute pops out, opens, and pulls out the drag chute. The drag chute is jettisoned by pulling aft on the handle to clear the detent, pressing the thumb button and lowering the handle. The release and jettison mechanism then returns to the normal position, permitting the drag chute to pull free.

NORMAL OPERATION

Normal operation of the drag chute system consists of deploying and jettisoning the drag chute. The drag chute is deployed by grasping the drag chute handle and rotating the handle aft. To jettison the drag chute, rotate handle further aft to clear detent, press the thumb button and then rotate handle full forward.

EMERGENCY OPERATION

There are no specific emergency operations pertaining to the drag chute system.

LIMITATIONS

Maximum airspeed for drag chute deployment is 200 KCAS.

DUAL CONTROLS CONFIGURATION

— NOTICE —
Some illustrations referred to within this system writeup may be located in appendix A.
These illustrations are referred to, within the text, as (figure A-, appendix A).

DESCRIPTION

Dual flight control kits are available for installation. The kit is in the aft cockpit, and can be easily removed to return the airplane to its primary configuration. The dual flight control kit provides a control stick, rudder pedals, throttle control for each engine, and an instrument panel which contains the additional instruments needed by the aft cockpit pilot. The following controls are not available in the aft cockpit: flaps, speed brakes, landing gear, arresting gear, wheel brakes, and nose wheel steering.

FLIGHT CONTROLS

The conventional type control stick and grip, controls the stabilator, ailerons and spoilers. The grip contains a trim button for aileron and stabilator trim. The rudder pedals are not linked to the brakes, nor are they adjustable. A rudder trim switch is on the instrument panel.

WARNING

The rear cockpit deck must be kept clear of obstructions that may prevent freedom of stick movement.

THROTTLES

Throttle controls for each engine are on the left side of the aft cockpit. The throttles have full throw between the range of IDLE and MIL, but they cannot be placed in the OFF or MAX positions. A microphone button with positions of ICS and UHF is the only electrical connection to the rear cockpit throttles. The dual throttle configuration incorporates a load limiter device which enables the pilot in the forward cockpit to overpower the throttle controls in the aft cockpit.

INSTRUMENTS

The dual control instrument panel contains the following instruments: vertical velocity indicator, turn and slip indicator, accelerometer, and engine tachometers. The aft cockpit instruments are powered from the same sources as those in the forward cockpit.

NORMAL OPERATION

Normal operation of the limited equipment as installed in the dual control configured airplane is the same as its counterpart installed in the forward cockpit with the exception of the throttles.

EMERGENCY OPERATION

Emergency operation of the equipment as installed in the dual control configured airplanes is the same as its counterpart installed in the forward cockpit.

LIMITATIONS

Limitations on the equipment as installed in the dual configured airplanes is the same as its counterpart installed in the forward cockpit.

EJECTION SEATS

— NOTICE —
Some illustrations referred to within this system writeup may be located in appendix A. These illustrations are referred to, within the text, as (figure A-, apprndix A).

DESCRIPTION - BEFORE AFC 307

The ejection seat system (figure 1-15) provides the occupant with a means of safe escape from the aircraft at practically all altitudes. The ejection seat is an automatic device that primarily regulates the opening of the personnel parachute at a predetermined altitude or deceleration G force which is within a safe limit for the occupant. The basic structure of the seat is the main beam assembly. The seat bucket is attached to the main beams and provides a mounting for the survival kit which forms the cushion for the occupant. The bucket is attached to the main beams by four lugs that ride in tracks on the main beams. The seat is equipped with two separate firing controls which are used to fire the seat during the ejection sequence. These two controls are the face curtain and lower ejection handle. The face curtain, above the head, provides head protection and promotes proper ejection posture during the ejection sequence. The lower ejection handle, between the occupant's knees on the seat bucket, provides an alternate method of firing the seat. Either control jettisons the canopy and fires the catapult gun. The canopy actuating cylinder guard is on the rear of the ejection seat. The top of the seat provides a mounting for the drogue chutes, face curtain, drogue chute restraining scissors and canopy interlock mecha-

nism. The drogue gun and time release mechanism are on either side of the seat near the top. Automatic operation of the seat is dependent upon these two units. They are equipped with trip rods that pull the sears from the units during the ejection sequence. A reel and snubber unit, used for retaining the upper harness, is at shoulder level and provides free forward and aft shoulder movement or, when locked, shoulder restraint during crash or bailout conditions. The seat is linked to the canopy by the interlock mechanism to prevent accidental ejection through the canopy plexiglas. Ejection through the plexiglas is not possible due to the high strength qualities of the plexiglas used on the canopy. The interlock mechanism is on the top aft portion of the seat and contains torque tubes and levers which are connected by mechanical linkage to the face curtain and lower ejection handle. The interlock mechanism is linked to the canopy by a cable. The drogue chutes, on the top of the seat stabilize the seat after ejection and deploy the personnel parachute. Three handles are on the seat bucket, which are the emergency harness release, the shoulder harness handle, and the leg restraint manual release handle. Two finger rings, adjacent to the leg restraint snubber units, release the snubbers on the leg restraint cords. The emergency harness release handle permits manual release of the harness during manual separation procedures. The shoulder harness handle controls the upper harness movement. The leg restraint manual release handle releases the leg restraint cords. A seat position switch, on the forward right side of the seat bucket, controls the seat adjusting motor.

DESCRIPTION - AFTER AFC 307

Ejection seats (figure 1-15) after AFC 307, contain a rocket pack on the bottom of the seat and an ejection sequencing system. Several of the previous components have been changed to give the ejection seat improved performance. The sequencing system (figure 1-16) provides an automatic ejection sequence if either crewmember actuates his ejection seat. This allows both crewmembers to eject in a shorter period of time, and precludes collisions between seats or a seat with a canopy. A command selector valve, installed in the aft cockpit, provides capability of selecting single ejection or dual automatic ejection. The shoulder harness snubber incorporates an inertial reel lock with a velocity retention system, and a powered retraction device to retract the crewmember to the back of his seat during ejection. The velocity retention system locks the inertial reel whenever the crewmember pitches forward faster than a predetermined rate. A hardshell container is provided for the 29.7 skysail parachute. On aircraft after ACC 176, the skysail chute is replaced by a 28 foot parachute which gives better performance at low airspeeds. The container rests on a bracket on the backrest part of the seat and is held in place by two parachute restraint straps and two lines attached to the bottom of the container. The lower lines are routed downward to loop around the sticker clips. The container separates from the crewmember after chute deployment. The catapult gun contains cartridges of reduced charge to lessen spinal forces during ejection. Except for the automatic ejection sequencing feature and small variations in the after ejection sequence, operation of the seat remains the same. Should the automatic sequencing system become inoperative, single ejection from either cockpit can be accomplished as before. Should the front canopy or both canopies be lost, the front canopy interlock block with its ejection sequence time delay is also lost. If ejection is then initiated from the front seat, this could expose the rear crewman to the front seat's rocket blast, and if conditions are right, a collision between seats could result. Should loss of the front canopy or both canopies occur, the rear crewman should be ordered to eject first by voice signal, eject light or visual signal. The front crewman can eject as soon as the rear seat leaves. With loss of the rear canopy only, normal sequenced ejection can be initiated from either cockpit.

WARNING

The rocket motor and igniter sear are under the seat. Do not use this area for stowage and exercise routine caution when performing any function in the vicinity of the rocket pack e.g., pulling rocket motor safety pin, adjusting leg restraint lines, etc. Even though a 15 pound downward pull force is required to actuate the igniter sear, inadvertent actuation could possibility occur as a result of lowering the seat on a foreign stowed object, jerking a leg restraint line that is entangled in the sear mechanism, etc.

MAIN BEAM ASSEMBLY

The main beam assembly is a strong lightweight structure built to withstand high G loads. This assembly is the main frame of the seat, and supports the seat pan, drogue chute container, drogue shackle scissors, drogue gun time release mechanism, and personnel parachute. It is composed of two vertical beams bridged by three cross-members. Each vertical beam has three slippers on the inner side. Upon ejection, these slippers slide in the guide rails of the cylinder barrel which is secured to the airplane structure. On the lower outboard side of each vertical beam are two seat bucket guide tracks. The seat bucket assembly rides in these tracks during seat height adjustment. The top latch mechanism is attached to the top of the left vertical beam and is used to secure the seat structure to the cylinder barrel.

CANOPY INTERLOCK MECHANISM

The canopy interlock mechanism is mounted across the top of the aft corners of the main beam on the seat. This mechanism provides proper sequencing between the canopy and ejection seat during the ejection sequence and also transmits the force of the face curtain ejection handle or lower ejection handle to the canopy initiator and catapult firing mechanism. The interlock block of the mechanism is connected to the canopy by a cable and is pulled from the interlock mechanism by the canopy during the ejection sequence. This block and various lever arrangements within the interlock mechanism prevent firing of the ejection seat before the canopy has been jettisoned from the aircraft. After ACC 187, a safety link connects the canopy interlock block to the ejection gun firing mechanism (interdictor) safety pin. The interdictor safety pin remains inserted in the ejection gun firing mechanism sear at all times except after canopy jettison. This gives added protection against inadvertent initiation due to foreign object damage.

Note

Although an ejection handle is pulled, ejection cannot occur if the canopy is fully opened. Since the canopy actuator is already at the top limit of its travel, the canopy will not jettison to remove the interlock block and will not allow the ejection gun to fire.

CANOPY ACTUATING CYLINDER GUARD

The canopy actuating cylinder guard protects the banana links in the event the canopy shear pin fails and the actuating cylinder falls against the seat. The guard is installed on the seat mounted initiator in the front cockpit only. After ACC 187, a guard is installed over the seat mounted initiator linkages in the rear cockpit to give added protection against inadvertent initiation due to foreign objects.

CATAPULT GUN

The catapult gun is on the ejection seat between the main beams and is attached to the bulkhead of the cockpit by two mounting lugs. The gun is attached to the seat by the seat slippers and top latch mechanism. It is used to jettison the seat from the cockpit during the ejection sequence and is operated by three pyrotechnic cartridges. The gun is composed of four major assemblies: the firing mechanism, inner tube, intermediate tube, and outer tube. During the ejection sequence, gas pressure produced by the primary and auxiliary cartridges, cause the tubes of the gun to telescope. When the inner and intermediate tubes are fully extended in the outer tube during upward travel of the seat, separation of the inner tube from the intermediate tube occurs. Separation of the tube is permitted by a shear rivet in the inner tube guide bushing which shears when the inner tube strikes the bushing. Water seals, on the gun around the primary and auxiliary cartridges and on the inner and intermediate tubes, prevent water from entering the gun during underwater ejection.

DROGUE GUN

The drogue gun is on the left side of the ejection seat headrest and is used to extract the controller drogue chute from its container 1/2 second after ejection. Upon ejection, a trip rod fixed to the airplane structure pulls a sear from the drogue gun to initiate the 1/2 second time delay. Effective airplanes 149403i and up, and all other airplanes after ACSEB 22-61, the drogue gun time delay is 1 second. After the time delay has elapsed, a cartridge is fired and the resultant gas pressures propel a piston out of the drogue gun barrel. Attached to this piston is a lanyard which pulls the controller drogue chute from its container. When deployed, the controller drogue chute pulls the stabilizer drogue chute from its container. After AFC 307, the drogue gun time delay is 0.75 second. On aircraft after ACC 56, a cocking indicator is installed on the bottom of the drogue gun. When the gun is cocked, the indicator extends approximately 1/2 inch below the gun housing with the indicator shaft showing. If the indicator is flush with the bottom of the gun housing without the shaft showing, the drogue gun is not cocked and will not fire during ejection.

DROGUE CHUTE RESTRAINING SCISSORS

The drogue chute restraining scissors are on the top of the seat, and are attached to the top crossmembers of the main beam assembly. This mechanism is used to connect the drogue chutes to the top of the seat when they are deployed during ejection. A movable jaw of the scissor is used to release the drogue chutes from the seat when the time release mechanism actuates. This mechanism allows the drogue chutes to deploy the personnel parachute when actuation of the time release mechanism occurs.

ROCKET MOTOR - AFTER AFC 307

A rocket motor is incorporated to provide a propulsion system for the rocket thrust phase of the ejection sequence. The rocket motor is on the bottom of the seat bucket and consists of a number of small

diameter combustion tubes containing solid propellant, screwed into a manifold containing nozzles. One of the combustion tubes is fitted with a mechanical firing mechanism and igniter cartridge. On aircraft after ACC 169, a fiberglass protector is installed on the bottom of the seat around the rocket sear and sear cable. The purpose of the protector is to prevent accidental pulling of the rocket sear. The protector breaks off during ejection when the sear cable becomes taut. As the ejection seat nears the end of the ejection gun stroke, a static line attached to the cockpit floor withdraws the sear from the firing mechanism allowing the springloaded firing pin to descend and fire the igniter cartridge, causing simultaneous ignition of the propellant. The rocket motor contains a thrust angle adjustment mechanism which is on the lower left side of the seat bucket. The mechanism consists of a track permanently attached to the seat beam and an arm welded to the rocket motor manifold. Seat CG location is a function of seat bucket position, so that whenever the seat is positioned with the seat positioning switch, the thrust angle adjustment mechanism changes the rocket motor angle to compensate for the new CG location. The ejection seat contains two leg guards mounted between the crewmember's legs and rocket motor. The guards prevent inadvertent contact between the crewmember's legs and the hot rocket tubes just after ejection.

ROCKET MOTOR INITIATOR-AFTER ACC 224

After ACC 224, the rocket motor sear and lanyard are removed from beneath the MK-H7 seats. Rocket motor ignition is then provided by a gas rocket motor initiator installed over the drogue gun firing mechanism on the left side of the seat. The initiator contains a cable lanyard which is attached to the drogue gun trip rod. During ejection the cable lanyard plays out from the initiator housing and, after reaching a height equivalent to rocket motor firing with the old configuration, pulls a lever assembly to withdraw a sear to fire the initiator. The initiator when fired produces a ballistic gas which is routed by a flexible hose to the rocket motor firing body on the bottom of the seat. The ballistic gas activates the firing pin in the firing body to fire the rocket motor. Removing the rocket motor sear and lanyard from the bottom of the seat makes the motor less suseptible to inadvertent firing. The new location of the initiator and cable lanyard allows for more convenient and complete visual inspection of the rocket motor initiating system. The flexible hose connecting the rocket motor firing body to the initiator is connected to the initiator by a quick disconnect. The quick disconnect must be pinned to the initiator body by a pin retained to the initiator body by a chain, or the spring-loaded disconnect will not remain connected to the initiator body. Ensure this pin is not inserted into the initiator sear.

TIME RELEASE MECHANISM

The time release mechanism is on the right side of the ejection seat headrest. Its function is to delay deployment of the personnel parachute and seat separation until the occupant has descended from the upper atmosphere, and/or has slowed enough to prevent excessive opening shock of the personnel parachute. The time release mechanism is armed upon ejection by a trip rod secured to the airplane. Initiation of the timing sequence follows immediately, providing the altitude is below 10,000 feet and the deceleration rate of the seat is less than 4.5 G. Initiation is delayed until these conditions are met. One and one-half seconds after initiation, the time release mechanism releases the drogue chutes from the restraining scissors allowing the personnel parachute to be pulled from its container. It unlocks the harness and leg restraint lines to allow the occupant to be pulled from the seat when the personnel parachute deploys. Effective airplanes 149403i and up, and all

other airplanes after ACSEB-22-61, the time release mechanism time delay is 1 3/4 seconds. After AFC 307, the 4.5 G limiter is eliminated and the time delay is set to 2 1/4 seconds. After ACC 94 or AFC 307, the time release mechanism is set to operate at 13,000 ± 1500 feet.

STICKER CLIPS

One sticker clip is on each side of the inner seat bucket. Each clip is made of spring steel with a detent point to hold the harness sticker strap lugs. The sticker clips clamp on the harness sticker strap lugs and retain the occupant in the seat until the personnel parachute blossoms and pulls the occupant clear of the seat. This prevents a collision between seat and occupant.

FACE CURTAIN EJECTION HANDLE - BEFORE AFC 307

A face curtain ejection handle (figure 1-15) is provided for normal seat ejection. The ejection handle at the top of the seat, projects forward and provides a gripping surface for the crewmember. When ejection is desired, a forward and downward pull on the handle fires an initiator. The expanding gases from the initiator operate the emergency canopy valve which directs emergency canopy system air to the canopy actuator and cockpit flooding doors actuators. The canopy opens and air loads separate the canopy from the cockpit. The canopy then removes the interlock from the seat firing mechanism. After the canopy has jettisoned, the handle can be pulled until full travel is reached. This pulls the face curtain over the face and removes the wedge-shaped sear from the ejection gun firing head, firing the main charge and ejecting the seat. Pulling the face curtain on the RIO's ejection seat also stows the RIO's radar scope, the radar set controls, and the radar antenna hand control, to provide more room for ejection from the cockpit. The canopy interlock in the firing mechanism of both seats prevents seat ejection before the canopy is jettisoned.

FACE CURTAIN EJECTION HANDLE - AFTER AFC 307

The face curtain ejection handle functions identically to the ejection handle used before AFC 307 except for the sequence of operation. When the face curtain ejection handle is pulled to the first position, the automatic ejection sequence is initiated. Previously this operation only jettisons the canopy. After canopy jettison during dual ejection initiated from either cockpit, the catapult gun can be fired by either the automatic sequencing system or the ejection handle. By continuing the pull on the handle it is possible to beat the sequencing system in firing the catapult gun. For single ejection from the rear cockpit, an additional pull on the handle is required since the catapult gun does not fire automatically. After AFC 482, the sequencing system is modified so that the rear seat fires automatically during single ejection, and that an additional pull on the ejection handle is no longer required. After AFC 500, the radar scope in the rear cockpit is moved forward and no longer stows on ejection. The radar set controls and antenna hand control still stow.

LOWER EJECTION HANDLE - BEFORE AFC 307

The lower ejection handle (figure 1-15) is on the seat bucket between the occupant's legs. This handle, connected to a cable assembly, routed under and behind the seat, initiates the same jettison and firing functions as the face curtain ejection handle. The lower ejection handle is guarded (by a plate) to prevent inadvertent actuation. The guard provides a mechanical stop to prevent the handle from moving, and must be rotated down before ejection.

LOWER EJECTION HANDLE - AFTER AFC 307

The lower ejection handle functions the same as the face curtain handle.

LOWER EJECTION HANDLE GUARD

The lower ejection handle has a guard that prevents inadvertent ejection. With the guard handle up, the lower ejection handle is locked and cannot be used for ejection. With the guard handle down, the ejection seat is armed.

COMMAND SELECTOR VALVE HANDLE - AFTER AFC 307

The command selector valve handle (figures A-1 and A-2) above the instrument panel on the left side of the aft cockpit, is used to select single or dual ejection. The vertical position of the handle is the single ejection position and the handle is normally kept in this position during flight. To select dual ejection, the handle is pulled directly out (without applying torque to handle) from the valve. During the pull, the handle rotates 90° clockwise to the locked open position through cam action.

Note

A cycle of the command selector valve handle is defined as movement from the vertical to horizontal to vertical position. Inspection of the valve will be in accordance with applicable maintenance directives.

COMMAND SELECTOR VALVE HANDLE - AFTER AFC 526

After AFC 526, the command selector valve is replaced by a more durable valve capable of 20,000 cycles. The new valve operates essentially like the old valve except for the following: the new valve is opened by applying torsion to the handle instead of a pulling action; the valve handle does not move away from the valve body when opening or closing; and the handle, if released in an intermediate position, will not always return to the vertical position, but to the vertical or 90° position depending on which side of the center of travel it is released.

SEAT POSITIONING SWITCH

The ejection seats may be adjusted vertically only. Fore and aft seat positioning is compensated for by adjusting the rudder pedals (front cockpit only). Vertical seat positioning is accomplished by actuating a momentary contact switch (figure 1-15) on the right forward side of the seat bucket. Each seat can be adjusted up or down through a total distance of 6 inches. It is not necessary to adjust the seat height before ejection; however, the seat should be low enough to afford adequate clearance between the helmet and face curtain ejection handle.

SHOULDER HARNESS LOCKING MECHANISM - BEFORE AFC 307

The shoulder harness locking mechanism is part of the seat center crossmember and is approximately at shoulder level. It is used to hold the occupant's upper torso against the seat back during all flight conditions and ejection. The mechanism consists of a strap wound on a spring-loaded reel, a snubbing unit, and an upper harness release pin. The strap wound around a spring-loaded retraction reel passes through a snubbing unit, and then through the occupant's upper harness roller fitting. The eye of the strap then returns back to the seat and through the rings to the two straps, securing the personnel parachute to the seat, and is anchored by the upper harness release pin. The snubbing unit prevents any forward movement of the strap unless the unit is unlocked. During ejection upon actuation of the time release mechanism, the upper harness release pin releases the eye fitting, thereby freeing the occupant's upper harness and the parachute securing straps.

SHOULDER HARNESS SNUBBER AND POWER RETRACTION UNIT - AFTER AFC 307

AFC 307 incorporates a new shoulder harness snubber utilizing a velocity retention system and a power retraction device. The snubber part of the unit, although somewhat different in construction from the previous snubber, functions essentially the same except that it is not used during ejection, and the automatic shoulder harness locking feature is based on rate of change of the crewmembers movement, or velocity, in the forward direction, instead of G forces on the aircraft. This modified feature is called the velocity retention system. The snubbing unit prevents any forward shoulder movement whenever it is locked. The powered retraction device retracts the shoulder harness loop straps to position and lock the crewmember's shoulder harness for ejection. The device is gas powered and can only be initiated by pulling the face curtain or lower ejection handles.

Shoulder Harness Handle - BEFORE AFC 307

The shoulder harness handle is mechanically linked to a two-position cam and must be mechanically moved to the unlocked (aft) position or the locked (forward) position. After placing the handle in the unlock position, the handle automatically returns to an unlocked neutral position. In this position, the shoulder harness automatically locks when the seat senses approximately 2.5 G in the vertical plane or approximately 4.0 G in the horizontal plane.

WARNING

The shoulder harness does not automatically lock when the harness movement exceeds a predetermined rate (such as an inertial reel system). The ejection seat must sense approximately 2.5 G vertically or approximately 4.0 G horizontally to automatically lock the shoulder harness.

Shoulder Harness Handle - AFTER AFC 307

The shoulder harness release handle has two positions, a forward or locked position, and an aft or unlocked position. The neutral position has been eliminated.

Note

Selecting the unlocked position of the shoulder harness release handle does not prevent the snubber from locking when the velocity reten-

tion system detects a high rate of velocity change of the crewmember in a forward direction. Once the shoulder harness is automatically locked, it must be manually unlocked by cycling the release handle full forward then full aft. G forces on the aircraft by itself does not lock the snubber. After AFC 217, the shoulder harness, after being locked automatically, can be unlocked by the crewmember relaxing tension on the harness, providing the shoulder harness is in the unlocked position.

LEG RESTRAINERS

A leg restraint assembly is provided on the seat to hold the occupant's legs in place and to prevent them from flailing during ejection. The leg restraint assembly consists of garters worn by the crewmember, leg restraint lines with lock pins, snubber unit, and shear fitting secured to the floor. The garters are strapped on to the legs level with the leg restraint lock-in hole, but not below the mid-calf position. The leg lines running from the shear fitting beneath the seat, pass through the snubber unit, through the garter, and then the lock pin on the leg lines, plug into the leg restraint lock-in hole on the front of the seat pan. When the seat is ejected, the slack in the leg restraint line is taken up by the upward travel of the seat, pulling the occupant's legs to the front face of the seat pan. When all the slack has been removed in the leg restraint lines, the tension of the line causes the shear fitting to fail. The occupant's legs are firmly held against the seat pan by the snubbing unit until the harness is released and the occupant is separated from the seat. Leg restraint disengage rings (figure 1-15) on the face of the seat pan are provided to adjust the amount of slack in the leg restraint lines. This slack may be adjusted by the occupant by pulling out on the appropriate finger ring. This allows more restraint line to be pulled out to provide sufficient slack. To take in excess slack, the occupant need only reach under the seat bucket and pull in the excess restraint line through the snubber unit. After AFC 307, a modified leg restraint assembly is incorporated. The modification changes the ratio of seat travel to leg restraint line withdrawal so that the legs are drawn to the seat at a faster rate during ejection. The modification also adds a spring to the leg restraint line leg lock mechanism. The spring ejects the lock pins whenever any of the following actions occur: the time release mechanism actuates, the emergency harness release handle is pulled, or the leg restraint release handle is moved to the unlocked position. After ACC 157, the leg restrainers utilize two garters on each restraint line, a calf garter worn above the flight boot and a thigh garter worn on the thigh just above the knee. Each garter contains a quick release device which allows the garter to be released and left in the aircraft without disturbing garter adjustment. The restraint line routing under the seat is changed to provide a slower leg withdrawal during ejection. The garter with the double ring is worn above the ankle and the

LEG RESTRAINERS

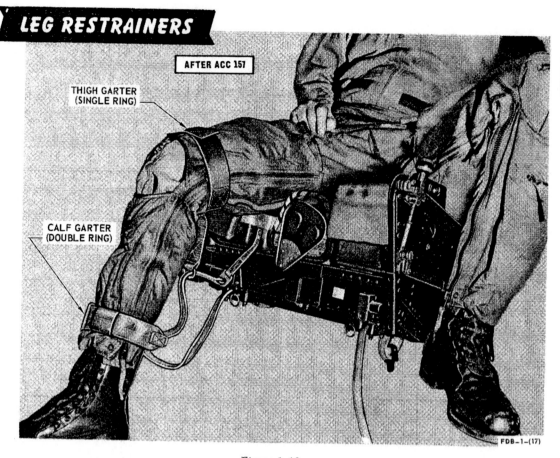

AFTER ACC 157

THIGH GARTER
(SINGLE RING)

CALF GARTER
(DOUBLE RING)

FDB-1-(17)

Figure 1-13

single ring garter is worn on the thigh. When routing the restraint lines through the garters, be certain the lines are not twisted and route first through the lower garter (route first through outboard ring of lower garter, then inboard ring) then through the thigh garter before inserting the lockpins in the snubber boxes (figure 1-13).

Leg Restraint Release Handle

The leg restraint release handle (figure 1-15) is on the left forward side of the seat bucket. When the handle is moved to the aft (unlocked) position, the lock pins on the leg lines are released from the leg lock mechanism. This allows the occupant to thread the leg lines back through the garter, enabling him to leave the seat without removing the garters.

GUILLOTINE ASSEMBLY

Components of the guillotine assembly (figure 1-15) are on the right side of the seat bucket and on the left side of the main beam assembly near the drogue gun. The guillotine is a pyrotechnically operated device used to sever the personnel parachute with-

drawal line during manual separation from the seat. The assembly consists of a firing mechanism gas line, and a guillotine blade assembly. The personnel parachute withdrawal line passes through a spring-loaded gate on the guillotine blade housing. Under normal ejection conditions, the parachute withdrawal line withdraws from the guillotine gate as the drogue chutes deploy the personnel parachute. During manual separation from the seat, guillotine actuation is accomplished when the emergency harness release handle is pulled. The action of the emergency harness release handle fires the guillotine cartridge, which supplies gas pressure to the guillotine blade assembly. The gas pressure forces the blade assembly upward, severs the withdrawal line and releases the personnel parachute from the drogue chutes.

INTEGRATED HARNESS

The integrated harness (figure 1-14) is a vest-like garment or a series of web straps worn by the crewmember. The harness, when used with the integrated type parachute, takes the place of a lap belt and shoulder harness. Both of the harness configurations have four buckles for attaching the parachute to the crewmember. The lower two buckles, when connected

INTEGRATED HARNESS

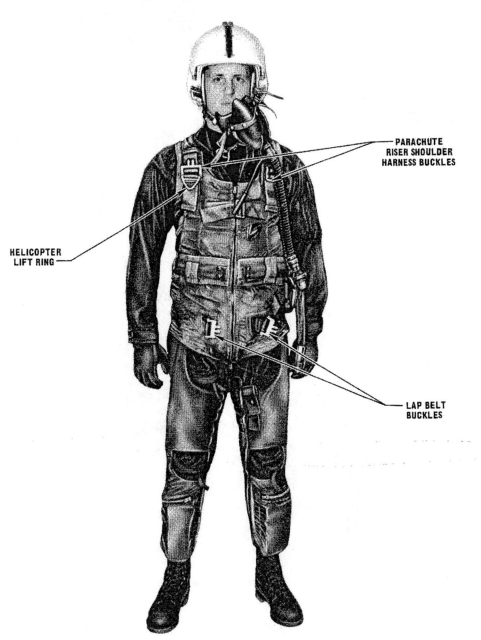

PARACHUTE
RISER SHOULDER
HARNESS BUCKLES

HELICOPTER
LIFT RING

LAP BELT
BUCKLES

FDB-1-(18)

Figure 1-14

EJECTION SEAT

TYPICAL

BEFORE AFC 307

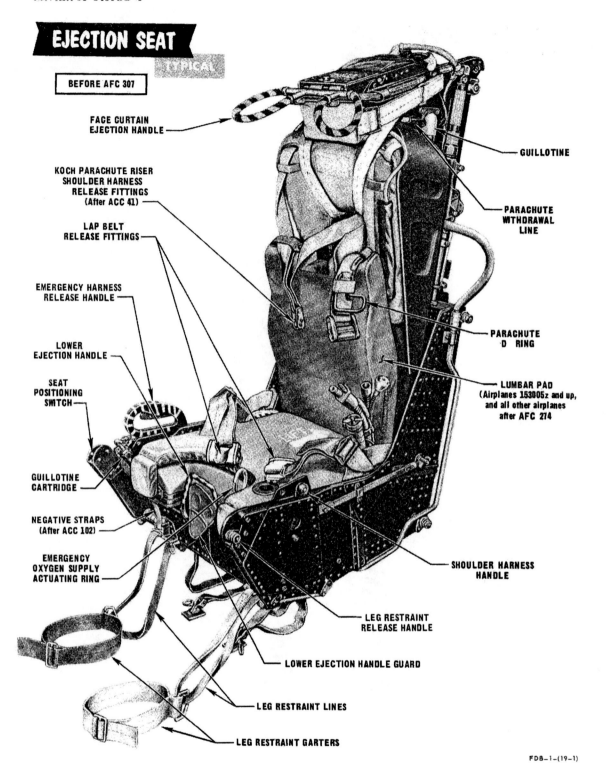

FACE CURTAIN
EJECTION HANDLE

KOCH PARACHUTE RISER
SHOULDER HARNESS
RELEASE FITTINGS
(After ACC 41)

LAP BELT
RELEASE FITTINGS

EMERGENCY HARNESS
RELEASE HANDLE

LOWER
EJECTION HANDLE

SEAT
POSITIONING
SWITCH

GUILLOTINE
CARTRIDGE

NEGATIVE STRAPS
(After ACC 102)

EMERGENCY
OXYGEN SUPPLY
ACTUATING RING

GUILLOTINE

PARACHUTE
WITHDRAWAL
LINE

PARACHUTE
D RING

LUMBAR PAD
(Airplanes 153005z and up,
and all other airplanes
after AFC 274

SHOULDER HARNESS
HANDLE

LEG RESTRAINT
RELEASE HANDLE

LOWER EJECTION HANDLE GUARD

LEG RESTRAINT LINES

LEG RESTRAINT GARTERS

FDB-1-(19-1)

Figure 1-15 (Sheet 1 of 2)

EJECTION SEAT

AFTER AFC 307

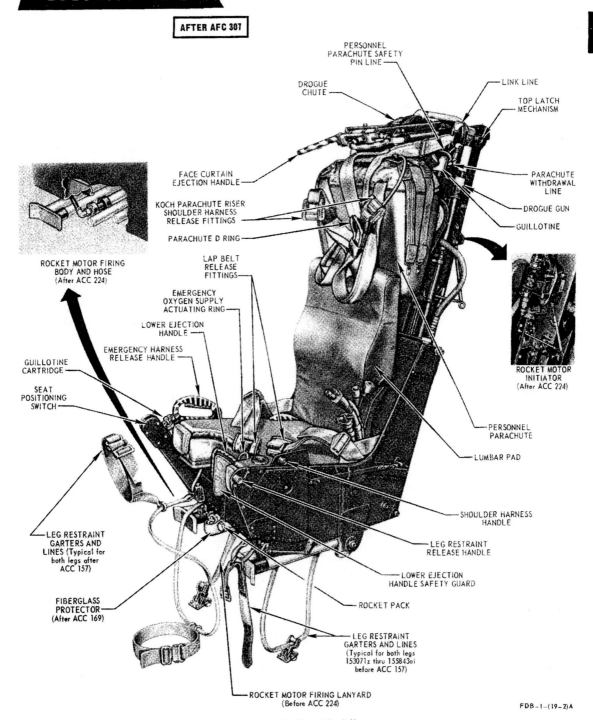

PERSONNEL
PARACHUTE SAFETY
PIN LINE

DROGUE
CHUTE

LINK LINE

TOP LATCH
MECHANISM

FACE CURTAIN
EJECTION HANDLE

PARACHUTE
WITHDRAWAL
LINE

KOCH PARACHUTE RISER
SHOULDER HARNESS
RELEASE FITTINGS

DROGUE GUN

GUILLOTINE

PARACHUTE D RING

ROCKET MOTOR FIRING
BODY AND HOSE
(After ACC 224)

LAP BELT
RELEASE
FITTINGS

EMERGENCY
OXYGEN SUPPLY
ACTUATING RING

LOWER EJECTION
HANDLE

EMERGENCY HARNESS
RELEASE HANDLE

ROCKET MOTOR
INITIATOR
(After ACC 224)

GUILLOTINE
CARTRIDGE

SEAT
POSITIONING
SWITCH

PERSONNEL
PARACHUTE

LUMBAR PAD

SHOULDER HARNESS
HANDLE

LEG RESTRAINT
GARTERS AND
LINES (Typical for
both legs after
ACC 157)

LEG RESTRAINT
RELEASE HANDLE

LOWER EJECTION
HANDLE SAFETY GUARD

FIBERGLASS
PROTECTOR
(After ACC 169)

ROCKET PACK

LEG RESTRAINT
GARTERS AND LINES
(Typical for both legs
153071z thru 155843oi
before ACC 157)

ROCKET MOTOR FIRING LANYARD
(Before ACC 224)

FDB-1-(19-2)A

Figure 1-15 (Sheet 2 of 2)

to the lap belt release fittings, which in turn are fastened to the seat, serve as the lap belt. The upper two buckles, when connected to the parachute riser-shoulder harness release fittings, which in turn are fastened to the locking reel assembly, serve as the shoulder harness. The integrated harness eliminates the need for the crewmember to wear his parachute to and from the airplane, and it eliminates a separate lap belt and shoulder harness with its inherent limited restraint capabilities.

Emergency Harness Release Handle

The emergency harness release handle (figure 1-15) is on the right side of the seat bucket. The handle is used by the occupant to manually separate from the seat in the event the automatic time release mechanism fails or in the event of ditching. Pulling aft on the handle operates a system of linkages which pulls the pins retaining the lap belt harnessing, pulls the pin from the shoulder harness, releases the leg restraint lines, and actuates the guillotine which severs the drogue chute from the personnel parachute. This handle performs the same functions as the time release mechanism. To actuate the handle, squeeze the trigger and pull up and aft. The handle is protected by a trigger that must be squeezed before the handle may be pulled. When the handle is pulled the lap belt harnessing, shoulder harness, and leg restraint lines are released. The guillotine is on the upper left side of the seat back. The emergency harness release handle should not be pulled in flight for the following reasons:

1. Actuating the emergency harness release handle creates a hazard to survival during uncontrollable flight, since negative G forces may prevent the occupant from assuming the correct ejection position.

2. Actuating the emergency harness release handle creates a hazard to survival if the pilot decides that he has insufficient altitude for ejection and is required to proceed with a forced landing. Once the emergency harness release handle has been pulled, the lap belt and shoulder harness cannot be refastened in flight.

3. Actuating the emergency harness release handle before ejection causes the occupant to separate from the seat immediately after ejection, and severe shock loads are imposed on the body.

SURVIVAL KIT

A modified PK-2 survival kit is packed within a two piece fiberglass container (figure 1-17) which, in turn, is attached to the occupant by strap-harnessing. The content of the survival kit is the same as for a normal issue PK-2, but the packing arrangement has been changed to suit the requirements of the container. The following is a list of contents of this kit:

Note

The emergency provisions included in the PK-2 survival kit are subjected to local option and may be altered at the discretion of the area commander.

Pararaft with inflation bottle, sleeve type sea anchor and lanyard
Shark repellent
Survival radio
De-salter kit (tablets)
Water storage bag
Signal mirror
Bailing sponge
50 feet of nylon line
2 packs dye marker
MK 73 Mod 0 smoke and flare signal
Canned rations
Can of sunburn ointment
Emergency code instruction sheets

All items except the pararaft and its associated gear are packed in a zipper enclosed bag which is attached to the pararaft by a lanyard. Both the pararaft and bag are packed into the survival kit container and the pararaft is attached by a lanyard to the upper half of the container. Aside from the PK-2 equipment packed in the lower half of the container, the upper half contains the emergency oxygen. A receptacle for the composite disconnect is in the left rear corner of the survival kit container, and a kit release handle is on the right rear side of the survival kit container. Pulling up on the kit releases handle, unlocks the container causing the lower container half and the life raft to drop below the crewmember on a drop line. The dropping action initiates inflation of the life raft. In the event of an over water ejection, the life raft should be inflated before entering the water since the kit release handle is accessible while still in the parachute harnessing and all survival equipment is secured to the crewmember. Should the crewmember enter the water before the survival kit release handle is pulled, the life raft can only be inflated by pulling the release handle and then reaching into the opened kit and pulling the life raft inflation bottle cable. After ACC 102, the survival kits contain four negative G straps. The straps, on each corner of the kit, prevent the kit raising above the seat pan during negative G flight. The front straps are held in place by the leg restraint line lock pins. Care should be taken whenever the lock pins are removed from the leg restraint line leg lock mechanism to resecure the front negative G straps by rethreading the lock pin through the strap lugs.

Composite Disconnect

The composite disconnect is used to connect aircraft oxygen, ventilating air, anti-G air and communications lines to the crewmember. The composite disconnect assembly consists of a lower block, an intermediate block, and an upper block. The intermediate block is fastened to the upper part of the survival kit and contains the tie-in between the crewman and the emergency oxygen supply. The disconnect is so designed that the aircrewman, during normal aircraft entrance or departure, is capable of quickly attaching or detaching all hoses and electrical lines leading from the aircraft to the survival kit and man. The lower block contains check valves in the ventilating air, anti-G and oxygen ports, that are open when the three sections of the disconnect are plugged in, and closed when either the upper or lower blocks are disconnected from the intermediate block. The check valves prevent gas leakage in the normal direction of flow when the valves are closed. The lower block is

AUTOMATIC SEQUENCING SYSTEM

MK-H7 SEAT AFTER AFC 307

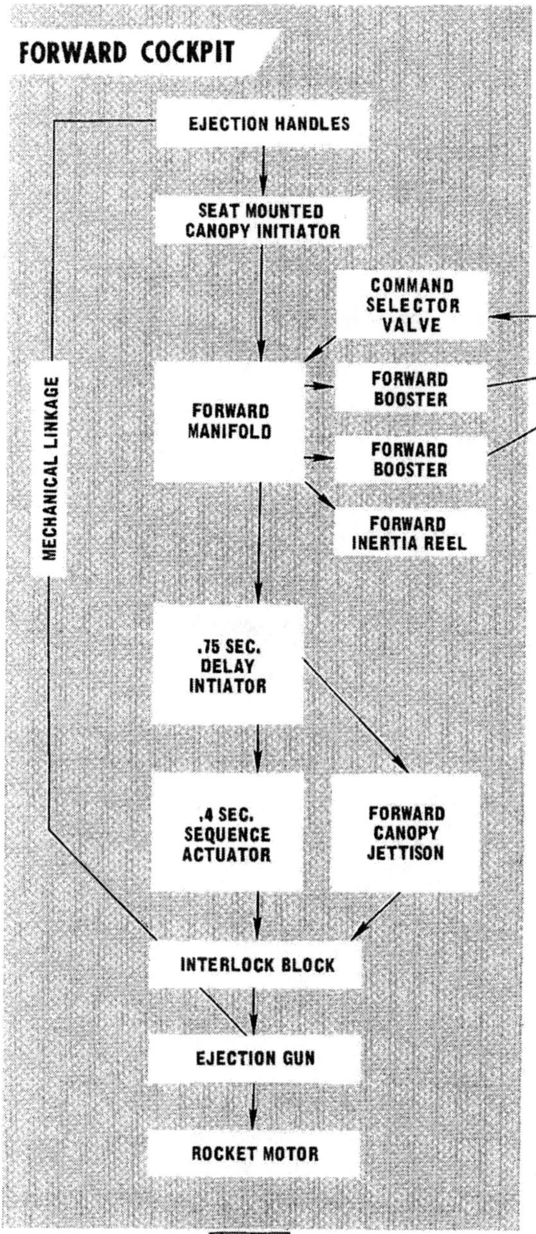

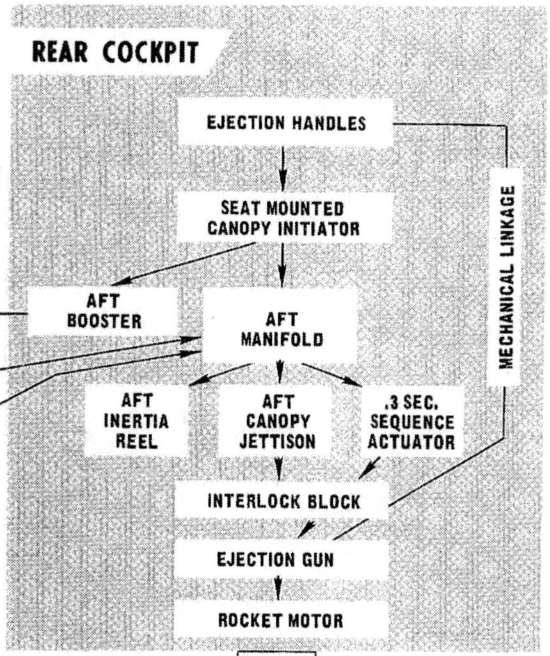

FORWARD COCKPIT

EJECTION HANDLES

SEAT MOUNTED CANOPY INITIATOR

COMMAND SELECTOR VALVE

FORWARD BOOSTER

FORWARD MANIFOLD

FORWARD BOOSTER

FORWARD INERTIA REEL

.75 SEC. DELAY INTIATOR

.4 SEC. SEQUENCE ACTUATOR

FORWARD CANOPY JETTISON

INTERLOCK BLOCK

EJECTION GUN

ROCKET MOTOR

MECHANICAL LINKAGE

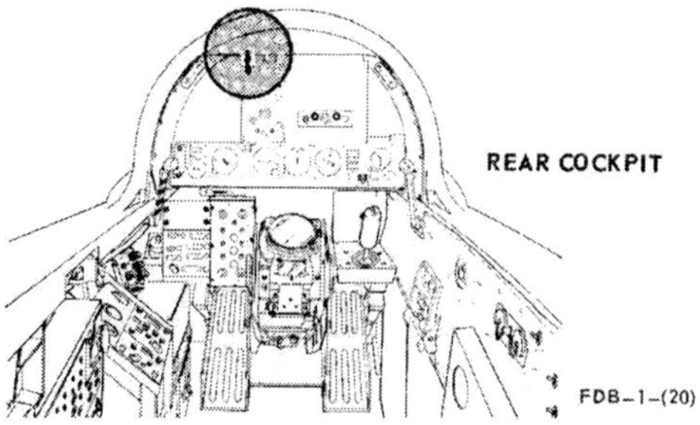

Note

ELAPSED TIME TO EJECTION GUN FIRING – 1.392 SECONDS.

REAR COCKPIT

EJECTION HANDLES

SEAT MOUNTED CANOPY INITIATOR

AFT BOOSTER

AFT MANIFOLD

AFT INERTIA REEL

AFT CANOPY JETTISON

.3 SEC. SEQUENCE ACTUATOR

INTERLOCK BLOCK

EJECTION GUN

ROCKET MOTOR

MECHANICAL LINKAGE

Notes

● ELAPSED TIME TO EJECTION GUN FIRING –0.54 SECONDS.

● BEFORE AFC 482, THE .3 SEC SEQUENCE ACTUATOR IS INOPERATIVE WITH SINGLE EJECTION SELECTED BY THE COMMAND SELECTOR VALVE. TO FIRE THE SEAT, THE EJECTION HANDLE MUST BE PULLED AFTER CANOPY REMOVAL.

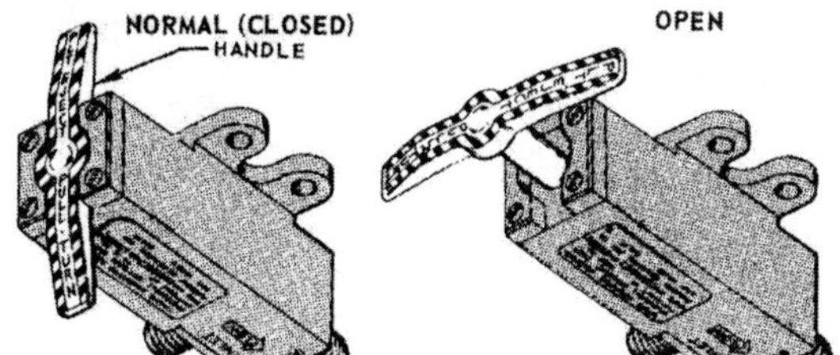

NORMAL (CLOSED) HANDLE

OPEN

COMMAND SELECTOR VALVE

REAR COCKPIT

FDB-1-(20)

Figure 1-16

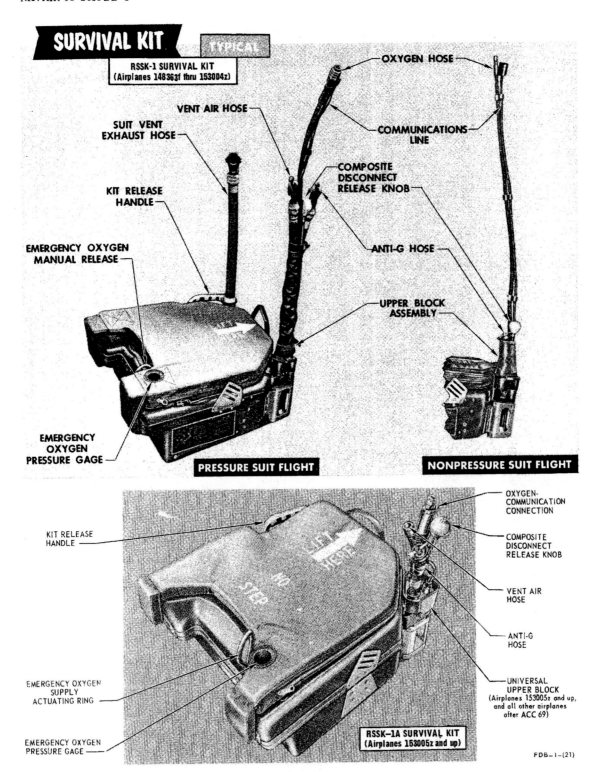

SURVIVAL KIT TYPICAL

RSSK-1 SURVIVAL KIT
(Airplanes 148363f thru 153004z)

OXYGEN HOSE

VENT AIR HOSE

SUIT VENT EXHAUST HOSE

COMMUNICATIONS LINE

KIT RELEASE HANDLE

COMPOSITE DISCONNECT RELEASE KNOB

EMERGENCY OXYGEN MANUAL RELEASE

ANTI-G HOSE

UPPER BLOCK ASSEMBLY

EMERGENCY OXYGEN PRESSURE GAGE

PRESSURE SUIT FLIGHT

NONPRESSURE SUIT FLIGHT

KIT RELEASE HANDLE

OXYGEN-COMMUNICATION CONNECTION

COMPOSITE DISCONNECT RELEASE KNOB

VENT AIR HOSE

ANTI-G HOSE

EMERGENCY OXYGEN SUPPLY ACTUATING RING

UNIVERSAL UPPER BLOCK
(Airplanes 153005z and up, and all other airplanes after ACC 69)

EMERGENCY OXYGEN PRESSURE GAGE

RSSK—1A SURVIVAL KIT
(Airplanes 153005z and up)

FDB-1-(21)

Figure 1-17

provided with a lanyard operating locking device, the free ends of the lanyard being attached to the airplane structure. As the seat is ejected, tension in the lanyard unlocks the device and separates the lower block from the intermediate block. The intermediate block serves as the connecting link between upper and lower blocks and, in addition, by means of a tee in the oxygen line, connects the emergency oxygen to the system. The upper block provides for attaching all service lines corresponding to those leading to the lower block. It also contains a manual disconnect device that permits the aircrewman to free himself from all kit connections during normal aircraft departure by single pull on the manual disconnect handle. This action simultaneously unlocks the upper block from the intermediate block and the vent exhaust hose from the kit. In aircraft 153005z and up, all others after ASC 69, all three blocks remain with the survival kit in the aircraft, and connection is made by inline connections in each of the leads and hoses connecting the survival kit with the pressure suit. Upper blocks with this change are called universal upper block assemblies.

NORMAL OPERATION - BEFORE AFC 307

Operation of the ejection seat consists of two phases: primary operation, and secondary operation. Primary operation of the seat includes all operating events that occur during the ejection sequence. This sequence begins when actuation of either the face curtain or lower ejection handle causes the canopy to jettison and the catapult gun to fire, and continues until a normal parachute descent of the occupant is accomplished. After the seat is initially fired during the ejection sequence, seat operation is completely automatic and requires no action by the occupant during the sequence. Secondary operation of the seat consists of controlling shoulder movement, seat bucket positioning, manual release of the leg restraint cords, and leg restraint cord adjustment with the finger rings. Shoulder movement is controlled by the positioning of the shoulder harness handle. Ejection from the aircraft is accomplished by propelling the seat from the aircraft with a pyrotechnically energized catapult gun. The ejection sequence is initiated by pulling the face curtain handle or the lower ejection handle. Actuation of either handle fires the canopy initiator which subsequently jettisons the canopy from the aircraft. When the canopy separates from the aircraft, the canopy interlock block which is attached to the canopy is pulled from the seat. Continued pull of the ejection handle fires the primary cartridge of the catapult gun. Gas pressure generated by the cartridge causes the inner and intermediate tubes of the gun to extend upward. The upward travel of the inner tube actuates the top latch mechanism, which releases the seat from the aircraft. Continued movement of the inner tube propels the seat up the tracks. During upward travel of the seat, the sears of the drogue gun and time release mechanism are pulled by trip rods. Also during upward seat movement, the auxiliary cartridges are fired when they become exposed to the hot propellant gases within the gun. Gas pressure generated by the auxiliary cartridges adds additional force to the gun during upward travel. Separation of the inner tube from the gun occurs when the inner and intermediate tubes are

fully extended in the outer tube. Upward seat travel after separation from catapult gun continues by the momentum of the seat mass. Staggered firing of the catapult gun cartridges furnishes even pressure within the gun during the power stroke eliminating high acceleration forces during ejection. Approximately 1 second after ejection, the drogue gun fires, deploying the controller drogue, which subsequently deploys the stabilizer drogue. The seat is stabilized and decelerated by the drogue chutes and the seat and occupant descend rapidly through the upper atmosphere. When an altitude of approximately 10,000 feet (13,000 feet after ACC 94) is reached, a barostat actuates the escapement mechanism, which in turn, releases the occupant's harnessing, leg restraint lines, and chute restraint straps. The drogue chute pulls a link line to deploy the personnel parachute. The occupant is held to the seat by sticker clips until the opening shock of the parachute snaps him out of the seat. If an ejection is made below 10,000 (13,000 feet after ACC 94), the preceding sequence of the events occurs approximately 1-3/4 seconds after the seat has decelerated to 4.5 G. If the time release mechanism fails to operate automatically after descending through 10,000 feet, actuate the emergency harness release handle on the right side of the seat to its full aft position. Reach over your shoulders and pull the parachute off of the horse-shoe fitting, push free of the seat, and pull the parachute rip cord.

NORMAL OPERATION - AFTER AFC 307

Three ejection sequences may be selected. Dual ejection may be initiated from the forward cockpit and dual or single ejection may be initiated from the aft cockpit (figure 1-16). A command selector valve is provided in the aft cockpit to select single or dual ejection. Ejection is initiated by pulling the face curtain or the lower ejection handle. The sequence of seat operation after the catapult gun is fired is the same as before except for the following: seat acceleration is slower due to the reduced catapult gun charges; the rocket pack fires to propel the seat to a greater height and is fired through the action of a 6-foot lanyard connected between the cockpit floor and the rocket initiator sear; the drogue gun cartridge firing delay is 0.75 second; and the time release mechanism operates at an altitude of 13,000 ± 1500 feet, the 4.5 G limiter is removed, and the time delay is set to 2.25 seconds. The lanyard is unwound during upward travel of the seat, and pulls the rocket motor firing mechanism sear to fire the motor when the lanyard is fully extended. In addition, the drogue chute pulls the personnel parachute safety pin line along with the parachute link line when the time release mechanism is released. The personnel parachute safety line is connected on one end to the parachute link line and the other end containing the pin secures the flap on the top of the personnel parachute. The purpose of the pin is to secure the parachute from the premature opening due to windblast during descent before time release mechanism actuation. If manual seat separation is required, there is no need to pull the parachute off the horse-shoe fitting. A pair of box springs, installed between the seat and the parachute, force the parachute forward from the seat when the parachute restraint and hold-down straps are released. After ACC 224, the rocket motor sear

and lanyard are removed from the bottom of the seat, and rocket motor initiation is provided by a gas initiator mounted on the left side of the seat. The initiator is triggered by a self-contained cable lanyard which is attached to the drogue gun trip rod. As the seat travels up the rails during ejection, the cable plays out from the initiator and, when the seat reaches a height equivalent to that reached in the old configuration, the played-out cable lanyard actuates a lever assembly to pull a sear to fire the initiator. The initiator then transmits ballistic gas through a flexible hose to the firing body on the rocket motor which activates the firing pin to fire the rocket motor.

DUAL EJECTION INITIATED FROM THE FORWARD COCKPIT

Only dual ejection can be performed from the forward cockpit. The dual ejection sequence is initiated whenever the crewmember pulls either the face curtain handle or the lower ejection handle to fire the forward seat mounted initiator. Gas pressure from the seat mounted initiator is routed to the sequencing system stowing the aft cockpit equipment and operating the forward seat inertial reel, the aft seat inertial reel, aft canopy pressure operated valve (jettisoning aft canopy and opening flooding doors), aft pressure operated sequence actuator (ejecting aft seat), forward canopy pressure operated valve (jettisoning forward canopy), and forward pressure operated sequence actuator (ejecting forward seat), in that order. It is possible to save part of the 0.4 second sequence actuator delay time by maintaining a continuous pull on the ejection handle so that the catapult gun sear is pulled as soon as the canopy interlock block is removed.

Single Ejection From the Forward Cockpit After Rear Cockpit Has Ejected Independently

Even though the rear cockpit has ejected independently, when the front seat occupant initiates the ejection sequence, the 3/4 second interlock delay is still present. This delay is designed to prevent collision between the front canopy and the rear seat in a sequenced ejection. When the ejection sequence is initiated by the crewmember, after a 3/4 second delay, gas pressure from the seat mounted initiator is routed to the forward canopy pressure operated valve (jettisoning the forward canopy), and then 0.4 seconds after canopy jettison the forward pressure operated sequence actuator operates to eject the forward seat. It is possible to save part of the 0.4 second sequence actuator delay time by maintaining a continuous pull on the ejection handle so that the catapult gun sear is pulled as soon as the canopy interlock block is removed. On aircraft after AFC 477, the system is modified such that the 3/4 second delay will be bypassed after the rear cockpit has ejected independently. That is, if the rear cockpit has ejected, the front seat will eject approximately 0.4 second after a front ejection handle is pulled. However, in order for the 3/4 second delay to be completely bypassed, the rear ejection handle must be pulled at least 3/4 of a second before ejection is initiated from the front seat. If the front ejection handle is pulled sometime within 3/4 seconds of the rear handle, the delay will be reduced proportionally. That is, if the front seat initiates ejection 0.5 second after the rear seat, the 3/4 second delay is reduced to 0.25 second and the front seat then ejects approximately 0.65 second after the front ejection handle is pulled.

DUAL EJECTION INITIATED FROM AFT COCKPIT

The aft crewmember initiates a dual ejection by opening the command selector valve and pulling either the face curtain or lower handle to fire the seat mounted initiator. Gas pressure generated by the initiator is routed to the sequencing system which operates the aft cockpit equipment stowage, the aft seat inertial reel, aft canopy pressure operated valve (jettisoning aft canopy and opening the flooding doors), aft pressure operated sequence actuator (ejecting aft seat), forward canopy pressure operated valve (jettisoning forward canopy), and forward pressure operated sequence actuator (ejecting forward seat), in that order. It is possible to save part of the 0.3 second sequence actuator delay time by maintaining a continuous pull on the ejection handle so that the catapult gun sear is pulled as soon as the canopy interlock block is removed.

Note

When opening the command selector valve, pull directly out on the valve handle without applying torque. The handle rotates 90° clockwise through cam action. After AFC 526, the handle is turned by the application of torque only, and there is no requirement to pull the handle.

SINGLE EJECTION INITIATED FROM AFT COCKPIT

Single ejection occurs when the aft cockpit crewmember pulls either the face curtain handle or lower ejection handle with the command selector valve in the normal (closed) position. Gas pressure generated by the aft seat-mounted initiator is routed to the sequencing system which operates the aft seat inertial reel, the aft cockpit equipment storage, and the aft canopy pressure operated valve (jettisoning the aft canopy and opening the flooding doors). An additional pull on the ejection handle then fires the seat catapult. On aircraft after AFC 482, the sequencing system will fire the seat and there is no need for the additional pull on the ejection handle. However, the ejection handle may be still pulled to save part of the 0.3 second sequence actuator delay time so that the catapult gun sear is pulled as soon as the canopy interlock block is removed.

EJECTION HANDLE SELECTION

Due to its greater accessibility and shorter travel when compared to the face curtain, the lower ejection handle should be used during situations requiring an expeditious ejection. Some of these situations are insufficient flying speed from catapult, ramp strike, parting of cross deck pendants during carrier arrestment, low altitude, uncontrolled flight, and under high G during spin or ACM maneuvers.

EMERGENCY OPERATION

There are no provisions for emergency operation of the ejection seats; however, if the ejection seats fail to eject, the crewmember can abandon the airplane by following the procedures outlined in Emergency Procedures.

LIMITATIONS

Assuming wings level and no aircraft sink rate, the ejection seats provide safe escape within the following parameters:

MK H5 seats - Before AFC 307

a. Ground level - 130 KCAS minimum
b. Ground level to 100 feet - 350 KCAS maximum
At airspeeds greater than 350 KCAS below 100 feet, the time required (altitude loss) for the G-limiter to function (seat deceleration) is not sufficient to complete parachute deployment before ground impact.
c. Above 100 feet - 400 KCAS maximum (based on human factors)
- 550 KCAS maximum (based on seat limitation)
At airspeeds greater than 400 KCAS, appreciable forces are exerted on the body which makes escape more hazardous.

MK H7 (rocket assist) seats - After AFC 307

a. Ground level (zero altitude) - zero airspeed (canopy must be closed)
b. Ground level and up - 400 KCAS maximum (based on human factors)
- 500 KCAS OR M equal 0.92 maximum, whichever is greater (based on seat limitations)
At airspeeds greater than 400 KCAS, appreciable forces are exerted on the body which makes escape more hazardous.

ELECTRICAL POWER SUPPLY SYSTEM

— NOTICE —
Some illustrations referred to within this system writeup may be located in appendix A. These illustrations are referred to, within the text, as (figure A-, appendix A).

DESCRIPTION

The airplane electrical power supply system consists of two engine driven ac generators, two dc transformer-rectifiers, an emergency ac generator, and a power distribution (bus) system. The generators supply ac power to the right main 115/200 volts ac bus, the right main 28 volt ac bus, the essential 115/200 volt ac bus, the essential 28 volt ac bus, the left main 115/200 volt ac bus, the left main 28/14 volt ac bus, and the transformer-rectifiers. The transformer-rectifiers convert 115/200 volt ac power to dc power, which is supplied to the essential 28 volt dc bus, the right main 28 volt dc bus, and the left main 28 volt dc bus. Refer to Electrical System, figures A-5 and A-6 appendix A, for the individual bus loading.

A-C ELECTRICAL POWER

Two 400 Hz, three phase, 115/200 volt ac generators are the primary source of all electrical power. Each generator (one on each engine) is capable of supplying the system with 20,000 volt-amperes of electrical power. On aircraft 152965y and up, each generator is rated at 30,000 volt-amperes (60 KVA system). The generators are driven by constant speed drive units, which utilize engine oil as a coolant and as the hydraulic media to regulate the generators at a constant speed of 8000 rpm. The CSD units incorporate a mechanical shaft disconnect feature which disconnects the CSD from the engine if a malfunction occurs in the CSD to cause it to lose oil or overheat. The left engine generator supplies power directly to the left main 115/200 volt ac bus, and the left transformer-rectifier. The right engine generator supplies power directly to the right main 115/200 volt ac bus, the essential 115/200 volt ac bus, the ignition bus and the right (essential) transformer-rectifier. On aircraft prior to 152965y, either generator is capable of supplying electrical power to the entire bus system through an auto-parallel controlled bus tie relay. When the generators are in phase and are operating at approximately the same frequency,

the auto-parallel control closes the bus tie relay, thereby connecting the left and right bus systems. This is called parallel bus operation (figure A-5, appendix A). If one of the generators becomes out of phase or frequency with respect to the other, the fault protection circuits deenergize the bus tie relay and each generator supplies power only to its own bus system. If one generator fails, the fault protection circuits drop the malfunctioning generator off the line and the bus tie relay closes, or remains closed, allowing the good generator to power the entire system. On aircraft 152995z and up, and all others after AFC 227, the auto-parallel feature is removed, and during normal operation the bus tie is open with each generator supplying its associated buses independently. This is called split bus operation (figure A-6, appendix A). If a generator fails, the bus tie closes and the remaining generator supplies power to the entire system, as is the case with parallel bus operation. Each generator may be manually disconnected from the bus system by placing its generator control switch OFF. Under maximum generator loads, a generator drops off the line at an engine rpm of approximately 53%. At less than maximum generator loads, a generator drops off the line at a lower engine rpm than for maximum generator loads. An emergency ac generator, when operating, supplies power to the essential 115/200 volt ac bus, the essential 28 volt ac bus, the ignition 115/200 volt ac bus, and the right transformer-rectifier. Auto-transformers reduce 115/200 volt ac power to 28 volt ac power, and the transformer-rectifiers convert 115/200 volt ac power to 28 volt dc power.

Emergency Generator

An emergency 400 Hz, three phase, 200/115 volt ac generator is provided as a source of electrical power if both engine driven generators go off the line. The emergency generator is capable of supplying the essential ac and dc buses with 3000 volt-amperes of electrical power. The generator is powered by a ram air turbine which is extended into the airstream pneumatically. When the emergency generator reaches its rated voltage, it energizes an ac relay which connects a generator output to the ignition 115/200 volt ac bus, the essential 115/200 volt ac bus, the essential 28 volt ac bus, and the essential 28 volt dc bus. The emergency generator ac relay does not become energized unless both engine driven generators are off the line, and the airplane airspeed is above approximately 90 knots CAS. If either engine driven generator is restored, or the aircraft airspeed drops below approximately 90 knots CAS, the emergency generator ac relay deenergizes and disconnects the emergency generator from the bus system. To extend the ram air turbine, place the ram air turbine control handle to RAT OUT (push down). If engine driven generators are restored, the ram air turbine may be retracted by placing the ram air turbine control handle to RAT IN (pull up). Based on NATC tests, the emergency generator delivers fully rated power for a minimum continuous period of 3 hours.

D-C ELECTRICAL POWER

Two 60 ampere transformer-rectifiers receive 400 Hz, three phase, 115/200 volt ac power, and supplies 28 volt dc power. On 152965y and up, each transformer-rectifier is rated at 100 amperes (60 KVA system). The left transformer-rectifier supplies power directly to the left main 28 volt dc bus. The right transformer-rectifier supplies power directly to the essential 28 volt dc bus, and through an essential dc line relay to the right main 28 volt dc bus. The output of both transformer-rectifiers is connected in parallel through a 60 ampere bus tie current limiter. If the transformer-rectifier fails, the remaining transformer-rectifier supplies power to the entire dc bus system. The emergency generator supplies power through the right transformer-rectifier to the essential 28 volt dc bus.

EXTERNAL ELECTRICAL POWER RECEPTACLE

To provide adequate power for ground operation of electrical equipment, an external power receptacle (figure 1-1) is on the bottom of the left air duct. The external power required is three-phase, 400 Hz, 115/200 volt ac and it is distributed through the entire electrical system in the same manner as generator output.

GENERATOR CONTROL SWITCHES

Two generator control switches, one for each generator, are on the generator control panel (figure A-1, appendix A). The switches, labeled R GEN - ON, OFF, ON - EXT and L GEN - ON, OFF, ON - EXT, are utilized to select the source of electrical power for the airplane bus system. With external electrical power applied, and with both generator control switches in EXT ON, electrical power is supplied to the entire bus system. When either engine driven generator is operating, its output may be connected to the entire bus system by placing its control switch to GEN ON.

Note

If either generator indicator light illuminates as a result of a temporary generator mal-

function, the generator may be reset. It is however, necessary to wait approximately 45 seconds to enable the generator control relays to reset. To reset the generator, place the generator control switch OFF, wait 45 seconds and reposition it to GEN ON. There is no waiting period in aircraft 152965y and up with 60 KVA systems installed.

CIRCUIT BREAKERS

Most of the circuits are protected by circuit breakers in the aft cockpit. The circuit breakers in essential circuits are on a panel (figure A-1, appendix A) on the outboard side of the right console in the forward cockpit. The majority of the remaining circuit breakers are on panels in the RIO's cockpit (figure A-2, appendix A).

GENERATOR INDICATOR LIGHTS

The LH GEN OUT and RH GEN OUT indicator lights, and the BUS TIE OPEN light are on the generator control panel (figure A-1, appendix A) in the front cockpit. One of the generator lights illuminates any time its generator is not on the line. The pilot may attempt to reset the generator by placing generator switch OFF and then placing it back to GEN ON. If a double generator failure occurs, both generator lights are illuminated as long as the generators are turning. The BUS TIE OPEN indicator light illuminates when the left and right generator bus systems are not paralleled. With split bus systems, the BUS TIE OPEN indicator illuminates only when a single generator is inoperative and the bus tie is open. The bus tie relay is open with both generators on the line but the BUS TIE OPEN light does not illuminate.

ESSENTIAL D-C TEST BUTTON

An essential dc test button and indicator light are on the right side of the rear cockpit (figure A-1, appendix A). When the essential dc test button is pressed the essential dc line relay is deenergized. Power then is supplied to the essential dc test light by the right (essential) transformer-rectifier. With external power on the airplane, illumination of the light indicates both transformer-rectifiers are delivering dc power. If the light does not illuminate, one or both transformer-rectifiers are inoperative or not receiving power. With one or both generator operating, illumination of the light indicates the right transformer-rectifier is delivering dc power.

AUTOPILOT GROUND TEST SWITCH

On aircraft 153049aa and up, and all others after AFC 203, with external power applied to the aircraft buses and the autopilot ground test switch in the NORM position, no electrical power can be applied to the AFCS circuits. To apply power to the AFCS, the autopilot ground test switch must be placed to the TEST, solenoid held position. The autopilot ground test switch, just aft of No. 2 circuit breaker panel (figure A-1, appendix A), remains in TEST until either external power is removed, a generator comes on the line, or the switch is manually placed to NORM. When either generator comes on the line, the autopilot ground test switch can no longer by used to remove power to the AFCS. The purpose of the switch is to prolong AFCS component life by removing power to the system while external power is applied to the aircraft for maintenance of other systems.

NORMAL OPERATION

Normal operation of the electrical system commences when external power is applied to the aircraft and the generator switches are in EXT ON, or when the engines are running and the generator control switches are in GEN ON.

EMERGENCY OPERATION

SINGLE GENERATOR FAILURE

Failure of one generator is noted by illumination of either the LH or RH GEN OUT light. The light determines which generator has failed. One generator in normal operation is sufficient to support the entire electrical demand or load. If a generator failure occurs, cycle the generator control switches from GEN ON to OFF, wait 45 seconds, and back to GEN ON. In aircraft 152965y and up, with the 60 KVA system installed, there is no waiting period. If the generator fault has been corrected, the generator is brought back on the line and the light goes out. If the light remains illuminated, monitor engine oil pressure and variable nozzle operation. If oil starvation is indicated secure the affected engine if practicable. On airplanes 153030aa and up, after PPC 62 and all others with AFC 252 and PPC 62, illumination of the applicable engine oil low warning light can be used as an indication of oil starvation.

```
CAUTION
```

Upon illumination of a generator indicator light, immediately check the corresponding oil pressure gage. The generator failure could have been caused by oil starvation which also affects the engine oil system.

DOUBLE GENERATOR FAILURE

Although a double generator failure is highly remote, the possiblity of a double failure is still present. It is more likely that one generator will fail, followed by the failure of the other generator. As previously stated in the paragraph on single generator failures, one generator out light is illuminated when one of the generators fail. When the other generator fails both generator out lights are illuminated. Although a double generator failure results in a complete electrical power failure, the permanent magnet generators (provided for field excitation and generator warning lights) continue to function while the generators are turning. Upon the loss of both generators, extend the ram air turbine and turn off all electrical equipment not necessary to maintain flight. Attempt to return the generators to the line by cycling the generator control switches OFF, wait 45 seconds

then back to GEN ON. In aircraft 152965y and up, after the 60 KVA system there is no waiting period. If the fault has been corrected, the generator lights are extinguished. With the loss of all electrical power in flight, the emergency pneumatic system should be utilized to extend the landing gear and flaps. If the gear has been lowered prior to loss of electrical power, the pneumatic system should still be utilized. Blowing the gear down assists the integral locks in keeping the gear down and locked since, with the loss of electrical power, the landing gear selector valve reverts to a neutral position. In the neutral position, both sides of the actuating cylinder are routed to utility return, resulting in no hydraulic pressure on the down side of the landing gear actuator. Therefore, by blowing the gear down, 3000 psi pneumatic pressure is exerted on the down side of the landing gear actuator to keep the gear down and locked. If all electrical power is lost while taxiing, the emergency pneumatic system should be actuated to assure that the gear remains locked. If the flaps had been lowered prior to electrical failure, air loads will return the flaps to a low drag position. The utility hydraulic system gage does not operate on RAT power.

BUS TIE OPEN

Because of design, it is possible to lose the essential buses as a result of a short in the right generator system. For airplanes with parallel bus systems, a short on the right generator bus is indicated by the illumination of the BUS TIE OPEN light followed in 5 seconds (3.8 seconds with the 60 KVA system) by the illumination of the RH GEN OUT light. The BUS TIE OPEN light then is extinguished. If the BUS TIE OPEN light remains illuminated, the short presents no problem since the left generator supplies the power to the right buses. However, if the BUS TIE OPEN light illuminates again within 2 seconds, all the buses supplied by the right generator are lost since the illumination of the BUS TIE OPEN light indicates that the bus tie relay has opened. Because the bus tie relay parallels the output of the two generators it can be seen that an open relay and an inoperative right generator automatically deprives the airplane the use of the right main ac and essential airplane buses. An attempt should be made to regain the right generator by placing the right generator control switch OFF, waiting 45 seconds, (no waiting period with 60 KVA systems) and placing the switch back to GEN ON. If the right generator comes on the line, the short is no longer present. The generators parallel and normal operation is resumed. If the right generator light does not go out, the short remains and the emergency generator must be used. The essential buses may be regained but this necessitates the loss of the left generator system, since the emergency generator does not come on the line as long as either main generator is in service. Extension of the ram air turbine must be followed by switching off the left generator in this circumstance. A short in the left generator or in any of the left generator system buses is not of such a serious nature due to the fact that the right main and essential buses still are in operation. For airplanes with split bus systems, under normal conditions, both generators operate independently of each other, with the bus tie relay open and without the BUS TIE OPEN light illuminated. But with certain electrical faults present in the system, it is possible to lose either of the generators while retaining the bus tie open. The result is a single generator operating to provide power to only part of the electrical buses with illumination of the BUS TIE OUT light and either the LH GEN OUT light or the RH GEN OUT light. An important example of this kind of fault is the loss of the essential buses due to a short in the generator system. A short on one of the right generator buses will be noted by the illumination of the RH GEN OUT light followed in 2 seconds by the illumination of the BUS TIE OPEN light. All the buses powered by the right generator, including the essential buses, will be lost. An attempt shall be made to regain the right generator by placing the right generator control switch OFF, and placing the switch back ON. If the right generator comes on the line, the short is no longer present. The generators will resume normal operation. If the lost generator fails to be restored, cycle the left generator control switch in an attempt to close the bus tie. If none of these procedures succeed the short is probably still present, and the emergency generator must be used to restore the essential buses. Exercise care after extending the RAT as the short might be on one of the essential buses. A short on one of the buses associated with the left

generator is not of such a serious nature because the right main and essential buses will still be in operation. The same procedure shall be followed, however, to attempt to restore the lost generator and, failing that, to close the bus tie. Refer to Emergency Procedures for action to be taken upon illumination of the BUS TIE OPEN light.

ELECTRICAL FIRE

If an electrical fire occurs, extend the ram air turbine and turn the generator control switches and all electrical switches OFF. When the fire subsides, place the generator control switches to GEN ON. If the fire still persists after turning the generator control switches ON, turn the generator control switches OFF. Operate essential equipment only, and land as soon as practicable. If no fire is apparent when the generator control switches are placed to GEN ON, individually reposition the electrical equipment switches ON, beginning with the most essential equipment first. If the malfunctioning piece of equipment is found, turn that equipment OFF, and pull the applicable circuit breaker.

LIMITATIONS

There are no specific limitations pertaining to the electrical system.

EMERGENCY EQUIPMENT

— NOTICE —
Some illustrations referred to within this system writeup may be located in appendix A. These illustrations are referred to, within the text, as (figure A-, appendix A).

DESCRIPTION

The airplane emergency equipment consists of a pneumatically extended and retracted ram air turbine, and a comprehensive set of warning and indicator lights.

RAM AIR TURBINE

A ram air turbine, in the upper left side of the aft fuselage, is a power source for an emergency ac generator. The turbine assembly consists of a housing that contains two variable pitch turbine blades, a governing unit that controls the pitch of the blades, and the gearing to transfer blade rotation to a vertical drive shaft. The gear box drives the generator on one end. When the ram air turbine is extended into the airstream, the turbine blades are at a maximum angle of attack. This results in a rapid acceleration of the turbine blades and governing unit. As the regulating speed of the governing unit is approached, the turbine blades decrease their angle of attack. Turbine blade angle of attack (as directed by the governing mechanism) then varies with respect

to the velocity of the airstream in order to maintain a constant 12,000 rpm. In effect, the ram air turbine functions as a constant speed drive unit for the emergency generator providing the airspeed is above approximately 90 knots. Refer to Electrical System, this section, for the operation of the emergency ac generator. Ram air turbine operating time shall be logged on the yellow sheet (OPNAV Form 3760-2).

Ram Air Turbine Control Handle

The ram air turbine is extended and retracted pneumatically by a ram air turbine handle (figure A-1, appendix A) in the forward cockpit. Pushing down on the handle extends the turbine, pulling up on the handle retracts the turbine. Air pressure for extension and retraction is taken from a 4.2 cubic inch air bottle (in reality, not a bottle but an enlarged air line) which is charged by the pneumatic system. If the pneumatic system loses pressure, the air line retains its pressure through the action of a check valve. However, after loss of pneumatic system pressure there is only enough charge left in the air line for a single actuation (extension or retraction).

WARNING

Minimum RAT extension pressure is 1000 psi. Therefore to ensure RAT extension in the event of an air bottle check valve failure, the RAT should be extended whenever pneumatic pressure begins dropping and RAT utilization is anticipated.

CAUTION

When retracting the ram air turbine, ensure at least 2000 psi pneumatic pressure in airplanes with Ronson 7U7161 ram air turbine sequencing valves, and at least 200 psi pneumatic pressure in airplanes with Ronson 7U7234 ram air turbine sequencing valves. If the ram air turbine is retracted when the pressure is less than that recommended, the ram air turbine doors close prematurely resulting in damage to the doors.

Note

During ram air turbine extension in airplanes 152216u and up, it is normal for the FIRE and OVERHT lights to flicker for a short time period until the RAT comes up to full operation. Disregard these lights unless they remain on after RAT extension.

Limitations

1. Maximum airspeed for operation of the ram air turbine is 515 KCAS or Mach 1.1, whichever is less. Acceleration limits with RAT extended are -1.0 to +5.2 G.
2. Based on NATC tests, the emergency generator delivers fully rated power for a minimum continuous period of 3 hours.

WARNING AND INDICATOR LIGHTS

Warning and indicator lights have been incorporated throughout the cockpits to reduce instrument surveillance to a minimum. The majority of the lights are in the front cockpit, with most of them being grouped on the telelight panel.

Telelight Panels

Telelight panels, on the front cockpit right vertical panel and the generator control panel (figure A-1, appendix A), contain the telelight bars. When a condition exists that requires corrective action, or is worthy of note, a telelight bar corresponding to the condition illuminates. Most of the lights on the telelight panels illuminate in conjunction with the MASTER CAUTION light. Indicator lights that do not illuminate in conjunction with the MASTER CAUTION light are: SPEED BRAKE OUT, L EXT FUEL, CTR EXT FUEL, R EXT FUEL and REFUEL READY. Electrical power to the telelights is supplied by the 28/14 volt ac warning lights bus. The light(s) will be extinguished when the condition that caused the light(s) to illuminate is corrected. Amplification of conditions that exist upon illumination of a telelight,

and its corrective action, can be found in Warning/Indicator Light Analysis, section V.

Master Caution Light

A MASTER CAUTION light operates in conjunction with lights on the telelight panel. It is only necessary to monitor the MASTER CAUTION light for an indication of a condition requiring attention, and then referring to the telelight panel for the specific condition. The MASTER CAUTION light may be extinguished by pressing the MASTER CAUTION RESET button, on the generator control panel. The illuminated lights on the telelight panel are not extinguished by the MASTER CAUTION RESET button, with the exception of the A/P DISENGAGED light, until their respective faults have been cleared. After the MASTER CAUTION light is cleared, and additional condition exists that requires attention the MASTER CAUTION light again illuminates.

CAUTION

When the MASTER CAUTION light illuminates with no other indications, activate the warning lights test switch to check for a burned out bulb in the telelight panel.

Warning Light Test and Dimmer Circuit

The warning light test and dimmer circuit checks the bulbs in the warning and indicator lights. All warning and indicator lights are included in the test and dimmer circuit which is powered by the left main 28/14 volt ac bus. In aircraft after AFC 287, the TANK ABOARD (TK) light is also included in this circuit. The circuit does not provide an operational check of any warning or indicator system, it merely checks the light bulbs. The warning and indicator lights may be illuminated by actuating the warning lights test switches on the interior lights control panels.

Eject Light

An EJECT LIGHT system is installed in airplanes 152266v and up, and 148363f through 152215t after AFC 165. The system provides for a positive visual ejection command from the pilot to the RIO. The lights can be actuated only from the front cockpit. The pilot's switch and monitor light are incorporated into a single unit, mounted under the left canopy sill just forward of the flap switch (figure A-1, appendix A). The switch is a push ON, push OFF type, with the push button being the lens of the light. The lens is recessed sufficiently to preclude an accidental actuation. The light in the rear cockpit is a rectangular press to test unit mounted at the bottom right of the instrument panel (figure A-2, appendix A). Pressing the lens of the rear light tests the rear light bulb and circuitry only. When the switch in the front cockpit is pressed, both EJECT lights illuminate. Pressing the switch again extinguishes both lights. The lights both incorporate red lenses with black lettering. Power for the system is supplied by a separate dry cell battery mounted in the front cockpit.

ENGINES

DESCRIPTION

The airplane is powered by two General Electric J79-GE-8 engines, a lightweight (approximately 4000 pounds), high thrust, axial flow turbojet engine equipped with an afterburner for thrust augmentation. At military power the engine develops 10,900 pounds thrust and with complete afterburner, total thrust is 17,000 pounds. The engine features a variable stator (first six stages), a 17-stage compressor, 10 annular combustion chambers, a three-stage turbine, a variable area exhaust nozzle and a variable thrust afterburner. An impingement type starter, supplied with air from an external auxiliary power unit, cranks the engine during starting. During operation, air enters the inlet of the engine and is directed into the compressor rotor by the variable inlet guide vanes. As it is compressed, the air is forced through the compressor rear frame into the combustion chambers. Fuel nozzles, projecting into the combustion chambers, eject a fuel spray which mixes with the compressed air. Ignition is provided by a spark plug located in the number 4 combustion chamber, the remaining nine combustion chambers are ignited through cross fire tubes. The gases resulting from combustion, flow from the combustion chambers into the turbine. The three turbine wheels move as a unit on a common shaft, which is directly splined to the compressor rotor. After passing through the turbine section, the exhaust gases flow into the afterburner where their flow is stabilized and then ejected through the variable exhaust nozzle. Additional fuel may be injected into hot exhaust gases for afterburner combustion, producing considerable thrust augmentation. The engine oil system is a dry sump type completely contained on the engine. The compressor inlet guide vanes and the stators in the first six compressor stages are variable, and are controlled by the variable stator system. The compressor blades are small fixed airfoils whose theory of operation is essentially that of a wing. It is highly advantageous to control the angle of attack of the early stage blades, and this is accomplished, in effect, by controlling the airflow to blade impingement angle through the variable stator system. The impingement angle is controlled within acceptable limits for low airflow (low speed and/or rpm) conditions and to permit high airflow with a minimum of restriction. Controlling the impingement angle reduces compressor stall problems at critical engine-airplane speeds, particularly during burst acceleration and deceleration. The variable stators and inlet guide vanes are interconnected externally and are positioned by two actuators which utilize high pressure engine fuel as the hydraulic medium. The variable nozzle system is hydromechanically controlled and schedules nozzle area by positioning the nozzle opening to obtain optimum thrust with respect to altitude and airspeed conditions. The purpose of the variable exhaust nozzles is to control the operating temperature of the engine as governed by the engine amplifier during military and maximum engine operation. Air bled from the 17th stage of each engine compressor is used by the auxiliary equipment cooling system, the boundary layer control system, the air data computer system, the cockpit air conditioning and pressurization system, the engine anti-icing system, the fuel tank pressurization system, the pneumatic system (air source), and the windshield rain removal system.

ENGINE FUEL CONTROL SYSTEM

The fuel control system (figure A-5, appendix A) for each engine is complete in itself and the two systems are identical. For simplicity of discussion, only one system or engine shall be discussed. The engine fuel control system transports fuel from the engine fuel inlet to the combustion chambers. This fuel is discharged in the proper state of atomization for complete burning. Varying engine power settings and conditions demand changes in fuel flow; therefore the engine fuel control system must also control fuel flow to obtain maximum engine efficiency within the design limits of the engine. Only the engine fuel system is discussed in the following paragraphs. The afterburner fuel system is discussed separately in this section.

Fuel Pump Unit

The engine fuel pump unit consists of a low pressure impeller-type pumping element, a high pressure gear-type main pumping element, a low pressure fuel filter, a fuel filter by-pass, and an output pressure relief valve. The centrifugal impeller performs a pressure boost function which assures pump operation at low inlet fuel pressures. Airplane boosted fuel from the main fuel manifold passes through the impeller-pump. The impeller boosted fuel then passes through the fuel filter to the main gear-pump, which delivers it to the main engine fuel control at approximately 1000 psi. If fuel pressure differential across the fuel filter exceeds approximately 33 psi, the fuel filter bypass opens, and a CHECK FUEL FILTERS light, on the pilot's right vertical panel, illuminates. If the discharge pressure of the gear-pump exceeds approximately 1125 psi, the output pressure relief valve opens to maintain safe fuel pressures. The output pressure relief valve reseats when discharge pressures reduce to approximately 1025 psi.

Engine Fuel Control

The main fuel control is a hydromechanical computer which uses engine fuel as the hydraulic controlling medium. The control performs the following functions: provides engine speed control by regulating main fuel flow; provides fuel surge protection; limits turbine inlet temperature to a safe value; provides a positive fuel shutoff; schedules variable stator vane angle to control airflow into the engine; and provides a hydraulic signal to initiate afterburning operation. High pressure fuel from the pump is delivered to the bypass valve and the metering valve in the main fuel control. The bypass valve senses the pressure differential across the metering valve, and maintains this pressure differential at a pre-determined value by bypassing varying amounts of fuel back to the main fuel pump inlet. The metering valve is positioned by various operating signals and meters fuel to the engine as a result of these integrated signals. From the metering valve fuel flows through the main fuel control cutoff valve. The cutoff valve cuts off fuel flow at engine shutdown.

Fuel Oil Heat Exchanger

Fuel, metered from the main fuel control, passes through the coolant tubes of the fuel-oil heat exchanger and then to the fuel nozzles. The fuel serves as the coolant for the scavenge oil which flows around the heat exchanger tubes. The heat exchanger incorporates a bypass valve to regulate the flow of oil, which in turn, controls the temperature of the oil and fuel. There are two fuel-oil heat exchangers on the engine, one utilizes normal engine fuel as a coolant while the other uses core afterburner fuel. Both fuel-oil heat exchangers serve the same purpose and their operation is the same.

Fuel Pressurization and Drain Valve

The fuel pressurization and drain valve prevents fuel flow to the engine until sufficient fuel pressure is attained in the main fuel control to operate the servo assemblies, which are used to compute the fuel flow schedules. It also drains the fuel manifold at engine shutdown to prevent post shutdown fires, but keeps the upstream portion of the system primed to permit faster starts. When the fuel pressure differential across the pressurizing valve drops below 80 psi, the pressurizing valve closes, cutting off fuel flow to the engine and the drain valve opens to drain the fuel manifold.

Fuel Nozzles

A flow-divider type fuel nozzle in each inner combustion chamber liner delivers metered fuel, in the proper state of atomization for maximum burning, into the compressor discharge air entering the combustion chamber. The nozzles produce a uniformly distributed, cone shaped, hollow fuel spray. High velocity compressor air is directed around the nozzle by an air shroud to provide a cooling action around the nozzle orifice and to reduce carbon deposits.

Check Fuel Filter Indicator Light

The CHECK FUEL FILTERS indicator light is on the telelight panel. The CHECK FUEL FILTERS indicator light, and MASTER CAUTION light illuminates when the low pressure fuel filter on either engine is being bypassed. The light circuit is completed through a pressure differential switch which senses filter inlet and filter outlet pressure. In the case of a partially clogged low pressure fuel filter, the CHECK FUEL FILTERS indicator light may be extinguished by reducing power on both engines. Check each engine individually by adding power to see if the light illuminates. In this manner, it can be determined if one or both engines are affected.

OIL SYSTEM

Each engine is equipped with a completely self contained, dry sump, full pressure oil system. Oil is stored in a 5.3 gallon pressurized reservoir, located at the 1 o'clock position on the engine compressor front casing. The oil pump is a positive displacement, dual element, rotary vane type unit. The lubrication element is capable of delivering 11.8 gpm at 60 psi. Each element contains a filter, through which the oil is pumped before distribution. Engine oil is used for engine lubrication, variable exhaust nozzle operation, generator lubrication and cooling, and constant speed drive unit control. After distribution to various points throughout the engine, the oil is picked up by three scavenge pumps, routed through a scavenge filter, through an air oil cooler and two fuel oil heat exchangers and then back to the tank. The pressurizing system maintains the proper relationship between ambient air pressure and air pressure in the bearing sumps, gear boxes, damper bearing and reservoir to ensure effective oil seal operation, and to prevent damage to the reservoir and sumps during high speed climbs and descents. Oil is also supplied directly from the reservoir to the constant speed drive unit, and is used as both the control and final drive medium for controlling generator speed.

Oil Quantity Indicator Lights

On airplanes 153030aa and up, and all others after AFC 252 and PPC 62, L ENG OIL LOW and R ENG OIL LOW lights have been added. The indicator lights on the telelight panel illuminate when a low level condition exists in either or both engine oil tanks. A detector, in the right missile well, detects a low level condition and provides a signal to illuminate the appropriate indicator light. There is an oil quantity sensor selector switch on the oxygen panel on the left console in the forward cockpit. During flight with the switch in NORM, the appropriate indicator light illuminates when the oil quantity drops to 3.2 gallons or less in either or both tanks. During ground checking operations, with the switch placed in SERV CHK the appropriate indicator light illuminates if the oil level in either or both tanks is 4.6 gallons or less. The ground check operation is only valid with external electrical power applied and engines off.

Note

On aircraft after AFC 252 but not PPC 62 the L ENG OIL LOW and R ENG OIL LOW lights are installed; however, the oil level sensor is not. The lights may flicker during test but do not indicate when a low oil level exists.

Lubrication

The lubrication element of the oil pump supplies oil to cool and lubricate bearings, gears and other rubbing or moving parts in the engine. Lubricating oil is also circulated through the engine driven generator for cooling purposes. Oil is drawn from the lowest standpipe in the reservoir by the constant displacement, rotary vane type lubrication element of the oil

ENGINE OIL SYSTEM

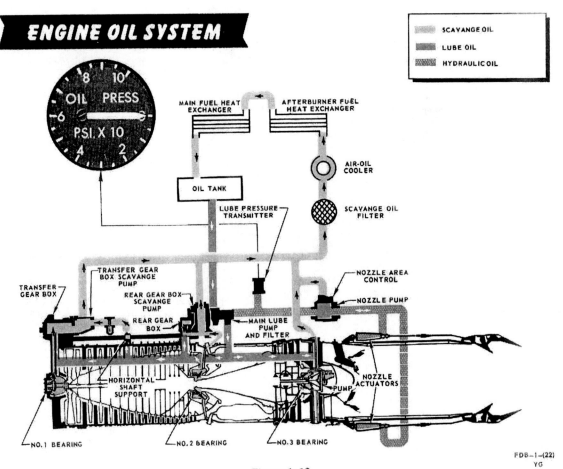

Figure 1-18

FDB-1-(22)
YG

pump, which is capable of delivering 11.8 gpm at 60 psi. By supplying the lubrication element from the lowest standpipe, oil is available for lubrication, should leakage occur in the nozzle control or constant speed drive unit. Lubricating oil is routed from the lubricating element, through the filter to three branch lines. The first branch distributes oil forward to the transfer gear box, intermediate damper bearing, No. 1 bearing, front gear box and the afterburner fuel pump. The second branch distributes to the No. 2 and 3 bearings and the rear gear box. The third branch distributes to the pressure transmitter and the pressure relief valve. The pressure relief valve protects the system and is set to relieve at approximately 95 psi. The oil is picked up from the bearing sumps by the scavenge pumps, which pumps the oil through the scavenge filter, the air oil cooler, the two fuel oil heat exchangers and returns it to the tank. Oil temperature is maintained by temperature regulators on the two fuel oil heat exchangers. A check valve, in the lubrication element outlet, prevents gravity flow of oil from the oil tank when the engine is not running.

Variable Nozzle Control

Engine oil is used as the hydraulic medium for positioning the variable nozzle flaps. During normal flight attitudes, oil flows through a gravity valve and into an accumulation compartment in the reservoir. During inverted flight, the gravity valve closes and oil for nozzle positioning is available for approximately 30 seconds. From this compartment, oil is drawn through a weighted, flexible standpipe, which stays submerged regardless of flight attitude, to the hydraulic element of the oil pump. This element is of the rotary vane type, and is capable of delivering 4.1 gpm at 70 to 110 psi. A relief valve in the pump protects the system by opening at approximately 70 psi. Oil is routed from the pump, through the hydraulic element filter to the nozzle pump. From here it may return directly to the scavenge system, or be boosted and directed to the nozzle actuators on command from the nozzle area control. From the actuators, oil is routed back to the nozzle pump and into the scavenge system. The scavenge system is the same as described in the preceding paragraph.

ENGINE AIR INDUCTION

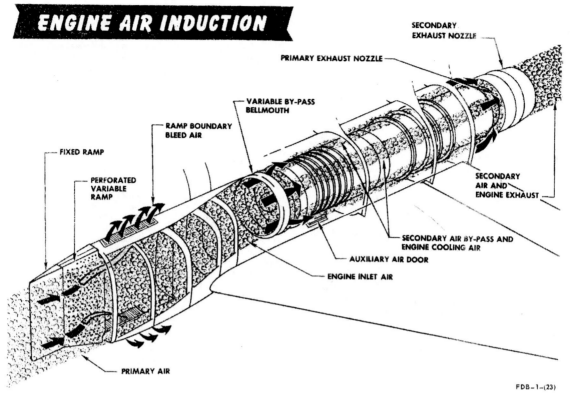

Figure 1-19

FDB-1-(23)

ENGINE AIR INDUCTION

There are two independent but identical air induction systems, one for each engine. The component units are fixed and variable ramps, which make up the primary air system, a variable bypass bellmouth and an auxiliary air door which make up the secondary air system.

Variable Duct Ramp

The variable duct ramp system provides primary air at optimum subsonic airflow to the compressor face throughout an extremely wide range of aircraft speeds. The ramp assembly consists of a fixed forward ramp and two variable ramps. The forward variable ramp is perforated to allow boundary layer air to be bled off and exhausted overboard. The aft variable ramp is solid. Movement of the aft ramp positions the forward variable ramp through mechanical linkage. The air data computer supplies a total temperature input to the ramp control amplifier, which in turn sends a signal to a utility hydraulic system servo unit which positions the ramps for optimum airflow at Mach 1.5 and above. The airplanes have a fixed forward ramp angle of 10 and a variable ramp angle of 0 to 14 relative to the fixed forward ramp.

RAMP SCHEDULING

Ramps begin scheduling at +52°C total temperature and stop at +146°C total temperature. The following schedule is representative of ramp opening:

RAMP SCHEDULE

40,000 FEET

OAT°C	RAMPS BEGIN TO OPEN AT APPROX. MACH
-40	1.40
-45	1.45
-50	1.50
-55	1.55
-60	1.60
-65	1.65
-70	1.70

Engine Inlet Temperature High Indicator Light

The engine inlet temperature high indicator light, marked ENG INLET TEMP HIGH, is on the telelight panel (figure A-1, appendix A). The light when illuminated, indicates that the temperature within the engine intake duct (compressor inlet) is beyond allowable limits for steady state engine operation.

The maximum steady state operation of the engine is limited to 121°C (250°F) compressor inlet temperature. Operating the engine at high altitudes, with the compressor inlet temperature above the prescribed limit, causes the life of the gears, bearings, and carbon seals to be reduced because the lubricating oil exceeds its design temperature. Exceeding the temperature also causes structural components of the engine (compressor rear frame and combustion casings) to exceed their design limit because of high temperatures and pressures.

Variable Bypass Bellmouth

The variable bypass bellmouth is an automatic unit which allows excess induction air from the compressor face to flow into the engine compartment. Air diverted in this fashion is referred to as the Secondary Air System. The variable bellmouth is a perforated ring between the airplane duct structure and the engine compressor inlet. Between .4 to .98 Mach the bellmouth is closed; however, a limited amount of bypass air flows into the engine compartment through the perforations in the bypass bellmouth and the engine air-oil cooler bleed. Above .98 Mach the bypass bellmouth controller senses the optimum airflow (based on duct air velocity) for induction into the engine. When this airflow is exceeded, (rapid throttle retardation) the controller signals a utility system hydraulic actuator which opens the bypass until the optimum airflow to the engine is established.

Auxiliary Air Door

Two auxiliary air doors, one for each engine compartment, are on the center underside of the fuselage. They are normally controlled by the landing gear handle and actuated open or closed by utility hydraulic pressure. When the landing gear handle is placed down, the doors open, making additional air available to the engine compartments for cooling purposes. When the landing gear handle is placed up, the doors close. The closing force applied to each door by its hydraulic actuator is equivalent to the area of the door times 13.3 psi. If the engine compartment pressures exceed the ambient pressure by approximately 13.3 psi, the door is forced open by an amount proportional to the overpressure. As soon as the overpressure is relieved, the actuator pulls the door closed.

CAUTION

Engine compartment pressures in excess of 13.3 psi are not normal. Therefore, in the event either auxiliary air door indicator light illuminates (other than momentary), corrective action should be taken as soon as possible. Refer to Auxiliary Air Door Malfunction section V.

Auxiliary Air Door Indicator Lights

The auxiliary air door indicator lights on the telelight panel (figure A-1, appendix A), marked L AUX

AIR DOOR and R AUX AIR DOOR respectively, illuminate, should the auxiliary air doors operate out of phase with the landing gear handle. The lights illuminate momentarily when engine compartment overpressures are relieved. Illumination of the auxiliary air door indicator lights cause the MASTER CAUTION light to illuminate. Refer to section V for operating instructions during auxiliary air door malfunction.

VARIABLE AREA EXHAUST NOZZLE

Two sets of cylindrical nozzles, operating together, make up the variable area exhaust nozzle system. The primary nozzle, hinged to the aft end of the tail pipe, controls the convergent portion of the nozzle, while the secondary nozzle, hinged to a support ring, controls the divergent portion of the nozzle. The two sets of nozzles are linked together and maintain a scheduled area and spacing ratio which is infinitely variable between full open and full closed. The nozzles are regulated by the nozzle area control. Movement of the nozzles is accomplished automatically by four synchronized hydraulic actuators. The exhaust gases leave the primary nozzles at sonic velocity and are accelerated to supersonic velocity by the controlled expansion of the gases. Control of this expansion is provided by the cushioning effect of the secondary airflow through the annular passage between the two sets of nozzles.

Exhaust Nozzle Control Unit

Throttle position, nozzle position feedback, and exhaust gas temperature are the parameters utilized to schedule the correct nozzle area. During engine operation in the sub-military region, nozzle area is primarily a function of throttle angle and nozzle position feedback. The nozzle is scheduled full open at idle and the area is decreased as the throttle is advanced toward the military position. However, during a rapid throttle burst from below 79% rpm to 98% rpm, a control alternator supplies engine speed information to the temperature amplifier which in turn schedules engine off speed inputs as a function of temperature limiting. This signal prevents the primary nozzle from closing down past a preset position, permitting a rapid increase in engine rpm. During engine operation in the military and afterburner region, it becomes necessary to limit the nozzle schedule as established by throttle angle and nozzle feedback to prohibit exhaust gas temperature from exceeding the design limits. Exhaust gas temperature is sensed by 12 thermocouple loops and the resulting millivoltage is transmitted to the magnetic temperature amplifier. The amplifier which receives its power supply from the control alternator, compares the thermocouple signal to a preset reference voltage, representing desired engine temperature. The difference is amplified and transmitted to the nozzle area control. Nozzle area control output signal directs the operation of the variable pressure, variable displacement nozzle pump.

Note

Spasmodic exhaust nozzle operation shall be logged on the yellow sheet (OPNAV Form 3760-2).

AFTERBURNER SYSTEM

The engine is equipped with an afterburner, where additional fuel may be injected into the hot exhaust gases for afterburner combustion, producing considerable thrust augmentation. The main components of the afterburner system are the afterburner fuel pump, afterburner fuel control, afterburner fuel manifold and spray bars, and the torch igniter.

Afterburner Fuel System

The afterburner fuel system (figure A-5, appendix A) provides the fuel for augmentation of the thrust produced by the engine. A separate, constant pressure drop, variable fuel control meters afterburner fuel. Ignition is by a separate AB ignition system. The airplane boost pumps supply fuel to the inlet of the afterburner fuel pump. The inlet valve is opened by a fuel pressure signal from the main fuel control when engine speed is above 91 percent rpm and throttle angle is above 76.5 degrees (in minimum AB range). Fuel passing through the check valve continues to the afterburner fuel control, is metered, separated into core and annulus flows, and directed to the afterburner pressurizing valve. The core fuel passes through the afterburner fuel/oil heat exchanger on the way to the control and pressurizing valve. The core and annulus flows are further subdivided into primary and secondary flows by the pressurizing valve. The flow sequence as the throttle is advanced in the afterburner range is to the primary core, secondary core, primary annulus and secondary annulus.

Afterburner Fuel Pump

The afterburner fuel pump is an engine-driven centrifugal pump. It operates continuously, but discharges fuel to the afterburner fuel system only when the inlet valve on the pump is open. To open the inlet valve to the afterburner fuel pump, the pilot must move the throttle into the afterburner modulation range and engine speed must be sufficiently high (above 91% rpm) to support combustion.

Afterburner Fuel Control

The afterburner fuel control is linked mechanically to the main fuel control through the use of teleflex cabling. Any movement of the throttle moves the main fuel control teleflex to the afterburner fuel control. Fuel entering the afterburner fuel control is metered and separated into core and annulus flows in response to throttle movement and changes in compressor discharge pressure. The control varies fuel flow between the minimum necessary for afterburner combustion for any flight condition and the maximum fuel flow allowable at the flight condition. The afterburner fuel control is designed to hold a constant pressure drop across an orifice while the area of that orifice is varied in accordance with throttle position and compressor discharge pressure.

Afterburner Fuel Distribution

The afterburner fuel pressuring valve delivers fuel to four separate fuel manifolds: primary annulus, primary core, secondary annulus, and secondary core. The fuel is distributed by these manifolds to 21 multi-jet afterburner fuel nozzles which are equally spaced around the perimeter of the afterburner section. Each multi-jet nozzle contains 4 tubes, one for each manifold, and holes in the sides of the tubes spray the fuel into the exhaust gases. When the throttle is first placed into the afterburner position, the pressurizing valve directs fuel to the primary core manifold. Further advancement directs fuel to the secondary core manifold which joins the primary core in delivering fuel for afterburner operation. Then the throttle is advanced still further, the pressurizing valve directs fuel to the primary annulus manifold. As the throttles are advanced to the maximum afterburner position, the fuel is directed to the secondary annulus thus joining the other three manifolds in delivering fuel to the nozzles; this is full full afterburner operation. The afterburner fuel manifolds and multi-jet nozzle system gives a smooth afterburner operation, with no appreciable acceleration surge between full military and minimum afterburner, or between minimum afterburner and maximum afterburner.

IGNITION SYSTEM

The ignition system consists of an ignition button (figure A-1, appendix A) on each throttle, a low voltage, high energy ignition unit on the engine, a spark plug in No. 4 combustion chamber and the necessary wiring. The main ignition system ignites the atomized fuel-air mixture in No. 4 combustion can. The remaining nine combustion cans are ignited through the cross fire tubes. The afterburner ignition system includes the torch igniter, an afterburner ignition switch, and a torch igniter fuel metering valve. The pilot burner, which includes an afterburner spark plug and a fuel nozzle, is continuously supplied with fuel during engine operation. The fuel, however, is not ignited until the throttle is first moved into the afterburner detent. After PPC 8, a torch igniter metering valve is installed. The metering valve supplies fuel to the torch igniter only during the time that afterburner operation is selected with the throttle. When the throttle is moved into the afterburner detent, fuel from the main engine fuel control is directed to the pressure actuated afterburner ignition switch. Electrical power from the left main 115/200 volt ac bus is then supplied to the afterburner spark plug which emits a continuous arc to ignite the fuel-air mixture in the torch igniter. Continuous ignition is provided as long as the throttle is in the afterburner detent. The torch igniter produces an intense flame which ignites the afterburner fuel.

Ignition Buttons

The ignition buttons are spring-loaded push button type switches on each throttle directly below the throttle grips. Pressing the ignition button causes the spark plug to discharge, igniting the fuel-air mixture as the throttle is moved from OFF to IDLE during engine start. The spark plugs fire only while the ignition button is pressed. The ignition duty cycle is 2 min. on, 3 min. off, 2 min. on, and 23 min. off.

The ignition circuits are completed anytime aircraft power is on, and ignition button is depressed.

STARTING SYSTEM

The impingement starting system consists of an assembly of ducting and valves which are airframe mounted and a manifold assembly which is mounted on the turbine frame of the engine. The single receptacle for connecting the air supply line is on the bottom left side of the fuselage aft of the main gear wheel well. Air from the external source is directed to the left or right selector valves which distribute the air to either the left or right engine, depending on cockpit selection. The engine manifold assembly distributes the starting air to seven impingement nozzles, which direct the air against the second stage turbine blades of the turbine wheel.

Engine Start Switch

The engine starter switch (figure A-1, appendix A) is on the left console in the pilot's cockpit just inboard of the throttles. The starter switch is a three-position switch and is marked L., OFF, and R. On aircraft prior to 151473s before AFC 176, the switch receives power from the 28 volt dc starter cart bus. On aircraft 151473s and up and all others after AFC 176, the switch receives power from the essential 28 volt dc bus, thereby eliminating the need for dc power from the APU. With APU air connected, actuating the starter switch to L energizes the left engine impingement nozzles. Selecting R energizes the right engine selector valve and permits air to flow to the right engine impingement nozzles. The OFF position closes both selector valves and stops airflow to the engines. For impingement starting a 5.5:1 pressure ratio gas turbine starting unit is desired.

ENGINE CONTROLS

Engine Master Switches

The toggle lock type two-position engine master switches (figure A-1, appendix A) are on the left console in the pilot's cockpit on the inboard engine control panel. Placing the switch ON directs power to the fuel boost pumps and fuel transfer pumps. The circuits for the fuel shutoff valves, which are normally operated by the throttles, are such that either valve is closed when its respective engine master switch is OFF regardless of the throttle position.

Throttles

A throttle (figure A-1, appendix A) for each engine is on the left console of the forward cockpit. Mechanical linkage and teleflex cables transmit mechanical motion from the throttle to those accessories requiring coordination to obtain the degree of trust desired. Movement of the throttle is transmitted by mechanical linkage to the main fuel control. The main fuel control unit incorporates a throttle booster which reduces the amount of effort needed to move the throttles. The boost power is supplied by fuel

from the engine driven fuel pump. Teleflex cables from the main fuel control link the nozzle area control and afterburner fuel control to throttle movement so that fuel flow and nozzle area are compatible throughout the full range of engine operation. A friction adjusting lever is mounted between the throttles which permits adjustment of throttle friction to suit individual requirements. The throttle mechanism is a gear shift type. Included on the throttles are the ignition buttons (one for each engine on the applicable throttle), speed brake switch and microphone button on the right throttle, and master lights control switch on the outboard side of the left throttle. On aircraft after AFC 448, a singles chaff button is added to the right throttle. Limit switches which control the main fuel shutoff valves are built into the throttle quadrant. Advancing the throttle from OFF to IDLE (with the engine master switch ON) actuates electrical switches which open the main fuel shutoff valve corresponding with the throttle moved. With further advancement of the throttle from IDLE to MIL, engine thrust increases proportionally. At the MIL position of the throttles, the engine should be delivering its rated military power. Afterburner light-off can be initiated anywhere within the afterburner modulation range by shifting the throttles outboard and moving forward toward MAX. Movement of the throttles from IDLE to OFF actuates a switch which closes the main fuel shutoff stopping fuel flow to the engine. Throttle movement through the cutouts is as follows: To move throttles from OFF to IDLE, push forward and then shift throttles inboard. To move from MIL to MAX shift throttles outboard, throttles can now be moved forward in the afterburner range.

Catapult Throttle Grips

Catapult throttle grips secured to the pilot's cockpit structure and above the MIL throttle detent and MAX throttle detent may be hinged upward to line up with the throttles at the MIL and MAX throttle positions. The grips and throttles may then be held together during catapulting to prevent inadvertently throttling back. The grips are automatically stowed when released.

ENGINE INSTRUMENTS

Engine Fuel Flow Indicators

The engine fuel flow indicators (figure A-1, appendix A) are on the right side of the pilot's instrument panel. The fuel flow indicating system indicates the amount of main fuel system flow, in pounds per hour, of fuel the engines are using at a particular power setting. The rate of fuel flow is shown in 1000 pounds per hour by a pointer moving over a scale calibrated from 0 to 12. Maximum fuel flow fluctuations are: 100 PPH for indicator readings of 0-3000 PPH; 750 PPH for readings of 3001-12,000 PPH. The flow is measured by transmitters mounted on the engines. Afterburner fuel flow bypasses the fuel flow transmitters and therefore is not shown on the indicators.

Tachometers

The electric tachometer system is composed of two tachometer indicators (figure A-1, appendix A)

Changed 1 March 1972

mounted on the pilot's instrument panel and one engine-driven tachometer generator mounted on each engine. The system is completely self-contained in that it requires no external source of power. The tachometer generator develops a poly-phase alternating current which is used to indicate percentage of maximum engine rpm. The indicator dials are calibrated from 0 to 110. Each indicator includes two pointers, a large one operating on the 0 to 100 scale and a small one operating on a separate scale calibrated from 0 to 10.

Exhaust Gas Temperature Indicators

The exhaust gas temperature indicators (figure A-1, appendix A) are on the pilot's instrument panel. The scale range on the indicators is 0 to 11 with the reading multiplied by 100°C. The system indicates the temperature of the exhaust gas as it leaves the turbine unit during engine operation. Twelve dual loop thermocouples are on each engine and are connected in parallel. The millivoltages produced by one of the sets of dual loop thermocouples is directed to an amplifier for temperature limiting. The millivoltages produced by the other set of 12 thermocouples is directed to the cockpit indicator. The indicator is a null-seeking potentiometer type. It balances a thermocouple voltage against a constant voltage source with a small servo motor simultaneously balancing a bridge circuit and operating the indicator pointers.

Exhaust Nozzle Position Indicators

Exhaust nozzle position indicators (figure A-1, appendix A) which show the exit area of the exhaust nozzle, are on the pilot's instrument panel. The instruments are placarded Jet Nozzle Position and are calibrated from CLOSE to OPEN in 1/4 increments. The nozzle position indicators enable the pilot to make a comparison of nozzle position between engines, and is also used to establish a relationship between nozzle position and exhaust gas temperature and nozzle position and throttle settings.

Oil Pressure Indicators

The oil pressure indicators (figure A-1, appendix A) are on the pedestal panel. The scale range on the indicators is 0 to 10 with reading multiplied by 10. The oil pressure indication system senses oil pressure downstream of the main lube pump in the main lube discharge line.

ENGINE ANTI-ICING SYSTEM

The engine anti-icing system is a compressor discharge air bleed type system, controlled by an on-off pressure regulating valve. Air for anti-icing purposes is supplied from the 17th stage of the engine compressor at pressures up to 275 psi, and temperatures up to 593°C. A regulator in the anti-icing valve reduces the incoming air to a pressure of approximately 14-20 psi. Air from the anti-icing valve is distributed through the first stage stator vanes, the compressor front frame struts, and the inlet guide vanes. On airplanes 150652o and up, and all others after ASC 69, engine anti-ice air is delivered to a port in the front gear box for engine nose dome anti-icing.

CAUTION

During subsonic flight, the anti-icing system should be used when icing conditions are anticipated. However, during supersonic flight, the anti-icing system should only be used when actual icing is noted.

Engine Anti-Icing Switch

A two-position engine anti-icing switch (figure A-1, appendix A) is on the outboard engine control panel. The switch is marked engine anti-icing and the switch positions are DE-ICE and NORMAL. Placing the switch in DE-ICE opens the regulator valve which starts anti-icing airflow. With the switch in NORMAL, no anti-icing operation is being performed.

Engine Anti-Ice Lights

Engine anti-ice lights have been installed on the tele-light panel in airplanes 150652o and up, and all others after ASC 69. The lights, marked L ANTI-ICE ON and R ANTI-ICE ON, operate from a pressure sensitive switch which is actuated by the pressure of engine bleed air when the system is turned on. During flight in the high Mach number region, a pressure build-up, caused by high dynamic pressures, may occur in the anti-icing system. This may cause the anti-icing lights to illuminate even though the anti-icing switch is in NORMAL, resulting in an erroneous indication. If the lights illuminate under these conditions, reduce speed. If the lights go out, high Mach flight may be continued. If the lights illuminate during low speed flight and the engine anti-icing switch is in NORMAL, check for proper system operation by placing the anti-ice switch to DE-ICE and observe a 10° rise (approximately) in exhaust gas temperature.

CAUTION

If the MASTER CAUTION light and the L ANTI-ICE ON and/or R ANTI-ICE ON lights illuminate during high Mach flight, and a speed reduction does not extinguish them, remain at a reduced speed. Continued operation in the high Mach range may cause engine damage.

FIRE AND OVERHEAT DETECTOR SYSTEM

Engine Fire/Overheat/Bleed Air Leakage Warning Lights

The fire and overheat detection system consists of three separate and independent systems: Engine Fire Detection System, Aft Fuselage Overheat system, and on aircraft after AFC 439, a Bleed Air Leakage Detection System. The FIRE and OVERHT warning lights, one for each engine, are on the upper right portion of the main instrument panel. The BLEED AIR OVERHT lights (3 each) are on the tele-light panel. In addition to the lights, each system consists of a control unit, and series of continuous sensing elements. The fire warning sensing elements are routed throughout the engine compartments. The right or left FIRE warning light illuminates if a temperature of approximately 765°F occurs in the corresponding engine compartment. The aft fuselage overheat sensing elements are routed in vertical recesses of the skin fairing on each side of the keel. These recesses are opposite the aft end of the secondary engine nozzle fingers. The left or right OVERHT warning light illuminates if a temperature of approximately 1050°F occurs at the corresponding aft fuselage skin. Do not use afterburner if an aft fuselage OVERHT warning light illuminates. This indicates a safety of flight condition such as an open engine compartment door or a damaged engine nozzle. Either of these conditions can lead to the loss of flight control if afterburner is used. The bleed air leakage sensing elements are routed along the bleed air ducts, and illuminate three different lights, depending on where the leak occurs. The elements routed under fuel cell 2 through the fuel/hydraulic bay (door 22) and then through the left and right refrigeration packages illuminates the FUS BLEED AIR OVERHT warning light if a temperature of approximately 410°F occurs in this area. The elements routed along each wing leading edge outboard to the BLC shut off valve illuminates the WING BLEED AIR OVERHT light if a temperature of approximately 410°F occurs in this area. The element routed along the engine bleed air duct, in the keel web, illuminates the ENG BLEED AIR OVERHT light if a temperature of approximately 575° occurs in this area. Illumination of any of the fire or overheat lights is a warning to initiate the appropriate emergency procedure(s). The MASTER CAUTION light illuminates in conjunction with any of the fire or overheat warning lights. The engine fire and aft fuselage overheat lights operate on RAT power, however the bleed air overheat lights do not.

Note

- When extending the ram air turbine in airplanes 152216u and up, it is normal for the FIRE and OVERHT lights to flicker for a short time period until the RAT comes up to full operation. Disregard these lights unless they remain on after RAT extension.

- Except for illumination resulting from RAT extension, illumination of the FIRE or OVERHT light shall be logged on the yellow sheet (OPNAV Form 3760-2).

Fire Detector Check Switch

The engine fire, aft fuselage overheat, and on aircraft after AFC 439, the bleed air overheat warning light system may be checked by depressing the fire detector check switch. The lights should first be checked by placing the warning light test switch, on the right console, to test. This action only checks the light bulbs. Depressing the fire detector check switch illuminates the FIRE, OVERHT, FUS BLEED AIR OVERHT, WING BLEED AIR OVERHT, and ENG BLEED OVERHT lights and also checks the continuity of their sensors and the operation of each system's control panel. The engine fire and aft fuselage overheat warning test circuit receives power from the right main 28 volt dc bus. Therefore, when op-

erating on RAT, these lights cannot be tested. The bleed air overheat warning lights do not operate on the RAT.

ENGINE BLEED AIR SYSTEM

The bleed air system supplies high temperature, high pressure air from the engines to the boundary layer control system, the cabin air conditioning system, the equipment air conditioning system, and the fuel cell pressurization system. The functional control of the bleed air is initiated by the requirements of each individual system and the flow, temperature, and pressure are regulated by the system. The system utilizes engine compressor bleed air tapped off the 17th stage compressor. Normally, both engines supply the air for the operation of these systems, but when necessary, single engine operation supplies sufficient air for their operation. On aircraft after AFC 440, during single engine operation trailing edge BLC will be lost on the wing adjacent to the inoperative engine. The system ducting routes the flow of bleed air from the engines to the systems and is insulated to protect the airframe structure from heat radiation. Check valves are installed in the ducting to prevent back flow into the nonoperating engine during starting and single engine operation.

Engine Bleed Air Switch

On aircraft 155903ap, and 157274ap and up, and all others after AFC 440, a lever-locked engine bleed air switch is installed on front cockpit right utility panel. The switch has two positions, NORM and OFF, and controls a bleed air shutoff valve installed in the keel Y duct between the engines. After AFC 550, the lever-locked engine bleed air switch is replaced by a simple toggle switch and a red guard. Actuation of the switch to OFF shuts off engine bleed air to all systems except trailing edge BLC. As a result, cabin refrigeration and pressurization, defog/foot-heat, fuel system pressurization and internal wing and external fuel transfer, pneumatic system charging, SPC, canopy seal and anti-G suit pressurization, and leading edge BLC will be lost. CNI equipment (TACAN, ADF, UHF, IFF and SIF), and radar will lose cooling air from the equipment refrigeration package, but will still have ram air cooling available. Ram air is also available for cabin temperature control. Under RAT power, bleed air will be delivered to all systems regardless of switch position.

| CAUTION |

When the engine bleed air switch is positioned to OFF, radar and CNI equipment should be placed in the OFF position unless safety of flight/operational necessity requires their use.

Bleed Air Off Light

After AFC 550, a BLEED AIR OFF light is added to the caution light panel. The light illuminates any time the bleed air shutoff valve is in the off position. The MASTER CAUTION light illuminates in conjunction with the BLEED AIR OFF light. The BLEED AIR OFF light is powered by the warning lights 28/14 volt ac bus through the BLC warning light circuit breaker.

Changed 15 August 1972

NORMAL OPERATION

STARTING ENGINES

OPERATING CHARACTERISTICS

T₂ Reset

During high compressor inlet temperature operation
(high speed flight) engine idle speed is rescheduled

ENGINE OPERATING ENVELOPE

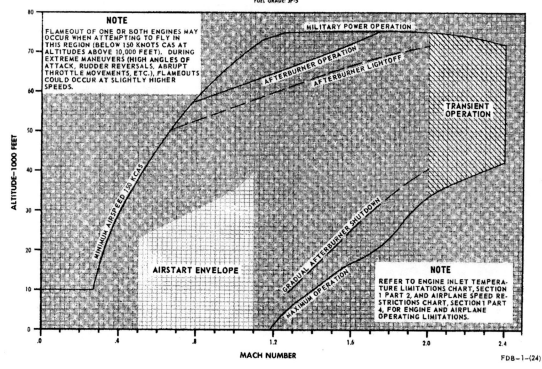

REMARKS
ENGINE(S): (2) J79-GE-8
ICAO STANDARD DAY
FUEL GRADE: JP-5

NOTE

FLAMEOUT OF ONE OR BOTH ENGINES MAY OCCUR WHEN ATTEMPTING TO FLY IN THIS REGION (BELOW 150 KNOTS CAS AT ALTITUDES ABOVE 10,000 FEET). DURING EXTREME MANEUVERS (HIGH ANGLES OF ATTACK, RUDDER REVERSALS, ABRUPT THROTTLE MOVEMENTS, ETC.), FLAMEOUTS COULD OCCUR AT SLIGHTLY HIGHER SPEEDS.

MILITARY POWER OPERATION

AFTERBURNER OPERATION

AFTERBURNER LIGHTOFF

TRANSIENT OPERATION

MINIMUM AIRSPEED 150 KCAS

AIRSTART ENVELOPE

GRADUAL AFTERBURNER SHUTDOWN

MAXIMUM OPERATION

NOTE

REFER TO ENGINE INLET TEMPERATURE LIMITATIONS CHART, SECTION 1 PART 2, AND AIRPLANE SPEED RESTRICTIONS CHART, SECTION 1 PART 4, FOR ENGINE AND AIRPLANE OPERATING LIMITATIONS.

ALTITUDE-1000 FEET

MACH NUMBER

FDB-1-(24)

Figure 1-20

upward to maintain sufficient airflow to prevent compressor stall. As compressor inlet temperature increases from 57° to 108°C, engine idle speed is raised from normal idle (65 percent) to 100 percent regardless of the throttle position. To reduce engine idle speed, once it has been reset, compressor inlet temperature must be reduced. This is effected by retarding the throttles out of afterburner to reduce thrust. Thrust can be further reduced by retarding the throttles below the military position so that the exhaust nozzles open, lowering exhaust gas velocity and temperature. As thrust decreases, compressor inlet temperature decreases as a result of lower airspeed, and engine speed control is returned to the throttle.

T_2 Cutback

When the compressor inlet temperature (T_2) falls below +4°C, the maximum engine rpm is limited to prevent excessive mass airflow through the engine. The rpm maximum speed reduction starts at +4°C and is reduced until at -54°C the maximum rpm is approximately 91.5 percent.

T_5 Reset

The engines incorporated an exhaust gas temperature (T_5) reset during military and full AB operation. This T_5 reset occurs at the same point as T_2 cutback and reduces EGT at the same time that T_2 cutback is reducing rpm. As a result of T_5 reset, the engines run at lower EGT, operate with larger nozzle areas, provide less net thrust and consume less fuel while operating in the speed cutback region at low CIT conditions.

ENGINE OPERATING ENVELOPE

The engine operating envelopes (figure 1-20) show pertinent engine operating data for an ICAO Standard Day. The various envelopes are plotted to show an approximate area of operation; therefore, airstarts, afterburner light-offs, minimum airspeed operation, etc. may occur, depending upon prevailing flight conditions, on either side of the plotted operational area. However, under 1 G level flight conditions, satisfactory engine operations can be expected within the plotted envelopes. The transient operation zone (Mach 2.0 to 2.4) and the maximum engine operation curve are standard day airspeed restrictions and are shown for reference only. In all cases the Airplane Speed Restriction Chart and Engine Airspeed Limit Chart in section I of this manual shall take precedence over any or all operations shown herein.

EMERGENCY OPERATION

ENGINE FAILURE

Jet engine failures in most cases are caused by improper fuel scheduling due to malfunction of the fuel control system or incorrect techniques used during certain critical flight conditions. Engine instruments often provide indications of fuel control system failures before the engine actually stops. If engine failure is due to a malfunction of the fuel control system or improper operating technique, an air start can usually be accomplished, providing time and altitude permit. If engine failure can be attributed to some obvious mechanical failure within the engine proper, do not attempt to restart the engine.

RUNAWAY ENGINE

There is no provision made on the main fuel control for stabilized engine rpm in the event the throttle linkage becomes disconnected from the control. If a disconnect occurs, vibration may cause the fuel control to hunt or assume any setting from idle to maximum power. Therefore, at the first indication of a runaway engine while on the ground, secure the engine with the engine master switch. If a runaway engine occurs in flight, shut it down before commencing the approach, or sooner if necessary.

AIRSTARTS

In general, airstart capability is increased by higher airspeeds and lower altitudes; however, airstarts can be made over a wide range of airspeeds and altitudes. Depending on airspeed and altitude, the engine starts at various low rpm indications. Above 12 percent rpm, however, is considered optimum. An airstart is accomplished by pressing the ignition button with the throttle at any position beyond IDLE. A start is indicated by a rapid increase in EGT followed by an increase in rpm. If light-off does not occur within 30 seconds after ignition, the engine does not continue to accelerate after light-off, the EGT exceeds maximum limitations, or the oil pressure does not attain 12 psi minimum at idle, retard the throttle to OFF. Wait 30 seconds before initiating a restart.

Note

• If one or both engines flame out, do not delay the airstart. If a mechanical failure is not immediately evident, press and hold the ignition button(s) to restart the engine(s) before excessive rpm is lost.

• If airstarts are attempted outside the airstart envelope (figure 1-20), a hung acceleration condition may result. RPM will hang between 65% and 71% while EGT will continue to rise

and the engine will not respond to throttle movement. To terminate this condition the throttle may have to be retarded to OFF. Restart attempt may be initiated as soon as RPM drops below 60%.

AFTERBURNER IGNITION FAILURE

If for any reason afterburner ignition is not available, afterburner light-offs can generally be obtained through turbine torching. If afterburner thrust is required and/or desired, slam accelerate the engine into afterburner range from 90% rpm or higher. If the first selection is not successful, an immediate slam reselection should achieve successful results.

OIL SYSTEM FAILURE

The standpipes which supply the three systems utilizing engine oil are in the reservoir such that the pipe for the constant speed drive unit is the highest, the one for the nozzle control is the next highest, and the lubricating system pipe is the lowest. Therefore, a leak in the constant speed drive unit probably causes a failure of that system only, while a leak in the nozzle control system may cause failure of that system and the constant speed drive unit. A leak in the lubricating or the scavenging system causes failure of the constant speed drive unit and the nozzle control system, and ultimately, engine bearing failure results. A GEN OUT light illumination, followed by sluggish exhaust nozzle action, are early indications of impending engine oil starvation. The engine oil pressure gage should be monitored closely subsequent to a generator failure. In general, it is advisable to shut the engine down as early as possible after a loss of oil supply is indicated, to minimize the possibility of damage to the engine and the constant speed drive unit. The engine operates satisfactorily at military power for a period of 1 minute, with an interrupted oil supply. However, continuous operation, at any engine speed, with the oil supply interrupted results in bearing failure and eventual engine seizure. The rate at which a bearing will fail, measured from the moment the oil supply is interrupted, cannot be accurately predicted. Such rate depends upon the condition of the bearing before oil starvation, temperature of the bearing and loads on the bearing. Malfunctions of the oil system are indicated by a shift (high or low) from normal operating pressure, sometimes followed by a rapid increase in vibration. A slow pressure increase may be caused by partial clogging of one or more oil jets; while a rapid increase may be caused by complete blockage of an oil line. Conversely a slow pressure decrease may be caused by an oil leak; while a sudden decrease is probably caused by a ruptured oil line, or a sheared oil or scavenge pump shaft. Vibration may increase progressively until it is moderate to severe before the pilot notices it. At this time, complete bearing failure and engine seizure is imminent. Limited experience has shown that the engine may operate for 4-5 minutes at 80-90 percent speed before a complete failure occurs. In the event of a drop in oil pressure or a complete loss of pressure, shut the affected engine down if power is not required or, set the engine speed at 86-89% if partial power is required. If partial power is required on the affected engine, avoid abrupt maneuvers causing high G forces and avoid unnecessary or large throttle bursts.

AUTO-ACCELERATION

If the auxiliary air doors fail to open when the landing gear is lowered, there is a possibility that the engines may automatically accelerate up to 100 percent rpm. A utility hydraulic system failure renders the variable bypass bellmouth and auxiliary air doors inoperative. Operation of an engine with an open variable bypass bellmouth and closed auxiliary air doors allows engine compartment secondary air to recirculate to the engine inlet. During low altitude or ground operation, the temperature of the recirculating air may be high enough to initiate T_2 reset. When T_2 reset is initiated the engines auto-accelerate. The auto-accelerated engines can be shut down if on the ground, by placing the throttles OFF. If engine operation is required, the thrust output can be regulated by modulation of the engine throttle. Modulation of the engine throttle repositions the exhaust nozzles. However, the engine rpm is not affected.

VARIABLE AREA INLET RAMP FAILURE

There are no provisions made for emergency operation of the inlet ramps. Malfunctions of the inlet ramp control or actuating system may cause the ramp to assume the fully retracted (maximum duct area) position or the fully extended (minimum duct area) position. A failure of the ramp to the retracted position has no effect on engine operating characteristics or performance below approximately 1.5 Mach. Engine compressor stalls may occur above 1.7 Mach. A failure of the inlet ramps to the extended position below approximately 1.5 Mach causes a substantial loss of thrust, and engine compressor stall and flameout may occur above approximately 18,000 ft. altitude. Extended inlet ramps may be detected by: observing the ramp position in the rear view mirror; significantly reduced fuel flow at power settings above 85% rpm; high pitched howl at airspeeds above 300 KCAS; and significantly reduced thrust (approximately 35%) at power settings above 90% rpm. Engine acceleration time and response to throttle movement are not affected by the extended ramp. No special procedures are required for throttle manipulation under these conditions. Jam accelerations to military and max AB power, stabilized high power operation, sideslips and airstarts may be performed without overtemperature or compressor stalls. Power settings above 94% rpm with the ramps extended produce increased fuel consumption without increasing engine thrust output. For this reason, cruising altitudes should be selected at which the recommended maximum range Mach number for existing configuration and gross weight can be maintained with 94% rpm or less. Refer to section V for flight procedures with ramps extended.

ENGINE SPEEDS

CONDITION	STATIC	INFLIGHT
NORMAL OPERATION	100 ± 0.5% RPM	100 ± 0.5% RPM
ALLOWABLE OVERSPEED NON TIME LIMITED	103% RPM	102% RPM
ALLOWABLE OVERSPEED TIME LIMITED	103-105% RPM FOR 3 MINUTES	102-103.6% RPM FOR 1 MINUTE
IDLE	65 ± 1% RPM	————

ANY RPM IN EXCESS OF THE ABOVE LIMITATIONS SHALL BE LOGGED ON THE YELLOW SHEET (OPNAV FORM 3760-2)

FDB-1-(25)

Figure 1-21

LIMITATIONS

RPM DROP

When entering afterburner from throttle settings less than military, the allowable rpm drop is 14%. When entering afterburner from stabilized military power allowable rpm drop is 10%. All exceeded engine speed limitations must be recorded on the flight forms (yellow sheets).

TEMPERATURE

Engine temperatures are limited by degree and time as shown on figures 1-22 and 1-23.

THROTTLE BURST

When operating with maximum engine compressor bleed air (flaps down and cockpit pressurized) in outside air temperatures of -37°C and below, rapid throttle bursts may result in an rpm hang-up. If a throttle burst into maximum afterburner is made, cyclic engine operation may result. When rapid throttle bursting is necessary under these conditions, it is recommended that the throttle be advanced to minimum afterburner first and the engine rpm be allowed to stabilize before advancing further into the afterburner range.

ENGINE EXHAUST TEMPERATURE LIMITATIONS

CONDITION	TEMP	TIME
Steady state temperature for continuous operation in military or maximum range.	625 ± 10°C	NO LIMIT
Maximum time at temperature during starting	1000°C 980°C 930°C 900°C Down to 733°C	3 sec 10 sec 1 min 1 min 30 sec
During all engine operations other than starting	750°C 635°C	3 sec NO LIMIT

Notes

● If any of the above limits are exceeded the aircraft will be aborted and written up. In addition, if 705°C is exceeded during start for any period of time, the engine will require corrective action to prevent recurrence. This is not an abort item.
● During all engine operations other than starting, temperature peaks above 750°C for a maximum of 3 seconds are acceptable.

FDB-1-(26)

Figure 1-22

ENGINE INLET TEMPERATURE LIMITATIONS

CONDITION	TEMP	TIME
ENG INLET TEMP HIGH Warning Light Illumination	121°C	Prohibited operation with light illuminated below 30,000 FT.
Transient Temperature Operation	121°C-193°C (max. temperature occurs approximately .4 Mach above illumination of DUCT TEMP HI warning light.)	5 min. per hour (noncumulative) above 30,000 FT.

FDB-1-(27)

Figure 1-23

WINDMILLING

Except for emergency shutdown, do not allow the engine to windmill below 7% rpm below 40,000 feet for periods greater than 10 minutes. Extended windmilling may result in engine damage from inadequate lubrication or oil depletion, and may cause internal engine conditions that are conducive to sump fires when re-lighting. Prior to non-emergency conditions, the engine should be decelerated to the coolest operating point (lowest EGT), and this speed maintained long enough to stabilize EGT. The number of 10 minute intervals below 7% rpm is not limited, providing the engine is operated above 7% rpm for a minimum of 10 minutes between intervals.

POWER

Maximum Power

Maximum power is obtained with full afterburning thrust and is time limited to 30 minutes below 35,000 feet, and 2 hours above 35,000 feet.

Military Power

Military power is obtained with full non-afterburning thrust and has the same limits as Maximum power i.e., 30 minutes below 35,000 feet, and 2 hours above 35,000 feet.

ENGINE IGNITION

The engine ignition duty cycle is as follows:

2 minutes ON - 3 minutes OFF
2 minutes ON - 23 minutes OFF

EMERGENCY FUEL

The engines may be operated on MIL-G-5572B 115/145 AVGAS if JP-4 or JP-5 is not available. When AVGAS is used the aircraft is restricted to one flight of no more than 5 hours duration at subsonic speeds. AVGAS has a specific gravity range between 0.730-0.685. The fuel control should be set to correspond to these values. The engine top speed should be adjusted as necessary. If the fuel control adjustments cannot be made, the aircraft may be flown; however, the pilot should be aware that the following degradations in engine performance will occur.

   a. Longer time to start and accelerate, with possible missed-starts or start-stalls.
   b. Maximum engine RPM and EGT may not be attained.
   c. Slow acceleration throughout the operating range.
   d. Lower than normal afterburner thrust.
   e. Reduced aircraft range.

GRADUAL AFTERBURNER SHUTDOWN

Gradual afterburner shutdown is required in certain areas of the airplane flight envelope, and is intended to allow the airplane to decelerate to a lower Mach number before the engine exhaust nozzles close. This, in turn, prevents the nozzles from becoming overpressurized and possibly damaged, due to peak transient pressures between Max and Mil power.

CAUTION

If a compressor stall occurs above approximately 630 kts, gradual afterburner shut down is required to prevent afterburner damage. See Airplane Speed Restrictions Chart, section I part 4 for specific speeds.

ENGINE G

Due to limited oil distribution to all systems utilizing engine oil for lubrication or operation during negative G or zero G flight, the airplane is limited to the following:

a. 30 seconds of negative G flight.
b. 10 seconds of zero G flight.

ENGINE OIL PRESSURE LIMITATIONS

The oil pressure limitations for the primary engine lubricating oil is 12 psi at idle, while for other static and inflight conditions, oil pressures vary with type of oil and aircraft effectivity. Refer to section I, part 4, for oil pressure limitations. Oil pressure fluctuations of ± 2.5 psi are allowed around a known steady state pressure. During steady state operation any erratic pressure change which exceeds 5 psi for more than 1 second must be investigated. During any engine speed reduction, indicated oil pressure will decrease approximately 1 psi per 1 percent reduction in rpm from 100%. Pressure changes resulting from airspeed increases or going ON/OFF afterburner are acceptable down to 40 psi minimum. From flight to flight, indicated pressure must repeat within 5 psi of the known normal pressure for a particular aircraft engine combination. When an alternate lubricating oil is utilized, refer to section I, part 4, of this publication for oil pressure limitations.

FLAPS

----- NOTICE -----
Some illustrations referred to within this system writeup may be located in appendix A. These illustrations are referred to, within the text, as (figure A- , appendix A).

DESCRIPTION

The wing flap system comprises two-position leading edge flaps and three-position trailing edge flaps. On aircraft 152995z and up, and all others after AFC 218, the ailerons deflect 16-1/2 degrees when the flaps are selected. The leading edge flaps are mounted on the inboard, center and outer wing panels. On airplanes 152995z and up, and all others after AFC 218, the leading edge flap on the inboard wing panel is fixed and does not extend. Trailing edge flaps are mounted on the inboard portion of the wing adjacent to the fuselage. Each flap has its own hydraulic actuator. The leading edge flaps are locked in the retracted position by over-center linkages. Trailing edge flaps are locked in the retracted position by internal locks in the cylinders. A check valve is provided as an integral part of the selector valve to prevent unlocking of over-center mechanisms and internal locks by back pressure in the return lines. A flow divider is provided to synchronize the trailing edge flaps. There is no synchronization between leading edge flaps or between leading edge, trailing edge flaps and ailerons.

WING FLAP SWITCH

The leading and trailing edge flap switch (figure A-1, appendix A) is on the wing flap control panel, which is mounted above the left console outboard of the throttles. The three-position toggle switch is marked UP, 1/2, and DN and is shaped like an airfoil for ease of identification. Selecting 1/2 moves the center and outboard leading edge flaps to the full down position (60°, 55° respectively), the inboard leading edge flaps to full down (30°), and the trailing edge flaps to

1/2 down (30°). On airplanes 152995z and up, and all others after AFC 218, the inboard leading edge flaps are fixed in the retracted position and do not extend. On these aircraft, the ailerons also move down (16 1/2°) when 1/2 flaps are selected. Selection of DN moves the trailing edge flaps to the fully extended position (60°). Selecting 1/2 after the flaps have been fully extended raises the trailing edge flaps to the 1/2 (30°) position. Placing the flap switch in UP simultaneously returns all the flaps (and ailerons in aircraft 152995z and up and all others after AFC 218) to the fully retracted position. There is no individual selecting of flaps.

EMERGENCY AILERON DROOP SWITCH

On aircraft after AFC 534, an emergency aileron droop switch is provided. This lever-locked switch replaces the emergency speed brake switch located on the left vertical panel and allows selection of aileron droop during emergency flap operation. The switch has positions of NORMAL and DISABLE; in NORMAL, the ailerons will droop when emergency flap is selected; in DISABLE, the ailerons will remain in the non-drooped position when emergency flap is selected or return the ailerons to a non-drooped position if already drooped during emergency flap operation. If emergency flap is selected during a utility hydraulic system failure with both PC systems operating normally, and the switch is in NORMAL, the ailerons will droop normally; however, if the utility and a single PC system fail simultaneously, an asymmetric aileron droop condition will result. In this condition, or anytime a non-drooped condition is preferred during emergency flap operation, place the switch to DISABLE and the ailerons will return to a non-drooped condition. Power for the emergency aileron droop control is supplied by the essential 28 volt dc bus.

EMERGENCY FLAP EXTENSION

Emergency extension of the wing flaps is accomplished pneumatically. Normally, the flaps are extended pneumatically only when a utility hydraulic system failure is indicated, since in most instances operation of the emergency flap system causes a utility hydraulic system failure. High pressure air (approximately 3000 psi), stored in a 300 cubic inch air bottle, may be released to extend the flaps by pulling the flap circuit breaker and pulling full aft on emergency flap extension handle (figure A-1, appendix A). The handle is airfoil shaped and is painted in alternating black and yellow stripes for ease of identification. Actuation of the emergency flap extension handle extends the leading edge flaps to the full down position, the trailing edge flaps to the one-half down position, and the aileron droop as follows: on aircraft 152995z and up, and all others after AFC 218, but prior to AFC 400, the ailerons are blown down with the flaps; on these aircraft after AFC 400, but before AFC 534, the ailerons remain in the non-drooped position (if normal flap extension preceded emergency extension, the ailerons would return to non-drooped condition); on aircraft after AFC 534, with the emergency aileron droop switch in NORMAL, the ailerons move to the drooped position. With the switch in DISABLE before emergency flap operation, the ailerons remain in the non-drooped position; however, if during emergency flap operation aileron droop is not desired, placing the switch to DISABLE will return the ailerons to a non-drooped condition. The air bottle contains sufficient air for one flap extension.

Note

The flaps, when extended pneumatically, will not be retracted by the flap blow-up switch.

FLAP POSITION INDICATOR

The leading edge and trailing edge flap indicators (figure A-1, appendix A) are on the left vertical panel in the pilot's cockpit. The indicators work in conjunction with position switches on the leading and trailing edge flaps. The position of the flaps as indicated by drum dials viewed through cutouts in the instrument panel. With flaps up, the word UP appears on the indicators, flaps in transit from up to 1/2 down are indicated by a barber pole. Half flaps are indicated by the letters DN on the leading edge indicator and the figure 1/2 on the trailing edge indicator. With flaps full down the letters DN appear on both indicators. There is no barber pole indication for flap transit from 1/2 to full down, or full down to 1/2 down. On aircraft after AFC 400, the trailing edge flap indicator shows barber pole when the flaps are extended with emergency air.

Note

On airplanes 148363f thru 148434h the leading edge flaps indicate down while in transient, or in the full down position.

LANDING GEAR WARNING LIGHT

The landing gear warning light, marked WHEELS, is on the upper left corner of the main instrument panel. The light flashes any time the flaps are down and the landing gear handle is up. An additional light is in the landing gear handle and it illuminates any time the gear is unlocked.

BOUNDARY LAYER CONTROL SYSTEM

The boundary layer control system utilizes air bled from the 17th stage of the engine compressor. This air passes through ducts attached to the rigid part of the wing between leading edge flaps and the spar and between the trailing edge flap and the flap closure beam. Slots along the ducts behind the outboard and center panel leading edge flaps and in front of the trailing edge flaps direct laminar air over the wing and flaps when the flaps have deflected sufficiently to expose the slots. The high temperature and high velocity laminar air directed over the wings and flaps will delay flow separation over the airfoil, hence reducing turbulance and drag. This results in a lower stall speed and therefore a reduction of landing speed. Leading edge BLC is operative in the 1/2 or full flap position. Trailing edge BLC is operative only when the flaps are in the full down position. BLC air is controlled by four valves, one in each leading edge duct and one in each trailing edge duct. On airplanes 152995z and up, and airplanes 149403i thru 152994y before AFC 218, the BLC valves are actuated by mechanical linkages connecting the valves to the flaps. The leading edge flap BLC valves open with the flap switch in the 1/2 or full flap position, and the trailing edge flap BLC valves open with the flap switch in the full flap position. On airplanes 149403i thru 152994y after AFC 218, the trailing edge BLC valves are still mechanically actuated but the leading edge BLC valves are opened by hydraulic actuators. For hydraulic actuation a sequence valve is opened to route fluid from the flapdown lines to the hydraulic actuator. The sequence valves are mechanically linked to the leading edge flaps which open the valves when the leading edge flaps are full down. When the flaps are blown down, air is routed thru the sequence valves to be utilized by the actuators to open the leading edge BLC valves when the leading edge flaps travel full down. On aircraft after AFC 440, leading edge BLC can be shut off by placing the engine bleed air switch OFF.

CAUTION

- Operation of the engine(s) with the flaps down and wings folded should be avoided, to protect the leading edge BLC bellows from unrestricted heat expansion. If engine operation must be accomplished, power setting should be kept at a minimum.

- On aircraft after AFC 440, if an engine is shut down trailing edge BLC will be lost on the wing adjacent to the shut down engine.

Changed 1 March 1972

BLC Malfunction Indicator Light

A BLC MALFUNCTION light (figure A-1, appendix A) is on the telelight panel. When any one of the four BLC valves is not fully closed, and the flaps are up, the BLC MALFUNCTION light illuminates. On airplanes 153030aa and up, and all others after AFC 263, the BLC MALFUNCTION light also illuminates in the 1/2 flap position if the trailing edge BLC valve opens. Illumination of the BLC MALFUNCTION light indicates only that a BLC valve has failed to close when the flaps are either 1/2 or up. No indication is provided for a completely inoperative system, nor is there an indication provided for a BLC valve failing to open when the flaps are down.

NORMAL OPERATION

The leading edge flaps are operated by the use of a manifold-mounted selector valve and single-acting actuators, while the trailing edge flaps employ the same manifold-mounted selector valve, a wing-mounted-selector valve, and dual-acting actuators. Placing the flap switch in 1/2 energizes the manifold-mounted selector valve allowing utility hydraulic pressure to lower the leading edge flaps full down, trailing edge flaps 1/2 down, and on aircraft 152995z and up and all others after AFC 218, the ailerons 16-1/2 degrees down. Further movement of the

switch to DN energizes the wing-mounted selector valve resulting in complete extension of the trailing edge flaps. Immediate movement of the switch from UP to DN causes both selector valves to become energized simultaneously, thereby completely extending the leading and trailing edge flaps (and the ailerons on aircraft 152995z and up). The limit switches provided on each flap are all connected in parallel to deenergize the electrical circuits to the selector valves after all flaps are retracted. The electrical circuits are continuously energized to maintain hydraulic pressure on flaps down. Should the cockpit switch inadvertently be left in the down position, the flaps retract through the action of an airspeed switch. This switch is set to automatically retract the flaps between the airspeeds of 230 and 244 knots during acceleration. During deceleration, the flaps automatically extend (providing the flap switch is down) between 234 and 210 knots. The extension speed is approximately 10 to 20 knots below the speed at which the flaps retracted. Flap extension is accomplished in approximately 8 seconds and retraction in approximately 6 seconds.

CAUTION

The airspeed switch receives its sensing pressure through the pitot system. Should the pitot tube become clogged erroneous indications are sensed by the flaps pressure switch as well as by the ADC. It is therefore possible to lower the flaps by the normal means at excessive airspeeds.

EMERGENCY OPERATION

If normal wing flap operation fails, the flaps (and dropped ailerons on aircraft 152995z and up and all others after AFC 218) can be lowered by pulling the flap circuit breaker, and pulling full aft and down on the emergency wing flap extension handle. The flap circuit breaker must be pulled before lowering the flaps by the emergency system. This causes the flap

hydraulic selector valve to return to its full trail position, blocking hydraulic pressure to the flap actuators and insuring that hydraulic fluid is not forced into the actuators on top of the pneumatic pressure. Should this occur, system hammering may result, with possible eventual rupture and loss of system integrity. Once the emergency wing flap extension handle has been pulled, it should be left in the full aft position. Returning the handle to its normal position allows the compressed air from the flap down side of the actuating cylinder to be vented overboard, and the flaps are blown up by the airstream. If the flaps are inadvertently extended in flight by emergency pneumatic pressure, they must be left in the extended position until postflight servicing. If retraction in flight is attempted, rupture of the utility reservoir will probably occur with subsequent loss of the utility hydraulic system. On aircraft 152995z and up and all others after AFC 400 the ailerons remain in the non-dropped position or return to the non-drooped position (if previously lowered) when emergency flap extension is selected.

CAUTION

Pull the flap circuit breaker prior to extending the flaps by the emergency system.

Note

• Any pneumatic extension of the wing flaps shall be logged on the yellow sheet (OPNAV FORM 3760-2).

• On aircraft after AFC 400, the trailing edge flap indicator will show barber pole following pneumatic flap extension.

LIMITATIONS

Do not attempt to lower flaps above 250 knots CAS.

FLIGHT CONTROLS

NOTICE
Some illustrations referred to within this system writeup may be located in appendix A. These illustrations are referred to, within the text, as (figure A-, appendix A).

DESCRIPTION

The airplane primary flight controls consist of the stabilator, rudder, ailerons, and spoilers. The stabilator, ailerons and spoilers are actuated by irreversible, dual power cylinders. The rudder is actuated by a conventional, irreversible power cylinder. Artificial feel systems provide simulated aerodynamic control stick and rudder pedal forces due to the lack of aerodynamic feedback forces from the power control cylinders. The feel systems have trim actuators which, through the power cylinders, move the entire control surface. Secondary controls are leading edge flaps, trailing edge flaps, and wing mounted speed brakes. Refer to figure 1-25.

LATERAL CONTROL SYSTEM

The lateral control system, a unique aileron-spoiler combination, basically consists of the control stick; left and right push-pull rod systems; left and right walking beam bellcranks; aileron dual power cylinders with integrated control valves; spoiler dual control valves; left and right autopilot series servos; left and right lateral feel trim actuators; and, in airplanes 152995z and up, and all others after AFC 218, a left and right aileron droop actuating cylinder. The ailerons travel downward 30 degrees from a full trail position. Upward travel is limited to 1 degree. The spoilers travel upward, 45 degrees from a flush contour position in the upper wing surface. Lateral movement of the control stick is transmitted mechanically by the push-pull rods through the walking beam bellcranks to the spoiler and aileron control valves. The control valves meter hydraulic fluid to their respective dual power cylinders in proportion to the mechanical displacement. An override spring cartridge is incorporated into the left and right push-pull rod systems. If one side becomes jammed, the override spring deflects under force, allowing operation of the other lateral control surfaces. The walking beam bellcranks receive control surface movement inputs from three sources; the control stick, the lateral trim system, and the autopilot series servos. A self-serviced hydraulic damper, attached to the aileron backup structure, is utilized as an up-stop for the aileron as well as a flutter damper. The control system uses dual power cylinders to allow simultaneous use of both power control hydraulic systems. If a single power control hydraulic system fails, the remaining system supplies adequate power for control. On aircraft after AFC 400, PC-1, PC-2, and utility hydraulic systems are modified (rerouted) to provide the ailerons and spoilers with three independent sources of hydraulic pressure. PC-1 and utility systems provide hydraulic pressure to the left aileron and spoiler, and PC-2 and utility systems provide hydraulic pressure to the right aileron and spoiler. The control system uses dual power cylinders to allow simultaneous use of PC-1, PC-2, and utility hydraulic systems. If a single hydraulic system fails, the remaining system(s) supply adequate power for control.

Aileron Control

The ailerons are controlled by dual, irreversible, power cylinders that receive metered hydraulic fluid from dual integrated control valves. The control valves, in turn, are controlled by the push-pull rods, through the walking beam bellcranks, and control stick. Each power cylinder contains four parallel inner cylinders with rods and pistons. The piston rods are joined at one end by a yoke attached to the airplane structure. The cylinder portion of the power cylinder is attached to the aileron. The two outer cylinders receive hydraulic fluid from PC-2, and the two inner cylinders receive hydraulic fluid from PC-1. This arrangement provides symmetrical loading of the yoke should one of the power control systems fail. On aircraft after AFC 400, the two outer cylinders of the left aileron and spoiler receive hydraulic fluid from the utility system, and the two inner cylinders receive hydraulic fluid from PC-1. The two outer cylinders of the right aileron and spoiler receive hydraulic fluid from PC-2, and the two inner cylinders receive hydraulic fluid from the utility system. This arrangement provides symmetrical loading of the yoke should one of the systems fail. In airplanes 152995z and up and all others after AFC 218, the ailerons deflect 16-1/2 degrees down when 1/2 or full flaps are selected. This is accomplished by utilizing an aileron droop actuating cylinder which repositions a bellcrank pivot point when flaps are selected. As the bellcrank pivot point is repositioned, linkage to the aileron control cylinder is deflected which, in effect, tells both ailerons that 16-1/2 degrees of travel is required. Even

though the ailerons are drooped, they continue to function as originally designed, except that the ailerons neutral point is 16-1/2 degrees down, and the aileron deflecting up for a particular maneuver travels as far as 16-1/2 degrees back to the streamlined position instead of 1 limit of up travel as in the case without the ailerons drooped. For instance, if the control stick is moved 5 degrees to the right with the flaps half or full down, requiring 6-7/8 degrees of aileron, the right aileron raises 8-1/4 degrees from the 16-1/2 degree position, while the left aileron deflects an additional 6-7/8 degrees and assumes a 23-3/8 degree down position. Therefore, the ailerons move essentially the same as the nondrooped ailerons; however, the aileron neutral point is 16-1/2 degrees lower. The aileron droop cylinder is positioned by hydraulic or pneumatic pressure through the flap normal and emergency systems. After AFC 400, the aileron droop cylinder is not actuated when the flaps are extended by the emergency pneumatic system.

Spoiler Control

Each wing contains two spoiler surfaces, spoiler power cylinders, and a dual spoiler control valve. Each surface has a dual, irreversible power cylinder, with a feedback linkage to a dual spoiler control valve. The spoiler control valve divides each power control system input into equal parts which is then distributed to each spoiler dual power cylinder. One portion of each power cylinder receives hydraulic pressure from PC-1, and the other portion receives hydraulic pressure from PC-2. If one of the power control hydraulic systems fail, the other supplies adequate pressure for spoiler control. On aircraft after AFC 400, one portion of each power cylinder of the right wing receives hydraulic pressure from PC-2, and the other portion receives hydraulic pressure from the utility system. One portion of each power cylinder of the left wing receives hydraulic pressure from PC-1, and the other portion receives hydraulic pressure from the utility system. If one of the systems fail, the other(s) supply adequate pressure for spoiler control.

Lateral Control Feel and Trim System

The lateral trim system consists of the trim switch (figure 1-24), a rotary power unit, two flexible drive shafts, and two screwjack actuators. When the trim switch is energized, the rotary power unit and flexible drive shafts position the screwjack actuators. The screwjack actuators are connected to the airplane structure on one end, and the walking beam bellcranks on the other end. As the screwjack actuators extend and retract, the lateral control are repositioned and the control stick follows the trim movements. Lateral control artificial feel is provided by double-action spring cartridges connected in tandem with the screwjack actuators. When the control stick is moved from neutral, the springs are compressed. The farther the control stick is moved from neutral, the greater the force required to compress the springs. The spring cartridges return the control stick to neutral when the force on the control stick is removed.

Aileron Position Indicator

An aileron position indicator (figure A-1, appendix A) is on the left vertical panel in the front cockpit. A transmitter is mechanically connected to the lateral control linkage in the left wing. As the control linkage moves, the mechanical input is converted into electrical impulses which are sent to the position indicator. The indicator, marked in units of percent of system travel, represents actual control surface position. A wings level indication is zero trim, and a full down left or right indication is maximum trim travel. The maximum lateral trim available is 33%.

STABILATOR CONTROL SYSTEM

Longitudinal control is provided by a single unit horizontal tail surface (stabilator), that is actuated by an irreversible dual power cylinder. In airplanes 152995z and up and all others after AFC 218, a slotted stabilator is provided to increase stabilator effectiveness, and thereby counter the nose down pitching moment caused by the drooped ailerons. The stabilator control system components include the control stick; push-pull rods; cables; bellcranks, integrated control valve; and an irreversible dual power cylinder. Additional components include a ram air bellows and bob weight for system artificial feel, a trim actuator, and an AFCS servo that is integral with the control valve. When the control stick is moved longitudinally, the motion is transmitted by push-pull rods to a bellcrank. It is then transmitted by a cable assembly to another push-pull rod set. The second push-pull rod set actuates the control valve which meters hydraulic fluid to the dual power cylinder. Hydraulic pressure to the stabilator power cylinder is supplied by both power control hydraulic systems. If one of the power control hydraulic systems fail, the remaining system provides adequate control response. A hydraulic AFCS servo is integrated into the stabilator dual servo valve. It positions the dual servo valve in the same manner as control stick inputs. As a result, when the autopilot signals for a pitch attitude change, the control stick follows the movement. The bob weight in the control linkage also increases stick forces proportionally to increases in G forces.

Stabilator Control Feel and Trim System

Artificial feel is provided by a dynamic (ram air) pressure bellows acting through a variable bellcrank on the stabilator trim actuator and a 5 pound/G bob weight. When the airplane is in trim, the ram air force on the bellows is balanced by a balance down-spring assembly and the bob weight. As the aircraft increases or decreases in airspeed, the pressure on the bellows changes causing the bellows-spring assembly to become off balance. The off balance condition is then transmitted through the trim actuator, control cables, and push-pull rods back to the control stick. Actuating the trim switch causes the stabilator trim actuator to move, balancing the forces between the bellows and the balance down-spring assembly

bob weight combination, thereby eliminating force on the control stick. On airplanes with AFC 308, the balance down-spring assembly is removed and only the bob weight acts upon the control stick when an out-of-trim condition exists. This causes the force on the control stick to be much less and increases the apparent trim effectiveness. A viscous damper, attached to the trim actuator, prevents abrupt control surface movements by increasing control stick forces with rapid stick movements. An override spring cartridge allows the feel and trim portion of the stabilator control system to be bypassed in the event of a nose up trim malfunction (runaway trim and/or bellows diaphram failure). On airplanes 151448r and up, and all others after ASC 153, a heater is installed in the bellows ram air inlet probe and venturi to prevent freezing of moisture which causes restriction of airflow in these units. The heaters are controlled by the pitot heat switch on the right console (figure A-1, appendix A).

Stabilator Trim Position Indicator

The stabilator trim indicator (figure A-1, appendix A) is on the left vertical panel in the front cockpit. It is directly controlled by a transmitter which is integral with the stabilator feel trim actuator. The indicator, marked in units of percent of trim, represents trim actuator position.

CONTROL STICK

The control stick, which consists of a strip grip and motional pickup transducer, is mounted in a yoke to permit left, right, fore and aft movement. The control stick grip contains five controls; a four-way trim switch, a bomb and centerline stores release button, a nose gear steering heading hold cutout button, a missile trigger switch, and an emergency disengage switch. After AFC 500, a target slave and acquisition button is added and the nose gear steering/heading hold cutout button is relocated. The emergency disengage switch can be used to disconnect the automatic pilot in the event of an emergency. The motional pickup transducer is utilized in conjunction with the automatic flight control system to provide control stick steering. The nose gear steering button also functions as a heading hold cutout button for the automatic flight control system. Refer to figure 1-24 for the location of the control stick grip controls.

RUDDER CONTROL SYSTEM

The rudder control system consists of the rudder pedals, push-pull rods, cable assemblies, bellcranks, a rudder feel trim system, an aileron-rudder interconnect actuator, a rudder damper, and an irreversible power cylinder with integral control valve. When the rudder pedals are moved, the motion is transmitted by the push-pull rods, bellcranks and cable assemblies to the control valve of the power cylinder.

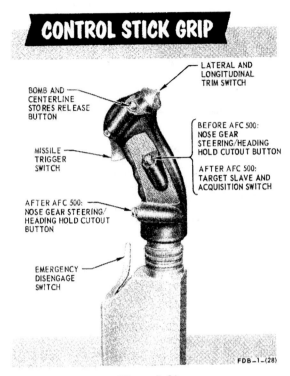

CONTROL STICK GRIP

LATERAL AND LONGITUDINAL TRIM SWITCH

BOMB AND CENTERLINE STORES RELEASE BUTTON

MISSILE TRIGGER SWITCH

AFTER AFC 500: NOSE GEAR STEERING/ HEADING HOLD CUTOUT BUTTON

EMERGENCY DISENGAGE SWITCH

BEFORE AFC 500: NOSE GEAR STEERING/HEADING HOLD CUTOUT BUTTON

AFTER AFC 500: TARGET SLAVE AND ACQUISITION SWITCH

FDB-1-(28)

Figure 1-24

The control valve meters utility system hydraulic fluid to the power cylinder which positions the rudder. It is possible to have limited mechanical authority over the rudder if a utility hydraulic system fails. A bypass valve in the power cylinder opens when system pressure is lost, allowing fluid to pass from one side of the cylinder to the other. Total amount of rudder deflection available is then a function of air loads on the rudder; however, under all speed conditions it requires a considerable amount of pilot effort to manually deflect the rudder. A hydraulic servo for yaw damping and AFCS operation is incorporated into the control valve of the power cylinder. Operation of the AFCS however, does not move the rudder pedals.

Rudder Feel Trim System

Artificial feel is supplied to the rudder pedals by an artificial feel trim system. A hydraulic cylinder with utility system hydraulic pressure on both sides of a differential area piston, provides a pedal force of approximately 2.6 pounds per degree of rudder deflection when the rudder airspeed pressure switch is in the low speed condition. When the rudder airspeed pressure switch is energized to the high speed condition, hydraulic pressure to the low area side of the differential area piston is cut off and the pedal force becomes approximately 11.5 pounds per degree of rudder deflection. The airspeed pressure switch is set to convert from the low to the high gradient at

airspeeds between 228 to 252 knots while accelerating. During deceleration, the airspeed pressure switch converts from the high gradient to the low gradient between 232 to 218 knots. A rudder trim switch is located on the left console. Normal trim range is 7.5 ± 1 degree of rudder deflection on each side of the neutral.

CAUTION

In the event of a loss of the right main 28 volt dc bus, while in the high range of the rudder airspeed pressure switch, the rudder feel force of approximately 11.5 pounds per degree of rudder deflection automatically reverts to approximately 2.6 pounds per degree of rudder deflection. As a result, rudder pedal forces become more sensitive, and excessive structural loads can be imposed on the airplane if full rudder deflection is commanded.

Rudder Trim Switch

The rudder trim switch (figure A-1, appendix A) is in the front cockpit on the inboard engine control panel. This switch controls the trim actuator in the rudder feel and trim system to trim the airplane directionally.

Rudder Position Indicator

A rudder position indicator (figure A-1, appendix A) is on the left vertical panel in the front cockpit. A transmitter is mechanically connected to the rudder control linkage. As the control linkage moves, the mechanical input is converted into electrical impulses which are sent to the indicator. The indicator is only marked for takeoff trim, which is zero degrees of rudder deflection.

Rudder Pedals

The rudder pedals are conventional type suspended units which are coupled to the rudder push-pull rod system by individual screwjacks. The screwjacks provide adjustment of the rudder pedals for comfort and are adjusted simultaneously by turning a crank on the pedestal panel. The pedals are also coupled to the power brake valves so that toe pressure on the pedal applies the brakes. The rudder pedals are also used to control the nose gear steering unit when the nose gear steering button on the control stick grip is pressed.

Stall Warning Vibrator

A stall warning vibrator is on the front cockpit left rudder pedal to warn of approaching stall conditions. The vibrator is electrically connected to a switch in the angle of attack indicator, which is set at 22.3 units on non-drooped aileron airplanes, and 21.3 units on drooped aileron airplanes. The stall warning vibrator motor is powered from the right main 28 volt

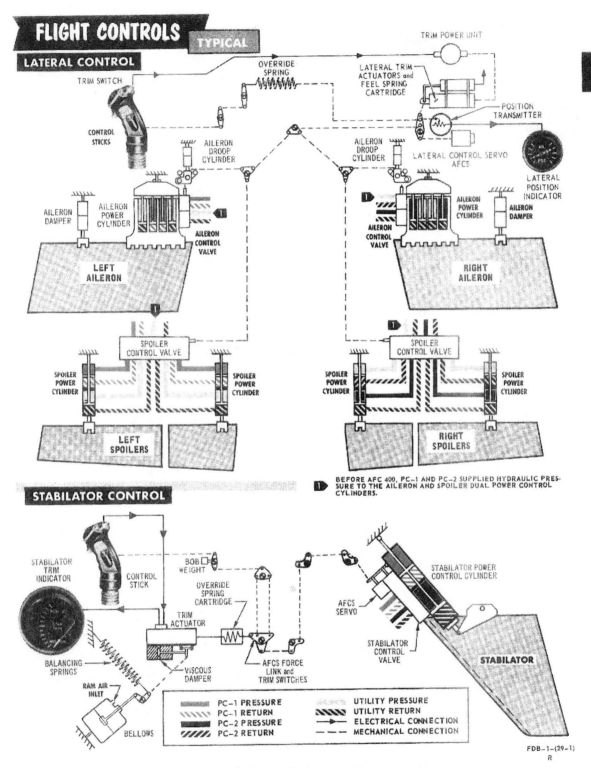

FLIGHT CONTROLS TYPICAL

LATERAL CONTROL

BEFORE AFC 400, PC-1 AND PC-2 SUPPLIED HYDRAULIC PRESSURE TO THE AILERON AND SPOILER DUAL POWER CONTROL CYLINDERS.

STABILATOR CONTROL

	PC-1 PRESSURE		UTILITY PRESSURE
	PC-1 RETURN		UTILITY RETURN
	PC-2 PRESSURE		ELECTRICAL CONNECTION
	PC-2 RETURN		MECHANICAL CONNECTION

FDB-1-(29-1)
R

Figure 1-25 (Sheet 1 of 2)

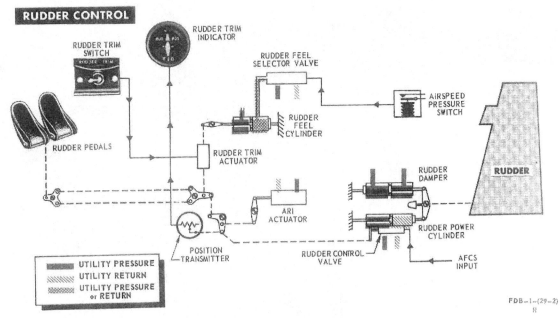

RUDDER CONTROL

Figure 1-25 (Sheet 2 of 2)

FDB-1-(29-2)
R

dc bus through the angle of attack probe heater circuit breaker (J11, No. 1 circuit breaker panel). If the vibrator runs continuously, it may be rendered inoperative by pulling this circuit breaker.

AILERON RUDDER INTERCONNECT (ARI)

The aileron-rudder interconnect system causes rudder displacement proportional to aileron displacement which provides coordinated turns at low airspeeds. The limits of the system are 15° of rudder displacement when the automatic flight control system is in the stability augmentation or autopilot mode, and 10° rudder displacement when the stab aug switch is disengaged. Components of the system include the control amplifier, the 10° servo actuator, acting through a walking beam, an airspeed pressure switch and two aileron transducers. In airplanes 148363f thru 150651n, the ARI system is actuated when the rudder airspeed pressure switch is in its low speed condition and full flaps are down. In airplanes 150652o and up, and 148363f thru 150651n after AFC 305, the ARI system is actuated with the flaps either one half or full down. When the flap switch is in DN or 1/2 and the flap airspeed switch is in the low speed condition, 28 volts dc is applied to the engage relay solenoids of the ARI system. This allows the hydraulic 10° servo actuator to move the control linkage (if aileron displacement is present) and cause rudder displacement. The system can be disengaged by depressing the emergency disengage switch on the control stick, this disengages the ARI only as long as it is held depressed. To regain the 5° of rudder authority the stab aug switch must be reengaged. On aircraft 153049aa and up and all others after AFC 203, the ARI system and the yaw stab aug is disengaged as long as the emergency disengage switch is held depressed; when the switch is released the

ARI (10°) and the yaw stab aug (5°) rudder authority will be regained. To permanently disengage the system, the circuit breaker on the left utility panel must be pulled, and the stab aug switch must be disengaged. Pulling the circuit breaker only, and keeping stab aug engaged still provides 5° of ARI rudder authority. To completely disengage the ARI while retaining complete stab aug pull the rudder trim circuit breaker (B1, No. 1 circuit breaker panel) in the rear cockpit.

Note

There are various inflight situations where rudder jump is experienced when the ARI system cuts in or out with a lateral input to the control stick. These rudder jumps are most apt to occur in situations where the flaps are put up or down during a turn, such as retracting the flaps during a climb out after takeoff or during a go-around. Assuming no manual rudder inputs, it is possible that after the flap switch is placed to UP during a go-around, the rudder can jump from a deflected position to neutral after the flap switch is actuated. Another jump displacing the rudder back from neutral then occurs when the right hand trailing edge one half down limit switch closes. When the flaps go above the limits of the one half down limit switch the rudder again deflects to neutral. Sometimes the first jump just described does not occur because the one half down limit switch is not open when flaps up is selected. Rudder jumps also occur whenever the flap airspeed switch is actuated when the flaps limit speed is exceeded, or by placing the flap switch to DN or 1/2.

NORMAL OPERATION

Normal operation of the flight controls is accomplished through the use of the control stick for longitudinal axis (ailerons) and lateral axis (stabilator) control, and the rudder pedals for vertical axis control.

EMERGENCY OPERATION

STABILATOR FEEL TRIM FAILURE

Partial Bellows Failure

Partial bellows failure is recognized by a mild nose down stick force proportional to the airspeed, unless the failure occurs during maneuvering flight at which time it may not be noticeable. Reduction of stick centering and pitch stability results. Should this failure occur, reduce airspeed to 250-300 knots CAS, retrim the airplane; avoid abrupt fore and aft stick movements and land as soon as practicable.

Complete Bellows Failure

A complete bellows failure is recognized by a heavy nose down feel force at the control stick. The maximum amount that this stick force can attain is 30 pounds dependent on the trim position. This force can be reduced to 5 pounds by applying full NOSE UP trim. On airplanes with balance down-springs removed (AFC 308), stick force never exceeds approximately 5 pounds and this force cannot be trimmed out. Should a complete bellows failure occur, reduce airspeed to 250-300 knots CAS; apply nose up stabilator trim as required; avoid abrupt fore and aft stick movements, and land as soon as practicable.

Ice/Water Blockage of Ram Air Line

On airplanes prior to 151448r before ASC 153, ice or water blockage can occur in the artificial feel bellows ram air line. Ice or water blockage of the artificial feel bellows ram air line results in conditions similar to a complete bellows failure. If ice or water blockage is suspected, longitudinal trim should not be applied to relieve control stick force. The intermittent nature of this condition and the suddenness of return to normal can cause violent pitch transients. When the ram airline is blocked no stick force gradient is felt by the pilot if a change in stick position is required. In the event of suspected ice or water blockage of the ram airline, reduce airspeed to 250-300 knots CAS; maintain attitude by pilot effort, and if practicable descend to air that is above freezing. If the above condition persists, land as soon as practicable.

Runaway Stabilator Trim

If stabilator trim appears to be running away, it is possible under certain conditions to lessen the situation. Runaway stabilator trim can be alleviated by engaging the auto pilot, providing the stab trim circuit breaker has been pulled immediately upon detection of runaway trim; runaway trim is in the nose up direction; nose down runaway trim has not exceeded 2-1/2 units; and airspeed is reduced to 300 knots CAS or less. If the above conditions are met, engage the autopilot. When the autopilot is used to alleviate a runaway trim condition, and excessive out of trim forces are present (full nose down runaway trim), the autopilot alternately disengages and re-engages. If this occurs, discontinue use of the autopilot and plan to land as soon as practicable. If the autopilot is still engaged when in the landing configuration (gear and flaps extended), grasp the control stick firmly and disengage the autopilot at 180 to 190 knots CAS. Depending upon the severity of the malfunction, the airplane may or may not be in trim; if out of trim the forces are not too high and the airplane can be landed with the out of trim condition, or the autopilot can be re-engaged, and the landing made with control steering. If the landing is made with autopilot engaged, disengage the autopilot immediately after touchdown to prevent damage to autopilot components.

ARI SYSTEM DISENGAGEMENT

The ARI system can be temporarily disengaged by depressing the AFCS/ARI emergency disengage switch; this disengages the ARI only as long as it is held depressed. On aircraft thru 153048aa before AFC 203, to permanently disengage the ARI system, the circuit breaker on the left utility panel must be pulled and the stab trim switch must be disengaged. On aircraft 153049aa and up and all others after AFC 203, to permanently disengage the ARI system, the yaw stab aug switch must be disengaged and the circuit breaker pulled. Pulling the circuit breaker only, and keeping the stab aug engaged still provides 5° of ARI rudder authority. To permanently disengage the ARI while retaining complete stab aug, pull the rudder trim circuit breaker on circuit breaker panel no. 1 in the rear cockpit. Pulling the rudder trim circuit breaker is the preferred method.

LIMITATIONS

There are no specific limitations pertaining to the flight controls.

FUEL SYSTEM

```
─────────────── NOTICE ───────────────
Some illustrations referred to within this system writeup may be located in appendix A.
These illustrations are referred to, within the text, as (figure A-, appendix A).
```

DESCRIPTION

Note

All fuel weights in this manual are based on JP-5 at 6.8 pounds per gallon.

The fuel system (figure A-7, appendix A), consists of six interconnected fuel cells in the fuselage, and two integral wet wing cells in the wing torque boxes. Provisions are made for two externally mounted droppable wing tanks and a droppable fuselage centerline external tank, which is interchangeable with a refueling tanker external store (referred to as buddy tank). Provisions are also made for an air refueling system. The function of fuselage cells 2, 3, 4, 5 and 6 is to keep cell 1 supplied with fuel. See figure 1-26, Fuel Quantity Data Table for fuel quantities. An air pressure fuel transfer system transfers wing and external tank fuel to the fuselage cells. Hydraulic and electric transfer pumps plus gravity feed are utilized to transfer fuel from the fuselage cells to cell 1 which is the engine feed tank. Single point ground pressure fueling at the rate of approximately 250 gallons per minute may be accomplished. Two point ground pressure fueling is available by using the air refueling probe. There are no gravity fueling or defueling provisions for the internal or external fuel systems. Single point defueling is accomplished by using the single point fueling receptacle. All internal fuel cells incorporate capacitance type fuel gaging units which continuously indicate the total fuel quantity in pounds in all internal cells. The fuel system is equipped with refueling level control valves which are float type valves that shut off the pressure fueling when predetermined fuel levels are reached. All internal and external fuel tanks are pressurized in flight by regulated engine bleed air which is also utilized to transfer wing or external fuel to the fuselage cells or to dump wing fuel. The internal cells and external centerline tank or buddy tank are all vented to a common manifold which dumps overboard from the fuel vent mast immediately below the rudder. The external wing tanks are vented to the wing cell dump lines. With the buddy tank installed, the airplane becomes a tanker with the capabilities of transferring in flight, a predetermined amount of its internal fuel supply (plus the buddy tank fuel supply) to a receiver airplane, or return transfer from the buddy tank to its own internal fuel supply.

FUEL BOOST SYSTEM

Fuel is supplied to the engine during all flight attitudes by two submerged electric motor-driven cen-

trifugal type boost pumps. The left pump is a two-speed unit. During normal operation, both pumps operate at high speed. In the event of a complete electrical or double engine failure, extending the ram air turbine automatically switches the left pump from high to low speed, thereby, reducing a high amperage load and conserving electrical power and at the same time maintaining positive fuel pressure at the engine inlet. The boost pumps are in the engine feed cell 1. Both pumps are mounted on the bottom of the cell and provide for negative G requirements. Due to internal cell baffling and check valves, which trap approximately 905 pounds of fuel in the lower third of the cell during inverted flight, the boost pumps always remain submerged and provide a continuous fuel flow to the engines. The two boost pumps operate when either engine master switch is ON, provided ac power is supplied to the system.

Note

- When the electrical fuel boost pumps are inoperative, gravity fuel is sufficient to maintain full military power at altitudes below 20,000 feet, provided no unusual attitudes and/or negative G conditions are present.

- In the event of a double engine failure and loss of electrical power, extending the ram air turbine automatically switches the left boost pump to low speed. The low speed boost pump plus gravity feed supplies enough fuel pressure to the engine driven fuel pumps to enable the engines to be started.

Boost Pump Pressure Indicator

The boost pump pressure indicators (figure A-1, appendix A) are on the left console in the front cockpit. The gage dials are calibrated from 1 to 5 with readings multiplied by 10. Pressure transmitters on the airplane keel in the engine compartment measure pressure in the aircraft fuel system as it enters the engine fuel pump. This signal is transmitted to the indicators in the cockpit.

Fuel Boost Pump Check

It is possible for the pilot to check the operation of the fuel boost pumps through use of the fuel pump check switches. The left and right boost pump check switches, with a CHECK position and a spring-loaded NORMAL position, are on the fuel control panel (figure A-1, appendix A). A boost pump check may be made only with external power applied to the aircraft and with the engine master switches OFF and the ground refueling switch, in the right main wheel well, OFF. Holding either check switch in CHECK operates the corresponding left or right engine shutoff valve, allowing a pressure transmitter to pick up boost pump pressure. Fuel boost pump pressure transmitters transmit an electrical signal to the applicable pressure indicator on the left utility panel. To perform a boost pump pressure check, operate each boost pump check switch individually and check for a reading of 30 ± 5 psi on the applicable pressure indicator. Should fuel in cell 1 be less than approximately 1000 pounds when the boost pump check is being performed, a low boost pump pressure reading may be experienced. With the fuel tanks pressurized, if a reading of more than 4 psig above the reading is noted, the fuel cells are overpressurized and a malfunctioning pressure regulator and/or fuel vent valve should be suspected. The system should be vented by slowing down and extending the probe. If it is not practicable to slow down, pull the refuel probe circuit breaker D15, No. 1 panel, and place the refuel probe switch to REFUEL.

FUEL TRANSFER SYSTEM

The electric transfer pumps in fuselage cells 4 and 6 commence transferring fuel to cells 1 and 2 with the selection of the ON position of either engine master switch. With hydraulic and electrical power supplied and either engine master switch on, the hydraulic transfer pumps in cells 4 and 6 will also be operating to deliver fuel to cells 1 and 2. On airplanes 152965y and up, and all others after AFC 273, the hydraulically driven fuel transfer pumps operate only when: hydraulic power is available with no electrical power on the airplane; when either engine is in afterburner operation; or when the fuel low level warning circuit is energized. The level control valves open to allow fuel from the transfer pump to enter cells 1 and 2 when the fuel level in these cells drops below that of the floats. Cell 2 transfers to cell 1 by gravity only, cell 3 gravity feeds cell 4; and cell 5 gravity feeds to cell 6. All internal and external tanks and cells are pressurized when the landing gear control is up or the wing transfer pressure switch is in EMERG and an engine is running. Wing fuel is now capable of being transferred by regulated air pressure to fuselage cells 1 and 3. Wing fuel will not normally enter cell 1 unless the fuel level in the cell 1 drops low enough to permit the transfer level control valve to open. Wing fuel is transferred to fuselage cell 3 as soon as the internal wing tanks are pressurized, providing the refueling level control valve in cell 3 opens. This action constitutes the automatic wing fuel transfer feature. Internal wing fuel is not transferred to cell 5 to prevent an aft CG condition. With an engine running, fuel from the external tanks commences transferring upon selection of the desired position (OUTBD or CENTER) on the external transfer switch (figure A-1, appendix A), provided the landing gear handle is up or the wing transfer pressure switch is in EMERG. On airplanes 153030aa and up, and all others after AFC 249, an automatic fuel transfer system is provided. The automatic fuel transfer system will be energized when the fuel level in fuselage cells 1 and 2 drops

below 1880 pounds. This system transfers all internal wing and external fuel (not previously transferred) into fuselage cells 1 and 3, regardless of switch settings on the fuel control panel. Internal wing and external fuel can be transferred when operating on the emergency generator.

Internal Wing Transfer Switch

The internal wing transfer switch (figure A-1, appendix A) is a two-position toggle switch on the fuel control panel. The switch positions are marked NORMAL and STOP TRANS. In NORMAL, internal wing fuel is transferred to fuselage cell 3 as soon as the internal wing tanks are pressurized, and the refueling level control valve in cell 3 opens. Internal wing fuel also transfers into cell 1 if space is available. Selecting STOP TRANS of the switch closes the internal wing fuel transfer valves, thus preventing further internal wing fuel transfer. On airplanes 153030aa and up, and all others after AFC 249, the internal wing fuel transfer valves are opened by the automatic fuel transfer system when the fuel level in fuselage cells 1 and 2 drops below 1880 pounds, regardless of the internal wing transfer switch position.

Wing Transfer Pressure Switch

The wing transfer pressure switch (figure A-1, appendix A) is a two-position switch on the fuel control panel. The switch positions are marked NORMAL and EMERG. When the landing gear handle is up and the wing transfer switch is in NORMAL, all internal and external tanks become pressurized by the pressure regulator valves being deenergized open and the pressurize relief valves energized closed. If the landing gear is down, internal wing or external fuel will not transfer unless the wing transfer pressure switch is in the emergency position. Placing the switch in EMERG performs the same functions as did the landing gear handle switch; all pressure regulators open and all pressure relief valves close; the tanks are pressurized and ready to transfer. To prevent external tank collapse during high altitude descent with wheels down, place wing transfer pressure switch to EMERG before lowering the landing gear. If the tanks have been deenergized in level flight, place wing transfer pressure switch to EMERG and continue in level flight for approximately 30 seconds to insure adequate re-pressurization before continuing descent. Place wing transfer pressure switch to NORMAL before landing.

External Transfer Switch

The external transfer switch (figure A-1, appendix A) is a three-position toggle switch on the fuel control panel. The switch positions are marked CENTER, OFF and OUTBD. Upon the selection of CENTER, the internal wing tank shutoff valves close, the centerline tank fuel shutoff and refuel shutoff valves are energized open, and fuel commences to transfer. Placing the switch in OUTBD closes the centerline shutoff valve, refuel valve, and opens the external wing tanks shutoff valves and fuel transfers to cell 3. External fuel also transfers to cell 1 if space is

NAVAIR 01-245FDB-1

available. On airplanes 149403i and up, and all others after ASC 84 (external fuel tank electrical revision), external fuel transfers to fuselage cells 1, 3, and 5. On airplanes 153030aa and up, and all others after AFC 249, external fuel automatically transfers to fuselage cells 1 and 3 when the fuel level in cells 1 and 2 drops below 1880 pounds, regardless of the external transfer switch position.

CAUTION

Catapult launching acceleration can force fuel out of the external tanks through the transfer lines to the fuselage cells at a rate beyond tank venting capability, thus creating a partial vacuum in the external tanks. Therefore, to prevent external tank collapse during a catapult launch, insure that the external transfer switch is OFF before launch.

Note

If external tanks are being carried, internal wing fuel does not transfer if the external transfer switch is in any position other than OFF. On aircraft 153030aa and up, and all others after 249, the internal wing fuel transfer valves are opened by the automatic fuel transfer system when the fuel level in fuselage cells 1 and 2 drops below 1880 pounds, regardless of the external transfer switch position.

AUTOMATIC FUEL TRANSFER

On aircraft 153030aa and up, and all others after AFC 249, an automatic fuel transfer circuit is added. Inflight, when the fuel level in cells 1 and 2 drops below 1880 ± 200 pounds, all internal wing fuel, external wing fuel and centerline fuel will simultaneously transfer to cells 1 and 3 regardless of fuel switch or landing gear positions. This fuel will not enter cells 5 and 6. On these aircraft, during landing approach or loiter, the automatic transfer circuit may activate early due to high AOA and a partially full cell 1. The automatic fuel transfer system is completely independent of the fuel quantity indicating system.

EMERGENCY FUEL TRANSFER

There are no provisions for an emergency fuel transfer system on this airplane. With hydraulic and electric fuselage transfer pumps working simultaneously, and the utilization of air pressure for wing and external tanks transfer, the possiblity of a complete fuel transfer system failure is highly improbable. On aircraft 152965y and up, and all others after AFC 273, the electric transfer pumps in cells 4 and 6 transfer fuselage fuel. The hydraulic transfer pumps operate only with loss of electric power, fuel low level circuit energized, or operation in afterburner.

PRESSURIZATION AND VENT SYSTEM

The pressurization and vent system provides regulated engine bleed air pressure to all internal, and

external tanks for pressurization, fuel transfer, and wing dump. The system also provides for venting of external tanks to prevent collapse during fast descents.

Wing Tank Pressurization and Vent

The wing cells and external tanks pressurization system utilizes pressure regulators and pressure relief valves which are set respectively at 15 ± 0.5 psi and 17.5 ± 0.5 psi. The wing cell pressure relief valves, which provide fuel tank pressure and vacuum relief, dump into a common manifold which is vented overboard under the rudder. The external wing tanks are vented through their pressure relief valves to the wing cell dump lines. The wing cells and external wing tanks are vented to the atmosphere when the landing gear is extended.

Fuselage Tank Pressurization and Vent

The fuselage tank pressure regulator, in conjunction with the flow limiter and pressure relief vent valve, maintains regulated air pressure at 2 ± 0.5 psi and pressure relief at 3.5 ± 0.5 psi. The fuselage cells and the buddy tank or centerline external tank are vented to the common fuel vent manifold and then dumped overboard through the fuselage pressure relief valve. When the landing gear is extended, all pressure relief valves are open, venting all tanks to the atmosphere.

WING FUEL DUMP

Wing fuel may be dumped in flight at any time regardless of any other transfer position by selecting DUMP on the internal wing dump switch (figure A-1, appendix A). The two position toggle switch marked NORMAL and DUMP is on the fuel control panel on the left console of the pilot's cockpit. Selecting DUMP opens the left and right wing dump shutoff valves and closes the wing transfer and vent valves (if not previously closed). The wing air pressure regulators open (if not previously open) allowing the wing tanks to pressurize and force fuel out the dump lines at the wing fold trailing edge. On airplanes 153030aa and up, and all others after AFC 249, a hex-head is installed on the internal wing dump switch to make it more easily recognized. At 85% rpm in level flight, the fuel dumping capability is approximately 100 gpm. The dumping rate varies directly with rpm and pitch attitude, i.e., lower rpm and/or nose pitched down decreases the dumping rate. Air pressure continues to bleed out the dump line until the internal wing dump switch is placed in NORMAL to close the dump valves.

Note

• Because the internal wing dump switch functions with the engine master switch ON or OFF, and the landing gear up or down, wing fuel is dumped on the deck when internal wing dump switch is placed in DUMP and external power is applied to the airplane.

• Wing fuel dump cannot be initiated on RAT power.

SMOKE ABATEMENT SYSTEM (FUEL ADDITIVE)

On aircraft after AFC 373 an engine exhaust smoke abatement system is incorporated to improve fuel combustion. The improved fuel combustion reduces the black smoky exhaust emitting from the engine exhaust while operating at miliary power settings at low altitudes. The system, when energized, injects a combustion improver CI-2 into the engine fuel manifolds. The system consists of two interconnected reservoirs, a pressure regulator and vent valve, a shutoff valve, flow restrictors, and a control switch. The reservoirs have a total capacity of approximately 2 gallons (approximately 30 minute duration) and are pressurized by 17th stage engine bleed air. Pressure within the reservoir is maintained between 46 and 55 psi by the pressure regulator and vent valve. The valve receives pressure from the fuel tank pressurization line and vents through the centerline tank vent line. The shutoff valve and flow restrictors, control and regulate flow from the reservoirs to the fuel manifolds. During afterburner operation the system is deactivated by the afterburner sensing relays regardless of the control switch position.

Smoke Abatement Control Switch

A two position smoke abatement control switch (figure A-1 appendix A) with positions of OFF and ON is on the engine control panel. When the switch is ON, the shutoff valve is energized open and additive is injected into the fuel manifolds. Additive injects into the fuel manifolds until the switch is placed OFF, or the reservoirs are depleted, or until afterburner is selected.

FUEL QUANTITY INDICATING SYSTEM

The fuel quantity indicating system is of the capacitance type and provides a reading in pounds of total internal fuel. The system components include the fuel quantity indicator, fuel check switch and a fuel level low indicator light. There are 13 fuel gaging units throughout the internal tanks which register at the one cockpit fuel quantity gage.

Fuel Quantity Indicator

A combination (counter-sector) fuel quantity indicator figure A-1, appendix A) is in upper right corner of the pilot's instrument panel. The counter unit of the gage continuously indicates the total usable fuel quantity (with readings multiplied by 10) in all internal tanks. The sector portion of the indicator simultaneously indicates the total usable fuel quantity in the fuselage cells only with readings multiplied by 1000. After all wing fuel has transferred, the counter and sector portions of the fuel quantity gage should read within 350 pounds of each other. There is a possibility that fuel quantity variations may be noted on the fuel quantity indicator during aircraft accelerations and decelerations. These variations are due to the high acceleration and deceleration rates. Transient increases in fuel quantity readings may be noted during deceleration, and transient decreases in fuel quantity readings may be noted during acceleration. Therefore, optimum fuel quantity gage indications are achieved with the aircraft in a straight and level attitude in conjunction with moderate stabilized power settings.

Note

At the low end of the fuel scale, the counter portion of the fuel quantity gage has a tolerance of ± 200 pounds, and the sector portion has a tolerance of ± 150 pounds. Therefore, if the FUEL LEVEL LOW light illuminates above an indicated 2080 pounds, the warning light should be used as the primary indication of a low fuel state, and continued aircraft operation should be judiciously considered.

Feed Tank Check Switch

The two-position feed tank check switch (figure A-1, appendix A), with switch positions of CHECK and NORMAL, permits the pilot to check the fuel quantity in the engine feed tank. When the switch is placed in spring-loaded CHECK, the sector portion and the counter portion of the fuel quantity gage indicate engine feed cell fuel quantity. In addition to checking feed cell fuel quantity, it is also an indication that there is power to the fuel quantity circuits and that the gage is functioning properly.

Fuel Level Low Indicator Light

The FUEL LEVEL LOW indicator light on the tele-light panel illuminates when the combined usable fuel in the engine feed cell and cell 2 is reduced to approximately 1880 ± 200 lb. level. The FUEL LEVEL LOW light illuminates at the above fuel quantities only if the airplane is in a perfectly level attitude and moderate stabilized power settings are being used. However, due to the various attitudes and power settings required during a normal flight the illumination of the FUEL LEVEL LOW indicator light is not an accurate indication of the amount of fuel remaining in cells 1 and 2. The illuminated light only indicates to the pilot that his fuel is low. In this system the unit which operates the low level indicator light is a thermistor sensing switch which is on the engine feed cell fuel quantity probe. When the fuel level in cells 1 and 2 is above the sensor switch, the resistance of the reference thermistor (which is enclosed in an air filled capsule) is much less than the resistance of the sensing thermistor, causing an unbalance in the bridge circuit. The relay is energized and the FUEL LEVEL LOW indicator light is out. When the fuel level drops below the sensor switch the thermistors are exposed to air, and resistances of the reference and sensing thermistors are equal, balancing the bridge circuit. The relay then becomes deenergized and allows current flow to the FUEL LEVEL LOW indicator light. The fuel level low light is completely independent of the fuel quantity indicating system. On airplanes 153030aa and up, and all others after AFC 249, when the fuel level low relay energizes the automatic fuel transfer feature is activated. On these aircraft a FUEL LEVEL low indicator light is also installed on the rear cockpit instrument panel.

FUEL QUANTITY DATA TABLE

TANK	FULLY SERVICED		USABLE FUEL			
			BEFORE AFC 352/288		AFTER AFC 352/288	
	GALLONS	POUNDS	GALLONS	POUNDS	GALLONS	POUNDS
FUSELAGE CELL 1	–	–	314	2135	231	1571
CELL 2	–	–	221	1503	221	1503
CELL 3	–	–	164	1115	164	1115
CELL 4	–	–	221	1503	221	1503
CELL 5	–	–	201	1367	201	1367
CELL 6	–	–	235	1598	235	1598
TOTAL FUSELAGE FUEL	1391	9391	1356	9221	1273	8657
INTERNAL WING TANKS	* 638	* 4338	* 630	* 4284	630	4284
TOTAL INTERNAL FUEL	* 2019	* 13729	* 1986	* 13505	1903	12941
EXTERNAL WING TANKS	744	5059	740	5032	740	5032
INTERNAL FUEL PLUS EXTERNAL WING TANKS	* 2763	* 18788	* 2726	* 18537	* 2643	17973
EXTERNAL CENTER TANK	607	4094	600	4080	600	4080
INTERNAL FUEL PLUS EXTERNAL CENTER TANK	* 2621	* 17823	* 2586	* 17585	2503	17021
MAXIMUM FUEL LOAD TOTAL INTERNAL PLUS ALL EXTERNAL TANKS	* 3365	* 22882	* 3326	* 22617	3243	22053
TOTAL UNUSABLE	39	265	–	–	–	–

* INTERNAL FUEL CAPACITIES AND TOTAL FUEL CAPACITIES ARE FOR AIRCRAFT 148411h AND UP BEFORE AFC 352/288. TO OBTAIN THE CORRECT CAPACITY ON AIRCRAFT 148363f THRU 148410g, ADD 7 GALLONS AND/OR 47 POUNDS.

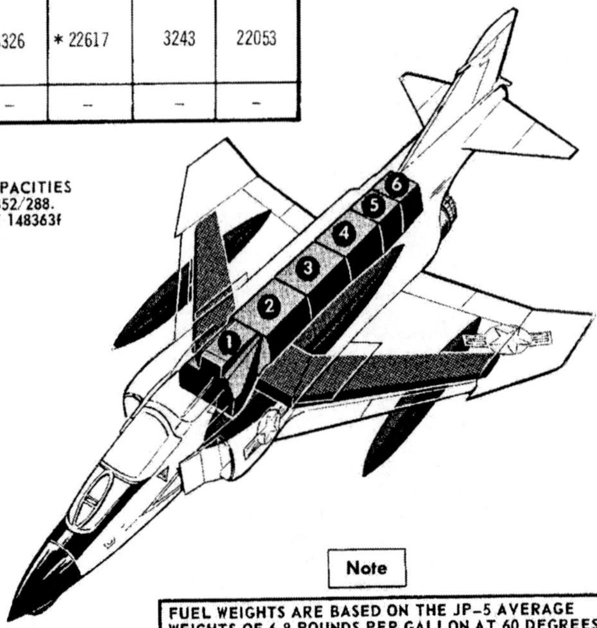

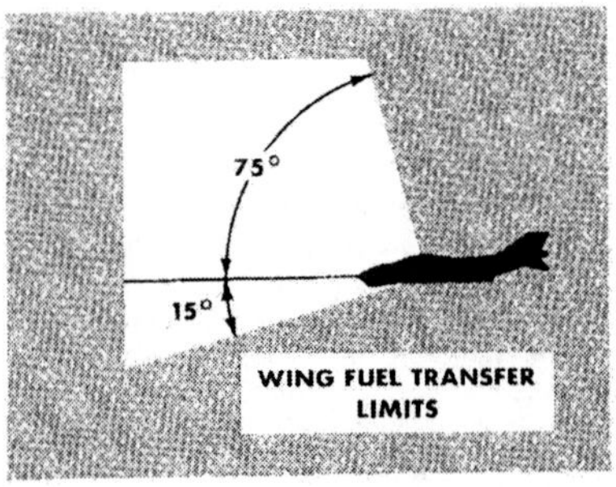

WING FUEL TRANSFER LIMITS

75°

15°

Note

FUEL WEIGHTS ARE BASED ON THE JP-5 AVERAGE WEIGHTS OF 6.8 POUNDS PER GALLON AT 60 DEGREES FAHRENHEIT.

FDB-1-(30)

Figure 1-26

Note

If automatic transfer is activated, and external tank(s) is/are installed and empty, the corresponding external fuel flow warning light(s) illuminates.

Left and Right External Fuel Lights

The L. EXT FUEL or R. EXT FUEL indicator lights on the telelight panel are provided to indicate an empty left or right outboard external tank with OUTB'D selected on the external transfer switch. One of the other external fuel indicator lights and the MASTER CAUTION light illuminate simultaneously when fuel flow from one of the external wing tanks ceases. This indicates to the pilot that the tank indicated is empty or flow is interrupted. Since external fuel transfer is intermittent rather than continuous the MASTER CAUTION light and the L. EXT FUEL, and the R. EXT FUEL indicator lights come on during a temporary halt of fuel flow. Although the MASTER CAUTION light is cleared and the external tanks fuel indicator lights have gone out, the lights again illuminate (approximately 10 to 30 seconds later) during the next interruption of fuel flow. On airplanes 150406L and up, and all others after ASC 97, the MASTER CAUTION light does not come on when the L. EXT FUEL or R. EXT FUEL lights are illuminated. Intermittent external fuel transfer is desired because the transfer rate is greater than engine consumption and fuselage fuel is being maintained at its highest possible volume. The L. EXT FUEL or R. EXT FUEL indicator lights also illuminate when the tanks are fueled during refueling operation. When selecting the outboard or refuel position on the fuel control panel, the L. EXT FUEL or R. EXT FUEL lights illuminate any time fuel flow is less than 5 gpm. On airplanes 153030aa and up, and all others after AFC 249, the R. EXT FUEL and L. EXT FUEL lights illuminate if automatic fuel transfer is initiated and the wing fuel tanks are empty, or MERs are installed on the outboard wing stations.

Centerline External Tank Fuel Light

The CTR EXT FUEL indicator light is provided to indicate an empty centerline tank with CENTER selected on the external transfer switch. The CTR EXT FUEL indicator light and the MASTER CAUTION light illuminates simultaneously when fuel flow ceases. On airplanes 150406L and up, and all others after ASC 97, the MASTER CAUTION light does not come on when the CTR EXT FUEL light is illuminated. The CTR EXT FUEL indicator light also illuminates when the tank is full during a refueling operation or when the tank flow stops during fuel transfer to the buddy tank. On airplanes 153030aa and up, and all others after AFC 249, the CTR EXT FUEL indicator light illuminates, if automatic fuel transfer is initiated and the centerline fuel tank is empty. When selecting the CENTER BUDDY FILL or REFUEL positions on the fuel control panel, the CTR EXT FUEL light illuminates any time fuel flow is less than 5 gpm.

TK Light

The TK light, on the missile status panel, is located on the lower left side of the main instrument panel.

The light illuminates when the centerline tank or any other store is installed on the centerline station. When the TK light is illuminated, the forward fuselage missiles cannot be fired.

EXTERNAL TANK JETTISON SYSTEM
External Tank Jettison Switch

The external wing tanks can be jettisoned by simply selecting JETT on the fuel control panel (figure A-1, appendix A) on the left console in the pilot's cockpit. The tanks can be jettisoned before or after the flow indicating light illuminates. Illumination of the flow light indicates flow has ceased and external tanks are empty. If the external transfer switch has been inadvertently left in either OUTB'D or CENTER and external tanks are not installed on the airplane, or the tanks have been jettisoned, the external wing tanks fuel shutoff valve closes and the switch is ineffective, allowing wing fuel to transfer in its normal manner.

> **CAUTION**
>
> The external wing tanks can be jettisoned by the external wing tank jettison switch any time power is on the airplane and the external tanks safety pins are removed. This circuit is not wired through the landing gear handle.

Note

Refer to External Stores Limitations chart (part 4 of this section) for external tanks jettison restrictions.

External Centerline Tank Jettison

Centerline external stores only are jettisoned (providing the landing gear handle is up) by selecting DIRECT on the bomb control switch and then pressing the bomb release button on the control stick grip. On airplanes 148363f thru 149474k after ASC 87, to jettison only the external centerline tank, the landing gear handle must be up; the centerline station safe switch, on the bomb control panel, must be in READY; and the bomb control switch, on the bomb control panel, must be in DIRECT. In addition, on airplanes 150406L and up, and all others after ASC 78 (Part I), the master arm switch, on the multiple weapons control panel must be in SAFE. On airplanes 152278w and up, and all others after AFC 241 the master arm switch is called the weapons (WPNs) switch and it is placed to CONV OFF - NUCL ON for centerline fuel tank jettison. When these switches are set, pressing the bomb release button on the control stick grip jettisons the external centerline tank.

External Stores Emergency Release Button

The external stores emergency release button (figure A-1, appendix A) is on the left vertical panel. This button when pressed, jettisons all external stores except missiles, carried on the airplane, provided the landing gear handle is up. On airplanes 150406L and up, and all others after ASC 78, 87 and 97, pressing the external stores emergency release button jettisons all external stores (including missiles and pylons) provided the landing gear handle is up or the main gear struts are extended.

AIR REFUELING SYSTEM

The air refueling probe is on the starboard side of the fuselage above the engine air inlet duct. The probe is equipped with an MA-2 refueling nozzle capable of receiving fuel from any drogue type refueling system. The refueling operation is actuated by the refuel probe switch on the fuel control panel. The refuel probe switch has three positions: REFUEL, EXTEND and RETRACT. The REFUEL position conditions the airplane fuel system for inflight refueling of all tanks and extends the inflight refueling probe. The EXTEND position retains the probe in the extended position, but returns the airplane fuel system to normal operation with the exception that fuselage cells 1 and 3 accept fuel from the tanker at full flow until they are full, then at a rate equal to fuel consumption. This position is used when it is necessary to replenish the fuel in the engine feed cell, either by normal fuel transfer or from the tanker. It is also used if the probe is damaged and cannot be retracted. The RETRACT position returns the fuel system to normal transfer operation and retracts the probe. On airplanes 152303w and up, and 151498t thru 152304w after AFC 213, when the refuel probe switch is placed in REFUEL, a REFUEL READY light, on the telelight panel, illuminates if the fuselage pressurization and vacuum relief valve opened properly. This assures that the fuselage cells are properly vented for refueling. On aircraft after AFC 370, the air refueling probe can be extended by pneumatic pressure from the canopy air bottle, when the normal extension system fails. Pneumatic extension is initiated by the emergency refuel probe control switch on the outboard engine control panel. The switch, marked NORMAL and EMER EXT, extends the probe when placed in EMER EXT. The refuel selection switch is on the fuel control panel. This is a two-position guarded switch with ALL TANKS and INT ONLY position. The ALL TANKS position opens the external tank fuel shutoff valves when refueling. The INT ONLY position closes the external tank fuel shutoff valves and allows only the internal tanks to be refueled during air refueling.

I.F.R. Probe Unlock Indicator Light

The IFR PROBE UNLOCKED indicator light on the telelight panel illuminates when the air refueling probe is not fully retracted. The illumination of the IFR PROBE UNLOCKED light also energizes the MASTER CAUTION light. The indicator light circuit is completed through a limit switch located within the air refueling probe latching actuator.

Air Refueling Probe Light

On airplanes 148411h and up, and all others after ASC 42, an air refueling probe light has been installed on the right side of the fuselage forward of the air refueling probe. The light is used during night air refueling operations to illuminate the refueling probe and the drogue from the refueling airplane. The light is controlled by the IFR switch and variable intensity control knob, both located on the exterior lights control panel.

GROUND REFUELING SYSTEM

The airplane is capable of either single point or two point pressure refueling. The single point refueling receptacle is on the right underside of the fuselage in the area below the aft cockpit. Single point pressure fueling at the rate of approximately 250 gallons per minute may be accomplished. Two point pressure fueling at the rate of approximately 480 gallons per minute may be accomplished by utilizing the inflight refueling probe with a special fitting attached. The system allows a controlled partial refueling capability. If desired, fuel is locked out of the left and right wing tanks, and fuselage cells 5 and 6. This allows the airplane to be partially refueled up to 920 gallons (approximately 6256 pounds) without creating an undesirable CG condition.

Cockpit Switch Positions

The switches on the fuel control panel on the left console in the pilot's cockpit should be in the following position before single point pressure fueling; external transfer switch OFF, wing transfer pressure switch NORMAL, refuel selection switch ALL TANKS buddy fill switch STOP FILL, refuel probe switch RETRACT. Refueling of the internal tanks only, with any or all external tanks installed may be accomplished by selecting INT ONLY on the refuel selection switch. The buddy tank is interchangeable with the centerline external tank and is refueled in the same manner as the centerline tank. The landing gear control handle must be down and master switches and throttle should be OFF. The generator control switches should be in EXT ON. If two-point pressure refueling is desired, the refueling probe switch should be placed in REFUEL.

REFUELING OPERATION

Apply external ac power to the airplane and place the generator control switches to EXT ON. Open filler door and attach fueling nozzle to service inlet valve. Set ground fueling switch in the right wheel well to REFUEL. (The ground fueling switch is only effective with the engine master switches OFF and ground electrical power applied.) With REFUEL selected on the ground fueling switch, all valves in the fuel system are closed with the following exceptions. The fuselage air pressure regulators are open, all internal tank vent valves are open, all external tank vent valves are open if their respective tanks are installed and the refuel selection switch is on ALL TANKS. All fuel level control valves are open to receive fuel until their respective tanks are filled at which time floats rise in the valves to shut off fuel. Outboard and centerline external tanks motor-operated shutoff valves are open allowing fuel to fill the external tanks installed. A fuel flow transmitter in each refueling line energizes a fuel flow warning light in the cockpit, corresponding to the tank not accepting fuel. Partial refueling is accomplished by actuating and holding the left and right wing tank and fuselage cell 5 fuel level control valves switches.

Functional Precheck of Electrical Transfer Pumps

Individual momentary type check switches for each electrically operated transfer pump and a pressure indicator light are on a panel in the left wheel well to provide a functional check for each electric transfer pump when on external electrical power only. When either switch is placed in CHECK, the primary circuit shuts off both fuselage fuel level control valves in fuselage cells 1 and 2, energizes the pressure transmitter switch and operates the applicable transfer pump in cell 4 or 6. The pressure transmitter switch energizes the green indicator light if the discharge pressure of the selected pump is normal. No light, while the pump is being checked, indicates a malfunction in the pump.

Functional Precheck of Hydraulic Transfer Pumps

A momentary type check switch is on a panel in the left wheel well to check the operation of the hydraulic transfer pumps. The switch works in conjunction with two indicator lights. The check switch, when placed in CHECK closes the transfer pump level control valves in fuselage cells 1 and 2, and opens the hydraulic shutoff valve to allow both pumps to operate and energize each pressure transmitter switch. Each pressure transmitter switch illuminates the green indicator light for each pump if their discharge pressure is normal. No light, with the switch in CHECK, indicates a malfunction of that pump. Hydraulic and electrical ground power must be connected to the airplane to conduct the above check. During the precheck of the electric and hydraulic transfer pumps, if the indicator light does not illuminate immediately, continue holding check switches for at least 1 minute, since the cell 1 must be full before the cell 1 fuel level control valve closes.

Functional Precheck of Refueling Level Control Valves

A double throw momentary type master check switch and seven individual momentary type check switches are in a panel in the right wheel well. The master switch has positions of CHECK NO. 1 and CHECK NO. 2. With fuel flow started from the fueling source, hole the master check switch to CHECK NO. 1. This position closes the motor operated shutoff valves of any external tank installed and energizes a solenoid in the primary float unit of the refueling level control valves, causing the primary floats to rise and shut off fuel flow to all internal tanks. Placing the master check switch in CHECK NO. 2, closes the motor operated shutoff valves of any external tank installed and energizes a solenoid in the secondary float unit of the refueling level control valves which causes the secondary floats to rise and shut off fuel flow to all internal tanks. When a malfunction occurs in the primary or secondary system, that respective position on the master switch shall be held. Malfunction of any refueling level control valve can then be isolated by operating the individual momentary type check switches one at a time to their respective position until fuel flow is stopped. The respective position of the individual switches energizes the solenoid in the circuit of each valve opposite to the circuit checked on the master switch. The individual switch that stops fuel flow indicates a malfunction of that valve in the primary or secondary unit respective to the circuit checked. Continuation of fuel flow with the master switch in CHECK NO. 1 or CHECK NO. 2 indicates a malfunction of one or more of the refueling level control valves and/or motor operated shutoff valves. In the event of an operational necessity, the aircraft may be refueled as follows: Pull the fuel transfer pump circuit breakers, on No. 1 circuit breaker panel, at approximately 6000 pounds total reading on the counter. Cut down the source pressure to 30 psig maximum until a counter reading of 9000 pounds is reached, then cut the source pressure down to 4-5 psig until the airplane is fully fueled.

NORMAL OPERATION

Operation of the fuel system is controlled through the fuel control panel. With no external tanks aboard, all switches on the fuel control panel should be in the inboard position, with the exception of the external transfer switch which should be OFF. With this switch arrangement, the fuel system is set up for automatic fuel transfer and no further switching is required. If external tanks are carried, switch positions are the same as with no external tanks except that the external transfer switch is placed in an appropriate external tank position. In this case, it is necessary to switch to another external tank position, or place the external transfer switch OFF when the fuel in the selected tank(s) is depleted. If the external tanks are carried in conjunction with conventional multiple weapons, special fuel manangement may be required. Refer to Fuel Management Requirements, part 1, this section. After all external fuel is expended and the external transfer switch is OFF, internal wing fuel transfers automatically and no further switching is required. The L. EXT FUEL, R. EXT FUEL and CTR FUEL warning lights illuminate when flow from the selected tank is interrupted, therefore, the only indication of completed external fuel transfer is the illumination of the external fuel warning lights accompanied by a decrease in internal fuel. Upon depletion of external tank fuel, the fuselage cells continue to supply fuel to the engine feed cell; however, internal wing fuel does not commence transferring until the external transfer switch is turned OFF. During carrier operation, manage internal wing fuel so as to arrive at the carrier with the maximum trap weight.

EMERGENCY OPERATION

FUEL BOOST PUMPS

If fuel boost pumps fail, fuel still is supplied to the engine by gravity feed if positive G is maintained. If both boost pumps fail above 20,000 feet and/or at a high power setting, flameout or an unstable rpm indication on one or both engines may occur. During gravity feed, high fuel flow rates required by afterburner operation cannot be met. A boost pump pressure indication of 0 psi indicates that both boost pumps are inoperative. If both engines have flamed out, reduce airspeed to 515 knots CAS or Mach 1.1 whichever is less and extend the ram air turbine. Extending the ram air turbine operates the left fuel boost pump at low speed. This supplies enough fuel to either engine to accomplish an airstart. If an airstart has been accomplished or the engines have not flamed out, reduce power and/or descend until stable engine operation can be maintained. Since the boost pumps feed into a common manifold before branching off to the engines and boost pump pressure transmitters, an operative pump is noted on both boost pump indicators. Therefore, a boost pump pressure reading below normal is a good indication that one of the boost pumps is inoperative. The power settings on each engine should be reduced as necessary until a boost pump pressure reading of 5 psi or greater is obtained.

INTERNAL TANKS TRANSFER SYSTEM

Transfer system failure can usually be attributed to failure of the fuel system to become pressurized. This will only affect external and internal wing fuel transfer. Fuselage fuel is transferred by two electrically driven transfer pumps that run continuously whenever electrical power is applied. In case of complete electrical failure, two hydraulically driven pumps take over. The hydraulically driven pumps will commence transferring fuel when hydraulic power is available with no electrical power (electrical system failure), when either engine is in afterburner or when the fuel low level warning circuit is energized. If the fuel system fails to become pressurized, place the wing transfer pressure switch in the EMER position. This performs the same functions as the landing gear handle switch, all pressure regulators open and all pressure relief valves close.

AIR REFUELING PROBE

On aircraft after AFC 370, the air refueling probe can be extended with pneumatic pressure by pulling the refuel probe circuit breaker D15, No. 1 panel, placing the probe switch to REFUEL, and placing the emergency refuel probe switch to EMER EXT. This extends the refueling probe with canopy air, and cycles the fuel system for refueling. After inflight refueling has been accomplished, the fuel system is pressurized by placing the refuel probe switch on the fuel control panel to EXTEND. The emergency refuel probe switch must be left in EMER EXT.

Note

To prevent possible damage to the utility reservoir and/or loss of utility pressure, the air refueling probe must be left in the extended position, once it has been extended with pneumatic pressure.

CENTERLINE TANK JETTISONING

Jettisoning the centerline tank when it is partially full, may result in aircraft damage and severe control problems. If release of the centerline tank is necessary proceed as follows:

1. Maintain flight integrity or attempt to rendezvous with an available aircraft if a single plane flight and conditions permit.
2. Maintain an altitude at or above 5,000 feet if possible.
3. Maintain a wings level attitude and 1 G flight.
4. Establish appropriate release airspeed determined from NATOPS publications.
5. Jettison tank according to the type of situation as defined below.
   a. If the tank is ruptured:
      (1) Wingman advise the extent of streaming fuel.
      (2) If fire hazard from streaming fuel is imminent, jettison the tank and be prepared for control difficulties.
      (3) If wingman indicates fire danger is not imminent, allow the tank to drain and land ashore with it empty. If landing ashore is not practicable, jettison the tank after it is empty.
      (4) Do not select afterburner power with fuel streaming from a ruptured tank.
   b. If the tank is not ruptured:
      (1) If the tank is partially full, attempt to fill it with fuselage fuel if total fuel available permits. If time or total fuel available preclude such procedures be prepared for aircraft damage and control difficulties after jettisoning the tank.
      (2) Completely empty or completely full tank - establish proper jettison airspeed and jettison the tank.

LIMITATIONS

WING FUEL TRANSFER

Internal wing fuel does not transfer above 75° nose up attitude, or below 15° nose down attitude.

HYDRAULIC POWER SUPPLY SYSTEM

— NOTICE —
Some illustrations referred to within this system writeup may be located in appendix A. These illustrations are referred to, within the text, as (figure A-, appendix A).

DESCRIPTION

Hydraulic power is supplied by three completely independent closed center hydraulic systems. They are Power Control System One (PC-1), Power Control System Two (PC-2), and Utility System. The systems have operating pressures of approximately 3000 psi, and are pressurized any time the engines are running. The power control system supplies hydraulic pressure to the dual power control cylinders of the ailerons, spoilers, and stabilator. The utility system supplies hydraulic pressure to the power control cylinder of the rudder, and to all other hydraulically operated systems. On aircraft after AFC 400, the utility system is modified (rerouted) to include the dual power control cylinders of the ailerons and spoilers. Each system can be pressurized by an external hydraulic power source.

POWER CONTROL SYSTEM ONE (PC-1)

PC-1 (figure A-8, appendix A) is pressurized to 3000 ± 250 psi, by a variable volume (18 to 26 gpm), constant pressure hydraulic pump mounted on the left engine. This system supplies hydraulic pressure to one side of the dual power control cylinders of the ailerons, spoilers, and stabilator. On aircraft after AFC 400, PC-1 is modified (rerouted) to supply hydraulic pressure to one side of the dual power control cylinders of the left aileron and spoiler. Actuation of the stabilator is the same as before AFC 400. Fluid is supplied to the pump by an airless, pressure loaded piston-type hydraulic reservoir that has a usable capacity of 0.83 gallons. The reservoir insures positive hydraulic pressure and fluid supply to the pump suction port, regardless of airplane altitude of flight attitude. A 50 cubic inch accumulator, precharged to 1000 psi, is utilized as a pump surge compressor, and as a limited source of hydraulic fluid and pressure when system demands exceed pump output. A pressure relief valve protects the system from pressure surges, and limits pressure build-up, by dumping pressures in excess of 3250 and up to 3850 psi to return. A pressure transmitter, for the PC-1 hydraulic pressure indicator (figure A-1, appendix A), is in a main pressure line. If a loss of system pressure occurs, a CHECK HYD GAGES indicator light and MASTER CAUTION light illuminate. The hydraulic fluid is maintained at a usable temperature by a fuel-hydraulic fluid heat exchanger. On aircraft prior to 152331x, before AFC 220, the system may be pressurized to 1400 ± 100 psi, by an emergency hydraulic pump that is driven by a ram air turbine if the engine driven pump fails.

POWER CONTROL SYSTEM TWO (PC-2)

PC-2 (figure A-8, appendix A), is pressurized to 3000 ± 250 psi, by a variable volume (18 to 26 gpm), constant pressure hydraulic pump on the right engine. This system supplies hydraulic pressure to one side of the dual power control cylinders of the ailerons, spoilers, and stabilator. On aircraft after AFC 400, PC-2 is modified (rerouted) to supply hydraulic pressure to one side of the dual power control cylinders of the right aileron and spoiler. Actuation of the stabilator is the same as before AFC 400. Fluid is supplied to the pump by an airless, pressure loaded, piston-type hydraulic reservoir that has a usable capacity of 0.83 gallons. The reservoir insures positive hydraulic pressure and fluid supply at the pump suction port regardless of airplane altitude or flight attitude. A 50 cubic inch accumulator precharged to 1000 psi, is utilized as a pump surge suppressor, and as a limited source of hydraulic fluid and pres-

sure when system demands exceed pump output. A pressure relief valve protects the system from pump surges, and limits pressure build-up, by dumping pressures in excess of 3250 and up to 3850 psi to return. A pressure transmitter, for the PC-2 hydraulic pressure indicator (figure A-1, appendix A), is in a main pressure line. If a loss of system pressure occurs, a CHECK HYD GAGES indicator light and MASTER CAUTION light illuminate. The hydraulic fluid is maintained at a usable temperature by a fuel-hydraulic fluid heat exchanger. There are no emergency hydraulic pump provisions associated with the PC-2 hydraulic system.

UTILITY SYSTEM

The utility hydraulic system (figure A-8, appendix A), is pressurized to 3000 ± 250 psi by two variable volume (22 to 30 gpm combined), constant pressure hydraulic pumps, one on each engine. To prevent the utility hydraulic pumps from resonating, check valves with different cracking pressures are installed on the pump output lines. As a result, the right engine utility hydraulic pump delivers 2775 ± 225 psi at idle rpm, while the left engine utility hydraulic pump delivers 3000 ± 250 psi at idle rpm. Fluid is supplied to the pumps by an airless, pressure loaded, piston-type hydraulic reservoir that has a usable capacity of 1.84 gallons. The reservoir insures positive hydraulic pressures and fluid supply at the suction ports of the pumps regardless of airplane altitude or flight attitude. A 50 cubic inch accumulator, precharged to 1000 psi, is utilized as a pump surge suppressor, and as a limited source of hydraulic fluid and pressure when system demands exceed the output of the pumps. A pressure relief valve protects the system from pump surges, and limits pressure build-up by dumping pressures in excess of 3250 and up to 3850 psi to return. A pressure transmitter, for the utility hydraulic pressure indicator, is in a main pressure line. If either pump fails, a CHECK HYD GAGES indicator light and MASTER CAUTION light illuminate. The hydraulic fluid is maintained at a usable temperature by two fuel-hydraulic fluid heat exchangers. The utility hydraulic system supplies hydraulic pressure to the:

Aileron Dampers
Aileron Power Control Cylinders - Aircraft after AFC 400
Aileron-Rudder Interconnect
Air Refueling Probe
Arresting Hook (retraction)
Auxiliary Air Doors
Flaps (leading and trailing edge)
Forward Missile Cavity Doors
Fuel Transfer Pumps (hydraulic)
Landing Gear
Lateral Control Servo (autopilot)
Leading edge flap BLC valves (drooped aileron aircraft)
Nose Gear Steering
Pneumatic System Air Compressor
Radar Antenna Drive
Rudder Feel/Trim

Rudder Power Control Cylinder
Speed Brakes
Spoiler Power Control Cylinders - Aircraft after
  AFC 400
Variable Engine Bellmouth
Variable Engine Intake Duct Ramps
Wheel Brakes
Wing Fold

HYDRAULIC PRESSURE INDICATORS

Three hydraulic pressure indicators (figure A-1, appendix A), are on the pedestal panel in the front cockpit. Pressure transmitters, one for each system, convert pressure impulses into electrical impulses which, in turn, are supplied to the indicators. The indicators are identical, and cover a pressure range of 0 to 5000 psi and are marked from 0 to 5 with readings multiplied by 1000. Electrical power for PC-1 and PC-2 indicators is supplied by the essential 28 volt ac bus. On aircraft 148363f through 152215t before AFC 262 the PC-2 indicator is powered by the left main 28 volt ac bus. Electric power for the utility hydraulic pressure indicator is supplied by the left main 28 volt ac bus.

Note

Electrical power to the utility hydraulic pressure indicator is supplied by the left main 28 volt ac bus; therefore, the utility hydraulic pressure gage will be inoperative on RAT power or when the left generator is inoperative and the bus tie is open.

HYDRAULIC PRESSURE INDICATOR LIGHT

An amber CHECK HYD GAGES indicator light is on the telelight panel (figure A-1, appendix A). This single light is utilized by both the power control systems and the utility system to indicate loss of hydraulic system pressure and direct the pilot's attention to the hydraulic pressure indicators. Illumination of the CHECK HYD GAGES indicator light is controlled by the hydraulic systems pressure switches. The CHECK HYD GAGES light illuminates when the pressure in any one system drops below 1500 ± 100 psi and/or when one of the utility hydraulic pumps fail. In all cases a loss of system pressure is noted on the applicable hydraulic pressure indicator, but, a failed utility hydraulic pump may not register a significant pressure drop on the utility pressure indicator. However, an illuminated CHECK HYD GAGES light with no noted pressure drop on any of the hydraulic pressure indicators signifies that the right utility hydraulic pump has failed. An illuminated CHECK HYD GAGES light with a utility hydraulic pressure drop of 200 psi signifies that the left utility pump has failed. The MASTER CAUTION light illuminates with the CHECK HYD GAGES indicator light. The MASTER

CAUTION light may be extinguished by pressing the reset button. The CHECK HYD GAGES light remains illuminated until the pressure in the faulty system increases beyond 1750 psi. If a failure occurs in one of the remaining hydraulic systems while the CHECK HYD GAGES light is already illuminated, the MASTER CAUTION light does not illuminate again and the pilot is not alerted to the second failure.

Note

The MASTER CAUTION light, AUX AIR DOOR light, and CHECK HYD GAGES light may illuminate momentarily when the landing gear is being lowered due to high system demands.

NORMAL OPERATION

Normal operation of the hydraulic system commences with engine operation.

EMERGENCY OPERATION

The loss of a hydraulic pump in either power control system or in the utility hydraulic system, is noted by the illumination of the CHECK HYD GAGES light. This single light serves all three systems, and the pilot should check the hydraulic gages to determine which system has malfunctioned. PC-1 and PC-2 are independent of each other, but each system satisfactorily functions as an emergency system for the other. On aircraft after AFC 400, the utility system is modified (rerouted) to include the dual power control cylinders of the ailerons and spoilers. Thus, each flight control hydraulic supply system serves as an emergency system for the other(s). If simultaneous loss of the utility system and one of the power control system, the operable aileron and spoiler provides adequate lateral control for an emergency landing. Thus each flight control hydraulic supply system serves as an emergency system for the other(s).

COMPLETE POWER CONTROL SYSTEM FAILURE

The pilot should, upon initial detection of hydraulic power loss, note the trend of failure as to whether the gages show a definite steady drop, or gage fluctuations. With a steady drop indication, hydraulic power will probably not recover. In the event of complete power control hydraulic failure, the aircraft will become uncontrollable.

UTILITY HYDRAULIC SYSTEM FAILURE

Failure of the utility system prevents/degrades the hydraulic operation of the following essential items:

a. Ailerons (some aircraft)
b. Air refueling probe
c. Auxiliary air doors

d. Arresting hook (retraction)
e. Flaps
f. Fuel transfer pumps
g. Landing gear
h. Leading edge BLC valves (drooped aileron aircraft
i. Nose gear steering
j. Pneumatic system air compressor
k. Rudder
m. Rudder feel/trim
n. Speed brakes
o. Spoilers (some aircraft)
p. Variable by-pass bellmouth
q. Variable engine intake ramps
r. Wheel brakes
s. Wing fold
t. Drooped ailerons (on aircraft 152995z and up, also aircraft with AFC 218

Of the above items emergency aircraft pneumatic operation is provided for the following:

a. Landing gear
b. Leading edge flap BLC valves (drooped aileron aircraft)

c. Wheel brakes
d. Wing flaps
e. Dropped ailerons
f. Air refueling probe

In addition to emergency (pneumatic) operation of the landing gear, wheel brakes, wing flaps, and air refueling probe, back-up or alternate operation is provided for the rudder, fuel transfer pumps, and speed brakes. The rudder can be manually operated; however, deflection is entirely dependent upon air loads on the rudder surface. The electric fuel transfer pumps continue to operate, if electrical power is available, even though utility pressure is not available to the hydraulic transfer pumps. The speed brakes can be retracted to a low drag trail position by placing the emergency speed brake switch to RETRACT. The power control hydraulic systems act as a back-up for the ailerons and spoilers.

LIMITATIONS

No specific limitations pertain to the hydraulic system.

INSTRUMENTS

---- NOTICE ----
Some illustrations referred to within this system writeup may be located in appendix A. These illustrations are referred to, within the text, as (figure A-, appendix A).

DESCRIPTION

Most of the instruments are electrically operated by power from the electrical system, see figure A-5, appendix A. Some instruments, such as the accelerometer, are self-contained and do not require external power. Only the instruments which are not covered under another system are discussed herein.

TRUE AIRSPEED INDICATOR

A true airspeed indicator (figure A-1, appendix A), is on the pilot's and RIO's instrument panels. The airspeed is indicated by a small counter which rotates to show a row of numbers through a window on the indicator face. The airspeed indicator indicates directly in knots TAS; the range of the instrument is from 0 to 1500 knots to the nearest knot. The true airspeed system calibrated range is 150 to 1500 knots. Therefore, true airspeed readings below 150 knots are not reliable. The true airspeed indicator may indicate between 108 and 150 knots while the airplane is motionless on the ground. The true airspeed outputs are produced from the signal from the total temperature sensor of the ADC by routing this signal through a potentiometer driven by one of the Mach number function cams. Thus, Mach number is translated into true airspeed.

ALTIMETER

An altimeter (figure A-1, appendix A), on the pilot's and RIO's instrument panel indicates the altitude of the airplane above sea level. This unit is of the counter pointer type which displays the whole thousands numbers in a counter window and indicates the increments of the whole number with a pointer which rotates on the face of the instrument. The pointer scale is graduated in 50 foot units with major 100 foot scale divisions from 1 to 10. The range of the altimeter is 0 to 80,000 feet. An adjustable barometric scale is provided so that the altimeter may be set to a sea level pressure. This scale range is from 28.50 to 30.90 inches mercury. The altimeter is positioned by a corrected static pressure supplied by the ADC, and no position error correction need be made to the indicated altitude as long as the static correction source is operative. In the event static correction monitors off, (illumination of STATIC CORR OFF light) the altimeter indications are in error.

CAUTION

To prevent stripping of barometric setting gear, do not force settings beyond 28.50 inches minimum and 30.90 inches maximum.

Note

Even though the ADC supplies corrected static pressure to the altimeters, it is normal for the altimeter to fluctuate when passing through the transonic speed range. Refer to NAVAIR 01-245FDA-6 for allowable tolerances.

SERVOED ALTIMETER

Aircraft 148411h and up and all others after AFC 353 have a servoed altimeter in each cockpit instead of the conventional pressure altimeter. The servoed altimeter uses both barometric and electrical inputs. The barometric function is used in both standby and normal modes. In the standby mode the servo mechanism is disabled and the altimeter functions as a standard barometric altimeter. In the normal mode the barometric portion of the altimeter positions the pointers to the indicated pressure altitude. If the indicated pressure altitude and the true pressure altitude, as determined by the air data computer, are the same there is no servo action. If there is a difference the synchro overrides the barometric mechanism and positions the pointer to indicate true altitude. A switch on the altimeter is spring loaded to the center position, and has momentary positions of RESET and STBY. After the switch is placed to RESET the electronic signal is applied to the altimeter (if required) and the system is in the normal mode. When RESET is selected and the system is functioning the STBY flag on the face of the altimeter disappears. If a failure occurs in the altimeter, altitude encoder unit, or the air data computer, the altimeter reverts to the standby mode immediately. This is indicated by the appearance of the standby warning flag on the face of the altimeter, and by the possible illumination of associated warning lights (see figure 1-8). The servoed altimeter is set and checked in the same manner as the conventional pressure altimeter.

WARNING

On aircraft after AFC 496, when operating aircraft with the servoed altimeter installed, the RESET position can be used. On aircraft before AFC 496 use the STBY mode only.

CAUTION

To prevent stripping of barometric setting gear, do not force settings beyond 28.50 inches minimum and 30.90 inches maximum.

AIRSPEED AND MACH NUMBER INDICATOR

The combination airspeed and Mach number indicator (figure A-1, appendix A) shows airspeed readings at low speeds and includes Mach number readings at high speeds. Both readings are provided by a single pointer moving over a fixed airspeed scale, graduated from 80 to 850 knots, and a rotatable Mach number scale graduated from Mach .4 to Mach 2.5. A movable bug is included as a landing speed reference and can be positioned by the knob on the face of the instrument. The same knob can position another bug on the Mach number scale for maximum indicated airspeed reference. The airspeed indicator pointer and the Mach number scale are synchronized so that a proper relationship between the two is assured throughout all altitude changes. Thus, at sea level and under standard conditions, the pointer indicates Mach 1 approximately 660 knots. Under the same conditions, but at 50,000 feet, if the same true airspeed is maintained the pointer indicates approximately 292 knots and a mach number of 1.15. The airspeed and Mach number indicator utilizes a corrected static pressure source from the ADC which eliminates the need for instrument position error correction. Therefore, the airspeed and Mach number indicator displays calibrated airspeed (CAS) and true Mach number (TMN) when the static pressure correction portion of the ADC is operative. If the static correction source is lost (illumination of STATIC CORR OFF light) the airspeed and Mach number indicator revert to displaying indicated airspeed (IAS) and indicated Mach number (IMN).

VERTICAL VELOCITY INDICATOR

A vertical velocity indicator (figure A-1, appendix A) is on the pilot's instrument panel. The indicator shows the rate of ascent or descent of the airplane, and is so sensitive that it can register a rate of gain or loss of altitude which is too small to cause a noticeable change in the altimeter reading. The upper half of the indicator face is graduated in 500 foot units from 0 to 6,000 feet with 100 feet scale divisions from 0 to 1,000 feet. The upper half of the instrument indicates rate of climb in thousands of feet per minute. The lower half of the indicator face is identical to the upper half except that it indicates rate of descent in thousands of feet per minute. The vertical velocity indicator is connected to the corrected static pressure system of the airplane and measures the change in atmospheric pressure as the airplane climbs or descends. Since the vertical velocity indicator utilizes corrected static pressure, a failure of the corrected static pressure source (illumination of STATIC CORR OFF light) may result in a slightly erroneous vertical velocity indication.

TURN-AND SLIP INDICATOR

A slip inclinometer and rate of turn needle is incorporated into the attitude director indicator (figure A-1, appendix A), on the front cockpit instrument panel of all airplanes. A conventional turn and slip indicator is on the rear cockpit instrument panel of dual control airplanes. The rear cockpit indicator displays a 90 degree per minute turn rate for a single needle width deflection (four minute turn). The turn indicator consists of an electrically driven gyro, linked to a pointer needle. When the needle is off center, it indicates that the airplane is turning in the direction shown by the needle. The amount the needle is off center is proportional to the rate of turn. The slip indicator is a ball type inclinometer. The ball is in a curved, fluid filled tube. When the airplane is flying straight and level, the ball is centered in the tube by its own weight. When the airplane is making a turn, the ball is acted upon by centrifugal and gravity forces. During a coordinated turn, both forces balance out to hold the ball centered in the tube. The ball indicates proper lateral attitude for any rate of turn as well as for straight and level flight. The front cockpit turn and slip indicator, however, displays turn rate about the vertical axis of the airplane, and as a result, does not provide an accurate indication of actual airplane rate of turn. When the airplane bank angle is increased, the rate of turn needle shows increased turn rate up to a point, beyond which the rate of turn around the vertical axis of the airplane decreases. This characteristic normally precludes obtaining a full needle width deflection at high altitudes and/or high airspeeds. Therefore, the front cockpit rate of turn needle should not be used as a primary turn rate instrument. At low airspeeds a single needle width deflection is approximately equivalent to a 2 minute turn. The turn needle is deflected electronically, and therefore an electrical failure renders the needle immediately inoperative, despite the fact that the gyro is still spinning.

ACCELEROMETER

An accelerometer, to measure and record positive and negative acceleration G loads, is on the front cockpit instrument panel (figure A-1, appendix A). The indicator has three movable pointers. One pointer moves in the direction of the G load being applied, while the other two (one for positive G and one for negative G) follow the indicator pointer to its maximum travel. These recording points remain at their respective maximum travel position of the G load being applied. Pressing a PUSH TO SET button, in the lower left corner of the instrument, allows the recording pointers to return to the one G position.

Note

Accelerometers may indicate as much as 1/2 G low; possibly lower if the pull-in rate is high.

STANDBY ATTITUDE INDICATOR

A standby attitude indicator is in the pilot's main instrument panel. The instrument is identical to the RIO's remote attitude indicator. The instrument supplies attitude information from the radar vertical gyro. A gyro erect switch, with positions of NORM and FAST, is on the main instrument panel, and may be used to increase the erection rate of the standby and remote attitude indicators as necessary. The indicators display an OFF flag when power is interrupted.

STANDBY COMPASS

A conventional magnetic compass on the cockpit windshield frame is provided for navigation in event of instrument or electrical malfunction. Compass deviation cards are above the canopy sill on the right side of the cockpit.

ELECTRONIC ALTIMETER SET AN/APN-141

The electronic altimeter set is a pulsed range-tracking radar, providing the pilot with accurate terrain

clearance information from 0 to 5000 feet, within ± 5 feet or ± 5 percent of the indicated altitude, whichever is greater. The set functions normally up to 30° bank angles and 50° pitch angles. The set consists of two identical antennas, a receiver-transmitter unit, an rf switching unit, and a height indicator. The receiving antenna is on the lower left front fuselage near the left inboard leading edge flap, and the transmitting antenna is on the corresponding spot on the starboard side of the fuselage.

Height Indicator

The height indicator, on the left side of the pilot's main instrument panel (figure A-1, appendix A) provides the read-out for the set. The face of the indicator contains a dual scale, an altitude pointer, a movable low altitude index pointer, and an OFF flag. The dial scale is logarithmic throughout its range. The OFF flag indicates that power is not supplied to the set, that the 5000 foot altitude range has been exceeded, or that the altitude indication is unreliable.

Function Control Knob

The function control knob, on the lower left side of the height indicator, provides complete control of the set. By rotating the knob clockwise past the off detent, power is supplied to the set. Rotating the knob further clockwise positions the low altitude pointer. Pushing in on the knob activates a self test function, when airborne, which supplies the set with an artificial return signal. The altitude pointer moves to 5 ± 5 feet. The test function is activated continuously on the ground by a scissors switch located on the right main landing gear.

Low Altitude Warning Light

A red, low altitude warning light is directly below the front cockpit true airspeed indicator. The light illuminates any time the aircraft descends below the altitude set on the low altitude index pointer.

NORMAL OPERATION

Electronic Altimeter Set AN/APN-141

With electrical power supplied, rotate the function control knob clockwise to turn the set on. Move the knob further clockwise to set the low altitude index pointer as desired. After a 3 minute warm-up period, the set is ready for operation. As the airplane ascends through 5000 feet (approximately), the OFF flag becomes visible and above 14,000 feet the transmitter is disabled by a barometric pressure switch. The set test function may be activated any time the airplane is airborne below 14,000 feet.

EMERGENCY OPERATION

There are no specific emergency operations pertaining to the instruments.

LIMITATIONS

ELECTRONIC ALTIMETER SET

The set is limited to 5000 feet altitude range and 30° bank angle/50° pitch angle.

High frequency radar waves can penetrate snow and ice fields. When operating in areas covered with snow and ice, the radar altimeter may indicate a greater terrain clearance than actually exists.

INSTRUMENT LANDING SYSTEM (AN/ARA-63)

DESCRIPTION

Aircraft after AFC 470 (Part II), contain an AN/ARA-63 instrument landing system (ILS). This system can be used for primary manual instrument landing approach, or it can be used to monitor the automatic landing performance of an automatic landing approach system. The ILS is used with carrier based azimuth and elevation transmitters. The major components of the AN/ARA-63 system are a receiver, decoder, and a control panel.

SURFACE TRANSMITTERS

The AN/ARA-63 ILS receives continuous coded angular guidance azimuth and elevation signals from the carrier based AN/SPN-41 transmitters. These signals maintain the aircraft on the approach path toward the touchdown point. The transmitted elevation scan pattern is from ground 0° to 10° looking up. Proportional angle steering in elevation is displayed ± 1.4° from the 3° glide slope. The azimuth channel sweeps ± 20° from an established reference. The reference used is the carrier deck centerline. For azimuth, proportional angle steering is displayed between ± 6°. At a range of 20 miles, the azimuth scanning beam sweeps an area approximately 8 miles wide, while the elevation of glide path is about 4 miles high.

ILS RECEIVER

The ILS receiver receives coded transmissions of azimuth and elevation guidance data from the surface transmitters. The receiver transforms these coded signals to video pulses suitable for processing in the decoder.

ILS DECODER

The ILS decoder receives the azimuth and elevation video pulses from the receiver, and converts them to azimuth and elevation command signals which drive the pitch and bank steering bars and their associated warning flags on the ADI.

Azimuth Command Signals

If the coder receives azimuth signals of sufficient strength for tracking, the signals control the movement of the bank steering bar, and the vertical director warning flag (at the 12 o'clock position) de-flects out of view. If the decoder receives weak azimuth signals or no signals, the bank steering bar deflects to the right side of the ADI, and the warning flag comes into view.

Elevation Command Signals

If the decoder receives elevation signals of sufficient strength for tracking, the signals control the movement of the pitch steering bar, and the horizontal director warning flag (at the 3 o'clock position) deflects out of view. If the decoder receives weak elevation signals or no signals, the pitch steering bar deflects to the upper portion of the ADI, and the warning flag comes into view.

ILS CONTROLS AND INDICATORS

The controls and indicators for the ILS are on the AN/ARA-63 control panel. The ADI and the navigation function selector panel on the front cockpit main instrument panel are used but are not part of the AN/ARA-63 system.

ILS CONTROL PANEL

The ILS control panel is on the right console in the front cockpit. The panel contains an on-off power switch, a power on indicator light, a built-in-test pushbutton, and a channel selector knob.

Power Switch

The power switch is a lock-type toggle switch with positions of ON and OFF. Placing the switch to ON applies power to the ILS and illuminates the green power on indicator light.

Built-In-Test

The BIT pushbutton is depressed to check for correct system operation. If the system is operating properly the bank steering bar on the ADI slowly oscillates one half scale to the left and then to the right. The pitch steering bar indicates the glide slope (3°).

Channel Selector Knob

The channel selector knob is a rotary type knob that can select any one of 20 channels.

NAVIGATION FUNCTION SELECTOR PANEL (ILS)

On aircraft after AFC 470 (Part II), the navigation function selector panel has a DL/ILS position added. Placing the mode selector knob to DL/ILS enables the ILS system to operate in a manual instrument landing approach, or to monitor an automatic landing approach during which the aircraft is receiving signals from the data link and AN/SPN-42 systems. At the time the automatic approach is being monitored the pitch and bank steering bars on the ADI are responding to signals from the AN/ARA-63 system.

NORMAL OPERATION

The AN/ARA-63 ILS is operational when the ILS power switch is placed to ON. To receive the transmitted azimuth and elevation signals from the surface transmitters, set the mode selector knob to DL/ILS and set the channel selector knob to the correct channel for receiving the incoming signals. When the aircraft is within the range of the transmitters, the bank steering bar and the pitch steering bar on the ADI indicate in which direction the aircraft must be flown to line up with the fixed approach path to the carrier deck. If the pitch steering bar is below the miniature wings on the ADI and the bank steering bar is to the right of center, the aircraft must be flown down and to the right to attain optimum glide path. When the aircraft is lined up in azimuth and elevation, both steering bars on the ADI are centered. When the aircraft reaches a point within 1/2 mile of the carrier deck at a 200 foot altitude, use the Fresnel Lens Optical System, or go visual with the deck as a reference.

LANDING GEAR SYSTEM

NOTICE

Some illustrations referred to within this system writeup may be located in appendix A. These illustrations are referred to, within the text, as (figure A-, appendix A).

DESCRIPTION

The airplane is equipped with fully retractable tricycle landing gear which are completely covered by flush doors when retracted. The gear is electrically controlled by the right main 28 volt dc bus and hydraulically actuated by the utility hydraulic system. The airplane is not equipped with a tail skid. Accidental retraction of the landing gear when the airplane is on the ground is prevented by safety switches on the main gear torque scissors, and ground safety locks.

MAIN GEAR

Each main gear is hydraulically retracted and extended. As the main gear retracts, the struts are mechanically compressed. They automatically return to the normally extended position when the gear is extended. The gear is locked down by an internal finger-type latch in the side brace actuator. The main gear retracts inboard and is enclosed by fairing doors that are flush with the underside of the wing. The gear is locked up by a hydraulically actuated mechanism. All main gear doors remain open when the gear is extended.

NOSE GEAR

The nose gear is hydraulically retracted and extended. The gear is locked down by an integral downlock mechanism within the gear actuating cylinder. A hydraulically operated nose gear uplock cylinder is in the nose gear wheel well, and is employed in the system as part of the nose gear up latch mechanism. The nose gear retracts aft into the fuselage and is covered by mechanically operated doors that close flush with the underside of the fuselage. The forward door is attached to the nose gear strut, and closes with retraction; the aft door is operated and latched closed by the gear uplatch mechanism. The nose gear is equipped with dual nose wheels, a combination shimmy damper steering actuator and a self-centering mechanism. The nose gear can be steered by differential braking of the main gear wheels in the event nose wheel steering is not utilized.

LANDING GEAR CONTROL HANDLE

Operation of the landing gear is controlled by a handle (figure A-1, appendix A) at the left side of the main instrument panel. The handle has a wheel shaped knob for ease of identification. Placing the handle up or down energizes a solenoid valve to connect system pressure to the landing gear. Placing the handle up energizes switches in the fuel tank vent and pressurization, jettison and armament circuit. A red warning light is in the landing gear control handle knob. This light comes on whenever the control handle is moved to retract or extend the gear and it remains on until the gear completes its cycle and locks.

Emergency Landing Gear Control

Two 100 cubic inch air bottles provide sufficient compressed air to extend the gear pneumatically if hydraulic system fails. Pulling the landing gear control handle full aft operates an air valve which directs 3000 psi compressed air to open all gear doors, release the uplocks, and extend all gear.

Landing Gear Position Indicators

The landing gear position indicators (figure A-1, appendix A) are on the left vertical panel in the front cockpit. The indicators operate by position switches on the landing gear. The position of the landing gear wheels is indicated by drum dials viewed through cutouts in the instrument panel. With gear up, the word UP appears on three indicators; gear in transient is indicated by a barber pole; and with gear down, a picture of a wheel is seen through the cutouts.

NOSE GEAR STRUT EXTENSION

The nose gear strut extension system is utilized to increase the airplane angle of attack for catapult launches. A nose gear extension switch in the left main gear wheel well operates a solenoid valve that ports high pressure air into a chamber above the nose gear shock strut piston. The shock strut piston is then forced down to extend the nose gear. The high pressure air is dumped when the left main gear strut extends after launching, or when the landing gear handle is moved up. The nose gear strut extension chamber may also be deflated by momentarily placing both generator control switches OFF.

CAUTION

- If the angle of attack indexer lights and approach lights are not illuminated during a landing approach, it may mean that the nose gear catapult extension is still pressurized. To preclude the possibility of exploding the nose gear strut upon touchdown, relieve the catapult extension pressure by cycling the landing gear.

- During normal operations, the airplane's pneumatic system must be fully charged (2750 psi minimum) before extending the nose gear strut and must indicate a minimum of 1475 psi after extension. Insufficient pneumatic pressure may allow the strut to bottom out causing damage to the strut or fuselage structure, and/or the proper angle of attack for a catapult takeoff may not be achieved.

- Do not allow the pneumatic system pressure to exceed 2300 psi with the nose gear strut extended. If the pneumatic pressure approaches this value, actuate the emergency air brakes as necessary to maintain the pressure below 2300 psi. If the pneumatic pressure exceeds 2300 psi the emergency brakes will not release the pressure in the nose strut. To release this excess pressure the nose strut will have to be deflated and then re-inflated. Allowing the pneumatic system pressure to exceed 2300 psi subjects the nose strut to excessive loads during catapulting.

Note

See Nose Strut Extension Pressure Minimums Chart, section III, for lower than normal launch weights.

NOSE WHEEL STEERING

An electrically controlled, hydraulically operated nose gear steering system is installed in the aircraft. It provides directional control of the aircraft during ground operation in two modes; nose gear steering and shimmy damping. For nose gear steering, the rudder pedals, through mechanical linkage, control a variable gain electrical output from the command potentiometer. Low gain (for fine, more precise steering) occurs near rudder pedal neutral and increases non-linearly in the command potentiometer to high gain (for coarse, quick steering) near full rudder pedal deflection. The first 5° of rudder pedal deflection from neutral deflects the nose wheel approximately 3°, but the last 5° of rudder pedal deflection deflects the nose wheel approximately 40°. Steering is limited to approximately 70° either side of center. The control unit receives the signal from the command potentiometer and electrically selects a servo valve setting in the utility hydraulic system. This electrical sub-system is energized and the servo setting is continually following the rudder pedals when there is electrical power in the aircraft, the nose gear is not locked up, and there is weight on the right main landing gear. Hydraulic pressure to turn the nose wheel is provided when the nose gear steering button on the control stick (figure 1-24) is depressed. This button energizes a relay which opens the selector valve in the hydraulic system. Hydraulic pressure is supplied to the servo valve which moves to the selected setting and ports hydraulic pressure to the power unit, a rotary vane hydraulic motor, on the nose gear strut. The power unit turns the nose wheel through a geared strut torque collar. As the nose wheel turns, the follow-up potentiometer on the power unit balances the electrical circuit in the control unit so that the servo valve closes as the nose wheel reaches the position commanded by the rudder pedals. Releasing the nose gear steering button also closes the servo valve and removes hydraulic pressure from the power unit. A failure detection circuit will shut-off hydraulic power to the system upon detection of an electrical short or open. Should the electrical fault be removed, nose gear steering will again be operative by depressing the nose gear steering button. Shimmy damping is automatically activated whenever the nose gear steering button is released. A restrictor, bypassing the selector valve, allows a balanced pressure of 275 psi (regulated by the compensator) to remain in the power unit. This pressure prevents cavitation of the rotary vane hydraulic motor as the nose wheel swivels. Fluid flow is metered through one-way restrictors in the power unit to damp wheel shimmy. The nose wheel can swivel to any direction in this mode.

CAUTION

To prevent the landing gear struts from being subjected to abnormal side loads, do not use nose wheel steering and brakes simultaneously while in a turn.

NORMAL OPERATION

Operation of the landing gear is controlled by the wheel shaped landing gear control handle. To lower the landing gear, push the handle down. A red warning light in the control handle knob illuminates and stays illuminated until the gear is fully extended and locked. To raise the gear, pull up on the landing gear handle; the warning light again illuminates until the landing gear is up and locked.

FLIGHT WITHOUT MAIN LANDING GEAR DOORS

If maintenance or operational consideration require flight without main landing gear doors, the airplane is limited as follows:

1. Below 20,000 feet - 250 knots CAS.
2. Between 20,000 and 35,000 feet - Mach 0.85.
3. Above 35,000 feet - 250 knots CAS or Mach 0.85, whichever is greater.
4. Descent - 250 knots CAS or onset of any buffet.
5. After each flight wheel wells should be inspected for evidence of cracks or malformed lines and fittings.

EMERGENCY OPERATION

If normal gear operation fails, the gear can be lowered by pushing the landing gear handle down, pulling the landing gear circuit breaker and then pulling aft on the landing gear handle. The landing gear circuit breaker must be pulled before lowering the gear by the emergency system. This causes the landing gear hydraulic selector valve to return to its full trail position, blocking hydraulic pressure to the landing gear and insuring that hydraulic fluid is not forced into the actuators on top of the pneumatic pressure. Should this occur, system hammering may result, with possible eventual rupture and loss of system integrity. Hold the handle aft until the gear indicates down and locked. Do not retract the landing gear following an emergency extension. If the landing gear is inadvertently extended in flight by emergency pneumatic pressure, it should be left in the extended position until post-flight servicing.

CAUTION

Hold handle in full aft position until gear indicates down and locked, and then leave the landing gear handle in the full aft position. Returning the handle to its normal position allows the compressed air from the gear down side of the actuating cylinder to be vented overboard. In this condition the main landing gear side brace integral mechanical latch is the only device preventing the landing gear from collapsing upon landing. Pull the landing gear circuit breaker before extending the landing gear by the emergency system.

Note

Any pneumatic extension of the landing gear shall be logged on the Yellow sheet (OPNAV form 3760-2).

LIMITATIONS

Maximum permissible airspeed for lowering of the landing gear is 250 knots CAS.

LIGHTING EQUIPMENT

—— NOTICE ——
Some illustrations referred to within this system writeup may be located in appendix A. These illustrations are referred to, within the text, as (figure A-, apprndix A).

DESCRIPTION

EXTERIOR LIGHTING

The exterior lights consist of the position lights (wing and tail), join-up lights (wing only) fuselage lights, anti-collision light, angle-of-roll light, and approach lights. An exterior lights master switch on the outboard left throttle grip which controls most of these lights is also utilized in the operation of night catapult launches. The exterior lights control panel contains all of the manual controls, with the exception of the master switch, for the exterior lights.

Exterior Lights Master Switch

The exterior lights master switch provides a master control for the following exterior lights: position lights, join up lights, fuselage lights, and anti-collision light. Before any of these lights can be operated, the master switch must be in either the ON or the SIGNAL position. Further control of these lights is accomplished from the exterior lights control panel. The switch, on the outboard throttle grip, has three positions; ON, OFF and SIGNAL. Placing the switch to ON energizes the switches on the exterior lights control panel for the above lights. The SIGNAL position functions identically to ON, except that it is spring-loaded to OFF. In addition to controlling the above exterior lights, the ON and SIGNAL positions dim the approach lights should they be illuminated. The master switch and exterior lights panel receive power from the right main 28 volt dc bus.

Position and Join Up Lights

The position lights include the wing tip position lights and the tail light. The join-up light consists of a red or green light on the trailing edge of the applicable wing tip. The wing tip position lights and join-up lights are both operated by the exterior lights master switch on the outboard throttle and the WING switch on the exterior lights control panel. With the exterior lights master switch ON or SIGNAL, the lights are controlled by BRT, DIM and OFF positions of the WING switch. The wing and join-up lights do not have flash capabilities. The tail light is controlled by the exterior lights master switch, TAIL switch, and FLASH switch on the exterior lights control panel. With the exterior lights master switch ON or held in SIGNAL the tail light can be controlled by the BRT, DIM and OFF positions of the tail switch. The tail light will flash or illuminate steady depending on whether the FLASH switch is in the STEADY or FLASH position. The dim circuit of the position and join-up lights is powered by the left main 14 volt ac bus. The bright lights circuit is powered by the right main 28 volt ac bus.

Fuselage and Anti-Collision Lights

Three semi-flush white lights are on the fuselage, one above the number two fuel cell and one below each of the engine air inlet ducts. In addition to the fuselage lights, one red anti-collision light is installed in the leading edge of the vertical stabilizer. The fuselage switch on the exterior lights control panel illuminates the three fuselage lights and the anti-collision light. The switch has three positions, DIM, MAN and BRT. The three fuselage lights illuminate in the DIM and BRT positions in conjunction with the exterior lights master switch. They illuminate steady or flashing depending on the position of the flasher switch. The anti-collision light illuminates only when the fuselage switch is in BRT and the exterior lights flasher switch is in FLASH. The light does not function in the steady condition or with the fuselage switch in MAN or DIM. The MAN position of the switch allows the fuselage lights to be energized by the manual key button. The fuselage lights are powered by the left main 28 volt ac bus. One of the two lamps in the anti-collision light is powered by the right main 28 volt ac bus, and the other from the left main 28 volt ac bus.

Exterior Lights Flasher Switch

The exterior lights flasher switch on the exterior lights control panel has two positions, FLASH and STEADY. If STEADY is selected, the tail light and fuselage lights produce a steady illumination, provided the FUS light switch and TAIL light switch are in DIM or BRT positions. Placing the flasher switch to FLASH causes the fuselage lights and tail light to flash, and anti-collision lights to flash if the FUS switch is in BRT.

Manual Key Button

The manual key button on the exterior lights control panel is used to energize the fuselage lights when the fuselage lights switch is in the MAN position. With the key button depressed and the exterior lights flasher switch in STEADY, the fuselage lights illuminate steady; with the flasher switch in FLASH, the fuselage lights flash. An indicator

light on the exterior lights panel glows when the manual key button is pressed. The manual key button receives its power from the left main 28 volt ac bus.

Angle of Roll Light

The low, swept wing design of the airplane prevents the landing signal officer from observing the right wing tip light during a normal carrier approach until the airplane is almost on final; therefore, a green angle of roll light is installed on the left side of the fuselage just above the trailing edge of the wing. This light illuminates steady during carrier approaches and field mirror landing practice only and serves as a roll reference for the landing signal officer until such time that the right wing tip is visible. The angle of roll light illuminates steady, in flight, with the landing gear down and locked, the flaps 1/2 or full down, and the arresting hook down. With the landing gear down and locked, the flaps 1/2 or full down, and the arresting hook up, the angle of roll light will flash (unless the hook bypass switch is in the BYPASS position). The angle of roll light receives power from the left main 28 volt dc bus.

Hook Bypass Switch

The hook bypass switch is on exterior lights control panel. The switch has two positions, NORMAL and BYPASS. This is the only operating control in the cockpit for the approach light and angle of roll system. The switch, when placed in BYPASS completes a circuit which causes the approach lights to illuminate steady without having the arresting hook extended. With the switch in the NORMAL position, and with the gear down and the flaps in full or half down, the approach lights flash unless the arresting hook is down. With the arresting hook down, the approach light illuminates steady.

Approach Lights

Refer to Angle-of-Attack system, this section.

Air Refueling Probe Light

On airplanes 148411h and up, and all others after ASC 42, an inflight refueling probe light has been installed on the right side of the fuselage forward of the air refueling probe. The light is used during night air refueling operations to illuminates the refueling probe, and the drogue from the refueling airplane. The light is controlled by the IFR switch and variable intensity control knob, both are on the exterior lights control panel. Power to the light is provided by the right 115 volt ac bus.

Taxi Light

The taxi light is adjacent to the approach light assembly on the nose gear door. The light is controlled by the taxi light switch on the exterior light control panel. Power to the light is supplied by the essential 28 volt ac bus. Power to the light is provided by the essential 28 volt ac bus on aircraft 148363f thru 152272v, and the left 28 volt ac bus on aircraft 152273w and up.

PILOT'S INTERIOR LIGHTING

Interior lighting in the airplane is powered by the ac electrical system, either from the engine driven generators or by the emergency generator. Most of the pilot's interior lighting controls are on the cockpit lights control panel (figure A-1, appendix A).

Instrument Lights

The instruments are illuminated by integral instrument lights. Variations in instrument lighting intensity on all airplanes is controlled by the instrument panel lights control knob on the forward inboard corner of the cockpit lights control panel. The control knob varies the brilliance of the instrument lights from OFF to BRT. Also, as the control is rotated from OFF to BRT, a switch within the control knob energizes the warning lights dimming relay, reducing the brilliance of the warning lights in both cockpits. After AFC 536 integral lighting for the following flight instruments is no longer controlled by the instrument panel lights control knob: altimeter, airspeed/mach indicator, vertical velocity indicator, angle of attack indicator, horizontal situa-

tion indicator, attitude director indicator and standby attitude indicator. Individual intensity control of the above lights is provided by seven controls on the flight instrument lights balance control panel added above the right console under the canopy sill. Prior to this change the intensity of the standby attitude indicator lighting is less than the other flight instrument lights. With the flight instrument lights balance controls installed, the standby attitude indicator lighting can be balanced with the other flight instrument lights. AFC 536 also installs the flight instrument lights knob on the engine control panel on the left console. The flight instrument lights knob simultaneously varies the intensity of the above seven lights so that they can be balanced with the remaining instrument lighting still controlled by the instrument lights knob on the right console. The flight instrument lights knob varies the flight instrument lights from OFF to BRT. In addition, a switch within the knob dims the HSI mode lights and also takes over the function of dimming the warning lights from the instrument lights knob. If the normal instrument lighting system fails, secondary instrument lighting is provided by red floodlights on the instrument panel glare shield. These floodlights are controlled by the instr panel emer flood switch mounted above the cockpit lights control panel. The three position switch is labeled OFF, DIM and BRT and provides only bright or dim positions.

Console Lights

Console lighting is used for combination edge and floodlighting. Variation in edge lighting intensity is controlled by the console lights control knob on the cockpit lights control panel. This knob controls all edge lighting on the left and right console, the pedestal panel and the armament control panel. The console control knob varies the brilliance of the console edge lights from OFF to BRT. Also, as the control is rotated from OFF to BRT, a switch within the control knob energizes the DIM position of the console floods switch, thus providing console floodlight illumination and edgelighting. The console floods switch above the console control knob selects BRT, DIM or MED brilliance for the red console floodlights. The console floodlights are off only when the console floods switch is in DIM and the console control knob is rotated OFF.

White Floods Switch

One white floodlight is above each console under the canopy sill. Control is by the white flood switch in the forward outboard corner of the cockpit lights control panel. This switch is of the lever-lock type to prevent inadvertent operation. No intensity variation is provided on these lights.

Standby Compass Switch

The standby compass switch on the cockpit lights control panel is used to turn the standby compass light on and off. The console lights control knob must be turned on before the standby compass switch is energized.

Warning Lights Switch

The warning lights test switch is a two position, spring-loaded, toggle switch on the cockpit lights control panel. The switch is spring-loaded to NORMAL and when placed to TEST illuminates all cockpit warning lights simultaneously. The test circuit for these warning lights receives power from the right main 28 volt dc bus.

Utility Light

A utility spot and floodlight on the right side of cockpit above right console includes an integral ON-OFF intensity control. Its color may be changed from red to white by depressing the latch button and rotating the lens housing. An additional plug-in socket for the light is provided on the right windshield sill aft of the instrument panel.

Spare Edge Lamps

Spare edge lamps are in a spring-loaded cylindrical container on the wingfold control panel on the right console.

Indexer Lights Control Knob

On airplanes 150436m and up, and all others after ASC 133, an indexer lights control panel has been added to the airplane. The panel is aft of the cockpit lights control panel (figure A-1, appendix A). The indexer lights control knob on the cockpit lights control panel controls the intensity of the angle of attack indexer lights. Rotation of the knob from OFF to BRT increases the intensity of the indexer lights.

RIO'S COCKPIT LIGHTING

The RIO's interior lighting is controlled from the RIO's main instrument panel (figure A-3, appendix A) and consists of an instrument lights control knob, an equipment lights control knob, a cockpit floods switch, and a warning light switch. In addition to these controls, a utility light is provided for auxiliary lighting. On aircraft 148411h and up after AFC 288 the flood lights switch is on the cockpit lights/data link control panel under the RIO's left canopy sill.

Instrument Lights

The instrument lights are controlled by a variable intensity control knob. As the control knob is rotated from OFF towards BRT, instrument light intensity increases.

Equipment Lights

The equipment lights utilize a variable intensity type control knob to control the intensity of the equipment panel edge lights. As the knob is rotated from OFF towards BRT, equipment light intensity increases.

Cockpit Floods Switch

The cockpit floods switch is a three-position switch, with the switch positions of OFF, DIM and BRT. The switch is used to select operation and intensity of four red floodlights in the RIO's cockpit. On aircraft 148363f and up and all others after AFC 355 the cockpit floods switch selects operation and intensity of six red flood lights.

Warning Lights Switch

The warning lights switch is a two-position switch on the instrument panel inboard of the cockpit floods switch. The switch positions are OFF and TEST and is spring-loaded OFF. When placed in TEST the CANOPY UNLOCK, LEFT WING PIN UNLOCK, RIGHT WING PIN UNLOCK, and RADAR CNI COOL OFF warning lights illuminate. The warning lights test circuit receives power from the right main 28 volt dc bus.

Utility Light

The utility light is above and to the left of the RIO's instrument panel. An additional plug-in socket for the light is provided on the upper structure aft of the instrument panel to provide an alternate location to illuminate the chartboard when it is being used. This light may be changed from red to white by rotating the lens housing. The light has an integral on-off and intensity control.

Spare Edge Lamps

Spare edge lamps are in a spring-loaded cylindrical container on the utility panel in the left forward section of the cockpit.

NORMAL OPERATION

Normal operation of the exterior lights and pilot's and RIO's interior lights are controlled by the various switches on their control panels.

EMERGENCY OPERATION

There are no provisions for emergency operation of the exterior or interior lighting. However, the pilot's insturment panel and consoles, and the RIO's cockpit floodlights can be illuminated when the ram air turbine is extended, by placing the respective flood light switches in BRT. The taxi lights, pilot's and RIO's instrument panel lights, and the warning lights also operate on RAT power. However, the warning lights cannot be dimmed.

LIMITATIONS

There are no limitations pertaining to the lighting equipment.

NAVIGATION EQUIPMENT

NOTICE
Some illustrations referred to within this system writeup may be located in appendix A. These illustrations are referred to, within the text, as (figure A-, appendix A).

DESCRIPTION

The three main navigational systems on the airplane consist of the loft bomb release computer set, the flight director group (HSI and ADI), and the navigation computer system. Each of these systems provides sufficient information to supply the crewmembers adequate navigational assistance.

LOFT BOMB RELEASE COMPUTER SET (AN/AJB-3A)

The loft bomb release computer set consists of the following components: (1) a three-axis attitude director indicator (ADI) on the pilot's insturment panel, (2) bomb control switches on the pilot's instrument panel, (3) an interval timer on the right side of the RIO's cockpit, (4) an amplifier-power supply unit, (5) a two-gyro reference unit, (6) a switching rate gyro, (7) a distribution box, (8) a bomb release angle computer, (9) a compass adapter unit, (10) a compass controller unit and (11) a magnetic flux valve. The set has two distinct functions. First, it furnishes the pilot with all the necessary information to perform LABS maneuvers. Second, it functions as a pitch and roll stabilized directional gyro compass system. The loft bomb release computer set also provides head-

ing, pitch and bank signals to the autopilot and navigation computer. The attitude director indicator display sphere is painted to give the illusion of visual flight. Heading is marked off in five-degree increments along the horizontal and in 30 degree increments at high or low pitch angles. Bank angle scale around the periphery is graduated in 10 degree increments up to 30 degrees. Use of a stabilized platform instead of conventional gyro compass and horizon gyro, provides unlimited pitch and roll axis maneuvering without gyro tumbling or discontinuity in pitch axis indication during an Immelmann turn. It also eliminates large heading errors at high pitch and bank angles, or during continuous turns. A turn and slip indicator is in the ADI, and on aircraft with dual controls a turn and slip indicator is on the main instrument panel in the rear cockpit. (For additional information see Instruments, this section). A flag on the face of the ADI indicates power on and off and phase reversal. The OFF letters disappear when power is on and phasing is correct. The single control on the indicator is a pitch trim knob which may be used to give normal indications for various angles of attack caused by gross weight airspeed combinations. The limits of pitch trim adjustment are $5°$ nose down to $10°$ nose up.

COMPASS CONTROLLER

A compass system controller on the pilot's right console provides the controls and indication to operate the gyro-magnetic compass system. This unit is used to select the mode of directional gyro control, indicate compass vs. heading data synchronization, control manual fast synchronization, and to set up latitude compensation slaving of the directional gyro. The controls include the following:

a. A three-position rotary mode switch labeled FREE, SLAVED and COMPASS.
b. An N-S hemisphere knob and a latitude compensation control wheel and readout window.
c. A push-to-turn heading set knob which controls the speed and direction of rotation of the output data shaft in the compass adapter. The speed may be controlled from 1/2 to 10 rpm.
d. A push-to-sync button which is used to synchronize the output data shaft with the magnetic heading.

The airplane may be equipped with either an MX-2826/AJB or MX-2826A/AJB compass adapter compensator. The sync and slew time of the compass varies depending on which compass adapter compensator is installed. Fast sync with the MX/2826/AJB compass adapter compensator is 170 degrees in five seconds, while fast sync with the MX-2826A/AJB is 170 degrees in 8 1/2 seconds. In the slaved mode, the compass card rotates quite slowly for the first 180 degrees, and then increases in speed for the next 180 degrees, during push-to-slew operation using the MX-2826A/AJB compass adapter compensator. Push-to-slew speed is the same all the way (faster during the first 180 degrees) using the MX-2826/AJB compass adapter compensator. In addition, the compass card drives to the magnetic heading if the compass is not in sync when the heading set knob is pressed (but not rotated) using the MX-2826A/AJB compass adapter compensator.

Free Mode

The free mode is used in north and south latitudes greater than 70° and in areas where the earth's magnetic field is appreciably distorted. When the free mode is initially selected, the magnetic heading of the airplane must be set into the system by positioning the attitude director indicator sphere to this known heading. This is accomplished by rotating the heading set knob on the compass system controller. The system uses this reference for all following heading indications. Apparent and real drift compensation is accomplished by a differential synchro driven at a predetermined rate. Random drift, which cannot be predicted, may cause small errors in this mode. For this reason, the free mode should be used only when necessary. During shipboard operation, place the compass controller in the FREE mode because of errors in the SLAVE mode due to the magnetic influence of the ship.

Slaved Mode

In the slaved mode, the azimuth system is primarily controlled by signals from the remote compass transmitter. In addition to this signal, bias signals are supplied to compensate for drift. Because system accuracy is dependent upon the earth's magnetic field, the slaved mode should only be used in latitudes under 70°, and in areas where the earth's field is not distorted. A visual indication of the synchronization between the azimuth system and the remote compass transmitter is provided by the sync indicator.

Compass Mode

The compass mode is considered an emergency mode in the AN/AJB-3A system. It should only be used if the displacement gyro fails, and the slaved or free mode cannot be used. The compass mode furnishes azimuth information to other systems when the attitude director indicator is disabled. It bypasses the dispalcement gyro completely and depends solely upon the remote compass transmitter for azimuth information. The interlock with the AFCS mode of operation of the automatic flight control system is automatically opened in the compass mode to prevent erratic magnetic heading signals from being applied to the autopilot. The sync indicator remains operational in the compass mode. The attitude director indicator is still coupled to the displacement gyro in the compass mode and should not be used.

GYRO ERECTION SWITCH

After AFC 478 there is a gyro fast erect switch on the front cockpit main instrument panel which, when placed to the momentary FAST position, causes a high erection voltage to be applied to the AN/AJB-3A displacement gyro roll and pitch torques. This provides fast erection after aircraft maneuvering. However, the aircraft must be in straight and level flight before going to fast erect. In the NORMAL position, low erection voltage is utilized and the gyro erects normally. During the time the erection switch is held in the FAST position, the power fail flag on the attitude director indicator is in view and the autopilot is disengaged.

CAUTION

Do not hold the gyro erection switch in the FAST position longer than 1 minute as damage to the gyro could result.

FLIGHT DIRECTOR GROUP

The purpose of the flight director group is to provide an integrated display of the navigation situation of the airplane. The flight director group consists of a flight director computer, the horizontal situation indicator (HSI), and a selector panel. Although the attitude director indicator (ADI) is not a component of the flight director group, it does receive some signals from the flight director computer and shall be discussed along with the flight director group.

Flight Director Computer

The flight director computer provides navigation information to the HSI, and steering information to the ADI. Except for the bearing and distance display on the HSI, all signals for the HSI, and signals for portions of the ADI pass through or originate in the computer. The flight director computer has no control over the three axis sphere portion of the ADI. Steering signals are computed to provide the pilot with flight direction information when flying either manually or remotely set headings and manually selected tacan radials. These computed signals, together with the required flag signals and off scale signals, are supplied by the computer to the ADI.

HORIZONTAL SITUATION INDICATOR

The HSI (figure 1-27) provides the horizontal or plan view of the aircraft with respect to the navigation situation. That is, the HSI is a platform picture of the aircraft's present situation, as seen from above the airplane. The aircraft symbol, in the center of the HSI, is the airplane superimposed on a compass rose. The compass card rotates so the aircraft's magentic heading is always under the lubber line. Index marks are provided every 45 degrees around the perimeter of the compass card, which can be used in holding patterns, procedure turns, etc. The bearing pointer provides magnetic bearing to a selected tacan or navigation computer station, depending on which is selected on the bearing distance selector switch. When ADF is selected on the bearing distance selector switch, the bearing pointer indicates relative bearing to the UHF Station. The heading marker is controlled by the heading set knob, except when navigation computer steering is desired at which time it is automatically set. The needle which reflects the steering asked for by the heading marker is the bank steering bar on the ADI. The heading marker is centered under the lubber line when ATT is selected on the mode selector knob, but indicates a command heading for the bank steering bar to steer to in any other mode. The course arrow has two functions. For tacan steering, it must be set (using the course set knob) to coincide with the desired tacan track. The course selector window always agrees with the course arrow when used for tacan. Just as the heading marker provides steering information to the bank steering bar on the ADI, the course arrow provides the course deviation indicator on the HSI with displacement information. When the navigation computer is being used for steering information, the course arrow automatically indicates the magnetic ground track presently being flown. The to-from indicator indicates whether the aircraft is approaching or going away from the tacan station on the course selected, providing tacan azimuth is locked-on. It doesn't indicate whether the aircraft is actually heading toward the selected station. If the to-from indicator points toward the head of the course arrow (equivalent to a TO indication), it indicates the tacan course selected will steer the aircraft toward the station and not away from it. The to-from indicator only operates when tacan mode is selected. The course deviation indicator operates in conjunction

with the course arrow and is only operative when in tacan mode. The course deviation indicator represents the selected tacan radial. The relationship between the aircraft symbol and the course deviation indicator is the same as an actual plan view of the selected tacan radial and the aircraft. The course deviation indicator indicates direction and angular relationship to the tacan radial. In addition, angular error from the tacan radial can be read up to five degrees. The two dots, on each side of center, each indicate two and one half degrees of angular error from the selected tacan radial. Once the course deviation indicator is fully deflected, angular error cannot be read directly, but up to five degrees on either side of the selected tacan radial can be read. Four mode-of-operation word messages are shown around the HSI display. These lights are illuminated internally to indicate the selected operating mode, provided the instrument panel lights control knob is ON. The intensity of the mode lights is also controlled by this knob.

ATTITUDE DIRECTOR INDICATOR

The primary function of the ADI (figure 1-27) is to provide aircraft attitude reference. The black and gray sphere is movable and stabilized through all attitudes so that the miniature aircraft wings, against the moving horizon line on the sphere, give the pilot attitude reference. Pitch angle increments of 10 degrees are marked on the sphere and can be set using the pitch trim knob. Heading indications are also provided around the sphere's horizon line. Ten degree bank increments, up to 30 degrees, are marked on the bottom of the instrument. The bank steering bar is the only bar used in conjunction with the flight director group. The bank steering bar indicates corrective action necessary to intercept the selected heading, tacan radial or navigation computer destination. The bank steering bar receives its bank information from the heading marker on the HSI, through the flight director computer. When the heading marker is positioned either manually or automatically, the bank steering bar deflects right or left to direct the pilot to the new heading. The bank steering bar does not indicate direction or displacement from the desired heading, but rather the corrective action required. The maximum bank angle that is commanded by the bank steering bar is 30 degrees. This is because the maximum heading error the computer will command is 90 degrees. If the heading marker on the HSI is set at 90 degrees or more from the present position, the bank steering bar indicates a maximum bank of 30 degrees. Any heading error of less than 90 degrees produces a bank angle indication of something less than 30 degrees. Obviously, there are times when more than 30 degrees of bank is desired to intercept the new heading or tacan radial and in these cases, the bank steering bar must be disregarded. The bank steering bar information is only reliable for tacan steering if the selected tacan track is within ± 60 degrees of the present heading. The course deviation indicator on the HSI is reliable regardless of the tacan track selected. The ± 60 degree limitation applies only to the bank steering bar. If,

ATTITUDE DIRECTOR AND HORIZONTAL SITUATION INDICATORS

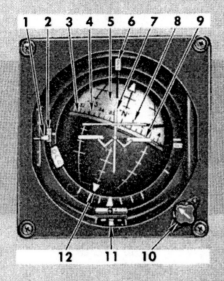

ADI

1. VERTICAL DISPLACEMENT POINTER
2. VERTICAL DISPLACMENT WARNING FLAG (TACAN, DATA LINK, ILS)
3. HORIZON BAR
4. HEADING REFERENCE SCALE
5. 3-AXIS SPHERE
6. VERTICAL DIRECTOR WARNING FLAG (TACAN, DATA LINK, ILS)
7. BANK STEERING BAR
8. PITCH STEERING BAR
9. MINIATURE AIRCRAFT
10. PITCH TRIM KNOB
11. TURN AND SLIP INDICATOR
12. BANK POINTER

HSI

1. COMPASS CARD
2. BEARING POINTER
3. LUBBER LINE
4. COURSE DEVIATION INDICATOR
5. COURSE ARROW
6. HEADING MARKER
7. COURSE SET KNOB
8. COURSE SELECTOR WINDOW
9. TO-FROM INDICATOR
10. AIRCRAFT SYMBOL
11. RANGE INDICATOR
12. HEADING SET KNOB

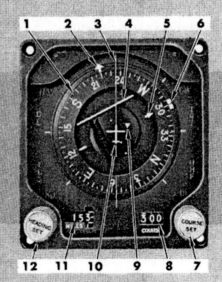

FDB-2-(31)

Figure 1-27

NAVIGATION FUNCTION SELECTOR PANEL

when on the selected tacan radial, it becomes necessary to establish a crab angle due to wind drift (aircraft heading different from selected radial), the bank steering bar indicates a heading error. To eliminate this apparent heading error, the heading marker on the HSI should be manually set to correspond to the new heading. Do not expect the bank steering bar to automatically correct for wind drift. The bank steering bar can also indicate erroneously due to a phasing problem, dependent upon which side of the AN/AJB-3 gyro was up upon original erection. A determination as to whether the gyro has erected correctly can be made in the heading mode by selecting a heading, other than the one the aircraft is presently on, with the heading set knob and banking toward the selected heading. The bank steering bar moves toward center. If it moves away from or remains away from center, the bank steering bar should be disregarded for the remainder of the flight. The error can be corrected in flight by performing a loop or similar maneuver which causes the gyro to flip. The bank steering bar then indicates correctly. Effective airplanes 151397p and up, this situation has been corrected. The vertical director warning flag (12 o'clock position) and the vertical displacement warning flag (9 o'clock position), normally out of view, appear if an unreliable signal is received from the tacan, data link (some aircraft), and the ILS system (some aircraft). The OFF power fail flag on the ADI appears if there is a failure of the AN/AJB-3 system, if the gyro is in the start cycle, if the gyro fast erect switch is held on, or if there is a power failure to the indicator.

NAVIGATION FUNCTION SELECTOR PANEL

The navigation function selector panel (figure 1-28) is on the pilot's main instrument panel. The panel contains a mode selector knob and a bearing distance selector switch. The mode selector knob and bearing distance switch control separate functions of the ADI and HSI, and do not necessarily have to be set up as a pair. The bearing distance switch activates only the bearing pointer and range indicator (and the mode word which reflects what is selected) on the HSI. The information displayed for the three positions of the bearing distance switch are shown in figure 1-32. The displays for the different mode selector knob settings are shown in figures 1-29 through 1-31.

NAVIGATION COMPUTER AN/ASN-39

The navigation computer is in airplanes 149403i and up, and in all others after ASC 76. It is a great circle computer and consists of a control panel and an amplifier-computer. The system furnishes the following information during flight:

a. The aircraft's present position latitude and longitude based on dead reckoning computations from an initial fix.

b. The continuous great circle magnetic bearing and distance to either of two preset targets. This is an instantaneous spherical trigonometric solution based on true north.

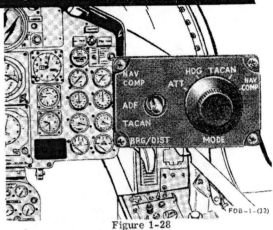

Figure 1-28

The dead reckoning computations are only as accurate as the wind vectors and magnetic variation references furnished the system by the RIO. Inputs of magnetic heading and true airspeed are automatically supplied by the AN/AJB-3 and ADC. For purposes of discussion, the navigation computer can be divided into two functional sections. The first is the present position computer section which performs the basic dead reckoning computation. The second is a course and distance computer section which provides a great circle course and distance to a target (or base).

PRESENT POSITION COMPUTER

The present position computer is a group of servomechanisms in the computer control panel with their amplifiers in the amplifier-computer. The present position computer receives magnetic heading from the AN/AJB-3 and true airspeed from the ADC. Magnetic variation, wind speed, wind direction, and the latitude and longitude of the starting position, the base, and destination are set manually by means of control knobs on the computer control panel. The present position computer resolves true airspeed and wind velocity to their north-south and east-west components and adds them algebraically to derive the components of aircraft ground speed. Ground speed is integrated with respect to time to attain distance which is then converted to a change of latitude and longitude. The north-south mileage covered is converted directly into degrees and minutes of latitude by the position latitude counter on the computer control panel, since 1 nautical mile is always equal to 1 minute of latitude. In the longitude channel an additional step is necessary since a direct conversion can only be made at the equator. At other latitudes, the east-west mileage covered is multiplied by the secant of the latitude at which the aircraft is traveling. The modified east-west mileage is then converted directly to degrees and minutes longitude by the position longitude counter on the computer control panel. The present position computer continuously computes the change in latitude and longitude from the aircraft's starting position (initial fix). These coordinate changes are applied to the corresponding position counters, both of which have been manually set

ATTITUDE AND HEADING DISPLAYS

ATT (Attitude)

THE COURSE ARROW, COURSE DEVIATION
INDICATOR AND HEADING MARKER ARE
SLAVED TO THE MAGNETIC HEADING OF
THE AIRPLANE (I. E. VERTICAL ON THE
FACE OF THE HSI). NO MODE LIGHT IS
ILLUMINATED.

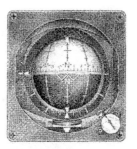

ALL POINTERS ARE DEFLECTED OUT OF
VIEW. ONLY ATTITUDE AND AZIMUTH
INFORMATION IS DISPLAYED.

HDG (Heading)

THE HEADING MARKER IS POSITIONED BY
THE HEADING SET KNOB TO PROVIDE
THE ADI BANK STEERING BAR WITH BANK
AND AZIMUTH INFORMATION IN ORDER
TO TURN TO THE SELECTED HEADING.
THE MAN MODE LIGHT IS ILLUMINATED.

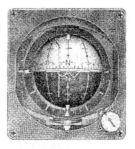

THE BANK STEERING BAR INDICATES
BANK ANGLE STEERING UP TO 30° OF
BANK TO APPROACH THE HEADING
SELECTED BY THE HEADING SET KNOB
ON THE HSI.

| Note |

THE BANK STEERING BAR CAN INDICATE ERRONEOUSLY
DUE TO A PHASING PROBLEM DEPENDENT UPON WHICH
SIDE OF THE AJB-3 GYRO WAS UP UPON THE ORIGINAL
ERECTION. A DETERMINATION AS TO WHETHER THE
GYRO HAS ERECTED CORRECTLY CAN BE MADE BY
SELECTING HDG ON THE MODE SWITCH. SELECT A
HEADING OTHER THAN THE ONE THAT THE AIRPLANE
IS PRESENTLY ON WITH THE HEADING SET KNOB, AND
BANK TOWARD THE SELECTED HEADING. THE BANK

STEERING BAR SHOULD MOVE TOWARD THE CENTER.
IF IT MOVES (OR REMAINS) AWAY FROM THE CENTER,
THE NEEDLE SHOULD BE DISREGARDED FOR THE
REMAINDER OF THE FLIGHT. THE ERROR CAN BE
CORRECTED IN FLIGHT BY PERFORMING A LOOP OR AN
IMMELMAN WHICH WILL CAUSE THE GYRO TO FLIP. THE
BANK STEERING BAR SHOULD THEN INDICATE COR-
RECTLY. EFFECTIVE AIRPLANES 151397p AN UP,
THIS SITUATION HAS BEEN CORRECTED.

FDB-1-(33)

Figure 1-29

NAVIGATION COMPUTER DISPLAYS

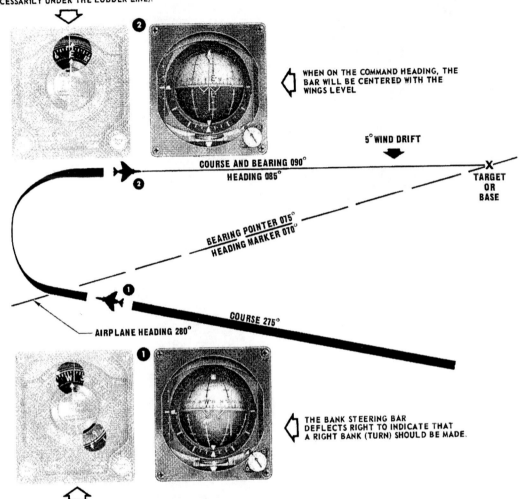

WHEN ON THE COMMAND HEADING, THE HEADING MARKER
WILL BE UNDER THE LUBBER LINE. THE COURSE ARROW
AND BEARING POINTER WILL BE ALIGNED (BUT NOT
NECESSARILY UNDER THE LUBBER LINE).

WHEN ON THE COMMAND HEADING, THE
BAR WILL BE CENTERED WITH THE
WINGS LEVEL

5° WIND DRIFT

COURSE AND BEARING 090°
HEADING 085°

TARGET
OR
BASE

BEARING POINTER 075°
HEADING MARKER 070°

COURSE 275°

AIRPLANE HEADING 280°

THE BANK STEERING BAR
DEFLECTS RIGHT TO INDICATE THAT
A RIGHT BANK (TURN) SHOULD BE MADE.

THE HEADING MARKER INDICATES THE MAGNETIC HEADING
THAT MUST BE FLOWN TO MAKE GOOD A COURSE DIRECT
FROM THE PRESENT POSITION OF THE AIRCRAFT TO THE
DESTINATION (TARGET OR BASE) SELECTED ON THE NAV
COMPUTER. WHETHER THE HEADING IS CORRECT OR NOT
IS DEPENDENT UPON THE ACCURACY OF THE WIND
DIRECTION AND VELOCITY, THE VARIATION, AND THE
ACCURACY OF THE PRESENT POSITION. THE COURSE
ARROW INDICATES THE TRACK THAT IS CURRENTLY BEING
MADE GOOD, ALSO DEPENDENT UPON THE ACCURACY OF
THE NAV COMPUTER SETTINGS. THE COURSE DEVIATION
INDICATOR IS SLAVED TO THE COURSE ARROW. THE
COURSE SELECTOR WINDOW WILL INDICATE THE SAME
TRACK AS THE COURSE ARROW. THE BEARING POINTER
INDICATES MAGNETIC BEARING TO DESTINATION. IN ORDER
TO OBTAIN NAV COMPUTER INFORMATION FROM THE
BEARING POINTER AND THE RANGE INDICATOR, THE BRG/
DIST SWITCH MUST BE IN THE NAV COMP POSITION.

FDB-1-(34)

Figure 1-30

TACAN DISPLAYS

TACAN STATION

WITH NO DRIFT, THE BANK STEERING BAR WILL BE CENTERED WITH THE WINGS LEVEL WHEN ON THE TACAN RADIAL.

WHEN ON THE TACAN RADIAL, THE COURSE DEVIATION INDICATOR WILL BE CENTERED UNDER THE AIRPLANE SYMBOL.

④

THE BANK STEERING BAR WILL DEFLECT RIGHT AT APPROXIMATELY 15° FROM THE TACAN RADIAL TO INDICATE A RIGHT BANK (TURN) IS NECESSARY TO MAKE AN ASYMTOTIC APPROACH TO THE TACAN RADIAL. TO INTERCEPT THE TACAN RADIAL AS SOON AS POSSIBLE, THE BANK STEERING BAR SHOULD BE DISREGARDED.

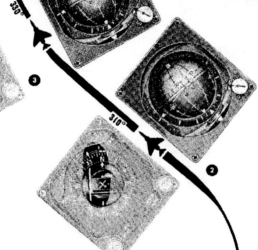

330°

310°

③

WHEN WITHIN 5° OF THE RADIAL. THE COURSE DE-VIATION INDICATOR BEGINS MOVING TOWARD THE CENTER (AIRCRAFT SYMBOL). THE PILOT CAN NOW READ ANGULAR DISPLACEMENT FROM THE RADIAL ON THE COURSE DEVIATION INDICATOR.

WHEN IN A LEFT BANK (TURN) WITH THE BANK STEERING BAR CENTERED, THE BAR WILL DEFLECT RIGHT TO INDICATE A ROLL OUT ON APPROXIMATELY A 50° ANGLE APPROACH TO THE TACAN RADIAL. TO INTERCEPT THE TACAN RADIAL AS SOON AS POSSIBLE DISREGARD THE BANK STEERING BAR AND INCREASE APPROACH ANGLE TO THE RADIAL.

180°

②

THE BANK STEERING BAR INDICATES BANK ANGLE STEERING UP TO 30° OF BANK TO APPROACH THE SELECTED TACAN RADIAL, HOWEVER, IN ORDER TO ATTAIN CORRECT STEERING INFORMA-TION, THE HEADING MARKER MUST BE ALIGNED WITH THE SELECTED TACAN RADIAL. A RELIABLE TACAN SIGNAL IS INDICATED BY THE RETRACTION OF THE TWO RED FLAGS LOCATED AT THE 9 AND 12 O'CLOCK POSITION.

THE COURSE DEVIATION INDICATOR REPRESENTS THE ACTUAL TACAN RADIAL AND THE AIRCRAFT SYMBOL REPRESENTS THE AIRCRAFT POSITION RELATIVE TO THE RADIAL. THE DESIRED APPROACH ANGLE CAN BE SET UP BY FLYING THE AIRCRAFT SYMBOL TOWARD THE DEVIATION INDICATOR.

THE COURSE SELECTOR WINDOW AND THE COURSE ARROW ARE POSITIONED BY SELECTING THE DESIRED COURSE (TACAN RADIAL) WITH THE COURSE SET KNOB. THE HEADING MARKER IS MANUALLY ALIGNED WITH THE SELECTED TACAN RADIAL. THE COURSE DEVIATION INDICATOR DEFLECTS TO INDICATE AIRPLANE DISPLACEMENT TO THE RIGHT OR LEFT OF THE SELECTED COURSE. THE TWO DOTS ON EITHER SIDE OF THE COURSE DEVIATION INDICATOR INDICATE 2 1/2° PER DOT OF ANGULAR TRACK ERROR. THE TO-FROM INDICATOR INDICATES WHETHER THE SELECTED COURSE IS TOWARD OR AWAY FROM THE STATION. THE BEARING POINTER INDICATES THE CURRENT MAGNETIC BEARING TO THE TARGET, PROVIDED THE BEARING DISTANCE SWITCH IS IN THE TAC POSITION.

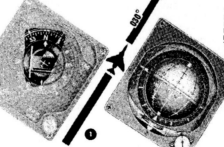

030°

①

THE BANK STEERING BAR DEFLECTS LEFT INDICATING THAT A LEFT BANK (TURN) IS NECESSARY TO CENTER THE POINTER.

Notes

THE AIRCRAFT HEADING MUST BE WITHIN 60° OF THE TACAN RADIAL IN ORDER TO OBTAIN RELIABLE BANK STEERING BAR STEERING INFORMATION.

FDB-1-(35)

Figure 1-31

HORIZONTAL SITUATION INDICATOR BEARING AND DISTANCE DISPLAYS

THE BEARING DISTANCE SWITCH CONTROLS ONLY THE INDICATIONS DISPLAYED BY THE BEARING POINTER AND RANGE INDICATOR OF THE HSI.

BEARING DISTANCE SWITCH
NAV COMP (Navigation Computer)

THE BEARING POINTER INDICATES MAGNETIC BEARING TO THE DESTINATION SELECTED ON THE NAV COMPUTER. THE RANGE INDICATOR INDICATES THE NAUTICAL MILES TO THE DESTINATION SELECTED ON THE NAV COMPUTER (TARGET OR BASE). THE NAV LIGHT WILL BE ILLUMINATED.

BEARING DISTANCE SWITCH
ADF (Automatic Direction Finder)

THE BEARING POINTER INDICATES RELATIVE BEARING TO THE UHF STATION SELECTED ON THE COMMUNICATION CONTROL PANEL (EITHER COMM OR AUX ADF POSITION MUST BE SELECTED). THE RANGE INDICATOR WINDOW WILL BE BLANK. THE UHF LIGHT WILL BE ILLUMINATED.

BEARING DISTANCE SWITCH
TACAN

THE BEARING POINTER INDICATES MAGNETIC BEARING TO THE SELECTED TACAN STATION. THE RANGE INDICATOR INDICATES THE SLANT RANGE NAUTICAL MILES TO THE TACAN STATION. FOR DISTANCE INDICATIONS, THE TACAN SELECTOR SWITCH MUST BE IN THE T/R POSITION. THE TAC LIGHT WILL BE ILLUMINATED.

FDB-1-(36)

Figure 1-32

to the coordinates of the starting position. Since the position counters add the change in coordinates to the starting coordinates, they provide continuous indication of the aircraft's present position.

COURSE AND DISTANCE COMPUTER

The basis of course and distance computation is the solution of the spherical triangle (each side of which is a segment of a great circle) formed on the earth's surface by the geographic north pole (true north), the present position, and the preselected target or base. The latitude and longitude of the base and the target are manually inserted into the system by means of the position and target counters on the computer control panel. The base coordinates are retained by memory circuits of the position counters. Since this information is known within the system, as is present position of the aircraft which is available continuously from the present position computer, two sides of the spherical triangle and the angle between them are known. This makes it possible to solve for the third side and angle using the information available. The third side represents the great circle distance and

the angle represents the great circle bearing or course angle.

COMPUTER CONTROL PANEL

The computer control panel (figure A-3, appendix A) contains the operating controls and counters which provide a readout of inserted information. The position counters also provide a continuous readout of present position during flight.

Function Switch

The function switch is a five-position rotary switch with positions of OFF, TARGET, BASE, STBY, and RESET. The OFF position removes all power from the navigation computer. The TARGET position selects output displays of target range, ground track relative to magnetic heading, and bearing relative to magnetic heading to the preselected target coordinates set on the target counters. The BASE position selects the same output displays as the TARGET position but is referenced to the preselected base or alternate target coordinates which are retained in the memory circuits of the position counters. The STBY position supplies filament power to the amplifire-computer and the latitude and longitude integrator channels of the system are inoperative. The RESET position is used to set base alternate target, or return point coordinates in the memory circuits of the position counters. Placing the switch to RESET causes the origianl memorized coordinates to be lost. A restriction on the switch prevents accidental switching to RESET. The switch must be pulled outward slightly to override the restriction when switching to OFF or RESET.

Wind Control Knobs

The wind control knobs consist of the wind velocity control knob and the wind from control knob. The wind velocity control knob is used to manually insert the wind velocity affecting flight into the system and is displayed on the wind velocity counter. The wind from control knob is used to manually insert the true wind direction. The true wind direction is expressed as an angle measured clockwise from true north and is presented in degrees on the wind from counter.

Magnetic Variation Control Knob

The magnetic variation control knob is used to manually insert the magnetic variation angle into the system. The magnetic variation is the angular difference between true north and magnetic north.

Position Control Knobs

The position control knobs are initially used to insert the base, alternate target, or return point latitude and longitude into the system. To insert these coordinates the function switch must be in RESET. With the function switch in any position but RESET, the position control knobs are used to manually insert present position latitude and longitude to establish an initial fix for the dead reckoning function of the navigation computer. The base, alternate target, or return point latitude and longitude are not displayed anywhere during flight; a memory of these coordinates is retained by the system so long as the function switch is not placed to RESET. The position latitude and longitude counters continuously indicate the aircraft present position in degrees and minutes during flight.

Target Control Knobs

The target control knobs are used to manually insert the target latitude and longitude into the system. These coordinates are displayed on the target latitude and longitude counters. The system provides output displays to fly to these coordinates when the function switch is placed to TARGET.

Output Displays

The navigation computer display information in the front cockpit is shown in figure 1-30. To display navigation computer information on the BDHI in the rear cockpit, select NAV COMP on the navigation selector switch. The displayed information on the BDHI is as follows:

Note

The placard for the No. 1 and No. 2 needle in NAV COMP of the navigation selector switch is incorrect and should be disregarded.

1. Magnetic bearing to target or base displayed on the No. 1 needle when read against the compass card. A relative bearing to the target or base can also be read by noting the number of degrees from the index clockwise to the No. 1 needle.
2. Magnetic ground track displayed on the No. 2 needle when read against the compass card. Left or right drift angle can also be read by noting the number of degrees left or right from the index.
3. Distance to the target or base displayed on the range counter.

To travel the great circle route to the target or base, the aircraft should be flown on a course that causes the two needles to be coincident. However, it is not necessary to fly the course shown by the coincidental needles. Departure from the route may be made, as a part of evasive maneuvers or to fly a search pattern, without affecting the operation of the system. Since computations are being made countinuously, the current position of the airplane is shown at all times on the position counters regardless of the path flown. As the target (or base) is approached, the distance on the range counter decreases. When the target is reached, uncertainty is exhibited by the No. 1 needle which turns 180° as the target is passed in order to indicate bearing to target. At any time during flight, the present position may be compared with a known check point or a fix obtained from radar, tacan, or GCI and the position counters change accordingly. This corrects errors in computation that have previously occured but does not disturb the memory of the base or target position.

NORMAL OPERATION

AN/AJB-3A GYRO COMPASS OPERATION

Free Mode

To establish the free mode of operation, place the bomb control switch OFF, the compass mode switch in FREE, the hemisphere knob to the proper north or south latitude, and set the proper latitude in the latitude read-out window. If necessary, set the ADI sphere and compass cards to the actual airplane magnetic heading and adjust the ADI for zero pitch attitude. Readjust the latitude control for each five degrees change in latitude.

Slaved Mode

To place the compass in the slaved mode, place the bomb control switch OFF and place the compass mode switch to SLAVED. Allow 10 seconds for automatic fast synchronization and check the sync indicator for a center scale indication. Slight deviation of the pointer from the center position is corrected by normal slaving. Adjust the ADI for zero pitch attitude.

FLIGHT DIRECTOR GROUP

Operation of the flight director group is shown in figures 1-29 through 1-32.

NAVIGATION COMPUTER

All controls required to operate the navigation computer are on the computer control panel. To simplify the procedure, it is understood that where a counter setting is specified, the control knob associated with the counter is rotated to set the counter. The position latitude and longitude control knobs must be pressed in to engage them with their associated counter. The initial flight plan may be set into the navigation computer at any time.

Navigation computer ground check (electrical power required): -

a. Set magnetic variation counter to 00.
b. Set wind velocity counter to 00.
c. Place function switch to RESET.
d. Set position and target longitude counters to the local longitudinal coordinates. Set position and target latitude counters to local latitude coordinates plus one degree.
e. Place function switch to STANDBY.
f. Set position latitude counter to local latitude coordinates.
g. Allow 1 minute warm-up period. Place function switch to TARGET. BDHI (No. 1 needle) should read $360° \pm 2°$ and the range counter should read 60 nm $\pm$ 2 nm.
h. Place function switch to BASE and repeat step g.

Navigation computer initial flight plan (electrical power not required): -

a. Set magnetic variation counter to local magnetic variation.
b. Set wind from counter and wind velocity counter to wind direction and wind speed that affects the flight.

Note

Weather stations may provide the magnetic wind direction which must be corrected for variation to obtain the true wind direction.

c. If memory base information is desired, place function switch to RESET and set latitude and longitude or alternate target, base, or return point on position counters.
d. Place function switch to any position but RESET and set local latitude and longitude in position counters.
e. Set latitude and longitude of the target or destination on the target counters.

f. Place function switch OFF until after starting engines.

Note

- Do not select an operating mode (TARGET or BASE) until after airspeed reaches 160 knots.

- The position counters should be checked for accuracy and updated if necessary during flight.

Updating Methods

The position counters should be checked and updated at each opportunity by one of the following methods:

a. Visual reference to a geographical position.
While in one of the operating modes or temporarily in STBY, adjust the position latitude and longitude to agree with the latitude and longitude of the visual fix. This latitude and longitude may be obtained from maps, charts, or publications.
b. Radar reference to a geographical position.
Use radar mapping to obtain a bearing and distance to a known geographical position. Set the latitude and longitude of this position in the target counters or in base memory. Adjust the position counters so that the No. 1 needle and the range counter on the BDHI agree with the radar bearing and distance.
c. Tacan fix.
Set the latitude and longitude of the acquired tacan station in the target counters or in base memory. Adjust the present position counters so that the No. 1 needle and the range counter on the BDHI agree with the tacan readout.
d. GCI or radar monitored fix.
Set the latitude and longitude of the controlling agency in the target counters or in base memory. Adjust the position counters so that the No. 1 needle and range counter on the BDHI agree with the bearing and distance provided by the controller.

Wind Finding Techniques

a. True wind utilizing a tacan fix.
This solution assumes that a constant altitude is maintained while the wind is being found. The wind velocity counter is set to zero; the latitude and longitude of the reference tacan station are set on the target counters; and the position latitude and longitude counters are set so that the tacan range and bearing and the computer range and bearing on the BDHI are identical. After a convenient time interval has elapsed, the tacan range and bearing and the computer range and bearing should be plotted, either on a chart, a grid such as that on an MB-4 computer, or pictured on the face of the BDHI itself. The difference between these two plotted positions gives the wind vector for the elapsed time interval. Applying variation, the direction of the wind vector is from the computer or fix to the tacan fix. Multiply the distance by the factor necessary for an hourly rate to produce an

accurate wind speed setting. For best results repeat this process as necessary and add the new vector to the original vector.

EMERGENCY OPERATION

AN/AJB-3A GYRO COMPASS

Compass Mode

The compass mode is considered an emergency mode in the AN/AJB-3A system. It should only be used if the displacement gyro fails and the slaved or free mode cannot be used. To place the system in the compass mode, place the bomb control switch OFF and place the compass mode switch in COMP.

Note

In the compass mode, the attitude director indicator is still coupled to the displacement gyro and is not receiving magnetic compass corrections. Therefore, the azimuth reading of the ADI may be in error and the HSI compass card should be used as the heading reference.

LIMITATIONS

NAVIGATION COMPUTER

Beyond 72°N or 72°S latitude, the navigation computer continues to operate but with a progressive loss of accuracy as either geographic pole is approached.

OXYGEN SYSTEM

NOTICE
Some illustrations referred to within this system writeup may be located in appendix A. These illustrations are referred to, within the text, as (figure A-, appendix A).

DESCRIPTION

The liquid oxygen (LOX) system consists of a 10 liter capacity vacuum insulated container, build-up coils, check valves, vent valves and quantity gages. The system is designed to deliver gaseous oxygen to the crew at a continuous rate of up to 120 liters per minute at 60 to 90 psi. From the container, the liquid oxygen flows to the build-up coils which are predetermined lengths of tubing wrapped around the outside bottom of the container. When the liquid flows through the build-up coil it absorbs heat from the the the surrounding area and becomes gaseous. The gaseous oxygen is then increased in pressure to assure 40 to 90 psi to the regulators. From the build-up coils, the oxygen flows into the warm-up plate in the rear cockpit aft of the ejection seat. The warm-up coils warm it to a temperature no colder than 20°F under the cockpit temperature. From the warm-up plate the oxygen is now ready for crew consumption. A system relief valve set at 110 psi vents excessive pressures that may occur due to the boil-off of the LOX when the system is not being used. A blow out patch in the oxygen container provides added safety if a relief valve should fail. An electrical capacitance type indicator provides the pilot and RIO with an accurate means of determining the amount of LOX remaining at any time. An OXYGEN LOW indicator light operated by the indicator circuit on the telelight panel alerts the pilot when the liquid oxygen gage indicates one liter of oxygen remaining in the system.

OXYGEN SUPPLY LEVERS

A two-position ON-OFF oxygen supply lever is on a panel in each cockpit. The pilot's supply lever (figure A-1, appendix A) is on the aft end of the left console. The RIO's supply lever (figure A-2, appendix A) is on the utility panel in the left forward section of the cockpit.

OXYGEN QUANTITY GAGE

An oxygen quantity gage is in each cockpit which reads 10 liters maximum. The pilot's oxygen gage (figure A-1, appendix A) is on the forward end of the left console. The RIO's oxygen gage (figure A-3, appendix A) is on the utility panel in the left forward section of the cockpit. See figure 1-33 for oxygen duration chart.

OXYGEN REGULATOR

The oxygen breathing regulator is personnel mounted and is used both in the inflight and bailout or emergency conditions. With an inlet pressure of 40 to 90 psi the regulator delivers 100% oxygen automatically to the user, between the altitudes of 0 to 50,000 feet. In addition, the regualtor incorporates automatic safety pressure build-up to a maximum of 2 inches of water below 35,000 feet and automatic pressure breathing for altitudes above 35,000 feet and is designed to integrate with the A13/A oxygen breathing mask.

OXYGEN CONNECTION (STANDARD FLIGHT SUIT)

There are two types of oxygen connection equipment presently in use. The first type requires that the crewmember carry the upper block with his personal gear since the oxygen supply line is not detachable. With this type equipment, the personal leads are routed from the upper block under the left arm and up to the oxygen regulator and communications connector. The second type (over the shoulder) utilizes a universal upper block which remains in the airplane.

OXYGEN DURATION CHART

	OXYGEN DURATION-HOURS							
Cabin Pressure Altitude Feet	Gage Quantity-Liters							Below 1
	10	8	6	4	2	1		
40,000 and Above	60.6	48.5	36.4	24.2	12.0	6.0		
35,000	37.0	29.6	22.2	14.8	7.4	3.6		
30,000	27.2	21.8	16.4	10.8	5.4	2.8		—EMERGENCY—
25,000	20.4	16.4	12.4	8.2	4.0	2.0		DESCEND TO
20,000	16.0	12.8	9.6	6.4	3.2	1.6		ALTITUDE NOT
15,000	12.8	10.2	7.6	5.2	2.6	1.2		REQUIRING
10,000	10.0	8.0	6.0	4.0	2.0	1.0		OXYGEN
5,000	8.4	6.6	5.0	3.2	1.6	0.8		
SEA LEVEL	7.0	5.6	4.2	2.8	1.4	0.6		

● DURATION TIME IS HALVED WHEN TWO CREW MEMBERS ARE USING OXYGEN

FDB-1-(37)

Figure 1-33

The oxygen-communication lead is an integrated single line. It is fastened to the back of the torso harness at the left waist and center shoulder areas with velcro fasteners. The line is then routed forward over the left shoulder and fastened permanently to the oxygen regulator. The line is clipped to the left side of the helmet. A communications lead plug is attached to the line where it is clipped to the helmet. The universal upper block features a locking indicator in the release handle. When securely locked, the indicator is flush with the handle.

WARNING

The over the shoulder oxygen-communication integrated line must be routed under the shoulder harness to preclude the possibility of the crewmembers helmet being jerked from the head after ejection. This action is caused by the left parachute riser (shoulder harness strap) snapping up against the integrated line with the opening of the personnel parachute.

OXYGEN CONNECTION (FULL PRESSURE SUIT)

There are two types of pressure suit oxygen connection equipment presently in use. The first type requires that the composite upper block be carried with the crewmember's personal gear since the personal leads are permanently attached to it. With this type connecting equipment, the personal leads are routed up the back of the life vest, and end in quick disconnects just below the helmet. When the helmet is in place the leads are hooked up to two corresponding helmet leads. The second type equipment utilizes a universal upper block which remains in the airplane. The personal lead is an integrated oxygen-communication line which is permanently attached to the left side of the helmet. After the helmet is in place, the personal lead is routed back over the left shoulder and attached to the center shoulder area of the life vest with a velcro fastener. It is then routed through a nylon channel sewn to the life vest pad along the lower left side. The line is then connected to the universal upper block. The vent air supply, and anti-G hose routings and connections are similar for both types of equipment.

EMERGENCY OXYGEN

Emergency oxygen is stored in a cylinder in the upper half of the survival kit container. The emergency oxygen cylinder is a coil assembly constructed of steel tubing closed at both ends with a volume of 100 cubic inches. The cylinder is normally charged to 1800 psi and supplies gaseous oxygen in emergencies for breathing and suit pressurization. The flow of oxygen from this coil is controlled and regulated by the pressure reducer manifold which is actuated either manually or automatically. The pressure reducer manifold is within the survival kit and is attached to the forward left corner of the upper half of the container. It is used to reduce the oxygen pressure within the emergency oxygen cylinder to 65 ± 15 psi with a flow up to 140 lpm. Components of the manifold include a toggle arm, pressure gauge, relief valve, filler valve, and safety plug. When the toggle arm of the manifold is in the cockpit position, flow of oxygen from the emergency oxygen cylinder is prevented by action of the pressure reducer valve within the manifold. When the toggle is tripped, emergency oxygen flows through the manifold at a reduced pressure to the intermediate block for suit pressurization and breathing. The emergency oxygen is delivered through the minature demand regulator, and duration of the supply depends upon altitude and demand. Under a normal workload, there is sufficient oxygen for 10 minutes at sea level. At 40,000 feet this supply would last approximately 50 minutes. The relief valve, attached to the manifold, prevents excessive pressure build-up in the system when manifold pressure regulation fails. The emergency oxygen filler valve is accessible through a hole in the upper half of the container which permits ease of servicing. The safety plug of the manifold prevents excessive pressure within the emergency oxygen cylinder due to overservicing or thermal expansion. A pressure gauge attached to the pressure reducer manifold provides pressure indication for the cylinder and is visible through a hole in the kit cushion.

Emergency Oxygen Manual Release Ring

The emergency oxygen manual release ring (figure 1-17) on the left forward end of the survival kit container is colored green and is in the ready position during all normal flight conditions. When emergency oxygen is needed for breathing, the release ring is pulled from the kit to actuate the emergency oxygen. The ring when pulled separates from the kit after the emergency oxygen has actuated.

> **WARNING**
>
> When pulling the emergency oxygen manual release ring, apply the force of the pull at an angle perpendicular to the horizontal plane of the survival kit. A pull at any other angle may cause the ring to malfunction, resulting in no emergency oxygen available to the crewmember.

NORMAL OPERATION

Operation of the oxygen system consists of turning the oxygen supply lever from OFF to ON.

EMERGENCY OPERATION

Emergency oxygen is obtained by pulling up on the emergency oxygen manual release ring until the ring separates from the seat.

LIMITATIONS

No limitations pertain to the operation of the oxygen system.

PITOT-STATIC SYSTEM

NOTICE
Some illustrations referred to within this system writeup may be located in appendix A. These illustrations are referred to, within the text, as (figure A-, appendix A).

DESCRIPTION

A conventional pitot-static system is used in the airplane, with a single pitot tube near the top of the vertical stabilizer and two static ports one on each side of the radome. The pitot-static system supplies both impact and atmospheric pressure to various instruments and system components. The pitot-static system is composed of two separate systems. Both pressures may be utilized by the same instruments but at no time do the pressures intermingle. Both pitot and static pressures are supplied to airspeed pressure switches that retract the flaps, cut out the emergency generator (on aircraft thru 152331x before AFC 220), actuate the rudder feel system, and actuate the aileron-rudder interconnect system. The pitot and static pressures are also directed to the air data computer where they are calibrated and corrected (static pressure only) and then sent to the various instruments and systems requiring pitot-static pressures.

PITOT HEAT SWITCH

A pitot heat switch on the right utility panel in the front cockpit (figure A-1, appendix A), has positions of OFF and ON. Placing the switch ON energizes the heating element in the pitot tube, to prevent formation of ice during flight.

EMERGENCY OPERATION

No emergency operations pertain to the pitot-static system.

LIMITATIONS

No limitations pertain to the pitot-static system.

PNEUMATIC SYSTEM

NOTICE
Some illustrations referred to within this system writeup may be located in appendix A.
These illustrations are referred to, within the text, as (figure A-, appendix A).

DESCRIPTION

The pneumatic system (figure A-9, appendix A), provides high pressure air for the normal and emergency operation of the canopies; normal operation of the ram air turbine (extension and retraction), the nose gear strut extension, and emergency operation of the landing gear, wing flaps, cockpit flooding doors, wheel brakes and after AFC 370, emergency extension of the inflight refuel probe. On aircraft after AFC 474, a secondary emergency canopy pneumatic system provides canopy jettison capability. Air for the pneumatic system is drawn from the engine bleed air supply, via the electronic equipment air conditioning system, and is compressed to 3100 +100, -50 psi by a hydraulic motor driven air compressor. A pneumatic pressure sensor in the system moisture separator opens a hydraulic shutoff valve, to activate the air compressor, when the system pressure falls below 2750 psi. When the pneumatic system pressure builds to 3100 +100, -50 psi, the pneumatic pressure sensor closes the hydraulic shutoff valve which deactivates the air compressor. The air compressor discharges through a moisture separator and chemical air dryer to the pneumatic system air bottles. Check valves prevent the air bottles from discharging back to the air compressor. Shutoff valves isolate the air bottles from their component systems until they are manually discharged. A pressure transmitter, for the pneumatic pressure indicator, is installed in a main pressure line.

PNEUMATIC PRESSURE INDICATOR

The pneumatic pressure indicator (figure A-1, appendix A) is on the pedestal panel and operates in

conjunction with the pneumatic pressure transmitter. The indicator has a range of 0 to 5000 pounds with calibrations of 0 to 50 and reads are multiplied by 100. Normal system pressures range from 2680-3270 psi due to pressure transmitter and pressure gage tolerances.

NORMAL OPERATION

Normal operation of the pneumatic system is automatic when the engines are running or by the application of external pneumatic power. A check of the pneumatic system cockpit pressure indicator or the basic system pressure gage denotes only the pressure in the supply line. Operating pressures for the emergency subsystems are indicated by their individual pressure gages. To de-activate the air compressor, pull out the pneumatic system control circuit breaker on the No. 2 circuit breaker panel.

EMERGENCY OPERATION

There is no emergency operation of the pneumatic system air compressor. However, all the normal and emergency systems have air storage bottles that assure adequate air pressure to the individual pneumatic subsystems. Operation of the normal and emergency subsystems is discussed under the applicable individual systems.

LIMITATIONS

The normal pneumatic system pressure as read on the cockpit indicator is 2680 to 3270 psi.

RADAR BEACON SYSTEM AN/APN-154

DESCRIPTION

Aircraft after AFC 363 have radar beacon AN/APN-154 equipment installed to enhance range tracking capabilities of certain ground-based radars. These are transportable, special purpose X-band radars which may be moved to forward areas and used to vector the interceptor to a specific target or target area. The radar equipment emits X-band signals which interrogate the AN/APN-154 radar beacon equipment in the aircraft; the AN/APN-154 in turn transmits a pulse reply to the interrogating radar. Hence, the radar site is actually receiving a transmitted signal which is considerable stronger than a radar echo. This improves target acquisition capabilities at the radar maximum ranges, especially in adverse environmental conditions. The AN/APN-

154 system is comprised of the following components: the receiver-transmitter, which includes the receiving, transmitting, decoding, and power supply assemblies; the duplexer, which permits signal reception and transmission with a single antenna, and the control panel (figure 1-34) which contains the only operating controls.

CONTROL PANEL

The control panel is in the aft cockpit and contains a power switch and a mode selector knob.

Power Switch

With the aircraft electrical system energized, placing the switch to STBY places the AN/APN-154 system in a standby (warmup) condition. To place the

RADAR BEACON CONTROLS AND SIGNAL FLOW

AN/APN-154

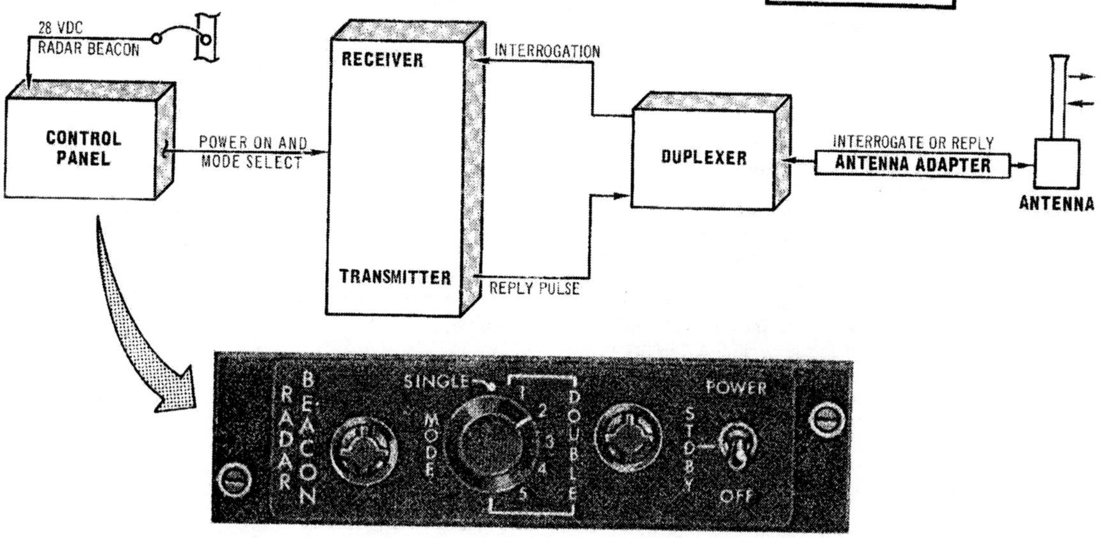

Figure 1-34

FDB-1-(38)

system into full operation, place the switch to POWER. For optimum performance, at least a 5-minute warmup period should be allowed in STBY.

Mode Selector Knob

The mode selector knob has a SINGLE position and five DOUBLE positions labeled 1, 2, 3, 4, and 5. With the knob in SINGLE the system responds only to single pulse interrogations. The double positions (codes 1 thru 5), enable the set to respond to double pulse interrogations. The mode the RIO selects should be determined either during mission briefing or by direct voice communication with the radar site.

NORMAL OPERATION

X-band pulse signals from an interrogating radar are received at the antenna and directed to the receiver portion of the receiver-transmitter by the duplexer. These signals may be single or double pulse trains,

depending on the selected operating mode at the radar site. The signals are amplified and decoded, and if the mode of the incoming signal matches the mode selected by the aircrew, the decoded signals trigger the transmitter. The transmitter output is directed by the duplexer to the antenna for transmission. There are no indicators that show system operation; the aircrew simply energizes the system and selects an operating mode. Vectoring information is obtained by normal voice communications between the interceptor and the interrogating radar.

EMERGENCY OPERATION

There is no emergency operation pertaining to the radar beacon system.

LIMITATIONS

There are no limitations pertaining to the radar beacon system.

SPEED BRAKES

DESCRIPTION

The hydraulically operated speed brakes are on the underside of the inboard wing panels and are hinged on the forward side permitting the brakes to open downward. The speed brakes are controlled from a switch on the throttle grip and may be positioned at any point in their travel. Due to the construction of the selector valve, the speed brakes do not close following a hydraulic pressure failure, unless the emergency speed brake switch on the left console is placed in RETRACT. This deenergizes a solenoid bypass valve to block the speed brake open and speed brake close lines from the selector valve and connects both sides of the cylinders to return. Air loads then close the speed brakes to the trail position. On airplanes 148412h and 150406L and up, a different speedbrake selector valve has been incorporated in the airplane. This valve differs from the old valve, in that placing the emergency speed brake switch in RETRACT results in the speed brakes being hydraulically closed rather than being closed by air loads. The emergency speed brake switch on these airplanes is only useful in the event of a failure of the throttle mounted speed brake switch. On aircraft after AFC 534, the emergency speed brake retract switch has been removed. The utility hydraulic system is used to operate the speed brakes.

SPEED BRAKE SWITCH

The speed brake switch (figure A-1, appendix A) on the throttle grip has three positions: IN, STOP and OUT. The STOP position is the normal position of the switch. Only the OUT position of the switch is momentary. Placing the switch in OUT operates the speed brakes toward the extend position. When the switch is released, it returns to STOP. The STOP position deenergizes the selector valve and blocks all ports giving a hydraulic lock for holding the speed brakes in any desired position. Selecting IN of the switch closes the speed brakes flush with the wing. The speed brakes take 2-3 seconds to fully open and 2-3 seconds to fully close. The speed brake switch IN position also serves as an emergency disengage switch for the approach power compensator system.

Note

The STOP position of the speed brake switch may not hold the speed brakes completely closed. This is noted by the illumination of the SPEED BRAKE OUT light. If this occurs, position the speed brake switch to IN and leave in that position.

OVERRIDE SAFETY SWITCH

On airplanes 148363f thru 148411h and 148413h thru 149474k, a two-position switch marked SAFE and NORMAL, is in the right wheel well. The SAFE position of the switch extends the speed brakes and prevents energizing the selector valve from the cockpit. This switch is provided for protection of personnel working in the speed brake well. The NORMAL position of the override switch permits normal speed brake operation.

Note

Speed brake safety switch should be checked in NORMAL before flight. If the switch is in SAFE, the speed brakes are inoperative.

SPEED BRAKE OUT LIGHT

An amber SPEED BRAKE OUT light (figure A-1, appendix A) on the telelight panel illuminates when either or both of the speed brakes are not fully closed.

Note

SPEED BRAKE OUT light does not light the MASTER CAUTION light.

NORMAL OPERATION

Normal operation of the speed brakes is through the three position throttle mounted speed brake switch. The IN position retracts the speed brakes, OUT extends the speed brakes, and STOP holds the speed brakes in any intermediate position. A SPEED BRAKE OUT light on the telelight panel illuminates any time the speed brakes are not closed.

EMERGENCY OPERATION

Should the selector valve or the utility hydraulic system fail, when the speed brakes are extended, they may be retracted by placing the emergency speed brake switch on the left console to RETRACT. This allows air loads to close the panels to a trailing position. On airplanes 148412h and 150406L and up, the speed brakes automatically close if an electrical failure occurs. However, if a hydraulic failure occurs, the speed brakes remain open until the throttle mounted speed brake switch is placed to IN. Air loads then close the speed brakes to a low drag trail position. If a failure occurs in the throttle mounted speed brake switch, the speed brakes can be closed by placing the emergency speed brake switch in RETRACT. On aircraft after AFC 534, the emergency speed brake retract switch is removed and emergency retraction is accomplished by pulling the SP BK (speed brake) circuit breaker, on the essential circuit breaker panel.

Note

In aircraft after AFC 392, the APCS may be disengaged at any time by moving the speed brake switch to IN, regardless of the position of the emergency speed brake switch or the speed brake circuit breaker.

LIMITATIONS

There are no specific limitations pertaining to the operation of the speed brakes.

TOW TARGET SYSTEMS

DESCRIPTION

The airplane can tow the Aero 35B banner, or can be equipped to tow the TDU-22/B or TDU-22A/B Tow Target with the RMU-8/A Reel Launcher or to launch the AQM-37A Missile Target (with the LAU-24/A Launcher).

AERO 35B BANNER

The standard 40 x 7.5 foot Aero 35B banner can be towed from the aircraft utilizing the existing aircraft systems. The banner is attached to the aircraft by 120 feet of 3/8 inch steel chain from the drag chute attachment fittings and 1800 feet of tow cable.

Note

The steel chain must be taut against the underside of the fuselage and attached to the centerline fitting with nylon webbing to allow taxiing. The 1800 feet of cable and the banner are attached to the aircraft when in position for takeoff.

RMU-8/A REEL/LAUNCHER

This jettisonable reel/launcher, mounted on the centerline station, is used to tow the TDU-22/B or TDU-22A/B tow targets. The reel/launcher (figure 1-36) is a ram air turbine driven power unit, with reversible pitch blades; capstans; a towline storage spool; a level wind mechanism; a target launcher boom and saddle; an emergency cable cutter, and an automatic control system. The automatic control system provides for automatic target launching and reel-out and reel-in to a preset towline length. The tow reel is capable of reel-out and reel-in speeds of 5200 feet per minute. The towline length normally carried on the tow reel is 40,000 feet, but it is capable of carrying up to 100,000 feet. Carriage of the RMU-8/A does not cause any adverse flight characteristics; however, the AC should expect to encounter the following phenomena:

1. Minor vibration during reeling operation, particularly during reel acceleration and deceleration.
2. High pitched whine (like a siren) during high speed reeling.
3. Torque effect during high speed reeling.

The launcher is down for launch and recovery only, and is up during target tow. The reel contains a nitrogen bottle to actuate the launcher and the pneumatic brakes. It uses the aircraft emergency bus to

provide power for stopping the reel and cutting the cable if aircraft ac power is lost.

Towline Length Sensing Unit

The towline length sensing unit (figure 1-36) contains pulsing switches used in sensing the amount of towline reeled out, three counter operated limit switches used in automatic sequencing during the launch operations, and a reset mechanism. The switches and switch functions are listed below:

OUT STOP	- Sets the maximum towline length required (minus stopping distance).
LAUNCH STOP	- Determines the point beyond which high speed reel-out action is permitted.
IN STOP	- Determines the point at which deceleration from high speed reel-in occurs. High speed reel-in may not be started; however, manually controlled target recovery may be started.
CABLE IN OUT/OFF	- Allows the ground crew to simulate a complete operating cycle. For inflight tow target operation, the switch is OFF.

Blade Pitch Change Actuator

The blade pitch change actuator consists of a reversible dc motor and a switch package containing six limit switches. The dc motor, through a gear train, rotates the power unit blades clockwise during recovery and counterclockwise during launching. The six limit switches are cam operated and determine the number of degrees rotation the blades turn and the direction of the turn.

Speed Monitor Switch Assembly

The speed monitor switch assembly consists of four switches. The operation of each switch is governed by the power unit speed. The switches are set to operate at 8600 to 9400 rpm (normal governing band), at 9900 rpm (ten percent overspeed), and at 10,800 rpm (twenty percent overspeed). The 8600 and 9400 rpm switches perform target reel-out/reel-in speed monitoring functions. The 9900 and 10,800 rpm switches are for emergency control.

Central Control Box

The central control box contains function control relays and an acceleration monitor. The relays are used to control the overall operation of the RMU-8/A. The acceleration monitor is used to automatically control change-rate of the towline speed during the operating cycle.

Power Unit

The power unit consists of eight reversible-pitch blades, each of which attaches to a central hub. The reversible-pitch blades are arranged in two rows of four blades each. The blade angle is controlled through the blade pitch change actuator which is mechanically coupled to the reversible-pitch blades and drives the blades on their individual axis. The power unit is driven by the wind force created by the forward speed of the aircraft. The unit rotates counterclockwise (as viewed from the rear) during reel-out and functions as a brake against the trailing towline and target. The power unit rotates clockwise (as viewed from the rear) during reel-in and functions as a turbine to furnish drive power to the transmission and spool during the recovery operation.

Transmission Assembly

The transmission assembly couples the driving power developed by the power unit through a gear train assembly to the capstan and through a slip-clutch mechanism to the towline spool. The transmission assembly houses the gear train, clutches, oil pump, scavenger oil-pump, and the oil dip stick.

Clutch Mechanism

The clutch mechanism consists of two, over-running, sprag-type clutches and a constant torque slip-clutch driven through a gear train. The arrangement of the clutch mechanism maintains towline tension between the capstan and the towline spool to prevent towline slipage on the capstans.

Spool and Levelwind

The spool and levelwind provides storage of the towline which is reeled-out or reeled-in. For convenience in rewinding, the spool is removable. The levelwind is driven by the spool and may be readily disengaged for purposes of synchronization and threading.

Lubrication

The lubrication system is a wet-sump type with automatic reversing, rotary, internal gear pumps located in the transmission assembly. Positive lubrication is furnished to the main drive gear mesh, capstan bearing, clutch assembly, and power unit. A separate pump scavenges the power unit and discharges the oil into the transmission assembly. The transmission assembly and clutch mechanism are capable of operating approximately 10 seconds with an interrupted oil supply. During the target launch and recovery operations, all oil is routed to the clutch assembly for cooling. There are also two oil pressure switches, an oil pressure indicator, and a temperature indicator in the system. The oil pressure switches and the oil temperature indicator are safety devices which provide a visual indication of low oil pressure and excessive oil temperature to the operator.

Pneumatic System

The pneumatic system provides the necessary power to extend and retract the launcher and to apply the brakes to the reel-launcher. A storage bottle contains compressed nitrogen at 3000 psi. The pressure is reduced to 300 psi before it is delivered to any of the operating mechanisms of the reel-launcher. This supply of nitrogen permits approximately four complete operating cycles. When the storage bottle pressure drops below 700 psi, a light in the control panel gives a low air indication. The latch that holds the launcher in the retracted position is also operated by nitrogen pressure. This latch is in series with the actuating cylinder that forces the launcher down. This is to assure that the latch is opened before the launcher boom is extended. The pneumatic system is designed so that towline tension is maintained at all times during launcher extension and retraction and so that the brakes are applied gradually to prevent snapping of the towline. During an emergency the brakes are applied instantly.

Launcher

A pneumatically operated target launcher is provided to launch and retrieve the target through the region of disturbed air flow around the RMU-8/A and the airplane. The launcher also acts as a shock absorber upon initial target contact during recovery. The launcher contains two mechanical clamps which hold the target when the launcher is fully retracted. These automatically open as the launcher is lowered.

Towline Cutter

An explosive cartridge operated towline cutter is mounted on the launcher support structure and provides for cutting the towline under any possible flight operating condition. The cutter is fired manually by actuation of the emergency stop and towline cut switch and is automatically fired under certain emergency conditions. The conditions under which the towline is cut automatically are: a 20% overspeed (towline reel rate of 6000 ft/min.) during any of the four operating cycles, or target approaching within 200 feet of the aircraft after failure to slow down and stop after passing through the preset in stop distance during the reel-in cycle (towline cutter is actuated by an anti-collision device).

Tension System

A strain gage bridge in the high tension sheave works in conjunction with a regulated power supply to present an indication of towline tension on the towline tension indicator.

Towline Speed Indicating System

A tachometer generator in the reel-launcher provides an indication of towline speed to the operator and a signal indicating the rate of change of speed to the acceleration monitor.

Control Circuit Sequencing

The normal stop and the emergency stop and towline cut functions can be initiated at all times. The normal stop function must be initiated to interrupt any cycle before initiating a new cycle. The following table illustrates cycles that can be initiated after the completion of a manual or automatic normal stop at various towline lengths relative to the towline length limit switch.

Target Position	Functions Possible
Target Stowed	Launch, Reel-Out
Target between stowed position and in-stop (2500 ft)	Reel-Out, Recover
Target between in-stop (2500 ft) and out-stop	Reel-Out, Reel-In
Past out-stop	Reel-In

TDU-22B AND TDU-22A/B TOW TARGETS

Both targets are center-of-gravity towed targets which measure 78 inches in length, 7 inches in diameter, and have a fin span of 22 inches. The TDU-22B weighs approximately 32 pounds and is radar augmented. The TDU-22A/B weighs approximately 40 pounds and is radar and infrared augmented. Radar augmentation consists of Luneberg lenses, and infrared augmentation consists of four flares with command radio receiver and battery pack. Flares are fired by a small tone generator mounted in the RIO's radio mic circuit.

RMU-8 A CONTROL PANEL

FDB-1-(39)

Figure 1-35

RMU-8/A CONTROL PANEL

The reel/launcher control panel may be mounted adjacent to the RIO's seat, or other accessible location. It has all of the instruments and switches required to control and monitor tow reel functions. Three instruments indicate reel-in or reel-out speed, tow cable tensions, and tow cable length. The switches include a master power switch, a target launch switch, a tow reel control switch, a turbine pitch control switch, a tow reel stop switch and a stop and cut switch. Indicator lights include an EMERG PWR light, a LOW AIR light, a TOW CUT light, a LAUNCHER DOWN light, a TARGET OUT light, and a SAFETY ARM light.

Master Power Switch

The master power switch, makred ON and OFF, is utilized to energize the tow target system.

Target Launcher Switch

The target launcher switch, with positions of LAUNCH and RECOVERY, is used during the first stage of target launch, and the last stage of target recovery. Placing the switch to LAUNCH extends the launching boom and allows the target to withdraw from the saddle. The LAUNCHER DOWN and TARGET OUT lights illuminate and the target begins to reel-out to approximately 100 feet. At 100 feet, the launching boom retracts, the LAUNCHER DOWN light goes out, and the tow reel is braked to a stop. During recovery, the reverse process takes place.

Tow Reel Control Switch

The tow reel control switch has positions marked REEL-IN and REEL-OUT, and is used after the target has been launched. Placing the switch to REEL-OUT releases the brake on the tow reel. The target then begins to reel-out at an increasing speed to a maximum of 5000 feet per minute. At a preselected cable length, the tow reel brake is applied to stop the target. Placing the switch in REEL-IN returns the target to a recovery position at reel-in speeds up to 5000 feet per minute.

Turbine Pitch Control Switch

The turbine pitch control switch, marked INCREASE SPEED and FEATHER, is used to manually control target recovery speeds. After the target has completed reel-in, actuating the turbine pitch control switch to INCREASE increases the target recovery speed approximately 150 feet per minute. Actuating the switch to FEATHER stops recovery procedures.

Tow Reel Stop Switch

The stop switch has two positions: STOP and a spring-loaded OFF position. The switch allows any operation in progress to be halted.

Stop & Cut Switch

The stop and cut switch has two positions: STOP & CUT and guarded OFF position. The switch provides an emergency means of stopping and cutting the towline at any time.

RMU-8/A REEL LAUNCHER

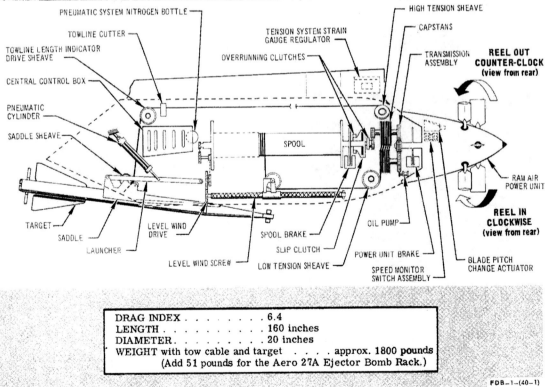

PNEUMATIC SYSTEM NITROGEN BOTTLE

TOWLINE CUTTER

TOWLINE LENGTH INDICATOR DRIVE SHEAVE

CENTRAL CONTROL BOX

PNEUMATIC CYLINDER

SADDLE SHEAVE

TENSION SYSTEM STRAIN GAUGE REGULATOR

OVERRUNNING CLUTCHES

HIGH TENSION SHEAVE

CAPSTANS

TRANSMISSION ASSEMBLY

REEL OUT COUNTER-CLOCK (view from rear)

SPOOL

TARGET

SADDLE

LAUNCHER

LEVEL WIND DRIVE

LEVEL WIND SCREW

SPOOL BRAKE

SLIP CLUTCH

LOW TENSION SHEAVE

OIL PUMP

POWER UNIT BRAKE

SPEED MONITOR SWITCH ASSEMBLY

RAM AIR POWER UNIT

REEL IN CLOCKWISE (view from rear)

BLADE PITCH CHANGE ACTUATOR

```
DRAG INDEX . . . . . . . . 6.4
LENGTH . . . . . . . . . 160 inches
DIAMETER . . . . . . . . . 20 inches
WEIGHT with tow cable and target . . . . approx. 1800 pounds
(Add 51 pounds for the Aero 27A Ejector Bomb Rack.)
```

FDB-1-(40-1)

Figure 1-36 (Sheet 1 of 2)

RMU-8/A REEL LAUNCHER

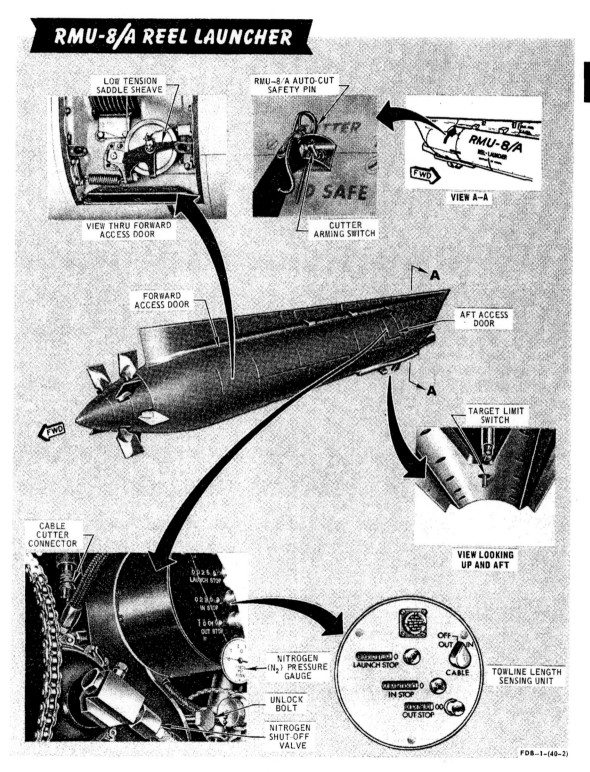

Figure 1-36 (Sheet 2 of 2)

FDB-1-(40-2)

Towline Length Indicator

The towline length indicator indicates the distance (in 10-foot increments) the target is from the reel-launcher assembly.

Towline Speed Indicator

The towline speed indicator provides an indication of the speed the towline is entering or leaving the RMU-8/A. The indicator is calibrated in feet-per-minute and consists of two scales: a lower scale with a range of 0 to 700 and an upper scale with a range of 700 to 6500. The upper scale has a green arc to indicate the normal operating range and a red line at 6000 feet per minute to indicate the maximum turbine speed. A neon light on the dial indicates which speed range is operative. The lower scale is operative with the light off and the upper scale is operative with the light on.

Towline Tension Indicator

The towline tension indicator provides an indication of the tension of the towline. The indication presented is calibrated in hundreds of pounds.

Target Out Light

The TARGET OUT light provides an indication that the target has been launched or is loose in the launcher because of lost towline tension.

Launcher Down Light

The LAUNCHER DOWN light provides an indication that the target launcher assembly is in the down position or is not locked.

Low Air Pressure Light

The LOW AIR PRESS light illuminates when the air storage bottle is depleted to an air pressure of 700 psi or lower.

Towline Cut Light

The TOWLINE CUT light functions in conjunction with the stop and cut sequence. When the stop and cut sequence is activated, the TOWLINE CUT light shows that the action of cutting the towline has been accomplished.

Emergency Power Light

The EMERG PWR light provides an indication of failure of the primary 28 volt dc supply.

Safety Arm Light

The SAFETY ARM light provides the operator with an indication that the anti-collision safety device is armed. The SAFETY ARM light illuminates during reel-in procedures and goes out during recovery.

AQM-37A MISSILE TARGET SYSTEM

The AQM-37A missile target system consists of a missile target, an LAU-24/A launcher, and a PEU-56/A missile firing control panel. The target and launcher are mounted only on the aircraft fuselage centerline station. Controls and indicator lights necessary for selecting, launching, and/or jettisoning the target, are in the forward cockpit. The target system installation utilizes components from existing aircraft systems as well as those specifically installed for the target.

AQM-37A MISSILE TARGET

The target is cylindrically constructed with a streamlined nose section and clipped delta wings which have a vertical fin on each tip. Control of the target is maintained through full span ailerons located on the trailing edge of the wings, and by movable canard surfaces on the forward nose section of the target. The target is propelled by a rocket engine that utilizes dual thrust chambers. The large chamber is used for initial boost and acceleration, while the smaller chamber is used for sustained power during target cruise operations. Stabilization and control of the target is maintained through a three axis gyro reference to pitch, roll, and yaw, regulated by a self-contained preset flight programmer. Mission capabilities of the target include supersonic flight operations in cruise altitude ranges up to 70,000 feet; however, operations are normally accomplished at altitudes between 30,000 and 40,000 feet.

PEU-56/A MISSILE FIRING PANEL

This panel is in the forward cockpit on the right console. The panel contains a PWR ON light, a READY light, and a target function selector switch with positions marked SELECT, OFF, and JETTISON. When the function selector switch is placed to SELECT, power is supplied to the target and the PWR ON light illuminates. The READY light illuminates when power has been applied to the target for 5 minutes. Placing the function selector switch to JETTISON immediately jettisons the target. Separation of the jettisoned target from the launcher provides a destruct signal to the target's destruct system. The target may also be jettisoned by actuating the external stores emergency release button.

Note

The READY light indicates only that 5 minutes have elapsed since power was applied to the target and does not indicate target operational readiness. The target may be launched without the READY light illuminated if the PWR ON light has been on for 5 minutes.

NORMAL OPERATION

Refer to section IV, Tow Target Procedures.

EMERGENCY OPERATION

Refer to section IV, Tow Target Procedures.

LIMITATIONS

Refer to section IV, Tow Target Procedures.

WING FOLD SYSTEM

─────── NOTICE ───────
Some illustrations referred to within this system writeup may be located in appendix A.
These illustrations are referred to, within the text, as (figure A-, appendix A).

DESCRIPTION

Each outer wing panel is folded upward to a vertical position by a conventional hydraulic actuator that receives hydraulic pressure from the utility hydraulic system. A mechanical locking system is installed in the airplane to lock wing pins in hinge fittings when wings are spread. A flush mounted control lever (figure A-1, appendix A) on the right console in the pilot's cockpit, is connected by push rods and push-pull cables to a pin locking device in the wing fold area. Pulling up on the lever unlocks wing pins, extends warning flags on the upper wing surfaces, illuminates amber L WING PIN UNLOCK and R WING PIN UNLOCK lights in both cockpits and energizes the wing fold. Wing fold is actually accomplished by a two-position toggle switch underneath the wing pin release lever and is exposed when the lever is raised. The switch is marked FOLD and SPREAD. As an added safety precaution, the wing fold hydraulic circuit receives its hydraulic pressure from the landing gear down pressure line; this prevents pressurization of the wing fold system when the landing gear is up. On some airplanes the wing pins are released by pulling up on a control handle that juts out of the wing fold panel. The wing fold switch on these airplanes is immediately forward of the pin pull handle. The wing pin pull handle, and wing fold switch operates the same controls as the previously described wing pin unlock lever and wing fold switch. When folding or spreading the outer panels, observe the following precautions:

a. Jury struts removed.
b. With jury struts removed, keep the wings spread when engine jet blast or high winds may buffet the wings.

c. Ensure wings are spread and locked, before taxiing or prior to being spotted directly aft of the jet blast deflector during launch operations.

NORMAL OPERATION

Normal operation consists of folding and spreading the wings, and is accomplished through the wing fold panel on the right console. To fold the wings, pull up on the wing pin lock lever, and place the wing fold switch in FOLD. To spread the wings, remove the jury struts, and place wing fold switch in SPREAD. After the panels have spread and pins have extended, push down on the wing pin lock lever. Red warning flags which are attached to the wing pin locks should be flush with the wing skin if the wing pin locks are fully inserted. The warning flags extend above the wing surface, inboard of the wing fold line, when the wing pin locks are not inserted. When the wing pin locks are fully inserted the L WING PIN UNLOCK and R WING PIN UNLOCK warning lights are extinguished.

EMERGENCY OPERATION

There is no emergency operation pertaining to the wing fold system.

LIMITATIONS

Whenever the aircraft is parked or towed with wings folded, jury struts must be installed. Taxiing with wings folded and jury struts not installed must be held to a minimum. Aboard ship, jury struts must be inserted any time wings are folded.

PART **3** SERVICING

For information pertaining to servicing (i.e., authorized AGE, consumable materials, capacities, pressures, and cockpit procedures), refer to the NATOPS Servicing Checklist (NAVAIR 01-245FDB-1C).

PART 4 OPERATING LIMITATIONS

AIRCRAFT

GENERAL

All airplane/systems limitations that must be observed during normal operation are covered or referenced herein. Some limitations that are characteristic only of a specialized phase of operation (i.e., emergency procedures, flight through turbulent air, starting procedures, etc.), are not covered here; however, they are contained along with the discussion of the operation in question.

INSTRUMENT MARKINGS

The limitation markings appearing on the instrument faces are shown in figure 1-37 and noted in the applicable text.

ENGINE LIMITATIONS

Refer to Engines, part 2 of this section.

AIRSPEED LIMITATIONS

The maximum permissible airspeeds in smooth or moderately turbulent air with arresting hook, landing gear, and wing flaps retracted, and with speed brakes retracted or extended are as shown in figure 1-38. Airspeed limitations for operation of various systems are as follows:

CAUTION

When flying at airspeeds in excess of 350 knots CAS below 10,000 feet with CG location aft of 32.0% MAC, avoid abrupt control motions. The CG location aft of 32.0% MAC normally occur whenever full internal fuel is maintained in conjunction with external stores. Prior to takeoff, refer to the Handbook of Weight and Balance Data (AN 01-1B-40) to determine CG location for the specific configuration.

a. With landing gear extended.	250 knots CAS
b. With flaps (leading and trailing edge) fully or partially extended.	250 knots CAS
c. With ram air turbine extended	515 knots CAS or Mach 1.1, whichever is less.
d. Air refueling probe extension or retraction.	300 knots CAS or Mach 0.9, whichever is less.
e. With air refueling probe extended.	400 knots CAS or Mach 0.9, whichever is less.
g. Boarding steps extended	400 knots CAS
h. With corner reflector extended	250 knots CAS
i. Chaff dispenser doors	Same as basic airplane*

*To preclude aircraft skin damage, flight time with chaff doors open should be limited unless tactical requirements dictate otherwise.

SYSTEM OPERATING RANGES

Refer to figure 1-39.

PROHIBITED MANEUVERS

1. Full-deflection aileron rolls in excess of 360°.
2. Intentional spins.
3. Abrupt control movements when carrying the 600-gallon external fuel tank or the D-704 air refueling store.
4. Lateral control deflections in excess of 1/2 of total stick travel when carrying the MK 104, the 600-gallon external fuel tank, the 370-gallon external wing tanks, or the D-704 air refueling store. This restriction does not apply when in takeoff and landing configurations.
5. With the AFCS engaged, intentional maneuvers that exceed the automatic disengagement limits of the AFCS.
6. Lateral control deflections in excess of 1/3 of total stick travel when carrying the RCPP-105 starter pod. This restriction does not apply when in takeoff and landing configurations.
7. Negative G in excess of 30 seconds.
8. Zero G in excess of 10 seconds.
9. Airborne deployment of drag chute except for emergency spin recovery.

CG LIMITATIONS

The center of gravity for all currently permissible gross weights and configurations must be kept between 27.0% and 36.0% of the mean aerodynamic chord (MAC). However, the maximum allowable aft CG will be forward of 36.0% MAC with certain external loading configurations. To maintain minimum acceptable longitudinal stability, the allowable aft CG must be moved forward as wing-mounted stores are added to the airplane. The minimum acceptable level of stability is based on airplane controllability. Refer to Longitudinal Stability (section IV) for a discussion of flight characteristics near the aft CG

INSTRUMENT RANGE MARKINGS

BASED ON JP-4 or JP-5 FUEL

	EXHAUST GAS TEMPERATURE	
635°C	▬ MAXIMUM STEADY STATE TEMP.	

	TACHOMETER	
102%	▬ MAXIMUM	

OIL PRESSURES AIRPLANES 148363f THRU 150435L PRIOR TO INCORPORATION OF ASC 115

MIL-L-7808 OIL		MIL-L-23699 OIL
65 PSI	MAXIMUM	75 PSI
35 PSI	MINIMUM AT MILITARY RPM	45 PSI
12 PSI	MINIMUM AT IDLE RPM	12 PSI
35-65 PSI	NORMAL OPERATION AT MIL POWER AND ABOVE	45-75 PSI

Notes

- PLACARD PRESSURE ON THE OIL PRESSURE GAGES IS CORRECTED TO 100 PERCENT RPM. AT MILITARY THROTTLE SETTING DURING T₂ CUTBACK, OR ANY OTHER SPEED REDUCTION. INDICATED PRESSURE WILL DECREASE BELOW PLACARD PRESSURE APPROXIMATELY 1 PSI PER 1 PERCENT REDUCTION IN RPM BELOW 100 PERCENT RPM.

OIL PRESSURES AIRPLANES 150436m AND UP AND ALL OTHERS UPON INCORPORATION OF ASC 115

MIL-L-7808 OIL		MIL-L-23699 OIL
60 PSI	MAXIMUM	70 PSI
35 PSI	MINIMUM AT MILITARY RPM STEADY STATE-GROUND OPERATION	45 PSI
12 PSI	MINIMUM AT IDLE POWER	12 PSI
30-60 PSI	INFLIGHT NORMAL OPERATION AT MIL POWER AND ABOVE	40-70 PSI

Notes

- INDICATED OIL PRESSURE CORRECTED TO 100 PERCENT RPM MUST REPEAT WITHIN 5 PSI OF THE PLACARDED OIL PRESSURE.

- ANY STEADY-STATE OPERATION, ERRATIC PRESSURE CHANGE, WHICH EXCEEDS 5 PSI FOR MORE THAN 1 SECOND MUST BE INVESTIGATED.

FDB-1-(41)
R

Figure 1-37

AIRPLANE SPEED RESTRICTIONS

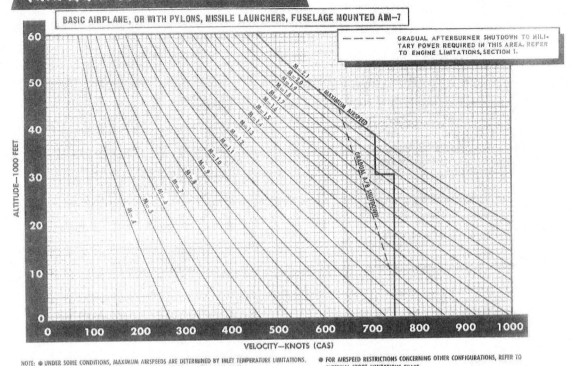

BASIC AIRPLANE, OR WITH PYLONS, MISSILE LAUNCHERS, FUSELAGE MOUNTED AIM—7

GRADUAL AFTERBURNER SHUTDOWN TO MILITARY POWER REQUIRED IN THIS AREA. REFER TO ENGINE LIMITATIONS, SECTION I.

NOTE: • UNDER SOME CONDITIONS, MAXIMUM AIRSPEEDS ARE DETERMINED BY INLET TEMPERATURE LIMITATIONS. REFER TO ENGINE INLET TEMPERATURE LIMITATIONS CHART, PART 2 OF SECTION I. • FOR AIRSPEED RESTRICTIONS CONCERNING OTHER CONFIGURATIONS, REFER TO EXTERNAL STORE LIMITATIONS CHART.

FDB—1—(42)

Figure 1-38

SYSTEM OPERATING RANGES

		PC-1	PC-2	UTILITY
HYDRAULIC PRESSURE PSI	R. ENG ONLY	0	2750 – 3250	2550 – 3000
	L. ENG ONLY	2750 – 3250	0	2750 – 3250
	BOTH ENGS	2750 – 3250	2750 – 3250	2750 – 3250
NORMAL FUEL FLOW – PPH		LIGHT OFF 225 – 800	IDLE 800 – 1400	MILITARY APPROX. 7000
MIN FUEL FLOW – PPH (THROTTLE CHOP)		COOL START CAM 330	HOT START CAM 445	
BOOST PUMP PRESS – PSI		30 ± 5		
PNEUMATIC PRESSURE – PSI		2680–3270		
MIN. PRESS FOR RAT EXTENSION		1000		

FDB—1—(43)

Figure 1-39

limit. Stability numbers for individual stores are contained in part 1 of section XI. After compiling the airplane stability index (sum of stability numbers) refer to the Aft CG Limits chart (figure 1-40) to determine maximum allowable aft CG. For precise loading and CG data, refer to the Handbook of Weight and Balance Data (AN 01-1B-40) for the specific airplane.

WEIGHT LIMITATIONS

The maximum allowable gross weights are as follows:

Field takeoff	54,800 pounds
Field landing minimum sink-rate (Before AFC 230)	38,000 pounds
(After AFC 230)	42,000 pounds
Catapulting	54,800 pounds
Barricade engagement	34,000 pounds
Arrested landing, touch-and-go, and FMLP (Before AFC 230)	34,000 pounds
(After AFC 230)	38,000 pounds

AFT CG LIMITS

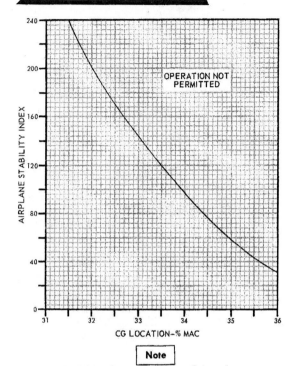

Note

The aft CG limit curve is based on inflight conditions. Before starting engines, initial CG positions up to 0.4% MAC aft of the limit curve are permissible, but shall not exceed 36% MAC. This assumes a corresponding forward shift in CG during ground operation.

FDB—1—(44)

Figure 1-40

ACCELERATION LIMITATIONS

The maximum permissible accelerations shown in figures 1-41 and 1-42 are for flight in smooth air. Moderate and heavy buffet should be avoided whenever possible. In conditions of moderate turbulence, it is essential that accelerations resulting from deliberate maneuvers be reduced 2.0 G below that shown in figure 1-43. This is to minimize the possibility of overstressing the airplane as a result of the combined effects of gust and maneuvering loads. Acceleration limitations for ram air turbine operation are 0 to +3.0 G for extension/retraction and -1.0 to +5.2 G with the RAT fully extended. Carriage and release acceleration limitations for the various external stores are shown in the External Stores Limitations charts, this section and appendix I of NAVAIR 01-245FDB-IT.

CAUTION

Normal accelerations of 8.5G are permissible only when gross weight and airspeed are equal to or less than 37,500 pounds and 0.72 Mach respectively. Acceleration to 8.5G at conditions outside these limitations will impose excessive stresses on aircraft structure. Since aircraft fatigue life depends largely on the number and magnitude of G application, accelerations above 6.5G should be used only as necessary in mission performance. Care should be taken to avoid G overshoot beyond authorized limits under all conditions.

FLIGHT STRENGTH DIAGRAM

The flight strength diagram (figure 1-42) is a composite presentation of the airplane's operating envelope at three different gross weights. Parameters of each envelope include maximum allowable Mach number, wings-level stall speed at sea level, and the positive and negative load factor limits. This diagram further restricts allowable negative load factors at speeds above 1.5 Mach, and allowable positive load factors at speeds above 1.8 Mach.

CARRIER OPERATIONS

For carrier arrested landings, total fuselage fuel shall not exceed 5100 pounds. This restriction does not apply to touch-and-go landings. For carrier approach and arrestment limitations, refer to applicable recovery bulletins.

Note

If an arrested landing is made with fuel in the internal wings, make a notation on the yellow sheet.

EXTERNAL STORES LIMITATIONS

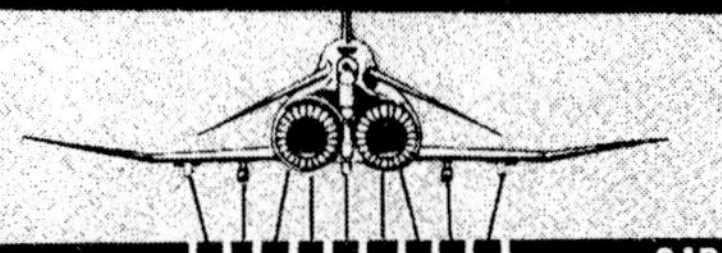

LBA – Limits of Basic Airplane
NE – Not Established

STORES		STATIONS 1 2 3 4 5 6 7 8 9	CARRIAGE MAX KCAS/MACH	CARRIAGE ACCELERATION SYM	CARRIAGE ACCELERATION UNSYM	JETTISON MAX KCAS/MACH	REMARKS
D-704 Air Refueling Store		X	500/1.1	0.0 to + 4.0	0.0 to + 3.2	300/0.9	See Notes 1 and 2. Buddy tank adapter pylon kit is required. Arrested landing, both shipboard and shore-based, are permitted only with empty tank. Catapulting with partially full tank is not permitted. AB operation is not permitted while dumping fuel. Maximum acceleration for operation is + 2.0G, and no abrupt maneuvers are permitted. Maximum airspeeds for operation are 300/0.8 with the hose extended and 250 KCAS for fuel dumping and hose retraction. Jettison in level flight.
AQM-37A Target System (KD-2B Target/LAU-24A Launcher)		X	550/0.95	0.0 to + 4.0	+ 1.0 to + 3.0	550/0.92	See Notes 1 and 2. Maximum bank angle not to exceed 60 degrees. Abrupt maneuvers not permitted. Avoid slipping and skidding. Buffet boundary operation not permitted except in landing configuration. Release in level flight.
AERO 43LM Reel/Launcher with AERO 36, 36A, 421R, or TDU-21 Targets	Target stowed, being launched or recovered	X	250/0.9	NE	NE	NE	See Notes 1 and 2. Refer to Tow Target procedures in Section IV for additional limitations.
	Target streamed 300 to 400 feet	X	300/0.9				
	Target fully streamed	X	400/0.9				
AERO 43LM Reel/Launcher Without Target		X	400/0.9	NE	NE	NE	
RMU-8A Reel/ Launcher with TDU-22 Target	Target reel-in, reel-out, or being launched	X	500/0.9	NE	NE	0.95	
	Target reel-in, reel-out, or fully streamed	X	500/1.6				
	Target being recovered	X	350/0.85				
RMU-8A Reel Launcher Without Target		X	500/1.6	NE	NE	0.95	

Notes

1. Below 10,000 feet, the following airspeed limitations shall be observed when carrying external stores other than Sparrow missiles:
   - Airplanes with C G location aft of 34% MAC – 0.70 Mach or external store limit, whichever is less.
   - Airplanes with C G location forward of 34% MAC – Basic aircraft limit as shown in Airplane Speed Restrictions Chart or the external store limit, whichever is less.

2. Refer to Acceleration Limitations Chart for additional acceleration limitations while carrying external stores.

3. Jettison, empty or full, in 1.0 G level flight with speed brakes, landing gear, and flaps retracted.

FDB-1-(46-2)

Figure 1-43 (Sheet 2 of 2)

SECTION II

INDOCTRINATION

FDB-1-(47)

TABLE OF CONTENTS

GROUND TRAINING

MINIMUM GROUND TRAINING SYLLABUS

The overall ground training syllabus for each activity varies according to local conditions, field facilities, requirements from higher authority, and the immediate Unit Commander's estimate of squadron readiness. The minimum ground training syllabus (pilot/RIO) for each phase is set forth below:

FAMILIARIZATION

Flight physiological training as appropriate

F-4B NAMT pilot's course

F-4B COT/WST. (within 10 days)

FLIGHT SUPPORT LECTURES

J79 engine

F-4B air induction system

Flight controls, flaps, BLC, and AFCS

Aircraft systems and emergency procedures

Aircraft operating limitations

Flight characteristics

No less than two preflight inspections utilizing the Preflight and Daily Maintenance Requirements Cards.

Cockpit/Pressure suit air conditioning and MK IV pressure suit

Ejection seat and survival kit

Cockpit procedures/checklists

BIT checks (RIO only)

Climb, loiter, and cruise performance

Fuel management/mission planning

Single-engine performance

F-4B CNI equipment

NATOPS Flight Manual (open and closed book) stressing normal and emergency procedures and aircraft/engine limitations.

INTERCEPT FLIGHT SUPPORT LECTURES

F-4B NAMT AERO-1A AMCS course

Naval Air Maintenance Training group instructions, Sparrow III missile

Naval Air Maintenance Training group instructions, Sidewinder missile

AN/APA-157 radar set group functions and computations, Sparrow III missile

AN/APA-157 radar set group computations, Sidewinder missile

AN/AAA-4-IR detectors operation procedures NTDS/ATDS operating procedures.

Tactical employment of the F-4B weapons system

Basic intercept procedures

Voice procedures

High altitude-high Mach intercepts

Low altitude intercepts

Sparrow III beam intercepts with Sidewinder re-attack

Forward hemisphere intercepts

Electronic Counter-countermeasures

Air intercept control techniques and procedures-broadcast control

Multiple intercept procedure

Missile firing procedures

Fighter vs fighter combat maneuvering

WEAPONS FIRING FLIGHT SUPPORT LECTURES

Arming/de-arming procedures

Firing procedures

Safety procedures

Jettison/dump areas

FMLP/CARQUAL FLIGHT SUPPORT LECTURES

Mirror and Fresnel's Lens optical landing system

Day landing pattern and procedures

Night landing pattern and procedures

Shipboard procedures and landing patterns

CCA procedures

Air refueling (Day/Night)

WAIVING OF MINIMUM GROUND TRAINING REQUIREMENTS

F/RF-4 qualified crewmembers shall be instructed on the differences from model in which qualified, and comply with those items listed below, as directed by the unit commanding officer.

Where recent pilot experience in similar aircraft models warrant, Unit Commanding Officers may waive the minimum ground training requirements provided the pilot meets the following mandatory qualifications:

Has obtained a current medical clearance

He is currently qualified in flight physiology

Has satisfactorily completed the NATOPS Flight Manual open and closed book examinations

Has completed at least one emergency procedure period in the COT/WST (if available)

Has received adequate briefing on normal and emergency operating procedures

Has received adequate instructions in the use/operation of the ejection seat and survival kit.

FLIGHT TRAINING SYLLABUS

AIRCREW FLIGHT TRAINING SYLLABUS

Prior to flight, all crewmembers will have completed the Familiarization and Flight Support Lectures previously prescribed. A qualified instructor pilot will be assigned for the first familiarization flight. The instructor pilot will occupy the rear seat. Dual control aircraft should be utilized if available. The geographic location, local command requirements, squadron mission, and other factors will influence the actual flight training syllabus and the sequence in which it is completed. The specific phases of training are:

FAMILIARIZATION

Military and afterburner power takeoffs

Buffet boundary investigation

Approach to stalls

Slow flight

Acceleration run to Mach 2.0

Subsonic and supersonic maneuvering

Investigate all features of the AFCS/Stab Aug

Formation flight

Aerobatics

Single engine flight at altitude and airstarts

Landings with and without drag chute

Nose gear steering on landing rollout

Simulated single-engine landing

Acceleration runs at various altitudes

INSTRUMENTS

Basic instrument work

Penetrations and approaches

Local area round robin (day and night) flights

WEAPON SYSTEM EMPLOYMENT

In accordance with existing training and readiness directives.

FIELD MIRROR LANDING PRACTICE AND CARRIER QUALIFICATION

Slow flight

Field mirror landing practice

Carrier qualifications flights

OPERATING CRITERIA

CEILING/VISIBILITY REQUIREMENTS

Prior to the pilot becoming instrument qualified in the airplane, field ceiling/visibility and operating area weather must be adequate for the entire flight to be conducted in a clear air mass according to Visual Flight Rules. After the pilot becomes instrument qualified, the following weather criteria apply:

Time-in-Model (hr)	Ceiling/Visibility (ft) (mi)
10-20	800/2; 900/1-1/2; 1,000/1
20-45	700/1; 600/2; 500/3
45 and above	Field minimums or 200/1/2 whichever is higher

Where adherence to these minimums unduly hampers pilot training, Commanding Officers may waive time-in-type requirements for actual instrument flight, provided crewmembers meet the following criteria:

Have a minimum of 10 hours in model

Completed 2 simulated instrument sorties

Completed 2 satisfactory Tacan penetrations

MINIMUM FLIGHT QUALIFICATIONS

Where recent crewmember experience in similar aircraft models warrant, Unit Commanding Officers may waive the minimum flight training requirements for basic qualifications. Minimum flight hour requirements to maintain pilot and RIO qualifications after initial qualification in each specific phase will be established by the Unit Commanding Officer. Crewmembers who have more than 45 hours in model are considered current subject to the following criteria:

Must have a NATOPS evaluation check with the grade of Conditionally Qualified, or better, within the past

12 months and must have flown 5 hours in model and made two takeoffs and landings within the last 90 days.

Must have satisfactorily completed the ground phase of the NATOPS evaluation check, including COT/WST emergency procedures check (if available), and be considered qualified by the Commanding Officer of the unit having custody of the aircraft.

REQUIREMENTS FOR VARIOUS FLIGHT PHASES
NIGHT

Pilot

Not less than 10 hours in model as first pilot

RIO

Not less than 3 hours in model as crewmember

CROSS COUNTRY

Pilot

Have a minimum of 15 hours in model as first pilot

Have a valid instrument card

Have completed at least one night familiarization flight

RIO

Have a minimum of 15 hours in model as crewmember

Have completed at least one night familiarization flight

AIR-TO-AIR MISSILE FIRING

Pilot

Have a minimum of 15 hours in model

RIO

Have a minimum of 15 hours in model as crew-member

Have satisfactorily completed a minimum of two intercept flights on which simulated firing runs were conducted utilizing the voice procedures and clear to fire criteria to be utilized in live firings

Be considered qualified by the Commanding Officer

CARRIER QUALIFICATION

Each crewmember will have a minimum of 50 hours in model, and meet the requirements set forth in the LSO NATOPS manual.

MINIMUM CREW REQUIREMENTS

The pilot and RIO (or 2 pilots) constitute the normal crew for performing the assigned mission for all flights. Unit commanders may authorize rear seat flights for personnel other than qualified pilots and RIOs provided such personnel have received thorough indoctrination in the use of the ejection seat and oxygen equipment and in the execution of rear seat checklist and emergency procedures. Where operational necessity dictates, unit commanders may authorize flights with the rear seat unoccupied provided the requirement for such flights clearly overrides the risk involved and justifies the additional burden placed on the pilot. Although a rear seat occupant is required in order to properly comply with the procedures in section V of the NATOPS manual, the infrequency of occurrence of these situations tends to justify judiciously selected instances of solo flight. Ferry squadron commanders may authorize solo ferry flights of F4 aircraft. In no case is solo flight authorized for shipboard operations, combat or combat training missions.

FERRY SQUADRONS

Training requirements, check-out procedures, evaluation procedures, and weather minima for ferry squadrons are governed by the provisions contained in OPNAVINST 3710.6.

CREWMEMBER FLIGHT EQUIPMENT

MINIMUM REQUIREMENTS

In accordance with OPNAVINST 3710.7, the flying equipment listed below will be worn by crewmembers on every flight. All survival equipment will be secured in such a manner that it will be easily accessible and will not be lost during ejection or landing. This equipment shall be the latest available as authorized by Aircrew Personal Protective Equipment Manual (NAVAIR 13-1-6).

Anti-buffet helmet modified in accordance with current aviation clothing and survival equipment bulletins

Oxygen mask

Anti-G suit (required on all flights where high G forces may be encountered)

Fire retardant flight suit

Steel-toed flight safety boots

Life preserver

Harness assembly

Shroud cutter

Sheath knife

Flashlight (for all night flights)

Strobe light

Pistol with tracer ammunition, or approved flare gun

Fire retardant flight gloves

Identification tags

Anti-exposure suit in accordance with OPNAVINST 3710.7

Personal survival kit

Other survival equipment appropriate to the climate of the area

Full pressure suit and MK 4 life preserver on all flights above 50,000 feet MSL

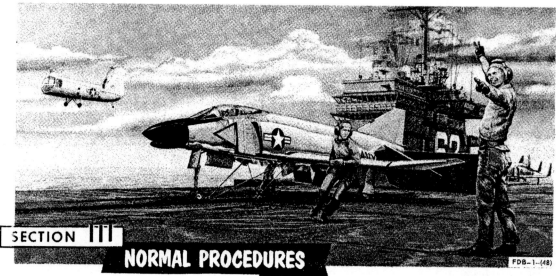

SECTION III

NORMAL PROCEDURES

FDB-1--(48)

TABLE OF CONTENTS

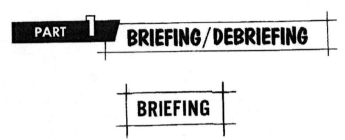

PART 1 BRIEFING/DEBRIEFING

BRIEFING

GENERAL

A briefing guide or syllabus card, as appropriate, will be used in conducting the briefing. Each crewmember will maintain a kneepad and will record all flight numbers, call signs, and all other data necessary to assume the lead and complete the assignment. However, this does not relieve the flight leader of the responsibility for briefing all crews in the operation and conduct of the flight. The briefing guide will include the following:

ASSIGNMENTS

Aircraft assigned, call sign, and deck spot when appropriate.

Engine start, taxi, and takeoff times

Visual signals and rendezvous instructions

MISSION

Primary

Secondary

Operating area

Control agency

Time on station or over target

WEAPONS

Loading

Safety

Arming, de-arming

Duds

Special routes with ordnance aboard

Minimum pull-out altitude

Jettison area

COMMUNICATIONS

Frequencies

Radio procedure and discipline

Navigational aids

Identification and ADIZ procedures

WEATHER

Local area

Local area and destination forecast

Weather at alternate

High altitude weather for the jet stream, temperature, and contrail band width

NAVIGATION AND FLIGHT PLANNING

Climb out

Mission route, including ground controlling agencies

Fuel/oxygen management

Marshal

Penetration

GCA or CCA

Recovery

EMERGENCIES

Aborts

Divert fields

Bingo and low state fuel

Waveoff pattern

Ready deck

Radio failure

Loss of visual contact with flight

SAR procedures

System failures

AIR INTELLIGENCE AND SPECIAL INSTRUCTIONS

Friendly and enemy force disposition

Current situation

Targets

Safety precautions

ECM and ECCM

OPERATING AREA BRIEFINGS

Prior to air operations in and around a new area, it is mandatory that a comprehensive area briefing be given including, but not limited to, the following:

Bingo Fields

Instrument approach facilities

Runway length and arresting gear

Terrain and obstructions

Emergency Fields

Fields suitable for landing but without required support equipment

Include information under Bingo fields

SAR Facilities

Type

Frequencies

Location

DEBRIEFING

GENERAL

Postflight debriefing is an integral part of every flight. The flight leader should review the entire flight from takeoff to landing including not only errors and poor techniques but also the methods of correct-ing them. Also, the flight leader shall cover com-pletely any deviations from standard operating pro-cedures. All intercepts should be reviewed using scope camera and controller information when avail-able.

PART 2 MISSION PLANNING

GENERAL

Refer to section XI, Performance Data, to determine fuel consumption, correct airspeed, power settings, and optimum altitude for the intended flight mission. Planning data for specialized missions is contained in the F-4B Tactical Manual, NAVAIR 01-245FDB-1T.

FLIGHT CODES

The proper Kind of Flight classification and codes to be assigned individual flights are established by OPNAVINST 3760.8 (Series). In order that a further amplification to the assigned codes may be utilized by squadron commanders, the following list of flight codes is recommended.

1A10	Aircraft Familiarization
1A11	Section Formation
1A12	Division Formation
1A13	Air Refueling Practice (Low Altitude)
1A14	Air Refueling Practice (High Altitude)
1A20	Basic Instruments
1A21	GCA/CCA Practice
1A22	Cross Country/Round Robin Navigation

1A3	Day FCLP
1A4	Day Carrier Qualification
1A60	CAP
1A61	Low to High/High to Low Intercepts
1A62	Low Altitude Intercepts
1A63	Medium/High Altitude Intercepts
1A64	Air Combat Maneuvering (Section)
1A65	Air Combat Manuevering (Division)
1A66	Escort Missions
1A67	Live Sidewinder/Live Sparrow Firing
1A68	Low Level/Radar Navigation
1A69	ECCM/EW
1A70	Angle Calibration
1A71	Bomb Drops
1A72	Rocket Firing
1A73	Radar Bombing (Simulated)
1A74	Radar Bombing (Actual)
1A75	Gun Pod Firing

The preceding list of codes reflect unit training (let-ter A) only. For appropriate letter codes for other flight purposes, refer to OPNAVINST 3760.8 (Series).

PART 3 SHORE-BASED PROCEDURES

PREFLIGHT

GENERAL

The yellow sheet must be checked for flight status, configuration, armament loading, and servicing before manning the aircraft. At least the 10 previous B sections should be reviewed for discrepancies noted and the corrective action taken. Weight and Balance clearance is the responsibility of the Maintenance Department.

AFT COCKPIT CHECK FOR SOLO FLIGHT

1. Canopy initiator safety pin (bulkhead mounted) - REMOVED
   Check pin removed to insure operation of forward initiator.

CAUTION

Exercise caution regarding hand movements in vicinity of airplane mounted canopy initiator linkages. Also, do not stow flight equipment or personal items in this area. Failure to comply could result in inadvertent jettisoning of the canopy.

2. Seat safety pins - INSTALLED
3. Circuit breakers - IN
4. Navigation computer function switch - OFF
5. Radar power switch - STBY
6. Pressure suit vent air valve - OFF
7. Oxygen supply lever - OFF
8. Cockpit light switches - OFF
9. Seat harness - STOWED
10. All loose gear - STOWED
11. Aft cockpit electrical test receptacle - ENSURE CAP TIGHTENED

Note

It is possible to trip both generators off the line if the electrical test receptacle 3P325 under the right canopy sill is loose. The generators cannot be restored until the cap is tightened.

After electrical Power -

12. Essential dc test button - DEPRESS
    Depress essential dc test button, and observe that essential dc test light illuminates. If light illuminates, both transformer-rectifiers are delivering dc power. If light does not illuminate, one or both transformer-rectifiers are inoperative or not receiving power.
13. Canopy - LOCKED

BEFORE ENTERING COCKPIT

1. Normal opening canopy lever - AFT/OPEN
2. Landing gear handle - DOWN
3. Emergency canopy release handle - FORWARD and SHEAR WIRED
4. Radar scope retaining bolts and secondary restraining device - CHECK
   Visually check for presence of safety wire passing across top of scope (AFC 166). Safety wire runs from a retaining bolt on one side of scope to a retaining bolt on other side of scope. Presence of safety wire indicates that radar scope retaining bolts are installed. On airplanes 152244v and up and all others after AFC 193, check that secondary restraining device is in place.
5. Center rear view mirror - CHECK
   Ensure mirror clears the windshield bow when canopy is closed.
6. Ejection seat and canopy rigging - CHECK

WARNING

After AFC 307, rocket motor igniter sear is under seat. Do not use area for stowage, and exercise caution when performing any function in vicinity of rocket pack, e.g., pulling rocket motor safety pin, adjusting leg restraint lines, etc.

a. Time release mechanism trip rod - Check time release mechanism trip rod secured to anchor beam and engaged in time release mechanism. Check for correct distance between the outer sleeve and the point where it bottoms against the clevis connection (approximately 1/2 inch). If the clevis connection (point where trip rod connects to the time release mechanism sear) on the inner shaft of the trip rod is bottomed down on the outer sleeve of the trip rod, the time release mechanism sear is probably not seated properly. In aircraft with locking indicator type top latch plunger, check that red color band on trip rods is not visible.

b. Seat mounted initiator firing link - Check seat mounted initiator firing link installed.

c. Banana links - Check banana links pin engaged in firing mechanism sear.

d. Canopy-seat interlock block - Check canopy-seat interlock block in place, and interlock block cable secure to canopy. After ACC 187, check interdictor pin is inserted in firing mechanism sear. The ejection seat will not fire if interlock block is not removed by canopy during ejection sequence.

e. Scissor shackle tie-down and scissor guard - Check that the scissor shackle tie-down passes under flap securing pin, around wire

EXTERIOR INSPECTION

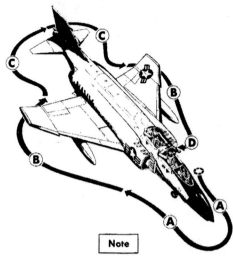

THE EXTERIOR INSPECTION HAS BEEN DIVIDED INTO FOUR AREAS AS SHOWN. FOR SIMPLICITY, THE INSPECTION BEGINS AT THE COCKPIT LADDER INCLUDING THE LEFT FORWARD NOSE AREA AND THEN ONLY THE RIGHT SIDE OF THE AIRPLANE IS DISCUSSED, EXCEPT FOR ITEMS SPECIFICALLY CALLED OUT AS LEFT SIDE (L).

Ⓐ NOSE

1. GENERAL AREA

A. REFRIGERATION UNIT INTAKE CLEAR
B. RADOME SECURE

2. UNDERSIDE OF NOSE

A. TIRE CONDITION, INFLATION, NOSE WHEEL NUTS SECURE
B. STRUT CONDITION, PROPER INFLATION, JACK PAD SECURE
C. GROUND LOCK REMOVED
D. GEAR DOORS SECURE, ROLLER FOR FREEDOM
E. APPROACH LIGHTS SECURE
F. WHEEL WELL CONDITION
G. PITOT STATIC VENT
H. EMERGENCY FLAP PRESSURE GAGE—2750 PSI TO 3100 PSI
I. RAM AIR TURBINE PRESSURE GAGE—2750 PSI TO 3100 PSI
J. EMERGENCY LANDING GEAR PRESSURE GAGE—2750 PSI TO 3100 PSI
K. EMERGENCY BRAKE AIR PRESSURE GAGE—2750 PSI TO 3100 PSI
L. WHEEL BRAKE ACCUMULATOR PRESSURE GAGE 1000 ± 50 PSI
M. FWD AND AFT CANOPY EMERGENCY JETTISON BOTTLES (INSIDE LOX SERVICE DOOR) 2750 TO 3100 PSI.

3. FORWARD FUSELAGE

A. ANGLE OF ATTACK PROBE COVER REMOVED
B. PROBE SECURE AND FREE TO ROTATE. ADJUST PROBE TO MID-RANGE.
C. ACCESS DOORS SECURE
D. INTAKE DUCT CONDITION, RAMPS SECURE

Ⓑ CENTER FUSELAGE AND WING

1. GENERAL AREA

A. CONDITION OF WING AND CENTER FUSELAGE
B. ACCESS DOORS SECURE

2. WING

A. WING FLAPS AND CONTROL SURFACES CHECK
B. EXTERNAL TANKS SECURE (VISUALLY CHECK LOCKED ON PYLON)
C. WING FOLD JURY STRUT REMOVED
D. NAVIGATION AND JOIN UP LIGHTS SECURE
E. AIR TURBINE DOOR SECURE L (TOP)

Ⓒ AFT FUSELAGE

1. GENERAL AREA

A. GENERAL CONDITION
B. ACCESS DOORS SECURE
C. PITOT COVER REMOVED
D. COLLISION LIGHT SECURE
E. AUX. AIR DOORS-CHECK THROTTLE LINKAGE SECURE
F. ENGINE ACCESS DOORS (96 L & R) SECURE
G. NOZZLE CONDITION, A/B SPRAY BAR CONDITION
H. ARRESTING HOOK UPLOCK REMOVED
I. ARRESTING HOOK CONDITION, SECURE
J. STABILATOR AND RUDDER CHECK

CHECK THE STABILATOR BY GRASPING THE STABILATOR TIPS AND PHYSICALLY ATTEMPT TO MOVE THE STABILATOR. IF THE AIRCRAFT HAS FLOWN WITHIN THE LAST TWELVE (12) HOURS AND STABILATOR TRAVEL IS GREATER THAN ONE (1) INCH, THE AIRCRAFT SHOULD BE GROUNDED FOR A MAINTENANCE CHECK.

WARNING

IF DROOPED AILERONS ARE INCORPORATED (Airplanes 152995z and up, and all others upon incorporation of AFC-218, THE AIRCRAFT MUST HAVE A SLOTTED STABILATOR INSTALLED.

K. NAVIGATION LIGHT SECURE
L. DRAG CHUTE DOOR SECURE
M. FUEL CAVITY DRAINS—DRY

Ⓓ UNDERSIDE OF FUSELAGE

1. GENERAL AREA

A. GENERAL CONDITION
B. ACCESS DOORS SECURE
C. EXTERNAL STORES SECURE
D. FUEL CAVITY DRAINS—DRY
E. PC HYDRAULIC RESERVOIRS—FULL (76 L & R)
F. MAIN PNEUMATIC GAGE, 2200 PSI MINIMUM

2. MAIN GEAR AND GEAR WELL

A. WHEELS CHOCKED
B. TIRE CONDITION, INFLATION
C. STRUT CONDITION, PROPER INFLATION, JACK PAD SECURE, SHRINK ROD STRAIGHT AND FASTENED
D. GROUND LOCK REMOVED
E. GEAR DOORS SECURE
F. SPEED BRAKE SAFETY SWITCH—NORMAL, (IF INSTALLED) GROUND FUELING SWITCH OFF (R)
G. #2 P.C.S. ACCUMULATOR PRESSURE GAGE—1000±50 PSI (R)
H. #1 P.C.S. ACCUMULATOR PRESSURE GAGE—1000±50 PSI (L)
I. SPEED BRAKES CONDITION, GROUND LOCKS REMOVED

FDB-1-(49)

Figure 3-1.

EJECTION SEAT AND CANOPY CHECK POINTS

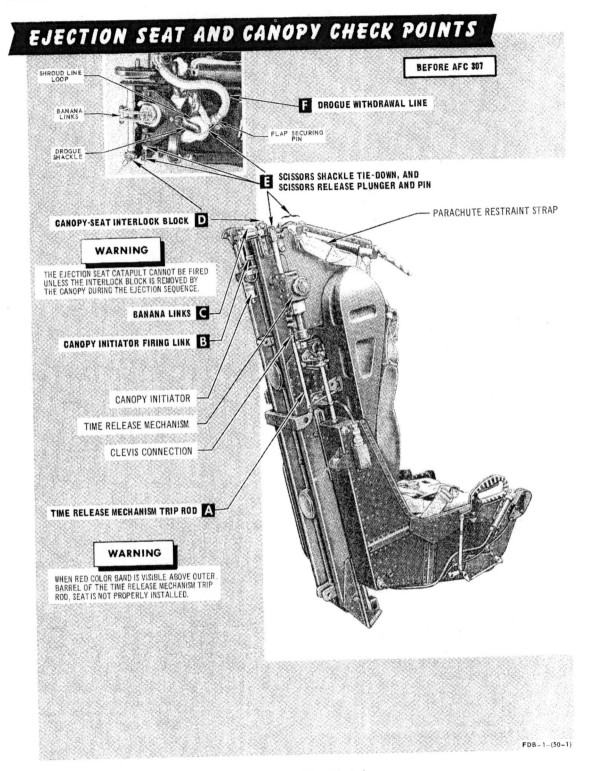

BEFORE AFC 307

SHROUD LINE LOOP

BANANA LINKS

DROGUE SHACKLE

F DROGUE WITHDRAWAL LINE

FLAP SECURING PIN

E SCISSORS SHACKLE TIE-DOWN, AND SCISSORS RELEASE PLUNGER AND PIN

PARACHUTE RESTRAINT STRAP

D CANOPY-SEAT INTERLOCK BLOCK

WARNING

THE EJECTION SEAT CATAPULT CANNOT BE FIRED UNLESS THE INTERLOCK BLOCK IS REMOVED BY THE CANOPY DURING THE EJECTION SEQUENCE.

BANANA LINKS **C**

CANOPY INITIATOR FIRING LINK **B**

CANOPY INITIATOR

TIME RELEASE MECHANISM

CLEVIS CONNECTION

TIME RELEASE MECHANISM TRIP ROD **A**

WARNING

WHEN RED COLOR BAND IS VISIBLE ABOVE OUTER BARREL OF THE TIME RELEASE MECHANISM TRIP ROD, SEAT IS NOT PROPERLY INSTALLED.

FDB-1-(50-1)

Figure 3-2. (Sheet 1 of 4)

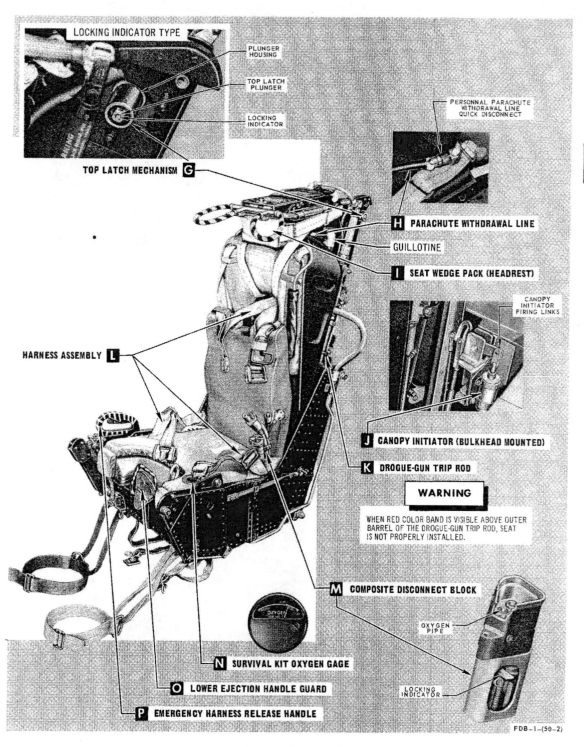

LOCKING INDICATOR TYPE

PLUNGER HOUSING

TOP LATCH PLUNGER

LOCKING INDICATOR

TOP LATCH MECHANISM **G**

PERSONNAL PARACHUTE WITHDRAWAL LINE QUICK DISCONNECT

H PARACHUTE WITHDRAWAL LINE

GUILLOTINE

I SEAT WEDGE PACK (HEADREST)

CANOPY INITIATOR FIRING LINKS

HARNESS ASSEMBLY **L**

J CANOPY INITIATOR (BULKHEAD MOUNTED)

K DROGUE-GUN TRIP ROD

WARNING

WHEN RED COLOR BAND IS VISIBLE ABOVE OUTER BARREL OF THE DROGUE-GUN TRIP ROD, SEAT IS NOT PROPERLY INSTALLED.

M COMPOSITE DISCONNECT BLOCK

OXYGEN PIPE

N SURVIVAL KIT OXYGEN GAGE

O LOWER EJECTION HANDLE GUARD

LOCKING INDICATOR

P EMERGENCY HARNESS RELEASE HANDLE

FDB-1-(50-2)

Figure 3-2. (Sheet 2 of 4)

EJECTION SEAT AND CANOPY CHECK POINTS

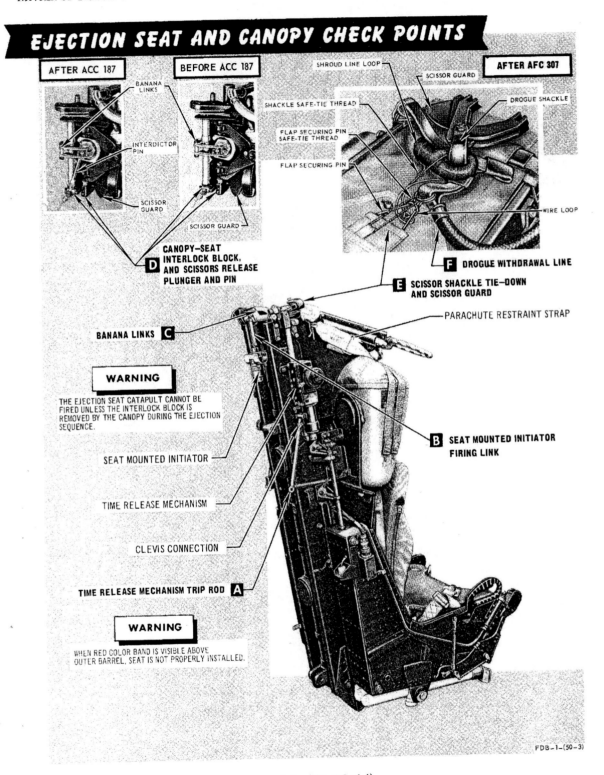

AFTER ACC 187

BANANA LINKS

INTERDICTOR PIN

SCISSOR GUARD

BEFORE ACC 187

BANANA LINKS

SCISSOR GUARD

SCISSOR GUARD

D CANOPY–SEAT INTERLOCK BLOCK, AND SCISSORS RELEASE PLUNGER AND PIN

SHROUD LINE LOOP

SCISSOR GUARD

SHACKLE SAFE-TIE THREAD

DROGUE SHACKLE

FLAP SECURING PIN SAFE-TIE THREAD

FLAP SECURING PIN

AFTER AFC 307

WIRE LOOP

F DROGUE WITHDRAWAL LINE

E SCISSOR SHACKLE TIE–DOWN AND SCISSOR GUARD

PARACHUTE RESTRAINT STRAP

BANANA LINKS **C**

WARNING

THE EJECTION SEAT CATAPULT CANNOT BE FIRED UNLESS THE INTERLOCK BLOCK IS REMOVED BY THE CANOPY DURING THE EJECTION SEQUENCE.

B SEAT MOUNTED INITIATOR FIRING LINK

SEAT MOUNTED INITIATOR

TIME RELEASE MECHANISM

CLEVIS CONNECTION

TIME RELEASE MECHANISM TRIP ROD **A**

WARNING

WHEN RED COLOR BAND IS VISIBLE ABOVE OUTER BARREL, SEAT IS NOT PROPERLY INSTALLED.

FDB–1–(50–3)

Figure 3-2. (Sheet 3 of 4)

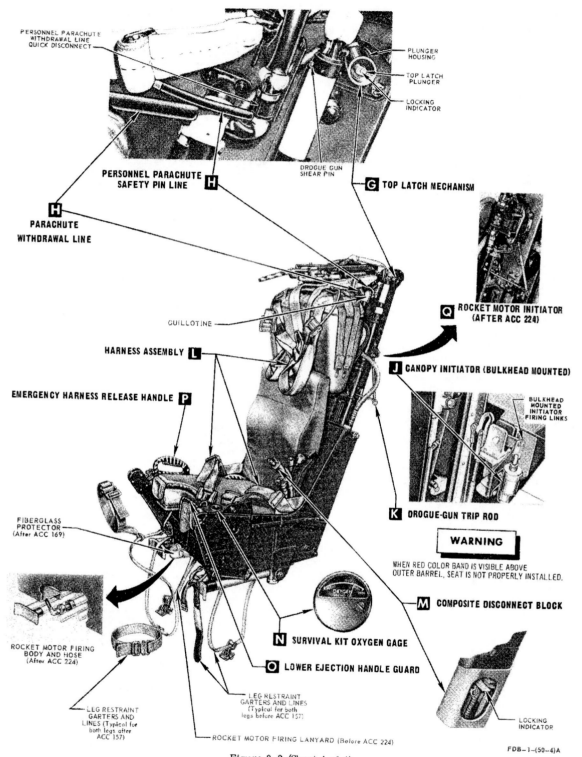

PERSONNEL PARACHUTE
WITHDRAWAL LINE
QUICK DISCONNECT

PLUNGER
HOUSING

TOP LATCH
PLUNGER

LOCKING
INDICATOR

DROGUE GUN
SHEAR PIN

PERSONNEL PARACHUTE
SAFETY PIN LINE **H**

G TOP LATCH MECHANISM

H PARACHUTE
WITHDRAWAL LINE

Q ROCKET MOTOR INITIATOR
(AFTER ACC 224)

GUILLOTINE

J CANOPY INITIATOR (BULKHEAD MOUNTED)

HARNESS ASSEMBLY **L**

BULKHEAD
MOUNTED
INITIATOR
FIRING LINKS

EMERGENCY HARNESS RELEASE HANDLE **P**

FIBERGLASS
PROTECTOR
(After ACC 169)

K DROGUE-GUN TRIP ROD

WARNING

WHEN RED COLOR BAND IS VISIBLE ABOVE
OUTER BARREL, SEAT IS NOT PROPERLY INSTALLED.

M COMPOSITE DISCONNECT BLOCK

ROCKET MOTOR FIRING
BODY AND HOSE
(After ACC 224)

N SURVIVAL KIT OXYGEN GAGE

O LOWER EJECTION HANDLE GUARD

LOCKING
INDICATOR

LEG RESTRAINT
GARTERS AND
LINES (Typical for
both legs before ACC 157)

LEG RESTRAINT
GARTERS AND
LINES (Typical for
both legs after
ACC 157)

ROCKET MOTOR FIRING LANYARD (Before ACC 224)

FDB-1-(50-4)A

Figure 3-2 (Sheet 4 of 4)

BEFORE ENTERING COCKPIT CONTINUED

loop, then aft under shroud line loop, through drogue shackle, over top of shroud line, and then forward and tied to other end of cord. Check drogue shackle engaged in scissors, and scissors plunger extended against moveable scissors arm with plunger pin visible on top of scissors plunger housing. Check the scissor guard (if applicable) on the lower right side of the scissor shackle assembly to ensure that the guard is not bent.

WARNING

A bent scissor guard could prevent the scissors jaw from opening during ejection and thereby preclude man/seat separation.

    f. Drogue withdrawal line - Check drogue withdrawal line (in wire braid sleeve) passes over and lays on top of all other lines.

    g. Top latch mechanism - Check that top latch plunger is flush with end of top latch mechanism housing. Locking indicator must be flush with end of top latch plunger.

WARNING

If top latch mechanism check does not meet outlined requirements, an inadvertent ejection could result.

    h. Parachute withdrawal line - Check that parachute withdrawal line passes through guillotine and is routed underneath parachute restraint strap. In addition check withdrawal line quick disconnect for proper connection and swivel action. On airplanes after AFC 307, check personnel parachute safety pin line not routed through guillotine, and check that both personnel parachute safety pin line and loop of personnel parachute withdrawal line pass through alignment ring on top of parachute pack.

    i. Seat wedge pack (headrest) - Check seat wedge pack has approximately 1 inch side play (H5 seats)

    j. Canopy initiator (bulkhead mounted) firing link - Check that bulkhead mounted canopy initiator firing link is installed.

CAUTION

Exercise caution regarding hand movements in vicinity of airplane mounted canopy initiator linkages. Also, do not stow flight equipment or personal items in this area. Failure to comply could result in inadvertent jettisoning of canopy.

    k. Drogue gun trip rod - Check drogue gun cocking indicator protruding approximately 1/2 inch from bottom of drogue gun (seats with ACC 56). Check drogue gun trip rod secured to anchor beam and engaged in drogue gun. In aircraft with locking indicator type of top latch plunger (ACC-19), check that red color band on trip rod is not visible.

    l. Harness assembly - Check that shoulder harness retaining pin is installed at retraction reel. Check that pins securing lap belt and survival kit to seat are in place.

    m. Composite disconnect block - Check that lower block locking indicator (yellow metal flag) is tight. Check that oxygen check valve pipe, in intermediate block, is extended. If universal upper block is being utilized, check that upper block is positively locked to intermediate block by pressing the yellow knob on composite disconnect release cable and noting that the indicator button is flush with top of knob. If the indicator button is protruding from top of knob, upper block assembly is not positively locked to intermediate block.

    n. Survival kit oxygen gage - Check survival kit oxygen gage for at least 1800 psi pressure.

WARNING

If RSSK-1A survival kit is installed in ejection seat, seat must also have a lumbar pad installed (AFC 274). If RSSK-1A Survival Kit and lumbar pad compatibility is not present, and ejection becomes necessary, seat occupant will most likely suffer a fractured vertebra.

    o. Lower ejection handle guard - Check lower ejection handle guard is in up (vertical) position.

    p. Emergency harness release handle - Check emergency harness release handle down, and firing sear installed in guillotine initiator.

    q. Rocket motor initiator and rocket motor firing body (if applicable) - check initiator cable lanyard connected to drogue gun trip rod without excessive cable hanging from initiator housing. Initiator sear installed with cable lever assembly link inserted. Initiator hose connected with hose pin in hose connection (not in initiator sear). On bottom of seat, rocket motor firing body installed and hose connected.

7. Check under seat for foreign objects, for rocket motor firing lanyard connected to floor fitting and ensure rocket motor sear is clear (H7 seats if applicable).
    On airplanes after AFC 307, ensure area beneath seat is clear of foreign objects before pulling rocket motor sear safety pin.

N E W

8. Seat safety pins, except face curtain pin and after ACC 187, the interdictor pin - REMOVE
   Check seat safety pins - ejection gun (before ACC 187), guillotine, seat mounted initiator, drogue gun, rocket motor (H7 seats after AFC 307 and before ACC 224), canopy initiator (bulkhead mounted), rocket motor initiator (after AFC 307 and ACC 224), and both dust covers removed (if applicable).

9. Aft cockpit electrical test receptacle - ENSURE CAP TIGHTENED.

BEFORE ENTERING COCKPIT CONTINUED

Note

It is possible to trip both generators off the line if the electrical test receptacle 3P325 under the right canopy sill is loose. The generators cannot be restored until the cap is tightened.

AFTER ENTERING COCKPIT
PILOT

Before electrical power -

1. Oxygen, communications, anti-G lines and helmet mounted sight (if applicable) - CONNECT

   On seats prior to universal upper block, check upper block properly inserted and locked into intermediate block by exerting an upward pull on block assembly after composite disconnect release knob is locked to cable housing. On seats with universal upper blocks, connect oxygen, communications and anti-G inline disconnects, as applicable, and check for positive lock. When the helmet mounted sight is utilized verify that the VTAS egress disconnect will operate normally. After connection, an upward motion from the snap location (seated) should effect release. Reconnect and verify that the movement flange is seated to preclude inadvertent disconnection during maneuvers. During disconnection, a taut lanyard moves the flange to release the lock.

   WARNING

   An improperly operating VTAS egress disconnect could cause serious injury during ejection.

   Note

   The composite disconnect should be carefully inserted with downward force parallel to seat ejection plane. After composite disconnect is fully inserted, push down on composite disconnect release knob to lock knob to cable housing and prevent release knob from laying over and dangling.

2. Pressure suit lines - CONNECTED (if applicable)

   WARNING

   When pressure suit is being worn without anti-G garment, anti-G hose must not be connected and corresponding port on pressure suit must be capped. Explosive decompression results upon ejection if anti-G hose is connected. If ejection over water or ditching, watertight integrity of pressure suit is nullified.

3. Pressure suit vent air valve - ON AS DESIRED (if applicable)
4. Oxygen - CHECK

   Turn oxygen selector on, check normal flow with mask held away from face. Put mask on, check normal breathing. Turn oxygen off, check no breathing.

   WARNING

   Do not pull emergency oxygen manual release before actual use. If emergency oxygen manual release is actuated prior to intended use, pressure reducer manifold may not prevent emergency oxygen from flowing to suit controller and/or oxygen regulator. If this happens, crewmember has no way of knowing how much, or if any, emergency oxygen remains and has no way of replenishing depleted supply.

5. Leg restraint lines - CONNECTED

   Pass leg lines through garters so that D-rings are on aft inboard side of calf and plugged into seat pin. Assure that leg lines are not twisted. For dual garter restrainers, route untwisted lines first through lower garter (double rings) and then through thigh garter (single ring) before inserting lock pins in snubber boxes.

   WARNING

   It is imperative that leg restraint system be hooked up at all times during flight to ensure legs are pulled aft upon ejection. This prevents leg injury and enhances seat stability by preventing legs from flailing following ejection. An unhooked leg restraint system necessitates pulling legs aft against seat to preclude hitting canopy bow. This action causes spine to flex and increases possibility of spinal injury during ejection.

6. Harnessing - FASTENED

   WARNING

   Make sure harness assembly is securely fastened to seat. Pins must be in their proper receptacles, one pin on each side of bucket seat and one pin on harness locking reel assembly. Emergency harness release handle must be down.

AFTER ENTERING COCKPIT CONTINUED
PILOT

> **WARNING**
>
> The over the shoulder oxygen-communication integrated line must be routed under shoulder harness to preclude possibility of crewmembers helmet being jerked from his head after ejection. This action is caused by left parachute riser (shoulder harness strap) snapping up against integrated line with opening of personnel parachute.

7. Shoulder harness handle - CHECK OPERATION
8. Face curtain pin - REMOVE

> **WARNING**
>
> • To prevent inadvertent firing of seat or canopy, all ejection seat safety pins must be either installed or removed and properly stowed before operating the canopy.
>
> • When removing or checking for removal of face curtain safety pin, make sure that safety pin shank has been removed from hole. Safety pin collar has been known to separate from pin shank upon attempted safety pin removal leaving pin shank in hole and face curtain safetied.
>
> • Do not pull down on face curtain ejection handle. Seat and canopy ejection systems are fully armed when safety pins are removed.

9. Lower ejection handle safety guard - AS DESIRED.

> **WARNING**
>
> Lower ejection handle safety guard, when lowered, can rebound to safe position if it is lowered too rapidly. This could consume critical time when lowering guard for a low altitude ejection.

10. Rudder pedals - ADJUST
11. Stick grip - SAFETY WIRED
12. Armament safety override switch - OUT

> **WARNING**
>
> If armament safety override switch is IN with landing gear handle down, and electrical power is applied to aircraft, landing gear armament safety feature is bypassed and power is supplied to armament bus relay. This could result in advertent dropping or firing of ordnance while aircraft is on ground.

13. Guns switch - OFF (some aircraft)
14. Strike camera mode switch - OFF (some aircraft)
15. Intercom control panel - CHECK
    a. Volume selector knob - AS DESIRED
    b. Function selector switch - HOT MIC
16. Fuel control panel - SET
    a. External tank jettison switch - NORMAL (guard closed)
    b. Buddy fill switch - STOP FILL
    c. Internal wing transfer switch - NORMAL
    d. Refuel selection switch - AS DESIRED
    e. Refuel probe switch - RETRACT
    f. Boost pump check switches - NORMAL
    g. External transfer switch - OUTBD or CENTER
    h. Internal wing dump switch - NORMAL
    i. Wing transfer pressure switch - NORMAL
17. Smoke abate switch - OFF
18. RAT handle - RETRACT AND SECURE
19. Wing flap switch - COINCIDES WITH FLAP POSITION
20. Wing flap emergency pull handle - UP
21. Communication antenna selector switch - UPR
    Electromagnetic interference (EMI) radiating from lower UHF antenna may interfere with nose wheel steering system. Therefore use of lower UHF antenna is restricted to inflight operation.
22. Engine anti-icing switch - NORMAL
23. Throttles - OFF
24. Master lights switch - OFF
25. Speed brake switch - STOP (NEUTRAL)
26. Throttle friction lever - SET AS DESIRED
27. Engine master switches - OFF
28. Engine start switch - NEUTRAL
29. ARI Circuit breaker - IN
30. Emergency speed brake switch - GUARD DOWN
31. Approach power compensator switch - OFF
32. Instrument light control knob - AS REQUIRED (some aircraft)
33. Emergency aileron droop switch - NORMAL (some aircraft)
34. Drag chute handle - DOWN
35. Landing gear handle - DOWN
36. VTAS power switch - OFF (some aircraft)
37. Radar altimeter - OFF
38. Missile jettison selector switch - OFF
39. Missile power switch - OFF
40. Missile arm switch - SAFE
41. Missile select switch - RADAR
42. Missile interlock switch - IN
43. Centerline station safety switch - SAFE (airplanes 150406L and up)
44. Bomb control switch - OFF
45. Multiple weapons master arm switch - SAFE (airplanes prior to 152278w before ASC 241)
46. Weapons switch - AS REQUIRED (airplanes 152278w and up and all others after ASC 241)
47. Data link bomb switch - MANUAL (some aircraft)
48. Multiple weapons nose and tail arm switch - SAFE
49. Multiple weapons station selector switch - OFF
50. Accelerometer - SET
51. Altimeter - SET

52. Vertical velocity indicator - CHECK
53. Clock - WIND and SET
54. Navigation function selector panel - SET
55. Manual canopy unlock handle - FWD
56. Arresting hook control handle - UP
57. Generator control switches - OFF
58. DCU-75/A arming switch - OFF
59. Emergency vent knob - IN
60. Defog footheat handle - AS REQUIRED
61. Rain removal switch - OFF/LOW
62. Pitot heat switch - OFF
63. Bleed air switch - NORM
64. Communications function selector switch - STBY
65. Tacan function selector switch - STBY
66. Compass system controller - SET
    a. Latitude compensator - SET
    b. Mode switch - SLAVE
67. Circuit breakers - IN
68. Cockpit temperature control panel - CHECK
    a. Heat knob - SET AS DESIRED
    b. Temperature control switch - AUTO

WARNING

MAN position of temperature control switch should not be used except as a back-up in case of failure in automatic system. The full hot manual position can produce temperatures in excess of 300°C at mil power settings.

69. Instrument panel emergency floodlights switch - OFF
70. ECM warning lights switch - OFF
71. IFF master knob - OFF/MODE SET
72. Cockpit lights - OFF
73. Exterior lights - AS DESIRED
74. Wing fold switch - COINCIDES WITH WING POSITION
75. Spare lamps - CHECK
76. KY-28 power switch - OFF (some aircraft)
77. KY-28 cipher switch - P (some aircraft)
78. ILS (ARA-63) power switch - OFF (some aircraft)
79. Flight instrument balance control panel - AS REQUIRED (some aircraft)
80. Flashlight, charts and reference material - CHECK

After electrical power -

CAUTION

Do not place generator control switch to EXT until external power has been connected and has had time to reach rated voltage and frequency.

81. Generator control switch - EXT ON
82. KY-28 (if installed) - AS DESIRED

83. Data link light control - AS DESIRED (some aircraft)
84. Cockpit lights - AS DESIRED
85. ECM warning lights switch - ON (some aircraft)
86. Seat - ADJUST
87. ICS - CHECK
88. Warning lights - CHECK
    Depress warning light test switch and note master caution light, warning lights panel, radar scope warning lights, missile status panel, arresting hook warning light, ECM warning lights (some aircraft) and land-gear warning lights are illuminated. Check warning lights dimming circuit by holding warning lights test button depressed and rotating instrument panel lights control knob from OFF to BRIGHT. Warning lights should dim and revert to bright when knob is returned to OFF.
89. Fire warning light - CHECK
    Depress the fire check button and note engine FIRE/OVERHT and the three BLEED AIR OVERHT warning lights illuminate.
90. Fuel quantity - CHECK
    Check fuel quantity indicators against known fuel quantity.
91. Fuel quantity gage - CHECK
    Actuate feed tank check switch and check fuel gage reads feed tank fuel (approx. 2100 lbs).
92. Landing gear indicator - CHECK
    Check landing gear position indicators indicate gear down.
93. Flap position indicator - SAME AS FLAPS
    Check flap position indicator corresponds with flap position.
94. Liquid oxygen gage - CHECK
95. Eject light system - CHECK
    Depress light switch and check that both front and rear cockpit EJECT lights illuminate. Depress switch again and check that both lights extinguish.
96. Master lights switch - AS REQUIRED
97. Boost pumps and engine fuel shutoff valve - CHECK
    Observe boost pump pressure indicators while actuating boost pump check switches one at a time. Normal pressure (30 ± 5) on side being checked indicates engine fuel shutoff valve open and boost pump running. Concurrent pressure on other indicator indicates other valve faulty (not properly closed). Lack of pressure on side being checked indicates faulty valve (not properly open) or pump inoperative. Also, note that zero fuel flow is registered on left fuel flow indicator.

CAUTION

Allow minimum of 3 seconds between release of one fuel boost pump test switch and actuation of other. Failure to do so could result in burning of switch contacts and subsequent engine flameout.

AFTER ENTERING COCKPIT CONTINUED
RIO

Before electrical power -

1. Composite disconnect or inline disconnects -
   INSERTED and LOCKED
   On seats prior to universal upper block,
   check upper block properly inserted and
   locked into intermediate block by exerting an
   upward pull on block assembly after composite disconnect release knob is locked to cable
   housing. On seats with universal upper blocks
   connect oxygen, communications and anti-G
   inline disconnects, as applicable, and check
   for positive lock.
2. Oxygen - CHECK
   Turn oxygen selector on, check normal flow
   with mask held away from face. Put mask on,
   check normal breathing. Turn oxygen off,
   check no breathing.
3. Pressure suit lines - CONNECTED (is applicable)
4. Pressure suit vent air valve - ON AS DESIRED
   (if applicable)
5. Leg restraint lines - CONNECTED
   Pass leg lines through garters so that D-rings
   are on aft inboard side of calf and plugged into the seat pan. Assure that the leg lines are
   not twisted. For dual garter restrainers,
   route untwisted lines first through lower garter (double rings) and then through thigh garter (single ring) before inserting lock pins in
   snubber boxes.
6. Harnessing - FASTENED
7. Shoulder harness handle - CHECK OPERATION
8. Face curtain pin - REMOVE
9. Lower ejection handle guard - AS DESIRED

WARNING

The lower ejection handle safety guard, when
lowered, can rebound to the safe position if
it is lowered too rapidly. This could consume
critical time when lowering guard for a low
altitude ejection.

---

10. Destruct circuit arm switch - PIN INSTALLED
    (some aircraft)
11. Data link radar display switch - OFF (some
    aircraft)
12. Data link BIT switch - NORM (some aircraft)
13. TACAN - STBY
14. UHF - STBY
15. Command selector valve handle - POSITION
    IN ACCORDANCE WITH TYPE COMMANDER/
    SQUADRON POLICY (After AFC 307)

CAUTION

Before AFC 526, when actuating the command
selector valve from the closed (vertical) to
open (horizontal) position, pull the handle

---

straight out allowing the cam action of the
valve to rotate the handle to the open position.
This procedure will prolong the service life
of the selector valve. After AFC 526, the
handle is turned by the application of torque
only, and there is no requirement to pull the
handle.

16. Navigational computer - OFF
17. Radar scope - AS DESIRED (some aircraft)
18. Radar set control panel - EXTENDED
19. Radar power switch - OFF
20. Radar Beacon power switch - OFF (some air-
    craft)
21. ALQ-91 function selector switch - OFF (some
    aircraft)

CAUTION

If AN/ALQ-91 function switch is not in OFF
when aircraft is switched to internal power,
damage to equipment or a blown fuse may
result.

---

22. Antenna hand control panel - EXTEND
23. Circuit breakers - CHECK
24. AN/AJB dc circuit breaker (E7) - PULL
    (Prior to 152273w before AFC 202)
25. Gyro cut-out switch - GYRO CUT OUT
26. Manual canopy unlock handle - FORWARD
27. AMCS BIT air data switch - SIMULATED
28. Altimeter - SET
29. Eject light - CHECK
30. Clock - CHECK
31. Intercom function selector switch - AS DESIRED
32. Navigation selector switch - CNI
33. Communication antenna selector switch -
    UPPER
34. Lights - AS DESIRED
35. Antenna switch - DISABLE (some aircraft)
36. Navigational computer - SET/STBY
37. AN/ALE-29A dispenser selector knob - OFF
    (some aircraft)
38. AN/ALQ-51A/100/126 mode selector knob -
    OFF (some aircraft)
39. APR-27/ALR-50 power switch - OFF (some
    aircraft)
40. DRSC power switch - OFF
41. Data link power switch - OFF (some aircraft)

After electrical power -

42. Destruct circuit arm switch pin - REMOVE
43. Oxygen quantity gage - CHECK
44. Nav command - AS DESIRED
45. Comm command - AS BRIEFED
46. Nav channel - AS BRIEFED
47. Aux channel - AS BRIEFED
48. Comm channel - AS BRIEFED
49. Essential dc bus test button - DEPRESS
    Depress button and check that essential dc
    bus indicator light illuminates. If light illu-
    minates, both transformer-rectifiers are
    delivering dc power. If the light does not il-
    luminate, one or both transformer-rectifiers
    are inoperative or not receiving power.
50. Radar set control switches - AS REQUIRED

51. Nav selector switch - NAV COMP
    Check DME runoff to zero, note error and
    return switch to CNI.
52. Warning lights - TEST
53. Seat - ADJUST
54. Circuit breakers - CHECK IN
55. Canopy - CLOSE and CHECK
    Close aft canopy first, report aft canopy light
    out.
56. Notify pilot - PRE-START CHECKS COM-
    PLETE - CIRCUIT BREAKERS IN

BEFORE STARTING ENGINES

PILOT

1. Wheels - CHOCKED
2. Fire bottle - MANNED
3. Intake and exhaust areas - CLEAR
4. Boarding steps - UP
5. External air supply - CONNECTED AND PRES-
   SURE UP
6. Rudder - CHECK MOVEMENT
7. Inform RIO - READY TO START

STARTING ENGINES

Whenever practicable, start and run up engines on
paved surface to minimize possibility of foreign objects being drawn into compressor with resultant
engine damage. Start engines with nose into or at
right angle to wind as exhaust temperatures may be
aggravated by tail wind.

| WARNING |

• Suction at intake is sufficient to kill or severely injure personnel drawn into or pulled
  suddenly against the duct.

• Danger areas aft of airplane are created by
  high exhaust temperature and velocities.
  The danger increases with afterburner operation.

Note

The procedure of performing an actual engine
start on the right engine first was adopted
to ascertain that both utility hydraulic system
pumps are operating. The right engine pump
delivers 2775 ± 225 psi at idle rpm, and the
left engine pump delivers 3000 ± 250 psi at
idle rpm. Therefore, the single needle utility
hydraulic pressure indicator cannot be used
to determine pump operation unless the right
engine is started first.

PILOT

| CAUTION |

With flaps extended, BLC ducts are open and
loss of engine bleed air while attempting to

start engines may result in a hot or false
(no-ignition) start. If it is imperative that
a start be made with flaps down, the starting
procedure recommended for starting with low
air pressure should be utilized with exception
that start should be initiated at normal starting rpm.

1. Throttles - OFF
2. External compressed air source - CONNECTED
3. Engine master switches - ON
4. Engine start switch - RIGHT

| CAUTION |

If there is no indication of engine rpm within
15 seconds, or no indication of oil pressure
within 30 seconds after start cycle begins,
shut down immediately and investigate.

Note

When attempting an engine start, there is a
possibility that starter air valve does not
open when start switch is actuated. This
does not mean that the solenoid operated
valve is completely inoperative, it may be
that the valve is only sticking closed. If the
valve does not open, have air shut off at the
starter cart and then actuate start switch.
The stuck valve, unopposed by air pressure,
may open.

5. At 10% rpm, right engine ignition button -
   DEPRESS
   At approximately 10% rpm, depress right
   engine ignition button and simultaneously
   advance the throttle half-way up the quadrant
   and then snap it back to the idle stop position
   while monitoring fuel flow. If the throttle is
   properly rigged, the snap-back will not affect initial starting fuel flow. However, if a
   momentary drop of more than 75 pph below
   minimum starting fuel flow is indicated, the
   throttle is out of rig. This can be confirmed
   by snapping the throttle forward and back
   several times while keeping ignition button
   depressed.

| CAUTION |

With normal starting air pressure available,
do not attempt to start engine before reaching 10% rpm. If the starting procedure is
initiated at a lower rpm, additional heat distress of the engine hot section is anticipated.
Overtemperature of turbine generally occurs
during a low rpm start if starter air is inadvertently interrupted during start cycle.
However, starting below 10% rpm may be
helpful with a hard-to-start engine in an
emergency situation.

STARTING ENGINES CONTINUED

PILOT

Note

The engine usually fires at approximately 10 to 16% rpm.

CAUTION

If engine does not light off by the time fuel flow reaches 800 pph or within 15 seconds after fuel flow or pressure is indicated, chop throttle to full OFF, release ignition button.

6. Release ignition button when light-off is indicated by a sudden increase in EGT.

CAUTION

If engine does not continue to accelerate after light-off, discontinue start.

7. Start switch - NEUTRAL
   When engine is operating at a self-sustaining rpm (usually about 45%), move starter switch to neutral position.
8. Exhaust temperature gage - CHECK WITHIN LIMITS (980°C max for 10 sec.)

CAUTION

• At no time, should EGT exceed temperature limits as defined in the Engine Exhaust Temperature Limitations Chart, section I, part 2, of this manual.

• With only one engine in operation, do not move control stick (surface controls) excessively. If stick is moved rapidly with hydraulic pressure on only one side of the tandem power cylinders, fluid that is in the other side of the cylinder is forced back through the return line to the reservoir, filling the reservoir, and either rupturing reservoir or forcing the excess fluid overboard. The seals within the tandem power cylinders may also be damaged due to ingesting and expelling of air and lack of lubrication. The power control hydraulic systems must be reserviced and checked.

Note

After engine reaches idle rpm and stabilizes, EGT should recede and stabilize.

9. Fuel flow indicator - CHECK
   Fuel flow should not exceed 800 pph at light-off, up to 2400 pph during transition to idle, and 800 to 1400 pph at IDLE.

Note

Fuel consumed while starting engines is approximately 65 pounds.

CAUTION

If fuel flow is in excess of 800 pph, a hot start likely results.

10. Oil pressure gage - CHECK
    Check oil pressure 12 psi minimum at idle rpm.

Note

• With right engine started, PC-2 and utility hydraulic pressure indicators should read within normal. CHECK HYD GAGES warning light remains illuminated until the other engine is started and all four hydraulic pumps (PC-1, PC-2 and utility) are operating properly.

• If throttles cannot be returned to OFF, engine may be shut down from any throttle setting by placing the respective engine master switch OFF. This closes corresponding fuel shutoff valve, thus depriving the engine of fuel. The engine(s) flame out in approximately 5 seconds from mil power.

CAUTION

After any wet start or false (no-ignition) start allow 1-minute or longer for the combustion system to drain before starting engine.

11. Generator control switches - GEN ON
    Left generator warning light is illuminated and bus tie warning light is out.

Note

Oil pressure should be below 50 psi before placing the generator control switches to GEN ON.

12. Start the left engine as per steps 4 thru 10.

Note

In the event of low ambient temperatures, the bus tie light (parallel bus airplanes only) may not immediately go out after left engine is started and left generator light goes out. This may be due to failure of generators to synchronize quickly because of cold oil in left generator CSD.

13. External/power/air - DISCONNECT
14. Cycle right generator control switch OFF.

WARNING

If both generator switches are placed OFF with engines running, auxiliary air doors close violently. On airplanes 148412h and 150406L and up, speed brakes also close when electrical power is removed.

15. Check both boost pump pressure gages for normal indications.
    a. Check that the right generator warning light illuminates and the bus tie warning light remains out.
16. Right generator control switch - GEN ON.
    a. With both generators in the GEN ON position, the generator warning lights and the bus tie light go out within 5 seconds.

Note

If the BUS TIE light does not extinguish within 18 seconds, (parallel bus airplanes only) accelerate either engine to approximately 70% rpm and re-cycle the right generator.

17. Notify RIO - BUS TIE LIGHT OUT

Note

• Non-start or abnormal starts shall be logged on the yellow sheet (OPNAV FORM 3760-2).

• Fuel consumption at idle rpm is approximately 42 ppm.

• After satisfactory starts are accomplished, engines do not require any warm-up time prior to placing throttles in any position.

RIO

1. Notify pilot of any emergency signals noted from ground crew.

STARTING WITH LOW AIR PRESSURE

If low pressure units are employed for operational necessity, and starting rpm seems to be hanging up, proceed as follows:

Note

When attempting an engine start, there is a possibility that starter air valve does not open when start switch is actuated. This does not mean that the solenoid operated valve is completely inoperative; it may be that the valve is only sticking closed. If the valve does not open, have air shut off at the starter cart and then actuate start switch. The stuck valve unopposed by air pressure may open.

At any rpm over 5%.-

1. Ignition button - DEPRESS, THROTTLE IDLE
2. Exhaust gas temperature - MONITOR
3. If EGT starts to move up rapidly as it passes 650°C - DISCONTINUE START, THROTTLE OFF
4. Let engine coast until EGT drops to 250°C - DEPRESS IGNITION BUTTON, THROTTLE IDLE

At 250°C the engine rpm should be approximately 12% rpm, so the second relight should be successful. If it is not successful, repeat procedure, cutting engine when it starts to overtemp and relighting when it cools to 250°C. A little rpm is gained each time.

CAUTION

Do not attempt to manually meter fuel flow with throttles between OFF and IDLE. This results in a premature hot section deterioration without any abnormal EGT indications.

BEFORE TAXIING

PILOT

1. IFF-SIF - STBY/ON
2. Compass system controller - SET
   a. Sync button - PUSH
   b. Sync indicator - CHECK

Note

Wings must be spread and locked prior to compass sync to prevent false bearing information.

3. Tacan - ON
4. Radios - ON
5. Altimeter and SPC - SET and CHECK
   a. Obtain field barometric pressure from tower and set altimeter barometric pressure correction dial. Altimeter pointer should indicate field elevation within ± 75 feet.
   b. With angle of attack set between 13-25 units. place SPC switch in RESET CORR position, the STATIC CORR OFF light should go out and remain extinguished. After reset, the altimeter should indicate within ± 40 feet of the before reset indication. Altimeter oscillations of any magnitude are unacceptable.

Note

On some aircraft altimeter may momentarily jump up to 90 feet before settling to actual engagement error. Disregard this initial momentary jump.

c. With static correction on (SPC engaged), set altimeter pointer to field elevation. Check difference between front and rear cockpit

BEFORE TAXIING CONTINUED
PILOT

altimeters. This difference should not exceed 0.06 inches Hg.

6. ADI and standby attitude indicator - SET
   On aircraft prior to 152273w before AFC 202 RIO must have reset AN-AJB-3A dc circuit breaker.

7. Electronic altimeter - ON & SET
   Turn altimeter on and set low altitude limit. On airplanes 152207t and up and all others after AFC 177 ensure that altitude pointer moves to 5 ± 5 feet after warm-up while on ground.

8. AFCS - CHECK

9. Trim switches - CHECK AND SET FOR TAKE-OFF
   Check operation of trim switches and set rudder and aileron trim to neutral. Set stabilator trim to 1 unit nose down. (Use 2 units nose down in airplanes which have downsprings removed, after AFC 308.)

Note

Before engaging stab aug, neutralize controls by using the force transducer to place control stick in the vertical position. Use of stick grip to neutralize controls introduces erroneous signals into system.

   a. Stab aug switch(es) - ENGAGE
   b. AFCS switch - ENGAGE

Note

● If stick is not off fwd or aft stops, AFCS may not engage.

● On airplanes 152331x thru 153048aa before AFC 203, engage altitude hold switch immediately after engagement of the AFCS. If altitude hold switch does not remain engaged, a malfunction or out of synchronization condition exists in pitch channel of AFCS. If pitch malfunction is indicated do not use AFCS. This malfunction does not affect stab aug operation.

   c. AFCS-ARI disengage switch - DEPRESS
      Check that all switches on AFCS panel return to OFF.

Note

In airplanes 153049aa and up, and in all others after AFC 203, only the AFCS switch moves to OFF when AFCS/ARI emergency disengage switch is depressed. The stab aug switches must be individually disengaged.

   d. Stab aug switches - DISENGAGE (if engaged)

Perform steps 10 thru 15 upon signal from plane captain:

10. Wings - SPREAD AND LOCKED

11. Speed brakes - CYCLE
    Ascertain from ground crew that speed brakes are fully closed and warning light is out.

12. Flap switch - CYCLE and CHECK
    Actuate the flaps to the 1/2 and DN position. While cycling flaps, have ground crew confirm that both trailing edge flaps extend together at the same rate and that both ailerons droop together at the same rate. Check that the BLC system is operating. Return flaps to 1/2.

13. Flight control surfaces and hydraulic systems - CHECK TRAVEL, NOTE PRESSURE DROP
    a. Cycle the flight controls and check corresponding movement of the control surface. While cycling the ailerons, check ARI (10° stab aug off, 15° stab aug on) by noting corresponding rudder movement.
    b. When checking the stabilator on airplanes with downsprings installed, pull stick full aft and release gently. The stick should return to its forward position. On airplanes with downsprings removed, set takeoff pitch trim (2 units nose down) and release the control stick from the full aft stop. The control stick should move forward to at least the 1/2 travel position, and further movement toward the forward stop should require no more than approximately one pound push force. Moderate stick movement should be smooth and free of any restrictions.

14. Flap switch - UP
    Actuate the flaps to UP and monitor the BLC MALFUNCTION light for a valve MALFUNCTION.

15. Close canopy and cycle probe and RAT - CHECK IFR PROBE UNLOCKED LIGHT OUT
    Prior to cycling probe, close canopy to preclude fuel being sprayed into the cockpits in the event the air refueling probe leaks.

16. Arresting hook - CYCLE (avoid abrupt movement)

17. Canopy rigging - CHECK and PREFLIGHT
    a. Engines - IDLE
    b. Cabin pressure vent knob - IN
    c. Foot heat/defog vent knob - AFT
    d. Cockpit temp control knob - SET AT 2 O'CLOCK
    e. Aft canopy - CLOSE, LIGHT OUT
    f. Front canopy - CLOSE (Closing and locking not to exceed 9 seconds)
       The canopy is closed when warning light is out, alignment marks aligned, and overcenter links moved over center.
    g. Open aft canopy, keep forward canopy closed and repeat timing check on aft canopy.
    h. If either canopy fails timing check, inflight loss of canopy may result.

18. Tune AIM-7 missiles (if aboard)
    Refer to section VIII of Classified Supplement for missile tuning procedures.

19. Perform VTAS test (some aircraft)
    Refer to section VIII of Classified Supplement and NATOPS Checklist for test procedures.

20. Perform dogfight computer BIT (some aircraft)
    Refer to section VIII of Classified Supplement
    and NATOPS Checklist for BIT procedures.
21. Anti-collision light - ON (day or night) and all
    external lights ON (dusk to dawn) during shore-
    based operations.
22. Perform digital and command display indicator
    BIT checks (some aircraft).
    Refer to Data Link System, section VIII,
    Classified Supplement.
23. Perform ILS (ARA-63) BIT (some aircraft)
24. Report - READY TO TAXI

RIO

1. Ascertain from the pilot that generator control
   switches are ON and bus tie and generator
   warning lights are out.
2. AN/AJB-3A dc circuit breaker (E-7) - IN
   (Prior to 152273w before AFC 202)
3. Vertical gyro cut-out (VGI) switch - NORMAL
4. Remote attitude indicator (VGI) - SET
5. Radios - TR + G
6. Tacan - T/R
7. Altimeter - SET and CHECK (in conjunction
   with pilot check)
8. Clock - SET
9. Radar power switch - STBY
10. Perform BIT as required.
    Refer to Section VIII, Classified Supplement,
    and NATOPS Checklist for BIT procedures.
11. Perform NavComp ground check, and set.
    Refer to section I, part 2.
12. Data link system operation - CHECK (some
    aircraft)
    Refer to Data Link System, section VIII,
    Classified Supplement for universal test mes-
    sage checks, data link BIT checks and digital
    display indicator BIT checks.
13. Data link BIT switch - NORM (some aircraft)

WARNING

Do not select BIT checks with the data link
BIT switch, on the cockpit lights/data link
control panel, while in flight. This could result in application of deflection signals to the
aircraft control surfaces.

14. ECM equipment operation - CHECK (some air-
    craft)
    Refer to section V, supplement to Tactical
    Manual for BIT procedures.
15. Vent air - AS DESIRED
16. Report - READY FOR TAXI

TAXIING

PILOT

High takeoff gross weight combined with the small
wheels and tires dictate that a positive technique be
used while taxiing this aircraft. After the chocks
have been pulled, add power as required on both engines and engage nose gear steering. After the aircraft has started rolling, check the brakes and reduce power. Taxi at the lowest practicable rpm and
use nose gear steering for directional control, where
possible, to minimize brake heating. Do not ride or
pump the brakes; use a steady pressure when needed.
Keep the taxi speed slow and make as few stops as
possible. Slow the aircraft before entering a turn to
reduce side loads while in the turn. Make turns as
wide as practicable, 75 foot radius if possible, at 12
to 13 knots. See figure 3-3 for minimum turning
radius and ground clearance.

RIO

1. Complete BIT Checks if not previously completed.
2. Radar power switch - STBY or OPR

TAKEOFF

BEFORE TAKEOFF

When in the run-up area, allow the aircraft to roll straight ahead to align the nose wheel. Apply brakes with a firm, steady pressure and assure flaps are up. Note idle RPM, EGT and fuel flow of both engines. Check engines individually at MIL power and observe that the RPM, EGT, exhaust nozzle, fuel flow, oil pressure and hydraulic pressure are within their normal operating ranges on the engine being checked; also check that the RPM, EGT and fuel flow on the idling engine remain stable and that ramps are fully retracted.

CAUTION

During engine run-up with flaps full up, a rise in rpm above 67.5 percent, a drop in EGT of more than 25°C, or a drop of more than 100 pph in fuel flow on the idling engine indicates a defective bleed air check valve on that engine. In cases where this check cannot be made at full military power, a valid check for an inoperative valve may be made at 80% rpm. Failure indications with such a check would be proportionally lower and should be verified at full military power if possible. This check performed with the flaps in any position other than full up is invalid.

To guard against possible engine flame-out during throttle chops at low altitude, check the throttle rigging and fuel control behavior by abruptly retarding each throttle from MIL power to IDLE. Monitor the fuel flow indicators. The momentary minimum acceptable fuel flow during this check is 445 pph on engines with fuel controls that do not have the cool start cam installed and 330 pph on engines with fuel controls that have the cool start cam. Observe that engine rpm returns to its originally noted value.

Note

- If fuel flow drops below 445 pph (without cool start cam) or 330 pph (with cool start cam), but engine recovers to original rpm, proceed with flight; however, do not snap decelerate these engines below 10,000 feet.

- Of engine rpm fails to recover to original idle rpm value, regardless of fuel flow reading, flight should be aborted.

- It is mandatory that an entry be made in OPNAV Form 3760-2 (Yellow Sheet) on all engines which drop below minimum fuel flow during snap deceleration and/or fail to recover to the original idle rpm.

Do not attempt to check the engine in the MAX power range and do not operate the engine at MIL power with the flaps down for a period longer than 1 minute.

When the engine checks are completed, complete the remainder of the takeoff checklist.

CAUTION

If canopy closure is attempted with engines running, engines should not be operating above a stabilized idle rpm. Attempted canopy closure with engine rpm above idle may result in canopy not fully locking due to back pressure caused by the aircraft pressurization system.

FLAP POSITIONS

Three flap positions are available for takeoff; half-flaps, full-flaps, and no-flaps. However, the half-flap configuration is recommended for all takeoffs. Full-flaps is not an acceptable takeoff configuration for field operations since it affords no advantages, and many disadvantages (increased drag, reduced thrust, reduced stabilator effectiveness and large trim change during transition to climb) over any other flap configuration. No flaps is not a recommended takeoff configuration. If a no-flap takeoff is attempted in a heavy or draggy aircraft in the same distance as a half-flap takeoff, the attitude of the aircraft at lift-off results in the airplane flying closer to the stall margin and aircraft control is more critical. In order to achieve the same takeoff attitude as that obtained with half-flaps, the airplane takeoff speed must be further increased. By increasing the takeoff speed, the takeoff distance and the airplane's kinetic energy are also increased proportionally, thereby making an abort more difficult. In addition, the increased takeoff speed begins to approach the rotational speed limitations of the tires, making the possibility of tire failure more probable. Stabilator effectiveness during a no-flaps takeoff is considerably greater than during a half-flaps takeoff, therefore, the stick must be programmed forward more rapidly to prevent overrotation beyond the desired 10 to 12 degree takeoff attitude. Since ARI is available only when flaps are used, increased adverse yaw may be expected in the no-flaps configuration. In airplanes 152995z and up, the slotted stabilator provides even greater stabilator effectiveness and results in increased sensitivity to overrotation during a no-flaps takeoff.

PILOT

1. Engines - RUN UP (one at a time)
   a. Variable area inlet ramps - CHECK FULLY RETRACTED
   b. Oil pressure - CHECK (relay reading to RIO)
2. Engine anti-ice - AS DESIRED
3. Radar horizon - SET
4. Stab aug/pitch aug - ENGAGE
5. Defog footheat handle - AS DESIRED
6. Pitot heat - ON
7. Compass - CHECK SYNC

MINIMUM TURNING RADIUS AND GROUND CLEARANCE

AIRCRAFT BEING TAXIED

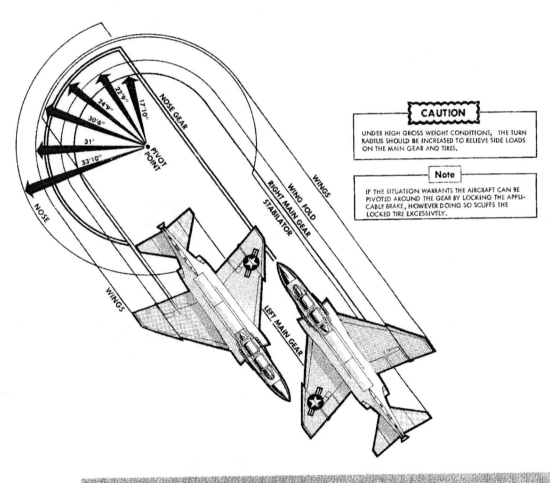

CAUTION

UNDER HIGH GROSS WEIGHT CONDITIONS, THE TURN RADIUS SHOULD BE INCREASED TO RELIEVE SIDE LOADS ON THE MAIN GEAR AND TIRES.

Note

IF THE SITUATION WARRANTS THE AIRCRAFT CAN BE PIVOTED AROUND THE GEAR BY LOCKING THE APPLICABLE BRAKE, HOWEVER DOING SO SCUFFS THE LOCKED TIRE EXCESSIVELY.

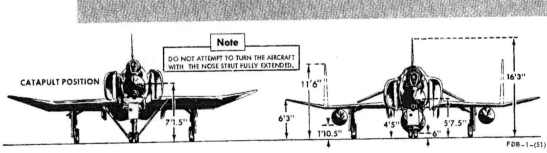

Note

DO NOT ATTEMPT TO TURN THE AIRCRAFT WITH THE NOSE STRUT FULLY EXTENDED.

FDB-1-(51)

Figure 3-3.

8. SIF - AS DESIRED
9. Suit vent air - LESS THAN 1/4 ON
10. Takeoff checklist - COMPLETE WITH RIO
    a. Controls - Checked
       Check controls for freedom of movement, normal pressure drop, and direction of movement.
    b. Wings - Locked
       Check wing pin unlock handle down, and WING PIN UNLOCK lights out.
    c. Trim - Set
    d. Flaps - 1/2
    e. Hook - Up
    f. Harness - Locked and lap belt secure
    g. Warning lights - Out
11. Seat pins - PULLED
12. Lower ejection handle guard - AS DESIRED.

RIO

1. Suit vent air - LESS THAN 1/4 ON
2. Compass heading sync - CHALLENGE PILOT
3. Circuit breakers - CHECK
4. Radar scope - STOWED
5. Takeoff checklist - COMPLETE
    a. Controls - Check
    b. Wings - Locked
       Visually check each wing lock pin down, and both WING PIN UNLOCK lights out.
    c. Trim - Check setting
    d. Flaps - Visually check
    e. Hook - Check up
    f. Harness - Locked and lap belt secure
    g. Warning lights - out
    h. Seat pins - PULLED
6. Lower ejection handle guard - AS DESIRED
7. Variable ramps - CHECK RETRACTED
8. Report flaps, ramps ready for takeoff.
9. Nav computer - TGT or BASE (when commencing takeoff roll)

TAKEOFF TECHNIQUE

For individual takeoff, the centerline of the runway should be used as a directional guide. When in position, roll forward slightly to align the nose wheel. If nose gear steering is desired, engagement must be made prior to commencing takeoff roll. Do not engage after the takeoff roll has started. The takeoff roll may be started with the engines in IDLE or the brakes can be applied until 80% rpm and 450-470°C EGT is reached on each engine. After the takeoff roll has begun, the throttles are advanced to MIL power and EGT and RPM are checked. If an afterburner takeoff is desired, afterburner is selected by moving both throttles into the afterburner detent and advancing smoothly to MAX power. If one afterburner fails to light, sufficient directional control is available with the rudder to continue the takeoff with asymmetric power. Very light braking or nose gear steering can be used to maintain directional control until the rudder becomes effective at approximately 70 knots. Nose gear steering should be disengaged when the rudder becomes effective. Nose gear steering must be disengaged prior to lift-off to ensure nose wheel centering and nose gear retraction. Optimum lift-off speeds are contained in the NATOPS Pocket Checklist and in section XI of this publication. Location of

the main landing gear a good bit aft of the normal CG prevents this aircraft from being rotated early in the takeoff roll.

In the normal rotation technique, full aft stick is applied at brake release and as the aircraft starts to rotate, the stick should be adjusted forward to maintain 10° to 12° of pitch. Concentrate on a smooth rotation and do not exceed 22 units angle of attack. This allows the airplane to fly off at optimum lift-off speed. The takeoff attitude of 10-12 degrees is identical in the half-flap and no-flap configurations. No-flap takeoff speed is 10-20 knots CAS faster than half-flap speed. Less than full aft stick at the start of rotation delays rotation and unnecessarily extends takeoff roll. The AUX. AIR DOOR, and MASTER CAUTION lights may illuminate momentarily as the landing gear and flaps controls are actuated. This is normal and should be no cause for alarm.

Note

Longitudinal stick forces during takeoffs in airplanes with downsprings removed (after AFC 308) are very light and care should be taken not to over control pitch attitude.

CAUTION

Due to the increased effectiveness of the slotted stabilator, a rapid nose-up pitching moment occurs during flaps up takeoff if the stick is held full aft, at rotation.

WARNING

From 30 knots CAS below takeoff speed until aircraft is normally airborne, rapid full aft stick movement may cause aircraft overrotation with resultant stalled flight condition, lift-off prior to reaching safe flying speed, or the stabilator striking the runway. With gear down and flaps down, do not exceed 22 units angle of attack. After gear retraction do not exceed 18 units angle of attack, since the angle of attack system indicates 3 to 4 units low with gear retracted.

MINIMUM RUN TAKEOFF

A minimum run takeoff in this airplane is the same as a normal afterburner takeoff.

CROSSWIND TAKEOFF

If nose gear steering is to be used, it must be engaged before commencing takeoff roll. Release brakes evenly, do not ride or keep pressure on the brakes during the initial part of the roll. The brakes should be used sparingly to prevent overheating. Excessive braking increases the takeoff roll. The rudder becomes effective at approximately 70 knots. Hold the nose wheel down until flying speed is reached. Fly the airplane off the runway at optimum lift-off speed. Do not assume an immediate wing low attitude to counteract for wind drift; the pilot cannot properly judge the wing tip ground clearance on a swept wing airplane.

FORMATION TAKEOFF

For formation takeoff, all aspects of the takeoff must be prebriefed by the flight leader. This should include flap settings; use of nose gear steering; power changes; power settings; and signals for actuation of landing gear, flaps, and afterburner. The leader will take position on the downwind side of the runway with other aircraft in tactical order maintaining normal parade bearing (normal parade is minimum safe aircraft separation). After pretakeoff checks are completed and the flight is in position, engines are run up to 80%, instruments checked and nose gear steering engaged (procedures for nose gear steering technique are the same as for single aircraft takeoff technique). On signal from leader, brakes are released, throttles are advanced to military power minus 2% rpm. (If afterburner is desired, the lead pilot may go into midburner immediately without stopping at military power, or he may select afterburner during the takeoff roll at a later time.) During the takeoff roll, the leader should maintain stick between center and three quarters aft position until reaching 120 KCAS, then smoothly rotate the aircraft to a 10°-12° nose high attitude. The lead should maintain this attitude until the flight is airborne. The wingman should strive to match the lead aircraft's attitude as well as maintain a position in parade bearing with wingtip separation. The gear and flaps are raised on signal. Turns into the wingman will not be made at altitudes less than 500 feet above ground level. The first section must be airborne before the second section commences its takeoff roll. Visual communication procedures are contained in section VII.

CAUTION

- In the event of an aborted takeoff, the aircraft aborting must immediately notify the other aircraft. The aircraft not aborting should add max power and accelerate ahead and out of the way of the aborting aircraft. This will allow the aborting aircraft to steer to the center of the runway and engage the arresting gear if required.

- It is imperative that the wingman always be alert for an over-running situation and take timely steps to preclude such an occurrence. Should an over-running/over-shooting situation develop after becoming airborne, the wingman should immediately move laterally away from the lead and, if feasible, reduce power in order to maintain wing position. Safe flight of both aircraft must not be jeopardized in an attempt to maintain formation. The leader should detach the wingman

if he is experiencing loss of thrust and flying speed. The wingman should detach and add power if unable to maintain a safe wing position on the lead.

AFTER TAKEOFF

When the aircraft is definitely airborne, perform the following:

PILOT

1. Ensure that aircraft is definitely airborne before retracting landing gear.
2. Raise landing gear.
3. Raise flaps at 300 feet or 200 knots CAS while maintaining a 10° to 12° nose-up attitude.
4. External transfer - AS DESIRED

Note

If boarding steps have inadvertently been left extended, or if they extend in flight, do not exceed 400 KCAS and land as soon as practicable.

5. Selective identification feature - AS DESIRED
6. Compass - SLAVED/SYNC

RIO

The RIO will challenge the pilot on the following:

1. Landing gear - UP
2. Flaps - UP
3. External transfer - AS DESIRED
4. Selective identification feature - AS DESIRED
5. Compass - SLAVED/SYNC
6. Lower ejection handle - AS DESIRED

TRANSITION TO CLIMB

When the airplane is definitely airborne, tap the wheelbrakes and raise the landing gear. Raise the flaps at 300 feet or 200 knots CAS while maintaining a 10° to 12° nose-up attitude.

CLIMB

A simplified MIL power climb at normal gross weights can be made by maintaining a 10° to 12° nose-up attitude until reaching 400 knots CAS. Vary the pitch attitude as necessary to maintain 400 knots CAS until reaching final cruise Mach. Then vary the pitch attitude as necessary to maintain cruise Mach until reaching cruise altitude. A simplified MAX power climb at normal gross weights can be made by maintaining a 10° to 12° nose-up attitude until reaching 250 knots CAS. At 250 knots CAS smoothly rotate to a 20° to 25° nose-up attitude and hold until reaching Mach 0.9. Vary the pitch attitude as necessary to maintain Mach 0.9 until reaching cruise altitude. For optimum climb performance, refer to section XI, part 3.

Note

The probability exists that engine flame-outs may occur while flying at altitudes above 35,000 feet in cirrus clouds. Such incidents have occurred and are generally believed to have been caused by excessive ingestion of ice crystals. Under such conditions, ice build-up on the duct lips or other parts of the aircraft are not likely to occur and flame-outs can, therefore, occur without warning. However, in all known incidents of this type, re-lights have been accomplished and maintained at lower altitudes. Therefore, if flame-out occurs at high altitudes in clouds, it is recommended that re-light attempts be deferred until descent to a lower altitude and, if possible, to a less dense part of the cloud.

Refer to Inflight Procedures, section IV, and Performance Data, section XI.

DESCENT/INSTRUMENT PENETRATION

PILOT

In all descents, care will be taken not to exceed any airframe limitations. See section I, part 4. In any descents from altitude, 5 minutes prior to letdown, select the desired DEFOG position on the defog lever and place the temperature control at the 2 o'clock (200 degrees of clockwise rotation) position. Since rapid descents cannot always be anticipated, the maximum comfortable interior temperature should be maintained. This aids in defrosting the windshield. Refer to section XI, part 7, for recommended descent. Before starting descent, perform the following:

1. Engine anti-ice - AS DESIRED
2. Radar gyro horizon - CHECK
3. SPC - CHECK
   At 9 units angle of attack, between 0.45 and 0.75 Mach and at an altitude between 5000 and 20,000 feet, check the SPC using the SPC Altimeter Tolerance Check chart. Refer to section XI or NATOPS Pocket Checklist. If SPC accuracy is in doubt, turn SPC off and use position error correction. Cross check all available altitude information; i.e., cockpit pressure altimeters, radar altimeter, and radar scope altitude line.
4. Electronic or radar altimeter - SET & CHECK
   On airplanes 151519t and earlier, before AFC 177, when below 10,000 feet, check unit is ON, altitude pointer is unmasked and desired low altitude limit is set. On airplanes 152207t and up, and all others after AFC 177, when below 5000 feet, ensure unit is ON, and that the OFF flag is masked. Depress and hold function control knob and check that altitude pointer goes to 5 ± 5 feet. Release knob and ensure desired low altitude warning is set.

5. Tacan and UHF homer - CROSS CHECK
6. ILS (ARA-63) power switch - ON and CHANNEL SET (some aircraft)
7. Defog/Footheat handle - DEFOG
8. Pitot heat - ON
9. Rain removal - AS DESIRED
10. Cabin heat - SET
11. Compass - SYNC (check against standby)
12. Missile power switch - OFF (STBY with AIM-7 missiles aboard)
13. Set IFF and SIF as directed by Approach Control.

Note

If it becomes necessary to dump fuel during a descent, thrust settings in excess of 85% rpm may be required to ensure rapid inflight dumping.

RIO

1. Altimeter - SET
2. Flight instruments - CHECK
3. Radar gyro horizon - CHECK (place gyro switch to out if horizon does not match aircraft attitude).
4. Challenge pilot as required for cabin heat, pitot heat, engine de-icing, compass sync, and electronic or radar altimeter.
5. Challenge pilot for all armament switches - OFF or SAFE

PATTERN ENTRY

Enter the traffic pattern at the altitude and airspeed prescribed by the local course rules. Whenever possible, pattern entry will be made in accordance with figure 3-4.

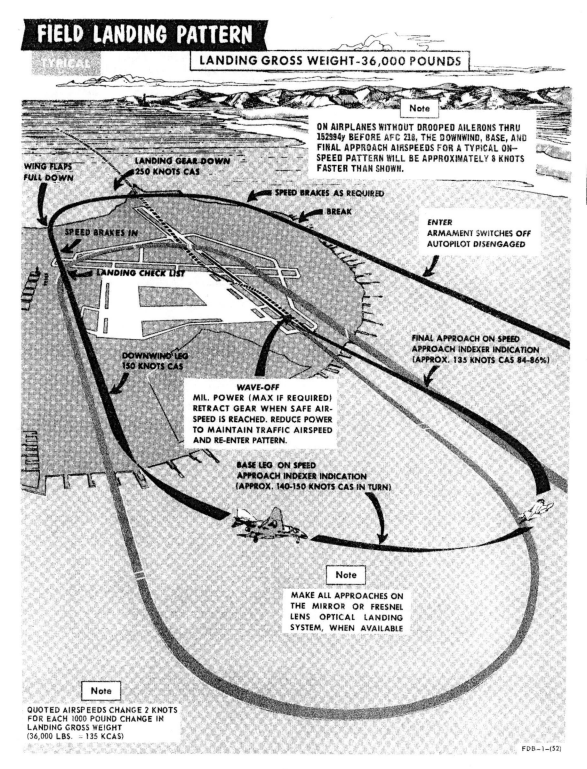

FIELD LANDING PATTERN

TYPICAL

LANDING GROSS WEIGHT-36,000 POUNDS

Note

ON AIRPLANES WITHOUT DROOPED AILERONS THRU 152994y BEFORE AFC 218, THE DOWNWIND, BASE, AND FINAL APPROACH AIRSPEEDS FOR A TYPICAL ON—SPEED PATTERN WILL BE APPROXIMATELY 8 KNOTS FASTER THAN SHOWN.

WING FLAPS FULL DOWN

LANDING GEAR DOWN 250 KNOTS CAS

SPEED BRAKES AS REQUIRED

BREAK

SPEED BRAKES IN

ENTER
ARMAMENT SWITCHES *OFF*
AUTOPILOT *DISENGAGED*

LANDING CHECK LIST

FINAL APPROACH ON SPEED APPROACH INDEXER INDICATION (APPROX. 135 KNOTS CAS 84-86%)

DOWNWIND LEG 150 KNOTS CAS

WAVE-OFF
MIL. POWER (MAX IF REQUIRED) RETRACT GEAR WHEN SAFE AIR-SPEED IS REACHED. REDUCE POWER TO MAINTAIN TRAFFIC AIRSPEED AND RE-ENTER PATTERN.

BASE LEG ON SPEED APPROACH INDEXER INDICATION (APPROX. 140-150 KNOTS CAS IN TURN)

Note

MAKE ALL APPROACHES ON THE MIRROR OR FRESNEL LENS OPTICAL LANDING SYSTEM, WHEN AVAILABLE

Note

QUOTED AIRSPEEDS CHANGE 2 KNOTS FOR EACH 1000 POUND CHANGE IN LANDING GROSS WEIGHT (36,000 LBS. = 135 KCAS)

FDB-1-(52)

Figure 3-4.

LANDING

PILOT

1. Landing checklist - COMPLETE
   a. Wheels
   b. Flaps
   c. Hook
   d. Armament
   e. Harness
2. UHF antenna - UPR
3. Lower ejection handle guard - AS DESIRED
4. Warning lights - CHECK
5. Wheel brakes - CHECK
6. Upon touchdown, throttles - IDLE
7. Drag chute - DEPLOY (as required)
8. Brakes - APPLY
9. Drag chute - RELEASE IN DESIGNATED AREA

Note

In airplanes with drooped ailerons (152995z and up and all others after AFC 218), an increase from the normal nose down pitching moment is noticed when flaps/ailerons are lowered. In addition, there is no synchronization between the left and right ailerons. Therefore, asymmetrical aileron extension and resulting rolling moment may occur as the flaps and ailerons are coming down.

RIO

1. Pilot's checklist - MONITOR
2. Communication antenna - UPR
3. Equipment - STOW
4. Harness - LOCKED
5. Lower ejection handle guard - AS DESIRED
6. Landing checklist - COMPLETE
7. Report - READY FOR LANDING

LANDING TECHNIQUE

For a field landing with a gross weight of approximately 36,000 pounds, fly the pattern as illustrated in figure 3-4. Enter the pattern as local course rules dictate, utilizing the throttles and speed brakes, as necessary, to maintain pattern altitude and airspeed. At the break, reduce thrust and extend the speed brakes (if required). As the airspeed decreases through 250 knots CAS, lower the landing gear and extend the wing flaps. Retract the speed brakes to decrease buffet; however, some buffet and noise comes from the nose wheel well as the landing gear extends. This noise and buffet disappears as approach speeds are reached. Continue to decelerate to, and maintain, 150 knots CAS. After the gear and flaps have been checked and reported, roll into the base leg and establish a mild rate of descent, maintaining on ON SPEED angle-of-attack indexer light (135 knots CAS). Use the angle-of-attack indexer and maintain the ON SPEED indication except that 125 knots is the minimum final approach speed. When on final approach, utilize a power setting of 84 to 86% rpm. This provides an ON-SPEED angle-of-attack indexer light with a 2 1/2° to 3° glide slope and a rate of descent of approximately 700 rpm. Attempt to land

within the first 1000 feet of runway whenever possible; however, do not chop power prior to touchdown as the sudden loss of boundary layer control air causes the airplane to settle immediately. At touchdown, retard the throttles to IDLE and deploy the drag chute. The nose will drop almost immediately due to the airplane center-of-gravity and stabilator location. When the nose gear is on the runway, hold full back stick to increase drag, and utilize the rudder, nose gear steering and wheel brakes, as necessary, to maintain directional control. When engaging the nose gear steering, be sure to have the rudder pedals centered, otherwise the nose gear will immediately cock in the direction and in proportion to rudder pedal displacement.

Note

The airspeeds quoted in the landing technique paragraph pertain to aircraft with drooped ailerons (aircraft after 152995z and AFC 218). In airplanes without drooped ailerons (before 152995z and AFC 218), the landing technique is the same; however, all quoted airspeeds are approximately 8 knots faster.

LANDING ROLL

The airplane is very clean on landing and even with fairly low residual thrust it will want to roll down the runway with little deceleration. Leave the flaps down to increase aerodynamic drag, and to decrease residual thrust by utilizing BLC air. Speed brake extension, full aileron and opposite rudder deflection may also be used to reduce landing roll. Aerodynamic controls are usually very effective in maintaining directional control of the aircraft during the early portion of the landing roll. If the drag chute is to be retained after the rudders and spoilers lose their effectiveness, employment of nose gear steering or differential braking must be utilized. Nose gear steering is the most effective of the two; however, differential braking may be desirable if the runway surface is dry and the aircraft is tracking relatively straight. Due to the powered brakes, differential braking must be judiciously used so as to preclude blowing a tire. If the runway surface is wet, it is recommended that nose gear steering be utilized to maintain directional control once the aerodynamic controls have lose their effectiveness. Exercise caution while using the brakes until you get the feel of them. They are fully powered rather than boosted and there is very little feel at the pedals. The tire pressures are very high and they will break loose and skid with heavy applications. Normally, wheel brakes should be used below 100 knots since the probability of blowing a tire decreases significantly with a like reduction in ground speed. Refer to Brake System, section I, part II for braking technique.

Note

Nose gear steering should be used to maintain runway alignment and supplemented with differential braking only if required.

DRAG CHUTE PROCEDURES

The drag chute will normally be deployed on all landings except for specified no-drag chute landings during the familiarization phase, or landings made with a known crosswind component equal to or greater than 20 knots. All landings should be planned and flown as no-drag chute landings. In case of drag chute nondeployment, a waveoff shall be initiated if conditions are not ideal to stop the aircraft. If a waveoff is initiated, the drag chute handle should be stowed immediately to preclude inadvertent chute deployment/jettison in the landing pattern. If committed for a no-drag chute landing, the pilot must be prepared to drop the hook and engage the arresting gear if there is any possibility that speed or runway condition will preclude stopping the aircraft on the runway. Caution must be exercised while taxiing with the drag chute deployed to ensure that the drag chute does not become entangled in the taxi lights, other aircraft, or other obstructions. The drag chute will be released on signal from the taxi-signalman in an area where the possibility of interference with other aircraft turning up or taxiing is least. The pilot must advise tower personnel if the drag chute is released elsewhere on the field.

CAUTION

Airborne deployment of the drag chute at approach power settings can result in chute main riser failure and subsequent chute collapse within as little as 5 seconds from time of deployment. During the time chute is fully blossomed, sink rate and AOA increase rapidly resulting in large deviations from optimum airspeed and glide path. Do not deploy the drag chute while airborne.

CROSSWIND LANDING (DRY RUNWAY)

Carefully compensate for crosswind in the traffic pattern to guard against undershooting or overshooting the final turn. Fly the final approach course with the aircraft ground track properly aligned with the runway. The crosswind may be compensated for either by using the wing low method, the crab method, or a combination of the two. When using the wing low method, the ARI can be overpowered by use of the rudder pedals. If the crab method is employed, the aircraft heading should be aligned with the runway just prior to touchdown. After touchdown, use rudder, aileron and spoiler, and nose gear steering as required to maintain directional control. Crosswind effect on the aircraft is not severe; however, rudder, differential braking, and/or nose gear steering must be used as required to maintain alignment with the runway. Use of the drag chute intensifies the weather vane effect for any given deployment condition. The weather vane effect increases as the forward velocity of the aircraft decreases, therefore, if the drag chute is to be used, it should be used at the initial portion rather than the latter portion of the landing roll. This also assures use of the drag chute in the speed region where it is most effective. If the drag

chute is used and excessive weathervaning is encountered, jettison drag chute. Since the nose gear will rapidly assume a position relative to the rudder pedals, nose gear steering should be initiated with the rudder pedals at or near the neutral position. For this reason the use of nose gear steering is advocated early in the landing roll rather than at a time when large amounts of rudder are required to hold the aircraft aligned on the runway. The most important aspect of directional control under crosswind conditions is keeping the aircraft precisely aligned with the runway rather than trying to correct back to the runway heading after it has deviated.

CROSSWIND LANDING (WET RUNWAY)

The problem of maintaining directional control on a wet runway is greatly intensified with an increase in effective crosswind. Refer to the Crosswing Landing Guide (figure 3-5) to determine the advisability of making a approach-end engagement. If a crosswind landing is to be made on a slippery runway, it should be done at the lowest practicable gross weight. Plan the pattern to be well established on final in a wings-level crab and with an ON SPEED indication. Plan to touch down on centerline within the first 500 feet. Make a firm touchdown while maintaining the wings-level crab. Touching down in the crab results in a continuation of a straight track down the runway. Immediately after touchdown retard throttles to IDLE, deploy the drag chute. As wheel-cornering capability overcomes aerodynamic effects, the nose of the aircraft will gradually assume the track down the runway. Nose gear steering is the primary method of maintaining directional control, and should be utilized as early as possible. Be ready to jettison the drag chute if the weathervaning effect begins to interfere with maintaining desired track. When directional control is firmly established, utilize normal braking.

HEAVY GROSS WEIGHT LANDING

As landing gross weight increases, the landing pattern should be expanded and approach and touchdown speeds should be increased accordingly. Follow procedures outlined in Landing Pattern Diagram, figure 3-4. To maintain an ON SPEED approach indexer indication, the airspeed is increased approximately 2 knots for each 1000 pounds over normal landing gross weight.

WET RUNWAY LANDING

If possible, a wet runway landing should be made with approximately 2000 pounds of fuel remaining. Fly a normal approach with an ON SPEED or slightly slow indexer indication. Plan to touch down on centerline with a maximum amount of runway remaining for deceleration. The drag chute should be deployed on touchdown and the flaps should be left in the down position in order to bleed off residual engine thrust by utilizing the BLC system. Light braking can be initiated at 100 knots IAS providing a smooth easy application is used. It is recommended that nose gear steering be used when a directional control problem is expected. Be prepared to engage the arresting

CROSSWIND LANDING GUIDE

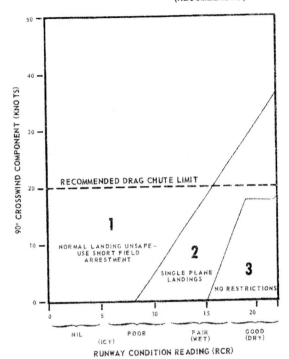

(RECOMMENDED)

Figure 3-5.

gear if the aircraft is not slowing down properly. The arresting gear should be engaged with feet off the brakes, flaps full down, and control stick full aft. During the high speed portion of the landing roll, particularly under wet or icy conditions, little deceleration will be felt because the braking potential is very low. Unless the pilot is familiar with the variables in braking potential of the aircraft, this low deceleration under high speed or adverse runway conditions might be mistakenly interpreted as brake failure. The following procedures are recommended when landing on a wet runway.

   a. Determine field condition prior to approach.
     (1) Braking action
     (2) Crosswind component

     (3) Type, status, and location of arresting gear
   b. Reduce landing weight as much as practicable.
   c. Land on runway centerline.
   d. On a flooded runway (0.1 to 0.3 inches of standing water), plan to make either a fly-in arrested landing or a roll-in arrested landing being sure to keep ground speed high enough to maintain effective directional control with aerodynamic control surfaces (ailerons, spoilers, and rudder). Braking and nose wheel steering may not be effective due to hydroplaning.
   e. When a crosswind exists, refer to Crosswind Landing Guide (figure 3-5) to determine the recommended drag chute deployment and arrested landing parameters.

SECTION LANDING

The leader should transition to optimum approach speed when the runway is sighted, touching down 500-1000 feet down the runway on his side. The wingman should avoid getting "sucked" and maintain a normal wing position except that as he approached the runway, he moves out to give additional wingtip clearances at touchdown. The wingman will call Good Chute or No Chute as the case may be.

MOREST LANDING

The techniques for engaging MOREST are essentially the same as for other types of arresting equipment and are as follows:

   1. Notify control tower as soon as possible of intention of engaging MOREST, and transmit estimated gross weight for touchdown.
   2. At the 180° position, receive clearance for a MOREST landing.
   3. Approach on mirror.
   4. Touchdown on centerline of runway and deploy drag chute as required.
   5. Lower arresting hook 1000 feet in front of MOREST gear.
   6. Longitudinal controls neutral prior to engagement.
   7. Engage wire with feet off the brakes.

WAVEOFF

The decision to take a waveoff should be made as early as possible. Advance the throttles to MIL or MAX as required to stop the sink rate. The landing gear should be raised only after the sink rate has been stopped and there is no possibility of the airplane contacting the ground. At a safe airspeed and altitude, raise the flaps.

POSTFLIGHT

POSTFLIGHT PROCEDURES

Before engine shutdown, it is recommended (but not required) that the engines be operated at IDLE power for 3 to 5 minutes to allow engine temperatures to stabilize. Landing roll and taxi time may be included. Carrier landings may require that the engines be shut down almost immediately after touchdown from high power settings. If the engines are shut down before the recommended idle time, a notation should be made on the yellow sheet. To shut down an engine, move the throttle OFF, the engine master switch OFF and the generator control switch OFF. With only one engine operating, do not move the control stick excessively. Excessive stick movement with hydraulic pressure on only one side of the tandem power control cylinders cause the hydraulic fluid that is in the unpressurized side of the cylinder to be forced back through the pressure lines to the reservoir, filling the reservoir, and causing the excess fluid to be dumped overboard. The seals within the power cylinders may also be damaged by air ingestion and lack of lubrication. If the above situation occurs, the power control hydraulic systems must be reserviced and checked. Perform the postflight checks as listed in the NATOPS Pocket Checklist, with the exception that during operations where temperature is below freezing or expected to drop below freezing the aircraft may be parked with wings spread and flaps in the full down position.

POSTLANDING

WARNING

- After flight, especially if negative G has been encountered, account for all loose items before opening canopy. Inadvertent seat ejection may occur if any foreign object in the cockpit becomes jammed between the canopy actuator and primary seat-mounted initiator or the ejection gun firing mechanism sear. If all known loose objects cannot be accounted for, leave the canopy closed until an inspection of the banana link area is made by a knowledgeable person.

- After flight, except in those instances where emergency ground egress is the primary consideration, remain completely strapped in until the canopy is fully raised.

PILOT

1. Flaps - UP (when clear of active runway)
2. Speed brakes - IN
3. Lower ejection handle guard - UP
4. Stab aub - OFF
5. Electronic altimeter - OFF

6. Missile power switch - OFF/STBY
7. VTAS power switch - OFF (some aircraft)
8. Pitot heat - OFF
9. Temperature control knob - FULL HOT
   Place temperature control knob to HOT to evaporate any water that may have collected in air conditioning system.
10. Defog/footheat handle - DEFOG
11. Suit vent - FULL OPEN
12. IFF - OFF
13. ILS power switch - OFF (some aircraft)
14. Ejection seat - RAISE (MK H7 seats)
    Elevate seat to gain clearance for insertion of rocket motor safety pin.
15. Notify RIO-READY FOR SHUTDOWN
16. Throttles - OFF
17. Engine master switches - OFF
18. Generator control switches - OFF
19. Seat pins - INSTALLED
20. All switches, levers and personal equipment - OFF or DISCONNECTED

RIO

1. Lower ejection handle guard - UP
2. Ejection seat - RAISE (MK H7 seats)
   Elevate seat to gain clearance for insertion of rocket motor safety pin.
3. Radar - PERFORM BITS/OFF
4. Nav computer - OFF
5. TACAN - STBY
6. Oxygen - OFF
7. UHF/COMM - OFF
8. Destruct circuit manual arm switch - SAFE (safety pin inserted; some aircraft)
9. AN/ALQ-91 function selector switch - OFF (some aircraft)

CAUTION

Failure to ensure AN/ALQ-91 function selector switch is turned OFF may result in damage to equipment or a blown fuse when external power is re-connected to aircraft.

10. Data link power switch - OFF (some aircraft)
11. AN/AJB-3A dc circuit breaker (E7) - PULL (Prior to 152273w before AFC 202)
12. Seat pins - INSTALLED (after engine shutdown)
13. Personal equipment - DISCONNECTED

HOT REFUELING

Prior to entering refueling pit -

1. Post Landing checklist steps 1 thru 13 - COMPLETED.
2. Air Refueling checklist - COMPLETED.

WARNING

Stop short of refueling pit for tire inspection. If notified of hot brakes, taxi clear of refueling area.

3. Monitor ground control frequency during refueling operation.

WARNING

- Do not operate any transmitter during refueling operations, except in an emergency.

- If fuel starts running from the wing dump masts or the fuselage vent mast, place the refuel selection switch to INT ONLY and discontinue refueling immediately.

When refueling is complete -

4. Air refuel switch - RETRACT.

REFUELING

ENGINES OFF, WITHOUT ELECTRICAL POWER

If operational expediencies dictate, the aircraft fuel system may be set up for refueling without electrical power. However, the transfer pumps and fuel level shutoff valves cannot be checked using this procedure.

Prior to engine shutdown -

1. Refuel probe circuit breaker - PULL (D15, No. 1 panel)
2. Refuel probe switch - REFUEL.
3. Refuel selector switch - AS REQUIRED.
4. Throttles - OFF.

After engine shutdown -

5. After generators drop off the line, engine master switches - OFF.
6. Refuel probe switch - RETRACT.
7. Refuel probe circuit breaker - RESET.

SCRAMBLE OPERATION

SCRAMBLE INTERIOR CHECK

PILOT

1. AIM-9 tone control - 1/4 TURN
2. ICS - HOT MIC
3. Fuel switches - SET FOR NORMAL OPERATION
4. Smoke abate switch - OFF
5. Flap switch - UP
6. Speed brake switch - STOP (NEUTRAL)
7. Engine master switches - ON
8. Engine start switch - RIGHT
9. Anti-ice switch - AS REQUIRED
10. Missile power switch - RADAR STBY
11. Electronic altimeter - ON & SET
12. Altimeter - SET
13. Generator control switches - OFF
14. Radio - ON (TR + G)
15. Tacan - ON (TR)
16. IFF - NORMAL
17. Pitot heat switch - ON
18. Bleed air switch - NORM
19. Light switches - AS REQUIRED

RIO

1. Radar power switch - OFF
2. All other radar switches set for immediate use after normal warm up.
3. Radio - ON (TR + G)
4. Tacan - ON (TR)
5. ICS - NORMAL

6. Light switches - AS REQUIRED
7. Black out curtain - AS DESIRED

SCRAMBLE ENGINE START

PILOT

1. Starting unit up to power - EXTERNAL POWER CONNECTED
2. Generator control switches - EXT ON
3. Signal plane captain to turn CNI ground power switch - ON
4. At 10% rpm, right ignition button - DEPRESS WHILE ADVANCING THROTTLE TO IDLE
5. At 35% on right engine, engine start switch - LEFT
6. At 53% on right engine, generator control switches - GEN ON
7. Signal to disconnect external ac
8. Static pressure compensator - RESET
9. Stab aug - ENGAGE
10. At 10% on left engine, left ignition button - DEPRESS WHILE ADVANCING THROTTLE TO IDLE
11. At 35% on left engine, engine start switch - NEUTRAL
12. Complete T.O. checklist.

RIO

1. Notify pilot of any emergency signals noted from ground crew.

SCRAMBLE TAKEOFF

Aircraft scrambles invariably take place under various conditions of radio silence (refer to NWP-41A, chapter 2). The following procedures will be followed for an alert which will probably result in the actual launching of the airplane. Normal preflight, start, and poststart checks will be conducted in accordance with the NATOPS Flight Manual and the NATOPS Pocket Checklist. Shut down the engines but leave the airplane as prepared as possible for takeoff. Remove all seat pins except the face curtain pin. If awaiting the scramble order requires the use of the aircraft radio, observe ground operating limitations. The ground equipment is positioned to provide rapid removal after starting. When the scramble order is received, start the engines, establish radio communications, determine that all ground locks and safety pins are removed, and that the ground crew and equipment are clear before taxiing. Taxi safely but expeditiously and energize all necessary electrical/electronic equipment. Complete the scramble checklist prior to scramble.

NIGHT FLYING

EXTERNAL LIGHT MANAGEMENT

During night operations, the external lights should be set as follows:

1. On the line - BRIGHT and STEADY.
2. When ready for taxiing - BRIGHT and FLASH
3. In flight
   a. Single aircraft - BRIGHT and FLASH (or as weather conditions dictate)
   b. Formations - AS REQUESTED BY WINGMAN.
      The last aircraft in formation flight should have his external lights on BRIGHT and FLASH unless tactical situation demands otherwise (actual penetrations etc.)

TAXIING

Night operation demands extra caution while taxiing. It is difficult to judge actual ground speed at night. Pilots can best judge their speed by frequently observing the runway or taxiway close to their aircraft as illuminated by the bottom fuselage light. Taxi slowly for it is possible that unlighted aircraft, vehicles, and/or obstructions are on the taxiways.

TAKEOFF

A night takeoff is accomplished in exactly the same manner as one outlined for daylight operations with the following addition:

Be prepared to transition to complete instrument flight immediately upon leaving the runway.

INFLIGHT PROCEDURES

See section IV of this publication.

LANDING

Night landing procedures are identical to day procedures with the following exceptions:

There is often a tendency to be fast. Be positive about checking angle of attack and airspeed. Determination of altitude and sink rate are difficult at night. This necessitates reference to the vertical velocity indicator. Rates of descent up to 750 feet per minute are acceptable, use mirror when available.

FIELD MIRROR LANDING PRACTICE

PREFLIGHT INSPECTION

A normal preflight inspection will be conducted with specific attention being given to tire condition, nose strut extension, angle of attack probe conditions, and windshield cleanliness. Check that the hook bypass switch is in BYPASS.

TAKEOFF

The takeoff will be individual using either MIL or MAX power depending on fuel weight, mission, etc.

RADIO PROCEDURES AND PATTERN ENTRY

It is advisable to call Paddles before pattern entry to confirm Charlie Time. Approaches to the field for break will be controlled by the tower and then switched to Paddles for FMLP pattern control. At no time will an aircraft remain in the pattern without a UHF receiver. On each succeeding pass, the following voice report will be made at normal meatball acquisition positions:

    Side Number
    Type aircraft
    Meatball or Clara (no meatball)
    Fuel State (nearest 100 lbs.)

PATTERN

The pattern is a race track pattern with the 180 approximately 1-1/4 miles abeam at 600 feet above field elevation. The length of the groove should be adjusted to give a wings-level descent on the glide slope of 20-25 seconds (approximately one mile). For maximum gross weight at touchdown, refer to section I, part 4. For a 36,000-pound airplane, an optimum ON SPEED indexer indication results in an airspeed of 135 knots CAS. The turn to downwind leg should be 30° angle of bank and 140-150 knots CAS, climbing to 600 feet above field elevation. Recommended airspeed at the 180° position is 140 to 150 knots CAS. Power is added to effect a level turn onto final. From the 180° to the 90° position, the airspeed should be corrected for the optimum angle of attack. At approximately the 45° position, the meatball appears on the mirror. A common error is to begin the descent upon first seeing the meatball. Maintain altitude until the meatball is centered on the mirror, then adjust power and angle of attack as necessary to start a rate of descent that keeps the meatball centered. When a Fresnel lens is used, care must be taken to avoid commencing descent until the airplane is aligned with the centerline, since an idiosyncrasy of this lens is to display a false meatball indication when viewed from the approach turn.

Note

Pattern airspeeds pertain to drooped aileron aircraft. In aircraft without drooped ailerons, quoted airspeeds will be approximately 8 knots faster.

APPROACH POWER COMPENSATOR TECHNIQUE

The technique required for an APC approach differs from a manual approach in that all glide slope corrections are made by changing airplane attitude. Since this technique violates the basic rule that altitude is primarily controlled by throttle, practice is required to develop the proper control habits necessary to use APC. For the APC to perform satisfactorily, smooth attitude control is essential. Large abrupt attitude changes result in excessive thrust changes. Close-in corrections are very critical. A large attitude correction for a high-in-close condition produces an excessive power reduction and can easily result in a hard landing. If a high-in-close situation develops, the recommended procedure is to stop meatball motion and not attempt to recenter it. A low-in-close condition is difficult to correct with APC and usually results in an over-the-top bolter. It may be necessary to manually override APC in order to safely recover from a low-in-close condition. Throughout the approach the pilot should keep his hand on the throttles in the event it is necessary to manually override the APC.

INTERVAL

The downwind turn should be commenced when the aircraft on the downwind leg is approximately in the 8 o'clock position. The turn should be made with a 30° angle of bank and 140-150 knots CAS, climbing to 500 feet above field elevation.

GLIDE SLOPE

A 2-1/4° to 3° glide slope is used, dependent upon wind conditions. This slope is chosen to give the same approximate rate of descent that would be used on the ship.

WAVEOFF TECHNIQUE

Any time the meatball is lost close-in, in the groove, the pilot initiates his own waveoff. Either MIL or MAX power is used to effect all waveoffs. Normally, waveoffs are taken straight ahead, especially when close-in. When using APC, waveoff technique is the same as for manual approaches except that the speedbrake switch should be moved to the closed position, thereby disengaging APC.

Note

If a waveoff is executed by manually over-riding the APC, and the APC is not disengaged, the throttles, when released, retard and attempt to re-establish the optimum approach angle of attack.

BINGO FUEL

No FMLP approach is commenced with 1500 or less pounds of fuel.

NIGHT FMLP

External lights steady - BRIGHT
Hook bypass switch - BYPASS

When comfortably situated in the pattern, simulated instruments should be flown as much as possible up to the 45° position.

SHORT AIRFIELD FOR TACTICAL SUPPORT (SATS) PROCEDURES

DAY OPERATIONS

GENERAL

Preflight, start, and poststart checks shall be accomplished in accordance with normal field procedures and the additions noted.

PREFLIGHT

1. Record the expected gross weight of the aircraft for catapult launch on the nose gear door.
2. Ensure that the tension bar retainer clip is installed securely and is in good condition.

START

1. Start engine sufficiently ahead of time to allow for taxi, catapult launches, and rendezvous before proceeding on the assigned mission.

POSTSTART

1. Set the emergency-jettison armament switch to the proper position prior to taxi.
2. Set trim and flaps as follows:
   a. Rudder: 0
   b. Aileron: 0
   c. Longitudinal:
      (1) Before/after both AFC 218 and AFC 308 - 1.5 units nose up.
      (2) After only AFC 308 - 1.0 units nose down.
   d. Flaps - DOWN

TAXI

1. Taxiing on advanced airfields presents little difficulty provided attention is given to keeping speed under control.
2. Wet or oily metal runway and taxiway surfaces require especially slow taxi speeds due to a greatly reduced coefficient of friction. Sharp turns cannot be made and the wheels will slide with moderate braking action.

SATS CATAPULT LAUNCHES

Proper positioning on the catapult is not easily accomplished due to surface irregularities in the holdback and arrester area. If the previously launched aircraft utilized afterburner, expect the area aft of the dolly arrester ropes to be wet and slippery. Approach the launch area slowly and be alert for signals from the taxi director.

WARNING

Do not taxi into the dolly arrester ropes area immediately following the launch of another aircraft until the dolly returns and is arrested. Failure of the arrester ropes may occur on dolly rebound. Wait until the dolly returns and is arrested.

1. Approximately 80 to 85 percent rpm is required to taxi up and over the arrester ropes and dolly ramp.

CAUTION

Keep speed under control.

2. As the main wheels roll over the arrester ropes be prepared for immediate braking and power reduction.
3. When the come-ahead signal is given by the taxi director, move ahead cautiously to prevent over-stressing the tension bar.
4. Ground handling crew will extend nose strut upon signal from plane director (prior to tensioning).

CAUTION

If pneumatic pressure approaches 2300 psi with nose strut extended, actuate emergency air brakes to keep pressure below 2300 psi. If the pneumatic pressure exceeds 2300 PSI the emergency brakes will not release the pressure in the nose strut. To release this excess pressure the nose strut will have to be deflated and then re-inflated. High pressures will subject nose strut to excessive loads during catapulting.

Note

Interruption of electrical power, such as cycling both generator switches simultaneously, will cause the nose strut to deflate.

5. After the aircraft is properly positioned and the holdback engaged, the taxi director will signal for the pilot to release brakes while the catapult is tensioned.

CAUTION

Ensure that the brakes are released before tension is taken.

6. After tension is taken the taxi director will transfer control of the aircraft to the launch officer who will signal the catapult for pre-launch turn-up. When the catapult is ready, the launch officer will signal the pilot for full power. Increase the throttle to MIL, observe acceleration time, and allow the engine to stabilize.
7. Recheck ADI and standby attitude indicator, engine instruments, trim indicators, and flap setting. Grip throttle and catapult handgrip firmly.
8. If launch is to be made at MAX A/B, nod to catapult officer after completing MIL power checks. When catapult officer signals, select MIN A/B and ease throttles forward to MAX A/B. Recheck engine instruments.

CAUTION

Failure to ease throttles from MIN A/B to MAX A/B may cause premature tension bar failure.

Note

Below 44,000 pounds gross weight, use MIL power. At 44,000 pounds gross weight or above, use MAX (AB) power.

9. When ready for launch, salute the catapult officer with the right hand, place head against the headrest, hold stick full aft, observe the green cutoff light, and wait. Launch will occur approximately 3 to 5 seconds after the catapult officer gives the launch signal.

CAUTION

After receiving the signal for full-power turnup, do not allow your hands to appear above the canopy rails unless you intend to salute as a launch signal. Unusual hand movements, such as lowering a helmet visor, will probably result in a premature launch.

TECHNIQUE

Maintain full aft stick until start of rotation. Upon perceiving the change in the cutoff light from green to amber, be prepared for rotation, as this is the signal that denotes catapult engine cutoff. Allow the aircraft to rotate to a liftoff attitude (10 - 12 degrees on the ADI) while maintaining positive control of rotation rate by easing stick forward. Do not exceed 21 units AOA (aircraft after AFC 218), or 22 units AOA (without AFC 218). The pilot must avoid gross control movements as the aircraft becomes airborne but should be prepared to make any attitude changes required. When safely airborne, retract gear and flaps as appropriate. Avoid turns until airspeed is well above takeoff speed.

WARNING

- Do not apply brakes during launch.
- Do not change power setting during launch.
- Avoid over-rotation. Over-rotation can result in stabilator contact with matting, excessive distance to clear obstacles, deceleration/stall.
- Rotation rates increase noticeably for CG positions aft of 32% MAC.

AIRCRAFT OR CATAPULT MALFUNCTION

1. If, after established at MIL power, the pilot determines that the aircraft is down, he so indicates to the launching officer by shaking his head from side to side. Never raise a hand into the catapult officer's view in order to give a "thumbs down" signal. Simultaneously broadcast "Suspend" to the tower. When the catapult officer observes the "No-Go" signal, he will immediately give a suspend signal.
2. If bridle shed or bridle failure occurs after holdback release, the pilot will note a sudden loss of acceleration; the dolly will continue to accelerate and move ahead of the aircraft. Wait until the dolly can be seen ahead of the aircraft, then maneuver to the side of the runway to avoid contact with the rebounding dolly. If safe abort or takeoff is not possible and ejection speed has been attained - EJECT.
3. A cold shot can result from inadequate catapult engine acceleration, early catapult cutoff, failure of the capstan brake to release completely, or failure of the dolly jaws. If an abort is attempted and the dolly moves ahead of the aircraft, maneuver to the side of the runway to avoid contact with the rebounding dolly. If safe abort or takeoff is not possible and ejection speed has been attained - EJECT.

LANDING PATTERN

Approach the break point either individually or in echelon, parade formation, at 250 to 300 KIAS. A 17- to 20-second break interval will provide a 35- to 40-second touchdown interval. Have the landing checklist completed, be at optimum AOA/approach speed by the 180-degree position.

APPROACH

Plan for and execute an optimum AOA, on-speed approach. Pay particular attention to maintaining the proper airspeed and correct lineup.

WAVEOFF

To execute a waveoff, immediately add full power, and maintain optimum attitude. Make all waveoffs straight ahead until clear of the landing area.

ARRESTED LANDING

The aircraft should be on runway centerline at touchdown. Aircraft alignment should be straight down the runway with no drift. Upon touchdown, maintain the throttle at the approach position. When arrestment is assured, retard the throttle to idle. Allow the aircraft to roll back to permit the hook to disengage from the pendant. When directed by the taxi director, apply both brakes to stop the rollback, raise the hook and flaps. If further rollback is directed, release brakes and allow the aircraft to be pulled back until a brake signal is given. Then apply brakes judiciously to prevent the aircraft from tipping or rocking back.

CAUTION

Use extreme caution when taxiing on a wet SATS runway.

BOLTER

Bolters are easily accomplished. Simultaneously apply full power and retract the arresting gear hook. Smoothly rotate the aircraft to a liftoff attitude and fly away.

WARNING

If landing on a runway with a SATS catapult installed, care must be taken to prevent engagement of the dolly arrester ropes with the aircraft's tailhook. Structural damage to the aircraft and catapult will result.

NIGHT OPERATIONS

GENERAL

This section covers only that portion of night operations significantly different from day operations.

POSTSTART AND TAXI

It is prudent to perform the poststart and taxi phase with the aircraft exterior lights and rotating beacon operating if allowed by local regulations and combat conditions. Wing lights should be on BRT/STDY.

CATAPULT LAUNCHES

Immediately prior to taxi onto the catapult, turn off all exterior lights using the master exterior light switch. Rely upon and follow closely the directions of the plane director. Upon receiving the signal from the plane director, release brakes as tension is applied. When given the turnup signal by the catapult officer, apply power, and check all instruments. When satisfied that the aircraft is ready for launch, so signify by placing the master exterior light switch in the ON position; fuselage light OFF. Be prepared to establish a wings level climbing attitude on instruments. An initial attitude of 10-12 degrees noseup is recommended. Retract gear when above 300 feet altitude, retract flaps at no lower than 500 feet. When climbing through 2500 feet, adjust lights and radio as briefed.

PART 4 — CARRIER-BASED PROCEDURES

PREFLIGHT

GENERAL

The CVA/CVS NATOPS Manual and the applicable Aircraft Launching Bulletins shall be read by all flight crewmembers prior to carrier qualification. A normal shore-based preflight inspection should be accomplished with particular attention given the landing gear, tires, hook, and underside of the fuselage for possible launching pendant or arresting cable damage. In the cockpit, particular attention should be given to the pilot's scope to ensure that the retaining devices have been installed. Tiedowns shall not be removed from the airplanes unless the emergency brake air pressure gage indicates at least 1000 psi. The pneumatic brake shall be used for stopping the aircraft anytime it is being moved while the engines are not running.

TAXIING

Any signal from the plane director above the waist is intended for the pilot. Any signal below the waist is intended for deck handling personnel. Taxiing aboard ship is much the same as on the land with the exception of additional power requirements. Nose gear steering is excellent and requires use of minimum power while taxiing. Taxi speed should be kept under control at all times especially on wet decks and approaching the catapult area. Be prepared to use the emergency air brake should normal braking fail. The lower ejection handle guard should be down while taxiing.

LAUNCH

PRIOR TO CATAPULT HOOK-UP

Prior to taxi onto the catapult, pilot and RIO shall ensure through verbal check-off that the takeoff checklists are complete, the compass controller is in the FREE mode, and the radar horizon is set for back-up attitude control. Errors are introduced into the SLAVED mode of the HSI due to the magnetic influence of the ship. To use the radar gyro horizon as an emergency back-up for attitude control if the ADI fails during launch, the pilot should set the radar horizon to zero. The RIO positions the elevation strobe to 17° down, the pilot should verify his el strobe is 17° down, and have the RIO make adjustments as necessary. Refer to applicable Launch Bulletin for temperature, gross weight, flap position, and trim setting considerations. Directional and lateral trim should be set at neutral in all cases, regardless of gross weight, flap position, or power settings.

> **CAUTION**
>
> Catapult launching acceleration can force fuel out of the external tanks through the transfer lines to the fuselage cells at a rate beyond tank venting capability, thus creating a partial vacuum in the external tanks. Therefore, to prevent external tank collapse during a catapult launch, insure that the external transfer switch is OFF before launch.

CATAPULT HOOK-UP

Proper positioning on the catapult is easily accomplished if the entry is made with only enough power to maintain forward motion and the plane director's signals are followed explicitly. All functional checks will be performed before taxiing onto the catapult, if practicable. The best technique for positioning is to approach the catapult track at a minimum amount of power utilizing nose gear steering. The pilot should sight down the catapult track, acquire the plane director and follow his signals very closely. The pilot should anticipate an initial hold after the nose wheel drops over the shuttle. After crossing the shuttle, prior to catapult tensioning, the nose strut will be extended (see figure 3-6 for nose strut extension pressure minimums). On signal of catapult tensioning, release brakes and advance power slowly to about 80%, anticipating a hand-off signal to the Catapult Officer. After catapult tension, recheck ADI and standby attitude indicator for desired pitch indications.

> **CAUTION**
>
> Do not allow the pneumatic system pressure to exceed 2300 psi with the nose gear extended. If the pneumatic pressure starts to build up above the value, actuate the emergency air brakes as necessary to maintain the pressure below 2300 psi. If the pneumatic pressure exceeds 2300 PSI the emergency brakes will not release the pressure in the nose strut. To release this excess pressure the nose strut will have to be deflated and then re-inflated. Allowing the pneumatic system pressure to exceed 2300 psi subjects the nose strut to excessive loads during catapulting.

WARNING

Once the nose strut is extended, any interruption of electrical power, such as cycling both generator switches simultaneously, causes deflation of the nose strut from the catapult extension condition.

PRELAUNCH

PILOT

1. External transfer switch - OFF
2. Stab aug - ENGAGE
3. Engine anti-ice - AS DESIRED
4. Trim-SET (refer to Pitch Trim Requirements chart)
5. Radar horizon - SET
6. Altimeters - CHECK
7. Pneumatic pressure indicators - CHECK
8. After nose extension - RECHECK PNEUMATIC PRESSURE
9. ADI and standby attitude indicator - CHECK AFTER NOSE EXTENSION
10. Defog/foot heat handle - AS DESIRED
11. Pitot heat - ON
12. Rain removal - OFF/LOW
13. Bleed air switch - CHECK NORM (some aircraft)
14. Bleed air off light - OFF (some aircraft)
15. Compass - DG MODE
16. Suit vent air - LESS THAN 1/4 ON
17. Lower ejection handle guard - DOWN
18. Complete panel mounted T.O. checklist
19. Engine run-up ON signal from catapult officer
20. Flight and engine instruments - CHECK

RIO

1. Suit vent air - LESS THAN 1/4 ON
2. Compass heading sync - CHALLENGE PILOT
3. Circuit breakers - CHECK IN
4. Radar antenna elevation strobe - 17° DOWN
5. Equipment - STOWED
6. Lower ejection handle guard - DOWN
7. Takeoff checklist - CHALLENGE PILOT FOR COMPLETION
8. Report circuit breakers in, flaps and ramps - READY FOR TAKEOFF
9. Navigation computer - TGT OR BASE (IMMEDIATELY PRIOR TO LAUNCH)

LAUNCH

MILITARY POWER

Upon receipt of a two finger turn-up signal from the Catapult Officer, advance throttle to MIL power, check engine instruments and trim settings. Ensure that the head is positioned firmly against the head rest. Use MIL power catapult hand grips or move throttles outboard into the afterburner detent and use as a throttle stop. When satisfied the aircraft is ready, give an exaggerated salute to the catapult offi-

cer. Place control stick aft. Control stick positioning during catapult launch is a function of aircraft gross weight and stabilator effectiveness. An increase in gross weight results in an aft CG shift with a resultant decrease in aft stick requirement. For normal-to-heavy gross weights, the control stick should be placed in the full aft position for initial positioning and then moved forward slightly reducing aft stick approximately one quarter. For carrier qualification weights, position the control stick full aft and hold in this position until rotation off the bow. Although the aircraft has no trimmed neutral stick position that meets the requirements for all gross weight launches, pilot experience is gained rapidly with a minimum number of launches, and stick positioning poses no problem. After launch, establish a 10° to 12° pitch angle on the ADI, cross checking the pressure instruments to ensure a positive rate of climb. If the ADI fails or is unreliable during launch, the standby attitude indicator and radar horizon are available for attitude reference. The altimeter, airspeed, and rate of climb may dip slightly during catapult stroke but recover shortly after shuttle release.

Note

- Holding the control stick fully aft during a high gross weight launch imparts a higher than desired airplane rotation rate. Although this overrotation may be stopped with forward stick, it creates an undesirable and unnatural control movement, especially during night or IFR conditions.

- In airplanes with the downsprings removed (AFC 308), longitudinal control feel which accompanies airspeed/pitch attitude change is reduced. Therefore, flight instruments must be closely monitored and care must be taken not to rely solely on stick forces for airspeed or attitude control following catapult launches, wave-offs, or bolters.

MAXIMUM POWER

When a MAX power launch is scheduled, the following signals will be used:

Two finger turn-up, advance power to MIL.

Catapult Officer responds with 5 fingers (open hand held towards pilot)

Pilot selects MAX power, checks instruments and positions himself, then gives an exaggerated salute to the Catapult Officer. An optional method of selecting the afterburner may be used by advancing the throttles to minimum AB and assuring an afterburner light-off by noting that the nozzles open slightly. After the catapult fires, advance the throttles to MAX.

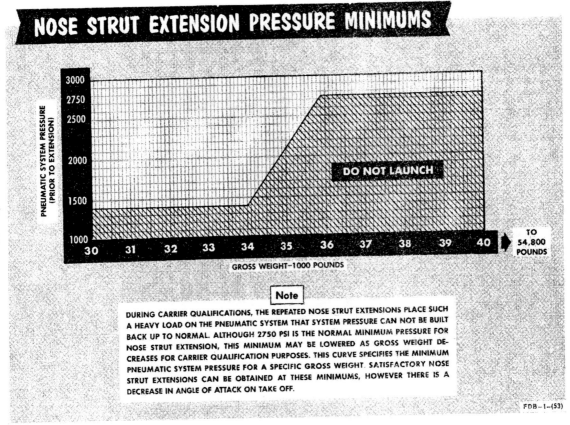

NOSE STRUT EXTENSION PRESSURE MINIMUMS

Note

DURING CARRIER QUALIFICATIONS, THE REPEATED NOSE STRUT EXTENSIONS PLACE SUCH A HEAVY LOAD ON THE PNEUMATIC SYSTEM THAT SYSTEM PRESSURE CAN NOT BE BUILT BACK UP TO NORMAL. ALTHOUGH 2750 PSI IS THE NORMAL MINIMUM PRESSURE FOR NOSE STRUT EXTENSION, THIS MINIMUM MAY BE LOWERED AS GROSS WEIGHT DECREASES FOR CARRIER QUALIFICATION PURPOSES. THIS CURVE SPECIFIES THE MINIMUM PNEUMATIC SYSTEM PRESSURE FOR A SPECIFIC GROSS WEIGHT. SATISFACTORY NOSE STRUT EXTENSIONS CAN BE OBTAINED AT THESE MINIMUMS, HOWEVER THERE IS A DECREASE IN ANGLE OF ATTACK ON TAKE OFF.

FDB-1-(53)

Figure 3-6.

LAUNCH ABORT PROCEDURES

If, after turn-up on the catapult, (day launch), the pilot determines that the aircraft is down, he so indicates by shaking his head from side to side. Never raise the hand into view to give a thumb down or make any motion that might be construed as a salute. After the Catapult Officer observes the no-go signal, he then crosses his forearms over his face. This signal is followed by the standard release-tension signal. When the bridle has dropped, the Catapult Officer then steps in front of the wing of the aircraft and gives the throttle-back signal. Then, and only then, will the power be reduced. If the aircraft is down after the go signal is given, transmit the words Suspend, Suspend.

Refer to Inflight Procedures, section IV, and Performance Data, section XI.

PITCH-TRIM REQUIREMENTS

AIRCRAFT WITH DOWNSPRINGS REMOVED

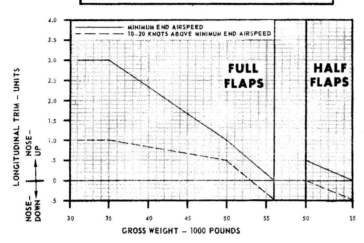

Figure 3-7.

FDB-1-(310)

CARRIER LANDING PATTERN

A carrier landing pattern (figure 3-8) starts with the level break at 800 feet, 300-350 KCAS, on the starboard bow of the ship. The break interval will be approximately one-half of the desired ramp interval time. Radio procedures will be in accordance with ship procedures. When established wings-level on the downwind leg, descend to and fly the pattern at 600 feet MSL. The 180° turn is commenced when abeam the LSO platform to arrive at the 45° position at approximately 450 feet MSL. Glide slope/meatball acquisition will occur at approximately 1 to 1 1/4 mile. On rollout to final, slightly overshoot the ship's wake. Optimum time on glide slope is approximately 30 - 35 seconds.

APPROACH POWER COMPENSATOR TECHNIQUE

Refer to Approach Power Compensator Technique, Field Mirror Landing Practice, this section.

GLIDE SLOPE

The technique of flying the glide slope is the same as FMLP except that more power may be required and

line-up is much harder to maintain. With rough seas and pitching decks, some erratic meatball movements may be encountered. If this is the case, average out the bouncing ball to maintain a smooth and safe rate of descent. In no case overcorrect if the ball moves to a high indication.

ARRESTMENT

Note

In the event of a blown tire on landing, do not raise the flaps until the flap area has been inspected.

ARRESTED LANDING AND EXIT FROM LANDING AREA

As the aircraft touches down, advance throttles to MIL. Upon completion of landing rollout, reduce power to IDLE, raise the hook and allow the aircraft to roll aft. Apply brakes on signal. Fold wings and have the RIO report wing fold position. Taxi forward on the come ahead, and keep the engines running until the CUT signal is given by the plane director. If, at anytime during this phase of operations, one or both brakes fail, utilize the emergency pneumatic brakes and call the tower and/or signal for chocks to be installed. Do not leave cockpit until tie-downs have been installed.

Note

After each arrested landing, inspect the stabilator leading edge for damage from arresting cable.

CARRIER CONTROLLED APPROACHES

GENERAL

Should conflict exist between these procedures and those contained in CVA/CVS NATOPS Manual (and augmenting ships instructions), the latter shall govern. Figure 3-9 illustrates a typical carrier controlled approach.

HOLDING PHASE

Five minutes before penetration, defogging shall be actuated and maximum comfortable interior temperature will be maintained to prevent possible fogging or icing on the windscreen and canopy.

LET-DOWN PROCEDURES

Note

If it becomes necessary to dump fuel during a descent, thrust settings in excess of 85% rpm may be required to insure rapid inflight dumping.

1. Before descent, check shoulder harness handle locked, set lights as dictated by existing weather, and lower arresting hook.
2. Turn on pitot heat and select engine anti-icing system as appropriate.
3. Accomplish final changes to radio and IFF upon departing Marshal or earlier. After these changes are made, pilot makes no further changes except under emergency conditions.
4. When commencing penetration, initiate a standard descent--250 knots CAS, 4000 feet per minute, speed brakes as desired.
5. Radar and barometric altimeters shall be cross checked continuously when below 10,000 feet.

PLATFORM

At 20 miles passing through 5000 feet, aircraft descent shall be slowed to 2000 feet per minute. At this point, a mandatory unacknowledged voice report will be broadcast by each pilot. The aircraft side number will be given, the word platform will be stated, and the SPC is rechecked if it has not been previously checked.

TEN MILE GATE

1. At 10 miles, call side number and 10-mile gate.
2. Commence transition to landing configuration, maintaining 1200 feet.
3. Gear down at 10 miles--flaps down at 195 knots CAS.
4. Complete the landing checklist. Check anti-ice, lights, rain removal, and pitot heat as desired.

SIX MILE GATE

When passing 6 miles, check exterior lights on, call side number, fuel state, and 6-mile gate. For a PAR approach, maintain 1200 feet at approach speed until intercepting the glide path at 2-3/4 miles unless otherwise directed. For an ASR approach, a gradual descent of 600 feet shall be commenced departing the 6-mile gate. In order that intervals remain constant, ship procedures as to when aircraft are slowed to final approach speed after passing 6 miles should be followed. Altitude of 600 feet is maintained until the Final Controller calls commence landing descent, or the meatball is observed to be centered. At 600 feet, aircraft intercepts the center of the glide slope at 1-1/4 miles on a four-degree slope. If ceilings or visibility preclude visual acquisition of the meatball at 1-1/4 miles, 500 to 700 feet per minute descent passing the following check points should be continued:

```
1    mile -- 500 feet
3/4 mile -- 400 feet
1/2 mile -- 300 feet
```

MEATBALL CONTACT

When ready to continue a visual approach, the pilot reports side number, F-4, meatball or clara (no meatball) and fuel state. The LSO acknowledges and instructions from the Final Controller cease. Because of this, pilots are cautioned against premature contact reports during night recoveries when visibility permits sighting the ship beyond 2 to 3 miles. There is little depth perception even under the most ideal conditions and it is difficult to judge distance from the ship without reference to tacan. During night VFR conditions, pilots must cross check tacan DME to ensure that they are actually at 1-1/4 miles, 600 feet,

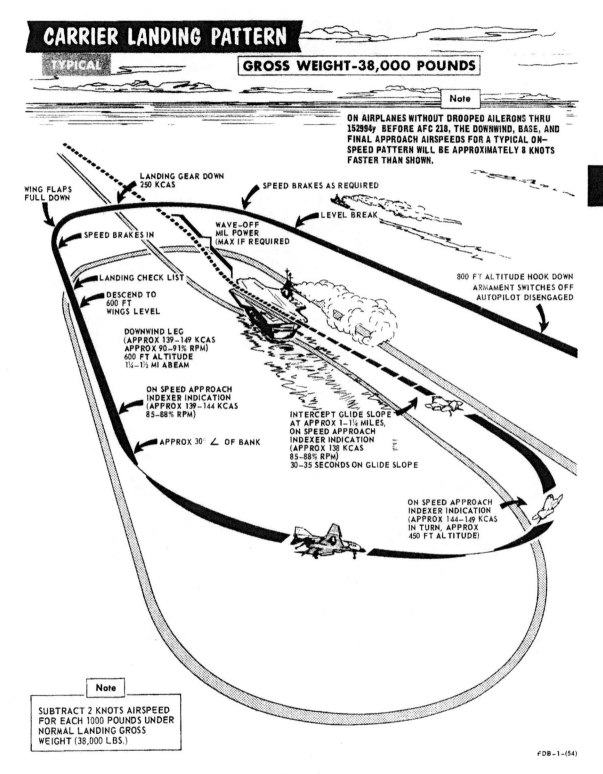

CARRIER LANDING PATTERN

TYPICAL

GROSS WEIGHT-38,000 POUNDS

Note

ON AIRPLANES WITHOUT DROOPED AILERONS THRU 152994y BEFORE AFC 218, THE DOWNWIND, BASE, AND FINAL APPROACH AIRSPEEDS FOR A TYPICAL ON-SPEED PATTERN WILL BE APPROXIMATELY 8 KNOTS FASTER THAN SHOWN.

LANDING GEAR DOWN
250 KCAS

SPEED BRAKES AS REQUIRED

WING FLAPS
FULL DOWN

LEVEL BREAK

SPEED BRAKES IN

WAVE-OFF
MIL POWER
(MAX IF REQUIRED)

LANDING CHECK LIST

800 FT ALTITUDE HOOK DOWN
ARMAMENT SWITCHES OFF
AUTOPILOT DISENGAGED

DESCEND TO
600 FT
WINGS LEVEL

DOWNWIND LEG
(APPROX 139–149 KCAS
APPROX 90–91% RPM)
600 FT ALTITUDE
1¼–1½ MI ABEAM

ON SPEED APPROACH
INDEXER INDICATION
(APPROX 139–144 KCAS
85–88% RPM)

INTERCEPT GLIDE SLOPE
AT APPROX 1–1¼ MILES,
ON SPEED APPROACH
INDEXER INDICATION
(APPROX 138 KCAS
85–88% RPM)
30–35 SECONDS ON GLIDE SLOPE

APPROX 30° ∠ OF BANK

ON SPEED APPROACH
INDEXER INDICATION
(APPROX 144–149 KCAS
IN TURN, APPROX
450 FT ALTITUDE)

Note

SUBTRACT 2 KNOTS AIRSPEED FOR EACH 1000 POUNDS UNDER NORMAL LANDING GROSS WEIGHT (38,000 LBS.)

FDB-1-(54)

Figure 3-8.

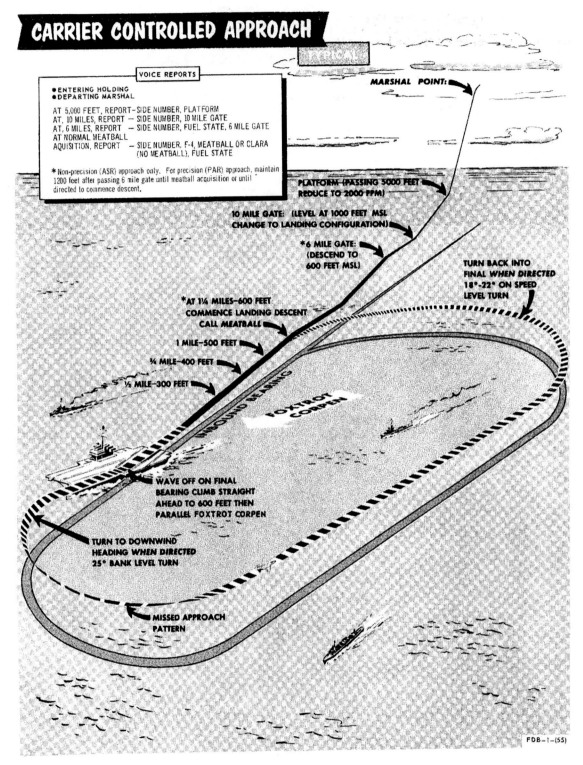

CARRIER CONTROLLED APPROACH

TYPICAL

VOICE REPORTS

● ENTERING HOLDING
● DEPARTING MARSHAL

AT 5,000 FEET, REPORT – SIDE NUMBER, PLATFORM
AT 10 MILES, REPORT – SIDE NUMBER, 10 MILE GATE
AT 6 MILES, REPORT – SIDE NUMBER, FUEL STATE, 6 MILE GATE
AT NORMAL MEATBALL
AQUISITION, REPORT – SIDE NUMBER, F-4, MEATBALL OR CLARA
(NO MEATBALL), FUEL STATE

* Non-precision (ASR) approach only. For precision (PAR) approach, maintain
1200 feet after passing 6 mile gate until meatball acquisition or until
directed to commence descent.

MARSHAL POINT:

PLATFORM (PASSING 5000 FEET
REDUCE TO 2000 PPM)

10 MILE GATE: (LEVEL AT 1000 FEET MSL
CHANGE TO LANDING CONFIGURATION)

*6 MILE GATE:
(DESCEND TO
600 FEET MSL)

TURN BACK INTO
FINAL WHEN DIRECTED
18°-22° ON SPEED
LEVEL TURN

*AT 1¼ MILES–600 FEET
COMMENCE LANDING DESCENT
CALL MEATBALL

1 MILE–500 FEET

¾ MILE–400 FEET

½ MILE–300 FEET

WINDWARD BEARING

FOXTROT CORPEN

WAVE OFF ON FINAL
BEARING CLIMB STRAIGHT
AHEAD TO 600 FEET THEN
PARALLEL FOXTROT CORPEN

TURN TO DOWNWIND
HEADING WHEN DIRECTED
25° BANK LEVEL TURN

MISSED APPROACH
PATTERN

FDB-1-(55)

Figure 3-9

prior to reporting meatball. The height, dimension of the lens or mirror optical beam at 1-1/4 miles is over 200 feet and the true center is difficult to distinguish. This, coupled with the relatively short length of the runway lights, gives the pilot the illusion of being on glide slope and high when, in fact, the aircraft may be 50 to 100 feet below the glide slope. An additional advantage of delaying the meatball report until reaching 1-1/4 miles--even though the ball is in sight--is that Final Control continues line-up instructions that can greatly assist the pilot in establishing satisfactory line-up. Use the vertical velocity indicator to set up a rate of descent of 500 to 700 feet per minute.

VOICE PROCEDURE

Detailed pilot/controller voice procedure must be established in accordance with each ship's CCA doctrine.

WAVEOFF AND BOLTER PHASE

WARNING

Due to stabilator ineffectiveness at low airspeeds the aircraft settles off the angle unless rotation to a takeoff attitude is commenced immediately upon leaving the deck. In order to avoid settling, position the stick well aft during the deck roll.

In the event of a waveoff or bolter, MIL/MAX power should be added as necessary, climb straight ahead to 600 feet, and maintain 150 knots CAS. When directed by CCA, initiate a level turn to the downwind leg. (If no instructions are received within 2 minutes or 4 miles distance on tacan, assume communications failure and initiate the downwind turn to the reciprocal of Foxtrot Corpen and report abeam. If no acknowledgement is received, re-enter the final through the 6-mile gate.) A 25-degree bank angle at 150 knots CAS on the upwind turn establishes the aircraft at the desired 1-3/8 to 1-1/2 miles abeam on the downwind leg. Aircraft that undershoot or overshoot a proper downwind leg may be vectored back to a proper abeam position. Slow to proper approach speed when approaching the abeam position. This position can be established by using a relative tacan bearing of 15 degrees aft of the wing at 1-3/4 to 3 miles on DME when on the downwind heading. Final Control clears the aircraft to turn back inbound to intercept the final bearing. A level, on speed approach turn of 18 to 20 degrees back angle from the normal abeam position allows the aircraft to properly intercept the final inbound bearing at 1-1/4 to 1-1/2 miles aft of the ship. Traffic spacing ahead may require that the aircraft continue on downwind leg well past the normal abeam position before being directed to turn to final bearing. No attempt should be made to establish visual contact with the ship when executing a CCA until the final approach turn has been executed. When fuel considerations become critical in an extended bolter pattern, 300 to 400 pounds per pass may be saved by raising the landing gear and selecting half flaps. Lower landing gear and full flaps on final. The WHEELS light on the pilot's instrument panel flashes with the gear up and the flaps down.

WARNING

Do not attempt to fly 19 units angle of attack with the flaps 1/2 or full down and the landing gear retracted. Gear up airspeeds at 19 units correspond to gear down airspeeds at 22 to 23 units (10 to 12 knots slow). This is especially critical in drooped aileron airplanes because landing configuration stalls occur at 24 units angle of attack.

FOULED DECK HOLDING

Detailed procedures for fouled deck holding are contained in the CVA/CVS NATOPS Manual. The best gauge for maximum endurance at any altitude is to fly 9 units on the angle of attack indicator, and utilize minimum bank angles. This pre-supposes that all aircraft in the landing configuration retract gear and flaps. If necessary, as fuel becomes critical with no Bingo field available, jettison external stores. In extreme emergency situations, a small amount of fuel (approximately 10 pounds per minute) can be saved by securing one engine at sea level with average landing gross weights. If holding must be accomplished with flaps fully extended, the normal endurance time is decreased by 4.5 minutes per 1000 pounds of fuel for average landing gross weights at sea level. Due to the increase in drag with flaps full down, and decreased efficiency due to the bleed air loss through the BLC system, this decrement increases with altitude. For example, at 25,000 feet the decrement is 9.0 minutes per 1000 pounds of fuel. It is, therefore, recommended that holding with flaps fully extended be accomplished at sea level.

ALL WEATHER CARRIER LANDING SYSTEM APPROACHES

All weather carrier landing system (AWCLS) approaches (data link approaches) apply to properly modified data link aircraft utilizing carrier or shore-based SPN-10, SPN-42, or MPN-T1 AWCLS facilities. Three approach modes are available; however, modes 1 and 1A are not presently authorized (refer to data link limitations, section VIII, Classified Supplement). In mode 1 approaches, data link/AWCLS control signals are coupled to the autopilot after automatic carrier landing (ACL) radar lockon and remain coupled until touchdown. Mode 1A approaches differ from mode 1 approaches in that the data link/AWCLS control signals are uncoupled 1/2 mile (approximately 200 feet altitude) from touchdown. Mode 2 approaches are similar to mode 1/1A approaches; however, data link/AWCLS control signals are not coupled to the autopilot.

AWCLS MODE 1 AND 1A APPROACH PROCEDURES

AWCLS mode 1 and 1A approaches are illustrated in figure 3-10. Mode 1 approaches require the APCS. The following steps describe typical mode 1 and 1A approach procedures. Light illumination and extinguishments (other than acknowledge button extinguishments) on the front cockpit digital display indicator (DDI), command display indicator (CDI), telelight panel, and HSI follow each step.

1. Position the following controls as indicated to prepare the aircraft for receiving data link/AWCLS signals. (Also refer to section VIII, Classified Supplement.)
   a. Navigation function selector panel.
      (1) Bearing/distance selector switch - TACAN
      (2) Mode selector knob - DL (HSI course deviation indicator is slaved to lubber line).
   b. DDI ACK button - PRESS WHEN ILLUMINATED
   c. Day-night controls - AS DESIRED
   d. Communications set control
      (1) Data link power switch - ON
      (2) Message selector switch - NORM
      (3) Frequency select dials - AS BRIEFED
   e. Data link BIT switch - NORM

       CDI - TILT
       HSI - DL, TAC (same throughout approach)

2. Before or while in Marshall, receive the universal test message (UTM) to check the data link system for proper operation. Refer to section VIII, Classified Supplement, for UTM procedures and displays.

       CDI - TILT (extinguished during testing)

3. Perform a normal CCA. At 10-mile gate, with aircraft level at 1200 feet MSL or as assigned, change to landing configuration.

       CDI - TILT

4. Engage APCS. While heading inbound, with aircraft in level flight at 1200 feet (or as assigned), stabilize approach speed.

Note

To fly mode 1 approaches, the APCS must be utilized. APCS is recommended but not required in mode 1A.

If APCS malfunctions, do not attempt to couple the aircraft. Execute a mode 2 (figure 3-11) or a mode 3 (talk-down) approach.

    CDI - TILT

5. Check that corner reflector is extended. Corner reflector extends when gear and hook are low-ered. If approach is made with hook up, place hook bypass switch to BY-PASS.

       CDI - TILT

6. Engage AFCS. It is desirable that the aircraft be flown in altitude hold prior to coupling. Altitude hold automatically disengages when aircraft is coupled.

       CDI - TILT

7. At approximately 6 miles, controller inserts aircraft address.

       CDI - TILT (extinguishes)
       DDI - LAND CHK

8. At approximately 4 to 6 miles, with aircraft level at 1200 feet (or as assigned) and on final bearing, controller reports "ACL lockon, report when coupled". The ADI pitch and bank steering bars commence providing glide slope line-up indications and the HSI heading marker displays the final bearing (command heading).

       CDI - CPLR ON (indicates aircraft is receiving autopilot engage/enable signal) or MANUAL (indicates aircraft not receiving autopilot engage/enable signal and aircraft cannot be coupled).
       DDI - ACL RDY

   a. A below glide slope indication by the pitch steering bar is normal. An above glide slope indication indicates passage of the glide slope extended and coupling should not be attempted.
   b. If the bank steering bar indicates the aircraft is not on the glide slope centerline extended (lateral error), establish a corrective cut before coupling. This reduces the initial lateral error command.
   c. With wings level at assigned altitude (vertical velocity indication less than ± 500 feet per minute) engage coupler switch on AFCS control panel.

Note

If aircraft is not coupled with wings level, it initially rolls to a wings level attitude upon coupling.

    CDI - CPLR ON
    DDI - ACL RDY

9. Report (side number) coupled.

       CDI - CPLR ON
       DDI - ACL RDY

AWCLS MODE 1 AND 1A APPROACHES

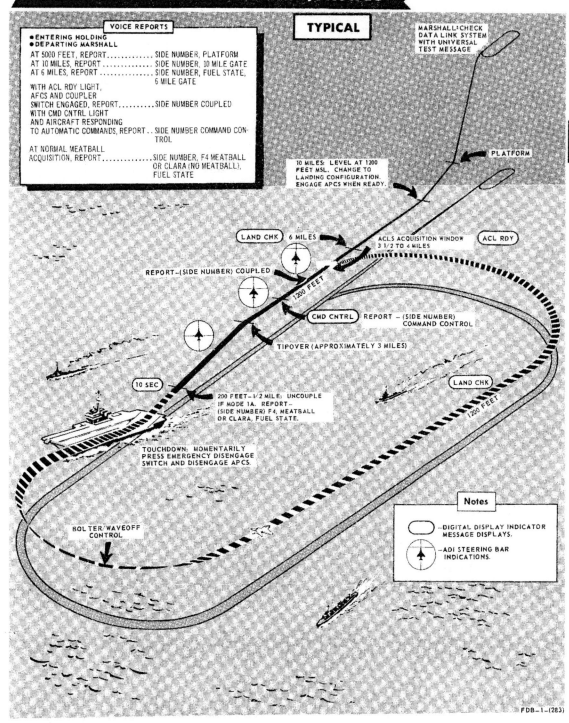

VOICE REPORTS

- ●ENTERING HOLDING
- ●DEPARTING MARSHALL

AT 5000 FEET, REPORT.............SIDE NUMBER, PLATFORM
AT 10 MILES, REPORT.............SIDE NUMBER, 10 MILE GATE
AT 6 MILES, REPORT.............SIDE NUMBER, FUEL STATE, 6 MILE GATE

WITH ACL RDY LIGHT, AFCS AND COUPLER
SWITCH ENGAGED, REPORT.........SIDE NUMBER COUPLED

WITH CMD CNTRL LIGHT AND AIRCRAFT RESPONDING
TO AUTOMATIC COMMANDS, REPORT..SIDE NUMBER COMMAND CONTROL

AT NORMAL MEATBALL
ACQUISITION, REPORT.............SIDE NUMBER, F4 MEATBALL OR CLARA (NO MEATBALL), FUEL STATE

TYPICAL

MARSHALL: CHECK DATA LINK SYSTEM WITH UNIVERSAL TEST MESSAGE

PLATFORM

10 MILES: LEVEL AT 1200 FEET MSL. CHANGE TO LANDING CONFIGURATION. ENGAGE APCS WHEN READY.

LAND CHK 6 MILES

ACLS ACQUISITION WINDOW 3 1/2 TO 4 MILES

ACL RDY

REPORT–(SIDE NUMBER) COUPLED

1200 FEET

CMD CNTRL REPORT – (SIDE NUMBER) COMMAND CONTROL

TIPOVER (APPROXIMATELY 3 MILES)

10 SEC

200 FEET–1/2 MILE: UNCOUPLE IF MODE 1A. REPORT– (SIDE NUMBER) F4, MEATBALL OR CLARA, FUEL STATE.

LAND CHK

1200 FEET

TOUCHDOWN: MOMENTARILY PRESS EMERGENCY DISENGAGE SWITCH AND DISENGAGE APCS.

BOLTER/WAVEOFF CONTROL

Notes

⬭ –DIGITAL DISPLAY INDICATOR MESSAGE DISPLAYS.

✦ –ADI STEERING BAR INDICATIONS.

FDB-1-(283)

Figure 3-10

10. Controller sends ACL commands. If radio fails, commands are sent 10 seconds after ACL lockon. Upon observing DDI CMD CNTRL light illumination and aircraft response to commands, report (side number) command control.

    CDI - CPLR ON
    DDI - ACL RDY (extinguishes)
          CMD CNTRL

11. Under certain circumstances the aircraft may become uncoupled. The cockpit indications and recommended pilot action for each instance are as follows:

a. Intentional disengagement by pilot. Pilot presses the AFCS/ARI emergency disengage switch on control stick and the AFCS and coupler switches disengage. The stab aug and ARI are disengaged as long as the AFCS/ARI emergency disengage switch is pressed.

    CDI - CPLR ON
    DDI - CMD CNTRL
    Telelight panel - AUTO PILOT DISENGAGE
    Windshield - COUPLER OFF (some aircraft)

(1) If disengagement occurs before intercepting the glide slope, continue the approach in mode 2/mode 3 or recouple (pilot's discretion). Recoupling is accomplished by re-engaging the AFCS switch and the coupler switch in that order. If the aircraft is uncoupled for an excessive length of time, large initial corrective commands may result when the aircraft is recoupled. Attempt to center the bank steering bar before recoupling. Never recouple if the ADI pitch steering bar indicates glide slope passage. Continue with a mode 2 approach.

(2) If disengagement occurs while on glide slope, continue the approach in mode 2/mode 3 or waveoff (pilot's discretion). No recoupling should be attempted at ranges less than 2 miles.

b. Unintentional disengagement.

(1) AFCS malfunction. The coupler switch disengages concurrently with the AFCS switch. Cockpit indications and pilot action are the same as with intentional disengagement.

    CDI - CPLR ON
    DDI - CMD CNTRL
    Telelight panel - AUTO PILOT DISENGAGE
    Windshield - COUPLER OFF (some aircraft)

(2) System malfunction. AFCS and coupler switches disengage. Continue approach in mode 2 or 3. The aircraft cannot be recoupled.

    CDI - CPLR ON (extinguishes)
          MANUAL (if malfunction due to loss of AFCS engage/enable signal) or

TILT (if malfunction due to termination of data link signals).
    DDI - CMD CNTRL
    Telelight panel - AUTO PILOT DISENGAGE
    Windshield - COUPLER OFF (some aircraft)

Note

If APCS disengages, it does not uncouple aircraft. Without APCS, a mode 2 or 3 approach should be flown.

c. System waveoff. A system parameter has been exceeded and the AFCS and coupler switches disengage. If waveoff is received after glide slope interception and in IFR conditions, execute a waveoff. The aircraft cannot be recoupled. Upon placing the speed brake switch to IN to cancel (extinguish) the flashing WAVEOFF lights, the APCS is disengaged.

    CDI - MANUAL
          WAVEOFF (flashing: extinguished when speedbrake switch is positioned to IN)
    DDI - CMD CNTRL
          WAVEOFF (flashing: extinguished when speedbrake switch is positioned to IN)
    Telelight panel - AUTO PILOT DISENGAGE
    Windshield - COUPLER OFF (some aircraft)
    Telelight panel/glareshield - APCS OFF

12. At 1/2 mile in mode 1A approaches, the controller downgrades the approach to mode 2. Although the AFCS and coupler switches automatically disengage, momentary actuation of the AFCS/ARI emergency disengage switch is recommended to ensure that the switches disengage.

    CDI - CPLR ON (extinguishes)
          MANUAL
    DDI - CMD CNTRL
    Telelight panel - AUTO PILOT DISENGAGE
    Windshield - COUPLER OFF (some aircraft)

13. In mode 1 approaches, the pilot receives the 10 seconds discrete 12.5 seconds before touchdown.

    CDI - CPLR ON
    DDI - CMD CNTRL (extinguishes)
          10 SEC

14. At touchdown in a mode 1 approach, momentarily actuate the AFCS/ARI emergency disengage switch to disengage the AFCS and coupler switches. Actuate speedbrake switch to disengage APCS. Do not hold the AFCS/ARI emergency disengage switch pressed after AFCS disengagement, since on a bolter or a touch and

go landing, the aircraft would depart the flight deck with stab aug disengaged.

```
CDI - CPLR ON
DDI - 10 SEC
Telelight panel - AUTO PILOT DISENGAGE
Windshield - COUPLER OFF (some aircraft)
Telelight panel/glareshield - APCS OFF
```

Note

Although the AFCS switch automatically disengages at touchdown on some aircraft, the AFCS/ARI emergency disengage switch shall be momentarily pressed to ensure switch disengagement.

15. If the aircraft bolters, the SPN-10/42 computer clears the data link discretes and terminates data link transmissions to the aircraft approximately 7 seconds after touchdown.

```
CDI - CPLR ON (extinguishes)
      TILT
DDI - 10 SEC (extinguishes)
Telelight panel - AUTO PILOT DISENGAGE
Windshield - COUPLER OFF (some aircraft)
Telelight panel/glareshield - APCS OFF
```

AWCLS MODE 2 APPROACH PROCEDURES

An AWCLS mode 2 approach is illustrated in figure 3-9. In a mode 2 approach, the ADI pitch and bank steering bars present vertical and lateral glide slope errors respectively in relation to the aircraft. The pilot flies the aircraft toward the steering bars as in an ILS approach. Light illumination and extinguishments are noted following the procedural steps as in AWCLS Mode 1 and 1A Approach Procedures.

1. Perform steps 1 thru 5 in the AWCLS Mode 1 and 1A Approach Procedures. APCS engagement is optional and at the pilots discretion.

```
CDI - TILT (extinguishes during testing)
HSI - DL, TAC (same throughout approach)
```

2. At approximately 6 miles, controller inserts aircraft address. Pilot rechecks landing checklist.

```
CDI - TILT (extinguishes)
      MANUAL
DDI - LAND CHK
```

3. ACL radar lockon. Pilot observes fly-up signal on ADI pitch steering bar and the final bearing on both the ADI bank steering bar and the HSI heading marker. Report (side number) needles. (A fly-down needle indicates erroneous information if further aft of the carrier than 3 miles at 1200 feet or indicates glide slope passage if within 3 miles at 1200 feet. If glide slope passage has occured, attempts to intercept it are at pilot's discretion.) Fly aircraft level as the pitch steering bar moves down from the top of the ADI. When the pitch steering bar approaches the ADI miniature wings, pitch the aircraft over onto the glide slope. Fly glide slope by keeping ADI steering bars centered.

```
CDI - MANUAL
DDI - ACL RDY or CMD CNTRL (refer to
      following steps a and b)
```

a. For approaches that were begun in mode 2, the DDI ACL RDY light illuminates and remains illuminated throughout the approach.

b. If a mode 1/1A approach was initiated and the pilot uncoupled and continued in mode 2, the CMD CNTRL light remains illuminated throughout the approach unless the controller recycles his console.

4. At 1/2 mile to touchdown or sooner (pilot's discretion), transfer to the standard visual approach and call the meatball.

```
CDI - MANUAL
DDI - ACL RDY or CMD CNTRL (Refer to
      previous remarks)
```

AWCLS MODE 2 APPROACH

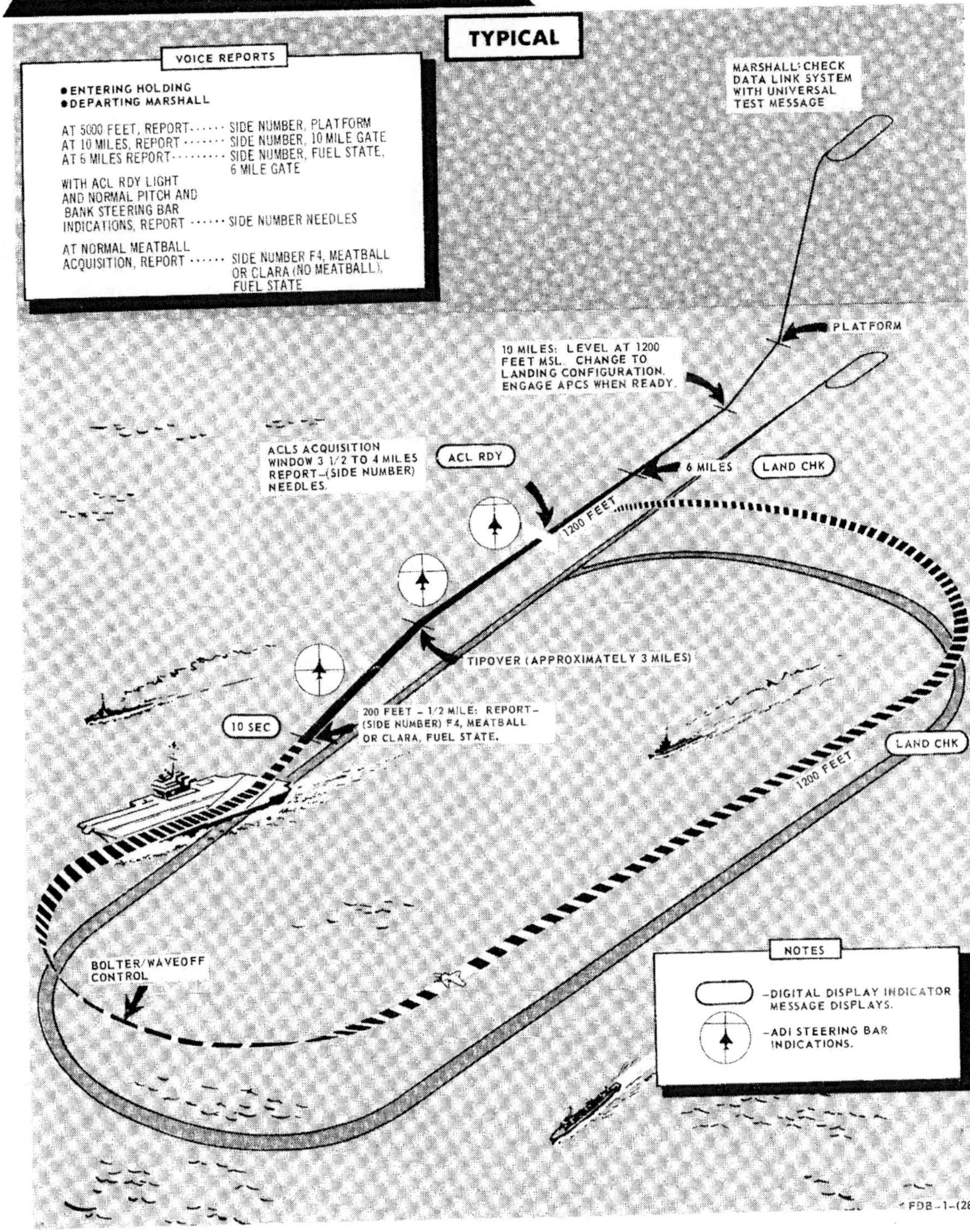

TYPICAL

VOICE REPORTS

- ENTERING HOLDING
- DEPARTING MARSHALL

AT 5000 FEET, REPORT · · · · · · SIDE NUMBER, PLATFORM
AT 10 MILES, REPORT · · · · · · SIDE NUMBER, 10 MILE GATE
AT 6 MILES REPORT · · · · · · · · SIDE NUMBER, FUEL STATE, 6 MILE GATE

WITH ACL RDY LIGHT
AND NORMAL PITCH AND
BANK STEERING BAR
INDICATIONS, REPORT · · · · · SIDE NUMBER NEEDLES

AT NORMAL MEATBALL
ACQUISITION, REPORT · · · · · SIDE NUMBER F4, MEATBALL
OR CLARA (NO MEATBALL),
FUEL STATE

MARSHALL: CHECK
DATA LINK SYSTEM
WITH UNIVERSAL
TEST MESSAGE

PLATFORM

10 MILES: LEVEL AT 1200
FEET MSL. CHANGE TO
LANDING CONFIGURATION.
ENGAGE APCS WHEN READY.

ACLS ACQUISITION
WINDOW 3 1/2 TO 4 MILES
REPORT—(SIDE NUMBER)
NEEDLES.

ACL RDY

6 MILES

LAND CHK

1200 FEET

TIPOVER (APPROXIMATELY 3 MILES)

10 SEC

200 FEET – 1/2 MILE: REPORT—
(SIDE NUMBER) F4, MEATBALL
OR CLARA, FUEL STATE.

LAND CHK

1200 FEET

NOTES

—DIGITAL DISPLAY INDICATOR
MESSAGE DISPLAYS.

—ADI STEERING BAR
INDICATIONS.

BOLTER/WAVEOFF
CONTROL

FDB-1-(282)

Figure 3-11

NIGHT FLYING

GENERAL

Night carrier operations have a much slower tempo than daylight operations and it is the pilot's responsibility to maintain this tempo. The procedure outlined here are different from, or in addition to, normal day carrier operations.

BRIEFING

Before initial night flight operations, all pilots should receive an additional briefing from the following persons.

Flight Deck Officer
Catapult Officer
Arresting Gear Officer
LSO

Individual flight briefings will include all applicable items outlined above, with particular emphasis on weather, and Bingo fuel. The ready room is lighted for night adaptation during briefings. In addition, pilots may wear night adaptation glasses from the ready room to the flight deck to prevent loss of night vision.

PREFLIGHT

External preflight will be made utilizing the red lensed flashlight. In addition to normal cockpit preflight, insure that external light switches are properly positioned for poststart light check. The general rule of not showing white lights on the flight deck at night should be observed.

POSTSTART

Adjust cockpit light intensity to desired level. When ready for taxi, indicate with appropriate signal.

TAXI

Night deck handling operations are of necessity slower than those used during the day. When a doubt arises as to the meaning of a signal from a taxi director, stop.

CATAPULT HOOK-UP

Maneuvering the aircraft for catapult hook-up at night, is identical to that used in day operation; however, it is difficult to determine your speed or degree of motion over the deck. The pilot must rely upon, and follow closely, the plane director's signals.

CATAPULT LAUNCH

On turnup signal from Catapult Officer, assure throttles in MIL and check all instruments. When ready to go, place external light master switch ON (dim/bright and steady), fuselage light OFF. After launch, establish a 10 to 12° pitch angle on the ADI, cross checking the pressure instruments to ensure a positive rate of climb. Retract the landing gear. Five hundred feet is considered to be minimum altitude for retraction of flaps. When well established in a climb, switch lights to bright and flashing or as applicable for an instrument climb-out. The standby attitude indicator or radar gyro should be used in the event of an ADI malfunction.

CATAPULT ABORT PROCEDURES

The pilot's no-go signal for night launches will be not to turn on his exterior lights. The pilot should also call on land/launch and advise with Side No., Cat No., is down. Maintain MIL power until the throttle-back signal is received from the Catapult Officer standing in front of the wing of the aircraft. In the event of a catapult malfunction, the above signals also apply. If the aircraft is down after the go signal is given, transmit the words Suspend, Suspend.

ARRESTMENT AND EXIT FROM LANDING AREA

During the approach, all lights shall be on bright and steady. At end of arrestment rollout, turn off external lights and follow director's signals.

FDB-1-(56)

SECTION IV **FLIGHT PROCEDURES**

TABLE OF CONTENTS

FLIGHT CHARACTERISTICS

ANGLE OF ATTACK

Flight characteristics of swept-wing high performance aircraft like the F-4 are predictable and repeatable. The most significant factors influencing flight characteristics are angle of attack and static margin. Angle of attack is defined as that angle formed by the chord line of the wing and the aircraft flight path (relative wind). Static margin is defined and discussed under Longitudinal Stability, this section.

LOW ANGLE OF ATTACK MANEUVERING

Induced drag is at a minimum at approximately 5 units angle of attack (nearly zero G); therefore, acceleration characteristics are exceptional. To achieve maximum performance acceleration from subsonic Mach numbers to supersonic flight, a 5 unit angle of attack pushover will provide minimum drag and allow gravity to enhance airplane acceleration. This technique provides the minimum time, fuel, and distance to accelerate from subsonic Mach numbers to the optimum supersonic climb schedule.

When confronted with a recovery from a condition of low airspeed and high pitch attitude, the angle of attack indicator becomes the primary recovery instrument. A smooth pushover to 5 units angle of attack will unload the airplane and reduce the stall speed to nearly zero. Recovery can be accomplished safely at any speed which will provide stabilator effectiveness (ability to control angle of attack). Smooth control of angle of attack is a necessity, and no attempt to control bank angle or yaw should be made. High pitch angles with rapidly decreasing airspeed will result in loss of stabilator effectiveness and subsequent loss of control of angle of attack.

MEDIUM ANGLE OF ATTACK MANEUVERING

Maneuvering at angles of attack from 5 to 15 units will produce normal airplane response to control movement.

HIGH ANGLE OF ATTACK MANEUVERING

Above 15 units angle of attack, airplane response and flight characteristics begin to exhibit the changes expected in swept-wing high performance aircraft. The primary flight characteristics exhibited at high angles of attack are adverse yaw (yaw due to roll) and dihedral effect (roll due to yaw).

Adverse Yaw

Attempts to roll the airplane with lateral stick deflections (ailerons and spoilers) will result in yaw opposite to the direction of the intended turn. This adverse yaw becomes more severe at high angles of attack. In the high angle of attack flight regime, aileron inputs provide very low roll rates. At very high angles of attack (near stall), aileron inputs cause increased adverse yaw and roll opposite to that intended. The natural tendency to raise the wing with aileron must be avoided. Aileron deflection at the point of departure from controlled flight will increase the probability of spin entry. At the first indication of adverse yaw, the ailerons must be neutralized.

Dihedral Effect

Attempts to yaw the airplane with rudder will produce roll in the same direction as yaw. This dihedral effect becomes more pronounced at high angles of attack. The use of rudder inputs to produce yaw and in turn generate roll, will provide the highest attainable roll rates at high angles of attack. Above 15 units angle of attack, desired roll should be generated primarily through use of the rudder. The rudder must be used judiciously, however, since excessive rudder inputs will induce excessive yaw.

LANDING

The optimum approach (ON-SPEED) indicated angle of attack with the landing gear down is 19.0 units, and stall warning (rudder pedal shaker) is set at 21.3 units (19.2 and 22.3 units respectfully on aircraft without drooped ailerons). The angle of attack reference changes with nose gear position in the approach speed range. The indicated angle of attack increases approximately 3 units when the nose gear is extended. This change in indicated angle of attack with nose gear position is due to a change in the airflow pattern over the fuselage mounted angle of attack probe with the nose gear retracted. All references to indicated angle of attack should take this factor into consideration. Optimum approach angle of attack is adequate for all allowable gross weight and flap configurations. No adjustment is required for gusting crosswinds, runway, or weather conditions.

MAXIMUM PERFORMANCE MANEUVERING

The three factors that determine maximum performance maneuvering capability are structural limitations, stabilator effectiveness, and aerodynamic limitations. Structural limitations are outlined in section I, part 4. The limit in stabilator effectiveness occurs at high altitudes and supersonic speeds where full aft stick can be attained without reaching aerodynamic or structural limits. Aerodynamic limitations (stall) are primarily a function of angle of attack. In this area of flight, maximum performance turns are achieved by maintaining 19 to 20 units angle of attack while utilizing afterburner as required. The adverse yaw produced by the use of aileron during high angle of attack maximum performance maneuvering has been discussed and is of paramount importance in Air Combat Maneuvering. If a high angle of attack must be maintained and a roll is necessary, rudder must be used to produce roll due to yaw as previously discussed. During maximum performance maneuvering, higher roll rates may be achieved by: momentarily unloading the airplane (reducing angle of attack to between 5 and 10 units), utilizing aileron to roll to the desired bank angle, then neutralizing aileron and reestablishing the required angle of attack. At the first indication of departure from controlled flight, controls must be neutralized to preclude aggravating the out of control condition. Maximum performance maneuvering must be fully understood and demonstrated by a qualified instructor pilot prior to attempting any practice in this area of flight.

STALLS

CRUISE/COMBAT CONFIGURATION

Normal Stalls

Normal (1G) stalls are preceded by a wide band of buffet. First noticeable buffet occurs at 12 to 14 units angle of attack and usually increases from moderate to heavy buffet immediately prior to stall or departure. The rudder pedal shaker is activated at 21.3 units on aircraft with drooped ailerons or 22.3 units on aircraft without drooped ailerons; however, it may not be recognizable due to heavy buffet. Wing rock, if encountered, will commence at approximately 23 units and variations in bank angle of up to 30° from wings level can be expected near the stall. The angle of attack at stall varies with loading and is normally above 25 units. The stall is characterized by a slight nose rise and/or yawing motion in either direction. Recovery from the stall is easily and immediately effected when angle of attack is reduced by positioning the stick forward, maintaining neutral ailerons and making judicious use of rudder to avoid inducing excessive yaw.

Accelerated Stalls

Only general stall characteristics are discussed herein; specific characteristics vary with airspeed, Mach number, loading, center of gravity position, G level, aircraft attitude, and control techniques. Accelerated stalls are preceded by moderate buffet which increases to heavy buffet immediately prior to the stall. Wing rock is unpredictable, but generally starts at about 22 to 25 units and progresses to a high frequency, large amplitude roll oscillation. The amplitude of the roll oscillations will be less with a heavy wing loaded aircraft. The angle of attack at stall varies considerably with loading, but is above 25 units for all loadings. Rapidly entered accelerated stalls may occur at lower indicated angles of attack. Increasing the rate of aft stick

STALL SPEEDS

ALL CONFIGURATIONS

ALTITUDES

10,000 FEET AND BELOW

POWER—ON STALL SPEEDS

AIRCRAFT THRU 152994y BEFORE AFC 218

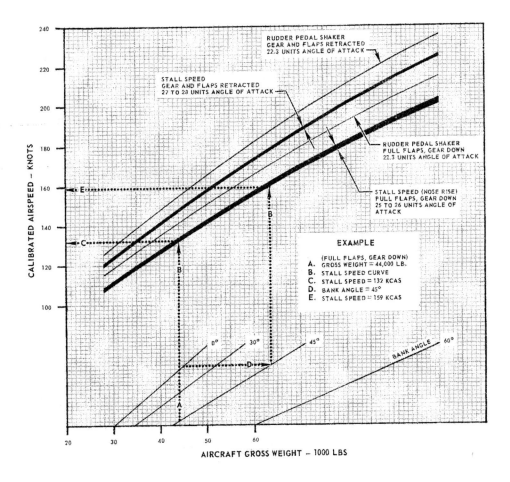

Figure 4-1

FDB-1-(57)

STALL SPEEDS

ALL CONFIGURATIONS

**AIRCRAFT 152995z AND UP, AND
ALL OTHERS AFTER AFC 218**

ALTITUDES

10,000 FEET AND BELOW

POWER—ON STALL SPEEDS

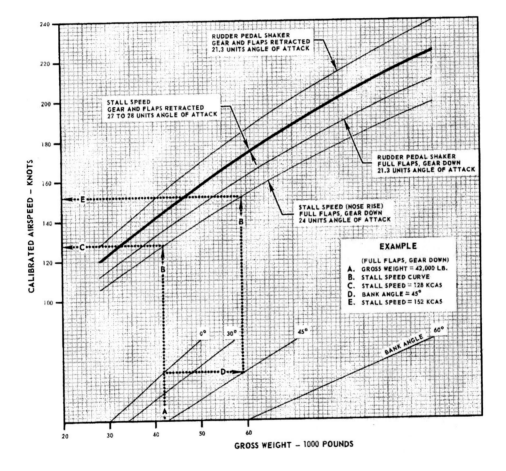

Figure 4-2

FDB-1-(287)

displacement increases the magnitude and rate of yaw and roll oscillations at the stall. Applying and holding full aft stick, even with ailerons and rudder neutral, can result in a spin. Prompt neutralization of controls will effect recovery from an accelerated stall. Oscillations in roll and yaw, which may be present during recovery, should be allowed to damp themselves out and should not be countered with ailerons or rudder.

Inverted Stalls

An inverted (negative angle of attack) stall can only be obtained with abrupt application of full forward stick in vertical maneuvers or an inverted climb of greater than 20° nose-up. Light to moderate buffet occurs at the stall and there are no distinct yaw or roll tendencies. Recovery from the inverted stall is effected by relaxing the forward stick pressure and maintaining an angle of attack between 5 and 10 units until recovered from the unusual attitude.

LANDING CONFIGURATION STALLS

Note

Do not practice landing configuration stalls above 10,000 feet. The effectiveness of the BLC system and engine bleed pressures decrease with altitude. Use of BLC above 10,000 feet may cause the systems using bleed air to become inoperative.

Aircraft With Drooped Ailerons

With the gear and flaps down, the stall occurs at approximately 24 units angle of attack, and is characterized by simultaneous nose rise and apparent loss of lateral stability. With the flaps down and the landing gear up (bolter configuration), the stall angle of attack will be approximately 3 units lower because of the different airflow pattern over the fuselage mounted angle of attack probe with the nose gear retracted. There is virtually no increase in general airframe buffet during stall approaches, and very little aerodynamic warning (stick force lightening and wing rock) is apparent prior to the stall. Stall warning is in the form of a rudder pedal shaker set at 21.3 units regardless of gear or flap position. With the gear and flaps down, the pedal shaker actuates approximately 8 knots prior to the stall. In the bolter configuration, the pedal shaker does not provide stall warning; the only stall warning being stick force lightening and slight wing rock just prior to the stall. The rate of increase of angle of attack above the stall is difficult to control and is a function of pitch rate and center of gravity position (aft CG most critical). Recovery from the stall is effected by placing the stick forward to reduce the angle of attack to below stall and increasing the throttles to MIL thrust. Recovery attitude is about 30° nose down. Stalls with one-half flaps are similar to full-flap stalls.

Aircraft Without Drooped Ailerons

With the gear and flaps down, the stall occurs at approximately 27 units angle of attack. With the flaps down and the landing gear up (bolter configuration), the stall angle of attack will be approximately 3 units lower because of the different airflow pattern over the fuselage mounted angle of attack probe with the nose gear retracted. Stall warning is in the form of a rudder pedal shaker set at 22.3 units angle of attack regardless of gear or flap position. With the flaps and gear down, the pedal shaker actuates approximately 17 knots above the stall and 9 knots before wing rock. At approximately 24 units, the airplane exhibits a slight nose rise accompanied by stick force lightening. At approximately 25 units, oscillations in roll (wing rock) begin that increase in intensity as speed is decreased, but normally do not exceed 30° of bank angle at the stall. If bank angles of 60° are experienced, the stall approach should be discontinued with application of forward stick and neutral ailerons. There is virtually no increase in general airframe buffet during stall approaches except a moderate buffet just prior to stall. If wing rock does not exceed 20°, the stall can be carried to the point of a second nose rise followed immediately by a nose down pitch. In all cases, recovery is effected by placing the stick forward to reduce the angle of attack to below stall and increasing the throttles to MIL. Recovery altitude is usually about 30° nose down. Stalls with one half-flaps are similar to full-flap stalls.

LOSS OF CONTROL

A loss of control or departure from controlled flight (departure) is best described as random motions about any or all axes. Departure characteristics are highly dependent on airspeed, Mach number, G level, type of entry, and loading. In addition to the stall warning discussed under Normal and Accelerated Stalls, a build-up in sideforces (tendency to move the pilot to the side of the cockpit) will be encountered immediately prior to a departure. The sideforces may not be detectable in a high speed, high G condition where wing rock will be the most positive indication of impending departure. If angle of attack is not reduced to below stall, departures can be expected to develop into spins. The angle of attack at departure is highly dependent upon loading. Clean or Sparrows-only airplanes will depart at slightly greater than 30 units, while heavy wing loaded air-to-ground configurations may depart as low as 27 to 28 units. Departures are best prevented by proper control of angle of attack. Although aileron deflection may aggravate the situation, excessive angle of attack is the primary cause of departure. Ailerons or excessive rudder deflection at departure increase the probability of spin entry following departure. Departures are characterized by a yawing motion with roll in the direction of yaw. The yawing motion at departure will be more violent when encountered during a high speed, high G condition than during a low speed, low G condition. At the first indication of departure, or when a nose high, rapidly decaying airspeed situation is encountered, attempt to reduce the angle of attack by moving the stick smoothly forward, simultaneously neutralizing ailerons and rudder. The throttles should be retarded to idle to reduce the probability of engine flame out unless, in the pilot's opinion, the altitude is so low that thrust will be required to minimize altitude loss during the recovery. The stick should be smoothly, yet positively, moved forward; not jammed forward. Forward stick should be applied until negative G is felt or until full forward stick is reached. An aircraft unloading (zero or negative G) is the most positive indication of recovery. The majority of recoveries will be effected before the stick reaches the forward stop. If recovery is not apparent after the application of full forward stick, deploy the drag chute without hesitation. Large roll and yaw oscillations may be present during recoveries from departures. Angle of attack indications will be erroneous during these oscillations and should not be used as a departure recovery indication. Apply full forward stick and neutralizing ailerons and rudder is the most effective means of damping the oscillations and should be maintained until the oscillations cease. An out of control situation may be reentered if stick movement off the forward stop is commenced prior to aircraft unloading and the oscillations ceasing. A series of rolls at 15 to 20 units angle of attack may be encountered with full forward stick; however, the unloading will not be present. Do not attempt to fly out of this condition; rather maintain full forward stick until negative G is felt. Do not confuse the rolls with a spin. Maintain 5 to 10 units until airspeed is sufficient for dive pull out (approximately 200 knots). Use angle of attack to minimize altitude loss and do not exceed 19 units during dive pull out. Recovery action upon departure from controlled flight is as follows:

1. Smoothly apply forward stick to reduce angle of attack (full forward if necessary), simultaneously neutralizing aileron and rudder, and reducing power to idle (altitude permitting).

2. If positive indications of recovery are not obvious after application of full forward stick, deploy the drag chute while maintaining full forward stick, and neutral ailerons and rudder.

3. Do not exceed 19 units during dive pull out.

Note

Engine flameouts may occur during departure; however, engine relights can be obtained with the throttles at idle even during a developed spin. Disengage the AFCS if in use.

If the angle of attack has been reduced to below the stall, the aircraft will not spin. The drag chute should produce recovery shortly after deployment, and will reduce the oscillations encountered during recovery. It is not necessary to jettison the chute since it will separate as airspeed builds up. The altitude loss following departure is dependent upon nose attitude at recovery, which is usually very nose low. Altitude loss pulling out of a 90° dive, initiated at 200

knots and utilizing 19 units, is approximately 5,000 feet. The out of control recovery procedure is summarized in figure 4-3.

SPINS

Spins have been entered from level flight stalls, accelerated turns, vertical climbs, 60° dive pullouts, and inverted climbs. Departure and spin characteristics were investigated with a clean aircraft, various heavy wing loadings, and with asymmetric loads. The angle of attack indicator is the primary instrument for verifying the type of spin (upright or inverted). During upright spins, the angle of attack indicator will be pegged at 30 units and during inverted spins will indicate zero (0) units. The direction of spin can easily be determined from visual cues if ground reference is available; however, the direction of spin should be verified by referencing the turn needle (not the ball). The turn needle will always be pegged in the direction of the spin.

Note

Angle of attack may momentarily indicate less than 30 units (off the peg) during a spin; however, a sustained yawing motion in one direction verifies the spin condition.

UPRIGHT SPINS

Steep Oscillatory Mode

The upright spin is oscillatory in pitch, roll, and yaw. The airplane pitch attitude may vary from slightly above the horizon to 90° nose down, and large roll angle excursions will be encountered. Yaw rate in the spin may vary between 10° and 80° per second, while airspeed will vary between 80 and 150 knots. The altitude lost during an upright spin is approximately 2000 feet per turn, and the spin turn rates average about 5 to 6 seconds per turn. Initially spin oscillations may produce slightly uncomfortable accelerations in the cockpit; however, the oscillations should not be confusing. If recovery from departure has not been effected after deploying the drag chute, and the airplane has been determined to be in an upright spin, POSITIVELY determine the spin direction and supply full aileron in the direction of the spin. Recovery from most spins will occur within two turns for a symmetrically loaded aircraft. The upright spin recovery procedure is:

1. Positively determine spin direction.
2. Maintain full forward stick and neutral rudder, and supply full aileron in the direction of the spin. (Right turn needle deflection, right spin, right ailerons.)
3. When the aircraft unloads (negative G) and/or yaw rate stops, neutralize the ailerons and fly out of the unusual attitude.
4. Do not exceed 19 units during dive pull out.
5. If still out of control by 10,000 feet above the terrain - eject.

The most positive indication of recovery from a spin is the aircraft unloading. Incidents have been encountered, however, where the yaw rate stopped and

OUT-OF-CONTROL RECOVERY

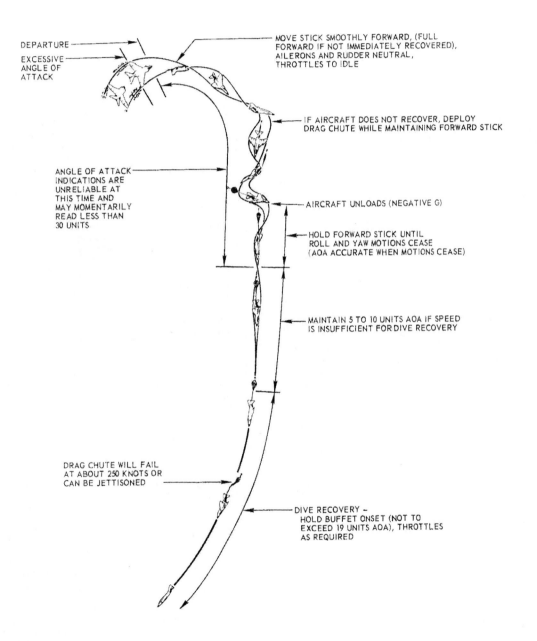

DEPARTURE

EXCESSIVE
ANGLE OF
ATTACK

MOVE STICK SMOOTHLY FORWARD, (FULL
FORWARD IF NOT IMMEDIATELY RECOVERED),
AILERONS AND RUDDER NEUTRAL,
THROTTLES TO IDLE

IF AIRCRAFT DOES NOT RECOVER, DEPLOY
DRAG CHUTE WHILE MAINTAINING FORWARD STICK

ANGLE OF ATTACK
INDICATIONS ARE
UNRELIABLE AT
THIS TIME AND
MAY MOMENTARILY
READ LESS THAN
30 UNITS

AIRCRAFT UNLOADS (NEGATIVE G)

HOLD FORWARD STICK UNTIL
ROLL AND YAW MOTIONS CEASE
(AOA ACCURATE WHEN MOTIONS CEASE)

MAINTAIN 5 TO 10 UNITS AOA IF SPEED
IS INSUFFICIENT FOR DIVE RECOVERY

DRAG CHUTE WILL FAIL
AT ABOUT 250 KNOTS OR
CAN BE JETTISONED

DIVE RECOVERY –
HOLD BUFFET ONSET (NOT TO
EXCEED 19 UNITS AOA), THROTTLES
AS REQUIRED

FDB-1-(58)

Figure 4-3

the aircraft entered 15 to 20 unit angle of attack rolls. If this occurs, the ailerons should be neutralized when the yaw rate stops and full forward stick maintained until the rolls cease and the aircraft unloads. Large excursions in roll and yaw may be encountered during recovery; do not mistake these excursions for a spin direction reversal. If the aircraft's nose remains on one spot on the ground or horizon, the aircraft is rolling, not spinning. Spin direction reversals are rare using the recommended recovery procedure; however, if reversal occurs, again positively determine the spin direction and reapply the upright spin recovery procedure. An out of control situation will be reentered if aft stick pressure is applied prior to aircraft unloading and the oscillations ceasing. Maintain 5 to 10 units until airspeed is sufficient for dive pullout (approximately 200 knots). Total altitude loss from a departure that develops into a spin until level flight is achieved can be as little as 10,000 feet; however, it will be closer to 15,000 feet if too much time is consumed determining spin direction. If the pilot considers that there is insufficient altitude for recovery, the crew should eject immediately. Figure 4-4 summarizes the upright spin recovery procedure.

Flat Mode

There have been isolated cases of the airplane exhibiting an upright flat spin mode. The flat spin can develop within one or two turns after departure from controlled flight or after several turns of an upright steep oscillatory spin. Oscillations in pitch and roll are not apparent in the flat spin. The spin turn rate is 3 to 4 seconds per turn, and the altitude lost per turn is 1,000 to 1,500 feet. There is no known technique for recovery from a flat spin. Tests indicate that a very high angle of attack, well in excess of 30 units, is required for flat spin entry. Proper use of controls at departure will preclude entering a flat spin.

INVERTED SPINS

The aircraft is highly resistant to an inverted spin entry and tests indicate that pro spin controls are necessary to maintain an inverted spin. The inverted spin is characterized by zero (0) units indicated angle of attack and negative G and is less oscillatory than the upright steep oscillatory spin. Spin direction can be determined visually by the yawing motion of the aircraft or more positively by the deflection of the turn needle which is always pegged in the direction of the spin. If recovery from uncontrolled flight is not effected by utilizing the out of control recovery procedure, and the airplane has been determined to be in an inverted spin, positively determine the spin direction and apply the following:

1. Full rudder against the spin (opposite the turn needle deflection).
2. Stick and ailerons neutral.
3. When the yaw rate stops, neutralize all controls and fly out of the unusual attitude.

ENGINE EFFECTS

Engine flameout (one or both) may occur during departure. The probability of engine flameout is greatest at MIL or MAX thrust, and least at IDLE thrust. The best indication of a flameout is a MASTER CAUTION light and one or both GEN OUT lights. Engine relights can be accomplished at idle throttle setting during a spin. Normal operation of the flight controls will deteriorate if a relight is not accomplished. The RAT will not be effective while in a spin, but will be an immediate source of electrical power following spin recovery.

ASYMMETRIC LOAD EFFECTS

Airplane departure and spin characteristics were tested to an asymmetric moment of 117,000 inch-pounds. An asymmetrically loaded aircraft will depart at a slightly lower angle of attack (approximately 25 to 27 units) and will always depart in the direction opposite the heavy wing. Asymmetric load spin characteristics are more oscillatory about all axes than spins with symmetric loads. With large asymmetric loads it may be impossible to prevent a spin if a departure occurs. The same procedures for recovery should be utilized for asymmetric load departures and spins as were presented for symmetric loads. Asymmetrically loaded configurations will require more turns for recovery than symmetrically loaded aircraft.

CAUTION

Angle of attack should be closely monitored when maneuvering with an asymmetric load because of the possibility of entering a spin immediately following departure from controlled flight.

STABILITY AND CONTROL

In discussing stability and control, it must be realized that a large variation exists throughout the flight envelope. Stability varies with Mach number and also CG location. Control effectiveness is also affected by Mach number, but just as much, if not more so, by Q (dynamic pressure).

LONGITUDINAL STABILITY

The forward CG limit is based on airplane strength and longitudinal control effectiveness. The aft CG limit is based on stability. For the clean airplane the aft limit is 36% MAC (Mean Aerodynamic Chord). This CG location provides an acceptable static margin. Refer to CG Limitations in part 4 of section I. Static margin is a physical measurement of longitudinal stability; the distance in % MAC between the CG and the aerodynamic center (AC), or nominal point of lift (A, figure 4-5). As we move the CG toward the AC, we reduce stability (B, figure 4-5). CG position alone does not define stability but rather the relative positions of the CG and the AC. The movement of the AC is a major contributor to stability. An actual shift in the AC can be felt during an accelerated transonic speed reduction where the AC moves from its aft supersonic location to a forward subsonic location, noticeably changing (reducing) the stability (C, figure 4-5). Attempting to maintain a constant stick force through this deceleration will produce a pitch-up or load factor increase when the AC shifts.

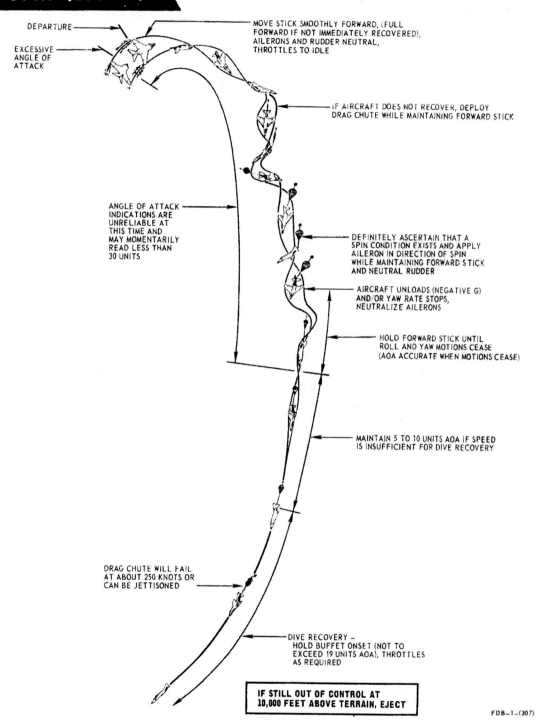

SPIN RECOVERY

DEPARTURE

EXCESSIVE ANGLE OF ATTACK

MOVE STICK SMOOTHLY FORWARD, (FULL FORWARD IF NOT IMMEDIATELY RECOVERED), AILERONS AND RUDDER NEUTRAL, THROTTLES TO IDLE

IF AIRCRAFT DOES NOT RECOVER, DEPLOY DRAG CHUTE WHILE MAINTAINING FORWARD STICK

ANGLE OF ATTACK INDICATIONS ARE UNRELIABLE AT THIS TIME AND MAY MOMENTARILY READ LESS THAN 30 UNITS

DEFINITELY ASCERTAIN THAT A SPIN CONDITION EXISTS AND APPLY AILERON IN DIRECTION OF SPIN WHILE MAINTAINING FORWARD STICK AND NEUTRAL RUDDER

AIRCRAFT UNLOADS (NEGATIVE G) AND/OR YAW RATE STOPS, NEUTRALIZE AILERONS

HOLD FORWARD STICK UNTIL ROLL AND YAW MOTIONS CEASE (AOA ACCURATE WHEN MOTIONS CEASE)

MAINTAIN 5 TO 10 UNITS AOA IF SPEED IS INSUFFICIENT FOR DIVE RECOVERY

DRAG CHUTE WILL FAIL AT ABOUT 250 KNOTS OR CAN BE JETTISONED

DIVE RECOVERY – HOLD BUFFET ONSET (NOT TO EXCEED 19 UNITS AOA), THROTTLES AS REQUIRED

IF STILL OUT OF CONTROL AT 10,000 FEET ABOVE TERRAIN, EJECT

FDB-1-(307)

Figure 4-4

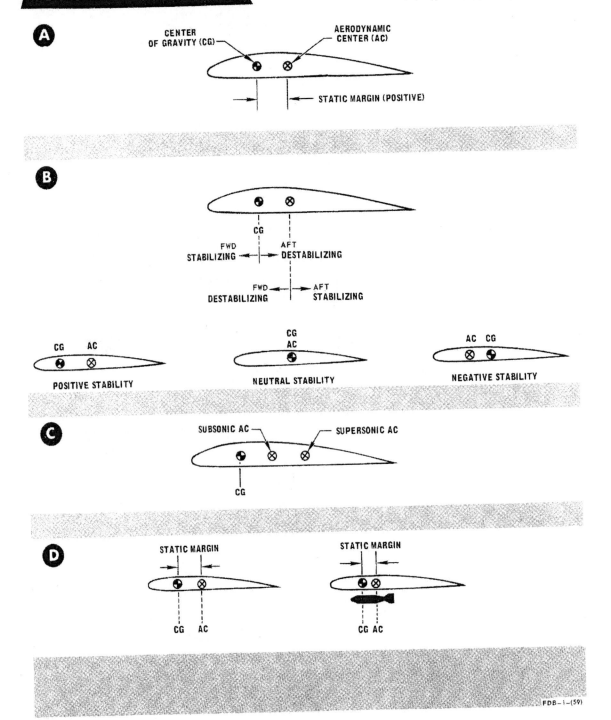

STABILITY EFFECTS

A

CENTER
OF GRAVITY (CG)

AERODYNAMIC
CENTER (AC)

STATIC MARGIN (POSITIVE)

B

CG

FWD
STABILIZING ← | → AFT
DESTABILIZING

FWD ← | → AFT
DESTABILIZING | STABILIZING

CG
AC

POSITIVE STABILITY

CG
AC

NEUTRAL STABILITY

AC CG

NEGATIVE STABILITY

C

SUBSONIC AC

SUPERSONIC AC

CG

D

STATIC MARGIN

STATIC MARGIN

CG AC

CG AC

FDB-1-(59)

Figure 4-5

C. G. TRAVEL DUE TO FUEL CONSUMPTION
APPROXIMATE

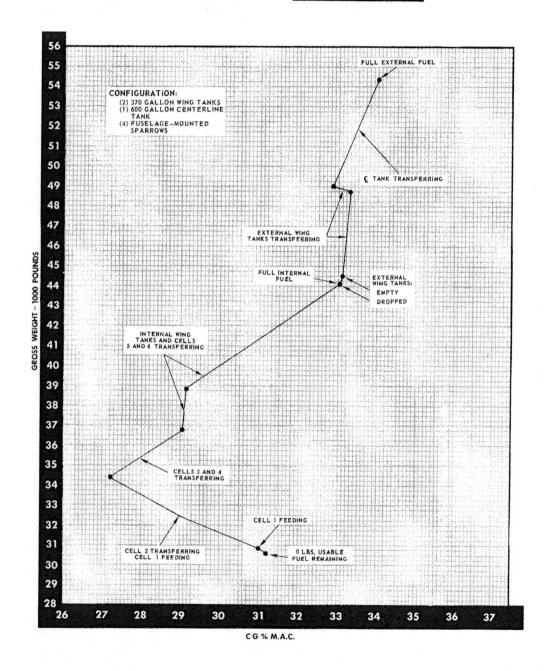

At high angles of attack, the AC moves forward when the wing tip stalls and, again, a reduction in stick force occurs. When a stores or tank is loaded under the wing, a change in the AC position results. The amount of AC movement is a function of the geometric characteristics of the store/tank, (D, figure 4-5). Centerline stores have essentially no aerodynamic effect on stability. The aerodynamic effect of any wing-mounted store/tank is always destabilizing. The static margin for a given configuration will change throughout the flight. Figure 4-6 illustrates CG travel due to fuel consumption for a specific configuration. Figure 4-7 illustrates the trend of CG travel during the initial phase of normal fuel transfer sequencing with two external wing tanks installed. During ground operation, the CG moves forward as fuselage fuel is transferred forward and consumed (A to B). When external fuel transfer is selected, the CG starts moving aft, and continues to move aft slowly throughout the climb (B to C). At level-off and throttle-back to cruise, the CG moves aft rapidly as the fuselage cells are refilled from the external tanks (C to D). During cruise, the CG remains near the aft starting point as external fuel continues to refill the fuselage cells (D to E). When the external tanks are empty and turned OFF (point E), the CG again moves forward as internal (wing and fuselage) fuel is consumed. In order to preclude flight with unacceptably low static margins, a Stabil-

INITIAL CG TRAVEL

NORMAL FUEL SEQUENCING

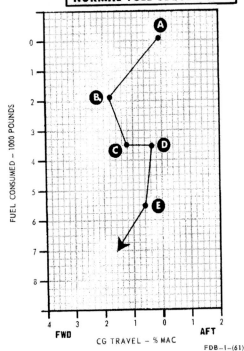

Figure 4-7

FDB-1-(61)

LONGITUDINAL STABILITY

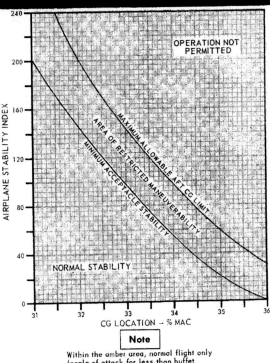

Note

Within the amber area, normal flight only (angle of attack for less than buffet onset) permitted. Only slow deliberate control movements allowed.

FDB-1-(62)
RGY

Figure 4-8

ity Index System has been established. Aerodynamic effects of stores, tanks, and associated suspension equipment are assigned unit stability numbers. For any given configuration, the stability index is the sum of the stability numbers of the tanks/stores and suspension equipment. Once the airplane stability index has been computed and the airplane CG location for the given configuration has been determined, figure 4-8 may be used to plot the point which represents these two numbers. If this point falls within the red area, flight is not permitted due to the excessive pitch attitude control caused by inadequate stability. If the point falls within the amber area, flight is permitted; however, smooth coordinated control inputs are required and the airplane is restricted to non-maneuvering flight (AOA below buffet onset). Within the amber area, longitudinal stick forces are very light and the possibility of overstressing the airplane or entering an accelerated stall prohibits air combat maneuvering. Pitch-up (where the nose of the airplane pitches up during maneuvering flight without additional back stick force) can also be encountered, again resulting in possible overstress and stall. High speed, low altitude flight should also be avoided in this area, since extremely sensitive pitch attitude control may lead to a dangerous pilot induced oscillation (PIO). If the point falls within the green area, maneuvering flight is permitted but maneuvering within 1 to 2%

MAC of the amber area must be undertaken with a reasonable degree of caution. The unsafe maneuvering characteristics present in the amber area are still present near the aft limit in the green area, but of a sufficiently reduced magnitude to allow safe operation. For flight in the green area, within approximately 1 to 2% MAC of the aft limit, every effort should be made to make smooth control inputs during all maneuvering. As the CG moves forward, the longitudinal stability characteristics improve and result in good flying qualities. The airplane exhibits satisfactory longitudinal stability characteristics for non-maneuvering flight in the amber and green area. The aft CG limits of figure 4-8 are based on operation with pitch aug engaged. Loss of pitch aug results in an apparent loss of longitudinal stability of at least 1% MAC. In this condition, maneuvering flight at the pitch aug ON limits should not be attempted. Individual pilot proficiency and operational necessity dictate whether to continue a mission upon failure of the pitch aug mode of the AFCS when near the aft CG limits for pitch aug ON operation.

Longitudinal Stability Improvement

Several approaches may be used to improve the longitudinal stability of the airplane. The primary method is by control of airplane CG through fuel management and external stores loadings. Selective loading of external stores can significantly affect airplane CG. All stores on stations 2 and 8 result in a forward CG shift, whereas the majority of stores on stations 1 and 9 result in an aft CG shift. Stores on the centerline station normally result in a slight aft CG shift. Maximum utilization of airplane stations 2 and 8 for external stores can thus result in more forward CG conditions. Fuselage mounted Sparrow III missiles can also be utilized to adjust CG location. Listed below are the approximate CG effects due to loading fuselage mounted AIM-7E missiles:

CONFIGURATION	CG SHIFT
2 Missiles forward (Stations 4 and 6 only)	Forward 1.48% MAC
2 Missiles Aft (Stations 3 and 7)	Aft 0.82% MAC
4 Missiles (Stations 3, 4, 6, and 7)	Forward 0.66% MAC

Fuselage fuel distribution is the primary in-flight CG position control. Burning down fuselage fuel provides improved stability as the aft tanks empty first. As previously shown (A to B in figure 4-7), holding external and internal wing fuel causes a favorable rate of forward CG movement. Obviously, sometime during the flight, external and internal wing fuel must be transferred and consumed with a resultant aft CG shift. Holding internal wing fuel, as opposed to simultaneous internal wing and fuselage transfer, will provide for a slightly more rapid rate of forward CG movement from the point of full internal fuel. Caution must be exercised during any non-standard fuel transfer sequence to preclude fuel

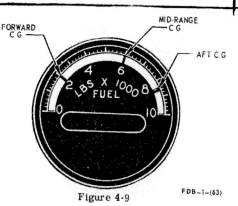

C G—FUEL REMAINING RELATIONSHIP

Figure 4-9   FDB-1-(63)

starvation due to not turning external tanks off. In order to transfer internal wing fuel, the external tanks must be turned off and internal wing transfer selected. Automatic fuel transfer should not be depended upon to correct for improper fuel switchology. Since the CG shifts due to fuel transfer and consumption, the fuel quantity gage (figure 4-9) can be used as an approximate indication of CG condition. A sector (fuel quantity of fuselage cells 1 thru 6) indication of 8500 pounds indicates an aft CG condition as all fuselage cells are full. At 6000 pounds on the sector, the CG is approximately mid-range of its possible travel (fuel cells 5 and 6 nearly empty and fuel distributed in cells 1 thru 4). The CG continues to move forward as the sector indication drops to approximately 2000 pounds.

SUBSONIC REGION

Takeoff Configuration

Takeoff performance is based on airplane gross weight and CG position. Lift-off speed is a function of gross weight and is essentially the speed at which the wings develop sufficient lift to raise the weight of the airplane. Nose wheel rotation speed is a function of CG and gross weight. Assuming that the full aft stick takeoff technique is utilized, a fully deflected stabilator provides nose wheel rotation when the downward lift on the tail exceeds the weight forward of the main gear. The full aft stick takeoff technique (full leading edge down stabilator) provides the shortest takeoff distance. The stabilator cannot be stalled in the takeoff maneuver. The rate of rotation is a function of airplane acceleration (rate of buildup of downward tail lift). CG position determines when the rotation begins; a lower speed than liftoff with an aft CG, and a higher speed than liftoff with a forward CG. In computing CG for takeoff, allowance must be made for the forward shift of CG during ground operation. The CG moves forward approximately 1% for every 1000 pounds of internal fuel used. In the forward CG range, nose wheel lift-off speed is increased approximately 4-5 knots for every percent of forward CG movement. The aft stick takeoff technique is used from 80 knots until liftoff. After liftoff, desired pitch attitude is maintained by using whatever control movement is required.

Landing Configuration

In this configuration, the aircraft exhibits positive longitudinal static stability except for an area about 10 knots before stall where a mild stick force lightening occurs. This is followed by a regaining of static stability after the stall so that if back pressure is released, the airplane recovers by itself. In the speed range between 130 - 180 knots, where most landing configuration flying is done, the airplane demonstrates almost neutral stick force stability up to about 150 knots and mild stick force stability above this speed. This is due to control system friction and rather weak stick centering at this low Q. Stabilator effectiveness is reduced with full flaps due to an aft center-of-pressure shift and a change in the downwash pattern over the tail. However, adequate effectiveness still remains for all known configurations. Since ground effect also decreases stabilator effectiveness, the aft stick-stop may be bumped during flare-out from a high sink rate landing. Stabilator effectiveness is not sufficient to hold the nose up after landing since the center of rotation is now about the main gear instead of the CG. Lateral directional control response in the landing configuration is good; however, adverse yaw generated by high roll rates produces a decrease in commanded roll due to strong dihedral effect. This strong dihedral effect can be utilized in the landing configuration to provide roll with rudder deflection. Judicious use of rudder in the landing configuration at approach angles of attack can provide desired roll response. The ARI (Aileron-Rudder Interconnect) feeds in rudder automatically to counteract yaw so that when large amounts of aileron are being used, the turns will be coordinated. Except for unusually asymmetrical external loadings or very rough, gusty air, only small lateral control motions are required for landing. The approach to stall is characterized by a decrease in lateral stability which becomes evident by a mild wing-rock (5 - 10 degrees) which gets progressively worse as speed is reduced.

Clean Configuration

Lateral and directional control response is good in the clean configuration and the aircraft exhibits good pilot feel. Rate of roll is quite high in this area and directional stability is strong enough so that ball-centered turns are made without the use of rudder. During abrupt aileron rolls, where some adverse yaw is experienced, the yaw damper is effective in keeping the ball centered.

TRANSONIC REGION

High Altitude

In the transonic region, longitudinal static stability becomes more positive and stabilator effectiveness somewhat reduced, resulting in slightly higher maneuvering stick force gradient. Transition from transonic to subsonic speeds while holding G on the aircraft results in a mild to moderate nose rise. If corrective action is not taken, this could place the aircraft in buffet at the higher altitude or cause a significant load factor increase at the lower altitudes. This is characteristic of most swept-wing aircraft and is a result of going from an area of higher stability and lowered stabilator effectiveness to an area of lowered static stability and higher stabilator effectiveness. Speed brakes increase the nose rise tendency during transition from transonic to subsonic speeds. Lateral and directional control in the transonic region is about the same as that experienced in the subsonic region except that roll rate capability is higher. Roll rates are highest in the transonic regions; however, in both transonic and subsonic regions, roll rate resulting from full aileron is much too great for any practical use.

Low Altitude

Transonic flight at low altitude presents low stick force gradient and high stabilator effectiveness which results in an area of high sensitivity and possible over-control. Even though the inherent dynamic stability of the aircraft is positive, it may be possible to create a short period longitudinal oscillation if the pilot's response becomes out of phase with the aircraft motion, thereby inducing negative damping. Such a condition is commonly known as pilot-induced oscillation (PIO). Since the dampers decrease stabilator response to rapid stick inputs, the possibility of inducing PIO is minimized with dampers on. It is recommended that the stability augmentation be used when flying at high speeds and low altitudes. The standard and most effective recovery technique from a pilot-induced oscillation is to release the controls. An out-of-trim condition is conducive to PIO and releasing controls while stick forces are present, because of an out-of-trim condition, could amplify the oscillation. Therefore, it becomes advisable to trim out longitudinal stick forces during a rapid afterburner acceleration at low altitudes. It should be noted, however, that if longitudinal forces are trimmed out while maneuvering, an out-of-trim condition will be present when returning to wings-level flight necessitating a push-force to hold altitude. In aircraft with the downsprings removed, the push force required is less than in the unmodified aircraft as a result of increased stabilator trim effectiveness. If the altitude of a mission is such that it is not desirable to release the flight controls, recovery from a PIO can be accomplished by making the arm and body as rigid as possible, even bracing the left hand against the canopy and either holding the stick in the approximate trim position or by applying slight positive G-loading. In addition, afterburner shutdown at high indicated airspeeds can produce a pitch transient. Abrupt pitch inputs could cause an oscillation to begin, therefore, all corrections should be performed smoothly. Always lock the shoulder straps when flying under conditions of high speed and low altitude. The body; from the lap belt up, could become the forcing function during an inadvertent pitch input if the shoulder straps are unlocked.

WARNING

A pilot induced oscillation can result if abrupt power change or pitch change is made while operating in the transonic region at low altitude.

SUPERSONIC REGION

High Altitude

Longitudinal static stability gets more positive as Mach number is increased in the supersonic region. Stabilator effectiveness decreases somewhat, so maneuvering stick forces become higher but do not exceed 10-12 pounds per G. Maneuvering capability is limited by stabilator effectiveness at the higher Mach numbers at higher altitudes; for example, full aft stick at Mach 2 at 50,000 feet will produce about 3.5 G. No abnormal lateral or directional control problems exist during supersonic flight. Directional stability remains strong and rate of roll, although decreasing with Mach number, remains quite adequate out to limit Mach numbers.

EFFECT OF EXTERNAL STORES

The effect on longitudinal stability and control is discussed under Longitudinal Stability. Inertial effects are evidenced during abrupt pitch maneuvers at very high angles of attack. The most noticeable effect is the increase in inertia about the longitudinal axis. This shows up as simply reducing roll rate and rolling acceleration. In other words, it takes longer to build up a given roll rate, but once a roll rate is established, it takes longer to stop it. Most restrictions on high-speed flight with external stores are based on structural considerations.

FLIGHT WITH ASYMMETRIC LOADINGS

Takeoff

Takeoff and landing with asymmetric loadings can be made with an asymmetric load equivalent to one full external wing tank loaded on a clean aircraft. The recommended technique is essentially the same as that used for a crosswind. A strong turning moment into the heavy wing will exist during takeoff roll. This characteristic becomes more prominent during rapid acceleration. Nose gear steering and rudder (when rudder becomes effective) should be used for directional control. As the aircraft breaks ground, there is a tendency to roll into the heavy wing. Therefore, trimming ailerons prior to takeoff roll is desirable. The actual lift-off should not be abrupt. Establish an attitude and allow the aircraft to fly itself off the ground using rudder and aileron as required.

Maneuvering

Caution must be exercised due to a rapid build up of asymmetric forces during maneuvering. Roll tendencies increase with load factor whereas control to counter this roll is a function of airspeed. Loss of lateral (roll) control can occur at angles of attack well below buffet and stall. Use of excessive lateral control (aileron) will produce adverse yaw. Control can be regained only when an airspeed is reached which will provide sufficient aerodynamic control to overcome the rolling force of the asymmetric load. The rolling moment produced by failure of one internal wing tank to transfer will be essentially undetectable in 1G flight. At higher load factors this rolling moment becomes significant. Every asymmetric condition has airspeed load factor combinations beyond which control cannot be maintained. Control can be regained only by an increase in airspeed and or reduction of load factor.

Landing

For airplanes with drooped ailerons (airplanes 152995z and up, and all others after AFC 218) approaches should be conducted with one-half flap at ON-SPEED AOA. Airplanes without drooped ailerons should approach with full flap at ON-SPEED AOA. If fuel permits fly, the airplane in the approach configuration prior to entering the pattern to become familiar with the lateral control characteristics. Execute a larger-than-normal or straight-in pattern, using a long groove to trim the airplane and establish line-up. Directional trim is important, particularly to eliminate any sideslip from the side opposite the heavy wing. For large asymmetric loadings, lateral trim may not be sufficient to trim the airplane for wings level flight at ON-SPEED AOA. However, for these conditions, lateral stick forces do not exceed 5 pounds and do not degrade the approach characteristics. If at any time lateral control becomes marginal, use rudder to obtain the roll response required and increase airspeed to increase lateral control effectiveness. During the approach avoid abrupt or accelerated maneuvers, particularly an abrupt landing flare since this may cause a strong roll into the heavy wing. Twin or single-engine emergency landings can be accomplished with asymmetric loadings up to the limits of section V. Single-engine approaches are slightly worse than two-engine approaches because of asymmetric thrust characteristics. In a left turn with the right engine at IDLE and the asymmetric load on the right wing, full MIL thrust and nearly full left stick are required for a 25° banked turn. Similarly, with the engine operating on a side opposite the asymmetric load, increases in thrust on final result in yaw and roll into the heavy wing which must be countered with additional lateral stick opposite and asymmetric load. This characteristic is especially noticeable during single-engine A/B wave-offs; however, the lateral control effectiveness increases rapidly with increasing airspeed. Approaches and landings can be accomplished in crosswinds up to 10 knots from the side opposite the heavy wing. To maintain maximum available lateral control in crosswind approaches, the technique of establishing a crab angle into the wind, rather than the wing down technique is recommended. If possible a runway should be selected such that the crosswind is from the same side as the asymmetric load. The airplane should be landed on the down wind side of the runway because the advantages of the crosswind from the heavy wing side are reversed during landing roll-out. The airplane tends to weathercock into the wind during normal landing roll-outs especially with the drag chute deployed. The vertical tail, the drag chute and the higher drag on the upwind wing (the asymmetric load) all tend to turn the airplane into the wind. This tendency is more pronounced than any tendency to turn away from the heavy wing because of differential braking conditions. The weathercocking into the wind can be satisfactorily countered with rudder and aileron opposite to the wind direction and with nose wheel steering as a last resort. For carrier operations the above techniques are equally applicable.

Note

Refer to section I, part 4, and section V for asymmetric load limitations.

HEAVY GROSS WEIGHT OPERATION

TAKEOFF

Consideration must be given to gross weight and CG effect on lift-off and nose wheel rotation speeds as discussed under Subsonic Region (Takeoff Configuration), this section. *Full aft stick takeoff is required to achieve handbook takeoff performance data.*

Maneuvering

Aft CG conditions are usually encountered during heavy gross weight operation. Also refer to Longitudinal Stability, this section. For any given indicated airspeed, the airplane is at a higher angle of attack. This condition reduces the margin of angle of attack prior to stall. A significant change in flight characteristics occurs during air refueling due to the immediate increase in gross weight; mission planning must consider this change in airplane flight characteristics.

Landing

Every reasonable technique must be pursued to attempt to reduce gross weight prior to an emergency landing. Excess weight reduces excess thrust, thereby narrowing the margin for recovery from any subsequent problem. Execute a larger-than-normal or straight-in landing pattern, and avoid abrupt or accelerated maneuvers. Utilize available power (including afterburner) as required to preclude excessive sink rates.

ZOOM CLIMB

A zoom climb can be performed by accelerating to a high energy condition and then slowly rotating to a pitch attitude higher than normal climb. Pitch angles in excess of 60° detract from the zoom climb capability and produce more uncomfortable recovery conditions. During a zoom climb to altitudes above 65,000 feet, the EGT must be monitored. Afterburner blowout will usually occur around 67,000 to 70,000 feet. When the afterburners blow out, the throttles should be taken out of the afterburner range to preclude unexpected or hard light-offs during descent. Above 70,000 feet, the engines must be shut down if they tend to over-speed or over-temp. Engine windmill speed at altitudes above 70,000 feet are high enough to maintain some cockpit pressurization and normal electrical power. Stabilator effectiveness decreases noticeably above 50,000 feet and an increased amount of aft stick is required to hold a given pitch attitude. Zoom climb recovery can be initiated at any time during the zoom maneuver by re-

laxing back pressure on the control stick and flying the aircraft over the top at a G loading which will prevent stall. Maintaining a constant value of angle of attack between 5 and 10 units properly decreases G with decreasing airspeed during the recovery while still maintaining a safe positive G loading on the aircraft. Negative G recoveries are not recommended due to aircraft and physiological limitations and lack of aircrew ability to detect impending stall. Two basic methods of recovering from the zoom climb are possible. A wings-level recovery can be effected by smoothly decreasing angle of attack to the minimum positive G value and holding this until the aircraft is diving. An inverted recovery can be effected by controlling angle of attack while rolling the aircraft to inverted and then increasing angle of attack to produce the maximum G loading on the aircraft. A comparison of the two techniques show that the positive G loading on the aircraft assists the recovery trajectory in the inverted case whereas it detracts from the recovery trajectory in the wings level case. The resulting flatter trajectory of the wings-level recovery produces a lower minimum airspeed and higher maximum altitude over the top in addition to a longer overall recovery time. Although the inverted recovery is superior from the standpoint of speed, altitude, and exposure time, it exhibits certain risks due to the capabilities required to properly control the angle of attack during the rolling maneuvers. All zoom climb recoveries demand smooth coordinated control action. The angle of attack indicator is the primary recovery aid regardless of recovery method. As speed decreases, the stabilator required to develop a given pitch command increases. Higher than normal stick displacement and rates are necessary to command or hold angle of attack at very low speeds. Inadvertent pitch inputs due to abrupt roll action or pilot inattention to required pitch control can quickly put the aircraft in a stalled condition. Zoom climb recoveries initiated from indicated airspeeds in excess of 250 knots CAS can be made inverted or wings-level. For the wings-level recovery, smoothly reduce angle of attack to 5 units and hold this value until the aircraft is in a recovery dive and speed has increased through 250 knots CAS. Attempts to hasten the recovery by pushing over to a value below 5 units of angle of attack will produce negative G on the aircraft and possible stall. Precise roll attitude is not important during the recovery. Any aileron used to correct or maintain roll attitude should be smooth and coordinated. For the inverted recovery, smoothly reduce angle of attack to 5 units and holding this value, smoothly roll the aircraft to inverted. Increase and hold angle of attack at 10 units to produce maximum safe G loading on the aircraft. When the aircraft is in an inverted recovery dive, the roll to wings-level must again be accomplished with smooth slow control action while holding angle of attack between 5-10 units. As before, angle of attack should be maintained in the recovery dive until airspeed builds up to 250 knots CAS. Zoom climb recoveries initiated at indicated airspeeds less than 250 knots CAS should be accomplished with the pilot's sole attention devoted to proper control of angle of attack between 5-10 units. Roll attitude should be completely ignored with aileron and rudder held generally neutral to maintain coordinated flight. If the pilot becomes confused or disoriented during any recovery, he should immediately concentrate only on angle of attack and ignore all other parameters. If angle of attack is maintained between 5-10 units the aircraft will recover safely to nose-down accelerating condition regardless of roll attitude.

FORMATION FLIGHT

PARADE FORMATION

The following description is a recommended guideline for pilots flying the aircraft in a basic parade position. This position is flown by the wingman placing the ramp hinge on the lead aircraft in line with the lead pilot's head, and placing his eye level directly abreast of the fuselage seam just aft of the wings on the lead aircraft. This triangulation should position the wingman at approximately a 6-foot stepdown with approximately 6 feet wing tip clearance. Refer to figure 4-10.

Note

When flying formation, do not use flaps at an airspeed greater than 200 knots CAS, since the variable actuation between flap airspeed pressure switches might cause unintentional retraction of one aircraft's flaps while the flaps of the other aircraft remain down.

INSTRUMENT WING FORMATION

The position for instrument wing is identical to the parade position. All turns are performed on the axis of the leader. It is important to maintain this position to avoid possible vertigo in actual instrument conditions. Refer to figure 4-11.

FREE CRUISE FORMATION

Free cruise formation allows for increased flight maneuverability and lookout coverage. The free cruise position is approximately one aircraft length nose-to-tail clearance, slightly stepped down (to avoid the leader's jet wash) and within a 60° cone aft of the leader. Power settings should be constant while maneuvering within the 60° cone. Refer to figure 4-12.

AIR REFUELING

Note

Before air refueling operations, each crewmember will become familiar with NATOPS Air Refueling Manual.

PROBE SWITCH OPERATION

The air refuel probe switch has three positions marked RETRACT, EXTEND, and REFUEL. Placing the switch to EXTEND merely extends the air refueling probe. However, with the switch in this position, fuselage cells 1 and 3 can accept fuel if/when space is available. Selecting REFUEL conditions the fuel system by venting all tanks to atmosphere, shutting off tank pressurization air, opening the refueling level control valves in cells 3 and 5 and the wing tanks, and by opening the fuel shutoff valves to the external tanks (providing the refuel selection switch is in ALL TANKS). Immediately after selecting REFUEL on the air refuel probe switch, monitor the sector portion of the fuel quantity gage. If the fuel quantity shown on the sector depletes more rapidly than the fuel quantity shown on the counter, it is a positive indication that the defuel valve has failed open and that fuselage fuel is transferring into the internal wing tanks. If the wing tanks are sufficiently empty, the fuselage fuel may be depleted completely. Should this indication occur, move the refuel probe switch to EXTEND, and allow fuel from the tanker to replenish the fuselage fuel tanks to approximately 6000 pounds to guard against flameout. Then move the switch to REFUEL and continue the air refueling. It is also possible to deplete the fuselage fuel supply

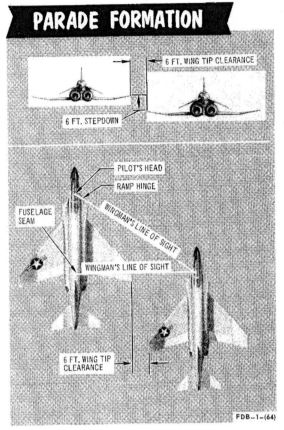

Figure 4-10

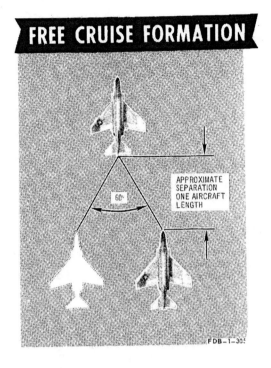

Figure 4-12

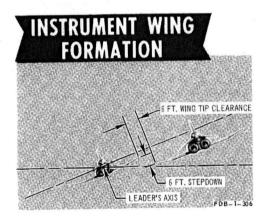

Figure 4-11

when attempting wet plug-ins. Since all tanks are vented, no internal wing or external fuel will transfer. If an excessive amount of time is used in attempting a plug-in, the fuselage cells may deplete to a low fuel state. In this event, place the air refuel probe switch to EXTEND. This permits the internal wing and external tanks to transfer to the engine feed tank. Once the engine feed tank is full, the air refuel probe switch may again be placed to REFUEL and air refueling resumed.

BEFORE PLUG-IN

The air refueling checklist should be completed before plug-in:

1. Radar master switch - STBY
2. Missile power switch - OFF (STBY with AIM-7D/E)
3. Arming switches - OFF/SAFE
4. Internal wing dump switch - NORMAL
5. Refuel probe switch - REFUEL (EXTEND for dry plug-ins).
6. Refuel selection switch - AS DESIRED
7. Check probe fully extended.
8. Check Refuel Ready light illuminated.
9. Visor recommended down.

Note

After selecting REFUEL, check for an indication of a failed open defuel valve. A failed open defuel valve is indicated by a rapid depletion of fuel quantity indications on the sector.

For night air refueling:

10. Exterior lights - STEADY BRIGHT
11. Air refuel probe light - ON
12. Tanker lights - AS DESIRED

REFUELING TECHNIQUE

Note

The following procedures, apply to tanker operation, refer only to single drogue refuelers.

WARNING

When receiving fuel from a KC-135 aircraft, the maximum total fuel received on board shall not exceed 11,800 pounds JP-4 or 12,500 pounds JP-5. Failure to observe these limitations may result in overpressurization and rupture of the fuel tanks.

Refueling altitudes and airspeeds are dictated by receiver and/or tanker characteristcis and operational needs, consistent with the tanker's performance and refueling capabilities. This, generally, covers a practical spectrum from the deck to 35,000 feet and 190 to 300 KCAS.

APPROACH

Once cleared to commence an approach, refueling checklists completed, assume a position 10 to 15 feet in trail of the drogue with the refueling probe in line in both the horizontal and vertical reference planes. Trim the aircraft in this stabilized approach position and insure that the tanker's (amber) ready light is illuminated before attempting an approach. Select a reference point on the tanker as a primary alignment guide during the approach phase; secondarily, rely on peripheral vision of the drogues and hose and supplementary remarks by the RIO. Increase power to establish an optimum 3 to 5 knot closure rate on the drogue. It must be emphasized that an excessive closure rate causes a violent hose whip following contact and/or increases the danger of structural damage to the aircraft in the event of misalignment; whereas, too slow a closure rate results in the pilot fencing with the drogue as it oscillates in close proximity to the aircraft's nose. During the final phase of the approach, the drogue has a tendency to move slightly upward and to the right as it passes the nose of the receiver aircraft due to aircraft-drogue airstream interaction. Small corrections in the approach phase are acceptable; however, if alignment is off in the final phase, it is best to immediately retire to the initial approach position and commence another approach, compensating for previous misalignment by adjusting the reference point selected on the tanker. Small lateral corrections with a shoulder probe are made with the rudder, and vertical corrections with the stabilator. Avoid any corrections about the longitudinal axis since they cause probe displacement in both the lateral and vertical reference planes.

MISSED APPROACH

If the receiver probe passes forward of the drogue basket without making contact, a missed approach should be initiated immediately. Also, if the probe impinges on the canvas lined rim of the basket and tips it, a missed approach should be initiated. Realization of this situation can be readily ascertained through the RIO. A missed approach is executed by reducing power and backing to the rear at an opening rate commensurate with the optimum 3 to 5 knot closure rate made on an approach. By continuing an approach past the basket, a pilot might hook his probe over the hose and/or permit the drogue to contact the receiver aircraft fuselage. Either of the two aforementioned hazards require more skill to calmly unravel the hose and drogue without causing further damage than to make another approach. If the initial approach position is well in line with the drogue, the chance of hooking the hose is diminished when last minute corrections are kept to a minimum. After executing a missed approach, analyze previous misalignment problems and apply positive corrections to preclude a hazardous tendency to blindly stab at the drogue.

CONTACT

When the receiver probe engages the basket, it seats itself into the drogue coupling and a slight ripple will be evident in the refueling hose. Here again the RIO can readily inform the pilot by calling contact. The tanker's drogue and hose must be pushed forward 3 to 5 feet by the receiver probe before fuel transfer can be effected. This advanced position is evident by the tanker's (amber) ready light going out and the (green) fuel transfer light coming on. The tanker's (green) fuel transfer light illuminates only when the receiver aircraft has REFUEL selected and the tanker has all required switches selected and other conditions met. While plugged-in, merely fly a close tail chase formation on the tanker. Although this tucked-in condition restricts the tanker's maneuverability, gradual changes involving heading, altitude and/or airspeed may be made. A sharp lookout doctrine must be maintained due to the precise flying imposed on both the tanker and receiver pilots. In this respect, the tanker can be assisted by other aircraft in the formation. The receiver RIO can also assist in maintaining a visual lookout since the receiver radar is in STBY.

Note

With gross weight above 48,000 pounds, when tanking in 190-210 knot region, high power settings and one-half flaps may be required. If tobogganing is used with one-half flaps, there is a possibility of flap blow-up.

DISENGAGEMENT

Disengagement from a successful contact is accomplished by reducing power and backing out at a 3 to 5-knot separation rate. Care should be taken to maintain the same relative alignment on the tanker as upon engagement. The receiver probe separates from the drogue coupling when the hose reaches full extension. When clear of the drogue, place the refueling probe switch in RETRACT. Ensure that the IFR PROBE UNLOCK light is extinguished on the telelight panel before resuming normal flight operations. At night, turn off the probe floodlight.

BUDDY TANK SYSTEM

BEFORE TAKEOFF

1. Buddy tank - SERVICED
   a. Filler cap - SECURE
   b. Guillotine cartridge - INSTALLED
2. Hose jettison switch - OFF
3. Power switch - OFF
4. Transfer switch - OFF
5. Hose control switch - RET
6. Light switch - AS REQUIRED
   For daylight refueling, place light switch to BRT; for night refueling, place light switch to DIM.
7. Buddy fill switch - STOP FILL

AIR REFUELING

1. Power switch - ON
2. Hose control switch - EXT

If airstream driven turbine is not at governed speed when hose control switch is placed to EXT, the drogue may momentarily delay ejection into airstream.
3. Buddy fill switch - AS DESIRED.
   To transfer buddy tank fuel only, buddy fill switch must be in STOP FILL. To transfer buddy tank fuel plus airplane (tanker) fuel, buddy fill switch must be held in FILL.
4. Drogue position indicator - EXT
   When hose and drogue are fully extended, amber READY light on tail cone illuminates, and drogue position indicator displays EXT.
5. Fuel transfer switch - TRANS
6. Drogue position indicator - TRA
   After engagement of drogue and hose has been retracted a minimum of 2 feet, green TRANSFER light on tail cone illuminates and drogue position indicator reads TRA.
7. Gallons delivered indicator - MONITOR
   Periodically check total gallons transferred. Do not transfer excessive amounts of internal fuel.
8. Fuel transfer switch - OFF
   Upon completion of refueling, place buddy fuel transfer switch to OFF. Fuel transfer may be discontinued at any time by placing transfer switch OFF.
9. Hose control switch - RET
10. Drogue position indicator - RET
    When hose and drogue is completely retracted, drogue position indicator reads RET.
11. Power switch - OFF

BUDDY TANK EMERGENCIES

Hose and Drogue Jettisoning

A violently whipping hose and drogue, or the inability to retract the hose for any reason, may require hose and drogue jettisoning. To jettison the hose and drogue, proceed as follows:

1. Hose jettison switch - CUT

| CAUTION |

Do not change the position of the hose jettison switch after being placed to CUT. If the switch is positioned to NORMAL after jettisoning, the buddy tank electrical system becomes energized.

Note

The guillotine may not fire immediately, since there is an electrical holding relay that does not close until the hose-reel mechanism is locked. Once the hose-reel mechanism locks, the guillotine hose cutter fires.

Buddy Tank Jettisoning

The buddy tank may be jettisoned individually from the centerline station or it may be jettisoned along with all external stores. Refer to external Stores Jettison Chart, section V.

TOW TARGET PROCEDURES

AERO 35B BANNER

PREFLIGHT CHECK

1. Drag chute handle - UP

Note

The drag chute handle must remain up until target release is desired.

2. Drag chute attachment and centerline fitting - SECURE

TAKEOFF AND CLIMB

1. Perform 1/2 flaps CRT takeoff.
2. Climb between 180 - 200 KCAS to desired altitude.
3. Reduce power to min-burner at 5000 feet and military power at 10,000 feet.
4. When level at desired altitude, raise flaps and accelerate to 220 KCAS. Do not exceed 220 KCAS while towing the 35B.

Note

In level flight, 30 feet of banner droop can be expected.

TARGET RELEASE PROCEDURES

1. Drag chute handle - DOWN
   Target release is positive and noticeable to the pilot.

TDU-22B TOW TARGET

No special procedures are required for this passive type target.

TDU-22A/B TOW TARGET

FLARE IGNITION

1. Set proper frequency on UHF.

Note

It is desirable to use cold mic when transmitting a flare tone. When hot mic is used, a tone is heard on the ICS as soon as tone is selected.

2. Select tone on tone generator box.
3. Depress mic button for at least 10 seconds, then release.
4. Turn off tone generator and listen for firing results.
5. If another flare is to be fired, wait at least 15 seconds between tone generator signals to allow stepping relay in target to actuate.

RMU-8/A REEL/LAUNCHER

CAUTION

Failure to adhere to the following preflight and post-start checks and flight procedures during any flight with an RMU-8/A reel/launcher installed may result in turbine over-speed and failure with extensive damage to the aircraft.

PREFLIGHT CHECK

After making sure that the proper tow line/target combination is installed, place the master power switch OFF, remove the tow reel access panels and check the following:

1. Target secure.
2. Launcher boom latched.
3. Tow line threaded through cable cutter and cartridge is installed in cutter and cutter assembly lockwired.
4. Pneumatic bottle charged to 2000 psi minimum, filler cap secure.
5. Tow line length limit switch assembly for desired settings. (Current LAUNCH STOP: 100, IN STOP: 3000, OUT STOP: 36,700).
6. Spool locks secure and lockwired.
7. Level-wind drive and adapter secure, and three cotter pins installed.
8. Tow line spool winding evenly wound with no snarls and insulated leader installed.
9. Oil level.
10. Remove power unit blade guard if used. Note condition of spinner and spinner nut lockwired.
11. Check propeller blades have no unacceptable nicks or scratches and they are feathered. Check brakes on.
12. Replace and secure access panels.
13. Remove safety flag, placing tow line cutter switch in spring-loaded ARM.

Note

For flight missions not involving target towing, if a target is not installed, accomplish all preflight items except 1, 3 and 8. In this case, the TARGET OUT light burns continuously when power is applied to the system. All other preflight and post-start items must be complied with in any case.

POSTSTART CHECK

1. Check all reel/launcher circuit breakers IN.
2. Check all press-to-test indicator lights on control panel.
3. Master power switch ON.
4. Check all the indicator lights OFF.
5. Pull RMU-8/A DC PWR circuit breaker and push IN.
6. Check EMERG PWR light ON.
7. Cycle master power switch OFF and ON.
8. Check EMERG PWR light OFF.

9. Reset tow line length indicator.
10. Leave master power switch ON during flight.

TAKEOFF AND CLIMB

1. Perform normal takeoff.
2. Do not exceed 0.90 IMN, 500 knots CAS, or the tension limit, whichever is less, with target in stowed position. See figure 4-9.

LAUNCHING PROCEDURES

Note

If Reel-Out Procedures are initiated first, Launch and Reel-Out procedures are automatically combined.

1. Maximum launch speed is 0.90 IMN, 500 knots CAS, or tension limit, whichever is less. Optimum launch at 250 to 300 knots CAS, sea level to 40,000 feet altitude.
2. In wings-level flight, actuate target launch switch to LAUNCH. When target launch switch is actuated, tow reel brakes are released, launching boom lowers, and target leaves saddle. LAUNCHER DOWN and TARGET OUT light then illuminates and target begins to deploy at approximately 400 feet per minute. When launch cycle is completed (present launch stop setting of approximately 100 feet of tow line out), launcher retracts, power brakes are applied, and LAUNCHER DOWN light goes out.

REEL-OUT PROCEDURES

1. Maximum reel-out speed is 0.75 IMN, 300 knots CAS, or the tension limit, whichever is less. See figure 4-14.
2. Actuate tow reel control switch to REEL-OUT. When switch is actuated to REEL-OUT, power brakes release and target begins to deploy at an increasing speed (up to a maximum of 5000 feet per minute). At preselected automatic stop setting, tow line speed decreases and power unit brakes are applied to stop reel-out.

┤ CAUTION ├

- To avoid tow line damage due to sheave scuffing, turns should be limited to 20-degree bank-angles while the tow reel is operating.

- To avoid tow line damage due to engine exhaust, with the tow reel stopped, 45-degree bank-angle turns are desirable (without A/B). If A/B is required for turns, use of outboard A/B is desirable. If turns are required with both engines in A/B, use of 60-degree bank-angles is desirable.

- If the tow reel should overspeed by 10 percent, a normal stop occurs. However, if normal 10 percent overspeed is observed (in excess of 5500 FPM) and a normal automatic stop is not observed, actuate the stop switch and reduce airspeed to minimum feasible. If overspeed continues immediately actuate stop and cut switch. If the overspeed persists, jettison the RMU-8/A reel launcher.

Note

- If the tow reel should overspeed by 20 percent, the power unit and tow reel brakes are immediately applied and the tow line cutter is actuated. The TOW CUT light then illuminates.

- Following a manual STOP command after launch and prior to automatic stop, Reel-In or Reel-Out procedures can be initiated. However, following the automatic stop function, only Reel-In procedures can be initiated.

TARGET PRESENTATION

1. Target can be offered for tracking or live firings within performance limits of target.
2. Tow line length may be altered; however, its length may never exceed the automatic stop setting (plus a stopping distance of 1500 to 2500 feet).
   a. If a stop has been commanded before reaching the automatic stop setting, automatic stop length may be reached by selecting REEL-OUT. If a length less than the automatic stop length is desired, tow reel control switch should be actuated to STOP.

Note

When commanding a stop before automatic stop, anticipate a stopping distance of 1500 to 2500 feet maximum, depending on reel-out speed.

   b. If a length less than automatic stop length is desired, actuate tow reel control switch to REEL-IN.

Note

When commanding a stop during reel-in, anticipate a stopping distance of 1500 to 2500 feet maximum, depending on reel-in speed.

REEL-IN PROCEDURES

1. Maximum reel-in speed is 0.75 IMN, 300 knots CAS, or tension limit, whichever is less. Anticipate a tension increase due to $0.1 \Delta M$ reel-in speed. See figure 4-14.
2. Actuate tow reel control switch to REEL-IN. When switch is actuated to REEL-IN, SAFETY-ARM light illuminates and power unit brakes are released. Reel-in speed increases to a maximum of 5000 feet per minute until automatic stop setting is reached at approximately 3000 feet. Power unit brakes are applied and target stops 500 to 2000 feet aft of tow plane.

┤ CAUTION ├

It is desirable to stabilize aircraft speed for cruise or descent before initiating reel-in procedure to reduce change of tow line failure.

TOWING LIMITATIONS

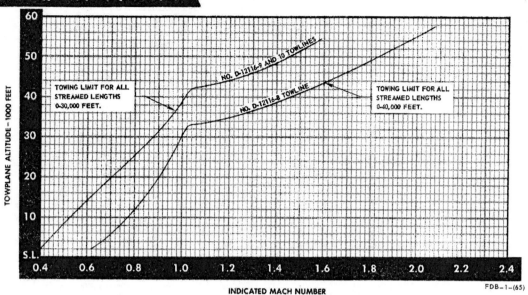

Figure 4-13

TENSION LIMITATIONS

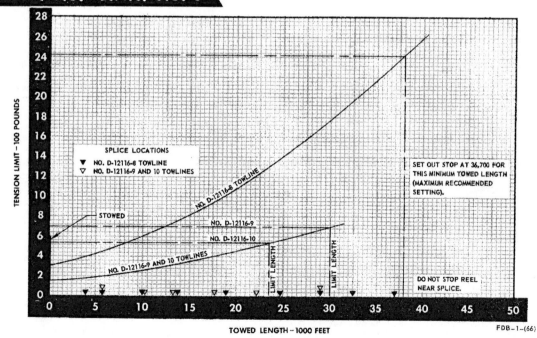

Figure 4-14

Note

● Following the reel-in command, some tow lines may reel-out until sufficient reel-in power is developed.

● Following a stop command before automatic stop, reel-in or reel-out can be initiated.

● Following an automatic stop, only recovery or reel-out can be initiated.

RECOVERY PROCEDURES

1. Maximum recovery airspeed is 0.85 IMN, 350 knots CAS, or tension limit, whichever is less. Optimum recovery occurs at 250 knots CAS, 15,000 feet altitude, 180 feet per minute.
2. Actuate target launch switch to RECOVER. When switch is actuated to RECOVER, SAFETY ARM light goes out, brakes are released, launcher extends, and LAUNCHER DOWN light illuminates.

Note

● Manual speed control is required to recover the target.

● Reel-in speed can be varied approximately 1000 feet per minute by actuating tow reel control switch to INCREASE SPEED and/or FEATHER.

● Increase speed is restricted to 0.5 degrees of pitch per actuation. The feather switch operates (while held) until feather pitch position is reached.

● For best recovery, final reel-in speed should be established before target is within 200 feet of the aircraft.

3. When the target seats in saddle, TARGET OUT light goes out. The launcher then retracts to stow target, and LAUNCHER DOWN light goes out. The power unit blades feather and brake is applied. Automatic stop length limits reset.

CAUTION

● Abort recovery if tension or speed fluctuation occurs. To abort, actuate stop switch, hold reel-out switch until reel-out occurs, reactuate stop switch at 500 feet. Repeat Recovery Procedure.

● When the recovery switch is actuated after stopping from reel-out mode, the increase speed switch must be actuated to energize the feather circuit.

EMERGENCY OPERATION

WARNING

If it becomes necessary for the crew to eject from the aircraft during towing operations, actuate tow reel stop switch to STOP & CUT before ejection.

Note

The RMU-8/A is a jettisonable store in all flight configurations up to 0.95 Mach.

LOW AIR LIGHT ILLUMINATED

If Based Ashore

1. Initiate reel-in and/or recovery procedure.

If Based Aboard Ship

1. During launch or recovery procedure, actuate tow reel control switch to STOP & CUT.
2. During reel-in or reel-out procedure, complete mission. When reel-in procedure is complete, actuate tow reel control switch to STOP & CUT.

TOW CUT LIGHT ILLUMINATED

No action required.

EMERGENCY POWER LIGHT ILLUMINATED

Wait until towline speed instrument indicates that the tow reel has stopped. Turn the master power switch OFF. Determine the cause of the airplane power failure and follow the electrical system emergency operation procedure. Place the master power switch ON. If the power trouble is corrected, continue operations. Anticipate a towline length instrument error due to use of emergency power.

Note

Actuation of the emergency power circuit may be caused by aircraft generator voltage transients.

SAFETY ARM LIGHT FAILS TO ILLUMINATE

Actuate the tow reel stop switch to STOP when the tow line length instrument indicates 03500. Initiate Recovery Procedure.

TOW LINE LENGTH INDICATOR ERROR

Use the launch stop, reel-out automatic stop, and reel-in automatic stop settings to determine target position.

TOW LINE FAILURE

Actuate the tow reel stop switch to STOP & CUT.

TARGET OUT LIGHT PRIOR TO LAUNCH

If tow line tension meter indicates zero, do not launch target. If normal tension is indicated, Reel-Out Procedure is required to launch the target.

LAUNCHER DOWN LIGHT ILLUMINATED

1. If target is at the launch stop position, complete mission.
2. After target recovery, and if based ashore with chase airplane, check to assure target is inside clamps. If target is inside clamps, actuate tow reel control switch to INCREASE SPEED, to increase tow line tension. Do not exceed tow line tension limits. Then place master power switch OFF. If target is outside clamps, actuate tow reel stop switch to STOP & CUT.
3. After target recovery, and if based aboard ship, or if a chase airplane is not available, actuate STOP, REEL-OUT, and STOP & CUT at 3-second intervals.

Field landings are permitted with the launcher down, with or without target. Minor damage to the target occurs.

PREMATURE FLARE IGNITION (TARGET STOWED)

Actuate reel control switch to REEL-OUT. If aircraft is on the ground, actuate tow reel stop switch to STOP & CUT and taxi clear of burning flare and target.

AQM-37A MISSILE TARGET SYSTEM

PREFLIGHT CHECK

1. Ascertain from ground crewman that three (3) target and launcher safety pins are installed.
2. Ascertain from ground crewman that centerline stores rack safety pin is removed.
3. Centerline station safe switch - SAFE.
4. External stores emergency release button - NORMAL.
5. Bomb control switch - OFF.
6. Master arm switch - SAFE.
7. Target function selector switch - OFF.

POSTSTART CHECK

1. Launcher no-voltage check - performed by ground crewman.
2. Ascertain that target safety pin removed by ground crewman.
3. Ascertain that launcher safety pins (2) are removed by ground crewman.

TARGET LAUNCH PROCEDURE

During Climb-Out to Launch Altitude

1. Target function selector switch - SELECT.
2. Target PWR ON light - illuminated.
3. Target READY light - illuminated (approximately 5 minutes after PWR ON light illuminates).

Note

• If the PWR ON light does not illuminate, place the target function selector switch OFF and execute mission abort procedures.

• The target READY light indicates only that power has been applied to the target for at least 5 minutes. If the target READY light does not illuminate, check lamp illumination with the press-to-test feature. Target launch may be executed without a READY light at the pilot's discretion.

At Launch Altitude

4. Launch altitude - CHECK.
5. Launch speed - CHECK.
6. Launch heading - CHECK.
7. Centerline station safe switch - SAFE.
8. Bomb control switch - OFF.
9. Centerline station safe switch - READY.
10. Bomb control switch - DIRECT.
11. Master arm switch - SAFE.
12. Bomb release button - depress until launch is confirmed (PWR ON and READY light extinguish).

Note

During the actual target launch operation, a slight thump is felt as the simultaneous action of launcher extension and target/aircraft separation occur. Immediately following this separation, it is considered standard practice for the pilot to initiate a hard-to-port turn. The pilot's signal for initiating this turn is when the PWR ON and READY lights on the missile firing panel are seen to extinguish, thus indicating that target launch has occurred.

13. Place all switches to OFF and SAFE.

GROUND CHECKS (AFTER FLIGHT)

1. Centerline stores rack safety pin - INSTALLED.

EMERGENCY OPERATION

PWR ON LIGHT FAILS TO ILLUMINATE

In Flight

1. Target function selector switch - OFF.
2. Bomb control switch - OFF.
3. Centerline station safe switch - SAFE.
4. Master arm switch - SAFE.

After Landing (Land or Carrier Based Operations)

1. Target safety pin - INSTALLED.
2. Launcher safety pins (2) - INSTALLED.
3. Centerline stores rack safety pin - INSTALLED.

JETTISON PROCEDURES

Master Jettison (All External Stores Including Target, Launcher, and Adapter)

1. External stores emergency release button - DEPRESS.

Centerline Station Jettison (Jettisons Target Only)

1. Target function selector switch - JETTISON.

FUNCTIONAL CHECKFLIGHT REQUIREMENTS

GENERAL

The functional checkflight will be performed after the completion of the calendar maintenance requirements using the applicable Functional Checkflight Checklist. This section contains a detailed description of the checkflight requirements, sequenced in the order in which they will be performed. The checkflight personnel will familiarize themselves with these requirements prior to the flight. NATOPS procedures will apply during the entire checkflight. Only those pilots designated in writing by the Squadron Commanding Officer shall perform squadron checkflights. Checkflight procedures will be accordance with the current edition of OPNAVINST 4790.2. For ready reference, excerpts from OPNAVINST 4790.2 are quoted below.

At the discretion of the Commanding Officer, checkflights may be flown in combination with operational flights, provided the operational portion is not conducted until the checkflight requirements have been satisfied and the results have been entered on the checkflight checklist. The general purpose code assigned to a combination check and operational flight will be the one that describes the primary purpose of the flight.

Pilots and crew members who perform checkflights are qualified in accordance with OPNAVINST 3710.7 Series and the applicable NATOPS manual, and are provided a thorough briefing by the Maintenance Officer or his designated representative (normally the QA Officer). This briefing should describe the requirements for that particular flight, the expected results, and corrective emergency action to be taken if required.

Checkflights are conducted with the minimum crew necessary to ensure proper operation of all required equipment.

Checkflights must be of sufficient duration to perform the prescribed checks and to determine whether any additional maintenance work is required.

Checkflights shall be conducted in accordance with the criteria established by OPNAVINST 3710.7 Series (NATOPS).

Checkflight forms must be properly completed and returned to the Maintenance Department.

Checkflights are required to determine whether the airframe, power plant, accessories, and items of equipment are functioning in accordance with predetermined requirements. Depending upon the maintenance performed, the functional checkflight will be either a complete or a partial checkflight. If a complete checkflight is to be flown, all the items contained in the Functional Checkflight Requirements must be accomplished. If a partial checkflight is to be flown due to engine change, flight control rigging, etc., only those items that directly relate to the equipment being checked need be accomplished. Therefore, some items contained in the Functional Checkflight Requirements are coded. This coding is intended to assist the FCF crew members in determining which items pertain to the various conditions requiring checkflights. Items coded (E) pertain to engine/fuel control maintenance as outlined in OPNAVINST 4790.2. Items coded (FC) pertain to flight control/rigging maintenance as outlined in OPNAVINST 4790.2. The uncoded items in conjunction with the coded items constitute a complete Functional Checkflight, requirements for which are outlined in OPNAVINST 4790.2. Coding shall appear adjacent to a paragraph title or a step. If it appears adjacent to a paragraph title, all steps following that paragraph title will apply. If the coding appears adjacent to a step, only that step and its subordinates will apply.

CHECKFLIGHT REQUIREMENTS (PILOT)

PREFLIGHT

Note

Due to expanded checks required by the Checkflight Requirements,
external intercommunication shall be used by the ground crew.

Exterior Preflight
The aircraft exterior preflight will be conducted in accordance with section III of this manual.
Particular attention shall be made to check for loose or improperly installed panels in those
areas where maintenance has been performed.

Interior Preflight
Internal inspection and proper switch positions will be accomplished in accordance with section
III of this manual.

(E)   ## STARTING ENGINES
Start engine in accordance with section III of this manual. Check normal indications for the
following:

- Fuel flow
  Fuel flow is 425 to 800 PPH at light off, up to 2400 PPH during the engine transition to
  idle.

- Light off (within 15 seconds)
  Ignition should occur within 15 seconds after fuel flow or oil pressure is indicated.

- EGT within limits

- Nozzle movement
  Afterburner nozzles should be monitored during start. Nozzle positions to full open at
  approximately 30% RPM and 7/8 to 3/4 open at idle.

- Idle RPM 65 ± 1%

- Boost pump pressure
  Pressure indicating 30 ± 5 psi at idle.

- Idle fuel flow 800 - 1400 PPH

- Idle EGT 220° - 420°

- Idle oil pressure 12 psi minimum.

- PC II pressure (R eng) 2750 - 3250 PSI.

- Utility pressure (R eng) 2550 - 3000 PSI.

- Extend refuel probe (R eng)
  This will ensure that the probe will extend on the reduced utility pressure.

(FC)   - Spoiler Check
  With right engine operating, slowly deflect control stick approximately 1-inch to left then
  return to center. Have ground crew verify that spoiler does not fully deflect. A fully
  deflected spoiler indicates a possible malfunctioning lateral series servo.

- PC I pressure (both eng) 2750 - 3250 psi

- Utility pressure (both eng) 2750 - 3250 psi

- Bus tie light out within 18 seconds.
  a. When the right generator is turned on, the RH GEN OUT light goes out. The BUS TIE
     light comes on momentarily, then goes out. When turning on the left generator, the
     LH GEN OUT light goes out and the BUS TIE light comes on and may stay on up to a
     maximum of 18 seconds, then goes out. The same indication occurs when the right
     generator is cycled.

●b. With both generators on the line, turn off right generator, note ADI, boost pump pressure gages and run seat motor up and down. If reverse phasing is present, these items will be malfunctioning and motors will run in reverse. Select right generator on.

● SPC light

STATIC CORR OFF light must go out and remain extinguished after placing SPC switch in the RESET CORR position. After reset, altimeter should indicate within ± 400 feet of the before reset indication. Altimeter oscillations of any magnitude are unacceptable.

● Wing fold

Operate the wing fold system. Check that the lights on the telelight panel operate and extension or retraction occurs in 12 to 16 seconds.

BEFORE TAXIING

(FC)

● Aileron trim 10-15 seconds

Move aileron trim left. Have ground crew confirm left spoiler up and right aileron down. Mark time and move aileron trim to the full right position. Maximum time to travel from full left to full right is 15 seconds. Insure stick moves from left to right, and have ground crew confirm that left spoiler going down and right spoiler up after passing neutral position. Move trim back to neutral and have ground crew confirm spoilers and ailerons neutral. Check control stick neutral position ± 1/4 inch.

a. Lateral control system checkout
  (1) Mechanical system checks.
    (a) With ailerons trimmed neutral; slowly trim the stick to the left until the left spoiler just breaks the stops. Have ground crew check that the right aileron is deflected down 1/4 to 1 inch.
    (b) Repeat this check on the opposite side to insure that when the right spoiler breaks the stop, the left aileron is down 1/4 to 1 inch.

CAUTION

If this check fails, the lateral controls must be re-rigged before flight, as large yaw angles and possible post-stall gyration can occur at high angles-of-attack since it will be impossible to neutralize the lateral controls.

  (2) Operation system checks.
    (a) With STAB AUG off, trim the lateral system as close to neutral as possible. Spoilers should be flush with the wing and ailerons aligned approximately with the trailing edge flaps.
    (b) Engage STAB AUG while observing both ailerons for movement. Ailerons should not move more than 1/4 inch.

● Tail hook/corner reflector (aircraft 148411h and up after AFC 288).

Extension of hook should be 5 seconds maximum. Reflector door opens, reflector extends and CORNER REFLECTOR OUT warning light remains out. Retraction of hook should be 10 ± 3 seconds. Reflector retracts and reflector door closes.

● Place hook by-pass switch in BY-PASS position; reflector door opens, reflector extends, and CORNER REFLECTOR OUT warning light remains out. The hook remains up and locked. Place hook by-pass switch in NORMAL position; reflector retracts and reflector door closes.

● Speed brakes

Should extend to full deflection in 2.5 ± 0.5 seconds and retract in 2.5 ± 0.5 seconds on the ground.

● RAT

Pneumatic pressure should not drop below 2200 ± 200 psi on extension and 1200 +400, -200 psi on retraction (when immediately following extension).

● Flaps/aileron droop/BLC/ARI

a. Full flaps
  (1) T.E. flaps extend within 8 ± 1 seconds.

(2) Ailerons droop within 3 seconds. (On aircraft 152995z and up, and all others after AFC 218).

(3) Check for presence of BLC at trailing edge.

(4) Check for presence of BLC at leading edge.

(5) Place engine bleed air switch OFF and ensure leading edge BLC is shut off. (On aircraft after AFC 440). On aircraft after AFC 550, ensure BLEED AIR OFF light illuminates and then goes out after bleed air switch is returned to NORM (guard down).

(6) Place engine bleed air switch NORM.

(7) Place YAW STAB AUG switch OFF and pull ARI circuit breaker. Move stick full left and check left spoiler up and right aileron down, rudder neutral. Place YAW STAB AUG switch ON and check for 5° left rudder, reset ARI circuit breaker and check for additional 10° left rudder. Repeat this procedure with full right stick.

b. 1/2 Flap

(1) Check for absence of BLC at trailing edge.

(2) Conduct left and right ARI check as checked with full flaps.

(3) Extend to full flaps.

(4) Flap switch up; retract within 6 ± 1 seconds.

(5) Ailerons return to neutral (after initial movement) within 6 seconds.

●Anti ice

Stabilize at 80% engine RPM or higher. Place anti-icing switch to ON and check for illumination of L ANTI-ICE ON and R ANTI-ICE ON lights. Observe approximate 10°C rise in EGT and slight rise in fuel flow. When switch is turned off, check drop in fuel flow, EGT, and that the lights go out.

TAXI

●Nose wheel steering

Engage the nose wheel steering after aircraft begins to roll and ascertain that nose wheel responds to steering command signals in both direction and magnitude.

●Air brakes

When a reasonable clear area is reached, move air brake lever slowly to on. Ascertain that both brakes are applied.

BEFORE TAKEOFF

(E) ●MIL power check

Check engines individually at MIL thrust and note any variation from the following limitations:

(E) ●Throttle check

Force required to move each throttle from IDLE to MIL requires approximately 5 pounds.

(E) ●EGT

Exhaust gas temperature at MIL power is 625° ± 10°C.

(E) ●Fuel flow

Fuel flow for each engine at MIL power is 7500 to 9000 pounds per hour (approx).

(E) ●Oil pressure

Engine oil pressure at MIL power for MIL-L-23699 oil is 40 to 70 psi, 45 to 75 prior to ASC 115.

(E) ●RPM

RPM at MIL power is 100% ± 0.5%.

(E) ●Nozzle position

Check and record nozzle position, ensure that both openings are approximately the same.

TAKEOFF

Perform a normal afterburner takeoff. Observe and record any variations to following limitations:

●EGT - 635°C MAX

(E) ●Nozzle position - 5/8 to 7/8 open.

(FC)

- Gear retraction - 4 to 6 seconds.

- Rudder switchover
  Accelerating - 228 to 252 KCAS
  Decelerating - Approximately 20 knots below accelerating switchover
  (Minimum 218 KCAS)

INFLIGHT

15,000 Feet

Climb to 15,000 feet and proceed with following checks:

- Cabin pressure (8000 feet)
  Check that both cockpit pressure altimeters read 8000 feet.

(FC)

- Flight control system
  a. Turn off stab aug. Trim aircraft for hands off flight and check position of spoiler and ailerons. Reengage each stab aug axis separately and check for transits.
  b. STABILATOR - Establish 350 knots and check for normal longitudinal feel. Establish a 2 G pull up and release the stick. Oscillations should dampen in 1/2 cycle. Trim full nose up, full nose down and check for 15 to 20 pounds of stick force. Return trim to neutral.
  c. AILERONS - Trim for hands off flight. Check ailerons and spoilers in trimmed position. Roll aircraft into a 60° bank and release the stick. Roll should stop and the stick should center. Repeat check in the opposite direction.
  d. RUDDER - With wings level trim aircraft so the yaw string is centered (if installed), or trim aircraft so the needle and ball on the ADI are centered. Displace rudder pedal to develop yaw. Release pedal, yaw should cease in 1/2 cycle. Repeat check in the opposite direction. Symmetrical flight should occur in 5 seconds following yaw input. Trim right and left ensuring rudder trims in proper direction.

- Compass system
  a. Standby, ADI, HSI - Heading accuracy (mode selector knob in SLAVED mode) within ± 5° of known magnetic heading. No more than 2-1/2° difference can exist between ADI and HSI headings. Standby compass headings should take into account corrections as noted on correction cards located in cockpit.
  b. ADF (PRI, AUX) - Accuracy is within ± 5° of heading toward or away from the transmitter. Bearings off wing tip are accurate with ± 20°. Needle oscillations must not exceed ± 3°.
  c. TACAN - Accuracy of all bearings will be within ± 1°; however, reading accuracy prompts an arbitrary tolerance of ± 2°. Distance accuracy will be ± 0.2 miles plus 0.1% of total distance to station. Course bar pointer and bearing pointer have no discernible difference in bearings. Erratic course bar movement is unacceptable except when close-in to the station.

(E)

- Engine idle power

  Reduce engine power to idle and observe the following limitations:

  a. EGT - 100° to 300°C.
  b. RPM - minimum 65% +0% -1% at 0.55 to 0.84 Mach.

(E)

- Engines military power

  Advance the throttles to military power and observe the following limitations:
  a. EGT - 625° ± 10°C
  b. RPM - 100% ± 0.5%
  c. Oil pressure - 40 to 70 psi, 45 to 75 prior to ASC 115.

(E)

- Engines (AB power)

  Advance the throttles to maximum power and observe the following limitations:
  a. EGT - 625° ± 10°C
  b. RPM - 100% ± 1.0%

• Cabin Vent

Perform a functional check of cabin vent by pulling up on emergency vent handle. Observe following action:
a. All air conditioning and pressurization air to cockpit and pressure suit is shut off.
b. Cabin pressure regulator and safety (dump) valve is opened and cockpit becomes depressurized.
c. Cabin and aircraft altimeter will read approximately same within 5 to 6 seconds after handle is pulled.
d. Ram air shutoff valve is opened and atmospheric air is allowed to enter cockpit through a port located just forward of pilot's feet.

• Wing fuel dump

Perform a check of wing fuel dump system, observing through rear view mirror that fuel actually dumps. RIO confirms dump with a visual check.

40,000 Feet

Climb to 40,000 feet and perform following checks:

(E)   • Engines (idle power)

Reduce engine power to idle, and observe following limitations:
a. EGT - 100° to 300°C
b. RPM - 80% (approx)

(E)   • Engines (MIL power)

a. EGT - 532° to 537°C at 91%; 619° to 635°C at 100.5%
b. RPM - 91% to 100.5%

(E)   • Engines (AB power)
a. EGT - 625° ± 10°C.
b. RPM - Military rpm ± 0.5%

(E)/(FC)   • VMAX
Maximum power Vmax is attained at 40,000 feet. Special instrumentation is required to check performance precisely; however, a check for minimum max-speed is felt to be a reasonable compromise. By using the appropriate maximum acceleration chart and subtracting 0.12 TMN from the Vmax given and a further correction for temperature (0.02 IMN/°C) from standard day, an acceptable figure is reached. An aircraft not meeting this minimum requirement may have malfunctioning bellmouth/ramp schedules for low-thrust engines and must be given a complete ground check. Thrust surging, directional oscillations and cyclic ramps are unacceptable characteristics.

• Pressure Suit
a. Suit vent air - Quantity and temperature of air will be fully controllable. Loss of manual cabin temperature control, with vent control ON, is normal.
b. Suit altitude indication - The cockpit altitude indicator will reflect altitude indicator with suit lines connected (unless suit has altimeter installed).
c. Suit controller - Dump cockpit pressure at 40,000 feet for a check of suit controller. Controller will maintain suit altitude of 35,000 +1500, -1000 feet at high aircraft altitudes and at the same time provides a check of the automatic switchover to oxygen for pressurizing the suit.

Descending From 40,000 Feet to 20,000 Feet

• Gyro horizon
Residual bank angle not to exceed ± 2° after erection period. Following 360° turn at a bank angle of 30° or more, the bank angle at roll-out will be no more than ± 2° from indication before beginning turn. Horizon is adjustable through minimum angle of 5° climb and 10° dive. A 360° roll will cause no precession in bank or pitch. Erratic motion of sphere is unacceptable. Cross check standby attitude gyro with ADI gyro; the maximum difference is ± 1%.

- Turn and bank indicator
  A single needle width turn results in turn rates of 165°-195° per minute.

- Vertical velocity indicator
  Must not exhibit erratic motion (except in transonic region where static pressure fluctuation normally occurs) and zeros in level flight.

- Accelerometer
  All needles return to within 1 ± 0.2G in 1G flight or on ground after reset button is actuated.

- Anti-G valve
  Commence air flow to G-suit connection at 1.5G. Flow rate may vary. At 2G a suit pressure of near 0 to 1.2 psi may be obtained. The suit pressure may vary between 2.9 and 4.3 psi at 4G. (Qualitative check only.)

- Altimeter

  The following lists allowable fluctuation in altitude with normal static pressure compensator operation.
  a. Mach range below 0.91 - Stable (25 feet random variation.)
  b. Accelerating through 0.91 to 0.93 - Two altitude breaks of ± 200 feet. Continuous oscillations should not exceed ± 50 feet.
  c. Acceleration through 0.93 to 1.05 - Two altitude breaks of ± 1000 feet. Continuous oscillation should not exceed ± 50 feet.
  d. 1.05 to Vmax - Stable (25 feet random variations).

Note

Static pressure compensator must continue to function through flight envelope. Occasional drop-outs (warning light ON) are unacceptable.

- True airspeed indicator
  The computation range is 150-1500 knots. Readings on ground of 108-150 knots are normal and will vary considerably. In-flight check requires free air temperature information.

- Air refueling probe (300 knots or 0.90 mach, whichever is less).
  Extend the air refueling probe and check READY light on. Check that reverse fuel transfer does not occur. (Rapid sector decrease.) Retract probe.

(FC)

- Lateral control check.
  At approximately 25,000 feet, disengage the stab aug (roll aug) and have the RIO visually check the ailerons for neutral trim. When neutral trim has been established, check the control stick for neutral position. Leave the roll aug disengaged. Slowly trim to establish a 3 to 5G pull out. Hands off stick and visually check aileron position. Accelerate to 350 knots, increase the angle-of-attack to 19 units and execute rudder rolls left and right (ailerons neutral). Large erratic yaw oscillations shall not occur. Establish a turn at 300 knots and 19 units AOA and gradually increase AOA until wing rock occurs, approximately 23 to 25 units. If any adverse characteristics are exhibited establish 5-10 units AOA. If the aircraft was not retrimmed, then hands off flight should again show the ailerons neutral.

- Automatic/manual temperature control
  Cockpit temperature is fully controllable over a range of -20°F to 100°F on AUTO setting. Manual selection may result in inlet temperature of -130°F to well above 220°F depending on flight conditions and techniques in using switch. For example, temperature limiter will limit the inlet air to 220°F ± 10°F when active; however, the unit is active only when manual switch is held in HOT position and does not react to higher temperatures that may occur as a result of speed and power changes. Pressure suit vent air control must be fully off to obtain control of the manual system.

- Defog foot heat control
  Defog air temperature is controllable from 85°F to 200°F, depending upon cabin temperature setting at time defog air is selected. Moving the defog lever through 50% travel position results in an increase in defog air temperature of approximately 100°F. In full defog position, 80% of available air is directed to windshield. In FOOT HEAT position only 10% of the air is directed to windshield.

●Horizontal situation indicator (HSI/TACAN)

The following functions will be checked for accuracy:

   (1) DME - Accuracy is ± 0.2 miles plus 0.1% of total distance from station; however, reading and flying accuracy will permit an accuracy check of no better than ± 1 mile.
   (2) Course indication - The course bar centers with ± 1° of known course of station. Erratic course bar movement is unacceptable. Course pointer and bearing pointer have no discernible difference in bearing in TACAN mode. Course selected in window and course pointer have no discernible difference in readings. Erratic movement of the bearing pointer is unacceptable, except for ± 3° jitter in ADF mode.

●TACAN

Volume control is sufficient to eliminate audible station identification signal. Lock-on normally occurs within 60 seconds following channel selection on T/R mode. This time will vary with bearing and distance from station.

●Attitude director indicator (ADI)

Vertical displacement pointer (VDP) moves opposite to direction of bank and centers with no discernible deviation when on selected heading.

●Antenna functional check.

●Gunsight functional check.

20,000 Feet

●Automatic flight control system.

Engagement of any mode or function of AFCS does not produce transients of sufficient magnitude to cause the aircraft to jump in pitch and/or roll. Performance of the system is unacceptable if an engagement jump occurs.

   a. Stability augmentation mode - Stab aug damps yaw inputs (rudder kicks) within 1/2 cycle to zero amplitude, and symmetrical flight (ball centered) will occur within 5 seconds following the yaw input. Transients in pitch and roll damp within 1/2 cycle; however, a slight residual pitch rate is considered normal because the stick longitudinal centering band may exceed the authority of the damper (± 2° stabilator travel) where excessive friction exists. Lateral inputs damp within 1/2 cycle. Random or cyclic transients about any axis are unacceptable.
   b. Control stick steering (CSS) - Control stick longitudinal breakout force will not exceed 4.0 pounds forward or 3.0 pounds aft, while lateral breakout force will not exceed 4.0 pounds. Self-induced lateral, longitudinal or directional transients, random or cyclic, are unacceptable. Control stick steering in excess of 70° ± 3° in pitch and bank will cause AFCS to disengage. While in a 0° to 70° bank, a reduction of stick force within these bank limits is unacceptable. Lateral return-to-level bank will not exceed 5° ± 2°. Heading hold error will not exceed ± 10° of the actual heading when return-to-level function becomes operative.
   c. Heading hold cutout - While operating in AFC mode, depress and release nose wheel steering button to activate heading hold cutout option. Minute heading changes between 0° and 5° angle of bank can then be made. Again depress and release nose wheel steering button and insure that AFCS heading hold function returns to normal operation.
   d. Altitude hold - Altitude hold function maintains altitude within ± 50 feet or 0.3% of reference altitude, whichever is greater, up to 0.9 Mach subsonic and above 1.0 Mach supersonic. While accelerating through transonic region, Mach jump may produce transients which will result in noticeably abrupt altitude hold corrections. This condition is considered normal as long as corrections do not become sharply erratic, and once this region is traversed aircraft settles down on reference altitude, or a new reference altitude and holds it. A change in altitude greater than 200 feet will cause reference altitude to slip by the amount that transient altitude limit (200 feet) is exceeded. Altitude hold function will become disengaged if control stick forces exceed 4.0 pounds maximum forward, or 2.75 pounds maximum aft for a period exceeding 0.5 seconds. When performing altitude hold function check, do not make initial engagement while in a climb which exceeds 1000 feet per minute. Engaging altitude hold mode in climbs greater than 1000 feet per minute may result in a reference altitude other than engage altitude.

e. Mach hold - (On aircraft 148363f thru 153029z before AFC 203.) The mach hold function shall hold the engage Mach number to within ± 0.3 of reference Mach. Response shall be smooth in all conditions and corrective action shall be noted within ± .01 Mach of the engage Mach number. Subsonic checks shall be made at .9 Mach, while supersonic checks may be made at any desired Mach number. Mach hold transients may be introduced in two ways. The airplane may be accelerated by adding throttle or the airplane may be decelerated by momentarily extending the speed brakes. In either case, there shall be a tendency towards altitude change with Mach remaining essentially constant. The transients introduced shall not exceed .05 Mach, since greater changes cause the reference (engage) Mach number to slip by the amount that the transient Mach limit (.05) is exceeded. The mach hold function will become disengaged when control stick forces exceed 4.0 maximum forward or 2.75 maximum aft for a period exceeding 0.5 seconds.

f. Emergency disengage - Disengaging the AFCS with emergency disengage switch will produce slight transients, but will not result in a G jump or more than ± 0.3G.

g. G-Limiter - Autopilot disengage at 4 ± 1/4 G (positive) and -1 ± 1/4 G (negative).

h. Automatic pitch trim
   (1) Assume flight conditions of 300 KCAS.
   (2) With AFCS switch off, manually trim aircraft for straight and level flight (make a mental note of stabilator trim position indicator).
   (3) Engage AFCS.
   (4) While holding control stick for straight and level flight, manually mistrim 2 units nose up.
   (5) Pull stab feel trim circuit breaker (pilot's right console) as trim indicator reaches 2 units out of trim.
   (6) In 2 to 15 seconds, A/P PITCH TRIM warning light shall illuminate.
   (7) Depress stab feel trim circuit breaker. The stabilator trim position indicator shall show a retrim toward the predetermined straight and level position.
   (8) The autopilot pitch trim indicator light shall go out when indicator is between 1 1/2 and 3/4 units from predetermined straight and level position.
   (9) Disengage AFCS, transient shall not exceed 0.3G.
      Repeat steps 2 thru 8 only in nose down direction.

10,000 Feet to Landing

Between 10,000 feet and landing, perform following checks:

- Angle of Attack
   a. Basic limitations and pictorial display of system will be found in section I of this manual. The following are additional tolerances.
   b. The airspeed will be within ± 4 knots except as noted in section I of this manual.
   c. Pedal shaker activates at 22.3 units angle of attack before AFC 218, and 21.3 units on aircraft 152995z and up, and all others after AFC 218.

- Flaps - Flap Blow Up Switch Test

Decrease airspeed below 205 knots and lower flaps. Slowly increase airspeed; the flaps will blow up at 215 to 242 knots. Slowly decrease airspeed; flaps will extend approximately (providing flap switch is down) 10 knots below noted retraction airspeed (minimum 215 KCAS). Flaps extend and retract within 8 ± 1 second and 6 ± 1 second, respectively.

- Ram air turbine
   a. Reduce airspeed to 250 knots.
   b. Secure TACAN, IFF, RADAR ALTIMETER and STAB AUG; (RIO) secure TACAN, RADAR.
   c. Extend RAT and check rotation.
   d. Secure right engine and relight.
   e. Secure both generators.
   f. Secure left engine and relight.
   g. Check normal operation of the following:
      (1) ICS
      (2) UHF (front and rear)
      (3) CADC RESET
      (4) Wing fuel transfer
      (5) Boost pump press 5-15 psi.
      (6) Landing gear/flap position indicators.
      (7) Longitudinal trim

(8) ADI/HSI

(9) Fuel quantity (fuel tank check switch also) and fuel flow indicators.

(10) RPM, EGT, nozzle indicators

(11) Oil/pneumatic pressure indicators

(12) Caution light reset

(13) Warning lights bright

(14) Instrument flood lights bright

(15) AOA indicator

(16) PC I/PC II pressure gauges.

(17) Check for electrical output at speeds down to 170 knots

h. Right and left generator - ON.

i. Accelerate, and retract RAT

(E) ●APCS functional check

> **WARNING**
>
> Do not engage the APCS unless all system components are installed
> and the landing gear is down.

a. Ensure speed brake switch is in STOP position, the APCS engine selector switch is in BOTH position, throttle friction lever is full aft, and emergency speed brake switch is in MAN position.

b. Engage APCS at approximate approach airspeeds and between 75% and MIL power rpm.

c. Move control stick forward and observe that throttles move aft and engine rpm decreases. Perform check with APCS air temp switch in HOT, COLD and NORM positions.

d. Move control stick aft and observe that throttles move forward and engine rpm increases. Perform check with APCS air temp switch in HOT, COLD and NORM positions.

e. Place air temp switch in applicable temperature position.

f. Neutralize controls, grasp throttles and override APCS. 20 to 40 pounds of force is required to override the APCS. Relax throttle pressure and observe that throttles return to their former position. APCS should be operating normally.

g. Select L position on APCS engine selector switch. Place right throttle between 77% and 82% rpm.

h. Move control stick fore and aft and observe that left engine throttle moves in opposite direction from control stick.

i. Neutralize controls and select R position of APCS engine selector switch. Place left throttle between 77% and 82% rpm. Move control stick fore and aft and observe that left engine throttle moves in opposite direction from control stick.

j. Neutralize controls and select BOTH position on APCS engine selector switch. Place speed brake switch to the IN position and observe that APCS engage switch moves to STBY and the APCS OFF and Master Caution lights illuminate. Throttles remain in the same position as when APCS was engaged.

●Radar altimeter

a. Drop-out altitude - Drop-out altitude is 5000 feet over land or water.

b. Low level warning - Accuracy is ± 5 feet of the selected altitude.

c. Drop-out angles - Occurs at no less than 30° bank angle and 50° pitch angle.

d. Accuracy - Will be ± 5 feet below 100 feet and ± 5% of terrain clearance between 100 and 500 feet.

●Speed brakes

Extend speed brakes and move emer speed brake switch to RETRACT. Speed brakes will be hydraulically closed and warning light extinguished.

●Landing gear

Landing gear extends in 5 to 7 seconds.

LANDING

(E)

●APCS disengagement
Prior to landing, engage APCS and check for disengagement on touch down.

●Drag chute
Force to deploy chute, approximately 50 pounds.

●Brakes
Check for spongy, draggy, or pulling brakes.

●Rain removal
During taxi with one or both engine(s) running, at or below 88% and flaps at 1/2 or down actuate the rain removal switch and check that air is coming from the rain removal ports in front of the windshield. Turn the switch off immediately and ensure the air flow decreases within a maximum of 6 seconds and stops within 17 seconds. If it does not stop, pull the EMERG VENT handle to prevent possible damage to the windshield.

●Fuel level low
Check that the FUEL LEVEL LOW light illuminates at 1880 ± 200 pounds. Check feed tank level at 1350 ± 200 pounds.

(E)

●Right engine shutdown.
With right engine stabilized at idle, place right throttle off. Check engine for smooth coast down.

(FC)

●Spoiler check
With left engine operating, slowly deflect control stick approximately 1 inch to right then return to center. Have ground crew verify that spoiler does not fully deflect. A fully deflected spoiler indicates a possible malfunctioning lateral series servo.

(E)

●Left engine
With left engine stabilized at idle, place left throttle off, check engine for smooth coast down.

AFTER FLIGHT

Pilot

●Before leaving aircraft, complete procedures in accordance with section III of this manual.

●All discrepancies or maintenance action requirements shall be properly posted on appropriate forms.

Ground Crew

Perform postflight inspection in accordance with applicable publications and as follows when applicable.

●Engines for audible bearing roughness; shrouds to turbine rotor seals for interference after shutdown; turbine wheels for contact with adjacent surfaces.

●Evidence of structural failure in areas where major structural modification or repair was accomplished prior to test flight.

●New or newly overhauled engine checks.
a. CSD and engine oil filter elements for metal particles.
b. Engine low and high pressure fuel filter elements for metal particles or foreign material.

●Remove emergency generator contact brush access cover.
a. Rotate RAT blades clockwise and observe armature for rotation. Failure of armature to rotate indicates probable quill shaft failure.

CHECKFLIGHT REQUIREMENTS (RIO)

TAXI

• AMCS
   a. Built In Test
      Perform Built-In-Test Function checks.

INFLIGHT

15,000 Feet

After climb to 15,000 feet, proceed with following checks.

• ADF
   Cross check ADF operation with front cockpit, allowable difference between instrument is ± 1°.

• TACAN
   Cross check TACAN operation with front cockpit, there should be no discernible difference between cockpit indicators.

• BDHI
   Cross check BDHI with HSI in front cockpit, allowable difference between instrument is ± 1°.

• Navigation computer
   Inflight check of NAV computer is basically a functional check because of inherent inaccuracy of the necessary high altitude wind information. Normal procedure is to set in your home field as a base, a TACAN station as a target and to utilize Weather Bureau altitude winds. System readouts are crosschecked with TACAN information during flight and unless an apparent error of appreciable magnitude is obvious, additional detailed checking is not performed. If closer checking is dictated by particular system performance, a leg of at least 12 minutes duration is flown (departing and exact fix) and all applicable parameters are noted at the departure and destination points; i.e., heading, TAS, computer settings and readouts. Resultant information is subsequently checked against the below tolerances.
   a. Present position latitude - ± 1 mile for each 12 minutes of elapsed time after start of problem or ± 1% of the distance travelled, whichever is greater.
   b. Present position longitude - Same tolerance as latitude.
   c. Aircraft ground track angle (relative to true heading) - ± 2° from ground speed of 150 to 1700 knots.
   d. Aircraft bearing (relative to true heading) - Bearing error shall not exceed an amount which is defined by a line passing through the present position and a point 5 miles to either side of the target or base (as selected), or ± 2° deviation from a line passing through the target or base, whichever tolerance is larger.
   e. Great circle distance (range) - The range error shall not exceed 5 miles ± 1% of the theoretical range.

40,000 Feet

After climb to 40,000 feet, proceed with the following checks.

• Airspeed and mach indicator
   Cross check the airspeed and mach indicator with the front cockpit, allowable airspeed difference at 1.4 Mach is ± 14 knots and allowable Mach difference at 1.4 Mach is ± 0.04 Mach.

Descending From 40,000 Feet to 20,000 Feet

• AMCS operational check.

20,000 Feet

- Attitude gyro

Cross check remote attitude gyro with ADI in front cockpit. Allowable error between instruments is 1°.

- Vertical velocity indicator

Cross check vertical velocity indicator with front cockpit (if installed). Maximum allowable deviation between instruments is 400 feet minimum.

- Altimeter

Cross check altimeter with front cockpit, allowable difference between instruments is 300 feet.

10,000 Feet to Landing

No check at this altitude.

SECTION V EMERGENCY PROCEDURES

FDB-1-(67)

TABLE OF CONTENTS

TABLE OF CONTENTS CONTINUED

GENERAL

This section contains procedures to be followed to correct an emergency condition. These procedures insure maximum safety for the crew and/or aircraft until a safe landing or other appropriate action is accomplished. Multiple emergencies, adverse weather and other peculiar conditions may require modification of these procedures. The mandatory items (ALL CAPITAL LETTERS) contained in the various emergency procedures cover the most adverse conditions. The nature and severity of the encountered emergency dictate the necessity for complying with the mandatory items in their entirety. It is essential, therefore, that aircrews determine the correct course of action by use of common sense and sound judgement. As soon as possible, the pilot should notify the RIO, flight/flight leader, and tower of any existing emergency and of the intended action.

When an emergency occurs, three basic rules are established which apply to airborne emergencies. They should be thoroughly understood by all aircrews:

1. Maintain aircraft control.
2. Analyze the situation and take proper action.
3. Land as soon as practicable.

When an airborne emergency occurs and the flight conditions permit, the pilot or RIO should record and/or broadcast all available information such as airspeed, altitude, power settings, instrument readings and fluctuations, warning lights illuminated, loss of thrust, and unusual noises. Flight leaders,

wingmen, other pilots, or any ground station receiving such information should copy it and forward it as soon as possible to the cognizant activity. Wingmen should also record their observations of vapor, smoke, flames or other phenomena. Whenever possible, an effort should be made to escort an aircraft with a declared emergency until it is safely landed. This escort will observe the distressed aircraft for any external indications or symptoms of the problem, to provide assistance or advice that may be required, and to assist in a SAR effort if required.

WARNING

In troubleshooting of a system discrepancy or in the accomplishment of an emergency procedure, the operation of a system control (such as flap lever, throttle, flight control, electrical control switch, etc.) is usually required. Due to the nature of some failures, and/or the occurrence of successive malfunctions, some control operations may occasionally result in undesirable aircraft responses, such as unexpected roll or pitch motions, smoke, unstable engine operation, etc. Often the most prudent action to take to eliminate such an undesirable response is to immediately return the operated control to its former setting. The pilot must be mentally conditioned to take that action promptly when appropriate.

AIR CONDITIONING/PRESSURIZATION

COCKPIT OVERPRESSURIZATION

1. Emergency vent knob - PULL

> **WARNING**
>
> Do not attempt to open the canopy by the normal method if the cockpit is overpressurized since this may cause the canopy to lift and separate from the aircraft and fall on the banana links resulting in an inadvertent ejection.

If vent knob does not relieve pressure -

2. Cockpit heat and vent circuit breakers - PULL (L7, M7, No. 2 panel)

> **WARNING**
>
> Inadvertent seat ejection may also occur if any foreign object in the cockpit becomes jammed between the canopy actuator and the primary seat mounted initiator or the ejection gun firing mechanism sear.

COCKPIT TEMPERATURE FAILURE

If the cockpit temperature remains full hot despite efforts to moderate the incoming air, the following corrective measures should be accomplished in sequence proceeding with the succeeding step only if the preceding effort fails to provide a tolerable environment. If corrective measures provide satisfactory results, land as soon as practicable.

1. Temp control auto-manual switch - MANUAL COLD (Hold for 5 seconds)
2. Cockpit heat and vent circuit breakers - PULL (L7, M7, No. 2 panel).
3. Emergency vent knob - PULL
4. Reduce altitude and reduce airspeed below flap blow up speed and lower flaps to full down. This utilizes max BLC air and thereby reduces cockpit air flow.
5. Bleed air switch - OFF (after AFC 440)
6. Jettison aft canopy.

EQUIPMENT COOLING TURBINE FAILURE

A malfunction of the equipment cooling turbine is evidenced by a high pitched whine and/or vibration forward and outboard of the pilot's left foot. The turbine may be secured by the steps listed below. This, in turn, shuts off equipment air conditioning and turns on emergency ram air cooling, but does not affect fuel tank pressurization and transfer, anti-G suits, etc.

To secure equipment cooling turbine.

1. Equipment cooling turbine circuit breakers - PULL (L6 & N6, No. 2 panel).

If undue delay is involved in locating the proper circuit breaker -

2. Extend RAT.
3. Turn off both generators to secure the cooling turbine.

After circuit breakers are located and pulled -

4. Turn on both generators.
5. Retract RAT.

AUXILIARY AIR DOOR(S)

GENERAL

The auxiliary air door warning light(s) illuminate any time the auxiliary air doors are out of phase with the landing gear handle (landing gear up, aux air door(s) open, or landing gear down, aux air door(s) closed). Neither of these situations constitutes a safety of flight condition if the problem is recognized and the appropriate action is taken. In the event of either a malfunction or failure, the appropriate corrective procedures must be utilized.

AUX AIR DOOR MALFUNCTION (GEAR UP, DOOR(S) OPEN)

1. Reduce pwr., slow to 250 KCAS or less
2. Landing gear - CYCLE

If light(s) remain on -

3. Bellmouth cont cb - PULL (J2 & J3, No. 1 panel).

If light(s) still remain on -

4. Maintain no more than cruise pwr

A cruise power setting will avoid engine compartment overheating.

> **CAUTION**
>
> Extended engine operation at high power settings will result in engine compartment and aft fuselage overheating.

5. Reset aux air door cb prior to lowering gear.

AUX AIR DOOR FAILURE (GEAR DOWN, DOOR(S) CLOSED)

If the auxiliary air doors fail to open when the landing gear is lowered, there is a possibility that the engines may automatically accelerate up to 100% rpm. A utility hydraulic system failure or double generator failure renders the variable bypass bellmouth and auxiliary air doors inoperative. Operation of an engine with an open variable bypass bellmouth and closed auxiliary air door allows engine compartment secondary air to recirculate to the engine compressor inlet. During low altitude or ground operation, the temperature of the recirculating air may be high enough to initiate T2 reset through normal detection by the compressor inlet temperature sensor. As T2 reset occurs, it increases the engine idle speed to maintain proper engine airflow and thrust under high temperature conditions, and can cause the idle speed to increase up to 100% rpm. The auto-accelerated engine can be shut down, if on the ground, by placing the throttle OFF. If a false reset occurs while airborne, a near normal landing can be made by modulating the exhaust nozzles of the affected engine(s).

1. Landing gear - CYCLE

AUTO-ACCELERATION OF ONE ENGINE

1. Throttle of affected engine - IDLE
2. Make an on speed approach
   Modulate throttle of unaffected engine for desired thrust. Under no conditions will the combined thrust of the auto-accelerated engine in idle, and the unaffected engine in idle, be in excess of that required to make an optimum on speed approach.
3. At touchdown, affected engine - SHUTDOWN

AUTO-ACCELERATION OF BOTH ENGINES

1. Throttle of either engine - IDLE
2. Modulate the exhaust nozzles of the remaining engine for desired thrust.
3. Make an on speed approach
4. At touchdown, left engine - SHUTDOWN
   Shutting down left engine at touchdown leaves you in a more favorable position (more systems available) in the event of a bus tie failure.

BLEED AIR SYSTEM

BLEED AIR DUCT FAILURE

Severe damage to the aircraft may result from a bleed air duct failure due to the high temperature produced by the bleed air system. The extremely hot air leaking from a failed duct may ignite flammables in the immediate vicinity of the duct failure. The following symptoms may be indictive of a bleed air system failure: a mild audible thump or bang on the airframe; complete or partial loss of cockpit pressurization; loss of pylons, missiles or other external stores; generator failure, popping of circuit breakers and illumination of fire/overheat warning lights, bleed air overheat warning lights with the MASTER CAUTION light, (on aircraft after AFC 439) and/or several other warning/indicator lights; erratic fuel quantity indication; mild stick transients; stiffness of throttles; hydraulic failure; smoke emitting from the intake duct louvers; fuel fumes in the cockpit; high fuel flow/erratic response to throttle movement (indicative of main fuel hose rupture).

| CAUTION |

Early analysis of a bleed air duct failure is required to prevent serious damage to, or possible loss of the aircraft.

If several of the preceding symptoms occur in close sequence -

Aircraft before AFC 440 -

1. Reduce power to lowest practicable setting.
2. Check for indications of fire.

If circumstances permit -

3. Lower flaps.
4. Land as soon as practicable.

Aircraft after AFC 440 -

1. Bleed air switch - OFF

Note

With the bleed air switch OFF, the following will be lost: cockpit air conditioning and pressurization, rain removal air, defog/footheat, equipment cooling air, external fuel and internal wing fuel transfer capability, automatic altitude reporting, pneumatic system charging, leading edge BLC, and SPC inputs to all systems.

2. Secure radar and CNI equipment, unless safety of flight/operational necessity dictates otherwise.
3. Check for indications of fire.
4. Land as soon as practicable.

Note

Without leading edge BLC, approaches can be made in the normal manner; however, handling characteristics will be slightly degraded and the airspeed indication will be approximately 7 knots higher than normal.

BLEED AIR CHECK VALVE FAILURE

No indication of a bleed air check valve failure will be noted in flight until the throttle is retarded and then readvanced on the engine with the failed bleed air check valve. If the throttle has been retarded and then readvanced, either rpm hangs up or a minor compressor stall and flame-out occurs at approximately 85% rpm. If a flame-out occurs, a restart can be made, but rpm will probably not go above 65%, EGT rises to approximately 625°, and nozzles go full

open. In either case, the engine can be regained as follows:

1. Normal operating engine - IDLE
   Idling normal operating engine equalizes pressure in bleed air line.
2. Accelerate engine with failed bleed air check valve.
3. Accelerate normal engine.
   Normal operating engine should not be accelerated to, or operated at, a rpm greater than that of affected engine for remainder of flight.

BOUNDARY LAYER CONTROL

BLC MALFUNCTION

A boundary layer control system malfunction is indicated by the illumination of the BLC MALFUNCTION warning light. The only type of malfunctions indicated by the light are: a leading edge BLC valve stuck open when the flaps are up, or a trailing edge BLC valve stuck open when the flaps are in any position other than full down. If the BLC MALFUNCTION indicator light flickers when flaps are raised, cycle the flaps to recheck valve operation. If the light fails to flicker again, the warning system may be burned out. If the BLC MALFUNCTION light flickers when the flaps are cycled the problem may be rigging. Either case should be handled as a BLC malfunction.

1. FLAPS - DOWN
2. Maintain airspeed consistent with gross weight and flap blow-up speed.
3. Land as soon as practicable.

CAUTION

Operating at normal power setting in excess of 30 seconds with the BLC MALFUNCTION light illuminated and flaps up or 1/2 may result in damage to the warning circuit wiring which extinguishes the warning light. Continued flight with the flaps up can then result in additional electrical, hydraulic, and structural damage to the wing from overheating. Hot BLC air can melt the insulation off the wiring to the flap up limit switch allowing the bare wire to short to ground. This short results in the same indication as a flaps down condition to the WHEELS light circuit, thereby, illuminating the WHEELS light. In view of the above, an illuminated WHEELS light with the landing gear handle and flaps switch up, or the gear handle DN and the flaps UP or 1/2, should be treated as a BLC malfunction.

BLC FAILURES

A boundary layer control (BLC) system failure effects the handling characteristics and approach

speeds of the airplane. This (BLC) system failure usually does not effect the complete BLC system, but rather a portion of the system, and is probably one of the following variations:

a. Trailing edge BLC inoperative on one side.
   This condition is characterized by a moderate roll when the flaps reach full down. Trim requirements vary only slightly as speed is reduced.
b. Leading edge BLC inoperative on one side.
   This condition is characterized by little or no lateral trim requirements when flaps are first lowered, followed by increased trim requirements as airspeed is reduced.
c. Leading and trailing edge BLC inoperative on the same side.
   With this condition, the initial flap down lateral trim requirements of the trailing edge is first apparent, followed by increased trim as airspeed decreases. Full lateral trim required well above approach airspeed.

The BLC failure will probably occur before or in the transition to flaps down during a landing approach, with the result being an asymmetric BLC condition. The asymmetric BLC condition has been found to be safe and easily controllable even with both leading edge and trailing edge BLC inoperative on the same side. There is no reason to raise flaps to avoid an asymmetrical BLC condition. In general, for these types of BLC failure, an on speed angle of attack gives satisfactory approach control.

1. Retrim airplane.
2. Fly on speed angle of attack.

Note

In the event of a simultaneous BLC and angle of attack failure, add 6 knots (with leading or trailing edge BLC failure on one side) or 18 knots (with both leading and trailing edge BLC failure on one side) to the approach airspeed obtained from the angle of attack conversion chart.

CANOPY

CANOPY MALFUNCTION

If either the front or aft CANOPY UNLOCK light remains on after an attempted closure, the canopy actuator shear pin may have failed, and the following procedures apply:

1. Do not actuate the normal canopy control selector, raise or lower the ejection seat, or allow external canopy control buttons to be operated.
2. Attempt to operate manual canopy release handle to full aft position. Apply approximately 20 pounds force.
3. If handle can be pulled full aft, canopy actuator shear pin has failed or pneumatic pressure has depleted. Egress can be made by pushing the canopy open manually.

WARNING

The crewmember leaving the affected seat should evacuate with extreme caution, taking care to stay clear of the canopy control lever.

4. If Canopy does not unlock, actuate normal canopy control lever to raise canopy. Further attempts to relock the canopy are not recommended.

CHARTS

GENERAL

The charts and illustrations in this sub-section contain procedures and information which complements the text in the rest of the section. These charts should be used as necessary, in conjunction with the text, in order to analyze and judiciously perform the emergency procedures in an expeditious manner.

LANDING GEAR MALFUNCTION — EMERGENCY LANDING GUIDE

FINAL CONFIGURATION	CARRIER LANDING	Notes	FIELD LANDING (ARRESTING GEAR) AVAILABLE	Notes	FIELD LANDING (NO ARRESTING GEAR) AVAILABLE	Notes
ALL GEAR UP	EJECT	2, 4, 5, 12	NO ARRESTED LANDING	5,7,8,12	LAND	5,7,8,12
NOSE GEAR UP	LAND	4,12	NO ARRESTED LANDING	5,7,8,12	LAND	5,7,8,12
STUB NOSE GEAR	LAND	4	NO ARRESTED LANDING	1,5,7,8,13	LAND	1,5,7,8
ONE MAIN GEAR UP	LAND	4,5	ARRESTED LANDING	5, 6, 14	LAND	1,5,7,8,10,11
ONE or BOTH STUB MAIN GEAR	LAND	4	NO ARRESTED LANDING	1,5,7,8,10,11	LAND	1,5,7,8,10,11
ONE MAIN GEAR UP NOSE GEAR UP	EJECT	1,2,4,5,12	NO ARRESTED LANDING	1,3,5,7,8,10,11,12	LAND	1,3,5,7,8,10,11,12
BOTH MAIN GEAR UP	LAND	3,4,5	NO ARRESTED LANDING	5,7,8,9	LAND	5,7,8,11

Notes

1. If wing tanks installed and landing gear can be actuated, retract all gear. Refer to All Gear Up Configuration.
2. Option to land if wing drop tanks installed.
3. Option to eject if wing drop tanks not installed.
4. Hook down barricade engagement in accordance with current aircraft barricade engagement recovery bulletin.
5. Retain drop tanks.
6. Foam runway beyond arresting gear if practicable.
7. Foam runway if practicable.
8. Deploy drag chute at touchdown in accordance with crosswind landing criteria.
9. Option of midfield arrestment if 4000 feet of runway plus overrun available. Secure engines on touchdown.
10. Land off-center to gear down side.
11. Keep engines operating in order to retain nose wheel steering and/or power boost brakes.
12. Angle of attack will indicate 3 to 4 units low with the nose gear up.
13. Remove all field arresting cables (for field landing with stub nose gear).
14. Jettison LAU-17 pylons.

 ● Multiple emergencies, adverse weather and other peculiar conditions may require modifications to these procedures.

 ● If available, an LSO is recommended for all field arrested landings.

 ● If a gear up landing is made with external tanks aboard, depressurize the external tanks by first pulling the landing gear circuit breaker, and then place the landing gear handle down.

 ● A field arrested landing should not be attempted during any gear malfunction involving a stub main gear due to the probability of severing the arresting cables with the stub.

 ● During some emergencies it is desirable to remove certain crossdeck pendants or field arresting cables. For additional information see applicable aircraft recovery bulletins.

 ● Jettison all external ordnance including missiles.

FDB-1-(68)

Figure 5-1

WARNING/INDICATOR LIGHTS

LIGHT	CAUSE	CORRECTIVE ACTION	REMARKS
WHEELS	FLAPS DOWN—GEAR UP.	LOWER LANDING GEAR OR RAISE FLAPS TO EXTINGUISH LIGHT.	AN ILLUMINATED WHEELS LIGHT WITH LANDING GEAR HANDLE UP AND THE FLAP SWITCH UP SHOULD BE TREATED AS A BLC MALFUNCTION.
FIRE → OVER HT	FIRE OR OVERHEAT CONDITION EXISTS IN INDICATED ENGINE COMPARTMENT.	CARRY OUT PRESCRIBED EMERGENCY PROCEDURE AS NECESSARY.	LIGHT INDICATES TEMPERATURE IN EXCESS OF 765°F IN AFFECTED ENGINE COMPARTMENT.
MASTER CAUTION	SOME SYSTEM HAS A CAUTION CONDITION.	CHECK TELELIGHT PANEL.	LIGHT ILLUMINATES WITH LIGHTS ON THE TELELIGHT PANEL EXCEPT: ● L/R/CTR EXT FUEL ● SPEEDBRAKES OUT.
L ENG OIL LOW / R ENG OIL LOW	APPLICABLE ENGINE OIL QUANTITY IS LOW.	NONE—INFO ONLY.	ENGINE OIL QUANTITY IS BELOW 3.2 GALLONS.
L WING PIN UNLOCKED / R WING PIN UNLOCKED	WING(S) UNLOCKED.	WING PIN HANDLE—LOCKED.	MAY BE NECESSARY TO RECYCLE THE WING FOLD SYSTEM.
L ANTI ICE ON / R ANTI ICE ON	SWITCH ON—NORMAL INDICATION.	INFO ONLY.	SWITCH OFF: ● IF LIGHT GOES OUT, ACCELERATE AND DISREGARD INDICATION. ● IF LIGHT STAYS ON, REMAIN AT REDUCED SPEED.
	SWITCH OFF—ERRONEOUS INDICATION.	REDUCE SPEED.	
IFF	MODE 4 HAS FAILED	NONE—INFO ONLY	LIGHT INOPERATIVE UNTIL MODE 4 IS INSTALLED.
L AUX AIR DOOR / R AUX AIR DOOR	DOOR(S) OUT OF PHASE WITH GEAR HANDLE.	CARRY OUT PRESCRIBED EMERGENCY PROCEDURES AS NECESSARY.	DISREGARD MOMENTARY LIGHT.
ALT ENCODER OUT	UNRELIABLE SIGNAL OR NO SIGNAL FROM ALTITUDE ENCODER UNIT	NONE—INFO ONLY	IF LIGHT STAYS ON: PERFORM THIS FUNCTION THROUGH VOICE COMMUNICATION.
IFR PROBE UNLOCKED	NORMAL INDICATION WITH PROBE EXTENDED.	INFO ONLY.	IF LIGHT STAYS ON: ● REFUEL PROBE SWITCH—EXTEND ● REMAIN BELOW PUBLISHED AIRSPEED LIMITATIONS.
	PROBE IS NOT FULLY RETRACTED.	REFUEL PROBE SWITCH—EXTEND, THEN RETRACT.	
CHK FUEL FILTERS	ONE OR BOTH LOW PRESSURE FUEL FILTERS ARE PARTIALLY CLOGGED.	NONE—INFO ONLY	LOG ON YELLOW SHEET (OPNAV 3760-2). MONITOR ENGINE OPERATION.
REFUEL READY	FUSELAGE PRESSURIZATION AND VACUUM RELIEF VALVE OPEN.	NONE—INFO ONLY	INDICATES THAT FUSELAGE TANKS ARE PROPERLY VENTED FOR REFUELING.
CABIN TURB OVERSPEED	TURBINE SUBJECTED TO EXTREME PRESSURE AND/OR TEMPERATURE.	● REDUCE THRUST. REDUCE SPEED.	IF LIGHT STAYS ON: ● EMERGENCY VENT KNOB—PULL
WINDSHIELD TEMP HIGH	WINDSHIELD IS OVERHEATED.	● RAIN REMOVAL SWITCH—OFF. ● EMER. VENT KNOB—PULL (IF NECESSARY)	INTERMITTENT ILLUMINATION DURING HIGH MACH FLIGHT, RAIN REMOVAL SYSTEM OFF, IS NORMAL.
CORNER REFL OUT	CORNER REFLECTOR EXTENDED	DO NOT EXCEED 250 KCAS	INTERMITTENT ILLUMINATION DURING FUEL TRANSFER IS NORMAL.
L EXT FUEL / R EXT FUEL / CTR EXT FUEL	● TANK IS EMPTY. ● FUEL FLOW HAS STOPPED. ● TANK IS FULL (DURING AIR REFUELING).	NONE—INFO ONLY	CORNER REFLECTOR EXTENDED AND THE NOSE LANDING GEAR IS UP
FUS BLEED AIR OVERHT	TEMP. IN EXCESS OF 410°F EXISTS IN FWD. FUS. AREA	● REDUCE POWER ● BLEED AIR SW. OFF	● MASTER CAUTION ILLUMINATES ● CONTINUED OPERATION WITH LIGHT(S) ON MAY RESULT IN EQUIPMENT DAMAGE
ENG BLEED AIR OVERHT	TEMP. IN EXCESS OF 575°F EXISTS IN KEEL WEB AREA.		WITH BLEED AIR SW OFF: ● LOSS OF L.E. BLC, FUEL PRESSURIZATION PNEUMATICS, CABIN & EQUIPMENT REFRIGERATION PACKS, & SPC.
WING BLEED AIR OVERHT	TEMP. IN EXCESS OF 410°F EXISTS IN WING L.E.		● LANDING SPEED INCREASES +15 KNOTS.
BLEED AIR OFF	BLEED AIR SHUT OFF VALVE IS CLOSED.	NONE — INFO ONLY	NONE

FDB-1-(69-1)A

Figure 5-2 (Sheet 1 of 2)

LIGHT	CAUSE	CORRECTIVE ACTION	REMARKS
RADAR CNI COOL OFF	EQUIPMENT COOLING TURBINE SHUTDOWN.	• AIRSPEED – REDUCE. • WAIT 15 SECONDS. • RESET – PUSH.	IF LIGHT STAYS ON: • REMAIN AT REDUCED AIRSPEED TO PREVENT EQUIPMENT DAMAGE. • IFF & RADAR – STBY. • TACAN – OFF.
AUTO PILOT PITCH TRIM	PITCH TRIM CIRCUIT IS NOT FUNCTIONING.	• STICK – GRASP FIRMLY. • AUTOPILOT – DISENGAGE.	DISREGARD A MOMENTARY LIGHT.
BLC MALFUNCTION	• FLAPS ARE UP AND AT LEAST ONE BLC VALVE IS STUCK OPEN. • FLAPS ARE 1/2 DOWN AND TRAILING EDGE BLC VALVE IS OPEN.	• REDUCE SPEED BELOW – 200 KTS CAS • FLAPS FULL DOWN.	CONTINUED FLIGHT WITH FLAPS UP AND LIGHT ON MAY RESULT IN ELECTRICAL HYDRAULIC AND STRUCTURAL DAMAGE TO AIRCRAFT.
ENG INLET TEMP HIGH	INLET TEMPERATURE IS ABOVE 121°C.	BELOW 30,000 FEET – REDUCE SPEED.	LIGHT ON OPERATION ABOVE 30,000 FEET: SEE ENGINE LIMITATIONS.
AUTO PILOT DISENGAGE	AUTOPILOT HAS DISENGAGED.	AUTOPILOT – RE-ENGAGE IF PRACTICAL.	NONE
OXYGEN LOW	SUPPLY DEPLETED TO 1 LITER.	DESCEND TO SAFE ALTITUDE.	REFER TO OXYGEN DURATION TABLE.
SPEED BRAKE OUT	SPEEDBRAKES ARE NOT CLOSED.	NONE – INFO ONLY	MASTER CAUTION WILL NOT ILLUMINATE.
PITCH AUG OFF	PITCH STAB AUG IS DISENGAGED.	NONE – INFO ONLY	ILLUMINATES ANY TIME BUSES ARE ENERGIZED AND PITCH STAB AUG IS DISENGAGED.
FUEL LEVEL LOW	1880 ± 200 POUNDS FUEL TOTAL REMAINING IN CELLS 1 & 2.	NONE – INFO ONLY	CHECK ALL FUEL TRANSFERRED TO THE FUSELAGE.
APCS OFF	APCS IS DISENGAGED.	NON – INFO ONLY	ILLUMINATES ANYTIME BUSES ARE ENERGIZED AND APCS BECOMES DISENGAGED.
CHK HYD GAGES	PRESSURE BELOW 1500 ± 100 PSI IN ANY SYSTEM.	ANALYZE SITUATION.	CARRY OUT PRESCRIBED EMERGENCY PROCEDURES.
STATIC CORR OFF	AIR DATA COMPUTER MALFUNCTION.	• AUTOPILOT – DISENGAGED. • STATIC COMPENSATOR SWITCH – RESET.	IF LIGHT STAYS ON: • STATIC COMPENSATOR SWITCH – CORR OFF. • USE INSTRUMENT POSITION CORRECTION DATA AS NECESSARY.
CANOPY UNLOCKED	FORWARD, AFT OR BOTH CANOPIES ARE UNLOCKED.	CARRY OUT PRESCRIBED EMERGENCY PROCEDURES AS NECESSARY	INSURE ADEQUATE PNEUMATIC PRESSURE FOR PROPER CANOPY OPERATION.
LH GEN OUT RH GEN OUT	CORRESPONDING GENERATOR IS OFF THE LINE.	AFFECTED GENERATOR SWITCH – CYCLE.	IF LIGHT STAYS ON: • CARRY OUT EMERGENCY PROCEDURES AS NECESSARY.
BUS TIE OPEN	WITH SPLIT BUS (ONE GEN OUT LIGHT ON) – FAULT ON INOPERATIVE GENERATOR BUSES.	CARRY OUT PRESCRIBED EMERGENCY PROCEDURES AS NECESSARY.	WITH LIGHT ON, INOPERATIVE GENERATOR BUSES WILL NOT BE POWERED.
	PARALLEL BUS (BOTH GEN OUT LIGHTS OUT) GENERATORS ARE OUT OF FREQUENCY PHASE, OR BOTH	CYCLE RIGHT GENERATOR	NO OPERATING RESTRICTIONS ARE IMPOSED WITH LIGHT ON.
	PARALLEL BUS (ONE GEN OUT LIGHT ON) – FAULT ON INOPERATIVE GENERATOR BUSES.	CARRY OUT PRESCRIBED EMERGENCY PROCEDURES AS NECESSARY.	WITH LIGHT ON, INOPERATIVE GENERATOR BUSES WILL NOT BE POWERED.
COUPLER OFF	DATA LINK COUPLER HAS DISENGAGED.	ASSUME MANUAL CONTROL OF AIRCRAFT.	INDICATES UNRELIABLE DATA LINK CONTROL SIGNALS OR INTENTIONAL DISENGAGEMENT

FDB-1-(69-2)

Figure 5-2 (Sheet 2 of 2)

EMERGENCY POWER DISTRIBUTION

LH GEN OUT-BUS TIE OPEN
INOPERATIVE EQUIPMENT

AFTERBURNER IGNITION
AIRBORNE MISSILE CONTROL SYSTEM
16 AN/ALQ-51/100
32 AN/ALQ-100/126
ANTI-ICE SYSTEM
3 BOMB FUZING (ELECTRICAL)
2 BUDDY TANK FUEL PUMP
2 BUDDY TANK HYD PUMP
4 CW RADAR
22 D/L (DATA LINK)
EQUIPMENT COOLING
5 FIRE DETECTOR
FUEL BOOST PUMP, RIGHT
FUSELAGE LIGHTS
5 HYD. PRESSURE IND, P.C.-2
26 INSTRUMENT LANDING SYSTEM
(AN/ARA-63)

8 MK 4 MOD 0 GUN POD
NOSE WHEEL STEERING
PILOT'S CONSOLE PANEL LIGHTS
PILOT'S CONSOLE RED FLOODS (MED & DIM)
PILOT'S INST. PANEL RED FLOODS (DIM)
10 RADAR
RIO'S COCKPIT FLOODS (DIM)
RIO'S EQUIPMENT LIGHTS
SEAT ADJUSTMENT
28 STRIKE CAMERA
11 TAXI LIGHT
TRANSFER PUMP, NO. 4 CELL
UTILITY HYD. PRESS. INDICATOR
UTILITY RECEPTACLE (A-C)
27 VTAS
WARNING LIGHTS (DIM)
WING & TAIL LIGHTS (DIM)

RH GEN OUT-BUS TIE OPEN
INOPERATIVE EQUIPMENT

AILERON FEEL TRIM
AILERON POSITION INDICATOR
AILERON RUDDER INTERCONNECT
21 AIMS
AIRBORNE MISSILE CONTROL SYSTEM
AIR DATA COMPUTER
AIR REFUEL PROBE LIGHT
ALTIMETER VIBRATORS
AN/AJB-3
29 AN/ALR-45
29 AN/ALR-50
19 APR-25
15 AN/APR-27 (Audio & Brt Warn Lts Lost)
18 AN/APR-30
20 APX-76A (AIR TO AIR IFF)
16 AN/ALQ-51/100 (Audio & Brt Warn Lts Lost)
13 ALQ-91 (TEASER)
ANGLE OF ATTACK INDICATOR
AOA HEATER
1 APPROACH POWER COMPENSATOR
ATTITUDE DIRECTOR INDICATOR
AUTOMATIC DIRECTION FINDER
AUTOPILOT
25 BLEED AIR OVERHEAT DETECTION SYSTEM
BUDDY TANK HOSE JETTISON
CENTERLINE STORES EMERG. JETTISON
COCKPIT HEAD AND VENT (CONTROL)
9 CW RADAR
EGT
31 EMER AIL DROOP DISABLE SELECT SW
24 EMER REFUEL PROBE
ENGINE IGNITION
14 ENGINE OIL LEVEL
ENGINE RAMPS
6 FIRE DETECTOR
FUEL BOOST PUMP (LOW SPEED), LEFT
17 FUEL CONTROL, MAIN
FUEL FLOW INDICATOR
FUEL LOW WARNING LIGHT
FUEL PRESSURE INDICATOR
FUEL QUANTITY INDICATOR
11 FUEL SHUTOFF VALVE, LEFT ENGINE
FUEL TRANSFER, EXT. WING (CONT)
FUEL VALVES (POWER)
30 FWD CKPT FLIGHT INSTR LIGHTS

GEAR AND FLAP POSITION INDICATOR
HYD. PRESSURE IND, P.C.-1
6 HYD. PRESSURE IND, P.C.-2
IFF
INTERCOM
12 KY-28
MASTER CAUTION LIGHT RESET
MISSILE JETTISON
NAV COMPUTER
NOZZLE POSITION INDICATORS
OIL PRESSURE INDICATORS
OXYGEN GAUGING
PILOT'S CONSOLE RED FLOOD (BRT)
PILOT'S INST. PANEL LIGHTS
PILOT'S INST. PANEL RED FLOODS (BRT)
PILOT'S & RIO'S UTILITY SPOT LIGHTS
PILOT'S WHITE FLOODS
PITOT HEATERS
PNEUMATIC SYSTEM PRESS. INDICATOR
9 RADAR
RADAR ALTIMETER (APN-41)
RADAR GYRO AND SIGHT RETICLE
RADAR SCOPE CAMERA
REFUEL PROBE
RIO'S COCKPIT FLOODS (BRT)
RIO'S INST. PANEL LIGHTS
RUDDER POSITION INDICATOR
23 SMOKE ABATEMENT SYSTEM
SPECIAL WEAPONS SAFETY
STABILATOR FEEL TRIM
STANDBY ATTITUDE INDICATOR
(EMER VERTICAL GYRO)
TACAN
7 TAXI LIGHTS
TRANSFER PUMP, NO. 6 FUEL CELL
TRIM, LATERAL AND LONGITUDINAL
TURN AND SLIP INDICATOR (PILOT)
UHF
WARNING LIGHTS (BRT)
WINDSHIELD TEMP SENSOR
WING AND TAIL LIGHTS (BRT)

FDB-1-(70-1)B

Figure 5-3 (Sheet 1 of 2)

Changed 15 August 1972

RAT OUT
OPERATIVE EQUIPMENT

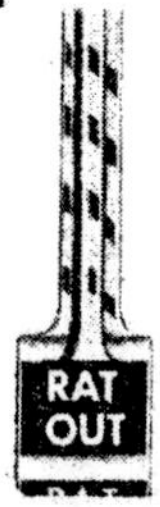

AILERON POSITION INDICATOR
AIR DATA COMPUTER
AN/AJB-3
ANGLE OF ATTACK INDICATOR
ATTITUDE DIRECTOR INDICATOR
BUDDY TANK HOSE JETTISON
EGT
31 EMER AIL DROOP DISABLE SELECT SW
24 EMER REFUEL PROBE
ENGINE IGNITION
14 ENGINE OIL LEVEL
EXT. STORES EMERG. RELEASE
EXT. WING TANK JETTISON
6 FIRE DETECTOR
FUEL BOOST PUMP (LOW SPEED), LEFT
FUEL BOOST PUMP PRESS. INDICATOR
17 FUEL CONTROL, MAIN
FUEL FLOW INDICATOR
FUEL LEVEL TK PRESS LTS
FUEL LOW WARNING LIGHT (BRT)
FUEL QUANTITY INDICATOR
11 FUEL SHUTOFF VALVE, LEFT ENG
FUEL TRANS, EXT WIND (CONTROL)
FUEL VALVES (POWER)
30 FWD CKPT FLIGHT INSTR LIGHTS
GEAR AND FLAP POSITION INDICATOR
HYD. PRESSURE IND, P.C.-1
6 HYD. PRESSURE IND, P.C.-2

IFF
INTERCOM
12 KY-28
MASTER CAUTION LIGHT RESET
MISSILE JETTISON
NOZZLE POSITION INDICATORS
OIL PRESSURE INDICATORS
PILOT'S CONSOLE RED FLOODS (BRT)
PILOT'S INSTRUMENT RED FLOODS (BRT)
PILOT AND RIO'S INSTRUMENT PANEL LIGHTS
PNEUMATIC SYSTEM PRESS. INDICATOR
REFUEL PROBE
RIO'S COCKPIT FLOODS (BRT)
RUDDER POSITION INDICATOR
23 SMOKE ABATEMENT SYSTEM
SPECIAL WEAPONS SAFETY
STABILATOR FEEL TRIM
STANDBY ATTITUDE INDICATOR (EMERG VERTICAL GYRO)
7 TAXI LIGHTS
TRIM, LONGITUDINAL
TURN AND SLIP INDICATOR (PILOT)
UHF (COMM)
WARNING LIGHTS (BRT)
WINDSHIELD TEMP. SENSOR
WING TANK JETTISON

1 Aircraft 152244v and up, and all others after AFC 172.
2 Aircraft 148363f thru 149450j.
3 Aircraft 150406L and up, and all others after ASC 78.
4 Aircraft 151427q and up, before AFC 227.
5 Aircraft 148363f thru 152215t, before AFC 262.
6 Aircraft 152216u and up, and all others after AFC 262.
7 Aircraft 148363f thru 152243u.
8 Aircraft 152278w and up, and all others after AFC 241.
9 Aircraft 152995z and up, and all others after AFC 227.
10 Aircraft 148363f thru 152994y before AFC 227.
11 Aircraft 152244v and up, and all others after AFC 268.
12 Aircraft 148412h and up after AFC 331 (Part I).
13 After AFC 334 or AFC 339.
14 Aircraft 153030aa and up.
15 After AFC 296 or AFC 339.
16 After AFC 333 or AFC 375 (Part II)

17 Controls right engine fuel shutoff valve on aircraft 152244v and up, and all others after AFC 268. On aircraft 148363f thru 152243u before AFC 268, controls right and left engine fuel shutoff valves.
18 After AFC 333 before AFC 375 (Part I).
19 After AFC 375 (Part I or II) before AFC 524.
20 After AFC 352 or AFC 539.
21 After AFC 353.
22 After AFC 288.
23 After AFC 373.
24 After AFC 370.
25 After AFC 439
26 After AFC 470 (Part II).
27 After AFC 500.
28 After AFC 518.
29 After AFC 524
30 After AFC 536
31 After AFC 534
32 After AFC 541

FDB-1-(70-2)B

Figure 5-3 (Sheet 2 of 2)

EXTERNAL STORES JETTISON CHART

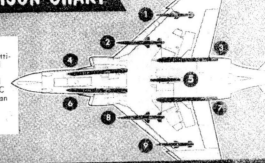

*Weight must be off gear.
†Missiles mounted on fuselage stations 4 and 6 cannot be jettisoned if a 600-gallon tank, MER, or buddy tank is installed on centerline station 5.
††After AFC 346, except for airplanes 151473s, 151496s, and 151497s, the ALL position is removed. However, after AFC 346 either the former ALL position or the RAFT position can be used to jettison the right aft missile.
†††Armament safety override button bypasses the gear handle switch and allows release with gear handle down.

EXTERNAL STATION	GEAR HDLE. POSITION	METHOD OF RELEASE
1, 5 & 9 (A/C 148363f thru 149474k prior to ASC 78, 87 & 97)	UP	External stores emerg release button – DEPRESS
1 thru 9 (A/C 150406L & UP and all others after ASC 78, 87 & 97)	UP or DOWN*	
1 & 9	UP or DOWN	External tanks jettison sw. – JETT
2 & 8	UP or DOWN	Missile jettison selector sw. – APPROPRIATE STATION (L. WING, R. WING) Missile jettison selector sw. – PUSH
3, 4 †, 6† & 7	UP or DOWN	Missile jettison selector sw. – APPROPRIATE STATION (L. FWD, R. FWD, L. AFT, R. AFT) Missile jettison selector sw. – PUSH
2, 3, 4 †, 6†, 7 & 8	UP or DOWN	Missile jettison selector sw. – ALL†† Missile jettison selector sw. – PUSH
5 (A/C 148363f thru 149474k)	UP	Bomb control sw. – DIRECT Bomb / ₵ store release button – DEPRESS
5 (A/C 148363f thru 149474k after ASC 87)	UP †††	Centerline station safe sw. – READY Bomb control sw. – DIRECT Bomb / ₵ store release button – DEPRESS
5 (A/C 150406L & UP and all others after ASC 78 Part I)	UP †††	Centerline station safe sw. – READY Bomb control sw. – DIRECT Multiple weapons master arm sw. – SAFE Bomb / ₵ store release button – DEPRESS
5 (A/C 152278w & UP and all others after AFC 241)	UP †††	Centerline station safe sw. – READY Bomb control sw. – DIRECT Weapons sw. – CONV OFF – NUCL ON Bomb / ₵ store release button – DEPRESS

FDB-1-(71)

Figure 5-4

AIRSPEED INDICATOR FAILURE

FLIGHT CONDITION	ANGLE OF ATTACK-UNITS

CATAPULT

Transition From Catapult
- (without drooped ailerons) Gear Down 22.0
- (without drooped ailerons) Gear Up 19.0
- (with drooped ailerons) Gear Down 21.0
- (with drooped ailerons) Gear Up) 18.0

MILITARY POWER CLIMB

Drag Index = 0 . . . . Sea level   5.5
  combat ceiling   7.6

Drag Index = 120 . . . . Sea level   7.6
  combat ceiling   8.5

MAXIMUM POWER CLIMB

All Drag Indexes . . . . Sea level   4.0
  combat ceiling   9.2

CRUISE AT ALTITUDES BELOW 20,000 FT. (all gross weights)

Drag Index = 0 . . . . 5.8
Drag Index = 130 . . . . 8.0

CRUISE AT OPTIMUM ALTITUDE

Drag Index = 0 . . . . 6.9
Drag Index = 130 . . . . 8.0

ENDURANCE AT OPTIMUM ALTITUDE

Drag Index = 0 . . . . 7.9
Drag Index = 130 . . . . 9.3

DESCENTS (low to medium gross weight)

250 KCAS, idle power 8.5
300 KCAS, 80% rpm 6.5

GEAR AND FLAPS EXTENSION

Safe Gear Extension (with flaps up) 9.0
Safe Flap Extension (with gear down) 13.0

STALL WARNING (pedal shaker)

Without drooped ailerons 22.3
With drooped ailerons 21.3

STALL

Gear Down, Flaps Down (without drooped ailerons) 27.0
Gear Down, Flaps Down (with drooped ailerons) 24.0
Gear Down, 1/2 Flaps (without drooped ailerons) 27.0
Gear Down, 1/2 Flaps (with drooped ailerons) 24.5
Gear Down, Flaps Up (without drooped ailerons) 27.0
Gear Down, Flaps Up (with drooped ailerons) 27.0
Gear Up, Flaps Down (without drooped ailerons) 24.5
Gear Up, Flaps Down (with drooped ailerons) 21.5
Gear Up, 1/2 Flaps (without drooped ailerons) 25.0
Gear Up, 1/2 Flaps (with drooped ailerons) 22.0
Gear Up, Flaps Up (without drooped ailerons) 27.0
Gear Up, Flaps Up (with drooped ailerons) 27.0

APPROACH

CCA/GCA Pattern (200 KCAS, gear up, half flaps)   without drooped ailerons 11.0
  with drooped ailerons 9.5

Final ON SPEED approach (gear down, all engine/flap
configurations) without drooped ailerons 19.2
  with drooped ailerons 19.0

Notes

- Due to the basic inaccuracy of setting up flight conditions (other than landing approach) by reference to the angle of attack indicator, the information included in this table should be used only in an emergency situation.
- The ranges shown for angle of attack versus drag index, while not entirely linear, may be interpolated linearly for practical purposes.

FDB-1-(72)

Figure 5-5

INTERCOM EMERGENCY PROCEDURES

PILOT'S INDICATION	PILOT'S ACTION	RIO'S INDICATION	RIO'S ACTION	RESULTS		HOT MIC
				PILOT'S	RIO'S	
Normal Operation	None	Headset Dead	Switch to EMER RAD	N	SR	NO
		No intercom sidetone other signals OK; Pilot can't hear RIO	Switch to EMER ICS	N	SR	NO
Headset Dead	Switch to EMER ICS	Normal	None	SR	N	YES
		No intercom sidetone other signals OK.	Switch to EMER ICS	SR	SR	NO
		Headset Dead	Switch to EMER RAD	SR	SR	NO
No intercom sidetone, other signals OK; RIO can't hear Pilot	Switch to EMER RAD	Normal	None	SR	N	YES
		No intercom sidetone other signals OK; Pilot can't hear RIO	Switch to EMER ICS	SR	SR	NO
		Headset Dead	Switch to EMER RAD	SR	SR	NO

Code: N—normal operation, SR = sidetone volume reduced; other intercom and audio signals normal. To eliminate feedback whistle during emergency operation by both cockpits, cut volume.

FDB-1-(73)

Figure 5-6

EMERGENCY VISUAL COMMUNICATIONS

MALFUNCTION AND EMERGENCIES

TYPE OF EMERGENCY	SIGNAL		RESPONSE	
	DAY	NIGHT	DAY	NIGHT
I am in trouble, I want to land immediately.	Arm bent across forehead, followed by landing motion with open palm.	Circular motion of flashlight shined at other aircraft.	Carry out squadron doctrine of escort for disabled planes. Assume lead if indicated, and return to base or nearest suitable field.	
Are you having difficulty?	Point to pilot and give series of thumb down movements.	Flash a series of dots using exterior lights.	Thumb up, I am all right. Thumb down, I am having trouble.	Lights off once then on steady, I am all right. Lights flashing, I am having trouble.
Initiation of HEFOE code.	Clench fist held to top of canopy.	Hold flashlight to top of canopy with steady light pointed at wingman, then flash exterior lights in accordance with code listed below.	Repeat signal to show acknowledgement.	

HEFOE SIGNALS

TYPE OF EMERGENCY	SIGNAL		RESPONSE	
	DAY	NIGHT	DAY	NIGHT
Hydraulic trouble.	One finger extended upward.	One flash of exterior lights.	Nod of head (I understand)	Series of Flashes (I understand)
Electrical trouble.	Two fingers extended upward.	Two flashes of exterior lights.	Nod of head (I understand)	Series of Flashes (I understand)
Fuel trouble.	Three fingers extended upward.	Three flashes of exterior lights.	Nod of head (I understand)	Series of Flashes (I understand)
Oxygen trouble.	Four fingers extended upward.	Four flashes of exterior lights.	Nod of head (I understand)	Series of Flashes (I understand)
Engine trouble.	Five fingers extended upward.	Five flashes of exterior lights.	Nod of head (I understand)	Series of Flashes (I understand)

FDB-1-(74)

Figure 5-7

EJECTION

GENERAL

Escape from the airplane in flight should be made with the ejection seat (figures 5-8 thru 5-15). For most conditions requiring ejection, it is the pilot's responsibility to give the Eject command and then remain with the airplane until the RIO has ejected. The reason for this is two fold; to avoid injury to the RIO and/or damage of his canopy, and to provide control of the aircraft in the event the RIO's seat fails to fire normally (i.e., to roll the aircraft inverted with a positive G and then pop the RIO out with a negative G). The only foreseeable deviations to this rule are: an out of control airplane in which the pilot has not been able to signal for ejection, or a double flameout in a dirty configuration at low altitude. In neither of these conditions can the pilot's presence in the aircraft be of any possible use to the RIO. If one of the conditions occur, the pilot should command Eject as he reaches for the ejection handle. A simultaneous ejection or one in which the pilot ejects slightly ahead of the RIO may be the only chance for survival of either crewmember. On airplanes after AFC 307, the above considerations are eliminated by an automatic sequencing system which ejects both cremembers. If the front canopy or both canopies are lost, the front canopy interlock block with its ejection sequence time delay is also lost. If ejection is then initiated from the front seat, this could expose the rear crewman to the front seat's rocket blast, and if conditions are right, a collision between seats could result. If loss of the front canopy or both canopies occurs, the rear crewman should be ordered to eject first by voice signal, eject light or visual signal. The front crewman can eject as soon as the rear seat leaves. With loss of the rear canopy only, normal sequenced ejection can be initiated from either cockpit. If at any time during an emergency, especially with loss of intercom, the RIO believes that the condition of the aircraft has reached or passed extremes, he must use his own judgement in ejecting. On airplanes after AFC 307, should a situation arise where it would be desirable for the RIO to eject singly, the command selector valve handle in the rear cockpit must be in the vertical (closed) position. It is vital that all pilots continuously keep the RIO informed during normal flight as well as in emergency conditions. The following signals will be used by the pilot to order the RIO to eject.

    a. DAY or NIGHT - WITH INTERCOM - WITH EJECT LIGHT
        Pilot actuates EJECT light and verifies light with an EJECT transmission.

    b. DAY - NO INTERCOM - WITH EJECT LIGHT
        Pilot actuates EJECT light and verifies light by repeatedly striking left side of his canopy.

    c. NIGHT - NO INTERCOM - WITH EJECT LIGHT
        Pilot actuates EJECT light and verifies light by moving his flashlight in a vertical motion over his left shoulder.

    d. DAY - NO INTERCOM - NO EJECT LIGHT
        Pilot will strike the left side of his canopy repeatedly.

    e. NIGHT - NO INTERCOM - NO EJECT LIGHT
        Pilot will move his flashlight in a vertical motion over his left shoulder.

    f. DAY or NIGHT - NO RIO RESPONSE (MK H5 seat)
        If RIO does not respond to any of the above signals, the pilot as a last resort signal, shall jettison his canopy if time/altitude permits.

    g. DAY or NIGHT - NO RIO RESPONSE (MK H7 seat).
        Initiate normal ejection sequence.

The study and analysis of escape techniques by means of the ejection seat reveals that:

    a. Ejection at airspeeds ranging from stall speed to 400 knots CAS results in relatively minor forces being exerted on the body, thus reducing injury hazard.

    b. Appreciable forces are exerted on the body when ejection is performed at airspeeds of 400 to 600 knots CAS rendering escape more hazardous.

    c. At speeds above 600 knots CAS, ejection is extremely hazardous because of excessive forces on the body.

When circumstances permit, slow the airplane before ejection to reduce the forces exerted on the body. The emergency harness release handle should never be actuated before ejection for the following reasons:

    a. Actuating the emergency harness release handle creates a hazard to survival during uncontrollable flight, since negative G forces may prevent the crew from assuming the correct ejection position. A full understanding of the particular situation must be established between crewmembers so that there is no erroneous or time consuming activity.

    b. Actuating the emergency harness release handle creates a hazard to survival if the pilot decides that he has insufficient altitude for ejection and is required to proceed with a forced landing. Once the emergency harness release handle has been pulled, the lap belt shoulder harnessing is released and cannot be refastened in flight.

    c. Actuating the emergency harness release handle before ejection causes the occupant to separate from the seat immediately after ejection, and severe shock loads will be imposed on the body.

When it is necessary to perform the actual ejection, the final judgement of which ejection handle to use is left up to the individual crewmember. There are circumstances which dictate the use of the lower ejection handle. The circumstances are: high G forces on the aircraft, bulky flight equipment worn by the crewmember, and narrow clearances between crewmember's helmet and the canopy due to seat adjustment or crewmember size. These factors could make actuation of the face curtain handle difficult if not sometimes impossible.

LOW ALTITUDE EJECTION

Low altitude ejection must be based on the minimum speed, minimum altitude and sink rate limitations of the ejection system (figures 5-8 thru 5-13). Figures 5-8, 5-9 and 5-10 show minimum ejection altitudes for a given sink rate, and figures 5-11, 5-12 and 5-13 show minimum ejection altitudes for a given airspeed and dive angle, such as encountered in a dive bombing run. Although these figures indicate minimum ejection altitudes based on seat capability and a representative pilot reaction time, the ultimate decision as to which altitude to eject must be made by the pilot. The H7 seat minimum ejection altitude charts are based on a 247 pound boarding weight which is defined to include the crewman, his clothing, and personnel equipment, excluding his parachute and seat pan survival kit. Ejection at low altitudes is facilitated by pulling the nose of the airplane above the horizon (zoom up maneuver). This maneuver affects the trajectory of the ejection seat providing a greater increase in altitude than if ejection is performed in a level flight altitude. This gain in altitude increases time available for seat separation and deployment of the personnel parachute. Ejection should not be delayed when the aircraft is in a descending attitude and cannot be leveled out. Assuming wings level and no aircraft sink rate, the ejection seats provide safe escape within the following parameters:

MK H5 seats – Before AFC 307

a. Ground level - 130 KCAS minimum

b. Ground level to 100 feet - 350 KCAS maximum
At airspeeds greater than 350 KCAS below 100 feet, time required (altitude loss) for G-limiter to function (seat deceleration) is not sufficient to complete parachute deployment before ground impact.

c. Above 100 feet - 400 KCAS maximum (based on human factors)
- 550 KCAS maximum (based on seat limitation)

At airspeeds greater than 400 KCAS, appreciable forces are exerted on the body which makes escape more hazardous.

MK H7 (rocket assist) seats – After AFC 307

a. Ground level (zero altitude) - zero airspeed (canopy must be closed)

b. Ground level and up - 400 KCAS maximum (based on human factors)
- 500 KCAS or M equal 0.92 maximum, whichever is greater (based on seat limitation)

At airspeeds greater than 400 KCAS, appreciable forces are exerted on the body which makes escape more hazardous.

MINIMUM EJECTION ALTITUDE vs SINK RATE

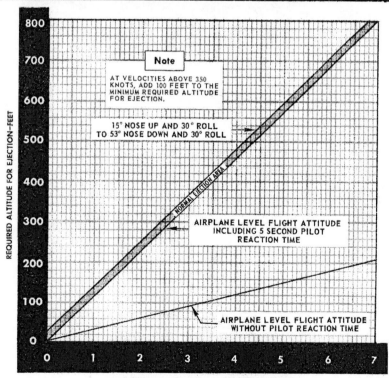

Figure 5-8

MINIMUM EJECTION ALTITUDE vs. SINK RATE

MK-H7 SEAT
AFTER AFC 307 AND BEFORE ACC 176 (SKYSAIL CHUTE)

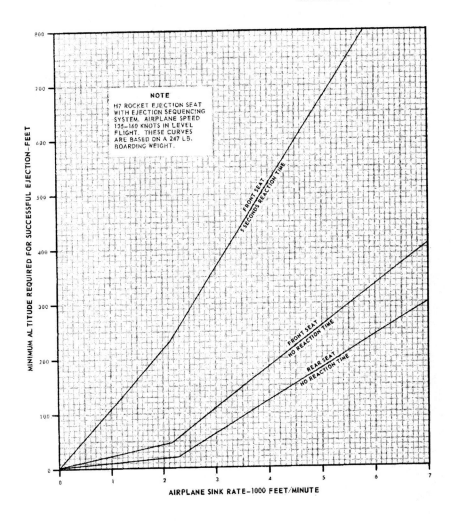

NOTE
H7 ROCKET EJECTION SEAT WITH EJECTION SEQUENCING SYSTEM. AIRPLANE SPEED 135-160 KNOTS IN LEVEL FLIGHT. THESE CURVES ARE BASED ON A 247 LB. BOARDING WEIGHT.

FRONT SEAT 5 SECONDS REACTION TIME

FRONT SEAT NO REACTION TIME

REAR SEAT NO REACTION TIME

MINIMUM ALTITUDE REQUIRED FOR SUCCESSFUL EJECTION-FEET

AIRPLANE SINK RATE-1000 FEET/MINUTE

FDB-1-(76)

Figure 5-9

EJECTION ALTITUDE vs. SINK RATE

MK H7 SEAT

**AFTER AFC 307 AND ACC 176
(28 FT CHUTE)**

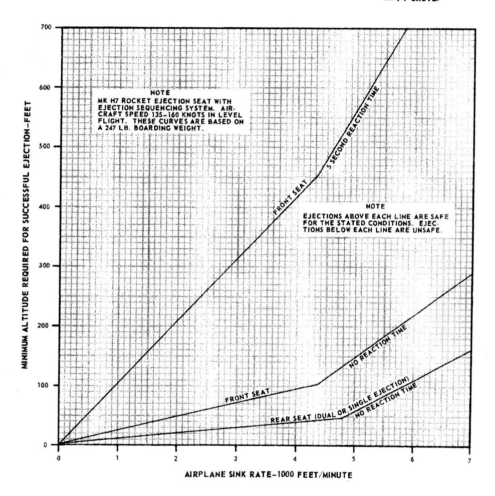

NOTE
MK H7 ROCKET EJECTION SEAT WITH EJECTION SEQUENCING SYSTEM. AIRCRAFT SPEED 135-160 KNOTS IN LEVEL FLIGHT. THESE CURVES ARE BASED ON A 247 LB. BOARDING WEIGHT.

NOTE
EJECTIONS ABOVE EACH LINE ARE SAFE FOR THE STATED CONDITIONS. EJECTIONS BELOW EACH LINE ARE UNSAFE.

FRONT SEAT — 5 SECOND REACTION TIME

NO REACTION TIME

FRONT SEAT

REAR SEAT (DUAL OR SINGLE EJECTION) — NO REACTION TIME

MINIMUM ALTITUDE REQUIRED FOR SUCCESSFUL EJECTION—FEET

AIRPLANE SINK RATE—1000 FEET/MINUTE

FDB-1-(77)

Figure 5-10

MINIMUM EJECTION ALTITUDE vs. AIRSPEED and DIVE ANGLE

MK-H5 SEAT

BEFORE AFC 307

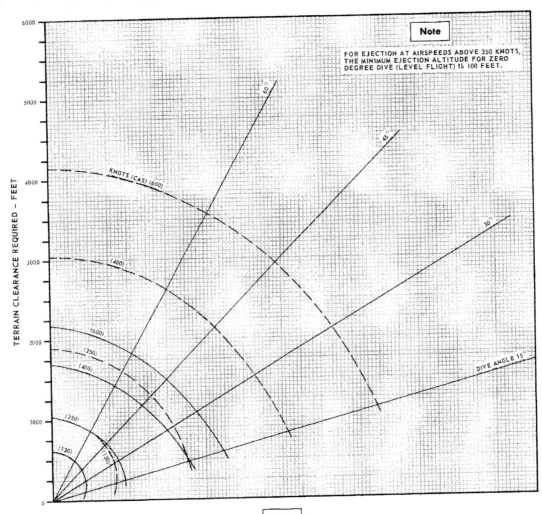

Note

FOR EJECTION AT AIRSPEEDS ABOVE 350 KNOTS, THE MINIMUM EJECTION ALTITUDE FOR ZERO DEGREE DIVE (LEVEL FLIGHT) IS 100 FEET.

Note

THE ALTITUDES SHOWN BY SOLID LINES ARE BASED ON EJECTION SEAT FIRING TIME AND MAKE NO ALLOWANCE FOR CANOPY DELAY OF CREWMEMBER REACTION TIME. THE ALTITUDES SHOWN BY DASHED LINES ARE BASED ON EJECTION SEAT FIRING TIME AND A TWO SECOND COMBINATION CANOPY JETTISON AND CREWMEMBER REACTION TIME. THE TWO SECOND CANOPY JETTISON AND CREWMEMBER REACTION TIME IS INTENDED AS A REPRESENTATIVE FIGURE. CREWMEMBER REACTION AND CANOPY JETTISON TIME BEGINS THE INSTANT THE CREWMEMBER STARTS THE EJECTION SEQUENCE (BEGINS TO ASSUME PROPER SEAT POSITION). THE CURVES DO NOT INCLUDE A CORRECTION FOR BAROMETRIC ALTIMETER LAG; FOR PROPER VALUES REFER TO PERFORMANCE DATA. THE CURVES ARE ALSO BASED ON THE FOLLOWING PARAMETERS:

DROGUE GUN DELAY	1 SECOND
TIME RELEASE DELAY	1 3/4 SECOND
G STOP MECHANISM	4 G'S
EJECTED WEIGHT	320 POUNDS

FDB–1–(78)

Figure 5-11

MINIMUM EJECTION ALTITUDE vs. AIRSPEED AND DIVE ANGLE

MK-H7 SEAT

AFTER AFC 307 AND
BEFORE ACC 176
(SKYSAIL CHUTE)

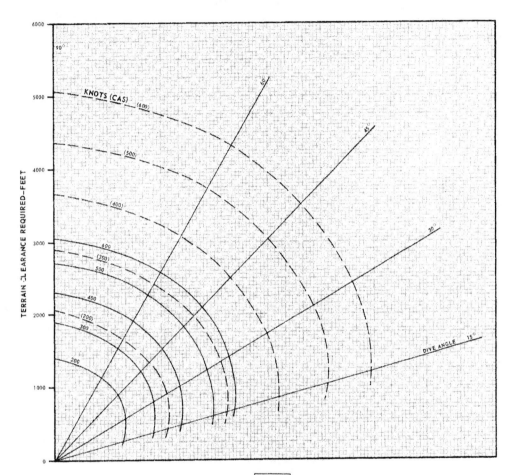

Note

THESE CURVES ARE BASED ON A 247 LB. BOARDING WEIGHT.
THE SOLID CURVES INDICATE MINIMUM TERRAIN CLEARANCE
WITH NO CREWMEMBER REACTION TIME. THE DASHED CURVES
INDICATE MINIMUM TERRAIN CLEARANCE WITH A TWO (2) SECOND
CREWMEMBER REACTION TIME. THE CURVES ARE BASED ON
WINGS LEVEL BANK ATTITUDE AND APPROPRIATE ANGLE OF
ATTACK. TIME REQUIRED FOR THE SEQUENCING SYSTEM TO
EJECT BOTH CANOPIES AND SEATS IS INCLUDED. THE CURVES
DO NOT INCLUDE A CORRECTION FOR BAROMETRIC ALTIMETER
LAG; FOR PROPER VALUES REFER TO PERFORMANCE DATA.

FDB-1-(79)

Figure 5-12

EJECTION ALTITUDE vs. AIRSPEED AND DIVE ANGLE

MK-H7 SEAT

AFTER AFC 307 AND ACC 176
(28 FT. CHUTE)

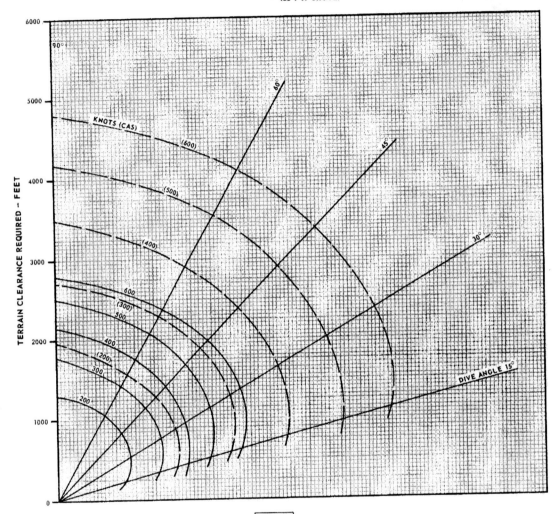

Note

These curves are based on a 247 lb. boarding weight. The solid curves indicate minimum terrain clearance with no crew member reaction time. The dashed curves indicate minimum terrain clearance with a two (2) second crew member reaction time. The curves are based on wings level bank attitude and appropriate angle of attack. Time required for the sequencing system to eject both canopies and both seats is included. It is assumed that the pilot initiates the sequencing system and continues pulling either ejection handle to fire the front seat as soon as the front canopy and interlock block are clear. If the pilot does not continue pulling, or the sequence is initiated by the rear crew member, relying on the front seat mounted time delay initiator to fire the front seat, an additional 250 feet altitude is required for a 90° dive angle at 600 knots, with proportionately less additional altitude required as dive angle and speed decrease. The curves do not include a correction for barometric altimeter lag; for proper values refer to part 1 of applicable index.

FDB-1-(284)

Figure 5-13

HIGH ALTITUDE EJECTION

For a high altitude ejection, the basic low level ejection procedure is applicable. Furthermore, the zoom up maneuver is still useful to slow the airplane to a safer ejection speed or provide more time and glide distance as long as an immediate ejection is not mandatory. If the aircraft is descending uncontrolled as a result of a mid-air collision, control failure, spin, or any other reason, the pilot and RIO will abandon the aircraft at a minimum altitude of 10,000 feet above the terrain if possible. If the pilot has decided to abandon the aircraft while still in controlled flight at altitude, the pilot and RIO will abandon the aircraft at a minimum altitide of 10,000 feet above the terrain with the aircraft headed to sea or toward an unpopulated area.

EJECTION HANDLE SELECTION

Due to its greater accessibility and shorter travel when compared to the face curtain, the lower ejection handle should be used during situations requiring an expeditious ejection. Some of these situations are insufficient flying speed from catapult, ramp strike, parting of cross deck pendants during carrier arrestment, low altitude, uncontrolled flight, and under high G during spin or ACM maneuvers.

SURVIVAL KIT DEPLOYMENT

During ground or low level ejection, the crewmember may not have time to deploy or remove the survival kit. However, if time permits, the kit should be deployed and the life preserver inflated during the parachute descent. The following options are available to the crewmember during parachute descent.

a. Land with survival kit intact.
b. Deploy survival kit prior to ground impact or water entry.
c. Remove survival kit and hold it by carrying strap to be dropped just prior to ground contact.

SURVIVAL KIT JETTISONING

If ground contact is anticipated among trees, rugged terrain, high tension wires, etc., it may be to the crewmembers advantage to remove the survival kit, hold it by the carrying strap and drop it just prior to impact. To jettison or hand carry survival kit, proceed as follows:

1. Open face visor or disconnect oxygen mask.
2. Composite disconnect release knob - PULL

3. Release left lap belt release fitting.
4. Take hold of survival kit, lifting rear kit handle with right hand.
5. Release right lap belt release fitting.

EJECTION SEAT FAILURE (BAILOUT)

If the canopy has been jettisoned but the ejection seat fails, proceed as follows:

1. Reduce speed as much as possible.
2. IFF - EMERG (SIF Mode 3 Code 77)
3. Emergency harness release handle - PULL
   Pull up on emergency harness release handle on right side of seat bucket to disconnect parachute harness and leg restraint harness from seat. This handle also fires cartridge actuated guillotine and severs link line between drogue chute and personnel parachute.
4. Reach over shoulders and grasp parachute risers and pull chute from horseshoe fitting on seat (MK-H5 seats)

WARNING

If the parachute risers are not grasped and chute pulled off horseshoe, chute will not clear protrusion at top of seat when attempting to leave.

5. Full nose down trim while holding airplane level.
6. Roll inverted, push stick forward and push sharply to fall clear of airplane.
7. When clear of airplane and at 10,000 feet or below, parachute D-ring - PULL

Note

Aircrews should rigidly hold left front riser with left hand and pull ripcord D-ring with right hand to ensure full travel of the lanyard.

WARNING

Aircrews using the manual method of seat separation and parachute deployment should immediately check for parachute actuation and be prepared to forcibly deploy the chute by hand after D-ring actuation.

BEFORE EJECTION SEQUENCE | TYPICAL BOTH COCKPITS

If time and conditions permit -
- IFF EMERGENCY
- MAKE RADIO DISTRESS CALL
- SLOW AIRPLANE AS MUCH AS POSSIBLE.

- STOW ALL LOOSE EQUIPMENT
- PULL EMERGENCY VENTILATING KNOB TO MINIMIZE DECOMPRESSION EFFECTS WHEN JETTISONING THE CANOPY.

1. ALERT RIO

2. ASSUME PROPER EJECTION POSITION

ADJUST SEAT POSITION SO TOP OF HELMET IS BELOW FACE CURTAIN HANDLES. BRACE THIGHS ON SEAT CUSHION, LEGS EXTENDED. SIT ERECT, BUTTOCKS BACK, SPINE STRAIGHT, HEAD BACK AGAINST HEADREST, AND CHIN IN.

If high speed ejection in aircraft without canopy bow thrusters -

3. JETTISON FRONT CANOPY BEFORE RIO EJECTS

| Note |

- THE LOWER EJECTION HANDLE SHOULD BE USED WHEN IT IS NECESSARY TO RETAIN CONTROL OF THE AIRCRAFT AND WHEN IT IS IMPRACTICABLE TO REACH THE FACE CURTAIN HANDLE.

WARNING

- IF CREWMEMBER ELECTS TO USE LOWER EJECTION HANDLE AFTER PULLING FACE CURTAIN HANDLE, THE FACE CURTAIN HANDLE SHOULD BE RETAINED WITH ONE HAND TO PREVENT THE POSSIBILITY OF ENTANGLEMENT WITH DROGUE GUN WHEN IT FIRES.

4. FACE CURTAIN HANDLE-PULL

REACH OVERHEAD, WITH PALMS AFT KEEPING ELBOWS TOGETHER, GRASP FACE CURTAIN HANDLE, PULL FACE CURTAIN AND MAINTAIN DOWNWARD FORCE UNTIL STOP IS ENCOUNTERED. WHEN CANOPY JETTISONS, CONTINUE PULLING FACE CURTAIN UNTIL FULL TRAVEL IS REACHED.

4. LOWER EJECTION HANDLE-PULL

GRASP THE LOWER EJECTION HANDLE, USING A TWO-HANDED GRIP WITH THE THUMB AND AT LEAST TWO FINGERS OF EACH HAND. PULL UP ON LOWER HANDLE UNTIL STOP IS ENCOUNTERED. WHEN CANOPY JETTISONS, CONTINUE PULLING UP ON LOWER EJECTION HANDLE UNTIL FULL TRAVEL IS REACHED.

WARNING

DURING THE SINGLE EJECTION FROM THE REAR COCKPIT USING THE MK-H7 ROCKET SEAT, THE SEAT CATAPULT WILL NOT FIRE AUTOMATICALLY AS IN DUAL EJECTION, AND THE CREW MUST CONTINUE PULL ON THE EJECTION HANDLE AFTER CANOPY REMOVAL TO FIRE THE SEAT GUN. AFTER AFC 482, THE SEQUENCING SYSTEM AUTOMATICALLY FIRES THE SEAT AND NO EXTRA PULL IS REQUIRED.

FDB-1-(80-1)

Figure 5-14 (Sheet 1 of 2)

BEFORE EJECTION SEQUENCE

TYPICAL BOTH COCKPITS

WARNING

IF CANOPY FAILS TO JETTISON RELEASE TENSION ON FACE CURTAIN HANDLE, AND
WHILE HOLDING HANDLE WITH ONE HAND, PERFORM THE APPROPRIATE FOLLOWING
PROCEDURE. WHEN CANOPY JETTISONS, AGAIN GRASP EJECTION HANDLE WITH
BOTH HANDS, AND PULL UNTIL FULL TRAVEL IS REACHED.

**If canopy fails to jettison in aircraft
with forward canopy bow thrusters**

5. Normal canopy control handle – OPEN • • • • • • • • • •

6. Manual canopy unlock handle – PULL • • • • • • • • • • • • • • •

MANUAL
CANOPY
UNLOCK
HANDLE

If canopy still fails to jettison -

7. Emergency canopy release handle – PULL • • • • • • • • • • • • •

EMERGENCY
CANOPY
RELEASE
HANDLE

If canopy still fails to jettison -

8. Put negative G on aircraft

When canopy separates -

9. Curtain/lower ejection handle – PULL

**If canopy fails to jettison in aircraft
without forward canopy bow thrusters**

5. For front canopy failure reduce airspeed below 500 knots or 0.8 mach

6. Emergency canopy release handle – PULL • • • • • • • • • • • •

EMERGENCY
CANOPY
RELEASE
HANDLE

If canopy still fails to jettison -

7. Normal canopy control handle – OPEN • • • • • • • • • •

8. Manual canopy unlock handle – PULL • • • • • • • • • • • • • •

MANUAL
CANOPY
UNLOCK
HANDLE

9. Put negative G on aircraft

When canopy separates -

10. Curtain/lower ejection handle – PULL

FDB-1-(80-2)

Figure 5-14 (Sheet 2 of 2)

AFTER EJECTION SEQUENCE

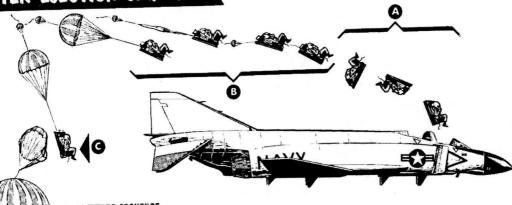

HIGH ALTITUDE SEQUENCE

PULL FACE CURTAIN TO INITIATE THE EJECTION SEQUENCE, CANOPY JETTISONS AND PULLS INTERLOCK BLOCK, PERMITTING CURTAIN TO EXTEND FULLY AND FIRE THE CATAPULT. AFTER AFC 307 THE SEAT ROCKET PACK FIRES.

A SEAT IS PROPELLED UP GUIDE RAIL. OCCUPANT'S LEGS ARE RESTRAINED, EMERGENCY OXYGEN IS ACTUATED, TIME RELEASE MECHANISM AND DROGUE GUN ARE TRIPPED, AND EMERGENCY IFF IS ACTUATED.

B DROGUE GUN FIRES APPROX. 1 SEC. (.75 SEC. AFTER AFC 307) AFTER EJECTION, DEPLOYS CONTROLLER DROGUE, WHICH IN TURN, DEPLOYS STABILIZER DROGUE. SEAT IS STABILIZED AND DECELERATED BY DROGUE CHUTES.

C SEAT AND OCCUPANT DESCEND RAPIDLY THRU UPPER ATMOSPHERE. WHEN AN ALTITUDE BETWEEN 13,000 FT. AND 10,000 FT. (14,500 FT. AND 11,500 FT. AFTER AFC 307 OR ACC 94) IS REACHED, THE BAROSTAT RELEASES THE ESCAPEMENT MECHANISM, WHICH IN TURN, ACTUATES TO RELEASE THE OCCUPANT'S HARNESSING, LEG RESTRAINT LINES, AND CHUTE RESTRAINT STRAPS. THE DROGUE CHUTES PULL THE LINK LINE TO DEPLOY THE PERSONNEL PARACHUTE.

BEFORE AFC 307 OR ACC 94
10,000 +3000 -0 FEET ...... IF NECESSARY PROCEED WITH ......

AFTER AFC 307 OR ACC 94
13,000 ±1500 FEET ...... IF NECESSARY PROCEED WITH ......

D OCCUPANT IS HELD TO SEAT BY STICKER CLIPS UNTIL OPENING SHOCK OF PARACHUTE SNAPS SEAT FROM HIM PERMITTING NORMAL DESCENT.

LOW ALTITUDE SEQUENCE

SAME AS CORRESPONDING STEPS **A - B** IN HIGH ALTITUDE SEQUENCE EXCEPT

C APPROX. 1¾ SEC. AFTER EJECTION AND DECELERATION FORCE ON THE SEAT HAVE DECREASED TO 4.5 "-G'S" OR LOWER, THE ESCAPEMENT MECHANISM ACTUATES TO RELEASE THE OCCUPANT'S HARNESSING LEG RESTRAINT LINES, AND CHUTE RESTRAINT STRAPS. THE DROGUE CHUTES PULL THE LINK LINE TO DEPLOY THE PERSONNEL PARACHUTE. AFTER AFC 307 THE 4.5 G LIMITER IS REMOVED AND THE TIME RELEASE MECHANISM IS SET TO 2¼ SEC.

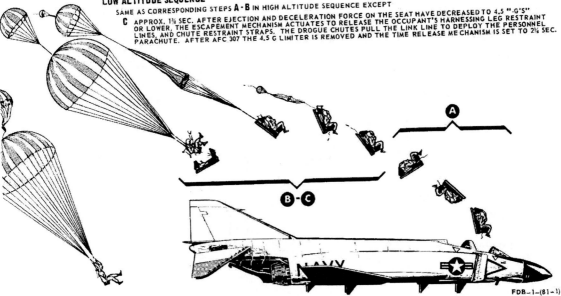

FDB-1-(81-1)

Figure 5-15 (Sheet 1 of 2)

SURVIVAL KIT DEPLOYMENT

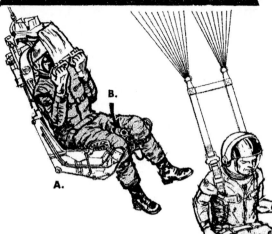

A. UPON EJECTION, SURVIVAL KIT EMERGENCY OXYGEN IS TRIPPED. THIS PROVIDES THE CREWMAN WITH BREATHING OXYGEN AS HE DESCENDS FROM HIGH ALTITUDES. THE OXYGEN IS ALSO USED TO PRESSURIZE THE SUIT ABOVE 35,000 FEET.

B. IF FOR SOME REASON THE OXYGEN FAILS TO TRIP AUTOMATICALLY, THE CREWMAN MUST PULL THE EMERGENCY OXYGEN RELEASE RING ON THE FRONT OF THE SURVIVAL KIT. CARE SHOULD BE TAKEN TO PULL THE RING DIRECTLY UPWARD, AS PULLING IT AT AN ANGLE INCREASES THE FORCE REQUIRED AND MIGHT BREAK THE RING LANYARD.

C. AFTER THE PARACHUTE HAS OPENED (ABOUT 10,000 FEET) OPEN FACE VISOR OR RELEASE OXYGEN MASK TO PREVENT SUFFOCATION WHEN EMERGENCY OXYGEN SUPPLY IS DEPLETED. IF OVER WATER, PULL UP ON KIT RELEASE HANDLE.

D. PULLING THE KIT RELEASE HANDLE RELEASES THE BOTTOM OF THE SURVIVAL KIT CONTAINER. THE CONTAINER BOTTOM AND RAFT DROP AND HANG FROM A 20 FOOT LINE SECURED TO THE CONTAINER TOP. THIS ACTION CAUSES THE LIFE RAFT TO INFLATE.

MANUAL SEPARATION

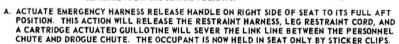

SHOULD THE TIME RELEASE MECHANISM FAIL TO OPERATE AUTOMATICALLY, THE OCCUPANT WOULD MANUALLY SEPARATE FROM THE SEAT AS FOLLOWS:

A. ACTUATE EMERGENCY HARNESS RELEASE HANDLE ON RIGHT SIDE OF SEAT TO ITS FULL AFT POSITION. THIS ACTION WILL RELEASE THE RESTRAINT HARNESS, LEG RESTRAINT CORD, AND A CARTRIDGE ACTUATED GUILLOTINE WILL SEVER THE LINK LINE BETWEEN THE PERSONNEL CHUTE AND DROGUE CHUTE. THE OCCUPANT IS NOW HELD IN SEAT ONLY BY STICKER CLIPS.

B. REACH OVER SHOULDERS AND GRASP PARACHUTE RISERS, AND PULL PARACHUTE OFF THE HORSESHOE FITTING ON THE SEAT, PUSH FREE OF STICKER CLIPS AND CLEAR OF SEAT. AFTER AFC 307, GRASPING THE RISERS IS NOT NECESSARY AS THE BOXSPRING WILL FORCE THE CHUTE AWAY FROM THE SEAT AFTER THE CHUTE RESTRAINT STRAPS ARE RELEASED.

C. PULL PARACHUTE RIPCORD D RING (LOCATED ON LEFT SHOULDER) AND MAKE A NORMAL PARACHUTE DESCENT TO THE GROUND.

WARNING

AIRCREWS USING THE MANUAL METHOD OF SEAT SEPARATION AND PARACHUTE DEPLOYMENT SHOULD IMMEDIATELY CHECK FOR PARACHUTE ACTUATION AND BE PREPARED TO FORCIBLY DEPLOY THE CHUTE BY HAND AFTER "D" RING ACTUATION

Note

AIRCREWS SHOULD RIGIDLY HOLD LEFT FRONT RISER WITH LEFT HAND AND PULL RIPCORD "D" RING WITH RIGHT HAND IN ORDER TO INSURE FULL TRAVEL OF THE LANYARD

FDB-1-(81-2)

Figure 5-15 (Sheet 2 of 2)

ELECTRICAL

GENERAL

If an electrical system failure occurs, various components of the combined aircraft systems are inoperative. Refer to (figure 5-3) for equipment that is lost/available with one or both generators inoperative.

Note

- With stability augmentation engaged, small transients in yaw and roll are experienced whenever power to the system is cut off and then reapplied. To prevent these transients, disengage the stab aug by the emergency disengage switch before turning on or cycling either of the generator switches.

- If the left engine fails on final and the bus tie remains open, afterburner ignition will not be available. However, if afterburner thrust is required, AB light-offs are generally obtainable through turbine torching by jam accelerating the right engine at 90% rpm or above.

SINGLE GENERATOR FAILURE OR INTERMITTENT GENERATOR OPERATION

If either generator malfunctions/fails with or without bus tie failure -

1. Failed generator switch - CYCLE
   OFF 45 seconds then ON for 40 KVA systems; no wait for 60 KVA systems.
2. Check generator warning light - OUT
3. If light remains illuminated, failed generator switch - OFF
4. Monitor engine oil pressure and nozzle operation - SECURE ENGINE IF NECESSARY
   If oil loss is indicated, secure engine.

Note

On airplanes 153030aa and up after PPC 62 and all others after AFC 252 and PPC 62 engine oil loss is indicated by the illumination of the applicable engine oil low warning light.

During night or IFR conditions prior to penetration and approach -

5. Extend RAT and place console floodlights switch to BRIGHT.
6. Land as soon as practicable.

Note

Multiple emergencies, adverse weather, and other peculiar conditions may require relighting of the engine. In this case, a relight should be initiated to ensure minimum time on the engine.

If BUS TIE OPEN light is illuminated -

7. Set throttles for cruise power or below.
   Throttles should be set for cruise power or below to prevent engine flame-out caused by power interruption to fuel boost pumps when operating generator is cycled.
8. Operating generator switch - CYCLE
9. Check BUS TIE OPEN light out.
10. If BUS TIE OPEN light remains illuminated, turn off all electrical equipment not essential to flight.

Note

During night flying, if the left generator remains inoperative with the bus tie open, there will not be power available to illuminate the warning lights while the instrument lights knob (the flight instrument lights knob after AFC 536) in the forward cockpit is in any position except OFF. To retain power for the warning lights, turn the instrument lights knob OFF and place the emergency instrument panel flood lights switch to BRT.

If right generator fails, bus tie open, and essential bus is desired -

11. Ram air turbine - EXTEND
    Reduce speed to RAT extension speed and extend RAT
12. Left generator control switch - OFF

CAUTION

With the BUS TIE OPEN light illuminated, cycling of the emergency generator should be done with caution. The original short/fault probably still exists and could be further aggravated by application of emergency power. If a short/fault exists on the essential buses, power can only be removed by RAT retraction.

DOUBLE GENERATOR FAILURE

1. Ram air turbine - EXTEND
   Reduce airspeed to RAT extension speed and extend RAT.
2. All unessential electrical switches - OFF
3. Generator control switches - CYCLE
   OFF wait 45 seconds then ON for 40 KVA systems, no wait for 60 KVA systems.
4. Check generator warning light(s) - OUT
5. If generator warning light(s) go out - RETRACT RAT.
6. Judiciously continue mission, be prepared to land as soon as practicable.

Changed 1 March 1972

7. If generator warning lights remain illuminated or re-illuminate, generator control switches - OFF

8. Console floodlights - BRIGHT
   During night or IFR conditions, turn console floodlights to BRT as it is the only source of console illumination on RAT power.

9. Landing gear - BLOW DOWN FOR LANDING

10. Flaps - BLOW DOWN (for carrier landing or if utility hydraulic failure is experienced)
    - UP (for field landings with utility hydraulic pressure available).

CAUTION

- Blow down gear even if lowered prior to the generator failure.

- Do not blow down the flaps unless making a carrier landing or a utility failure has been experienced. Emergency pneumatic extension of flaps may result in a hydraulic system failure.

11. Land as soon as practicable.

BUS TIE OPEN BOTH GENERATORS OPERATING (PARALLEL BUS SYSTEMS)

In airplanes equipped with a parallel bus system, a BUS TIE OPEN light with both generators operating should not necessitate aborting the mission. In most cases, the bus tie can be closed by cycling a generator. If the bus tie remains open after generator cycling, the out of phase/frequency condition still exists and, because the CADC and AFCS utilize outputs from both generators, altimeter and airspeed oscillations may occur and portions of the AFCS may be inoperative. The unreliable AFCS and the altimeter/airspeed oscillations may be eliminated by turning the SPC off and applying the necessary corrections, or a generator may be turned off to supply the same phase/frequency to all portions of the AFCS and ADC. In view of the above, proceed as follows:

1. Continue mission

2. Right generator switch - CYCLE
   OFF wait 45 seconds then ON for 40 KVA systems; no wait for 60 KVA systems. Cycle right generator so as not to interrupt power to AMCS. Once power to the AMCS is interrupted it requires a 3.5 minute warm-up time before re-engaging.

3. If light remains illuminated and altimeter and airspeed indicators are unreliable, SPC or right generator switch - OFF

ENGINE

GENERAL

Jet engine failures in most cases are caused by improper fuel scheduling due to malfunction of the fuel control system or incorrect techniques used during certain critical flight conditions. Engine instruments often provide indications of fuel control system failures before the engine actually stops. If engine failure is due to a malfunction of the fuel control system or improper operating technique, an air start can usually be accomplished, providing time and altitude permit. If engine failure can be attributed to some obvious mechanical failure within the engine proper, do not attempt to restart the engine.

SINGLE ENGINE FLIGHT CHARACTERISTICS

Single-engine flight characteristics are essentially the same as normal flight characteristics due to proximity of the thrust lines to the center of the airplane. With one engine inoperative, slight rudder deflection is required to prevent yaw toward the failed engine. Thus, good control is assured in the single-engine range. Minimum single-engine control speed varies with gross weight, flap setting, and landing gear position. The aircraft design is such that no one system (flight control, pneumatic, electrical, etc.), is dependent on a specific engine. Thus, loss of an engine does not result in a loss of a complete system.

ENGINE FAILURE DURING TAKEOFF

If an engine fails before leaving the ground, the continuation of takeoff is dependent on length of remaining runway, gross weight, airspeed, field elevation and ambient temperature.

Note

- During takeoff using Military power, where takeoff is not aborted, immediately advance both engines to maximum power and follow Engine Failure During Flight Procedures this section, as soon as possible.

- If a single-engine failure occurs using maximum power and takeoff is not aborted, retard dead engine throttle from afterburning range after safely airborne and follow Engine Failure During Flight procedures, this section, as soon as possible.

- On aircraft after AFC 440 with flaps down, an engine failure causes a subsequent loss of trailing edge BLC on same side. Due to asymmetric lift (wing adjacent to failed engine drops), mild trim control is necessary to correct this condition.

If decision to stop is made -

1. ABORT TAKEOFF
   Refer to Aborted Takeoff this section.

If takeoff is continued -

If an engine fails immediately after takeoff, lateral and directional control of the airplane can be maintained if airspeed remains above stalling speed. However, the ability to maintain altitude or to climb depends upon airplane gross weight and airspeed. If level flight cannot be maintained:

1. BOTH ENGINES - MAX (AFTERBURNER)
2. EXTERNAL STORES - JETTISON (IF NECESSARY)
   If altitude cannot be maintained, jettison external stores.
3. Gear - UP
4. Flaps - UP
5. Failed engine - SHUTDOWN
6. Non-mechanical failure - INITIATE AIRSTART
7. Land as soon as practicable.

ENGINE FAILURE DURING FLIGHT

1. Non-mechanical failure - INITIATE AIRSTART
2. Mechanical failure - SHUTDOWN FAILED ENGINE
3. Land as soon as practicable.

DOUBLE ENGINE FAILURE DURING FLIGHT

With double engine failure, flight below glide speed results in degraded flight control response due to insufficient hydraulic pressure from the windmilling engines.

1. RAM AIR TURBINE - EXTEND

Extend the ram air turbine to provide engine ignition and also to operate the left fuel boost pump at low speed. This supplies enough fuel to either engine for an airstart.

Note

On airplanes prior to 152695y before AFC 220 maintain airspeed above 195 knots CAS to prevent the emergency generator pressure switch from disconnecting the emergency generator from the essential buses. This results in a complete loss of electrical power, except for the engine ignition systems. On airplanes 152695y and up, and all others after AFC 220 the emergency generator remains on the line down to approximately 90 knots CAS.

2. EITHER THROTTLE - OFF
3. OTHER ENGINE - INITIATE AIRSTART
   To provide maximum fuel flow for airstart, retain throttle of remaining engine in OFF
4. If no start within 30 seconds, throttle - OFF
5. Remaining engine - ATTEMPT AIRSTART
6. If neither engine can be started - NOTIFY RIO AND EJECT

AIRSTARTS

In general, airstart capability is increased by higher airspeeds and lower altitudes; however, airstarts can be made over a wide range of airspeeds and altitudes.

Note

If one or both engines flameout, do not delay the airstart. If no engine mechanical failure is immediately evident, depress and hold the ignition button(s) to restart the engine(s) before excessive rpm is lost.

1. IGNITION BUTTON - DEPRESS (MORE THAN 12% RPM OPTIMUM)
2. THROTTLES - ANY POSITION BEYOND IDLE
3. Engine EGT and rpm - MONITOR

Note

Be sure to give the engine sufficient time for a re-light to occur before placing the throttle off and deciding that the engine is not going to start.

4. If unsatisfactory lightoff occurs due to any of the following, retard throttle to OFF.
   a. Lightoff does not occur within 30 seconds after ignition.
   b. Engine does not continue to accelerate after lightoff.
   c. EGT exceeds maximum limitations.
   d. Oil pressure does not attain 12 psi minimum at idle.
5. Wait 30 seconds before initiating another re-start.

ENGINE RE-START FAILURE

It may be necessary to shut down an engine in flight by placing the throttle to cutoff, for example, clearing a compressor stall. If the engine cannot be re-started, it is possible that the fuel shutoff valve of the affected engine is not opening due to a faulty throttle cutoff switch. A faulty engine master switch also prevents the fuel shutoff valve from opening. It may be possible to open the faulty fuel shutoff valve by cracking the throttle and placing the applicable boost pump switch to CHECK, and holding it in CHECK until a start is made. If the engine starts and then quits when the boost pump switch is released, the fault is probably due to a malfunctioning throttle cutoff switch. If the engine quits running when the boost pump switch is released, again restart the engine by utilizing the applicable boost pump switch. However, this time hold the switch in CHECK and on aircraft prior to 152244v before AFC 268, have the RIO pull the main fuel control circuit breaker (E13, No. 1 panel). On aircraft 152244v and up, and all others after AFC 268, have the RIO pull the left engine fuel shutoff valve circuit breaker (G1, No. 1 panel), or the main fuel control circuit breaker, whichever is applicable. Pulling the circuit breaker removes power to the fuel shutoff valve, and it remains in the open position. Pulling the main fuel control circuit breaker also causes loss of fuselage tank pressurization and loss of automatic fuel transfer in those airplanes that have the capability. If an engine does not start after the throttle has been placed in OFF, perform the following:

1. Throttle - CRACK
2. Boost pump switch - CHECK and HOLD
3. Ignition button - DEPRESS

After Engine Starts - Aircraft thru 152244v Before AFC 268

4. Main fuel control circuit breaker - PULL (E13 No. 1 panel)
5. Boost pump switch - RELEASE

After Engine Starts - Aircraft 152244v and up; all others after AFC 268

4. Main fuel control circuit breaker, or left engine fuel shutoff valve circuit breaker, whichever is applicable - PULL (E13 or G1, No. 1 panel).
5. Boost pump switch - RELEASE

RUNAWAY ENGINE

There is no provision made on the main fuel control for stabilized engine rpm if throttle linkage becomes disconnected from the fuel control. If a disconnect occurs, vibration may cause the fuel control to hunt or assume any position between idle and maximum power. In the event of a runaway engine while on the ground, shut down the engine by turning the engine master switch OFF. For an inflight runaway engine, proceed as follows:

1. Secure engine before entering pattern.

VARIABLE AREA INLET RAMP FAILURE

RAMPS RETRACTED AT SPEEDS ABOVE 1.5 MACH

If the inlet ramps fail to move toward the extended (minimum duct area) position while accelerating between 1.5 and 1.8 Mach, reduce airspeed to below 1.5 Mach and continue the mission. Engine performance and operating characteristics with the ramps failed to the retracted (maximum duct area) position are normal below 1.5 Mach.

CAUTION

Compressor stalls may occur at airspeeds above 1.7 Mach with the inlet ramps in the retracted position.

Note

A gradual failure of the inlet ramp to the extended position at any power setting from idle to max AB at airspeeds from 400 KCAS to landing approach speed does not cause unstable engine operation. However, a sudden failure of the inlet ramp to the extended position at high power settings and low airspeeds disrupts inlet flow and may cause compressor stalls.

RAMPS EXTENDED AT SPEEDS BELOW 1.5 MACH

Note

It may be possible to retract a ramp which has failed in the EXTENDED position by cycling the applicable ramp control circuit breaker, (H4R eng, H3L eng, No. 1 panel).

If the inlet ramps fail to the fully extended position reduce engine power to below 80% rpm and descend to below 18,000 feet. Engine operation is unaffected below 18,000 feet, but a substantial loss of thrust occurs at all power settings. Jam accelerations, afterburner operation and airstarts may be performed without overtemperature conditions or compressor stalls below 18,000 feet.

CAUTION

Compressor stall and flameout may occur at power settings above 80% RPM at 18,000 ft. altitude and above with the inlet ramps in the extended position.

Range, and waveoff performance are degraded. Power settings above 94% rpm produce increased fuel flow without increasing engine thrust output. If the inlet ramps fail to the extended position, (minimum duct area) maintain the highest altitude below 18,000 feet at which the maximum range Mach number recommended for existing gross weight and configuration can be maintained with 94% rpm or less.

Note

With the inlet ramps extended, the reduction in maximum range varies from 5% at 10,000 feet to 18% at 30,000 feet. Single-engine range is reduced by 10% at all attainable altitudes.

CAUTION

Sustained power settings above 90% rpm at subsonic airspeeds above 30,000 feet with the inlet ramps in the extended position may result in a faintly glowing fire warning light. Altitude and power setting should be reduced to extinguish the warning light.

LANDING

If both engines are operating, full-flap landings (both field and carrier) can be safely made with the inlet ramp fully extended. Normal power settings must be increased 1% to 2% rpm to maintain an on speed approach. Safe waveoffs can be performed with Military power at gross weight up to 33,000 pounds. At higher gross weights, afterburner may be required for a late waveoff.

SINGLE ENGINE LANDING

Single-engine carrier landings should not be attempted with the inlet ramps fully extended. Thrust necessary to maintain approach angle-of-attack and rate of descent would require a throttle setting between MIL and MIN AB. Waveoff performance, at all gross weights, is marginal under these conditions. Approximately 100 feet of altitude and 15 seconds are required to stop a normal rate of descent after MAX AB has been attained. Field landings at minimum gross weight can be made with 1/2 flaps. However, afterburner is required occasionally to maintain normal approach angle of attack and rate of descent.

COMPRESSOR STALL

A compressor stall is an aerodynamic disruption of airflow through the compressor, and is caused by subjecting the compressor to a pressure ratio above its capabilities at the existing conditions. The compressor capability may be reduced by FOD, corrosion, misrigged or malfunctioning inlet guide vanes, or the compressor may be subject to abnormal operating conditions as a result of a malfunction of the ramp or bellmouth system. Compressor stalls may be self clearing, may cause the engine to flameout, or may result in a steady state, fully developed stall. The first case requires no immediate action. In the second case, the flameout clears the stall and an airstart is required. The third case requires recognition and corrective action to restore thrust and prevent engine damage by overtemperature. The stall can be recognized by the simultaneous existence of high EGT, low rpm, low fuel flow, open nozzle, loss of thrust, and lack of engine response to throttle. Compressor stalls may be accompanied by muffled bangs. The most positive stall clearing procedure is to shut down the engine and perform an airstart. A throttle chop to IDLE may clear the stall if a significant fuel flow reduction from the stalled condition is achieved. If a compressor stall occurs, proceed as follows:

CAUTION

If a compressor stall occurs above approximately 630 knots, gradual afterburner shutdown is required to prevent afterburner damage. See Airplane Speed Restriction chart, section I, part 4, for specific speeds.

1. Ignition - HOLD DEPRESSED
2. Throttle bad engine - OFF
3. Throttle - ANY POSITION BEYOND IDLE
4. RPM, EGT, and fuel flow - MONITOR

Note

If stall is cleared but desired thrust cannot be obtained because of repeated stalling, the engine may be operated at any obtainable rpm, as long as EGT is within limits.

EXHAUST NOZZLE FAILED OPEN

If an exhaust nozzle fails to the full open position, a significant loss of thrust is noted; however, it is not necessary that the engine be shut down. Continued engine operation with a fully open nozzle does not damage the engine. The majority of exhaust nozzle failures result from engine oil starvation, but, because the CSD oil standpipe is above that of the nozzle control, oil starvation is usually first indicated by a generator warning light. If a failed open nozzle occurs, proceed as follows:

1. Throttle (engine indicating failed open nozzle) - IDLE.
2. Do not advance thrust on affected engine unless necessary.
3. Monitor oil pressure.
4. Land as soon as practicable.

BOTH EXHAUST NOZZLES FAILED OPEN

If both exhaust nozzles fail to the full open position, the thrust available above 80% rpm is approximately equal to the thrust available during normal single-engine operation. Afterburner lightoff above 15,000 feet is marginal; however, afterburner lightoff probability increases with a decrease in altitude.

1. Follow single-engine procedures.

EXHAUST NOZZLE FAILED CLOSED IN AFTERBURNER

Upon initiating afterburner, a rapid increase in exhaust temperature and a drop in rpm indicates that the exhaust nozzle has not opened. If an overtemperature condition exists:

1. Immediately move throttle to MIL range or below.

CAUTION

Do not attempt to relight afterburner. Damage to engine and airframe structure could result.

AFTERBURNER BLOW-OUT DURING FLIGHT

If an after burner blowout or loss of afterburning occurs, proceed as follows:

1. Throttle of failed afterburner - MIL RANGE
   Failed engine afterburner throttle should be moved inboard immediately to terminate fuel flow to afterburner nozzles.
2. If no obvious overheat is discernible - RELIGHT AFTERBURNER
   If cockpit indications of resumed afterburner are normal, continue afterburner operation.

OIL SYSTEM FAILURE

An oil system failure of either engine is indicated by a drop in oil pressure or a complete loss of pressure. Since the constant speed drive unit which drives the generator is supplied with oil under pressure by the engine oil system, a GEN OUT light, followed by sluggish exhaust nozzle action, are early indications of impending engine oil starvation. The engine oil pressure gage should be monitored closely after a generator failure. On aircraft 153030aa and up with PPC 62, and all others after AFC 252 and PPC 62, L and R ENG OIL LOW lights are provided to give an indication of impending oil starvation. In general, it is advisable to shut the engine down as early as possible after a loss of oil supply is indicated, to minimize the possibility of damage to the engine and the constant speed drive unit. The engine operates satisfactorily at military power for period of 1 minute with an interrupted oil supply. However, continuous operation, at any engine speed, with the oil supply interrupted results in bearing failure and eventual engine seizure. The rate at which a bearing fails, measured from the moment the oil supply is interrupted, cannot be accurately predicted. Such rate depends upon the condition of the bearing before oil starvation, temperature of the bearing and loads on the bearing. Malfunctions of the oil system are indicated by a shift (high or low) from normal operating pressure, sometimes followed by a rapid increase in vibration. A slow pressure increase may be caused by partial clogging of one or more oil jets; while a rapid increase may be caused by complete blockage of an oil line. Conversely, a slow pressure decrease may be caused by an oil leak; while a sudden decrease is probably caused by a ruptured oil line or a sheared oil or scavenge pump shaft. Vibration may increase progressively until it is moderate to severe before the pilot notices it. At this time, complete bearing failure and engine seizure is imminent. Limited experience has shown that the engine may operate for 4-5 minutes at 80 to 90% rpm before a complete failure occurs. In view of the

above, the following operating procedures are recommended:

1. If a minimum oil pressure of 40 psi (MIL-L-23699 oil) at Military rpm cannot be maintained, throttle - IDLE.
2. If a minimum of 12 psi at idle rpm cannot be maintained or if the oil pressure change is accompanied by vibrations, engine - SHUTDOWN

CAUTION

Increasing vibration is an indication of bearing failure. Severe vibration indicates that engine seizure will occur within a few seconds. Chop the throttle to OFF to prevent major engine, and possible aircraft damage.

3. If engine shutdown is not feasible - REDUCE THRUST

   Shut the engine down when partial power is not required from the affected engine. Where mission or flight requirements demand partial power from the affected engine, set engine speed at 86-89%.

4. Avoid abrupt maneuvers causing high G forces.
5. Avoid unnecessary or large throttle movements.

Note

To keep bearing temperatures and loads at a minimum, do not use high thrust settings.

6. In either of above instances - LAND AS SOON AS PRACTICABLE.

OIL LEVEL LOW LIGHT ILLUMINATED

1. Monitor oil pressure.
2. Monitor exhaust nozzle position indicators
3. Monitor generator warning lights
4. Avoid high G maneuvers.

GENERAL

The pilot's first indication of a fire is noted by the steady illumination of the FIRE/OVERHEAT warning light. However, a momentary illumination of the FIRE or OVERHEAT warning light should not be completely ignored. A momentary illumination should be followed by a check of the fire test circuit to determine if a fire actually exists and has burned through the fire detector wiring.

ENGINE FIRE DURING START

1. THROTTLES - OFF
2. ENGINE MASTER SWITCHES - OFF
3. GENERATOR CONTROL SWITCHES - EXT ON

4. CONTINUE TO CRANK ENGINE
5. Leave airplane as quickly as possible.

ENGINE FIRE OR OVERHEAT DURING TAKEOFF

If FIRE or OVERHT warning light illuminates during takeoff roll, it is preferable to abort immediately if sufficient runway is available to stop safely. Refer to Critical Field Length Charts, section XI, part 2.

If decision to stop is made -

1. ABORT TAKEOFF
   Refer to Aborted Takeoff, this section.

If takeoff is continued -

1. NORMAL OPERATING ENGINE - MAX (AFTERBURNER)
2. EXTERNAL STORES - JETTISON (IF NECESSARY)
3. THROTTLE (ENGINE INDICATING FIRE OR OVERHEAT) - IDLE
4. Landing gear - UP
5. Wing flaps - UP
6. Climb to safe ejection altitude and investigate. After reaching safe ejection altitude, proceed with Engine Fire or Overheat During Flight procedures.

ENGINE FIRE OR OVERHEAT DURING FLIGHT

1. THROTTLE (ENGINE INDICATING FIRE OR OVERHEAT) - IDLE
2. If warning light goes out - CHECK FIRE DETECTION SYSTEM
   Depress fire test button to determine that fire detecting elements are not burned through.
3. If fire detection system check is normal, land as soon as practicable; do not advance thrust on affected engine unless absolutely necessary.

CAUTION

Advancing thrust on the affected engine after the throttle has been retarded and the warning light has been extinguished may cause fire or overheat damage, and/or possible burn through the fire detecting elements.

4. If light remains on and/or fire is confirmed - SHUTDOWN ENGINE
   Shutdown engine if FIRE/OVERHEAT warning light remains illuminated after reducing thrust; if fire detection system has been found to be inoperative; or fire is apparent.
5. If fire persists - EJECT
   If fire continues after engine is shutdown, notify RIO and eject.
6. If fire ceases - LAND AS SOON AS PRACTICABLE.

AFT SECTION FUEL LEAK/FIRE

In-flight fires may be caused by fuel or hydraulic leaks in the aft fuselage/empennage sections without the engine or overheat warning circuits being activated. Hence, secondary indications must be used to detect this condition. Such fires often relate to maneuvering flight conditions and afterburner use. Discovery of any fluid leaking in the aft sections prior to a fire being ignited is critical. Any indication of abnormal (i.e., prolonged or continuous) fuel streaming from the fuselage fuel vent, empennage, or engine nozzle areas must be considered a potential aft section fire situation.

If fuel streaming occurs -

1. Disengage AB. Do not re-engage.
2. Cease fuel transfer. Do not allow subsequent fuel transfer to exceed 5000 pounds fuselage fuel.
3. Land as soon as practicable.

Indications that an aft section fire has already occurred include: fuel streaming, noises similar to compressor stalls, utility hydraulic failure, pronounced lateral control stick transients, loss of rudder control, loss of the rudder position indicator, or the popping of any rudder-associated circuit breakers.

If fire indications are evident -

1. Disengage AB. Do not re-engage.
2. Reduce speed to below 300 KCAS.
3. Prepare for ejection.
4. Land as soon as possible.

WARNING

With an aft section fire, simultaneous loss of PC1 and PC2 pressure to the stabilator is imminent. This will cause a violent nose-up pitching condition and loss of flight control.

ENGINE FIRE DURING SHUTDOWN

1. THROTTLES - OFF
2. MASTER SWITCHES - OFF
3. With external power available, generator control switches - EXT ON
4. Engine start switch - LEFT or RIGHT (engine indicating fire)
5. Leave airplane as soon as possible.

ELECTRICAL FIRE

1. Ram air turbine - EXTEND
2. Generator control switches - OFF
3. All electrical switches - OFF
4. When fire subsides, generator control switches - ON
5. If fire still persists when generator control switches are turned ON, turn generator control switches OFF.
   The RAT supplies power to essential buses only.
6. Land as soon as practicable.
7. If no fire is apparent when generator control switches are turned ON, individually reposition only mission essential electrical equipment first.
8. If malfunctioning item is found, turn electric power switch OFF and pull applicable circuit breaker.

ELIMINATION OF SMOKE AND FUMES

1. Descend to below 34,000 feet.
2. Emergency ventilating knob - PULL
3. Front canopy - JETTISON (IF NECESSARY)

WARNING

In aircraft with AFC 307 incorporated, the rear cockpit must eject first with the front canopy off. A possibility of seat to seat collision exists if the ejection is sequenced from the front cockpit with the front canopy off.

FLIGHT CONTROLS

GENERAL

Upon initial detection of any abnormal flight control movement, immediately depress the paddle switch to determine if the stab aug ARI or AFCS was causing the abnormality.

RUNAWAY STABILATOR TRIM

If stabilator trim appears to be running away, it is possible under certain conditions to lessen the situation. Runaway stabilator trim can be alleviated by engaging the AFCS, providing:

a. The trim cont circuit breaker has been pulled immediately upon detection of runaway trim.

b. The runaway trim has not exceeded 2-1/2 units nose down.

If the above conditions are met:

1. Reduce airspeed - 300 knots CAS or less
2. AFCS - ENGAGE

Note

- The A/P PITCH TRIM light may illuminate when AFCS is engaged.

- When AFCS is used to alleviate a runaway trim condition and excessive out of trim forces are present (full nose down runaway trim), the AFCS alternately disengages and re-engages. If this occurs, discontinue use of AFCS.

3. Plan to land as soon as practicable.
4. Before landing disengage AFCS.
   When in landing configuration (gear and flaps extended) and at 180 to 190 knots CAS, grasp stick firmly and disengage AFCS. Depending upon severity of malfunction, airplane may or may not be in trim; if out of trim, forces should not be too high and airplane can be landed with out-of-trim condition, or AFCS can be re-engaged and landing made with control stick steering.
5. If landing is made with AFCS engaged, disengage immediately after touchdown -
   Immediately after touchdown disengage AFCS to prevent damage to AFCS components.

In aircraft with downsprings removed, extremely high stick forces are not required to overcome nose down trim. If runaway stabilator trim has exceeded the limits at which the AFCS can be engaged:

6. Reduce airspeed - 300 KCAS or less
7. Land as soon as practicable.

STABILATOR FEEL TRIM FAILURE

PARTIAL BELLOWS FAILURE

Partial bellows failure is recognized by a mild nose down stick force proportional to the airspeed unless the failure occurs during maneuvering flight at which time it may not be noticeable. Reduction of stick centering and pitch stability results. Should this failure occur:

1. Reduce airspeed - 250-300 knots CAS
2. Retrim airplane.
3. Avoid abrupt fore and aft stick movements.
4. Land as soon as practicable.

COMPLETE BELLOWS FAILURE

A complete bellows failure is recognized by a heavy nose down feel force at the control stick. The maximum amount that this stick force can attain is 30 pounds, dependent on the trim position. This force can be reduced to 5 pounds by applying full nose up trim. In aircraft with feel system downsprings removed (AFC 308) the maximum amount the nose down stick force can attain is approximately 5 pounds. This force cannot be trimmed out on the modified airplanes. Should a complete bellows failure occur:

1. Reduce airspeed - 250-300 knots CAS
2. Stab trim - NOSE UP AS REQUIRED
3. Avoid abrupt fore and aft stick movements.
4. Land as soon as practicable.

ICE/WATER BLOCKAGE OF RAM AIR LINE

In airplanes 148363f thru 151447q before ASC 153, ice or water blockage of the artifical feel bellows ram air line could occur. This results in conditions similar to a complete bellows failure. If ice or water blockage is suspected, longitudinal trim should not be applied to relieve control stick force. The intermittent nature of this condition and the suddenness of return to normal can cause violent pitch transients. When the ram air line is blocked, no stick force gradient is felt by the pilot should a change in stick position be required. If a suspected ice or water blockage of the ram air line occurs:

1. Check pitot heat switch - ON
2. Reduce airspeed - 250-300 knots CAS
3. Maintain attitude by pilot effort.
4. If practical, descend to air that is above freezing.
5. If this condition persists, land as soon as practicable.

AILERON RUDDER INTERCONNECT (ARI) SYSTEM DISENGAGEMENT

The ARI system can be temporarily disengaged by depressing the AFCS/ARI emergency disengage switch; this disengages the ARI only as long as it is held depressed. To permanently disengage the ARI system, the circuit breaker on the left utility panel must be pulled and the stab aug switch must be disengaged. Pulling the circuit breaker only, and keeping the stab aug engaged still provides 5° of ARI rudder authority. To permanently disengage the ARI while retaining complete stab aug, pull the rudder trim circuit breaker on circuit breaker panel no. 1 in the rear cockpit. If an ARI system malfunction occurs, proceed as follows:

1. To temporarily disengage system, depress AFCS/ARI emergency disengage switch. Depressing the emergency disengage switch disengages ARI system only as long as switch is held depressed.
2. ARI circuit breaker - PULL (left utility panel)
3. To permanently disengage system, pull rudder trim circuit breaker (B1, No. 1 panel).

FUEL

FUEL BOOST PUMP FAILURE

The possibility of a simultaneous mechanical failure of both boost pumps is highly remote; however, double failure may occur as a result of an electrical malfunction. Provisions are made to supply fuel to the engines by gravity flow in the event of a double boost pump failure. This allows engine operation at a reduced power setting. If both boost pumps fail above 20,000 feet and/or at a high power setting, flameout or an unstable rpm indication on one or both engine may occur.

If both boost pumps fail:

1. If both engines have flamed out, execute procedure for double engine failure.
2. If airstart has been accomplished, or engines have not flamed out, adjust engine thrust or descent until a stable rpm can be maintained.

Note

Afterburner operation is not recommended. Military power operation is unrestricted at any airspeed from sea level to 20,000 feet.

3. Land as soon as practicable.

For single boost pump failure:

1. Adjust throttle to maintain a minimum of 5 psi boost pump pressure, if practicable.

Note

Afterburners may have to be modulated or shut off, depending on airspeed and altitude to maintain 5 psi boost pressure.

FUEL TRANSFER FAILURES

INTERNAL WING FUEL FAILS TO TRANSFER

Failure of internal wing fuel to transfer can be caused by either the wing tanks failing to pressurize, or the wing transfer valves failing to open. If internal wing fuel is not transferring, check the following switch and circuit breaker positions:

1. External transfer switch - OFF
2. Internal wing transfer switch - NORMAL
3. Refuel probe switch - RETRACT
4. Wing transfer control circuit breaker - IN (E3, No. 1 panel)

To ensure wing tank pressurization:

5. Wing transfer pressure switch - EMERG Continue in level flight for 30 seconds.

Note

If fuel transfers when the wing transfer pressure switch is placed in EMERG, leave the switch in this position for remainder of flight. Pressurization has been obtained and fuel can be transferred.

CENTERLINE FUEL FAILS TO TRANSFER

Failure of the centerline fuel to transfer can be caused by either the defueling shutoff valve failing to the open position, the refueling valve failing to the closed position, the tank shutoff valve failing to the closed position, or the tank failing to become pressurized. If the centerline fuel fails to transfer, check the following switch and circuit breaker positions:

1. Buddy tank switch - STOP FILL
2. External transfer switch - CENTER

3. External wing fuel control circuit breaker - IN
   (F14, No. 1 panel)
4. Fuel valve power circuit breaker - IN
   (E14, No. 1 panel)
5. Refuel probe switch - RETRACT

To ensure tank pressurization:

6. Wing transfer pressure switch - EMERG
   Continue in level flight for 30 seconds.

Note

If fuel transfers when the wing transfer pressure switch is placed in EMERG, leave the switch in this position for remainder of flight. Pressurization has been obtained and fuel can be transferred.

EXTERNAL WING FUEL FAILS TO TRANSFER

Failure of the external wing fuel to transfer can be caused by either the external wing tank shutoff valve failing to the closed position or the tanks failing to become pressurized. If the external wing tanks fail to transfer, check the following switch and circuit breaker positions:

1. External wing transfer switch - OUTBD
2. External wing fuel control circuit breaker - IN
   (F14, No. 1 panel)
3. Refuel probe switch - RETRACT
4. Fuel valve power circuit breaker - IN
   (E14, No. 1 panel)

To ensure tank pressurization:

5. Wing transfer pressure switch - EMERG

Note

If fuel transfers when the wing transfer pressure switch is placed in EMERG, leave the switch in this position for remainder of flight. Pressurization has been obtained and fuel can be transferred.

Note

If the above procedures fail to produce fuel transfer from either centerline or wing external tanks, it may still be possible to effect transfer by using high power settings for a period of time and/or climbing to an altitude of 35,000 feet or higher.

REVERSE TRANSFER OF FUSELAGE FUEL TO CENTERLINE TANK

Reverse fuel transfer from the fuselage tanks to the centerline tank is indicated by a rapid decrease in both the sector and counter and is caused by an open defuel valve or loss of tank pressurization (from combat damage, bridle slap etc.). Boost pump pressure forces fuel from the engine fuel manifold through the open defuel valve to the centerline tank when the defuel valve is failed open. The pressure differential on the refuel/transfer fuel level control valve caused by fuselage tank pressure allows fuselage fuel to reverse transfer through the open defuel valve and open centerline tank shutoff valve (provided centerline transfer is selected) into the centerline tank when tank pressurization is lost. On aircraft after AFC 412, a relief valve is added to the refuel/transfer fuel level control valve to prevent a pressure differential from occurring, thus preventing reverse transfer due to loss of centerline tank pressure. If reverse fuel transfer occurs, proceed as follows:

1. Buddy tank switch - STOP FILL
2. External tank transfer switch - OFF
3. Sector and counter readings - MONITOR

If the sector and counter readings continue to decrease, the centerline tank shutoff valve has also failed to the open position.

4. Centerline tank - JETTISON

REVERSE TRANSFER OF FUSELAGE FUEL TO INTERNAL WING TANKS

Reverse fuel transfer from the fuselage cells to the internal wing tanks is indicated by a rapidly decreasing sector reading with a normal counter, and is caused by an open defuel valve and a failed open internal wing fuel level control valve. If external wing tank fuel is available, and transferring, the counter may slowly increase. Boost pump pressure forces fuel from the engine fuel manifold through the open defuel valve to the internal wing tanks. If reverse fuel transfer occurs, proceed as follows:

1. Buddy tank switch - STOP FILL
2. Ram air turbine - EXTEND
3. Generators - OFF
4. Wing transfer control circuit breaker - IN
   (E3, No. 1 panel)
5. Boost pump control circuit breakers - PULL
   a. L.H. Boost pump norm cont - E12, No. 1 panel
   b. L.H. Boost pump emer cont - F12, No. 1 panel
   c. R.H. Fuel boost pump control - D12, No. 1 panel

Note

With boost pump circuit breakers pulled, it is recommended that flight operations be accomplished at altitudes of less than 20,000 feet.

6. Generators - ON
7. Ram air turbine - RETRACT

OPEN DEFUEL VALVE DURING REFUELING

When the refuel probe switch is placed to REFUEL and there is an indication of a failed open defuel valve, proceed as follows:

1. Buddy tank switch - STOP FILL
2. Refuel probe switch - EXTEND
3. External transfer switch - OFF
4. Refuel selector - INT ONLY

5. Boost pump control circuit breakers - PULL
   a. L.H. boost pump norm cont - E12, No. 1 panel
   b. L.H. boost pump EMER Cont - F12, No. 1 panel
   c. R.H. fuel boost pump control - D12, No. 1 panel

Note

With boost pump circuit breakers pulled, it is recommended that air refueling be accomplished at altitudes of less than 20,000 feet.

6. Refuel probe switch - REFUEL
7. Commence refueling.

When approximately 6000 pounds is indicated on the sector:

8. Boost pump control circuit breakers - RESET
9. Refuel selector - ALL TANKS
10. Continue refueling.

FUSELAGE FUEL DUMP

Transfer of Fuselage Fuel to Internal Wings for Dumping

To allow expedious reduction to landing weight, excess fuel can be transferred from fuselage cells 1 and 2 to the internal wings allowing it to be dumped using normal dump procedures. Reverse transfer can be accomplished by the following procedures:

1. Wing transfer control circuit breaker - PULL E3, No. 1 panel
2. Buddy fill switch - FILL
3. Internal wing dump switch - DUMP

Note

* Fuel transfers at approximately 1000 lbs per minute, and dumps at approximately 680 lbs per minute.

* Care must be exercised when using reverse transfer, for it is possible to deplete the fuel supply in fuselage cells 1 and 2.

* With centerline tank aboard, some fuel is transferred into the centerline tank using reverse fuel transfer.

After fuel is transferred/dumped -

4. Buddy fill switch - STOP FILL
5. Internal wing dump switch - NORMAL

REVERSE TRANSFER OF FUSELAGE FUEL TO EXTERNAL WING TANK

Reverse fuel transfer from the fuselage tanks to the external wing tanks can occur in aircraft before AFC 412 if external wing tank pressurization is lost (i.e., from combat damage), and is indicated by a rapid decrease in both sector and counter reading. The pressure differential on the refuel/transfer fuel level control valves caused by fuselage tank pressure opens the valves and allows fuselage fuel to reverse transfer to the external wing tanks. On aircraft after AFC 412, a relief valve is added to the refuel/transfer fuel level control valve to prevent a pressure differential from occurring thus preventing this reverse transfer. If reverse fuel transfer occurs, proceed as follows:

1. External tank transfer switch - OFF
2. Sector and counter readings - MONITOR
   If sector and counter readings continue to decrease, external wing tank shutoff valve has also failed open.
3. External tanks jettison switch - JETTISON

EMERGENCY EXTENSION AND OPERATION OF AIR REFUEL PROBE

On aircraft after AFC 370, if the air refueling probe can not be extended with normal utility hydraulic pressure, the probe can be extended pneumatically:

1. Pull refuel probe circuit breaker D15, No. 1 panel
2. Refuel probe switch - REFUEL
3. Emergency refuel probe switch - EMER EXT

After refueling has been accomplished:

4. Refuel probe switch - EXTEND

Note

To prevent possible damage to the utility reservoir and/or loss of utility pressure, the emergency refuel probe switch must be left in EMER EXT.

AIR REFUELING FUSELAGE TANKS ONLY

If the internal wing tanks become damaged and cannot hold fuel, emergency refueling of the fuselage tanks only can be accomplished as follows:

1. External transfer switch - OFF
2. Refuel selector switch - INT ONLY
3. Pull fuel valve power circuit breaker (E14, No. 1 panel)
4. Refuel probe switch - REFUEL
5. Commence refueling.

Note

Do not attempt to refuel external tanks. Damage to internal wing tanks may prevent external wing tanks from transferring. The centerline tank cannot be refueled using the above procedure.

HYDRAULIC

GENERAL

The loss of hydraulic pumps in power control systems no. 1, no. 2 or in the utility hydraulic system, is noted by the illumination of the CHECK HYD GAGES warning light. This single light serves all three systems, and the pilot should check the hydraulic gages to assure which system has malfunctioned.

SINGLE POWER CONTROL SYSTEM FAILURE

A hydraulic pump failure of either PC-1 or PC-2 presents no immediate problem, since either system is capable of assuming the full demand of the other system. On aircraft after AFC 400, a hydraulic pump failure of either PC-1 or PC-2 presents no immediate problem, since the utility system is capable of assuming full demand of either system.

Note

With no PC-1 system pressure available, the pitch axis of the stab aug system is lost; if the AFCS is engaged, the AFCS remains operative except that stabilator authority is lost. No indication of a stab aug failure is noted since the STAB AUG DISENGAGED light only illuminates upon switch disengagement, and in case of a PC-1 failure the switch remains engaged. The AFCS, if engaged, should be immediately disengaged since erratic AFCS operation may occur due to the loss of AFCS stabilator authority. Aircraft control is no problem and can be maintained through manual mode of operation which is powered by the PC-2 hydraulic system. On aircraft after AFC 400, aircraft control can be maintained by the PC-2 and utility hydraulic systems.

Note

If the CHECK HYD GAGES indicator light illuminates and remains illuminated, monitor the hydraulic system gages for the remainder of the flight, since warning of a second hydraulic system failure is not given.

PC-1 FAILURE

1. Land as soon as practicable.

PC-2 FAILURE

1. Land as soon as practicable.

SINGLE POWER CONTROL AND UTILITY SYSTEM FAILURE

On aircraft after AFC 400, the utility system is modified (rerouted) to include the dual power control cylinders of the ailerons and spoilers. Thus, each flight control hydraulic supply system serves as an emergency system for the other(s). In the event of simultaneous loss of the utility system and one of the power control systems, the operable aileron and spoiler provides adequate lateral control for an emergency landing:

1. Reduce speed to below 500 KCAS as soon as possible and discontinue mission.

WARNING

Do not allow airspeed to drop below 220 KCAS.

2. Jettison any asymmetric load.
3. Proceed to a suitable divert field.
4. Emergency aileron droop switch - DISABLE (some aircraft)

WARNING

If emergency aileron droop switch is not placed to DISABLE or essential 28 volt dc bus power is not available, a split aileron condition will occur if flaps are lowered pneumatically.

5. Extend gear and flaps pneumatically at a minimum altitude of 5000 feet.

Note

Ailerons do not droop during emergency flap operation and approach airspeed will be 10 knots faster than normal.

6. Investigate landing approach characteristics before descending for a landing.
7. Enter a wide and extended downwind leg.
8. Plan early line-up for straight-in approach (select runway to minimize crosswind, if possible). Full lateral stick displacement may be necessary to provide adequate roll response.
9. Make field arrested landing - fly 17 units AOA for final approach and touchdown.

> **CAUTION**
>
> In the event the arresting gear is missed and the decision is made to go around, the airplane should not be rotated until the airspeed is at least that corresponding to the angle of attack used during the approach.

> **WARNING**
>
> In the two engine, half flaps, one wing disabled configuration, it is probably feasible to make a carrier landing, utilizing 17 units AOA, under ideal (day VFR) conditions.

10. Carrier landing - Fly on speed and do not exceed 20 units AOA or wave-off performance will be degraded.

DOUBLE POWER CONTROL SYSTEM FAILURE

The pilot should, upon initial detection of hydraulic power loss, note trend of failure as to whether the gages show a definite steady drop, or gage fluctuations. With a steady drop indication, hydraulic power will probably not recover. If complete power control hydraulic failure occurs, the aircraft becomes uncontrollable. Before this occurs, proceed as follows:

1. If hydraulic pressure does not recover - EJECT
2. If hydraulic pressure recovers - LAND AS SOON AS PRACTICABLE.

UTILITY HYDRAULIC SYSTEM FAILURE

Failure of the utility hydraulic system prevents/degrades hydraulic operation of the following essential items:

a. Aileron Power Control Cylinders - (some aircraft) - PC-1 and and PC-2 assumes full demand of aileron power control cylinder.
b. Air Refueling Probe
   Emergency pneumatic operation of refueling probe is provided on aircraft after AFC 370. Refer to Emergency Extension and Operation of Air Refuel Probe, this section.
c. Auxiliary Air Doors
   There are no alternate or emergency provisions for opening auxiliary air doors. Refer to Auxiliary Air Door Malfunction, for procedures to follow in the event of auxiliary air door failure.
d. Arresting Hook (retraction)
   There are no alternate or emergency provisions for arresting hook retraction.

e. Flaps (leading and trailing edge)
   Emergency pneumatic operation is provided. Refer to Wing Flap Emergency Lowering, this section.
f. Fuel Transfer Pumps (hydraulic)
   There are no alternate or emergency provisions for hydraulic transfer pump operation.
g. Landing Gear
   Emergency pneumatic operation of landing gear is provided. Refer to Landing Gear Emergency Lowering, this section.
h. Leading Edge BLC Valves (aircraft prior to 152994y with AFC 218)
   Emergency pneumatic operation of leading edge BLC valves is provided. Refer to BLC malfunction, this section.
i. Nose Gear Steering
   There are no emergency provisions for nose gear steering.
j. Pneumatic System Air Compressor
   There are no alternate or emergency provisions for operation of pneumatic system air compressor.
k. Rudder Power Control System
   Limited manual control of rudder is available; however, pedal forces are much higher than normal.
m. Speed Brakes
   There are no alternate or emergency provisions for speed brake extension; however, they may be retracted to a low drag trail position. Refer to Speed Brake Emergency Operation, this section.
n. Spoiler Power Control Cylinder - (some aircraft) - PC-1 and PC-2 assumes full demand of the spoiler power control cylinder.
o. Variable Bypass Bellmouth
   There are no alternate or emergency provisions for operation of variable bypass bellmouth. Refer to Auxiliary Air Door Malfunction for side effects of simultaneous variable bypass bellmouth and auxiliary air door failures.
p. Variable Engine Intake Ramps
   There are no alternate or emergency provisions for operation of the variable engine intake ramps.
q. Wheel Brakes
   Emergency pneumatic and hydraulic operation of wheel brakes is provided. Refer to Wheel Brake Emergency Operation, this section.
r. Wing Fold
   There are no emergency provisions for folding wings.
s. Drooped Ailerons (before AFC 400)
   Emergency pneumatic operation of drooped ailerons is provided. Refer to Wing Flap Emergency Lowering, this section.
t. Rudder Feel Trim
   There are no alternate or emergency provisions for rudder feel trim.

If utility hydraulic system fails, proceed as follows:

Note

If the CHECK HYD GAGES indicator light illuminates and remains illuminated, monitor the hydraulic system gages for the remainder of the flight, since warning of a second hydraulic system failure is not given.

1. Land as soon as practicable.
2. Landing gear and flaps - BLOWN DOWN WHEN READY FOR LANDING.
3. Make a short field arrestment if available.
4. Shut down engines.

DIRECTIONAL CONTROL WITH UTILITY HYDRAULIC SYSTEM FAILURE

Without utility hydraulic pressure nose gear steering is lost and rudder control reverts to manual operation. Only small rudder deflections are available at landing speeds because of the high pedal forces required to overcome the air loads. Therefore, differential braking becomes the primary heading control during landing and is accomplished through the use of the brake hydraulic accumulator pressure (several applications normally are available), or through application of the emergency brakes (pneumatic) in conjunction with manual braking (which required high pedal forces and large pedal deflections) or differential control. Use of accumulator pressure provides braking action and feel identical to the normal utility system but the number of applications are limited. For this reason the pilot should hold steady pedal pressure to obtain braking action, once pedal force has been applied, even though differential pedal force may be required. If accumulator pressure becomes depleted through consecutive brake applications or a system malfunction, manual brakes must provide any differential braking required to maintain heading while using emergency pneumatic brakes to stop the aircraft. It should be re-emphasized that the normal brake system accumulator is capable of providing sufficient brake power to stop the aircraft while providing heading control through differential braking. Ailerons and spoilers provide some directional control and are more effective at higher speeds. The drag chute should be used with caution in a strong crosswind if the utility hydraulic system has failed. A deployed drag chute in a strong crosswind increases substantially the requirement for differential braking. This is especially applicable when the hydraulic accumulator pressure has been depleted and the emergency pneumatic brakes are employed to brake the aircraft, which leaves only the manual brake, with associated high pedal forces and deflections, for heading control.

LANDING GEAR UNSAFE

An unsafe gear indication does not necessarily constitute an emergency. The unsafe indication could be caused by a malfunction within the indicating system, or the result of incorrect gear lowering procedure coupled with a low pressure condition of the utility hydraulic system. Upon initial detection of unsafe gear indication, proceed as follows:

1. Airspeed - 250 knots CAS or BELOW
2. If utility hydraulic pressure is normal, recycle landing gear.
3. Landing gear position indicators - CHECK
4. If unsafe condition still exists, place landing gear handle up.
5. Apply negative G to airplane.
6. While under negative G, place gear handle down.
   Negative G helps if unsafe gear is caused by high break-out forces.
7. If unsafe condition still exists, utilize landing gear emergency lowering procedure.

LANDING GEAR EMERGENCY LOWERING

If normal gear operation fails, the gear can be lowered by utilizing the following procedures:

CAUTION

After a utility hydraulic failure, if the pneumatic pressure begins to drop and fuel remaining permits, extend the landing gear before the pressure drops below 2000 psi. If emergency extention is delayed, and there is a leak in the emergency gear air bottle, sufficient pressure to lower the gear will be lost.

1. Airspeed - BELOW 250 KNOTS CAS
2. Landing gear handle - DOWN
3. Landing gear circuit breaker - PULL (do not reset)
4. Landing gear handle - PULL AFT AND HOLD
   Pull handle full aft, (full limit of travel) and hold in full aft position until gear indicates down and locked.

CAUTION

- Hold handle in full aft position until gear indicates down and locked, and then leave the landing gear handle in the full aft position. Returning the handle to its normal position allows compressed air from the gear down side of the actuating cylinder to be vented overboard.

- If the landing gear is inadvertently extended in flight by emergency pneumatic pressure, it must be left in the extended position until post-flight servicing. If retraction in flight is attempted, rupture of the utility reservoir will probably occur with subsequent loss of the utility hydraulic system.

Note

It is possible to actuate the landing gear emergency system by pulling the landing gear control handle aft while the handle is in any position from UP thru DOWN. If the handle cannot be pulled aft while down, slowly raise the handle while continuing to pull aft. Once the handle moves aft, hold the handle in full aft position until the landing gear indicates down and locked; then continue to hold back pressure on the handle and return it to the full down position. If the handle is returned to its normal (IN) position, compressed air from the gear down side of the actuation cylinder is vented overboard.

5. Landing gear position indicators - CHECK

CAUTION

To prevent drop tank collapse during high altitude descent with wheels down, place wing transfer pressure switch to EMERG. Before landing, return wing transfer pressure switch to NORMAL.

If landing gear is still unsafe -

6. Yaw airplane to assist locking main gear, or bounce airplane on main gear to assist lowering/locking the nose gear.
7. If one main gear is still unsafe and the utility system pressure is within limits, refer to Landing Gear Emergency Retraction this section.
8. If gear is still unsafe and the utility system pressure is not within limits, refer to Landing Gear Malfunction-Emergency Landing Guide, figure 5-1.

Note

Any pneumatic extension of the landing gear shall be logged in the yellow sheet (OPNAV FORM 3760-2).

LANDING GEAR EMERGENCY RETRACTION

If gear retraction is desired after an attempted Landing Gear Emergency Lowering and the utility system pressure is within limits, retract the gear using the following procedures:

Note

Unless operational necessity dictates, this procedure should be used only when an unsafe gear condition exists after an attempted Landing Gear Emergency Lowering. It should not be used if the emergency gear was inadvertently actuated and all three gear are down and indicating locked.

1. Return the emergency gear handle to the normal position.
2. Wait a minimum of 1 minute.

3. Landing gear handle - UP
4. Landing gear circuit breaker - RESET

CAUTION

The landing gear circuit breaker must not be reset until the emergency handle is returned to normal, maintained in that position for a minimum of 1 minute, and the landing gear handle placed UP. Only then may the circuit breaker be safely reset.

5. After gear is retracted, refer to Landing Gear Malfunction - Emergency Landing Guide, figure 5-1.

WING FLAP EMERGENCY LOWERING

When contemplating a field landing, where arresting gear is not available, the flaps should be lowered pneumatically only when a utility hydraulic system failure is indicated, since in most instances operation of the emergency flap system causes a utility hydraulic system failure with loss of nose wheel steering and normal wheel brakes. For carrier landings, or field arresting landings where nose wheel steering and wheel brakes are not required, if extension of the flaps by the normal operation is unsuccessful, then the flaps should be extended by the pneumatic system, even if there is no indication of utility hydraulic failure. On aircraft after AFC 400, the trailing edge flap indicating circuit is wired through the aileron droop down limit switch and the trailing edge flaps will indicate barber pole following pneumatic flap extension. Therefore, there is no positive indication the trailing edge flaps have reached 1/2; however, the barber pole indication may be used as an indirect indication of trailing edge flap extension. The leading edge flap indications are not affected by aileron droop position and should read DN. Approach speed will be approximately 18 knots higher than approach speed with full flaps and drooped aileron. On all aircraft after AFC 534 selective emergency aileron droop is available through the emergency aileron droop switch. The flaps can be lowered utilizing the following procedures:

1. Airspeed - BELOW 200 KNOTS CAS
2. Flap circuit breaker - PULL (do not reset)

If only electrical or utility hydraulic system failure has occurred -

3. Emergency aileron droop switch - NORMAL (some aircraft)

If a single PC and utility hydraulic system failure has occurred -

4. Emergency aileron droop switch - DISABLE (some aircraft)

WARNING

If emergency aileron droop switch is not placed to DISABLE or essential 28 volt dc bus power is not available, a split aileron condition will occur if flaps are lowered pneumatically.

5. Emergency wing flap extension handle - PULL AFT

   Pull emergency wing flap extension handle full aft and down (full limit of travel).

Note

• Failure to pull the flap circuit breaker can result in an asymmetrical flap condition with some flaps extended and the others retracted. Emergency extension of the flaps after pulling the flap circuit breaker may still cause an asymmetrical extension and momentary aircraft roll. However, this can be easily countered by normal application of aircraft controls.

• Leave the emergency wing flap extension handle in the full aft position. Returning the handle to its normal position allows the compressed air from the flap down side of the actuating cylinder to be vented overboard, and the flaps will be blown up by the wind stream.

CAUTION

If the flaps are inadvertently extended in flight, by emergency pneumatic pressure, they must be left in the extended position until post-flight servicing. If retraction in flight is attempted, rupture of the utility reservoir will probably occur with subsequent loss of the utility hydraulic system.

6. Wing flap position indicators - CHECK

Note

Any pneumatic extension of the wing flaps shall be logged on the yellow sheet (OPNAV FORM 3760-2).

WHEEL BRAKE EMERGENCY OPERATION

If a utility hydraulic system failure occurs, or loss of brake action, the airplane can be stopped by using the emergency brake system. However, if arresting gear is available, plan to make a short field arrested landing.

1. Hydraulic wheel brakes - APPLY

   Depress brakes and keep a constantly increasing brake pressure. Do not pump

brakes. There may be brake applications available from emergency hydraulic accumulator.

Note

With no utility hydraulic system pressure available, the manual hydraulic brakes are still capable of furnishing flow and pressure to accomplish a limited amount of differential braking. Manual braking utilized with the emergency brake system becomes the primary method of maintaining directional control of the airplane. The number of such applications is limited, and higher pedal travel and higher brake pedal forces will be necessary.

2. If unable to stop airplane, pull emergency brake handle.

   The emergency brake system meters air pressure in proportion to applied pilot effort but does not provide differential braking.

Note

There is a time lag between pulling the emergency brake handle and the application of pneumatic pressure to the wheel cylinders.

3. Manual braking (heavy pedal forces) - AS REQUIRED

   Manual braking may be required for directional control as asymmetrical braking is prevalent when using emergency brake handle. Asymmetrical braking could be due to runway crown or crosswinds as well as unequal brake torque.

4. Do not taxi with emergency brakes.

SPEED BRAKE SYSTEM EMERGENCY OPERATION

On airplanes 148353f thru 148411h and 148413h thru 149474k, if the selector valve or the utility hydraulic system fails when the speed brakes are extended, they may be retracted by placing the emergency speed brake switch on the left console to RETRACT. Air loads close the panels to a trail position. On airplanes 148412h and 150406L and up, the speed brakes retract hydraulically upon the actuation of the speed brake emergency switch to RETRACT. If utility hydraulic failure occurs when the speed brakes are extended, placing either the speed brake switch to IN or the emergency speed brake switch to RETRACT, allows air loads to close the panels to the trail position. After AFC 534 the emergency speed brake switch is removed.

1. Emergency speed brake switch - RETRACT

If switch fails or after AFC 534 -

2. Speed brake circuit breaker - PULL

LANDING EMERGENCIES

LANDING GEAR MALFUNCTION

Refer to Landing Gear Malfunction - Emergency Landing Guide, figure 5-1.

FIELD ARRESTING GEAR

The various types of field arresting gear in use are the anchor chain cable, water squeezer, and the morest type. All of these types require engagement of the arresting hook in a cable pendant rigged across the runway. Location of the pendant in relation to the runway will classify the gear as follows:

A. Midfield Gear - Located near the half way point of the runway. Usually requires prior notification in order to rig for arrestment in the direction desired.

B. Abort Gear - Located 1500 to 2500 feet short of the upwind end of the duty runway and usually will be rigged for immediate use.

C. Overrun Gear - Located shortly past the upwind end of the duty runway, and is usually rigged for immediate use.

All pilots should be aware of the type, location, and compatibility of the arresting gear in use with the aircraft, and the policy of the local air station with regard to which gear is rigged for use and when. The approximate maximum permissible engaging speed, gross weight, and off-center engagement distance for field arrestment of aircraft are listed in figure 5-16.

WARNING

- Under no circumstances should a pilot's decision to abort a takeoff be delayed because of knowledge that an emergency arresting gear is available at the end of the runway. Decision to abort should be based on the usual parameters of remaining runway and distance required for stopping, using wheel brakes. The arresting gear will then serve as an assist to stop the aircraft from rolling off the runway onto unprepared surfaces.

- If off center just prior to engaging the arresting gear, do not attempt to go for the center of the runway. Continue straight ahead parallel to the centerline.

As various modifications to the basic type of arresting gear are used exact speeds will vary accordingly. Certain aircraft service changes may also affect engaging speed and weight limitations. Severe damage to the aircraft is usually sustained if an engagement into the chain gear is made in the wrong direction.

In view of the existing emergency runway conditions i.e., weather, time, fuel remaining and other considerations it may be impractical or impossible to adhere strictly to the following general recommendations. In an emergency situation, first determine the extent of the emergency by whatever means are possible (instruments, other aircraft, LSO, RDO, tower or other ground personnel). Next determine the most advantageous arresting gear available and the type of arrestment to be made under the conditions which prevail. Whenever deliberate field arrestment is intended, notify control tower personnel as much in advance as possible and state estimated landing time in minutes. If gear is not rigged, it will probably require 10 to 20 minutes to prepare it for use. If foaming of the runway or area of arrestment is required or desired it should be requested by the pilot at this time. In general the arresting gear is engaged on the centerline at as slow a speed as possible. Burn down to 1500 pounds of fuel or less. While burning down, make practice passes to accurately locate the arresting gear. Engagement should be made with feet off the brakes, shoulder harness locked, and with the aircraft in a 3-point attitude. After engaging the gear, good common sense and existing conditions now dictate whether to keep the engines running or shut down and abandon the aircraft.

SHORT FIELD ARRESTMENT

If at any time prior to landing, it is known that a directional control problem exists or a minimum rollout is desired, a short field arrestment should be made and the assistance of an LSO requested. He should be stationed near the touchdown point and equipped with a radio. Inform the LSO of the desired touchdown point. A constant glide slope approach to touchdown is permitted (mirror or Fresnel Lens Landing aid utilized) with touchdown on centerline at or just prior to the arresting wire with the hook extended. The hook should be lowered while airborne and a positive hook-down check should be made (observe light in the hook control handle). If midfield gear or morest type is available, it should be used. If neither are available, use abort gear. Use an approach speed commensurate with the emergency experienced. Landing approach power will be maintained until arrestment is assured or a waveoff is taken. Be prepared for a waveoff if the gear is missed. After engaging the gear, retard the throttles to IDLE or secure engines and abandon aircraft, depending on existing conditions.

1. Nofity tower and request LSO assistance.
   Notify tower of intended action, request LSO assistance (if required) and supply required information, e.g., type of emergency, estimated landing time, gross weight, etc.

2. Reduce gross weight.
   Dump and/or burn fuel to reduce gross weight to lowest practicable.

FIELD ARRESTMENT GEAR DATA

| ARRESTING GEAR | SHORT FIELD LANDING (g) | | LONG FIELD LANDING | | ABORTED TAKE-OFF | | MAXIMUM OFF-CENTER ENGAGEMENT (FEET) |
	AIRCRAFT GROSS WEIGHT (f)	MAXIMUM ENGAGING SPEED (KNOTS)	AIRCRAFT GROSS WEIGHT	MAXIMUM ENGAGING SPEED (KNOTS)	AIRCRAFT GROSS WEIGHT	MAXIMUM ENGAGING SPEED (KNOTS)	
M-2	36,000	101 (d)	38,000	98 (d)	54,800	84 (d)	20
E-14-1	36,000	160 (d)	38,000	160 (d)	54,800	142 (d)	50
E-27	36,000	151 (d)	38,000	149 (d)	54,800	132 (d)	35
E-15 (200'SPAN)	36,000	160 (d)	38,000	160 (d)	54,800	160 (d)	35
E-15 (300'SPAN)	36,000	160 (d)	38,000	160 (d)	54,800	160 (d)	50
M-21	36,000	150 (d)	38,000	145 (d)	54,800	135 (d)	10
E-28	36,000	160 (d)	38,000	160 (d)	54,800	160 (d)	40
E-5 (STD CHAIN)	36,000	150 (d)	38,000	150 (d)	54,800	133 (d)	(e)
E-5-1 (STD CHAIN)	36,000	156 (d)	38,000	153 (d)	54,800	133 (d)	(e)
E-5 (HVY CHAIN)	36,000	150 (d)	38,000	150 (d)	54,800	150 (d)	(e)
E-5-1 (HVY CHAIN)	36,000	165 (d)	38,000	165 (d)	54,800	163 (d)	(e)
BAK-6	36,000	156 (d)	38,000	154 (d)	54,800	141 (d)	15
BAK-9	36,000	160 (d)	38,000	160 (d)	54,800	150 (d)	30
BAK-12	36,000	160 (d)	38,000	160 (d)	54,800	160 (d)	50

(a) Maximum engaging speed limited by aircraft arresting hook strength.
(b) Maximum engaging speed limited by aircraft limit horizontal drag load factor (mass item limit "G").
(c) Maximum engaging speed limited by aircraft landing gear strength.
(d) Maximum engaging speed limited by arresting gear.
(e) Off-center engagement may not exceed 25% of the runway span.
(f) Recommended approach airspeed for 36,000 pounds is 135 CAS knots.
(g) 3.0 Degree glide slope setting.

FDB-1-(83)

Figure 5-16

3. Fly pattern as dictated by emergency.
4. Arresting hook - DOWN.
5. Fly final approach on LSO or for touchdown just short of wire. If LSO is available fly final approach and touchdown as directed. If LSO is not available, fly final approach touchdown on centerline and just short of the crossdeck pendant.
6. Maintain landing approach power until arrestment is assured.
7. Longitudinal control neutral until engagement.
8. Engage wire with feet off brakes.
9. Throttles IDLE or OFF at engagement as desired.

Note

Placing longitudinal control to neutral reduces the possibility and limits the severity of stabilator slaps.

LONG FIELD ARRESTMENT

The long field arrestment is used when a stopping problem exists with insufficient runway remaining (i.e. aborted take-offs, icy or wet runways, loss of brakes after touchdown, etc.). Lower the hook, allowing sufficient time for it to extend fully prior to engagement. Do not lower the hook too early and weaken the hook point. Line up the aircraft on the runway centerline. Inform the control tower of your intentions to engage the arresting gear so that aircraft landing behind you may be waved off. If no directional control problem exists (crosswind, brakes out, etc.), secure the engine.

1. ENGINES - IDLE
2. ARRESTING HOOK - DOWN
   Lower the tail hook at least 1000 feet ahead of the wire; 5 seconds are required for full extension.
3. DRAG CHUTE - DEPLOY
4. Aim for center of wire.
   Steer to engage the wire near the center and at a 90 degree angle.
5. Release brakes 100 feet ahead of wire.
6. Control stick - FULL AFT

ABORT-GEAR ENGAGEMENT

An abort gear arrestment is used when a stopping problem exists with insufficient runway remaining i.e., aborted takeoff, icy or wet runways, loss of brakes after touchdown. Lower the hook allowing sufficient time for it to extend fully (normally 1000 feet prior to reaching the arresting gear). Do not lower the hook too early and weaken the hook point. Line up the aircraft on the runway centerline and inform the control tower of your intention to engage the arresting gear, so that aircraft landing behind you may be waved off. After engagement, when no directional control problems exist, secure the engines. Any time the airplane cannot be stopped safely on the runway, attempt to engage the abort gear, executing as many of the following steps as time permits.

1. ARRESTING HOOK - DOWN
   Lower tail hook at least 1000 feet ahead of wire; 5 seconds are required for full extension.
2. CONTROL STICK - FULL AFT
3. Aim for center of wire.
   Steer to engage wire near center and at 90° angle.
4. Release brakes 100 feet ahead of wire.

BARRICADE ENGAGEMENT

1. Jettison all missiles.
2. Lower hook if possible.
   Lowering arresting hook assists barricade in stopping aircraft and helps to keep aircraft on deck at barricade entry.
3. Fly a normal on speed approach, on centerline and on meatball. Anticipate loss of meatball for a short period of time late in approach due to barricade stanchions obscuring meatball.

EXPENDING HUNG ORDNANCE

Before making an arrested landing with hung ordnance on a MER/TER, the following should be accomplished in an effort to expend ordnance.

1. Re-select station on which ordnance is hung and again depress bomb button.
2. Rock wings and/or pull positive G load.

LANDING WITH HUNG ORDNANCE

For emergency landing conditions only, the following asymmetric moments due to external stores loading are permitted:

Field landing (minimum sink-rate)	379,000 inch-pounds
twin or single-engine	2870 lbs. total on stations 1 or 9 or 4650 lbs. total on stations 2 or 8.
Field arrested landings and FMLP	212,000 inch-pounds
twin or single-engine	1600 lbs. total on stations 1 or 9 or 2610 lbs. total on stations 2 or 8.
Carrier landing, twin-engine	212,000 inch-pounds
	1600 lbs. total on stations 1 or 9 or 2610 lbs. total on stations 2 or 8.

Carrier landings, single-engine   60,000 inch-pounds

450 lbs. total on
stations 1 or 9
or
740 lbs. total on
stations 2 or 8.

The above asymmetrics are defined as the asymmetric load at the outboard wing stations (1 or 9) x 1325 plus the asymmetric load at the inboard wing stations (2 or 8) x 81.5.

CAUTION

- The hung ordnance restrictions of the TACTICAL Manual (NAVAIR 01-245FDB-1T, appendix I, page A1-21, Notes 19 and 20) apply and take precedence over the above limits.

- If a landing must be made with an asymmetric load, refer to Flight With Asymmetric Loadings, section IV for handling characteristics.

BLOWN TIRE

The situation may occur when a landing with a blown tire must be made, or a tire may rupture during the landing ground roll. A blown tire and high speed require immediate corrective action to keep the airplane aligned with the runway, therefore:

LANDING WITH A KNOWN BLOWN TIRE

1. Plan to make a short field arrestment (if available).

If short field arresting gear is not available -

2. Make a normal on-speed approach.
3. Land on side of runway opposite blown tire.
4. Touchdown with weight on good tire.
5. Use nose gear steering to maintain directional control.
   If nose gear steering is inoperative, use of aerodynamic steering should be considered.
6. Drag chute - DEPLOY
7. Use light opposite braking to slow aircraft.

CAUTION

Avoid braking on the wheel with the blown tire. Heavy braking could cause a flat spot on the wheel which could prevent further wheel rotation and make aircraft control more difficult.

8. Do not retract flaps.
   The wing flap seals may have been damaged by pieces of broken tire and retracting the wing flaps will increase the damage.
9. If fire equipment is available, throttles - OFF
   If possible, do not shut down engines until adequate fire fighting equipment is available.

WARNING

The damaged wheel may either be on fire or very hot, and fuel drained overboard during engine shutdown could contact the hot wheel and cause a fire.

BLOWN TIRE DURING LANDING ROLLOUT

1. **NOSE GEAR STEERING – ENGAGED (RUDDER CENTERED)**
2. **HOOK – DOWN FOR FIELD ARRESTMENT (IF ARRESTING GEAR AVAILABLE)**
3. Use light opposite braking to slow aircraft.

CAUTION

Avoid braking on the wheel with the blown tire. Heavy braking could cause a flat spot on the wheel which could prevent further wheel rotation and make aircraft control more difficult.

If arresting gear is not available -

4. Drag chute - DEPLOY
5. Do not retract flaps.
   The wing flap seals may have been damaged by pieces of broken tire and retracting the wing flaps will increase damage.
6. If fire equipment is available, throttles - OFF
   If possible, do not shut down engines until adequate fire fighting equipment is available.

WARNING

The damaged wheel may either be on fire or very hot, and fuel drained overboard during engine shutdown could contact the hot wheel and cause a fire.

CAUTION

If nose wheel tires are blown on landing, secure both engines as soon as possible to preclude portions of the tire entering either or both intake ducts.

Note

The airplane can be safely taxied or towed with a flat tire on either main or nose gear.

SINGLE ENGINE FAILURE ON FINAL

At the first indication of engine failure, the throttle of the operating engine must be advanced to obtain full military or afterburner thrust and the flaps immediately raised to the one-half position. Any unnecessary delay in applying power to the good engine results in excessive sink rates and/or airspeed bleed-off that you may not be able to overcome (even with full afterburner thrust) prior to ground impact.

The excessive sink rate condition develops if the angle of attack is allowed to increase beyond 20 units. If the angle of attack reaches 22 units, even the use of full afterburner thrust will not stop the sink rate before ground impact, unless the angle of attack is again reduced to 20 units or below. Raising the flaps to one-half while flying full flap on speed reduces drag and minimize power loss to the BLC system, but an altitude loss of 100 to 300 feet can be expected. Do not attempt to immediately level the aircraft; accept a continued rate of descent and maintain aircraft control with smooth coordinated attitude corrections being careful not to exceed 20 units angle of attack. External store drag is negligible at low airspeeds and has little effect on aircraft performance, the aircraft's gross weight dictates the thrust required to continue the approach or execute a go-around. At normal landing gross weights, once the situation is stabilized, i.e., flaps at one-half and the sink rate stopped or under control, afterburner thrust is no longer required. Very little yaw rate is induced by military thrust on one engine, however, a slight asymmetrical control problem is created by use of afterburner thrust on one engine. These yaw rates must be controlled with the rudder, since excessive aileron inputs could induce additional adverse control conditions. You can normally continue the approach, and land the aircraft on the runway, from a situation created by a single engine failure on final.

1. THROTTLE OF OPERATING ENGINE - MIL/ AFTERBURNER

Note

If the left engine fails on final and the bus tie remains open, afterburner ignition is not available. However, if afterburner thrust is required, afterburner light-offs are generally obtainable through turbine torching, by jam accelerating the right engine at 90% rpm or above.

2. FLAPS - RAISE TO 1/2
3. LAND OR WAVEOFF

If decision to Waveoff is made:

4. LANDING GEAR - UP
5. Initiate waveoff - climb to safe altitude
6. Non-mechanical failure - INITIATE AIRSTART
7. Mechanical failure - SHUTDOWN FAILED ENGINE
8. Land as soon as practicable.

SINGLE ENGINE LANDING

A single-engine landing is basically the same as a normal landing except that the pattern is expanded to avoid steep turns, final approach speeds are increased for better lateral control, and 1/2 flaps are used in lieu of full flaps.

1. Turn off non-essential electrical equipment.
2. Reduce gross weight to 34,000 pounds or less.
3. Variable area inlet ramp on operating engine - CHECK FULL OPEN

Note

If the inlet ramp on the operating engine is in the closed position, the afterburner must be utilized to make a safe approach.

4. Cycle afterburner of operating engine to insure rapid lightoff for possible afterburner operation.
5. Ram air turbine - EXTEND
6. Wing flap switch - 1/2

Note

● Full flaps are not recommended during a single-engine approach and landing, since the engine bleed air that would be utilized for the trailing edge BLC system deprives the engine of fully rated thrust. Also, the full flaps configuration increases drag appreciably over the 1/2 flaps configuration. In the 1/2 flaps configuration, trailing edge BLC is inoperative and the operating engine can deliver fully rated thrust if a waveoff is necessary.

● If the generator on the operating engine is lost, the flaps solenoid operated selector valves revert to a full trail position and the flaps will be blown up by the airstream.

Note

On airplanes 150642L and up, and all others, after AFC 125, the ARI system is inoperative with flaps retracted.

7. Landing gear handle - DOWN
8. For field landing fly 17 units angle of attack until landing is assured. For carrier landing fly an on-speed approach. Do not exceed 20 units AOA or waveoff performance is degraded.
9. In the event of waveoff, place throttle of operating engine to MAX.
10. In the event of carrier landing, place throttle of operating engine to MAX AB upon main gear touchdown.

Note

If the left engine is shutdown, and the bus tie is open, afterburner ignition is not available. However, if afterburner is required, afterburner light-offs are generally obtainable through turbine torching, by jam accelerating the right engine at 90% rpm or above.

Single engine landing with utility hydraulic failure after AFC-400

1. Reduce airspeed to 220 - 500 KCAS.
2. Jettison asymmetrical load.
3. Turn off non-essential electrical equipment.
4. Do not attempt carrier landing.
5. Reduce gross weight to 34,000 pounds or less.
6. Cycle AB of operating engine.
7. Check inlet ramp of operating engine.
8. If inlet ramp closed, AB must be used.

9. Ram air turbine - EXTEND
10. Extend gear and flaps pneumatically at minimum altitude of 5000 feet (AGL).
11. Investigate landing approach characteristics.
12. Enter a wide and extended downwind leg.
13. Plan a straight-in approach with 17 units AOA to touchdown.
14. Make an arrested landing.

LANDING WITH BLEED AIR SWITCH OFF (NO LEADING EDGE BLC) (WITH DROOPED AILERONS)

1. Jettison any asymmetric load.
2. Investigate landing approach characteristics before descending for a landing.
3. Enter a wide and extended downwind leg.
4. Plan for early line-up and straight in approach.
5. Field/carrier landings fly 18 units AOA for final approach and touchdown. Approach airspeed will increase 7 knots.

WARNING

- Actual stall occurs before the rudder pedal shaker is activated in the no leading edge BLC configuration. The aircraft stalls at approximately 20 units AOA and is characterized by a nose rise.

- In the single engine, half flap, leading edge BLC off configuration, the pilot-task during a carrier landing and approach is considerable. The decision to recover the aircraft aboard ship should be made only when conditions are optimum. Suitability of a divert field should be considered.

ARRESTING HOOK MALFUNCTION

If the arresting hook fails to extend when the control handle is placed down, deenergize the solenoid selector valve by pulling the arresting hook control circuit breaker (H5, No. 2 panel). Pressure is then removed from the upside of the arresting hook actuating cylinder and the hook extends. There are no provisions for arresting hook retraction in the event of a utility hydraulic failure or double generator failure.

DAMAGED AIRCRAFT

During any inflight emergency, when structural damage or any other failure is known or suspected that may adversely affect aircraft handling characteristics, a controllability check should be performed as follows:

1. Reduce gross weight to minimum practicable.
2. Proceed to a safe altitude.
3. Perform controllability check required by the type of emergency.

If aircraft has sustained structural damage -

4. Perform controllability check in the gear down, flap-up configuration.
5. Investigate approach and landing characteristics at 17 units AOA.
6. If adequate control is available, maintain configuration, plan a field landing, and make a straight-in approach with 17 units AOA at touchdown.

APPROACH POWER COMPENSATOR SYSTEM DISENGAGEMENT

If a malfunction occurs in the system, APCS disengagement should be attempted in the following sequence:

1. Emergency speed brake switch - MANUAL (in aircraft before AFC 392).
2. Speedbrake circuit breaker - IN (in aircraft before AFC 392).
3. Speedbrake switch - IN
   In aircraft after AFC 392, the APCS may be disengaged at any time by moving speedbrake switch to IN, regardless of position of emergency speedbrake switch or speedbrake circuit breaker.

If this fails -

4. APCS power switch - OFF or STBY.

If this fails -

5. Auto throttle circuit breakers - PULL. Pull three auto throttle circuit breakers (K1, K2, and K3, No. 2 panel).

This should ensure positive disengagement, but if it still remains engaged -

6. Manually override throttles. Pilot can manually override throttles by exerting 20 to 25 pound force per throttle. In this case, throttles must be held in desired position.

If time does not permit the accomplishment of the preceding steps -

1. RAT - OUT
2. Generators - OFF
3. Climb to a safe altitude
4. Auto throttle circuit breakers - PULL (K1, K2, and K3, No. 2 panel).
5. Generators - ON
6. RAT - IN

Note

When using the above procedures, discretion must be used as the flaps may blow up.

NO FLAPS LANDING

A no-flaps landing is basically the same as a normal landing except that the pattern is expanded to avoid steep turns; the downwind, base leg, and final approach speeds are increased to provide adequate lateral control.

1. Fly 17 units angle of attack.

HOT BRAKE PROCEDURES

Hot brake procedures are contained in BUAER/BUWEPS INST 13420.1. In view of the varied climatic conditions, field conditions, and safety devices available, specific procedures must be covered in local squadron/field SOP.

LANDING WITH BOTH ENGINES INOPERATIVE

Landing with both engines inoperative will not be attempted.

GLIDE DISTANCE

The aircraft will glide approximately 6 nautical miles for every 5000 feet of altitude. The recommended glide airspeed is 215 knots CAS. Below 50,000 feet, 215 knots CAS provides near maximum glide distance and allows the windmilling engines to maintain power control hydraulic pressures within safe limits.

PRECAUTIONARY EMERGENCY APPROACH

The standard precautionary emergency approach for the aircraft is the straight-in GCA/CCA approach modified to accommodate single-engine, half-flap, or no-flap approach speeds as power available dictates. The precautionary emergency approach depicted in figure 5-17 is used for field landings if one engine has failed and the remaining engine has suffered a malfunction that results in only partial power. This procedure may be used day or night, provided ceiling and visibility are such that visual contact can be maintained with the field. Although the approach depicted is the classic overhead entry to a left hand pattern, the precautionary approach may be initiated from any check point, using either a left or right hand pattern. The pilot must select a check point in either the straight-in or overhead approach at which the decision to continue the approach or eject must be made. Sink rate, power available, configuration, and position relative to the runway or obstructions must be considered. The flaps may have to be blown down due to airspeed being above flap blow-up speed. The check point selected must be early enough to permit safe ejection and in such a position so as not to compromise or endanger the safety of populated areas, military installations or other aircraft. In no case should this check point be lower than 1000 feet AGL for the straight-in approach, or 3000 feet AGL for the overhead approach. The pilot should plan the approach to utilize available field arresting gear. If the success of the approach and landing appear to be marginal to the pilot, consideration should be given to heading the aircraft into a clear area and ejecting instead of attempting the approach.

FORCED LANDING

WARNING

All forced landings on land shall be made with the landing gear extended, regardless of terrain. A greater injury hazard is present whenever emergency landings are made with the landing gear retracted. Increased airspeed or nose high angle of impact during landings with landing gear retracted is common practice and contributes greatly to pilot injury and damage to the airplane. This nose high attitude causes the airplane to slap the ground on impact, subjecting the pilot to possible spinal injury. Less airplane damage results with the gear extended.

It is recommended that a landing on unprepared terrain not be attempted with this airplane; the crew should eject. If a forced landing is unavoidable, proceed as follows:

1. Ram air turbine - EXTEND
2. If time and conditions permit, dump or burn excess fuel.
3. Notify RIO of existing emergency and intended action.
4. Shoulder harness - LOCK
5. Canopies - JETTISON (forward canopy first)
   The aft canopy should be jettisoned last to preclude possibility of forward canopy entering aft cockpit when jettisoned.
6. Armament - JETTISON
7. Landing gear - DOWN AND LOCKED
8. Wing flaps - DOWN
9. External tanks - RETAIN IF EMPTY AND UNPRESSURIZED
   Empty external tanks should be retained to absorb shock of landing.

Note

If gear is not lowered, external tanks can be unpressurized by pulling the landing gear circuit breaker and placing the landing gear handle down.

10. Make normal approach.
11. Drag chute - DEPLOY AFTER TOUCHDOWN
12. Engines - SHUTDOWN
    a. Throttles - OFF
    b. Engine master switches - OFF
13. As soon as stopped - EVACUATE AIRPLANE

PRECAUTIONARY EMERGENCY APPROACH PROCEDURE

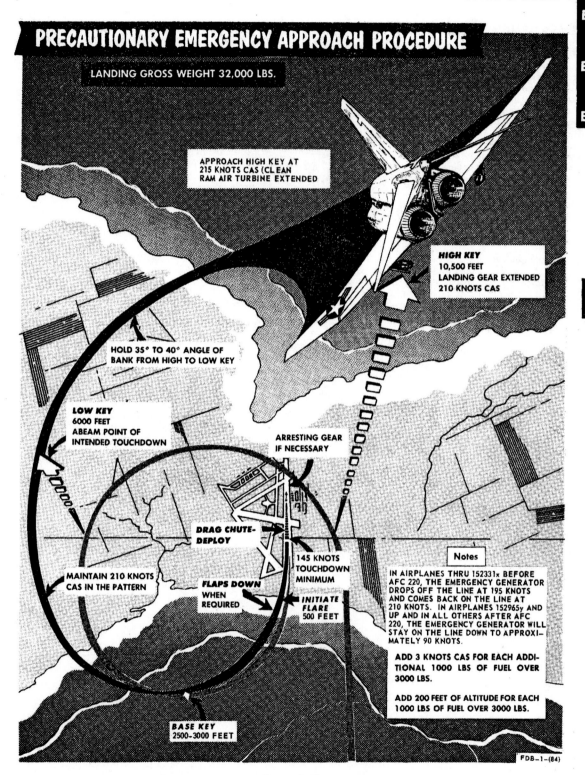

LANDING GROSS WEIGHT 32,000 LBS.

APPROACH HIGH KEY AT 215 KNOTS CAS (CLEAN RAM AIR TURBINE EXTENDED

HIGH KEY
10,500 FEET
LANDING GEAR EXTENDED
210 KNOTS CAS

HOLD 35° TO 40° ANGLE OF BANK FROM HIGH TO LOW KEY

LOW KEY
6000 FEET
ABEAM POINT OF INTENDED TOUCHDOWN

ARRESTING GEAR IF NECESSARY

DRAG CHUTE- DEPLOY

145 KNOTS TOUCHDOWN MINIMUM

MAINTAIN 210 KNOTS CAS IN THE PATTERN

FLAPS DOWN WHEN REQUIRED

INITIATE FLARE 500 FEET

BASE KEY
2500-3000 FEET

Notes

IN AIRPLANES THRU 152331x BEFORE AFC 220, THE EMERGENCY GENERATOR DROPS OFF THE LINE AT 195 KNOTS AND COMES BACK ON THE LINE AT 210 KNOTS. IN AIRPLANES 152965y AND UP AND IN ALL OTHERS AFTER AFC 220, THE EMERGENCY GENERATOR WILL STAY ON THE LINE DOWN TO APPROXIMATELY 90 KNOTS.

ADD 3 KNOTS CAS FOR EACH ADDITIONAL 1000 LBS OF FUEL OVER 3000 LBS.

ADD 200 FEET OF ALTITUDE FOR EACH 1000 LBS OF FUEL OVER 3000 LBS.

FDB-1-(84)

Figure 5-17

EMERGENCY EGRESS

Due to forced landing, ditching or landing emergency such as barricade engagement or runway overrun, rapid egress is essential. The most rapid method of egress is by divestment of both the seat survival kit and the parachute. On land, if the aircraft is burning, the extra time required to egress retaining the seat kit could cause serious injury or death. After safely egressing, return to the aircraft and retrieve the survival kit (conditions permitting). If ditching, the parachute should be divested and the seat kit retained to allow for underwater breathing and use of the raft/survival equipment.

WARNING

During emergency egress from aircraft with the H-7 rocket assist ejection seat, actuation of the emergency harness release handle allows the personnel parachute to slide down and wedge against the seat survival kit causing serious difficulty in egressing with the seat survival kit attached.

To evacuate cockpit without survival kit and parachute -

1. Canopy - OPEN
   a. Normal
   b. Canopy emergency release handle
   c. Manual unlock handle

Note

If circumstances dictate, open canopy after remaining steps are performed.

2. Rotate lower ejection handle guard - UP
3. Leg restraint release handle - PULL AFT

WARNING

On H5 seats, if the handle is allowed to return to the down position, the leg restraint lines may be relocked.

4. After arching back to apply tension to lap belt, fittings - RELEASE
5. Oxygen mask (open face plate if wearing full pressure suit) - RELEASE
6. Composite disconnect - RELEASE
7. Shoulder harness release fittings - RELEASE

To evacuate cockpit with survival kit only, refer to ditching chart, this section.

DITCHING

Ditching the airplane should be the pilot's last choice. All survival equipment is carried by the crewmember, thus ejection is advisable. However, if altitude and situation demand ditching, the procedures set forth on the ditching chart (figure 5-18) should be observed.

Note

In the event of ditching and sinking in water when immediate escape is impossible, it is possible for the crewmember to survive under water with oxygen equipment until escape can be made. The oxygen regulator is a suitable underwater breathing device since the regulator is always on 100% oxygen. If a pressure suit is not being worn it is essential that the mask be tightly strapped in place.

DITCHING CHART

WARNING
THE AIRCRAFT SHOULD BE DITCHED ONLY WHEN
ALL OTHER ATTEMPTS OF EGRESS HAVE FAILED.

CREW MEMBER	DUTIES BEFORE IMPACT	POSITION	DUTIES AFTER IMPACT	EQUIPMENT	EXIT
PILOT	1. RIO—ALERT. 2. Make radio distress call. 3. IFF—EMERGENCY 4. External stores—JETTISON. 5. Landing Gear—UP. 6. Wing Flaps—DOWN. 7. Arresting Hook—DOWN. 8. Leg restraint release handle—PULL AFT. Release leg restraint lines before ditching to expedite egress from the cockpit. 9. Visor—DOWN. 10. Oxygen mask or face visor—TIGHTEN or SEAL. 11. Canopy—JETTISON (forward canopy first). **Note** In the event of a ditching following such situations as catapult shots or bolters, attempt to jettison the canopy prior to hitting the water. Once the aircraft is immersed under water the canopy might not jettison until water introduced by the flooding doors equalize pressures between the inside and outside of the canopy, an event which would occur at a considerable water depth. 12. Lower seat, assume position for ditching. 13. Shoulder Harness—LOCK. 14. Fly parallel to swell pattern. 15. Attempt, to touch down along wave crest. 16. When hook contacts water— SHUT DOWN ENGINES.	1. In Seat. 2. Feet on rudder pedals knees flexed.	1. Lower ejection handle guard – UP 2. Shoulder harness release fittings – RELEASE 3. Emergency harness release handle – LOCK UP **WARNING** Before AFC 370, if handle is allowed to return to the down position, the leg restraint lines will be relocked. 4. Stand straight up without twisting to release survival kit sticker clips from the seat. **Note** The Bail-Out Bottle will actuate when the crewmember stands up. In the event of ditching and sinking in water when immediate escape is impossible, it is possible to survive under water with oxygen equipment or full pressure suit until escape can be made. 5. Abandon aircraft. **WARNING** Should aircraft be abandoned under water, exhale while ascending to the surface to prevent bursting of lungs due to pressure differential between lungs and outside of body. 6. Inflate life vest. 7. See that RIO is clear. 8. Inflate life raft and secure Emergency equipment. 9. Proceed away from aircraft and tie rafts together.	1. One man raft and Emergency equipment. 2. Life vest 3. Flash light.	Over canopy sill.
RADAR INTERCEPT OFFICER	1. Acknowledge pilots ditching order. 2. Radar equipment—STOW. 3. Leg restraint release handle—PULL AFT. Release leg restraint lines before ditching to expedite egress from the cockpit. 4. Visor—DOWN. 5. Oxygen mask or face visor— TIGHTEN or SEAL. 6. Canopy—JETTISON (Aft canopy last). **Note** In the event of a ditching following such situations as catapult shots or bolters, attempt to jettison the canopy prior to hitting the water. Once the aircraft is immersed under water the canopy might not jettison until water introduced by the flooding doors equalize pressures between the inside and outside of the canopy, an event which would occur at a considerable water depth. 7. Lower seat, assume position for ditching. 8. Shoulder Harness—LOCK.	1. In Seat. 2. Feet on deck knees flexed.	Same as for Pilot Except: 7. See that Pilot is clear.	1. One man raft and Emergency equipment. 2. Life vest. 3. Flash light.	Over canopy sill.

FDB-1-(85)

Figure 5-18

OPERATIONAL EMERGENCIES

GENERAL

Operational emergencies such as downed plane or lost aircraft are outlined in NWP and the current IFR Supplements. Emergency procedures associated with carrier operations are outlined in the CVA/CVS NATOPS manual and the individual ship's CATCC manual.

PILOT/RIO EMERGENCY COMMUNICATIONS

It is assumed that any communication required between the pilot and RIO concerning any emergency will be carried out on the intercom. If the intercom is inoperative for any reason, the following procedures will be utilized:

1. Check mikes and earphone plugs.
2. Check upper block connections.
3. Use Emergency ICS and Emergency Radio positions in conjunction with override switch.
4. Try intercommunication with UHF transceiver.
5. Check all circuit breakers visually and depress transformer rectifier circuit breaker to ensure their engagement.

Note

If operating on the RAT with the right transformer rectifier circuit open, the following essential equipment is inoperative; AN/AJB-3, ADC, CNI, gear and flap indicators, stabilator feel trim, and ICS.

PILOT/RIO ATTENTION SIGNALS

The following may be used as pilot/RIO attention signals under emergency conditions with no method of communicating.

1. The pilot will attract the RIO's attention by a rapid rocking of the wings.
2. The RIO will attract the pilot's attention by slamming home his radar scope to the stow position, or actuate the hand control to the limits of the antenna.
3. Acknowledgement of the attention signals will be a thumbs-up and future communications will be conducted by visual signals.

HEFOE signals (figure 5-7) may be utilized by the pilot and RIO. The pilot will be signaling over his left shoulder and looking in his left mirror for the return signals. The same signals will apply at night except that a flashlight must be held up to outline the fingers. If the RIO's upper block is unplugged as indicated by the 4-finger signal, the pilot will maintain a cockpit altitude of 10,000 feet or below for the duration of the flight. If the RIO desires an immediate landing, he will give a thumbs-down signal to the pilot.

DOWNED PLANE PROCEDURES

DECLARATION OF AN EMERGENCY

When flying without a wingman or section leader, it is critically important that the pilot advise someone of his trouble and location. Even a deferred emergency can develop into a first rate emergency. The initial radio contact should be preceeded with the word PAN when the situation requires urgent action, but is not an actual distress; the word MAYDAY should be used when threatened by serious or imminent danger and immediate assistance is required. If a serious emergency has arisen, shift immediately to EMERGENCY IFF; Set up Mode 3, Code 7700, place UHF to GUARD; and broadcast MAYDAY. The following information should be relayed to a ground station immediately:

1. PAN or MAYDAY (depending upon situation)
2. Identification
3. Model aircraft
4. Position
5. Situation
6. Intentions

Single Aircraft

If the situation permits, before ejection or crash landing:

1. Switch IFF to EMERGENCY; Mode 3, Code 7700
2. Transmit MAYDAY over guard channel.

Conditions existing following the ejection or crash landing dictate whether to remain near the scene of the crash or attempt to find assistance.

Section

If one member of a section goes down, the other member should:

1. Establish contact with a ground station, preferably a GCI site or RADAR control agency. Switch IFF to EMERGENCY and UHF to GUARD.
2. Make every effort to follow other aircraft or crew during descent. It is of primary importance to keep crew in sight at all times, while on ground or in water. Note as accurately as possible, bearings, distances from known prominent landmarks or navigational aids, to direct rescue planes or boats to scene.
3. Establish a RESCAP.
4. Maintain sufficient altitude to assure radio contact with rescue facility.
5. Leave area with sufficient fuel to POSITIVELY ensure return to base or alternate field.

Division

Everything mentioned earlier holds true if there are more than two members to the flight. Some additional procedures can be followed which insure a greater likelihood of a successful rescue. The other member of the section in which the downed crew has been flying, should:

1. Follow aircraft/crew and circle them at low altitude, making every effort to keep downed crew in sight.

Other members of the flight:

1. Remain at altitude.
2. Alert appropriate facilities.
3. Relay communications.
4. Conserve fuel.

NAV-COMM EMERGENCY PROCEDURES

These procedures deal with communication emergencies. Other types of emergencies where navigation and communication aids are available should be handled according to the individual circumstances under which they arise and as the factors involved indicate. An aircraft with running lights flashing usually indicates that an emergency condition exists.

LOST AIRCRAFT (WITHOUT NAVIGATIONAL AIDS)

The pilot will have navigated to best position by dead reckoning. The following procedures apply.

With radio receiver -

1. Fly minimum of 2 triangular patterns to the right with 1-minute legs. Repeat pattern at 20-minute intervals.
2. Conserve fuel and maintain altitude.
3. Squawk mode II and be alert for aircraft vectored to join.

Without radio receiver -

1. Fly minimum of 2 triangular patterns to the left with 1-minute legs. Repeat pattern at 20-minute intervals.
2. Conserve fuel and facilitate radar pickup by maintaining highest feasible altitude consistent with situation.
3. Squawk mode II and be alert for aircraft vectored to join.
4. After joining, inform good aircraft of all emergency conditions by appropriate hand signals to prevent separation during penetration/letdown.

LOST AIRCRAFT (WITH NAVIGATION AIDS)

1. Squawk mode II, proceed to alternate marshal.
2. Energize I/P function at least once each minute.

3. Commence penetration/letdown at EAC as briefed.
4. Be alert for aircraft vectored to join.
5. If immediate assistance is required, energize emergency IFF.

PENETRATION/LETDOWN NAV-COMM EMERGENCIES

Even though communication aids have failed, if navigation equipment is still available:

1. Continue approach.
   Regardless of weather, any jet aircraft having passed Platform must continue its approach.
2. If no contact has been made after 2 minutes past individual expected ramp time, conduct lost aircraft (without navigation aids, and without radio receiver) procedures.

If all communication and navigation equipment is lost, and last known weather at the ship was 800 feet with 2 miles visibility or better:

1. Continue approach by dead reckoning.
2. Maintain dead reckoning until 2 minutes past individual expected ramp time.
3. Conduct lost aircraft (without navigation aids, and without radio receiver) procedures.

If last known weather at ship was below 800 feet with 2 miles visibility or better:

1. Level off.
2. Conserve fuel.
3. Execute a one-half standard rate timed turn to a heading of 90 degrees to the right of previous penetration heading.
4. Maintain new heading for 2 minutes.
5. Conduct lost aircraft (without navigation aids, and without radio receiver) procedures.

LANDING WITHOUT UHF (WINGMAN ESCORTING)

Exact procedures to be followed in the event one aircraft in a flight experiences communication failures must be covered in detail on every pre-flight brief. In general, the following procedures are recommended for the approach and landing:

1. Escorting aircraft determine the escorted (no radio) aircrafts fuel state through hand signals.
2. Escorting aircraft determine escorted aircrafts UHF guard and auxiliary receiver status.
3. Escorting aircraft establishes flight for a straight-in approach, lowers gear and flaps through hand signals, and passes the lead to the escorted aircraft after clearance to land is received.
4. Passing of the lead should ideally be done at about 1 mile from touchdown. At this time the flight should be lined up with the runway with the proper rate of descent established.

SECTION CARRIER CONTROLLED APPROACH

Should a section approach become necessary because of radio or instrument failure:

1. Place wingman on right side before commencing descent.
2. Reduce speed to 145 knots during last part of final approach so as to be approximately on speed when meatball is sighted.
3. Indicate meatball to wingman (blink external lights at night) to indicate carrier in sight.
4. Wingman will continue approach and land.

5. Leader will make definite turn to port and parallel final bearing to be in position should wingman bolter.

6. Following wingman trap/bolter, leader will execute normal CCA waveoff procedure and be vectored in for an additional section approach or final landing.

CARRIER EMERGENCY NAV-COMM SIGNALS

Refer to CVA/CVS NATOPS Manual.

TAKEOFF EMERGENCIES

ABORTED TAKEOFF

Where an aircraft takeoff must be aborted, a roll-in type engagement of all arresting gear is recommended to prevent overrun. The aircraft is cleared up to the maximum takeoff gross weight specified in the aborted takeoff column (figure 5-16). Additionally, the data provided in the long field landing column may be used for light weight aborted takeoff, where applicable.

Note

The taxi light may be of use in locating arresting/abort gear at night.

ABORT - GEAR ENGAGEMENT

An abort gear long arrestment is used when a stopping problem exists with insufficient runway remaining, i.e., aborted takeoff icy or wet runways, or loss of brakes after touchdown. Lower the hook allowing sufficient time for it to extend fully (normally 1000 feet prior to reaching the arresting gear). Do not lower the hook too early, the hook scraping on the runway will weaken the hook point. Line up the aircraft on the runway centerline and inform the control tower of your intention to engage the arresting gear, so that aircraft landing behind you may be

waved off. After engagement, when no directional control problems exist, secure the engines.

1. ENGINES - IDLE
2. ARRESTING HOOK - DOWN
   Lower the tail hook at least 1000 feet ahead of the wire; 5 seconds is required for full extention.
3. DRAG CHUTE - DEPLOY
4. CONTROL STICK - FULL AFT
5. Aim for center of wire.
   Steer to engage the wire near the center and at a 90° angle.
6. Release brakes 100 feet ahead of wire.

AFTERBURNER FAILURE DURING TAKEOFF

If the afterburner(s) fail during takeoff, the resulting loss of thrust is significant. Takeoff need not be aborted if remaining runway is compatible with power available. After failure, the variable area exhaust nozzle continues to function as directed by exhaust gas temperature. In this circumstance, the nozzle moves as a function of temperature limiting only. If afterburner fails, proceed as follows:

1. Throttle of failed afterburner - MIL RANGE
2. If exhaust nozzle is operating properly, relight when desired.

BLOWN TIRE ON TAKEOFF

A situation may occur when the main wheel tire(s) or nose wheel tire(s) blow on takeoff roll. If the nose wheel tire(s) blow on takeoff, it is likely that one or both engines will receive FOD.

If decision to stop is made -

1. ABORT TAKEOFF
   Refer to Aborted Takeoff, this section.
2. LEAVE FLAPS IN POSITION SET FOR TAKEOFF.
   Leave flaps in their takeoff position to prevent additional damage to wing flap seals if they have been damaged by pieces of broken tire.

If takeoff is continued -

1. LEAVE LANDING GEAR DOWN, AND FLAPS IN POSITION SET FOR TAKEOFF.
   Leave landing gear extended to preclude fouling blown tire(s) in wheel well(s). Leave flaps in their takeoff position to prevent additional damage to wing flap seals if they have been damaged by pieces of broken tire.
2. Monitor engine instruments.
   If any abnormal indications, such as RPM, EGT, or engine vibrations are noted, it is possible that FOD is present.
3. Plan to make a short field arrested landing.
   Refer to Short Field Arrestment, this section.

FLAP RETRACTION AND/OR BLC LOSS DURING FIELD OR CATAPULT TAKEOFF

Inadvertent flap retractions and/or BLC loss during field and catapult takeoffs may occur. The above failures can be caused by any one or combination of the following: loss of electrical power, utility hydraulic failure, or failure of the flap blowup switch.

FIELD TAKEOFF

If takeoff is continued -

1. ENGINES - MAX AB
2. External stores - JETTISON (IF NECESSARY)

CAUTION

Avoid tendency of over rotation beyond desired 10° to 12° takeoff attitude.

If decision to abort is made -

1. Employ aborted takeoff procedures, this section.

CARRIER TAKEOFF

Crewmember decisions will be based on when the failure occurs during the takeoff phase. If the failure occurs during the catapult stroke or shortly thereafter -

1. EJECT IMMEDIATELY.

If the failure occurs at a time after the cat shot such that airspeed, altitude, and sink rate will allow the aircraft to be flown straight and level at less than 27 units AOA (above stall speed for gross weight), proceed as follows:

1. Engines - MAX AB
2. External stores - JETTISON
3. Flaps - BLOW DOWN
4. Attempt to maintain level flight or climb
5. Eject if above steps fail to effect minimum flight control and recovery.

FDB-1-(86)

SECTION **VI**

ALL-WEATHER OPERATION

TABLE OF CONTENTS

SIMULATED INSTRUMENT PROCEDURES

GENERAL

Instrument flight is primarily a problem of time and distance navigation wherein all, or part, of the flight is conducted under instrument conditions. To complete a successful instrument flight, crewmembers must be properly prepared and have conducted the necessary planning. All pilots will be current in latest instrument flight rules and regulations published by higher authority and, when operating aircraft under instrument flight conditions, will be guided by the current OPNAV INSTRUCTION 3710.7, (General Flight and Operating Instructions for Naval Aircraft) NATOPS Instrument Flight Manual and Federal Aviation Regulations.

SAFETY PRECAUTIONS

It is the responsibility of the chase pilot to insure that the flight is clear of other aircraft at all times.

The instrument pilot shall not go hooded on departure until reaching a minimum of 2000 feet above the terrain.

At a minimum of 500 feet above terrain, the instrument pilot goes contact on any hooded penetration or ground controlled approach.

The chase pilot conducts communications checks with the instrument pilot and receive an acknowledgement at 1-minute intervals below FL 240 and at 3-minute intervals above FL 240, if not under positive control.

In the event of loss of radio contact, the instrument pilot shall immediately go contact and remain VFR until radio contact is re-established. If necessary, the chase pilot passes to the right and pulls ahead/ in front to attract the instrument pilot's attention to go contact. Lighting afterburner when passing the instrument pilot usually gets his attention.

Radio contact will be positively established immediately before and after any channel or frequency change.

Unless under positive control, the instrument pilot shall call the indicated altitude at each 5,000-foot interval during descent and at level-off.

HOODED RADAR INTERCEPTS

a. All hooded intercept flights will be pre-briefed before launch.
b. Positive UHF communication must exist before going hooded and commencing intercepts. All aircraft in the flight will have UHF set on T/R + G. The chase and target aircraft has the tactical frequency with comm command in one

cockpit. The other cockpit has Guard set in the comm channel, allowing the pilots to take comm command and transmit on guard, if the need arises.

c. If the chase or target pilot does not have a Tally Ho before 5 miles, the hooded pilot shall go contact.

d. If the hooded aircraft does not have a Judy by 10 miles, the target aircraft shall call his altitude and the intercept pilot shall go contact, and remain so, for the completion of the run, even if a Judy is subsequently obtained.

e. Minimum altitude above all terrain is 2000 feet.

f. Target aircraft will not jink in altitude.

CHASE PLANE PROCEDURES

The chase pilot's duties on instrument flights are to act as lookout and to be a flight monitor. The best position for this is a loose tactical wing position where airspeed, attitude, and altitude may be monitored while maintaining a good lookout. During GCA approaches, the chase flies a position as directed by GCA. This position is normally about 4 or 5 o'clock from the GCA aircraft, 500 feet away, and slightly stepped-up.

CHASE PLANE RADIO PROCEDURES

The chase aircraft sets up its radios in the following manner: the frequency in use with comm command in one cockpit, and the guard position set in the comm channel of the other cockpit. The instrument airplane shall monitor the TR + G position. If the chase pilot suspects radio failure or cannot burn through transmissions by GCA or other controlling agencies, he can take command and transmit instructions to the instrument pilot on guard channel.

ACTUAL INSTRUMENT PROCEDURES

INSTRUMENT FLIGHT

This is an all-weather airplane that performs operational missions in all extremes of weather. Rapid acceleration rates and high pitch angles during climb, of necessity dictate some modification of standard instrument procedures.

INSTRUMENT FLIGHT PLANNING

On instrument flights, delays in departure and descent and low climb rates to altitude are often required in high density control areas. These factors make fuel consumption and flight endurance critical. All instrument flights should be carefully planned and consideration given to the additional time and fuel which may be required. A complete weather briefing for all pilots on the flights will be obtained and the appropriate flight plan will be filed.

BEFORE STARTING ENGINES

When practical, an ATC clearance should be obtained from the tower before starting engines. When the radios are operating on external power, they are limited to 10 minutes of accumulated operation in a 1-hour span. This limitation applies to all CNI equipment except the intercom, which is hot any time power is on the airplane.

BEFORE TAKEOFF

It is essential that the instrument and navigation equipment be thoroughly checked prior to takeoff. If a climb through precipitation or clouds is anticipated, place the pitot heat switch ON and the engine anti-ice switch to DE-ICE. At idle rpm, the operation of the engine de-icers can be checked by noting a slight rise (approx. 10°C) in EGT and a slight increase in fuel flow. The ADI wings symbol should be set with the wings 1° above the horizon and the compass should be aligned with the runway heading. The stab aug should be engaged.

INSTRUMENT TAKEOFF

Same as normal Takeoff.

INSTRUMENT CLIMB

The simplified climb schedules described in part 3 of section III can be used with minimum sacrifice in fuel consumption and climb rates. Turns should be kept to a minimum during climb due to the difficulty of determining bank angles and rates of turn while at high pitch angles. Upon reaching clear air, turn off the engine anti-icing and the pitot heat. Follow the clearance exactly as given. If unable to comply with the clearance, it is mandatory that ATC be advised immediately. Climb speed will conform to local procedures, but should be a comfortable airspeed with transition to the published climb schedule accomplished at a comfortable altitude above the terrain.

PENETRATION PROCEDURES

At 3 to 5 minutes before making a descent, the cabin temperature control should be set at the maximum comfortable level and the defog/footheat lever to DEFOG. Contact approach control 10 minutes prior to EAT or as directed by ARTC, and conform to the provision of section 2, Flight Planning Document. At 3 minutes before entering holding, adjust power to arrive at the holding fix with maximum endurance airspeed (265 knots CAS maximum). Before descent, the pilot will check missed approach procedures and obtain the latest weather information at the destination and at the alternate if required. Refer to Descent/Instrument Penetration procedures, section III.

PENETRATION WITH GEAR AND FLAPS EXTENDED

Under certain conditions, it may be necessary to penetrate with the gear and flaps extended. If such is the case, advise approach control that the approach will be executed with a non-standard approach speed.

Before commencing the approach, slow to below 250 knots CAS and lower the landing gear and flaps. If external tanks are carried, place the wing transfer switch to EMERG before extension of the landing gear to avoid de-pressurizing the fuel tanks. Commencing penetration, reduce the pitch attitude to maintain 195 knots CAS. This attitude seems extremely nose low. Make throttle adjustments as necessary to maintain a 3500 fpm rate of descent. Initiate a round-out in order to reach GCA pick-up or TACAN gate altitude at a speed of 150-160 knots CAS. If the descent has been made with the wing transfer switch in EMERG, return the switch to NORMAL prior to landing.

RADAR CONTROLLED PENETRATION

The approaches are basically the same as previously described with the following additions. The controlling activity normally asks for turns or specific IFF squawks for positive identification. The controlling activity advises turns or headings which produce the desired flight path. They also advise as to distance from the destination and direct a descent to lower minimum altitudes as traffic and terrain permit.

GCA (PAR) APPROACHES

This airplane handles exceptionally well in the GCA pattern. It is very stable directionally and is very responsive to minor corrections about all axes. When directed, descend to GCA pickup altitude and transition to landing configuration. Slow to 150-160 knots CAS which requires approximately 88-92%. Trim required is approximately 3 units nose-up. When the pilot is told to commence a normal rate of descent for his aircraft, he should retard the power to approximately 82-84%. Allow the plane to slow to 145 knots CAS minimum (section). If alone, adjust the nose to maintain 140 knots CAS or a donut on the angle-of-attack indexer, whichever is greater. While holding the attitude constant, make smooth but positive power adjustments to maintain a desired rate of descent of approximately 600-800 feet per minute or as directed. For heading corrections after starting descent, recommended bank angle is 10°. Up to 3° heading corrections may be made by using rudder alone. When the controller announces "minimums have been reached", the pilot looks up. If the runway is not in sight, he immediately executes a missed approach. If the pilot has the runway in sight, he adjusts power to establish optimum angle-of-attack/airspeed and complete the landing.

GCA BOX PATTERN

To enter the GCA pattern from other than a penetration, contact Approach Control and proceed as follows. The downwing leg is flown at 230-250 knots CAS with gear and flaps retracted. The base leg is flown at 150 knots CAS with gear and flaps down. After completing the turn on final and slowing to 140 knots CAS, the normal GCA procedures apply. If entering the GCA pattern after a touch-and-go landing, aircraft will comply with Approach Control instructions.

TURBULENT AIR AND THUNDER-STORM OPERATION

Intentional flight through thunderstorms should be avoided, unless the urgency of the mission precludes a deviation from course, due to the high probability of damage to the airframe by impact ice, hail, and lightening. The radar provides an excellent means of navigating between or around storm cells and the airplane is capable of climbing over the top of small and moderately developed thunderstorms.

PENETRATION

If necessary to penetrate, the basic structure of the airplane is capable of withstanding the accelerations and gust loadings associated with the largest thunderstorms. The airplane is exceptionally stable and comparatively easy to control in the severe turbulence; however, the effects of turbulence becomes noticeably more abrupt and uncomfortable at airspeeds above optimum cruise and below 35,000 feet. The airplane is not displaced significantly from the intended flight path and desired heading. Altitude, airspeed, and attitude can be maintained with reasonable accuracy.

Penetration Airspeeds

The optimum thunderstorm penetration speeds, based on pilot comfort, controllability, and engine considerations are between optimum cruise and 280 knots CAS below 35,000 feet, and no less than 300 knots CAS above 35,000 feet. The afterburner should be utilized if necessary to maintain airspeed.

APPROACHING THE STORM

If the storm cannot be seen, it may be located by radar. Adjust power to establish the recommended approach speed. Note stabilator trim position. Place the pitot heat switch ON, the engine anti-ice switch to DE-ICE, and the autopilot OFF. The seat should be lowered to view the instruments and to minimize the buffeting due to turbulence. Do not try to top thunderstorms at subsonic speeds above 40,000 feet; the stall margin of both the airframe and engines becomes critical in this region. Flight through a thunderstorm at the proper airspeed and attitude is much more advantageous than "floundering" into the storm at a dangerously slow airspeed while attempting to reach the top. If the penetration is made at night, the daylight floodlights should be ON, and the console and instrument lights should be full bright.

IN THE STORM

Maintain a normal instrument scan with added emphasis on the attitude gyro (ADI). Attempt to maintain a constant pitch attitude and, if necessary, accept moderate altitude and airspeed fluctuations. In heavy precipitation, a reduction in engine rpm may be necessary due to the increased thrust resulting from water ingestion. If compressor stalls or engine stagnation develops, attempt to regain normal engine operation by momentarily retarding the throttle to IDLE then advance to the operating range. If the stall persists, shut down the engine and attempt a relight. If the engine remains stagnated at reduced power and the EGT is within limits, maintain reduced power until clear of the thunderstorm. While in the storm, the longitudinal feel trim, angle of attack, total temperature, windshield overheat, static pressure correction, and cabin pressurization systems may experience some abnormalities due to rain, ice, or hail damage. No difficulty should be encountered in maintaining control of the airplane; however, the rapid illumination of numerous warning lights may be somewhat distracting to the pilot if he is not prepared.

Longitudinal Feel Trim Failure

Longitudinal feel trim system failures are caused by ice blockage of the ram air bellows venturi located in the vertical fin. The failure is characterized by either a complete or intermittent failure of the feel system. The failure can also be verified by noting that the pointer on the stab trim indicator has moved from the previously noted position.

Angle of Attack System Failure

The angle of attack system may become temporarily inaccurate due to probe icing, or it may permanently fail due to structural damage of the probe from ice or hail. Icing of the probe is usually characterized by a zero angle of attack indication which returns to normal in clear air. Structural damage may cause erroneous readings or fail the system completely.

Total Temperature System Failure

The total temperature sensor may fail due to water or ice damage. This failure is characterized by a flashing or steady ENGINE INLET TEMP light, erroneous airspeed indications, and possible cycling of the engine intake ramps.

Windshield Overheat Sensor Failure

The windshield overheat sensor may fail in heavy rain or icing conditions. The failure is characterized by a steady W SHIELD TEMP HI light.

SPC Failure

The SPC system monitors off during thunderstorm penetrations between speeds of 0.93 to 1.0 Mach. Immediately prior to SPC disengagement, the altimeter, airspeed indicator, and vertical velocity indicator are highly erratic. Attempts to reset the SPC in precipitation is usually unsuccessful; however, the SPC can be reset for normal operation upon reaching clear air.

Cabin Pressurization System Failure

Cabin pressurization fluctuation occurs in precipitation above the freezing level. This is evidenced by a significant decrease in available cabin pressuriza-

tion flow and is caused by ice at the pressure suit heat exchanger.

ICE AND RAIN

The possibility of engine and/or airframe icing is always present when the airplane is operating under instrument conditions. Icing is most likely to occur when takeoffs must be made into low clouds with temperature at or near freezing. Normal flight operations are carried on above the serious icing levels, and the airplane's high performance capabilities usually enable the pilot to move out of the dangerous areas quickly. When an icing condition is encountered, immediate action should be taken to avoid further accumulation by changing altitude and/or course and increasing the rate of climb or airspeed. When icing conditions are anticipated, actuate the engine anti-ice switch to DE-ICE and the pitot heat switch ON.

WINDSHIELD RAIN REMOVAL

The following precautions must be observed when contemplating the use of the windshield rain removal system.

1. Do not operate on a dry windshield.
2. Turn system OFF immediately if W SHIELD TEMP HI indicator light illuminates.
3. Do not operate above Mach 1.0.

LONGITUDINAL FEEL TRIM

When flying through areas of precipitation, partial or complete failure of the longitudinal control artificial feel system may result due to ice and/or water blockage of the bellows ram air line. If this condition occurs, excessive stick force is required to maintain the desired airplane attitude. Since sudden longitudinal trim changes may occur several minutes after flying through freezing precipitation (especially during descent to altitudes below the freezing level), the application of corrective longitudinal trim when a blocked bellows inlet is suspected is not recommended.

AIR DATA COMPUTER

The air data computer may malfunction during flight through ice and/or due to impact forces imposed by water and ice on the ADC total temperature sensor. A momentarily flashing ENGINE INLET TEMP warning light usually indicates that the sensor probe has been blocked or shorted by ice accumulation.

HYDROPLANING

Operations on wet or flooded runways may produce three conditions under which tire traction may be reduced to an insignificant value. They are:

a. Dynamic hydroplaning
b. Viscous hydroplaning
c. Reverted rubber skids

DYNAMIC HYDROPLANING

As the tire velocity is increased, the hydrodynamic pressure acting on the leading portion of the tire footprint will increase to a value sufficient to support the vertical load acting on the tire. The speed at which this occurs is called total hydroplaning speed, and can be computed using the empirically derived relation $V_H = 9 \sqrt{p}$, where V_H is the total hydroplaning speed in knots and p is the tire inflation pressure in pounds per square inch. Any increase in ground speed above this critical value lifts the tire completely off the pavement, leaving it supported by the fluid alone. Since the fluid cushion is incapable of sustaining any appreciable shear forces, braking and sideforce coefficients become almost non-existent. Total hydroplaning speed of the F-4B main landing gear tires at 365 psi is 170 knots; the nose gear tire inflated to 125 psi is 100 knots.

VISCOUS HYDROPLANING

Viscous hydroplaning occurs due to the inability of the tire to penetrate the very thin fluid film found under damp runway conditions. This condition is aggravated when more viscous fluids such as oil, or road dust and water mixed are present, and is improved in the presence of a coarse textured runway surface. Viscous hydroplaning occurs at medium to high speed with rolling or skidding tires, and the speed at which it occurs is not dependent on tire pressure.

REVERTED RUBBER SKIDS

Reverted rubber skids occur after a locked-wheel skid has started on a wet runway, when enough heat may be produced to turn the entrapped water to steam. The steam in turn melts the rubber. The molten rubber forms a seal preventing the escape of water and steam. Thus the tire rides on a cushion of steam which greatly reduces the friction coefficient and may continue to do so to very low speeds.

EXTREME WEATHER PROCEDURES

COLD WEATHER OPERATION

PREFLIGHT

Check that the airplane is free of frost, snow, and ice. These accumulations present a major flight hazard resulting in loss of lift and increased stall speeds. Do not allow ice to be chipped or scraped from the airplane; damage to the airframe may result. Shock struts, actuating cylinders, pitot-static sources, and fuel vents should be inspected for ice and dirt accumulation. In addition to the above checks, the BLC duct tape (if applied) should be removed.

In addition to normal walk-around check that:

1. Shock struts, pitot tube, fuel vents, and actuating cylinders are free of ice or dirt.
2. Fuel drain cocks free of ice and drain condensation and insure that all pneumatic bottles have been adequately serviced.
3. All exterior covers and BLC duct tape (if applied) removed.
4. Closely inspect nozzle shroud flaps for any signs of ice deposits. If any ice is present apply heat to nozzle control feedback housing area for 5 to 10 minutes just prior to engine start.

INTERIOR CHECK

If the oxygen mask is not fastened, keep it well clear of the face to prevent freezing of the inhalation valves. Due to the bulk of arctic flying clothes, difficulty may be experienced in getting strapped in and in removing the face curtain safety pin. Assistance from the crew chief may be required.

ENGINE START

During engine start operation, depress ignition buttons at approximately 6% rpm; however, do not advance the throttles until approximately 10% rpm is reached. Depressing the ignition buttons prior to throttle advance dries out the igniter plugs, enhancing a successful start. If any abnormal sounds or noises are present during starting, discontinue starting and apply intake duct preheating for 10 to 15 minutes. Immediately after starting the engine at extremely low temperatures, the engine oil pressure indication becomes excessive and may peg out at 100 + psi. When this condition occurs, allow the oil to warm-up and the pressure to drop below 50 psi before placing the generator control switch to GEN ON. Insure that GEN OUT and BUS TIE OPEN lights go out. The maximum amount of time that the engine can run at IDLE rpm 100 + psi before discontinuing the start is; 2 minutes below 0°F, and 4 minutes below -30°F.

WARM-UP AND GROUND CHECK

If the airplane has been parked in heavy rain when subsequent freezing has been anticipated, a protective pressure-sensitive tape should have been applied to the trailing edge wing/flap junctures to prevent precipitation and ice from accumulating in the BLC ducts and valves. If the tape has not been applied and it is suspected that ice has formed in the ducts and valves, the flap actuating check should not be performed until the engines have been running for 12 to 15 minutes at 85% rpm. This permits hot BLC air to thaw any ice which may have accumulated in the BLC valves. After it is felt that the valves have been thawed:

1. Flap switch - CYCLE AND CHECK
   Actuate the flaps to the 1/2 and full down positions. Check that the BLC system is operating. Actuate the flaps to up and monitor the BLC MALFUNCTION light for a malfunction indication.

CAUTION

A BLC MALFUNCTION light illumination with flaps up or 1/2 constitutes a flight hazard. Refer to Boundary Layer Control Malfunction, section V of this manual.

Note

A BLC MALFUNCTION light with flaps in any position other than up or 1/2, indicates that the flap-up limit switches are not returning to their normal open position. By cycling the flaps three or four times to allow circulating hydraulic fluid to warm the actuators, the switches may be freed so that the BLC malfunction indicating system functions normally.

TAXIING

Avoid taxiing in deep or rutted snow; frozen brakes will probably result. Increase the interval between taxiing airplanes to insure a safe stopping distance and to prevent icing of the airplane surfaces by the snow and ice melted by the jet blast of the preceding airplane.

BEFORE TAKEOFF CHECK

During the engine runups, an ice-free area should be selected if possible. The engine thrust is noticeably greater at low temperatures and the probability of skidding the airplane is likely. If icing conditions are encountered or expected, place the engine anti-ice switch in DE-ICE and the pitot heat ON.

Note

If inflight freezing within the longitudinal control system is experienced, excessive stick forces may be required to move the control stick. Normal airplane control is available but requires higher force inputs. Normal control forces and AFCS operation returns at lower (warmer) altitudes.

LANDING

If snow and ice tires are installed, use brakes intermittently to keep the tire tread from filling and glazing. As soon as practicable after the landing roll the flaps should be placed full up. This shuts off the BLC air which otherwise causes the loose snow to swirl and be drawn in through the auxiliary air doors and pass along the engine. If this happens, the snow melts and deposits of ice form shortly after engine shut down. The ice can cause binding of the nozzle feedback housing and possible result in nozzle failure upon the next engine start.

AFTER LANDING

During operations where the temperature is below freezing with heavy rain, or expected to drop below freezing with heavy rain, the aircraft may be parked with wings spread and flaps full down.

BEFORE LEAVING AIRPLANE

Weather permitting, leave the canopy partially open to allow for air circulation. This helps to prevent canopy cracking from differential cooling and decreases the possibility of windshield and canopy frosting. Check that all protective covers are installed.

HOT WEATHER OPERATION

TAXIING

While taxiing in hot weather, the canopies may be opened, if necessary, to augment crew comfort. Do not operate the engines in a sand or dust storm if avoidable. Park the airplane crosswind and shut down the engines to minimize damage from sand or dust.

TAKEOFF

When operating from runways which are covered with excessive water, snow or slush, high-speed aborts may result in engine flame-out due to precipitation ingestion. The probability of flame-out is highest when throttles are chopped from afterburner to IDLE at speeds above 100 knots. With a double flame-out, normal braking, and nose gear steering is lost. After takeoff from runways covered with snow or slush, packed snow/slush in the auxiliary air door area may make throttle movement difficult until the snow/slush can be melted. Check applicable takeoff distance charts, part 2 of section XI.

FDB-1-(87)

SECTION VII COMMUNICATIONS PROCEDURES

TABLE OF CONTENTS

RADIO COMMUNICATIONS

GENERAL

It is the responsibility of the pilot to ensure that all radio and electronic transmissions from the aircraft are in compliance with applicable directives and squadron doctrine. It is mandatory that the pilot and RIO be thoroughly indoctrinated in all communications equipment, methods and procedures including hand signals. Radio communications will be in accordance with procedures set forth in NWIP 41-1A, NWP 41A, ACP 165, JANAP 119 and local fleet/shore instructions.

PILOT/RIO INTERCEPT COMMENTARY

DESCRIPTIVE COMMENTARY

Descriptive commentary is given in a specific order when existing conditions allow; i. e., azimuth, elevation, closing rate. Under certain conditions, it is impossible to give the description in the desired sequence since adhering rigidly to the sequence may interfere with positive control of target movement. The description of target action or position is normally given in a conversational tone of voice. Upon initial contact, the RIO will immediately start giving descriptive commentary. It is apparent that if the RIO gives "CONTACT" followed immediately by a range reading, the pilot is aware of the urgency or need of positive action by the RIO. The RIO also, upon initial contact, will give any directive commentary that is necessary to insure that the target does not exceed the limitations of the set. Descriptive commentary is not required to be particularly accurate at long ranges, but as the fighter approaches visual or attack range, the description must be accurate, and still not interfere with commands to the pilot. Sufficient descriptive commentary should be given to keep the pilot constantly informed of the position of the target in terms of azimuth angle, range, elevation angle, and overtaking speed.

Contact Report

Contact reports will be given to the controlling agency in the following manner:

"CONTACT" followed by AZIMUTH - Degrees followed by LEFT or RIGHT.

RANGE - Nearest mile

Example: CONTACT, 25 LEFT, 30 MILES.

Target Position Reporting

Position reports will be given in a specific order, i.e., azimuth angle, range, elevation angle, and overtaking speed. The following items shall be used:

AZIMUTH - Degrees followed by LEFT or RIGHT

RANGE - In miles (yards may be used when appropriate)

ELEVATION - Degrees followed by above, below, or level

OVERTAKING SPEED - Knots

Examples:

10 RIGHT, 8 MILES, LEVEL, OVERTAKE 300.
20 LEFT, 12 MILES, 5 ABOVE, OVERTAKE 50.

Judy

"JUDY" is given to the controlling agency when assuming responsibility and control of the intercept.

DIRECTIVE COMMENTARY

Directive commentary is divided into three categories and is used when the situation calls for a change of the aircraft's direction, speed, or elevation. A considerable amount of information as to the urgency may be obtained from the inflection of the RIO's voice as well as speed with which one command follows the other. Voice modulation properly employed gives flexibility to commentary. If the RIO places empha-

sis in his voice commands, he insures that the pilot hears each and every command and also causes the pilot to react accordingly. Directive commentary shall at all times take precedence over descriptive commentary. The pilot will also inform the RIO whenever the limitations of the aircraft are reached. Upon achieving a speed change, leveling off, or resuming straight and level flight, the pilot will inform the RIO with commentary such as "SPEED SET", "STEADY AND LEVEL", or "ALTITUDE SET".

Heading Change Commands

"EASY PORT" or "EASY STARBOARD"	15° angle of bank.
"PORT" or "STARBOARD"	30° angle of bank.
"PORT HARD" or "STARBOARD HARD"	45° angle of bank.
"HARD AS POSSIBLE"	Maximum possible turn, maintaining airspeed and altitude.
"EASE"	Roll out slowly toward steady.
"HOLD"	Maintain present bank angle.
"STEADY"	Roll out of turn.
"HARDER"	Increase angle of bank to next higher increment. Example: if at 30° angle of bank, pilot increases bank angle to 45°; if at 15° bank, increase to 30°, etc.
"WRAP IT UP"	Maximum possible turn within aircraft acceleration limitations.
"REVERSE"	Immediate identical turn in opposite direction.

Note

Turns may be given as a specific number of degrees. For example: "PORT HARD 40", etc.

Elevation Commands

"GO DOWN_____"	Descend a specified number of feet designated by RIO.
"CLIMB_____"	Climb as directed by RIO (GATE, BUSTER, or specified number of feet).
"NOSE-UP"/-"DOWN"	Change pitch angle until given "HOLD" by RIO. Leave throttles at same setting.
"DIVE"	Maximum rate descent until given "HOLD DIVE" by RIO or until maximum permissible rate of descent is established.
"LEVEL OFF"	Return to level flight.

Speed Commands

"BUSTER"	Full military power.
"GATE"	Maximum power.
"BUSTER____" or "GATE____"	Military or maximum power to CAS or indicated Mach number specified.
"SPEED UP____"	Increase airspeed by amount specified (CAS or IMN).
* "THROTTLE BACK_____"	Decrease speed by amount specified (CAS or IMN).
* "THROTTLE RIGHT BACK"	Decrease airspeed as rapidly as possible until minimum airspeed reached or RIO gives "HOLD SPEED".
"HOLD SPEED"	Maintain present airspeed.

*Speed is normally reduced as rapidly as possible utilizing speed brakes and/or throttles as appropriate.

Less Frequent Commands

"BREAK STARBOARD" or "BREAK PORT"

Immediate maximum possible turn, within aircraft acceleration limitations, in direction indicated.

"COMPASS RECOVERY"

Immediate, hard as possible, turn 30° beyond target's last known heading.

VISUAL COMMUNICATIONS

GENERAL

Communications between aircraft will be conducted visually whenever practicable, provided no sacrifice in operational efficiency is involved. Flight leaders shall ensure that all pilots in the formation receive and acknowledge signals when given. The visual communications section of NWP 41 must be reviewed and practiced by all pilots and RIO's. For ease of reference, visual signals applicable to flight operations are contained figure 7-1 and deck/ground handling signals are contained in figure 7-2.

VISUAL COMMUNICATIONS

GENERAL CONVERSATION

MEANING	SIGNAL	RESPONSE
Affirmative (I understand).	Thumb up, or nod of head.	
Negative (I do not know).	Thumb down, or turn of head from side to side.	
Question (repeat). Used in conjunction with another signal, this gesture indicates that the signal is interrogatory.	Hand cupped behind ear as if listening.	As appropriate.
Wait.	Hand held up with palm outward.	
Ignore last signal.	Hand waved in an erasing motion in front of face, with palm turned forward.	
Numerals, as indicated.	With forearm in vertical position, employ fingers to indicate desired numerals 1 through 5. With forearm and fingers horizontal, indicate number which, added to 5, gives desired number from 6 through 9. A clenched fist indicates zero.	A nod of the head (I understand). To verify numerals, addressee repeats. If originator nods, interpretation is correct. If originator repeats numerals, addressee should continue to verify them until they are understood.

CONFIGURATION CHANGES

MEANING	SIGNAL	RESPONSE
Lower landing gear.	Rotary movement of hand in cockpit, as if cranking wheels.	Execute.
Lower arresting gear hook.	Leader lowers hook.	Wingman lowers arresting gear hook. Leader indicates wingman's hook is down with thumb up signal.
Extend or retract flaps or speed brakes as appropriate.	Open and close four fingers and thumb.	

FUEL AND ARMAMENT

MEANING	SIGNAL	RESPONSE
How much fuel have you?	Raise fist with thumb extended in a drinking position.	Indicate fuel in hundreds of pounds by finger numbers.
1—Arm or safety missiles as applicable; 2—how much ammo do you have? 3—I am unable to fire.	1—Pistol cocking motion with either hand; 2—followed by question signal; 3—followed by nose-held signal.	1—Execute and return signal; 2—thumb up, over half; down, less than half; 3—nod head (I understand).
1—Arm or safety tanks as applicable; 2—how many tanks do I have? 3—I am unable to drop.	1—Shaking fist; 2—followed by question signal; 3—followed by nose-held signal.	1—Execute and return signal; 2—indicate with appropriate finger numerals; 3—nod head (I understand).

FDB-1-(88-1)

Figure 7-1 (Sheet 1 of 2)

VISUAL COMMUNICATIONS

FORMATION

MEANING	SIGNAL	RESPONSE
1) I have completed my takeoff check list and am, in all respects ready for takeoff; 2) I have completed my takeoff check list and am, in all respects, ready for a section takeoff; 3) Takeoff path is clear, I am commencing takeoff.	1) Section takeoff leader raises arm (either) over head; 2) Wingman raises arm over head; 3) Leader lowers arm.	1) Stands by for reply from wingman, holding arm over head until answered; 2) Wingman lowers arm and stands by for immediate section takeoff; 3) Executes section takeoff.
Leader shifting lead to wingman. (Day)	Leader pats self on head points to wingman.	Wingman pats head and assumes lead.
Leader shifting lead to wingman. (Night)	1) Two aircraft — lead aircraft puts external lights on bright and flash. 2) More than two aircraft — leader places flight in echelon and then use two aircraft procedures.	Wingman turns external lights to DIM and STEADY and assumes lead.
	3) With external light failure — leader shines flashlight on hardhat, then shines at Wingman.	Wingman turns external lights to DIM and STEADY and assumes lead. With external light failure — Wingman shines flashlight at leader, then on his hardhat.
Leader shifting lead to division designated by numerals.	Leader pats self on head points to wingman and holds up two or more fingers.	Wingman relays signal; division leader designated assumes lead.
Take cruising formation.	Thumb waved backward over the shoulder.	Execute.
I am leaving formation.	Any pilot blow kiss.	Nod (I understand).
Aircraft pointed out leave formation.	Leader blows kiss and points to aircraft.	Execute.
Directs plane to investigate object or vessel.	Leader beckons wing plane, then points to eye, then to vessel or object.	Wingman indicated blows kiss and executes.
Refers to landing of aircraft, generally used in conjunction with another signal; 1) I am landing; 2) Directs indicated aircraft to land.	Landing motion with open hand: 1) Followed by patting head; 2) Followed by pointing to another aircraft.	1) Execute; 2) Execute.
a) Join up or break up, as appropriate. b) On GCA/CCA final: Leader has runway/ship in sight.	Flashing external lights.	a) Comply. b) Wingman repeats, indicating runway/ship in sight. Ship: Leader waves-off wingman lands. Field: When runway conditions preclude a safe section landing leader will wave-off.
Leader desires wingman to cross under to other side.	Arm held vertically with clinched fist against canopy.	Wingman executes. Section lead — maintains position or allows Number 2 to slide into position as appropriate.
Leader desires section to cross to other side.	Arm held vertically with clinched fist and pumps up and down.	Number 2 wingman maintains position. Section executes.

FORMATION SIGNALS MADE BY AIRCRAFT MANEUVER

COMBAT OR FREE CRUISE

MEANING	SIGNAL	RESPONSE
Single aircraft cross under in direction of wing dip.	Single wing dip.	Execute.
Section cross under.	Double wing dip.	Execute.
Close up.	Series of small zooms.	Execute.
Join up; join up on me.	Series of pronounced zooms.	Expedite join-up.

FDB-1-(88-2)

Figure 7-1 (Sheet 2 of 2)

DECK/GROUND HANDLING SIGNALS

ACKNOWLEDGEMENT

A CLENCHED FIST WITH THUMB POINTING STRAIGHT UP INDICATES SATISFACTORY COMPLETION OF A CHECK ITEM. A CLENCHED FIST WITH THUMB POINTING STRAIGHT DOWN INDICATES UNSATISFACTORY COMPLETION AND/OR DO NOT CONTINUE.

INSERT/PULL EXTERNAL AIR

PILOT INSERTS/PULLS INDEX FINGER TO/FROM OPEN PALM, SIGNALMAN RESPONDS WITH SAME SIGNAL.

INSERT/PULL ELECTRICAL POWER

PILOT INSERTS/PULLS INDEX AND MIDDLE FINGER TO/FROM OPEN PALM, SIGNALMAN RESPONDS WITH SAME SIGNAL.

GROUND INTERCOM

CUP HANDS OVER EARS OR POINT WANDS TO EARS.

START ENGINES

PILOT EXTENDS FINGERS TO INDICATE WHICH ENGINE IS READY FOR START. IF ALL CLEAR, SIGNALMAN RESPONDS WITH SIMILAR GESTURE POINTING AT PROPER ENGINE WHILE ROTATING OTHER HAND IN CLOCKWISE MOTION.

ENGINE RUN-UP

PILOT MOVES INDEX FINGER IN CIRCULAR MOTION INDICATING HE IS READY TO RUN UP ENGINES. SIGNALMAN RESPONDS WITH SIMILAR SIGNAL WHEN ALL CLEAR.

CUT ENGINES

HAND DRAWN ACROSS NECK IN "THROAT CUTTING" MOTION.

PULL CHOCKS

PILOT MAKES SWEEPING MOTION OF FISTS WITH THUMBS EXTENDED OUTWARD. SIGNALMAN SWEEPS FISTS APART AT HIP LEVEL WITH THUMBS EXTENDED OUTWARD.

NEED PNEUMATIC SYSTEM CHARGING

PILOT HOLDS HAND PALM UP IN FRONT OF MOUTH AND SIMULATES BLOWING ON HAND.

AM I CLEAR UNDERNEATH

WITH LEFT HAND OPEN, PALM OUT, PILOT MAKES SWEEPING MOTION ACROSS COCKPIT FROM RIGHT TO LEFT.

LOWER WING FLAPS

HANDS FLAT TOGETHER, THEN OPENED WIDE FROM WRISTS. ARMS IN CLOSE TO BODY.

HALF FLAPS

LOWER HALF FLAPS FOR BLC CHECK.

RAISE WING FLAPS

HANDS, OPENED WIDE FROM WRIST, SUDDENLY CLOSED, ARMS IN CLOSE TO BODY.

FOLD WINGS

ARMS, FROM STRAIGHT OUT SWEPT IN TO HUG SHOULDER.

WING LOCK

EXTEND ARM TO SIDE, LEVEL WITH SHOULDER. BEND ARM UPWARD, AND SLAP ELBOW.

SPREAD WINGS

ARMS IN HUGGING POSITION, THEN SWEPT OUT TO SIDES.

FDB-1-(89-1)

Figure 7-2 (Sheet 1 of 3)

Figure 7-2   (Sheet 2 of 3)

FDB-1-(89-2)

COME AHEAD
HANDS AT EYE LEVEL, EXECUTE BECK-ONING MOTION, RATE OF MOTIONS INDICATES DESIRED SPEED OF AIR-CRAFT. FOR NIGHT OPERATION, WAVE WANDS SIDE TO SIDE.

RIGHT TURN
PULL DESIRED WING AROUND WITH REGULAR "COME AHEAD"-POINT AT OPPOSITE BRAKE.

LEFT TURN
PULL DESIRED WING AROUND WITH REGULAR "COME AHEAD"-POINT AT OPPOSITE BRAKE.

TURNOVER OF COMMAND
BOTH HANDS POINTED AT NEXT SUCCEEDING TAXI SIGNALMAN.

SLOW DOWN
DOWNWARD PATTING MOTION, HANDS OUT AT WAIST LEVEL.

STOP
ARMS UPRAISED, FISTS CLENCHED AND HELD IN SIMPLE "POLICEMAN'S STOP".

EMERGENCY STOP
ARMS CROSSED ABOVE HEAD, FISTS CLENCHED.

HOT BRAKES
MAKE RAPID FANNING MOTION WITH ONE HAND IN FRONT OF FACE. POINT TO WHEEL WITH OTHER HAND.

ENGINE FIRE
DESCRIBE A LARGE FIGURE EIGHT WITH ONE HAND AND POINT TO THE FIRE AREA WITH THE OTHER HAND.

DRAG CHUTE
RELEASE DRAG CHUTE OR CHECK DRAG CHUTE HANDLE POSITION.

GROUND REFUELING ALL TANKS, NO EXTERNAL POWER
CIRCULAR MOTION PARALLEL TO THE HORIZON WITH HAND EXTENDED FOLLOWED BY A DRINKING MOTION (THUMB TO MOUTH)

GROUND REFUELING INTERNAL TANKS, NO EXTERNAL POWER
CIRCULAR MOTION WITH THE PALM OF HAND TOWARD STOMACH (AS RUBBING STOM-ACH), FOLLOWED BY A DRINK-ING MOTION (THUMB TO MOUTH)

NIGHT SIGNALS

NIGHT SIGNALS ARE THE SAME AS DAY SIGNALS EXCEPT AS NOTED. FLASHLIGHTS OR WANDS WILL SUBSTITUTE FOR HAND AND FINGER MOVEMENTS DURING NIGHT OPERATIONS.

CARRIER FLIGHT DECK PERSONNEL COLOR CODING

RED SHIRTS —ORDNANCE, FUEL HANDLING and CRASH CREW
YELLOW SHIRTS—PRI FLY, PLANE DIRECTORS, CATAPULT OFFICER and ARRESTMENT OFFICER
BLUE SHIRTS —PLANE HANDLERS (Pushers, Chock Men, etc.)

GREEN SHIRTS —AIRCRAFT MAINTENANCE, CATAPULT CREW, ARRESTMENT CREW
BROWN SHIRTS—PLANE CAPTAINS
WHITE SHIRTS —MEDICAL

FDB-1-(89-3)

Figure 7-2. (Sheet 3 of 3)

SECTION VIII
WEAPONS SYSTEMS

FDB-1-(90)

TABLE OF CONTENTS

AIRBORNE MISSILE CONTROL SYSTEM

Refer to section VIII, classified supplement.

BOMBING EQUIPMENT

Refer to NAVAIR 01-245FDB-1T for description and operation of the bombing equipment.

DATA LINK SYSTEM

Refer to section VIII, Classified Supplement.

DIRECT RADAR SCOPE CAMERA

Refer to section VIII, Classified Supplement.

ELECTRONIC COUNTERMEASURES EQUIPMENT

NOTICE
Some illustrations referred to within this system writeup may be located in appendix A.
These illustrations are referred to, within the text, as (figure A-, appendix A).

DESCRIPTION

The aircraft can be equipped with various countermeasures equipment which includes the chaff dispenser set MX-900, the chaff dispenser set AN/ALE-29A, the countermeasures sets AN/ALQ-51A/100/126, the countermeasures set AN/ALQ-91, the interrogator set AN/APX-76A, the radar homing and warning set AN/APR-25, the radar receiving set AN/APR-27, the speed security unit KY-28, the countermeasures receiving set AN/ALR-45(V), and the radar receiving set AN/ALR-50(V).

COUNTERMEASURES RECEIVING SET (AN/ALR-45)

On aircraft after AFC 524, provisions for the installation of the countermeasures receiving set AN/ALR-45(V) are provided. Refer to Supplement to Tactical Manual, NAVAIR 01-245FDB-1T(A) for description and operation.

COUNTERMEASURES SETS (AN/ALQ-51A/100)

Aircraft after AFC 333 or AFC 375 part II have the capability of having the countermeasures set AN/ALQ-51A or the countermeasures set AN/ALQ-100 installed. Refer to the Supplement to Tactical Manual, NAVAIR 01-245FDA-1T(A) for description and operation.

COUNTERMEASURES SET (AN/ALQ-91)

On aircraft after AFC 339 or on aircraft after AFC 296 and AFC 334, the countermeasures set AN/ALQ-91 is installed. Countermeasures set radar scope displays are provided on radar systems after AVC 664. Refer to the Supplement to Tactical Manual, NAVAIR 01-245FDB-1T(A) for description and operation.

COUNTERMEASURES SET (AN/ALQ-126)

On aircraft after AFC 541, the countermeasures set AN/ALQ-126 may be installed in place of the countermeasures set AN/ALQ-51A/100. Refer to the Supplement to Tactical Manual, NAVAIR 01-245FDB-1T(A), for description and operation.

INTERROGATOR SET (AN/APX-76A)

On aircraft after AFC 352 or AFC 539, the interrogator set AN/APX-76A is installed. Interrogator set radar scope displays are provided on radar systems after AVC 664. Refer to the Supplement to Tactical Manual, NAVAIR 01-245FDB-1T(A) for description and operation.

RADAR HOMING AND WARNING SET (AN/APR-25)

On aircraft after AFC 375, the radar homing and warning set AN/APR-25 is installed. Refer to the Supplement to Tactical Manual, NAVAIR 01-245FDB-1T(A) for description and operation.

RADAR RECEIVING SET (AN/ALR-50)

On aircraft after AFC 524, provisions for the installation of the radar receiving set AN/ALR-50(V) are provided. Refer to Supplement to Tactical Manual, NAVAIR 01-245FDB-1T(A) for description and operation.

RADAR RECEIVING SET (AN/APR-27)

On aircraft after AFC 296 or AFC 339, provisions for installing the radar receiving set AN/APR-27 are provided. Refer to the Supplement to Tactical Manual, NAVAIR 01-245FDB-1T(A) for description and operation.

SPEECH SECURITY UNIT (KY-28)

On aircraft after AFC 331, a speech security unit KY-28 is provided. Refer to the Supplement to Tactical Manual, NAVAIR 01-245FDB-1T(A) for description and operation.

DESTRUCT CIRCUITS

Certain electronic countermeasures (ECM) equipment, including the radar receiving set AN/APR-27, the countermeasures set AN/ALQ-91, and the countermeasures set AN/ALQ-100, have various destruct circuit provisions depending on the incorporated AFC. On aircraft after AFC 333, the radar receiving set AN/APR-27, if installed, is automatically destroyed whenever the pilot ejects, or an impact box initiates set destruction whenever the aircraft experiences a 50 G acceleration force. The aircraft altitude must be less than 20,000 feet and the landing gear must be up to complete the destruct circuits. On aircraft after AFC 334 or AFC 339, the countermeasures set AN/ALQ-91 may be destroyed by one of two methods. Set destruction is initiated whenever the pilot ejects or when the destruct switch on the interim control panel is ON, provided the nose landing gear is up. On aircraft after AFC 334 or AFC 339 with AFC 386, an impact box is added to the destruct circuits and the destruct switch on the interim control panel is replaced with a destruct safety switch. On these aircraft, provided the landing gear is up and the destruct circuit is armed (safety pin removed from destruct safety switch), an impact box initiated AN/ALQ-91 set destruction whenever the aircraft experiences a 50 G acceleration force. Set destruction is also initiated when the pilot ejects, provided the aircraft altitude is less than 20,000 feet, the destruct circuit is armed, and the landing gear is up. On aircraft after AFC 334 or AFC 339 with AFC 333 or

☆ U.S. GOVERNMENT PRINTING OFFICE: 1972--769646/1020   **Changed 15 August 1972**

AFC 375 part II, the interim control panel is replaced with the integrated control panel. On aircraft with AFC 333, the destruct switch is inoperative and AN/ALQ-91 set destruction may be initiated only by the impact box, provided the landing gear is up. On the aircraft with AFC 375 part II, with the AN/ALQ-91 set installed, set destruction may be initiated by two methods. Set destruction is initiated whenever the aircraft experiences a 50 G acceleration force, provided the destruct circuit is armed (safety pin pulled on integrated control panel) and the landing gear is up. The set is also destroyed whenever the pilot ejects, provided the aircraft altitude is less than 20,000 feet, the destruct circuit is armed, and the landing gear is up. On aircraft after AFC 390 (incorporated on aircraft after AFC 386 or on aircraft after AFC 333 with AFC 334 or AFC 339), an AN/ALQ-91 safe arm control panel is added. On aircraft after AFC 390 with AFC 386, the AN/ALQ-91 set destruction is initiated whenever the pilot ejects, provided the aircraft altitude is less than 20,000 feet, the destruct safety switch on the interim control panel is in ARM, the landing gear is up, and the manual arm switch on the safety switch panel is in ARM. The impact box initiates set destruction whenever the aircraft experiences a 50 G acceleration force provided the destruct safety switch is positioned to ARM, the landing gear is up, and the manual arm switch is positioned to ARM. On aircraft after AFC 390 with AFC 333, only the impact box initiates the AN/ALQ-91 set destruction, provided the landing gear is up and the manual arm switch is positioned to ARM. On aircraft after AFC 401, an AN/ALQ-91/100 manual arm switch is provided on the safety switch panel and the safety switch is removed from the integrated control panel. On these aircraft, AN/ALQ-91 set destruction is initiated whenever the pilot ejects, provided the aircraft altitude is less than 20,000 feet, the landing gear is up, and the AN/ALQ-91/100 manual arm switch is positioned to ARM. Also, an impact box initiates set destruction whenever the aircraft experiences a 50 G acceleration force, provided the landing gear is up and the AN/ALQ-91/100 manual arm switch is positioned to ARM. The countermeasures set AN/ALQ-100 also has various destruct capabilities depending on the particular AFC. The destruct circuits are the same as the AN/ALQ-91 set destruct circuits for the applicable AFC.

CHAFF DISPENSER SET MX-900

On aircraft with AFC 233, the bomb control monitor panel on the right console in the forward cockpit is removed and replaced by a chaff dispenser control panel for the chaff dispenser MX-900. The panel contains a dispensing rate selector knob which determines the rate at which the chaff is released from the dispenser. There is also a dispensing selector switch with positions of DISP, OFF, and HOLD. Placing the switch to DISP causes the chaff to begin dispensing. The OFF (center) position is used when all packages have been dispensed, or when more than one dispensing run is required and level flight is expected. The HOLD position is used when more than one dispensing run is required and maneuvering flight is expected, or when some chaff packages have not been dispensed and the airplane is going to land. The

dispenser can dispense from one package every 3 seconds to four packages every 1 second. The rate depends on the type materials from which the chaff is made.

CHAFF DISPENSER SET AN/ALE-29A

On aircraft after AFC 333 or AFC 375 part II, the AN/ALE-29A chaff dispenser set is installed in the aircraft. The set ejects countermeasure materials into the air to enable the aircraft to evade an air-to-air attack. The countermeasure materials consist of metallic chaff packages or flares contained within plastic cartridges. The cartridges are carried in the discharge tubes of the two dispensers mounted beneath hydraulic operated doors in either side of the fuselage in the area above the wing flaps. There are 30 tubes in each dispenser. The countermeasure materials are ejected from the cartridges by electrical signals controlled by the RIO. On aircraft after AFC 448, an AN/ALE-29A singles chaff button is provided in the front cockpit and countermeasures material may also be ejected by the pilot. The countermeasure material may be ejected in single or multiple salvos. A salvo consists of a series of burst ejected at specific intervals. Provisions are also provided for ejecting a single burst within a salvo. The salvo or salvos can be ejected from a single dispenser or simultaneously from both dispensers. Salvos with a single burst interspersed within the salvo can be ejected from a single dispenser, or salvos can be ejected from one dispenser while single bursts are ejected from the other dispenser. If one dispenser empties in the middle of a salvo sequence or if an empty dispenser is selected for a single salvo, the system cascades to the loaded dispenser from which the remaining bursts of the salvos or the single salvo are ejected. The number of salvos, time interval between salvos, number of burst per salvo, time interval between bursts, and the desired dispensers are selected by controls in the rear cockpit. Upon ejection, the chaff disperses aft of the aircraft to confuse and lessen the effectiveness of the enemy radar. The flares ignite aft of the aircraft to deceive heat-seeking (infrared) sensor devices. Controls and indicators for the chaff dispenser set are on the integrated control panel and programmer control panel in the rear cockpit (right console). On aircraft after AFC 448, a singles chaff button is installed on the right throttle control in the front cockpit.

INTEGRATED CONTROL PANEL

The integrated control panel (figure A-4, appendix A) provides the following controls and indicators: the dispenser selector knob, the single salvo selector button, the auto salvo selector button, the PORT and STBD doors open lights, and two cartridge counters.

Dispenser Selector Knob

This knob has four positions; OFF, PORT, STBD, and BOTH. When set to a position other than OFF, the knob provides electrical power to simultaneously open both dispenser doors. When both doors are fully opened, the PORT and STBD doors open lights illuminate. Placing the dispenser selector to PORT, STBD, or BOTH provides selection of the chaff dispensers for chaff or flare ejection.

Single Salvo Selector Button

This button is pressed to initiate ejection of one salvo of chaff or flares from either chaff dispenser depending on whether the dispenser selector knob is placed to PORT or STBD. If the knob is placed to BOTH, each dispenser ejects a single salvo of chaff or flares simultaneously. The number of bursts within the salvo and the interval between the bursts is determined by the settings of the burst selector knob and the burst interval selector knob on the programmer control panel.

Auto Salvo Selector Button

This button is pressed to initiate automatic ejection of chaff or flares in salvos. The number of salvos is determined by the setting of the salvo selector knob, and the quantity of bursts in each salvo is determined by the position of the burst selector knob. These knobs are on the programmer control panel.

Cartridge Counters

Two counters, labeled PORT and STBD, count down from the initial quantity of 30 cartridges to indicate the remaining number of unfired cartridges in each chaff dispenser. These counters are reset before flight.

PROGRAMMER CONTROL PANEL

The programmer control panel (figure A-4, appendix A) provides the following controls: the bursts selector knob, the burst interval selector knob, the salvo selector knob, the salvo interval selector knob, and the reset switch. The controls on the panel allow selection of the quantity of cartridges to be fired and the interval between ejections.

Bursts Selector Knob

The positions of 1, 2, 3, 4, and C (continuous) determine the quantity of chaff packages or flares ejected during one salvo. Selecting C permits continuous dispensing of individual bursts at the rate shown on the burst interval switch. Dispensing continues until all chaff has been expended or until the dispenser selector knob is positioned OFF. With the burst selector knob in C, the position of the salvo and salvo interval knobs are meaningless.

Burst Interval Selector Knob

The positions of .2, .3, .4, and .5 determine the interval in seconds between ejection of each chaff package or flare within a salvo.

Salvos Selector Knob

The positions of 4, 8, 12, 16, 20, 24, 28, and C determine the number of salvos ejected with each actuation of the auto salvo selector button. Selecting C

permits continuous dispensing of salvos. Dispensing continues until all chaff has been expended or until the dispenser selector knob is positioned OFF. With the salvo selector knob in C, the number of bursts per salvo, the burst interval, and the salvo interval can still be programmed.

Salvo Interval Selector Knob

The positions of 2, 4, 6, 8, 10, 12, and 14 determine the interval in seconds between ejection of salvos.

Reset Switch

Actuating this switch resets the sequencing switches to the number one position. In flight, the landing gear handle must be up. On the ground, the electrical power must be on and the armament override switch pressed.

AN/ALE-29A SINGLES CHAFF BUTTON

On aircraft after AFC 448, an AN/ALE-29A singles chaff button is provided on the right throttle control. This provides the pilot with the capability of dispensing countermeasures material. The button parallels the single salvo selector button on the programmer control panel and initiates the same functions when actuated.

NORMAL OPERATION

CHAFF DISPENSER SET (MX-900)

The operation of the chaff dispenser is accomplished as follows:

1. Master armament switch - ON
2. Dispensing rate selector knob - DESIRED DISPENSING RATE
3. Dispensing selector switch - DISP
   This is only setting necessary to begin dispensing chaff material
4. Leave switch in DISP for time necessary to dispense chaff packages.

CAUTION

Do not leave the dispensing selector switch in the DISP position after the dispenser is emptied.

Note

Station 5 of the airplane is the only station that is compatible with the MX-900 chaff dispenser.

CHAFF DISPENSER SET (AN/ALE-29A)

The countermeasures chaff dispenser set is turned on by placing the dispenser selector knob to any position other than to OFF. This opens both dispenser doors and enables the firing circuits of the selected dispenser if PORT or STBD is selected, or enables both firing circuits if BOTH is selected. When both dispenser doors are fully opened, the PORT and STBD doors open lights illuminate, and the safety interlock relays energize to provide cascade operation of the dispensers. Countermeasures material can then be deployed manually by utilizing the single salvo selector button or singles chaff button, or it may be deployed automatically by utilizing the auto salvo selector button.

CAUTION

Do not actuate the reset switch when safety pins are installed in the chaff dispenser doors as the set will become inoperative due to diodes burning out in the sequencing switches.

Note

Ensure that the dispenser door open lights are illuminated, indicating that the dispenser doors are open, before attempting to dispense the chaff.

Manual Operation

After a dispenser has been selected with the dispenser selector knob and the dispenser doors are fully opened, a single salvo of countermeasures material can be fired by pressing the single salvo selector button or singles chaff button. If the selected dispenser is empty, the system cascades to the loaded dispenser and the salvo is fired from that dispenser. If both dispensers are selected, a single salvo is fired from each dispenser. Selecting C with the burst selector knob permits continuous dispensing of countermeasures material at the rate selected on the burst interval knob. Continuous dispensing can only be terminated by positioning the dispenser selector knob OFF. The appropriate cartridge counter indicates a cartridge has been fired by showing the remaining unfired cartridges in the dispenser. Placing the dispenser selector knob OFF causes both dispenser doors to close and the countermeasures set to turn off.

Automatic Operation

To fire automatically, the number of bursts per salvo are selected by positioning the bursts selector knob, the interval between bursts on the burst interval selector knob, the number of salvos on the salvos selector knob, and the interval between salvos on the salvo interval selector knob. Selecting C with the bursts selector knob permits continuous dispensing

of individual bursts at the rate shown on the burst interval switch. Dispensing continues until all chaff has been expended or until the dispenser selector knob is positioned OFF. The position of the salvo and salvo interval switches are meaningless with the burst selector knob in the C position. Selecting C with the salvo selector knob also permits continuous dispensing of salvos. Dispensing continues until all chaff has been expended or until the dispenser selector knob is positioned OFF. With the salvo selector knob in C, the number of bursts per salvo, the burst interval, and the salvo interval is established by their respective switch positions. The set is then turned on by selecting a dispenser with the dispenser selector knob. After checking that the PORT and STBD lights are illuminated, the selected salvos are ejected by pressing the auto salvo selector button. If the selected dispenser empties during a salvo, the system cascades to the other dispenser from which the remaining bursts in the salvo or salvos are ejected. If both dispensers are selected, the selected number of salvos are ejected from both dispensers. If a single burst interspersed within a selected automatic salvo sequence is desired, pressing the single salvo selector button during the sequence causes a burst to be ejected from the selected dispenser. If it is desired to eject a single burst from the nonselected dispenser during an automatic salvo sequence, select the other dispenser with the dispenser selector knob and press the single salvo selector button. Pressing the single salvo selector button during an automatic sequence with both dispensers selected ejects a single burst from each dispenser. During any of the above sequences the system automatically cascades to the loaded dispenser if one dispenser empties, and the counters count each fired cartridge to indicate the number of unfired cartridges in each dispenser. After the desired sequence is completed, the dispenser doors are closed and the set is turned off by placing the dispenser selector knob OFF.

EMERGENCY OPERATION

There are no special provisions for emergency operation of the chaff dispenser.

LIMITATIONS

Extended flight time with the dispenser doors open may result in damage to the aircraft skin aft of the doors. Flight time with the doors open should be limited unless tactical requirements dictate otherwise.

GUNNERY EQUIPMENT

Refer to NAVAIR 01-245FDB-1T for description and operation of the gunnery equipment.

STRIKE CAMERA SYSTEM

— NOTICE —
Some illustrations referred to within this system writeup may be located in appendix A.
These illustrations are referred to, within the text, as (figure A-, appendix A).

DESCRIPTION

After AFC 518, the airplane is equipped with a strike camera system. The system consists of a camera pod LB-30A mounted in the left forward fuselage missile cavity. The camera pod contains a panoramic camera KB-18B and a forward looking motion picture camera KB-19A. The panoramic camera provides continuous film documentation of the strike area throughout an air-to-ground armament delivery. The forward looking camera provides motion picture coverage of the area forward of the aircraft along the boresight line during air-to-air or air-to-ground armament delivery. Both cameras operate simultaneously when energized by automatic or manual control circuits.

KB-18B CAMERA

The KB-18B camera components contained in the pod are the camera body with an accessory magazine LB-29A, and a camera control LB-17A. The camera has a 3-inch focal length f/2.8 lens. The shutter speeds range from approximately 1/100 second to 1/4000 second depending on limits established by a cycle rate switch and an aerial exposure index (AEI) switch. The accessory magazine accommodates 250 feet of film (300 exposures) and produces photographs with a format size of 2.25 by 9.40 inches. Panoramic photography is accomplished by rotating a double dove prism in front of the lens while the film is advanced across a narrow slit at the focal plane of the camera. Film advance is synchronized with prism rotation, projecting the panoramic image of the strike area on the film as the prism scans 180° fore and aft. Side coverage is 20° either side of the airplane vertical axis. The automatic exposure control senses variations in the light source and initiates compensatory aperture adjustments. The camera control contains switches for ground testing the camera and preselecting camera operating functions required for the mission. The controls include the ground test switch, cycle rate switch, overrun dial, and the AEI switch.

Overrun Dial

The overrun dial setting determines the time the camera will run (automatic mode only) after the trigger switch or bomb button is released. Dial settings are calibrated in 2-second increments from 0 to 20 seconds plus an additional setting of 32 seconds.

Cycle Rate Switch

The cycle rate switch permits selection of 1, 2, or 4 frames per second during camera operation. The switch is set in accordance with the planned mission altitude/airspeed combination.

AEI Switch

The AEI switch is set as determined by the type of film in the camera. Film speeds (exposure sensitivity) of 40, 64, 80, or 200 are selectable.

KB-19A CAMERA

The KB-19A camera mounted in the forward fairing of the pod, provides 16mm motion picture coverage of the area forward of the aircraft along the boresight line. The film magazine attached to the camera contains 100 feet of film. An automatic exposure control (AEC) controls the shutter sector opening to assure proper exposure.

Overrun Switch

The overrun switch controls the time the camera continues to operate after trigger or bomb button release and provides the following overrun selections: 0, 5, 10, or 15 seconds. An overrun indicator light marks the film at the release of the trigger or bomb button and continues marking until completion of the overrun period.

Test Switch

The test switch on the rear of the camera is utilized by the ground crew to test operation of the camera.

STRIKE CAMERA CONTROL PANEL

The strike camera control panel on the left console (figure A-2, appendix A), controls the operating modes of the strike camera system. The panel labeled CAMERAS contains a mode switch and a PAN OPERATE light. The mode switch has three positions: OFF, AUTO, and MANUAL. With the mode switch in AUTO, when the armament circuits are energized and the pilot presses the trigger switch or the bomb button the cameras begin operating. When the trigger switch or bomb button is released the cameras continue operating for the preselected overrun time. MANUAL is a momentary position and the cameras operate as long as the switch is held in MANUAL. The manual mode does not involve the armament systems and enables film coverage of specific terrain without armament delivery. The PAN OPERATE light blinks on for each cycle of operation of the KB-18B camera (i.e., illuminates during each panoramic scan and extinguishes between scans). If a film failure occurs or the film supply is exhausted in the KB-18B camera, the PAN OPERATE ceases to blink. This light may be tested by pressing the light.

NORMAL OPERATION

With the camera mode switch in AUTO, the cameras operate automatically during armament delivery; i.e., with the specific arming circuits energized, both cameras operate when the trigger switch or bomb button is pressed. Furthermore, camera operation continues for the preselected overrun time. The pilot may operate the cameras without expending armament by holding the mode switch in MANUAL.

EMERGENCY OPERATION

There are no special provisions for emergency operation of the strike camera system.

LIMITATIONS

No limitations have been established.

FDB-1-(91)

SECTION IX
FLIGHT CREW COORDINATION

PILOT/RIO RESPONSIBILITIES

GENERAL

The duties of the Pilot/RIO team are necessarily integrated, and each must support and contribute to the performance of the other. In this section, specific responsibilities are delineated; however, in the event of aircraft system malfunction, emergency, or unfamiliar circumstances where assistance is desired, cooperation and initiative become paramount. The pilot is the aircraft commander and is responsible for the successful completion of any mission assigned to his aircraft. The RIO should constitute an extension of the pilot's observation facilities. By intercommunication, the RIO should anticipate rather than await developments. A challenge and reply system will be used between pilot and RIO when using the checklist.

SPECIFIC RESPONSIBILITIES

FLIGHT PLANNING

Pilot

The pilot shall be responsible for the preparation of required charts, flight logs, navigation computations including fuel planning, checking weather and NOTAMS, and for filing required flight plans.

RIO

The RIO, when directed by the pilot, shall be required to prepare charts, flight logs, navigation computations including fuel planning, checking

NOTAMS, and obtaining weather for filing purposes, and for completing required flight plans.

BRIEFING

Pilot

The pilot/flight leader is responsible for briefing all crewmembers on all aspects of the mission to be flown.

RIO

The RIO shall assist the pilot/flight leader in preparing required flight or briefing forms and may, if applicable, brief that portion of the mission pertaining to the RIO.

PREFLIGHT

Pilot

The pilot is responsible for accepting and preflighting the aircraft assigned in accordance with this manual and appropriate preflight checklists contained in the F-4B NATOPS Pocket Checklist (NAVAIR 01-245FDB-1B).

RIO

The RIO shall assist the pilot as directed but in any case will be capable of, and proficient in, performing a complete aircraft preflight, including all armament. Normally, the preflight inspection is conducted with the pilot.

PRESTART

Pilot

The pilot shall execute pre-start checks prescribed by the NATOPS Pocket Checklist and, when external power is applied and checks requiring external power are completed, shall inform the RIO PRE-START CHECKS COMPLETED - READY TO START.

RIO

The RIO shall execute pre-start checks prescribed by the NATOPS Pocket Checklist and, when external power is applied, shall inform the pilot PRE-START CHECKS COMPLETE.

STARTING

Pilot

The pilot shall start engines as prescribed in part 3 of section III and shall keep the RIO informed of any unusual occurrences.

RIO

The RIO shall remain alert for any emergency signals from the ground crew and shall inform the pilot if such signals are observed.

POSTSTART

Pilot

After switching to internal power, the pilot shall inform the RIO ON INTERNAL POWER; BUS TIE CLOSED/OPEN. The pilot shall then complete all post start checks prescribed by the NATOPS Pocket Checklist. When post start checks are completed, he will inform the RIO READY TO TAXI. The pilot shall turn the missile power switch ON when requested by the RIO and shall acknowledge by APA-157 ON.

RIO

When informed that the aircraft is on internal power and the bus tie closed, the RIO shall complete the post start checks prescribed by the NATOPS Pocket Checklist. The RIO shall request the pilot to turn on the APA-157 and may take command of radio and navigation equipment, select appropriate frequencies, and advise the pilot READY TO TAXI. The RIO may call for taxi clearance as directed by the pilot.

PRE-TAKEOFF

Pilot

The pilot shall execute pre-takeoff, instrument, and takeoff checklists prescribed in the NATOPS Pocket Checklist and as posted in the aircraft. The pilot shall report to the RIO engine oil pressures noted on run-up, instrument checklist, and takeoff checklist items. The pilot will receive the READY FOR TAKE-OFF report from the RIO and shall advise him of the type/configuration takeoff planned prior to rolling or

catapulting. The pilot shall report ROLLING or salute as appropriate to the RIO.

RIO

The RIO shall execute pre-takeoff checklists prescribed by the NATOPS Pocket Checklist and shall report READY FOR TAKEOFF; CIRCUIT BREAKERS IN to the pilot. The RIO shall record oil pressures reported by the pilot and shall be alert to challenge the pilot if any item on the instrument checklist or the takeoff checklist is not reported as completed. The RIO shall assist in communications as directed by the pilot.

TAKEOFF/DEPARTURE

Pilot

The pilot shall ensure that the intercom remains in the HOT MIKE position for normal flight operations and will report GEAR UP and FLAPS UP to the RIO insofar as safety permits. The RIO should be advised of lift-off and any unusual occurrences such as over temperature, overspeed, or BLC malfunction. The pilot shall request, copy, and acknowledge all clearances.

RIO

Where departures are made in actual instrument conditions, the RIO shall monitor the published or clearance departure procedures and will inform the pilot of any deviation from the prescribed flight path. The RIO shall copy all clearances received and be prepared to provide the pilot with clearance information of navigational information derived from his instruments. BIT checks are not conducted during instrument climbouts.

INFLIGHT (GENERAL)

Pilot

The pilot shall inform the RIO of any unusual occurrences and ensure that the aircraft is operated within prescribed operating limitations at all times. The pilot normally requests, copies, and acknowledges all clearances. The pilot should afford the RIO ample opportunity to practice in requesting and copying clearances and in position reporting. The pilot shall inform the RIO whenever a descent commences and the altitude where the descent will terminate.

RIO

The RIO shall inform the pilot of the weapon system status. The RIO shall assist the pilot in changing communications frequencies, and shall request, copy, and acknowledge clearances or make position reports in normal or emergency situations as directed by the pilot. During descent, the RIO shall inform the pilot 1000 feet before reaching the intended level-off altitude.

INTERCEPT

Pilot

The pilot shall maneuver the aircraft as directed by GCI/CIC until radar contact is obtained by the RIO. The pilot shall maneuver or coordinate maneuvers of aircraft with or as directed by the RIO, observing normal operating limitations. The pilot shall inform the RIO of weapons status, weapons selected and armed, and when the target is sighted visually. The pilot shall make all missile away reports. Pilots shall monitor aircraft position from initial vector through breakaway by pigeons information or navigational display.

RIO

The RIO normally handles all communications from initial vector through breakaway, excluding missile away transmissions. The RIO shall provide the pilot with descriptive commentary including weapon status and target aspect if available. The RIO shall direct and coordinate aircraft maneuvers with the pilot as necessary to complete the intercept.

INSTRUMENT APPROACHES

Pilot

The pilot is responsible for the safe control of the aircraft, the decision to commence the approach with existing weather, and the selection of the type approach to be made. The pilot, before commencing any penetration, shall report to the RIO the completion of each item of the instrument checklist. In addition, the pilot shall challenge the RIO as to approach plate availability and corrected altimeter setting.

RIO

The RIO shall monitor aircraft instruments and the appropriate approach plate during holding, penetration, and approach and shall be ready to provide the pilot with any required information. He shall be particularly alert to advise the pilot of deviations from the course or minimum altitudes prescribed on the approach plate. The RIO shall assist with communications as directed by the pilot. BIT checks shall not be conducted in actual instrument conditions. The RIO shall inform the pilot of the status of the radar gyro horizon and shall do nothing to cause the display to be lost. During penetrations and/or descents (VFR or IFR), the RIO shall report to the pilot the aircraft descending through each 5000 feet of altitude above 5000 feet and each 1000 feet of altitude loss below 5000 feet, until reaching the desired altitude. The RIO shall report when altitude error exceeds either 10 percent of actual altitude or ± 300 feet.

LANDING

Pilot

The pilot shall utilize the landing checklist and shall report each item to the RIO before reporting GEAR DOWN; HOOK DOWN to the final controller/tower/prifly. The pilot shall receive a READY TO LAND report from the RIO.

RIO

In the landing pattern the RIO shall challenge the pilot on gear, flap, and hook position if the report is not received. The RIO shall attempt to check the position of the gear handle by looking through the opening on the left side of the instrument panel. The RIO shall complete the landing checklist and shall report READY TO LAND to the pilot. BIT checks shall not be conducted in the traffic pattern.

POSTFLIGHT

Pilot

The pilot shall inform the RIO of any unusual occurrences on the landing roll or arrestment. The pilot shall report flap position to the RIO when clear of the runway/landing area, and shall report when the wingfold is actuated. The pilot shall inform the RIO when shutting engines down. The pilot shall conduct a postflight inspection of the aircraft.

RIO

The RIO shall challenge the pilot on flap position if the report is not received. When informed by the pilot that the wingfold has been actuated, the RIO shall immediately respond with the position of the wings. The RIO shall complete the BIT checks remaining and will secure the rear cockpit for shutdown. The RIO shall assist the pilot in conducting a postflight inspection of the aircraft.

DEBRIEFING

The pilot and RIO shall complete the Yellow Sheet and all required debriefing forms.

Note

The RIO shall vacate the aircraft first and when he is on the ground/flight-deck/hangardeck, the pilot will exit. This is particularly important during shipboard operations.

PROCEDURES, TECHNIQUES, AND CHECKLISTS

GENERAL

Even though some of the procedures, techniques, and checklist are specifically designated for the individual pilot or RIO, the entire contents of the Flight Manual and the Pocket Checklist should be thoroughly read, understood, discussed, and agreed upon collectively by the Pilot/RIO team. Discrepancies in existing procedures, or the need for additional procedures, should be brought to the attention of your NATOPS Evaluator/Instructor. Most of the procedures (individual and coordinated) are contained in this volume and sub-divided into flight phases/categories. Aircraft systems description, with their individual operating criteria, is contained in section I. Classified systems description and procedures, and some limitations information are contained in the classified supplement. The Pocket Checklist contains the Pilot's and RIO's individual check-items for Preflight, Pre-Start, Start, Post-Start, Takeoff, Built-In Test (BIT), Instrument /Descent, and Post-flight.

FDB-1-(92)

SECTION X NATOPS EVALUATION

TABLE OF CONTENTS

NATOPS EVALUATION PROGRAM

CONCEPT

The standard operating procedures prescribed in this manual represent the optimum method of operating the F-4B aircraft. The NATOPS Evaluation is intended to evaluate compliance with NATOPS procedures by observing and grading individuals and units. This evaluation is tailored for compatability with various operational commitments and missions of both Navy and Marine Corps units. The prime objective of the NATOPS Evaluation program is to assist the unit commanding officer in improving unit readiness and safety through constructive comment. Maximum benefit from the NATOPS Program is achieved only through the vigorous support of the program by commanding officers as well as flight crewmembers.

IMPLEMENTATION

The NATOPS Evaluation program shall be carried out in every unit operating naval aircraft. The various catagories of flight crewmembers desiring to attain/retain qualification in the F-4B shall be evaluated initially in accordance with OPNAV Instruction 3510.9 series, and at least once during the twelve months following initial and subsequent evaluation. Individual and unit NATOPS Evaluations will be conducted annually; however, instruction in and adherence to

NATOPS procedures must be on a daily basis within each unit to obtain maximum benefits from the program. The NATOPS Coordinators, Evaluators, and Instructors shall administer the program as outlined in OPNAVINST 3510.9 series. Evaluees who receive a grade of unqualified on a ground or flight evaluation shall be allowed 30 days in which to complete a re-evaluation. A maximum of 60 days may elapse between the date the initial ground evaluation was commenced and the date the flight evaluation is satisfactorily completed.

DEFINITIONS

The following terms, used throughout this section, are defined as to their specific meaning within the NATOPS program.

NATOPS EVALUATION

A periodic evaluation of individual flight crewmember standardization consisting of an open book examination, a closed book examination, an oral examination, and a flight evaluation.

NATOPS RE-EVALUATION

A partial NATOPS Evaluation administered to a flight crewmember who has been placed in an Unqualified status by receiving an Unqualified grade for any of his ground examinations or the flight evaluations. Only those areas in which an unsatisfactory level was noted need be observed during a re-evaluation.

QUALIFIED

Well standardized; evaluee demonstrated highly professional knowledge of and compliance with NATOPS standards and procedures; momentary deviations from or minor omission in non-critical areas are permitted if prompt and timely remedial action is initiated by the evaluee.

CONDITIONALLY QUALIFIED

Satisfactorily standardized; one or more significant deviations from NATOPS standards and procedures, but no errors is critical areas and no errors jeopardizing mission accomplishment or flight safety.

UNQUALIFIED

Not acceptably standardized; evaluee fails to meet minimum standards regarding knowledge of and/or ability to apply NATOPS procedures, one or more significant deviations from NATOPS standards and procedures which could jeopardize mission accomplishment or flight safety.

AREA

A routine of preflight, flight, or postflight.

SUB-AREA

A performance sub-division within an area, which is observed and evaluated during an evaluation flight.

CRITICAL AREA/SUB-AREA

Any area or sub-area which covers items of significant importance to the overall mission requirements, the marginal performance of which would jeopardize safe conduct of the flight.

EMERGENCY

An aircraft component, system failure, or condition which requires instantaneous recognition, analysis, and proper action.

MALFUNCTION

An aircraft component or system failure or condition which requires recognition and analysis, but which permits more deliberate action than that required by an emergency.

GROUND EVALUATION

GENERAL

Prior to commencing the flight evaluation, an evaluee must achieve a minimum grade of Qualified on the open book and closed book examinations. The oral examination is also part of the ground evaluation but may be conducted as part of the flight evaluation. To assure a degree of standardization between units, the NATOPS instructors may use the bank of questions contained in this section in preparing portions of the written examinations.

OPEN BOOK EXAMINATION

The open book examination shall consist of, but not be limited to, the question bank. The purpose of the open book examination portion of the written examination is to evaluate the crewmember's knowledge of appropriate publications and the aircraft.

CLOSED BOOK EXAMINATION

The closed book examination may be taken from, but not limited to, the question bank and shall include questions concerning normal/emergency procedures and aircraft limitations. Questions designated as critical will be so marked.

ORAL EXAMINATION

The questions may be taken from this manual and drawn from the experience of the Instructor/Evaluator. Such questions should be direct and positive and should in no way be opinionated.

COT/WST PROCEDURES EVALUATION

A COT may be used to assist in measuring the crewmember's efficiency in the execution of normal operating procedures and his reaction to emergencies and malfunctions. In areas not served by the COT facilities, this may be done by placing the crewmember in an aircraft and administering appropriate questions.

NAMT SYSTEMS CHECK

If desired by the individual squadron, Naval Air Maintenance Trainer facilities may be utilized to evaluate pilot and RIO knowedlge of aircraft systems and normal and emergency procedures.

GRADING INSTRUCTIONS

Examination grades shall be computed on a 4.0 scale and converted to an adjective grade of Qualified or Unqualified.

Open Book Examination

To obtain a grade of Qualified, an evaluee must obtain a minimum score of 3.5.

Closed Book Examination

To obtain a grade of Qualified, an evaluee must obtain a minimum score of 3.3.

Oral Examination and OFT Procedure Check (If conducted)

A grade of Qualified or Unqualified shall be assigned by the Instructor/Evaluator.

FLIGHT EVALUATION

GENERAL

The flight evaluation may be conducted on any routine syllabus flight with the exception of flights launched for FMLP/CARQUAL or ECCM training. Emergencies will not be simulated.

(*) The number of flights required to complete the flight evaluation should be kept to a minimum; normally one flight. The areas and subareas to be observed and graded on a flight evaluation are outlined in the grading criteria with critical areas marked by an asterisk (*). Sub-area grades will be assigned in accordance with the grading criteria. These sub-areas shall be combined to arrive at the overall grade for the flight. Area grades, if desired, shall also be determined in this manner. At the discretion of the squadron or unit commander, the evaluation may be conducted in a WST, OFT, or COT.

OPERATIONAL DEPLOYABLE SQUADRONS

Pilots and RIO's assigned to operational deployable squadrons will normally be checked as a team with the flight evaluation being conducted by the check-crew flying wing. RIO commentary will be transmitted on the GCI/CIC control frequency in use.

TRAINING AND EVALUATION SQUADRONS

Units with training or evaluation missions that are concerned with individual instructor pilot/RIO standardization, rather than team standardization, may conduct the flight evaluation with the check-crew/pilot flying wing or on an individual basis. A pilot may be individually checked with the Instructor/Evaluator conducting the flight evaluation from the rear seat. The RIO may be individually checked by flying with the Instructor/Evaluator as his crewmember.

FLIGHT EVALUATION

The areas and sub-areas in which pilots and RIO's may be observed and graded for adherence to standardized operating procedures are outlined in the following paragraphs.

Note

If desired, units with training missions may expand the flight evaluation to include evaluation of standardized training methods and techniques.

(*) The IFR portions of the Flight Evaluation shall be in accordance with the procedures outlined in the NATOPS Instrument Flight Manual.

MISSION PLANNING/BRIEFING

   a. Flight Planning (Pilot/RIO)
   b. Briefing (Pilot/RIO)
(*)c. Personal Flying Equipment (Pilot/RIO)

PREFLIGHT/LINE OPERATIONS

In as much as preflight/line operations procedures are graded in detail during the ground evaluation, only those areas observed on the flight check will be graded.

   a. Aircraft Acceptance (Pilot/RIO)
   b. Start
   c. Before Taxiing Procedures (pilot)

TAXI/RUN-UP

(*) TAKEOFF/TRANSITION

   a. ATC Clearance (Pilot)
   b. Takeoff (Pilot)
   c. Transition to Climb Schedule

CLIMB/CRUISE

   a. Departure (Pilot)
   b. Climb and Level-Off (Pilot)
   c. Procedures Enroute (Pilot)

(*) APPROACH/LANDING

   a. Radar, ADF (Pilot)
   b. Recovery (Pilot)

COMMUNICATIONS

   a. R/T Procedures (Pilot/RIO)
   b. Visual Signals (Pilot/RIO)
   c. IFF/SIF Procedures (Pilot)

(*) EMERGENCY/MALFUNCTION PROCEDURES

In this area, the pilot/RIO will be evaluated only in the case of actual emergencies, unless evaluation is conducted in the COT/WST.

POSTFLIGHT PROCEDURES

   a. Taxi-in (Pilot)
   b. Shutdown (Pilot/RIO)
   c. Inspection and Records (Pilot/RIO)
   d. Flight Debriefing (Pilot/RIO)

(*) Critical Area

CREW COORDINATION
MISSION EVALUATION

This area includes missions covered in the NATOPS Flight Manual, F-4B Tactical Manual, and NWP/NWIP's for which standardized procedures/techniques have been deployed.

APPLICABLE PUBLICATIONS

The NATOPS Flight Manual contains the standard operations criteria for F-4B aircraft. Publications relating to environmental procedures peculiar to shorebased and shipboard operations and tactical missions are listed below:

F-4B Tactical Manual	ATC/CATCC Manual
NWP's	Local Air Operations Manual
NWIP's	Carrier Air Operations Manual

FLIGHT EVALUATION GRADING CRITERIA

Only those sub-areas provided or required will be graded. The grades assigned for a sub-area shall be determined by comparing the degree of adherence to standard operating procedures with adjectival ratings listed below. Momentary deviations from standard operating procedures should not be considered as unqualifying provided such deviations do not jeopardize flight safety and the evaluee applies prompt corrective action.

FLIGHT EVALUATION GRADE DETERMINATION

The following procedure shall be used in determining the flight evaluation grade: A grade of Unqualified in any critical area/sub-area will result in an overall grade of Unqualified for the flight. Otherwise, flight evaluation (or area) grades shall be determined by assigning the following numerical equivalents to the adjective grade for each sub-area. Only the numerals 0, 2, or 4 will be assigned in sub-areas. No interpolation is allowed.

Unqualified 0.0
Conditionally qualified . . 2.0
Qualified 4.0

To determine the numerical grade for each area and the overall grade for the flight, add all the points assigned to the sub-areas and divide this sum by the number of sub-areas graded. The adjective grade shall then be determined on the basis of the following scale.

0.0 to 2.19 - Unqualified
2.2 to 2.99 - Conditionally Qualified
3.0 to 4.0 - Qualified

EXAMPLE: (Add Sub-area numerical equivalents)

$$\frac{4+2+4+2+4}{5} = \frac{16}{5} = 3.20 \text{ Qualified}$$

FINAL GRADE DETERMINATION

The final NATOPS Evaluation grade shall be the same as the grade assigned to the flight evaluation. An evaluee who receives an Unqualified on any ground examination or the flight evaluation shall be placed in an Unqualified status until he achieves a grade of Conditionally Qualified or Qualified on a re-evaluation.

RECORDS AND REPORTS

A NATOPS Evaluation Report (OPNAV Form 3510-8) shall be completed for each evaluation and forwarded to the evaluee's commanding officer only.

This report shall be filed in the individual flight training record and retained therein for 18 months. In addition, an entry shall be made in the pilot/RIO flight log book under "Qualifications and Achievements" as follows:

Qualification			Date	Signature
NATOPS EVAL.	(Aircraft Model)	(Crew Position)	(Date)	(Authenticating Signature) (Unit which administered Eval.)

In the case of enlisted crewmembers, an entry shall be made in the Administrative Remarks of his Personnel Record upon satisfactory completion of the NATOPS Evaluation as follows:

(Date) Completed a NATOPS Evaluation in (Aircraft Designation) as (Flight crew position) with an overall grade of (Qualified or Conditionally Qualified).

CRITIQUE

The critique is the terminal point in the NATOPS evaluation and will be given by the Evaluator/Instructor administering the check. Preparation for the critique involves processing, reconstructing data collected, and oral presentation of the NATOPS Evaluation Report. Deviations from standard operating procedures will be covered in detail using all collected data and worksheets as a guide. Upon completion of the critique, the pilot/RIO will receive the completed copy of the NATOPS Evaluation Report for certification and signature. The completed NATOPS Evaluation Report will then be presented to the Unit Commanding Officer.

NATOPS EVALUATION QUESTION BANK

The following bank of questions is intended to assist the unit NATOPS Instructor/Evaluator in the preparation of ground examinations and to provide an abbreviated study guide. The questions from the bank may be combined with locally originated questions in the preparation of ground examinations. The closed book exam will consist of no less than 50 questions nor more than 75 questions. The time limit for the closed book exam is 1 hour and 30 minutes. The requirements for the open book exam are the same as those for the closed book exam, except there is no time limit.

F-4B NATOPS QUESTION BANK

1. An operating procedure, practice, or condition, etc., which, if not strictly observed, may damage equipment are indicated in the NATOPS manual by_____.

2. An operating procedure, practice, or condition etc., which may result in injury or death if not carefully observed or followed are indicated in the NATOPS manual by_____.

3. The eight circuit breakers in the front cockpit are:

   a._____

   b._____

   c._____

   d._____

   e._____

   f._____

   g._____

   h._____

4. List the warning lights in the RIO's cockpit: (152244v and up)

   a._____

   b._____

   c._____

   d._____

   e._____

   f._____

5. The cockpit will begin to pressurize at_____ feet. At 40,000 feet, the cabin altitude should be approximately_____.

6. The rain removal system directs_____ over the center windshield panel.

7. Pulling the emergency vent knob accomplishes the following:

   a._____

   b._____

   c._____

   d._____

   e._____

8. The RIO can select his own pressure suit temperature. T / F

9. The only control the RIO has over his pressure suit environment is the volume of airflow. T / F

10. With cabin pressure system inoperative above 35,000 feet, the pressure suit will be pressurized with_____ .

11. The first indication of composite disconnect separation from the seat pan will be free and easy breathing with a fitted oxygen mask. T / F

QUESTION BANK continued

12. Illumination of the RADAR CNI COOL OFF light shall be logged on the yellow sheet. T / F

13. Either the pilot or RIO can reset the CNI cooling reset button. T / F

14. Prior to resetting the CNI cooling reset button, what action must be taken?

    a._____

    b._____

15. If the CNI COOL OFF light cannot be extinguished, high speed flight should be avoided. T / F

16. Suggested angle of attack settings are:

    Climb (400 KCAS)_____ units

    Max Endurance_____units

    Stall Warning_____ units

17. The arresting hook is lowered by_____ and_____ . It is raised by_____ .

18. The arresting hook up latch is mechanically operated. T / F

19. With a loss of electrical power, the arresting hook cannot be extended. T / F

20. The two modes of operation of the automatic flight control system are:

    a. _____

    b. _____

21. In the AFCS mode of operation, the pitch limits are_____degrees, and the roll limits are _____ degrees.

22. The autopilot will disengage when acceleration forces exceed plus _____or minus _____ G's.

23. In the AFCS mode pitch trim corrections will be made automatically, within a range of____ to _____ G's.

24. Only_____ maximum effort brake applications should be anticipated when utility hydraulic pressure is lost.

25. Actuation of the emergency pneumatic braking system will introduce air into the wheel brake hydraulic system. T / F

26. The emergency pneumatic brake system does not provide differential braking. T / F

27. The canopies can be stopped at any intermediate position. T / F

28. Before actuating the canopy manual unlock handle, the normal canopy control handle must be in the _____ position.

29. The pilot's CANOPY UNLOCKED indicator light will illuminate if the RIO's canopy is jettisoned. T / F

30. The canopy is designed to remain in the full open position up to_____knots and to separate from the airplane at_____ knots.

31. Canopy closure should not be attempted with engines running above a stabilized idle rpm. T / F

32. Actuation of the canopy emergency system also actuates the cockpit flooding doors. T / F

33. On ejection, the radar indicator and the control box stow automatically; however, the hand control remains out. T / F

QUESTION BANK continued

34. When airspeed is below 160 KIAS with the STATIC CORR OFF light illuminated, actual altitude will usually be _____ than indicated by the altimeter.

35. Four sensor inputs to the ADC are:

    a. _____

    b. _____

    c. _____

    d. _____

36. The ADC supplies corrected information to the following instruments and systems:

    a. _____

    b. _____

    c. _____

    d. _____

    e. _____

    f. _____

    g. _____

    h. _____

37. The static pressure compensator will automatically reset during engine start. T / F

38. When in the CNI mode, the RIO's #1 needle on the BDHI will indicate_____ bearing, and the #2 needle will indicate_____ bearing.

39. The RIO can select the UHF antenna to be utilized when the pilot has control of the CNI equipment.
    T / F

40. Emergency operation of the intercom system is provided by placing the amplifier selector knob in the EMER ICS or Emergency RAD position, thereby by-passing the faulty amplifier. T / F

41. If the pilot selects emergency intercom operation, it is necessary for the RIO to also select emergency in order to regain satisfactory intercom communications. T / F

42. What effect does the RADIO OVERRIDE position of the intercom control have on UHF radio operation?

43. The CNI system is limited to___ minutes of ground operating time without external coolant air applied.

44. The items that are released or disconnected when the emergency harness release handle is actuated are:

    a. _____

    b. _____

    c. _____

    d. _____

45. The primary source of all electrical power is two, _____ cycle, _____ phase, _____ volt ac generators.

QUESTION BANK continued

46. With external electrical power connected, and either generator control switch in the EXT position, the aircraft buses will be energized. T / F

47. If the left generator is inoperative, the BUS TIE OPEN light is illuminated all dc buses will be energized. T / F

48. When operating on RAT electrical power, the following items of CNI equipment will be lost or operate on reduced power.

    a. _____

    b. _____

    c. _____

    d. _____

49. When operating with emergency power warning light illuminated, the following items of CNI equipment will be lost.

    a. _____

    b. _____

50. In airplanes 152965y and up, and in all others after AFC 220 the emergency generator will drop off the line at approximately_____ knots.

51. Pilot action, upon the illumination of a generator warning light, is to_____the generator control switch. If the generator does not come back on the line, secure the_____ and_____ as soon as practicable. (CSD without shaft disconnect only)

52. After a complete electrical failure, landing gear and flaps should be lowered by_____ .

53. The BUS TIE OPEN light will remain illuminated when one generator goes off the line. T / F

54. Prior to retracting the RAT, insure at least _____ psi on the pneumatic gage.

55. The sea level, standard day, static thrust ratings for the J79-8 engine are,_____ pounds in MIL, and_____ pounds in MAX.

56. The torch igniter plug will operate momentarily each time the throttles are moved to afterburner. T / F

57. The Engine Start switch should be moved to_____when the engine reaches_____ rpm.

58. In the event of a generator or exhaust nozzle failure, the pilot should immediately check the corresponding_____ pressure gage.

59. The ignition duty cycle is_____minutes ON,_____ minutes OFF,_____ minutes ON and _____ minutes OFF.

60. Operation with the DUCT TEMP HI warning light illuminated is prohibited below_____ feet.

61. MIL and MAX thrust are time limited to_____ minutes below 35,000 feet, and_____ hours above 35,000 feet.

62. Due to limited oil distribution to the variable nozzle system during negative G and zero G flight, the aircraft is limited to the following:

    a. _____ seconds of negative G flight.

    b. _____ seconds of zero G flight.

QUESTION BANK continued

63. The emergency flap system air bottles store enough air for _____ extension(s) of the wing flaps.

64. The wing flaps airspeed limit switch is/is not operative when the flaps are extended utilizing the emergency system.

65. When lateral trim corrections are made, the control stick moves in proportion to the amount of trim applied. T / F

66. The stabilator system utilizes a _____ to increase stick forces during rapid fore and aft stick movement.

67. To temporarily disengage the ARI:

   1. _____

   To permanently disengage the ARI:

   1. _____

   2. _____

68. The stall warning vibrator is set at:

   a. _____ units angle of attack (non-dropped aileron airplanes).

   b. _____ units angle of attack (drooped aileron airplanes).

69. Disengagement of the stability augmentation mode decreases the ARI authority by $5°$. T / F

70. Normal rudder trim range is ____ ± _____ degrees of rudder deflection.

71. It is possible to gravity fuel the fuselage tanks. T / F

72. Two electrically operated fuel boost pumps are located in fuselage fuel cell number _____ . In the event of an electrical failure, the left pump, which is a _____ speed pump, will operate on low speed when _____ .

73. The internal and external wing tanks are vented to the atmosphere when the landing gear is down and the wing transfer pressure switch is in the EMERG position. T / F

74. Two methods available to pressurize the internal fuel cells and the external wing tanks are:

   a. Landing gear handle - _____

   b. Wing transfer pressure switch - _____

75. With the engine running, fuel from the centerline tank will start transferring upon selection of the _____ position of the external transfer switch provided that the landing gear handle is in the _____ position or the wing press switch is in the _____ position.

76. When operating on RAT electrical power, external tanks may be transferred normally. T / F

77. The internal wing tanks can be pressurized on the ground by moving the wing transfer pressure switch to the _____ position. Transfer of internal wing fuel can then be accomplished by moving the internal wing transfer switch to the _____ position if the external tanks transfer switch is in the OFF position.

78. The internal wing tanks will be pressurized any time the wing transfer pressure switch is placed to EMERG and an engine is running. T / R

79. Fuel transfer pumps are located in fuselage cells _____ and _____ . Two are _____ and two are _____ operated.

80. 17th stage engine bleed air is used to transfer _____ and _____ fuel. Fuel in fuselage cells _____ , _____ and _____ is transferred by _____ only.

QUESTION BANK continued

81. Wing fuel may be dumped in flight any time, regardless of any other transfer switch position, by selecting the DUMP position on the internal wing dump switch. T / F

82. Wing fuel will be dumped on the deck if the internal wing dump switch is in the DUMP position and external electrical power is applied to the airplane. T / F

83. The fuel quantity indicator counter indicates fuel quantity in the_____and_____. The tape indicates fuel quantity in the_____cells only.

84. To prevent external tank collapse during high altitude descent with the gear down, place the_____ _____ in the_____position.

85. The internal wing dump control operates normally on RAT electrical power. T / F

86. Internal wing fuel can be dumped, regardless of the landing gear handle position. T / F

87. Illumination of the external fuel telelight is an indication of no flow, rather than low fuel quantity. T / F

88. When the air refueling probe is fully extended, the IFR PROBE UNLOCK warning light will not be illuminated. T / F

89. The FUEL LEVEL LOW warning light will illuminate any time the combined fuel in fuselage cells_____ and_____reaches_____pounds.

90. The total serviced internal fuel capacity, for airplanes 148411h and up, is approximately_____ pounds.

91. Fuel boost pump pressure limits on preflight check is_____to_____psi.

92. Wing fuel transfer limits are_____degrees nose-up, and_____degrees nose-down.

93. When carrying external tanks, internal wing fuel will not transfer unless the external transfer switch is in the_____position.

94. If both fuel boost pumps fail while operating above_____feet, flameout of both engines may occur.

95. Fuel will be supplied to the engines by gravity feed, if a failure of both fuel boost pumps occur. T / F

96. In the event one fuel boost pump fails, engine thrust settings should be reduced until a minimum boost pump pressure of_____psi can be maintained.

97. The power control systems supply hydraulic power to the_____,_____and_____.

98. There are three independent hydraulic systems in the airplane; they are the_____, the_____and the_____systems.

99. The utility hydraulic pumps utilize the same reservoir. T / F

100. The right engine utility hydraulic pump pressure is_____, the left utility pump pressure is_____ psi.

101. The three hydraulic systems operate in a pressure range of_____PSI. The CHECK HYD GAGES light will illuminate when any system pressure drops below_____± 100 PSI, and will go out when system pressure recovers to above_____PSI.

102. A PC-1 or a PC-2 failure will limit full travel of the lateral control surfaces and the stabilator at high airspeeds. T / F

103. A CHECK HYD GAGES warning light, with all three gages indicating 3000 PSI, indicates_____ _____.

104. The PC-1 and PC-2 hydraulic systems utilize the same accumulators and reservoirs. T / F

105. The rudder will be completely inoperative in the event of a utility hydraulic system failure. T / F

QUESTION BANK continued

106. There is no safety feature incorporated in the landing gear system to prevent retraction on the ground.
T / F

107. Nose gear steering is limited to _____ degrees either side of center.

108. Two possible ways to deflate the nose gear strut while airborne are:

a. _____

b. _____

109. The nose gear steering system also functions as a _____.

110. Actuation of the warning lights test switch by the RIO will illuminate the pilot's master caution light.
T / F

111. List the data that should be pre-set into the navigation computer:

a. _____

b. _____

c. _____

d. _____

e. _____

112. The OXYGEN LOW telelight will illuminate when the gage indicates one liter or less, regardless of supply. T / F

113. The normal pneumatic system pressure range on the cockpit indicator is _____ to _____ psi.

114. The systems operated with pneumatic system pressure are:

a. Normal system operation:

1. _____

2. _____

3. _____

b. Emergency system operation: (after AFC 370)

1. _____

2. _____

3. _____

4. _____

5. _____

6. _____

115. If the SPEED BRAKE OUT indicator light illuminates, the MASTER CAUTION light will also illuminate.
T / F

QUESTION BANK continued

116. The authorized fuels for the airplane are:

    a. Ashore - _____

    b. Afloat - _____

    c. Emergency - _____

117. To refuel the airplanes internal tanks on the ground engines running, place the refuel probe switch in the _____ position.

118. For ground pressure refueling, with engines off and external electrical power connected, list the fuel control panel switch positions:

    a. External transfer switch - _____

    b. Wing transfer pressure switch - _____

    c. Refuel selection switch - _____

    d. Buddy fill switch - _____

    e. Refuel probe switch - _____

    f. Wing fuel dump - _____

119. When you are pressure refueling on the ground, engines not running and electrical power connected, the engine master switches should be in the _____ position.

120. The ground fueling switch is located in the _____ wheel well.

121. The main and afterburner fuel controls should be adjusted for the specific density of the fuel grade being used. T / F

122. The maximum airspeed for drag chute deployment is _____ knots CAS.

123. List the airspeed limitations for:

    a. Landing gear extended - _____

    b. Wing flap extended - _____

    c. Canopy open - _____

    d. RAT extension - _____ Knots CAS or _____ Mach, whichever is less.

124. The center of gravity limitations for all current permissible gross weights and configurations are between _____ % and _____ % of the Mean Aerodynamic Chord.

125. The weight limitations for the following conditions are: (after AFC 230)

    a. Field takeoff - _____ pounds.

    b. Field landing (minimum sink rate) - _____ pounds.

    c. Catapulting - _____ pounds.

    d. Arresting landing, touch-and-go, and FMLP - _____ pounds.

126. What is the maximum airspeed and Mach number for the air refueling probe:

    a. Extension _____ knots CAS or _____ Mach, whichever is less.

    b. Fully extended _____ knots CAS or _____ Mach, whichever is less.

QUESTION BANK continued

127. List eight prohibited maneuvers:

a. _____

b. _____

c. _____

d. _____

e. _____

f. _____

g. _____

h. _____

128. Full pressure suits will be worn on all flights above _____ feet.

129. The pressure altimeter should be set and checked prior to engaging the static pressure compensator. T / F

130. The limiting wind velocity for crosswind drag chute deployment is:

a. 45° _____ Knots

b. 90° _____ Knots

131. The FMLP pattern altitude is _____ above ground level.

132. The pilot's NO-GO signals for catapult abort are:

a. Day - _____

b. Night - _____

133. If a BLC failure is experienced, approach and landing speeds must be increased. T / F

134. The day signal for HEFOE code commencing is _____
_____.

135. The RIO has just given you a HEFOE signal - four fingers - followed by a thumbs down. What pilot action is required? _____

136. The HEFOE signals and meanings are:

FINGERS -	ONE	TWO	THREE	FOUR	FIVE
MEANING -	____	____	____	____	____

137. Before AFC 307, the RIO will normally eject before the pilot. According to the NATOPS manual, what are the only foreseeable deviations from this?

a. _____

b. _____

QUESTION BANK continued

138. The ejection signals given to the RIO if the intercom is inoperative with no eject light are:

        MK-H5 Seat   MK-H7 Seat

    a. day _____   a. day _____

    b. night _____   b night _____

    If there is no response to either (a) (b):

    c. _____   c. _____

139. You are attempting to eject but the canopy fails to jettison. What would you do to manually jettison the canopy?

    a. _____

    If the canopy still fails to jettison:

    b. _____

    c. _____

140. After ejection, the crewmember must manually actuate his oxygen supply. T / F

141. The recommended maximum airspeeds for ejection are:

        MK-H5 Seat   MK-H7 Seat

    a. _____ knots below 100 feet   a. _____ knots

    b. _____ knots above 100 feet

142. List minimum ejection altitude for MK-H5 and MK-H7 seat in a 500 knot 45 degree dive, with reaction time.

    H5 _____ H7 _____

143. During a normal approach-full flaps, gear down, gross weight 34,000 pounds, the minimum safe ejection altitude for a seat having ground level capability is approximately _____ feet. This includes normal sink rates and pilot reaction time.

144. List the procedures required to obtain the use of the essential bus when the right generator failed and the BUS TIE OPEN light is illuminated.

    a. _____

    b. _____

145. List the NATOPS procedure for engine failure during takeoff, takeoff continued.

    a. _____

    b. _____

    c. _____

    d. _____

    e. _____

    f. _____

    g. _____

QUESTION BANK continued

146. List the NATOPS procedure for double engine failure during flight.

   a. _____

   b. _____

   c. _____

   d. _____

   e. _____

   f. _____

147. List the NATOPS air start procedure.

   a. _____

   b. _____

   c. _____

148. List the NATOPS procedure for engine fire during start.

   a. _____

   b. _____

   c. _____

   d. _____

149. After the gear and flaps are extended, using the emergency systems, their respective control handles should be reset by the pilot to ready the systems for normal operation. T / F

150. The emergency procedure for lowering the landing gear is:

   a. _____

   b. _____

   c. _____

   d. _____

151. The flap position for a single-engine landing is _____ flaps.

152. If a forced landing on unprepared terrain is unavoidable, land with the wheels_____ .

153. If it becomes necessary to jettison both canopies, jettison the_____ canopy first.

154. If it is necessary to ditch the airplane, ditch with the wheels_____ .

155. What steps should be taken in the event the intercom became inoperative:

   a. _____

   b. _____

   c. _____

   d. _____

   e. _____

QUESTION BANK continued

156. The pilot/RIO attention signals, under emergency conditions, with no other means of communication are:

    a. Pilot - _____

    b. RIO - _____

157. If you are lost and have an operative radio receiver, you should fly two triangles to the_____, repeating the pattern at _____ minute intervals.

158. If you are lost and have no operative radios, you should fly two triangles to the_____, repeating the pattern every _____ minutes.

159. The minimum altitude above the terrain at which a pilot may go hooded on departure is_____feet.

160. Instrument chase planes will make checks with the hooded plane at _____minute intervals above flight level 240, and at _____minute intervals below this level.

161. The minimum altitude a pilot may remain hooded on a descent is_____feet.

162. Supply the bank angles for the following directive commentary:

    a. EASY _____

    b. PORT (STBD)_____

    c. HARD_____

    d. HARD AS POSSIBLE _____

    e. WRAP IT UP_____

163. The proper sequence for information given in descriptive commentary is:

    a. _____

    b. _____

    c. _____

    d. _____

164. The pilot will echo all directive commentary given by the RIO. T / F

165. Supply the interpretation of the following directive commentary:

    a. Ease - _____

    b. Hold - _____

    c. Harder - _____

    d. Break _____

    e. Compass recovery - _____

    f. Buster - _____

    g. Gate - _____

166. The term JUDY informs the controlling agency that the aircraft radar is locked on the target. T / F

167. The daylight, emergency stop signal is raised crossed arms with clenched fists. T / F

QUESTION BANK continued

168. BIT checks should not be conducted during:

   a. _____

   b. _____

169. In the landing pattern, the RIO will challenge the pilot on the gear, flaps, and hook positions if a report is not received. T / F

170. The RIO will monitor all instrument departures and approaches, and will advise the pilot of any course or minimum altitude deviations. T / F

171. What are the airspeed and/or Mach limitations for a basic airplane:

   a. Below 10,000 feet, C.G aft of 30% MAC on airplanes 148363f thru 151447q before AFC 190 Mach.

   b. 10,000 to 30,000 feet _____ knots CAS.

   c. 30,000 feet and above _____ knots CAS or _____ Mach, whichever is less.

172. A gradual afterburner shutdown must be made at speeds above _____ knots CAS or _____ Mach, whichever is less, when operating at 40,000 feet.

173. The maximum limiting Mach number for a clean airplane is _____ and begins at _____ feet on a standard day.

174. The maximum allowable airspeed for a clean airplane below 10,000 feet with C.G forward of 30% MAC is _____ knots CAS.

175. Maximum allowable acceleration limits of the McDonnell (excluding the short fairing) centerline tank are:

   a. Full _____ to _____ .

   b. Empty to 3/4 Full _____ to _____ .

176. Maximum allowable acceleration limits of the external wing tank are:

         McDonnell or Sargent Fletcher   Royal Jet

   a. Full _____ to _____ .   a. Full _____ to _____ .

   b. Empty to 3/4 full _____ to _____ .   b. Empty to 3/4 full _____ to _____ .

177. The maximum speed for jettisoning:

   a. Wing tanks - _____ knots CAS below 35,000 feet and _____ knots CAS above 35,000 feet.

178. Jettisoning the centerline tank between _____ KCAS and _____ KCAS below _____ feet may result in airplane damage.

179. The maximum speed at which an LAU-17A launcher may be jettisoned is _____ knots CAS or Mach, whichever is less.

180. The four major groups of equipment which comprise the AERO 1A missile control system include:

   a. _____

   b. _____

   c. _____

   d. _____

QUESTION BANK continued

*181. The APQ-72 radar will detect targets and track them in _____ and _____ during normal conditions or in _____ alone in a counter measure environment.

182. The IN RNG light will be illuminated in the radar mode when the range to the target is less than maximum launch range, but greater than minimum launch range, regardless of the position of the aim dot with respect to the allowable steering error circle. T / F

183. The HOLD ALTITUDE light will illuminate when the interceptor altitude is greater than _____ feet, antenna elevation angle is greater than _____ degrees, and target range is greater than computed snap-up range.

184. The horizon bar, on the RIO's radar scope, may be moved vertically by the adjustment of the horizon adjustment knob on the pilot's radar scope. T / F

185. Lock-on in the EXP mode display can be accomplished in the AI ranges only. T / F

186. When in the MAP mode, the radar scan is single-bar with feed horn nutation. T / F

187. When the power switch on the radar set control panel is in the OPR position, the APQ-72 and the APA-157 transmitters are in operation. T / F

188. When the power switch on the radar set control panel is placed in the EMER position, the 3.5 minute protective delay relay of the APQ-72 will be overridden. T / F

189. The Break light will illuminate when the computed minimum range at which a missile can be effectively launched is reached. T / F

190. With the Vc switch in the 1 position, and the Vc gap at the seven o'clock position, the rate of closure is _____ knots.

191. Any target appearing below the altitude line must be airborne. T / F

192. The AMCS BIT air data switch must be in the ACTUAL position before a Sparrow III missile can be fired. T / F

193. The range selector, on the hand control, switches the radar range between _____ miles.

194. Two methods of differentiating between the ranges selected by the hand control range selector are:

    a. _____

    b. _____

195. The three inputs that AMCS system receives from the ADC are:

    a. _____

    b. _____

    c. _____

196. The OUT position of the gyro switch removes the horizon line from the radar scope indicator presentations, and positions the _____ and _____ servos to zero-zero; thus referencing the radar antenna to airplane coordinates.

197. Sparrow III missiles cannot be normally launched from the forward fuselage stations while carrying a centerline external tank (TK light illuminated). T / F

198. When the missile power switch is in the RADAR STBY position, the RIO should monitor the CW cooling. T / F

199. When the SELECTED and READY lights for a Sparrow III missile have initially been illuminated, both lights will remain illuminated even though the missile is no longer tuned. T / F

* CONFIDENTIAL WHEN FILLED IN

QUESTION BANK continued

200. If there are two sidewinder missiles aboard, and the missile select is in the HEAT position, there will be two SW lights illuminated on the missile status panel. T / F

201. With two sidewinder missiles aboard, a loaded station will be selected each time the missile select switch is moved to the HEAT REJECT position. T / F

202. The Sparrow III SELECTED lights will illuminate only after the missile has been tuned. T / F

203. The centerline tank will be automatically jettisoned when the forward fuselage missiles are fired. T / F

204. The flap interlock switch will prevent Sparrow III missiles from being launched from the wing stations when the flap switch is down. T / F

205. In the HEAT mode, the computer interlock functions are bypassed and Sidewinder missiles may be fired at any time. T / F

206. The HEAT REJECT position of the missile select switch is a momentary position which causes the computer to return to a Sparrow III mode of operation. T / F

207. Placing the missile arm switch to the ARM position when the missile select switch is in the HEAT position, will cause the wing station_____lights to illuminate if Sidewinders are being carried.

208. With missile power switch in PWR ON, missile arm switch in SAFE, and missile select switch in RADAR, the_____ light monitors Sparrow III missile tuned status. When missile select switch is positioned to HEAT, the_____light monitors Sparrow III tuned status.

209. With 6 Sparrow III missiles aboard and indicating SELECTED and READY, the first station to fire will be the_____station.

210. The wing missile stations may carry either Sparrow III AIM-7D, Sparrow III AIM-7E, Sidewinder AIM-9B, or Sidewinder AIM-9D missiles. T / F

211. When the wing missiles are jettisoned, the missiles remain attached to the pylon and the pylon is jettisoned. T / F

*212. The sidewinder IR seeker unit field of view is:

Sidewinder AIM-9B_____degrees

Sidewinder AIM-9D_____degrees

*213. The sidewinder IR seeker unit gimbal limits are:

Sidewinder AIM-9B_____degrees

Sidewinder AIM-9D_____degrees

214. The sidewinder missile is composed of the following major sections.

1._____

2._____

3._____

4._____

5._____

215. The normal clutter receiver channel of the APQ-72 provides maximum receiver sensitivity for maximum detection ranges. T / F

216. With a target return above the threshold level, power level mode switching should be accomplished in 2 seconds. T / F

* CONFIDENTIAL WHEN FILLED IN

217. Elevation coverage in the 3-bar radar scan is approximately_____1-bar radar_____1-bar map
_____ .

218. In the Sidewinder missile (HEAT) mode, the ASE circle is fixed in diameter. T / F

219. Head aim voltage is supplied to the Sparrow III missile immediately prior to launch. T / F

220. The Sparrow III provides its own radar signal. T / F

221. The missile power switch must be ON when performing valid BIT checks in BIT check number_____ .

222. The Vc memory circuit in the APQ-72 should maintain lock-on for at least 20 seconds. T / F

223. The time delay, prior to normal operation, for the following components is:

a. APQ-72_____min.

b. APA-157_____sec.

224. When a Sparrow III missile is fired, the missile select switch must not be switched to the HEAT position before the Sparrow III intercepts the target. In the HEAT position the Sparrow III will no longer have a guidance signal. T / F

225. If a Sparrow III missile misfires, the next missile in the firing sequence will be launched automatically after a 2 second delay. T / F

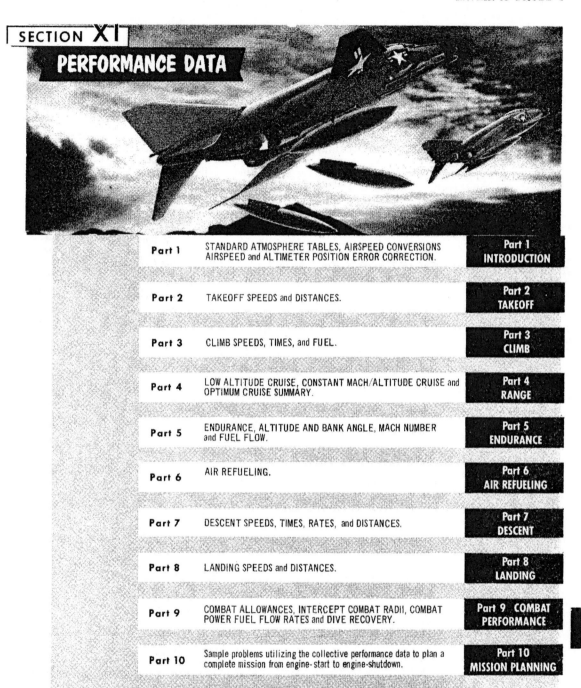

SECTION XI

PERFORMANCE DATA

FDB-1-(93)

PART 1 INTRODUCTION

CHARTS

This section is divided into parts (1 through 10) to present performance data in proper sequence for preflight planning. Two concepts of data presentation are utilized to show drag effects on aircraft performance; i.e., specific configuration charts and drag index charts. The drag index concept presents subsonic climb data, nautical miles per pound for cruise/endurance, and descents. All other data are presented as a specific configuration per chart. All performance data is based on flight tests or the contractor's estimate, ICAO standard day conditions and/or provisions to correct for non-standard temperatures, and J79-GE-8 engines using JP-5 fuel.

Note

The indication of the fuel quantity indicator presents the readings of actual fuel weight remaining. This is accomplished by means of compensator capacitors which provide accurate readings regardless of changes in the dielectric value of the fuel or variations in specific density due to temperature changes. Therefore, adjustment for various fuel densities is not necessary.

ARMAMENT ATTACHMENT ASSOCIATION CHART

The information necessary to determine the total weight of the stores loaded on the airplane, and their effect on the aircraft center-of-gravity is contained in the Armament Attachment Association chart (figure 11-1) and the Station Loading chart (figure 11-2). The Armament Attachment Association chart lists the various attachment (launcher, pylons, racks, and adapters) that are needed to carry an external store on any one particular station.

STATION LOADING

The Station Loading chart (figure 11-2) lists the individual weight, drag number, stability number, stations location and incremental center-of-gravity shift, of the various pylons, adapters, racks and external stores. It also lists the average operating weight with its corresponding center-of-gravity and the basic takeoff gross weight with its corresponding center-of-gravity for various airplanes. The chart does not intend to list the quantity and total gross weight of the external stores that can be carried on each station. However, the takeoff gross weight and approximate takeoff center-of-gravity can be computed by first referring to the Armament Attachment Association chart and determining the various attachments necessary to carry the particular stores that are to be loaded. Next refer to the Station Loading chart to find the individual weights and incremental center-of-gravity shifts of the selected stores and attachments. Once the individual weights have been noted, multiply the individual weights by the quantity to be carried (this figure will be the total external store weight). The external store weight, added to the airplane basic takeoff weight will result in a close approximation of the takeoff gross weight. The takeoff center-of-gravity can be computed by adding the incremental center-of-gravity values for each station that the various pylons, adapters, racks and external stores are intended to be carried on. The summation of the center-of-gravity values, added or subtracted as necessary from the center-of-gravity corresponding to the basic takeoff weight will result in a close approximation of the actual takeoff center-of-gravity.

INCREMENTAL CG SHIFT

Sample Problem

Configuration: 6 LAU-3/A rocket packs on aircraft stations 1 & 9 (FULL) (3 each station).
6 MK 82 LDGP bombs on aircraft station 5.

Estimated CG of 33.8% MAC (estimated operating weight plus weight of full internal fuel)

A. LAU-3/A (station 1 & 9)		
Forward cluster	(-0.02 x 6)	= -0.12
B. Suspension equipment (station 1 & 9)		
Wing tank pylon	(+0.04 x 2)	= +0.08
MER adapter	(+0.01 x 2)	= +0.02
MER (shifted aft)	(+0.12 x 2)	= +0.24
C. MK-82 LDGP (station 5)		
Forward cluster	(-0.31 x 3)	= -0.93
Aft cluster	(+0.26 x 3)	= +0.78
D. Suspension equipment (station 5)		
MER adapter	0	= 0.00
MER (shifted forward)	(-0.01 x 1)	= -0.01
E. Incremental CG shift		+0.06
F. Estimated takeoff CG	(33.8% +0.06)	= 33.86%

DRAG INDEX SYSTEM

The drag number for each externally carried store and its associated suspension equipment is listed. The drag index for a specific configuration may be found by multiplying the number of stores carried by its drag number and adding the drag number of the applicable suspension equipment (if not included). The total drag index may then be used to enter the planning data charts. Charts applicable for all loads and configurations are labeled ALL DRAG INDEXES. Charts labeled INDIVIDUAL DRAG INDEXES contain data for a range of drag numbers; i.e., individual curves/columns for a specific drag number. Supersonic data is not compatible to the drag index system: therefore, each chart is labeled for a specific configuration.

Sample Problem

Configuration: 6 LAU-3/A rocket packs on aircraft stations 1 & 9 (FULL) (3 each station).

6 MK 82 LDGP bombs on aircraft station 5.

A.	LAU-3/A drag number	4.2 x 6 = 25.2
B.	Wing tank pylon, MER adapter, MER	2(1.5 + 8.0) = 19.0
C.	MK 82 LDGP drag number	1.1 x 6 = 6.6
D.	MER centerline adapter, MER	2 + 8 = 10.0
E.	Total drag index	60.8

STABILITY INDEX SYSTEM

With the many possible external loading configurations and their resulting aerodynamic effects, it is possible to load the airplane past the aft CG limit. Adding wing-mounted stores tends to shift the aerodynamic center forward toward the CG of the aircraft, thereby reducing the longitudinal maneuvering stability. To be assured of an acceptable static margin, it is necessary to consider stability effects in conjunction with CG location. Each wing-mounted store and its associated suspension equipment is assigned a unit stability number corresponding to its aerodynamic effect. Each stability index (sum of stability numbers) has a corresponding aft CG limit.

After the loading configuration has been determined, compute the airplane stability index. Enter the Aft CG Limits chart (part 4 of section I) with the airplane stability index to obtain maximum allowable aft CG location. The CG location is determined in the normal manner by using a Weight and Balance Clearance Form F in conjunction with the Handbook of Weight and Balance Data, AN-1-1B-40.

Note

- In some cases where the originally desired configuration is not within the allowable envelope, an acceptable static margin may be achieved through rearrangement of wing-mounted stores.

- Tandem-mounted weapons count as a single weapon when computing the airplane stability index.

- Fuselage-mounted stores are not used in determining airplane stability index but they are used in computing takeoff CG location.

- Unit stability numbers are assigned for single mounted and cluster mounted weapons. The cluster mounted unit stability number will be used when two or more weapons are mounted on the same rack, with each weapon being assigned this number.

Sample Problem

Configuration: 6 LAU-3/A rocket packs on aircraft stations 1 & 9 (FULL) (3 each station).

6 MK 82 LDGP bombs on aircraft station 5.

A.	LAU-3/A (cluster mounted- stations 1 & 9)	13.5 x 6 = 81.0
B.	Wing tank pylon, MER adapter, MER	2 (4.3 + 7.1) = 22.8
C.	Stability index	103.8
D.	Aft CG limit based on stability index	34.3% MAC

DRAG DUE TO ASYMMETRIC LOADING

This chart (figure 11-3) provides the drag number that results from trimming out an asymmetric store loading. The drag number is added to the computed drag of the airplane to obtain the drag index. Asymmetric drag varies with Mach number and altitude.

USE

Find the net asymmetric load on stations 2 and 8 (stations 2 and 8 are indicated on the left vertical axis, and stations 1 and 9 are indicated by the diagonal parallel lines) by subtracting the lighter from the heavier weight. Attach to this net load the position, RWH (right wing heavy) or LWH (left wing heavy) as appropriate. In the same manner, find the net asymmetric load on stations 1 and 9. Enter the chart with the net asymmetric load for stations 2 and 8 corresponding to the load position. Proceed horizontally to the right to the net asymmetric load on stations 1 and 9 and its position. Proceed vertically downward to the altitude, horizontally to the right to the Mach number, and then vertically downward to obtain the incremental drag number.

Sample Problem

A. Load on station 2 = 1000 Lbs.
   Load on station 8 = 3000 Lbs.
   Net asymmetric load on stations 2 & 8 = 2000 Lbs. RWH
B. Load on station 1 = 2500 Lbs.
   Load on station 9 = 2000 Lbs.
   Net asymmetric load on stations 1 & 9 = 500 Lbs. LWH

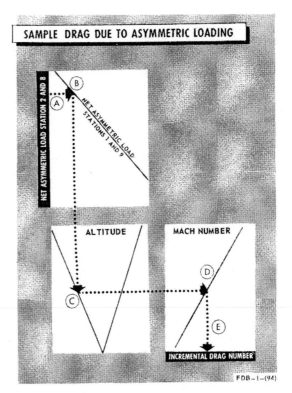

SAMPLE DRAG DUE TO ASYMMETRIC LOADING

FDB-1-(94)

C. Altitude   25,000 Feet
D. Mach number   0.7
E. Incremental drag   5.8
    number

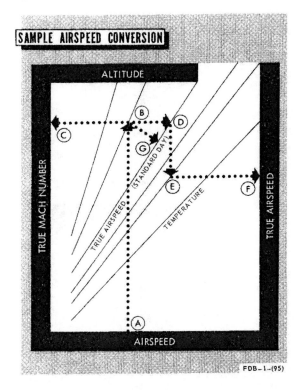

SAMPLE AIRSPEED CONVERSION

FDB-1-(95)

AIRSPEED CONVERSION

The Airspeed Conversion chart (figure 11-4) provides a means of converting calibrated airspeed to true Mach number and true airspeed.

USE

Enter the chart with the calibrated airspeed and proceed vertically to intersect the applicable altitude. From this point, proceed horizontally to the left to read true Mach number. From the calibrated airspeed-altitude intersection, proceed horizontally to the right to intersect the sea level line. From this point descend vertically to intersect the applicable flight level temperature. Then proceed horizontally to the right to read true airspeed. To obtain the standard day true airspeed, parallel the curved dash lines from the calibrated airspeed-altitude intersection to the sea level line.

Sample Problem

A.	Calibrated airspeed	330 Kts.
B.	Altitude	25,000 Ft.
C.	True Mach	0.782
D.	Sea level line	
E.	Flight level temperature	-20°C
F.	True airspeed	486 Kts.
G.	True airspeed (Standard Day)	472 Kts.

INDICATED AIRSPEED

Indicated airspeed (IAS) is the uncorrected airspeed read directly from the indicator when the ADC is inoperative.

CALIBRATED AIRSPEED

Calibrated airspeed (CAS) is indicated airspeed corrected for static source error. In this airplane, the ADC automatically compensates for this error so that calibrated airspeed may be read directly from the indicator.

EQUIVALENT AIRSPEED

Equivalent airspeed (EAS) is calibrated airspeed corrected for compressibility effect. There is no provision for reading EAS; however, it may be obtained by multiplying the TAS by the square root of the density ratio.

TRUE AIRSPEED

True airspeed (TAS) is equivalent airspeed corrected for atmospheric density. Refer to Airspeed Conversion, (figure 11-4).

SPC/ALTIMETER TOLERANCE CHART

The SPC/Altimeter Tolerance Check chart (figure 11-5) provides a means of checking the accuracy of the static pressure compensator in flight. The chart is plotted for 9 units angle of attack between 5000 and 20,000 feet. The Δ altitude between the curves represents the allowable tolerance of the system.

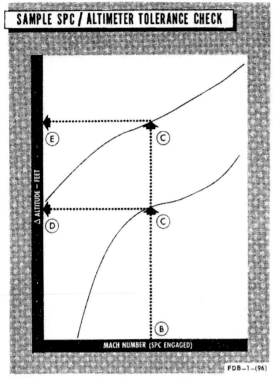

SAMPLE SPC / ALTIMETER TOLERANCE CHECK

FDB-1-(96)

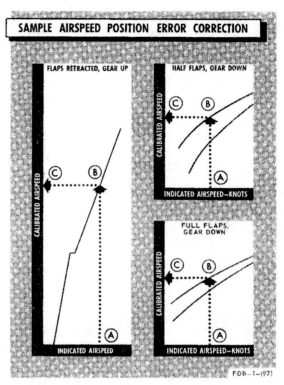

SAMPLE AIRSPEED POSITION ERROR CORRECTION

FDB-1-(97)

USE

With the static pressure compensator on and operating, establish the airplane at 9 units angle of attack between 5000 and 20,000 feet at a constant Mach number. Record the Mach number and altitude. Enter the chart with the Mach number and proceed vertically to intersect both curves. From these intersections, proceed horizontally to the left and record the two corresponding Δ altitudes. Add these to the indicated altitude to obtain the upper and lower allowable limits. Move the static pressure compensator switch (labeled CADC), on the pilot's left console to OFF. The altimeter must jump. Note and record the indicated altitude. If the indicated altitude, with the static pressure compensator turned off, falls on or between the previously computed limits, reset the static pressure compensator and ensure STATIC CORR OFF light is extinguished.

WARNING

If the altimeter does not jump, or the indicated altitude with the static pressure compensator off does not fall within the limits established by the SPC/Altimeter Tolerance chart, leave the static pressure compensator off during the remainder of the flight and utilize the Altimeter and Airspeed Position Error Correction charts (STATIC CORRECTION OFF).

Sample Problem

A.	Altitude	15,000 Ft.
B.	Mach	0.6
C.	Intersect both curves	
D.	Lower Δ altitude	225 Ft.
E.	Upper Δ altitude	375 Ft.
F.	Lower limit (A + D)	15,225 Ft.
G.	Upper limit (A + E)	15,375 Ft.

AIRSPEED POSITION ERROR CORRECTION

Under normal conditions, airspeed position error is automatically compensated for by the air data computer system (ADC). However, if a malfunction of the ADC occurs, position error must be applied to the cockpit indication. These charts (figures 11-6 thru 11-8) provide a direct-reading conversion from indicated to calibrated airspeed, and from indicated to true Mach number.

Sample Problem

Aircraft With Drooped Ailerons

Configuration: Gear and Flaps Up

A.	Indicated airspeed	400 Kts.
B.	Altitude	40,000 Ft.
C.	Calibrated airspeed	385 Kts.

Configuration: Gear and Flaps Up

A.	Indicated Mach number	1.4
B.	Indicated altitude	40,000 Ft.
C.	True Mach number	1.31

ALTIMETER POSITION ERROR CORRECTION

Under normal operating conditions, compensation for the static source position error, as it affects the altimeter, is provided by the ADC. If the ADC fails in flight (STATIC CORR OFF), the altimeter must be corrected by means of the Altimeter Position Error Correction chart (figures 11-9 and 11-10). The chart contains three altitude correction (Δ H) plots; one cruise configuration and two landing configurations. The altitude correction (Δ H) must be added (algebraically) to the assigned altitude to obtain indicated altitude.

Note

Assigned altitude + Δ H = indicated altitude. Fly indicated altitude.

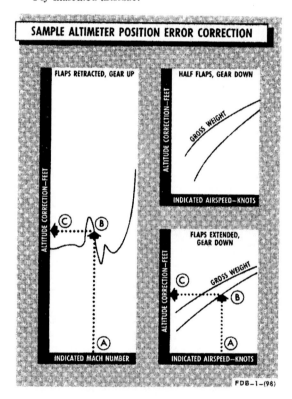

SAMPLE ALTIMETER POSITION ERROR CORRECTION

FDB-1-(98)

USE

Enter the cruise plot with the indicated Mach number. Proceed vertically upward to intercept the assigned altitude curve, then horizontally to the left to read out the altitude correction (Δ H). Enter either of the landing plots with the indicated airspeed, proceed vertically to the applicable gross weight reflector, then horizontally to the left to read altitude correction (Δ H). Apply Δ H to the assigned altitude to obtain the indicated altitude.

Sample Problem

Aircraft With Drooped Ailerons

To maintain 35,000 feet at 1.4 Mach (cruise plot), proceed as follows:

A.	Indicated Mach number	1.4
B.	Assigned altitude	40,000 Ft.
C.	Altitude Correction (Δ H)	+2900 Ft.
D.	Fly indicated altitude (B +C)	42,900 Ft.

ALTIMETER LAG CHART

These charts (figures 11-11 and 11-12) provide a means of obtaining the altimeter lag (difference between indicated altitude and actual altitude) resulting from diving flight. Data is provided for dive angles up to 60° and airspeeds up to 600 knots TAS.

USE

Enter the chart with dive airspeed, and project horizontally to the right to intersect the dive angle curve. From this point, project vertically downward to read the resulting altimeter lag. Add the altimeter lag data to desired/required pullout altitude to obtain indicated altitude for pullout.

Sample Problem

Aircraft With SPC Operative

1.	Dive airspeed (TAS)	400 Kts.
2.	Dive angle	45°
3.	Altimeter lag	92 Ft.

WIND COMPONENTS CHART

A standard Wind Components chart (figure 11-14) is included. It is used primarily for breaking a forecast wind down into crosswind and headwind components for takeoff and landing computations. It may, however, be used whenever wind component information is desired. To determine effective wind velocity, add one-half the gust velocity to the steady state velocity; e.g., reported wind 050/20G 30, effective wind is 050/35.

USE

Reduce the reported wind direction to a relative bearing by determining the difference between the wind direction and the runway heading. Enter the chart with the relative bearing. Move along the relative bearing to intercept the wind speed arc. From this point, descend vertically to read the crosswind component. From the intersection of relative bearing and wind speed, project horizontally to the left to read headwind component.

Sample Problem

Reported wind 050/35; runway heading 030.

A.	Relative bearing	20°
B.	Intersect windspeed arc	35 Knots
C.	Crosswind component	12 Knots
D.	Headwind component	33 Knots

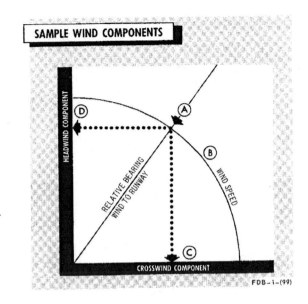

SAMPLE WIND COMPONENTS

FDB-1-(99)

ARMAMENT ATTACHMENT ASSOCIATION

STORES TO BE CARRIED	STATIONS AND ARMAMENT ATTACHMENTS								
	1	2	3	4	5	6	7	8	9
370 GAL. EXT. WING TANK	1								1
M117A1, MK 81, MK 82, MK 83 LDGP BOMB, MK 86, MK 87, MK 88, MK 124 PRACTICE BOMB	2 14	4			10 15			4	2 14
ADSID I (NORMAL) SENSOR	2 14	4						4	2 14
MK 81, MK 82 SNAKEYE I BOMB, MK 36, MK 40 DST.	2 14	4			10 15			4	2 14
MK 77 MOD 4 FIRE BOMB	2 14	4			10 15			4	2 14
ROCKEYE II	2 14	4			10 15			4	2 14
MK 12 SMOKE TANK	14	4						4	14
LAU-3A/A, LAU-60/A, LAU-61/A, LAU-69/A, AERO 7D ROCKET POD	2 14	4			10 15			4	2 14
LAU-10/A, LAU-10A/A ROCKET POD	2 14	4			10 15			4	2 14
LAU-32A/A, LAU-32B/A, LAU-56/A, AERO 6A-2 ROCKET POD	2 14	4			10 15			4	2 14
MK 76, MK 106, MK 89 PRACTICE BOMB	2 3 14	4 8			10 11 12 15			4 8	2 3 14
CNU-169/A BAGGAGE POD		17							17
600 GAL. EXT. TANK					9				
CBU-24, -29, -49 DISPENSER	2 14	4			10 15			4	2 14
NAMAR CAMERA POD		17							17
CTU-1/A DELIVERY CONTAINER	2 14				10				2 14

STORES TO BE CARRIED	STATIONS AND ARMAMENT ATTACHMENTS								
	1	2	3	4	5	6	7	8	9
SUU-40, -44 FLARE DISPENSER	2 14								2 14
LM-119A AERIAL FILM DELIVERY CONTAINER					9				
D-704 AIR REFUELING STORE					9				
RCPP-105 STARTER POD					9				
AERO 8A-1 PRACTICE BOMB CONTAINER					9				
SPARROW III AIM-7 MISSILES		5	16	16		16	16	5	
SIDEWINDER AIM-9B MISSILE		6 7					6 7		
SIDEWINDER AIM-9D/G MISSILE		6					6		
B43, B57, B61 SPECIAL STORES					9				
MK 24, MK 45 PARAFLARE	2 3 14	4 8			10 11 15			4 8	2 3 14
BDU-11E, BDU-6, BDU-20/C TRAINING SHAPE, MK 104					9				
AERO 43 LM REEL/LAUNCHER					9				
RMU-8/A REEL/LAUNCHER					9				
AQM-37A TARGET SYSTEM					9				
MK 4 MOD 0 GUN POD					13				

1 WING TANK PYLON

2 WING TANK PYLON, OUTBOARD MER ADAPTER, OUTBOARD MER

3 WING TANK PYLON, OUTBOARD MER ADAPTER, A/A37B-3 PMBR

4 LAU-17/A WING MISSILE PYLON, TER ADAPTER, TER

5 LAU-17/A WING MISSILE PYLON

6 LAU-17/A WING MISSILE PYLON, LAU-7/A MISSILE LAUNCHER

7 LAU-17/A WING MISSILE PYLON, MODIFIED AERO-3A LAUNCHER

8 LAU-17/A WING MISSILE PYLON, TER ADAPTER, A/A37B-3 PMBR

9 AERO-27A RACK

10 AERO-27A RACK, CENTERLINE MER ADAPTER AND, CENTERLINE MER

11 AERO-27A RACK AND A/A37B-3 PMBR

12 AERO-27A RACK AND AERO 8A-1 PBC

13 AERO-27A RACK, CENTERLINE MER ADAPTER AND TWO HUGHES ADAPTERS

14 WING TANK PYLON, OUTBOARD MER ADAPTER, TER

15 AERO-27A RACK, CENTERLINE MER ADAPTER AND TER

16 NO ADDITIONAL EQUIPMENT REQUIRED

17 LAU-17/A WING MISSILE PYLON, TER ADAPTER

FDB-1-(100)

Figure 11-1

STATION LOADING

WARNING

For precise external store and attachment information, refer to charts C and E of the Weight and Balance Data Handbook (AN-01-1B-40) for your airplane.

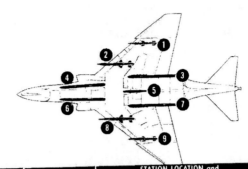

STORES BOMBS	UNIT WEIGHT (LBS)	UNIT DRAG	STABILITY NUMBER SINGLE MOUNTED	STABILITY NUMBER CLUSTER MOUNTED	BOMB RACK or BOMB CLUSTER POSITION		1	2	3	4	5	6	7	8	9
CBU-24/29/49 DISPENSER	835	4.2	7.4	9.9	MER	FWD CLUSTER	-.26				-.52				-.26
					MER	AFT CLUSTER	+.63				+.42				+.63
						TER	+.37	-.55			+.11			-.55	+.37
M-117A1	823	3.0	7.3	9.7	MER	FWD CLUSTER	-.26				-.52				-.26
					MER	AFT CLUSTER	+.63				+.37				+.63
						TER	+.37	-.57			+.11			-.57	+.37
MK-40 DESTRUCTOR (WITH SNAKEYE FIN)	1057	3.9	NE	NE	MER	FWD CLUSTER									
					MER	AFT CLUSTER									
						TER									
MK-81 LDGP	270	0.8	1.8	2.4	MER	FWD CLUSTER	-.10				-.15				-.10
					MER	AFT CLUSTER	+.21				+.16				+.21
						TER	+.11	-.15			+.05			-.15	+.11
MK-81 SNAKEYE	300	1.2	1.8	2.4	MER	FWD CLUSTER	-.09				-.18				-.09
					MER	AFT CLUSTER	+.25				+.14				+.25
						TER	+.13	-.19			+.05			-.19	+.13
MK-82 LDGP, MK-36 DESTRUCTOR (WITH CONICAL FIN)	531	1.1	2.8	3.7	MER	FWD CLUSTER	-.15				-.31				-.15
					MER	AFT CLUSTER	+.42				+.26				+.42
						TER	+.26	-.36			+.05			-.36	+.26
MK-82 SNAKEYE, MK-36 DESTRUCTOR (WITH SNAKEYE FIN)	570	2.4	2.8	3.7	MER	FWD CLUSTER	-.15				-.36				-.15
					MER	AFT CLUSTER	+.47				+.31				+.47
						TER	+.26	-.36			+.11			-.36	+.26
MK-83 LDGP	985	1.8	4.6	6.1	MER	FWD CLUSTER	-.05				-.62				-.05
					MER	AFT CLUSTER					+.47				
						TER	+.42	-.67			-.16			-.67	+.42
MK-77 (MOD 4)	520	3.5	14.3	19.1	MER	FWD CLUSTER	-.16				-.19				-.16
					MER	AFT CLUSTER	+.41				+.41				+.41
						TER	+.24	-.36			+.07			-.36	+.24
ROCKEYE II (MK 20)	475	2.9	NE	NE	MER	FWD CLUSTER	-.15				-.31				-.15
					MER	AFT CLUSTER	+.37				+.21				+.37
						TER	+.21	-.31			+.05			-.31	+.21

STORES MISSILES		UNIT WEIGHT (LBS)	UNIT DRAG	STABILITY NUMBER SINGLE MOUNTED	STABILITY NUMBER CLUSTER MOUNTED	BOMB RACK or BOMB CLUSTER POSITION	1	2	3	4	5	6	7	8	9
SPARROW III	AIM-7D	402	FUSELAGE MOUNTED 1.3 / WING MOUNTED 2.6	FUSELAGE MOUNTED NA / WING MOUNTED 2.7	NA	—		-.28	+.37	-.67		-.67	+.37	-.28	
	AIM-7E	455			NA	—		-.31	+.41	-.74		-.74	+.41	-.31	
	AIM-7E-2	427			NA	—		-.31	+.41	-.74		-.74	+.41	-.31	
	AIM-7F	515			NA	—									
SIDEWINDER	AIM-9B	157	1.3	1.0	1.4	—		-.10						-.10	
	AIM-9D/G	197	1.3	1.0	1.4	—		-.12						.12	

FDB-1-(101-1)

Figure 11-2 (Sheet 1 of 5)

STATION LOADING (CONTINUED)

A NOSE AND TAIL CONES ON
B NOSE CONE OFF TAIL CONE ON
C NOSE AND TAIL CONES OFF – FULL
D NOSE AND TAIL CONES OFF – EMPTY

STORES / ROCKETS	F/E	UNIT WEIGHT	UNIT DRAG A/B	UNIT DRAG C/D	STABILITY SINGLE MOUNTED	STABILITY CLUSTER MOUNTED	BOMB RACK or BOMB CLUSTER POSITION		1	2	3	4	5	6	7	8	9
AERO-7D, LAU-3A/A	F	431	4.2	13.5	10.1	13.5	MER	FWD CLUSTER	-.02				-.17				-.02
	E	73	12.5	12.0				AFT CLUSTER									
								TER	+.19	-.29			+.04			-.29	+.19
LAU-10/A, LAU-10A/A	F	533	3.6	11.2	8.0	10.6	MER	FWD CLUSTER	.00				-.21				.00
	E	105	10.2	10.0				AFT CLUSTER									
								TER	+.26	-.36			-.05			-.36	+.26
LAU-32A/A	F	174	2.7	6.8	3.9	5.2	MER	FWD CLUSTER	0				-.06				0
	E	51	6.3	6.2				AFT CLUSTER									
								TER	+.08	-.11			+.03			-.11	+.08
LAU-32B/A	F	175	2.7	6.8	3.9	5.2	MER	FWD CLUSTER	0				-.06				0
	E	53	6.3	6.2				AFT CLUSTER									
								TER	+.08	-.11			+.03			-.11	+.08
LAU-33A/A	F	286	F	2.2	NE	NA											
	E	72	E	2.2													
LAU-59/A	F	188	2.7	6.8	3.9	5.2	MER	FWD CLUSTER	.00				-.06				.00
	E	60	6.3	6.2				AFT CLUSTER									
								TER	+.08	-.11			+.03			-.11	+.08
LAU-60/A	F	434	4.2	13.5	10.1	13.5	MER	FWD CLUSTER	.00				+.36				.00
	E	74	12.5	12.0				AFT CLUSTER									
								TER	+.26	-.36			-.11			-.36	+.26
LAU-61/A	F	502	4.2	13.5	10.1	13.5	MER	FWD CLUSTER	.00				-.36				.00
	E	115	12.5	12.0				AFT CLUSTER									
								TER	+.26	-.36			+.11			-.36	+.26
LAU-68/A	F	200	2.7	6.8	3.9	5.2	MER	FWD CLUSTER	-.05				-.15				-.05
	E	58	6.3	6.2				AFT CLUSTER									
								TER	+.11	-.15			+.05			-.15	+.11
LAU-69/A	F	483	4.2	13.5	10.1	13.5	MER	FWD CLUSTER	.00				-.31				.00
	E	95	12.5	12.0				AFT CLUSTER									
								TER	+.21	-.36			+.11			-.36	+.21

STORES / PRACTICE BOMBS & ROCKETS	UNIT WEIGHT (LBS)	UNIT DRAG	STABILITY SINGLE MOUNTED	STABILITY CLUSTER MOUNTED	BOMB RACK or BOMB CLUSTER POSITION		1	2	3	4	5	6	7	8	9
MK 76	24	0.3	1.0	1.0	PMBR WITH (6) UNITS		+.11	-.15			+.05			-.15	+.11
MK 76	24	0.3	NE	NE	MER	FWD CLUSTER									
						AFT CLUSTER									
						TER									
MK 86 (WET SAND FILL)	200	0.8	1.8	2.4	MER	FWD CLUSTER	-.07				-.13				-.07
						AFT CLUSTER	+.18				+.12				+.18
						TER	+.42	-.14			+.03			-.14	+.42
MK 87 (WET SAND FILL)	330	1.1	2.8	3.7	MER	FWD CLUSTER					-.21				
						AFT CLUSTER	+.27				+.17				+.27
						TER		-.22			+.03			-.22	
MK 88 (WET SAND FILL)	750	1.8	4.6	6.1	MER	FWD CLUSTER	-.03				-.52				-.03
						AFT CLUSTER					+.32				
						TER		-.53			+.12			-.53	
MK 89	56	0.2	NE	NE	PMBR WITH (6) UNITS		+.21	-.31			-.05			-.31	+.21
MK 89	56	0.2	NE	NE	MER	FWD CLUSTER									
						AFT CLUSTER									
						TER									
MK 106	5	0.4	1.0	1.0	PMBR WITH (6) UNITS		+.05	-.05			.00			-.05	+.05
MK 106	5	0.4	NE	NE	MER	FWD CLUSTER									
						AFT CLUSTER									
						TER									
MK 124	565	2.8	NE	NE	NE										

FDB-1-(101-2)

Figure 11-2 (Sheet 2 of 5)

STATION LOADING (CONTINUED)

STORES			UNIT WEIGHT (LBS)	UNIT DRAG	STABILITY NUMBER		BOMB RACK or BOMB CLUSTER POSITION	STATION LOCATION and INCREMENTAL CG SHIFT FOR INDIVIDUAL UNIT								
TANKS, RACKS AND PODS					SINGLE MOUNTED	CLUSTER MOUNTED		1	2	3	4	5	6	7	8	9
370 GALLON EXTERNAL WING TANKS (INCLUDES PYLON)	MCDONNELL	E	340	4.8	29.8 ①	NA		+.05								+.05
		F	2856		20.0 ②			+.25								+.25
	SARGENT FLETCHER	E	308	6.4	29.8 ①	NA		+.05								+.05
		F	2824		20.0 ②			+.25								-.25
	ROYAL JET	E	NE	6.4	NE	NE										
		F	NE													
600 GALLON EXTERNAL CENTERLINE TANK	MCDONNELL	E	249	9.6	NA	NA						+.03				
		F	4329									+.33				
	ROYAL JET	E	304	9.6	NA	NA						+.03				
		F	4384									+.33				
MK-4 GUN POD		E	787	11.6	NA	NA						+.00				
		F	1390									+.31				
MK 12 MOD 0 SMOKE TANK		E	350	3.3	8.0	10.6	TER									
		F	1000	3.3												
LM-119A AERIAL FILM DELIVERY CONTAINER		E	180	5.5	NA	NA						+.05				
		F	450													
EXTERNAL WING TANK PYLON			92	1.1	4.3	NA		+.04								+.04
LAU-17/A GUIDED MISSILE LAUNCHER			150	2.4	6.9	NA			-.06						-.06	
MER ADAPTER			24	0.4	NA	NA		+.01								+.01
TER ADAPTER			24	0.3	NA	NA			-.02						-.02	
MER/TER ℄ ADAPTER			55	2.0	NA	NA						0				
LAUNCHER LAU-7/A, AERO 3A			87	0.4	2.2	NA			-.05						-.05	
MER	℄ STATION		215	8.0	NA	NA	RACK SHIFTED FWD / RACK SHIFTED AFT					-.01 / .06				
	WING STATION		225	8.0	7.1	NA	RACK SHIFTED FWD / RACK SHIFTED AFT	+.06 / +.12								+.06 / -.12
TER	℄ STATION		95	5.5	NA	NA						+.01				
	WING STATION		95	5.5	6.6	NA		+.05	-.05						-.05	+.05
℄ BOMB RACK AERO-27A			51	NA	NA	NA						0				
RCPP-105 STARTER POD (FULLY SERVICED)			2016	7.4	NA	NA										
D-704 AIR REFUEL STORE		E	733	10.0	NA	NA										
		F	2773	10.0	NA	NA										
CNU-169/A BAGGAGE POD		E	185	4.4	18.0	NA										
		F	435													
LB-30A STRIKE CAMERA POD			126	NA	NA	NA										

① WING TANK AND PYLON (WITH WEAPONS OR PYLONS INSTALLED ON STATIONS 2 & 8)
② WING TANK AND PYLON (WITHOUT WEAPONS OR PYLONS INSTALLED ON STATIONS 2 & 8)

FDB-7-(101-3)

Figure 11-2 (Sheet 3 of 5)

STATION LOADING (CONTINUED)

STORES FLARES, SPECIAL WEAPONS, SENSORS		UNIT WEIGHT (LBS)	UNIT DRAG	STABILITY NUMBER SINGLE MOUNTED	STABILITY NUMBER CLUSTER MOUNTED	BOMB RACK or BOMB CLUSTER POSITION		STATION LOCATION and INCREMENTAL CG SHIFT FOR INDIVIDUAL UNIT 1	2	3	4	5	6	7	8	9
MK-24, MK 45 PARAFLARE		27	1.0	1.0	1.3	MER	FWD CLUSTER	.00				.00				.00
							AFT CLUSTER	.00				.00				.00
							TER	.00	.00			.00				.00
SUU-40/44 FLARE DISPENSER	F	365	3.6	NE	NE	MER	FWD CLUSTER									
	E	125	3.6				AFT CLUSTER	+.37				+.21				+.37
							TER	+.16	-.31			+.11			-.31	+.16
B-43 BOMB	MOD. 0	2060	4.1	NA	NA	-						+.26				
	MOD. 1	2125	4.1	NA	NA	-						+.22				
B-57 BOMB		500	2.2	NA	NA	-						+.13				
MK-104 BOMB		2100	4.1	NA	NA	-						+.31				
BDU-20/C		500	NE	NE	NE	-										
BDU-6		2125	NE	NE	NE	-										
BDU-11E		500	2.2	NA	NA	-						+.16				
B-61		715	2.2	NE	NE	-										
AERO-8A-1 PRACTICE BOMB CONTAINER	F	504	3.3	NA	NA	-						+.11				
	E	354														
ADSID (NORMAL) SENSOR		26	4.5	NE	NE	-										
SUU-40/44 DISPENSER WITH AN/GSQ-117/-117LS/-141 SENSOR		NE	3.6	NE	NE	-										
			3.6													
NAMAR CAMERA POD		275	3.8	NE	NE	-										
CTU-1/A DELIVERY CONTAINER (EMPTY)		230	4.9	NE	NE	MER	FWD CLUSTER									
							AFT CLUSTER									
							TER									

FDB-1-(101-4)

Figure 11-2 (Sheet 4 of 5)

STATION LOADING, (CONTINUED)

Notes

- THE DRAG INDEX OF THE CLEAN AIRPLANE IS ZERO.

- INDIVIDUAL STORE DRAG X NUMBER OF STORES TO BE CARRIED + SUSPENSION EQUIPMENT DRAG (IF NOT INCLUDED) = DRAG INDEX

- DRAG NUMBERS FOR SINGLE STORES ARE SLIGHTLY CONSERVATIVE. INTERFERENCE DRAG BETWEEN MULTIPLE STORES HAS BEEN CONSIDERED.

- FUSELAGE-MOUNTED STORES ARE NOT USED IN DETERMINING AIRPLANE STABILITY INDEX BUT THEY ARE USED IN COMPUTING TAKEOFF CG LOCATION.

- TANDEM-MOUNTED WEAPONS COUNT AS A SINGLE WEAPON WHEN COMPUTING THE AIRCRAFT STABILITY INDEX.

- UNIT STABILITY NUMBERS ARE ASSIGNED FOR SINGLE MOUNTED AND CLUSTER MOUNTED WEAPONS. THE CLUSTER MOUNTED UNIT STABILITY NUMBER WILL BE USED WHEN TWO OR MORE WEAPONS ARE MOUNTED ON THE SAME RACK, WITH EACH WEAPON BEING ASSIGNED THIS NUMBER.

- NE = NOT ESTABLISHED

- NA = NOT APPLICABLE

- E = EMPTY, F = FULL

Estimated Operating Weight (Basic airplane plus the weight of oil, unusable fuel, and two (2) crew members)
AIRPLANES: 153912ab   29,000 LBS   32.4% M.A.C.

Estimated Take-off Gross Weight (Estimated operating weight plus weight of full internal fuel)
AIRPLANES: 153912ab   42,505 LBS   33.8% M.A.C.

NOTE: The incremental C.G. shift effects are in terms of % MAC (+ = AFT C.G. Shift), (- = FWD C.G. Shift). These unit store increments are approximations only, and will vary depending on the airplane gross weight and C.G. The above data is based on the estimated takeoff gross weight clean, for airplanes 153912ab and is considered more representative on F-4B aircraft.

FDB-1-(101-5)

Figure 11-2 (Sheet 5 of 5)

DRAG DUE TO ASYMMETRIC LOADING

REMARKS
ENGINE(S): (2) J79—GE-8
ICAO STANDARD DAY

GUIDE

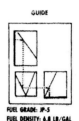

FUEL GRADE: JP-5
FUEL DENSITY: 6.8 LB/GAL

DATE: 1 MAY 1968
DATA BASIS: ESTIMATED (BASED ON FLIGHT TEST)

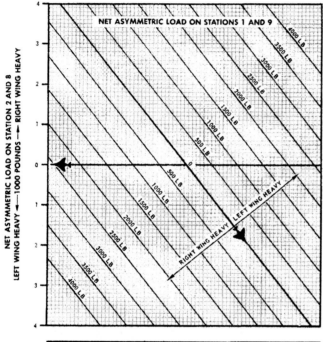

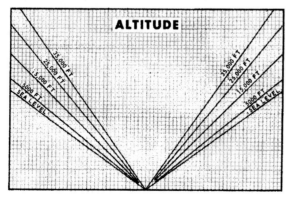

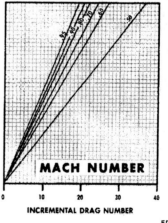

Note

● INCREMENTAL DRAG NUMBER IS INDEPENDENT OF TOTAL AIRCRAFT GROSS WEIGHT

● INCREMENTAL DRAG NUMBER VARIES WITH MACH NUMBER AND ALTITUDE

FDB-1-(102)

Figure 11-3

11-15

AIRSPEED CONVERSION

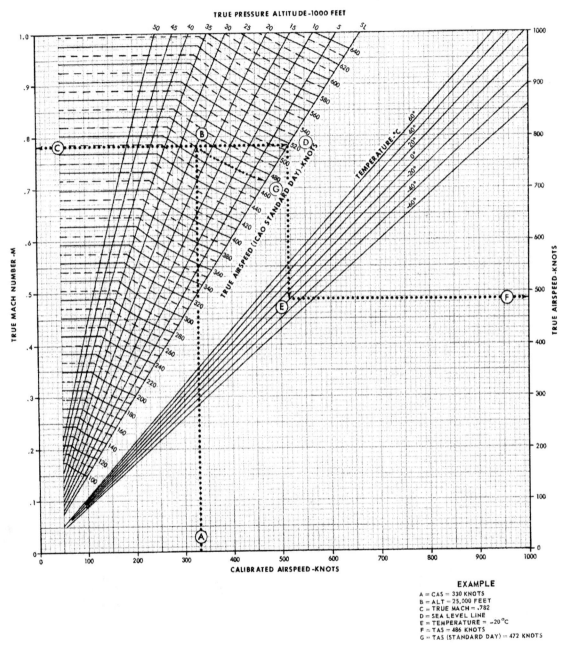

EXAMPLE

A = CAS = 330 KNOTS
B = ALT = 25,000 FEET
C = TRUE MACH = .782
D = SEA LEVEL LINE
E = TEMPERATURE = −20°C
F = TAS = 486 KNOTS
G = TAS (STANDARD DAY) = 472 KNOTS

FDB-1-(103-1)

Figure 11-4 (Sheet 1 of 2)

AIRSPEED CONVERSION

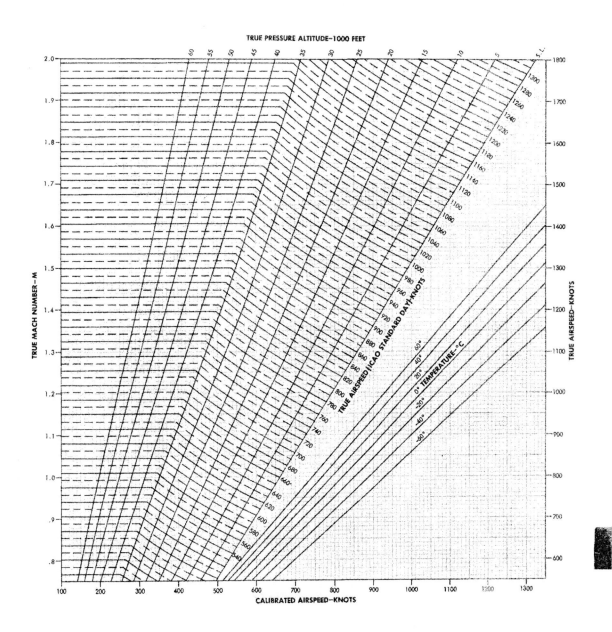

Figure 11-4 (Sheet 2 of 2)

SPC / ALTIMETER TOLERANCE CHECK
5,000 TO 20,000 FEET

AIRPLANE CONFIGURATION
FLAPS RETRACTED, GEAR UP

REMARKS
ENGINE(S): (2) J79-GE-8
ICAO STANDARD DAY

GUIDE

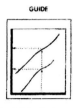

DATE: 15 MARCH 1966
DATA BASIS: **ESTIMATED** (BASED ON FLIGHT TEST)

FUEL GRADE: JP-5
FUEL DENSITY: 6.8 LB/GAL

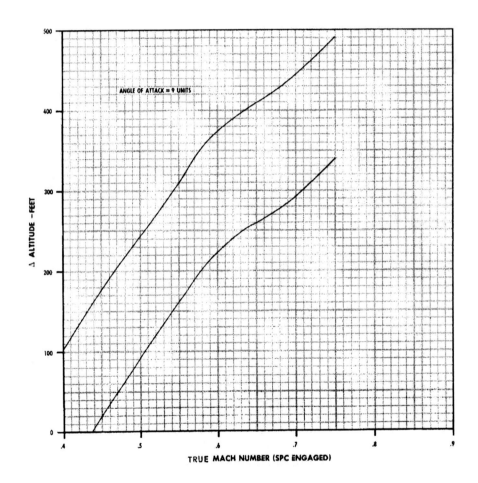

FDB-1-(104)

Figure 11-5

AIRSPEED POSITION ERROR CORRECTION
STATIC CORRECTION OFF

AIRPLANE CONFIGURATION
ALL DRAG INDEXES
FLAPS AND GEAR AS NOTED

REMARKS
ENGINE(S):(2) J79-GE-8

GUIDE

FUEL GRADE: JP-5
FUEL DENSITY: 6.8 LB/GAL

AIRCRAFT WITH DROOPED AILERONS

DATE: 15 OCTOBER 1967
DATA BASIS: FLIGHT TEST

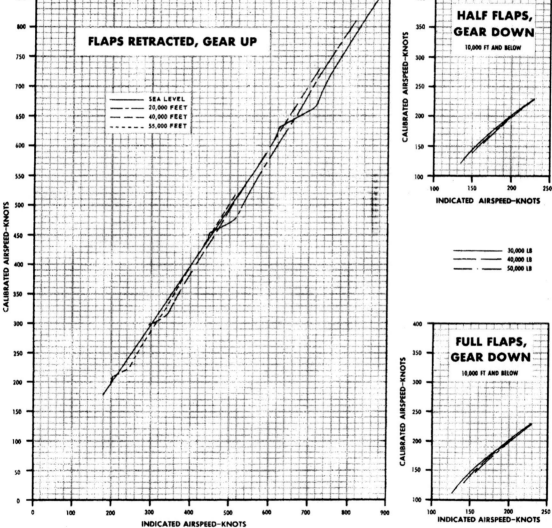

Figure 11-6

FDB-1-(105)

AIRSPEED POSITION ERROR CORRECTION
STATIC CORRECTION OFF

AIRPLANE CONFIGURATION
ALL DRAG INDEXES
FLAPS AND GEAR AS NOTED

REMARKS
ENGINE(S): J79-GE-8

GUIDE

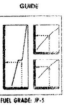

FUEL GRADE: JP-5
FUEL DENSITY: 6.8 LB./GAL

AIRCRAFT WITHOUT DROOPED AILERONS

DATE: 15 OCTOBER 1967
DATA BASIS: FLIGHT TEST

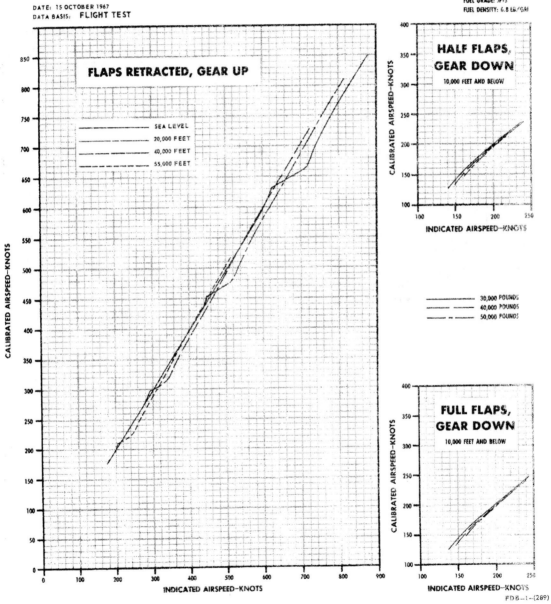

Figure 11-7

AIRSPEED POSITION ERROR CORRECTION
STATIC CORRECTION OFF

AIRPLANE CONFIGURATION

ALL DRAG INDEXES
FLAPS RETRACTED, GEAR UP

REMARKS
ENGINE(S): (2) J79-GE-8

GUIDE

AIRPLANES WITH OR WITHOUT
DROOPED AILERONS

DATE: 15 OCTOBER 1967
DATA BASIS: FLIGHT TEST

FUEL GRADE: JP-5
FUEL DENSITY: 6.8 LB/GAL

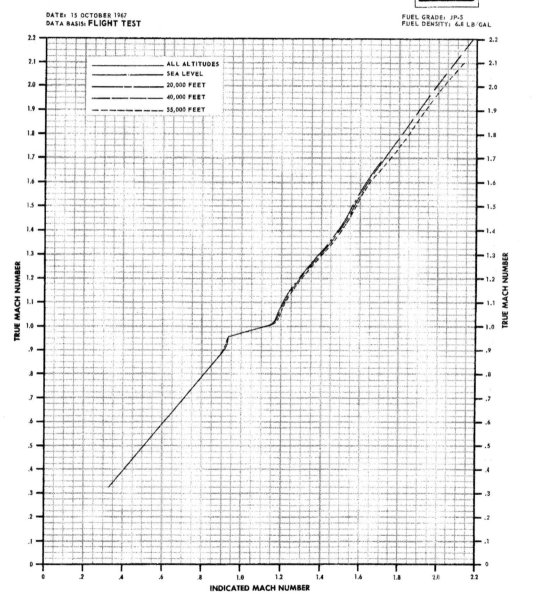

FDB-1-(290)

Figure 11-8

ALTIMETER POSITION ERROR CORRECTION
STATIC CORRECTION OFF

AIRPLANE CONFIGURATION
ALL DRAG INDEXES
FLAPS AND GEAR AS NOTED

REMARKS
ENGINE(S):(2) J79-GE-8

NOTE: ASSIGNED ALTITUDE + Δ H = INDICATED
ALTITUDE . FLY INDICATED ALTITUDE.

GUIDE

FUEL GRADE: JP-5
FUEL DENSITY: 6.8 LB/GAL

AIRCRAFT WITH DROOPED AILERONS

DATE: 15 OCTOBER 1967
DATA BASIS: FLIGHT TEST

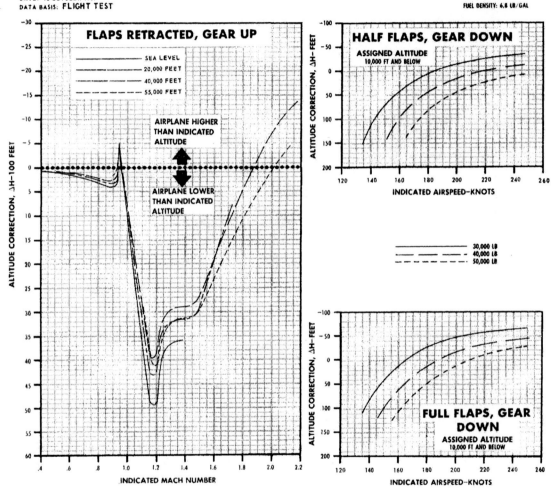

Figure 11-9

FDB-1-(106)

ALTIMETER POSITION ERROR CORRECTION
STATIC CORRECTION OFF

AIRPLANE CONFIGURATION
ALL DRAG INDEXES
FLAPS AND GEAR AS NOTED

REMARKS
ENGINE(S): (2) J79-GE- 8

NOTE: ASSIGNED ALTITUDE + ∆H = INDICATED
ALTITUDE . FLY INDICATED ALTITUDE.

GUIDE

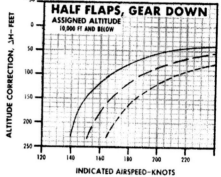

AIRCRAFT WITHOUT DROOPED AILERONS

DATE: 15 OCTOBER 1967
DATA BASIS: FLIGHT TEST

FUEL GRADE: JP-5
FUEL DENSITY: 6.8 LB/GAL

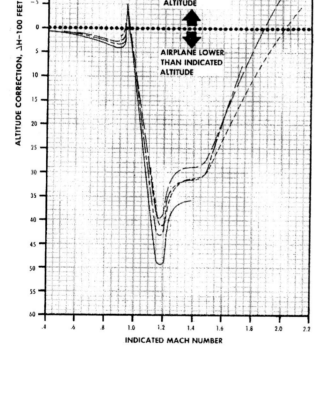

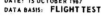

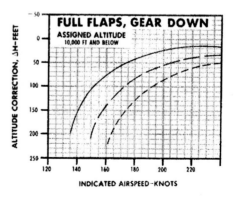

FDB-1-(291)

Figure 11-10

ALTIMETER LAG

AIRPLANE CONFIGURATION
ALL DRAG INDEXES

REMARKS
ENGINE(S): (2) J79-GE-8

GUIDE

WITH SPC INOPERATIVE

DATE: 1 AUGUST 1969
DATA BASIS: ESTIMATED

FUEL GRADE: JP-5
FUEL DENSITY: 6.8 LB/GAL

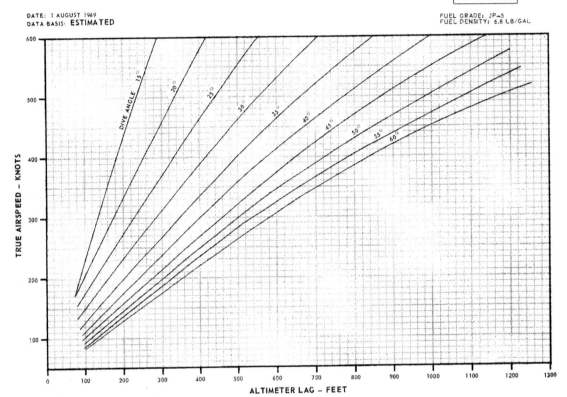

FDB-1-(288)

Figure 11-11

ALTIMETER LAG

AIRPLANE CONFIGURATION
ALL DRAG INDEXES

REMARKS

ENGINE(S): (2) J79-GE-8

WITH SPC OPERATIVE

DATE: 15 DECEMBER 1968
DATA BASIS: **FLIGHT TEST**

GUIDE

FUEL GRADE: JP-5
FUEL DENSITY: 6.8 LB/GAL

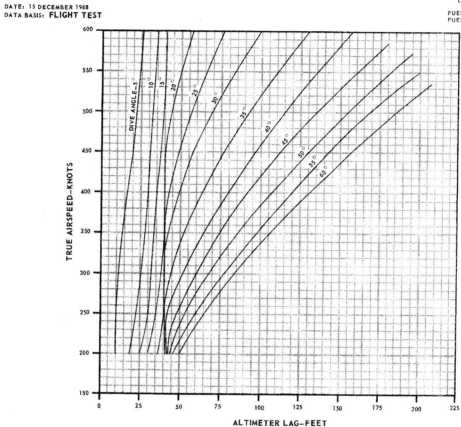

Figure 11-12

FDB-1-(107)

STANDARD ATMOSPHERE TABLE

Standard Sea Level Air:
T = 15°C.
P = 29.921 in. of Hg.

W = .07651 lb/cu. ft. ρ_0 = .002378 slugs/cu. ft.
1" of Hg. = 70.732 lb/sq. ft. = 0.4912 lb/sq. in.
a_0 - 1116 ft./sec.

This table is based on NACA Technical Report No. 218

ALTITUDE FEET	DENSITY RATIO ρ/ρ_0	$\frac{1}{\sqrt{\sigma}}$	TEMPERATURE		SPEED OF SOUND RATIO a/a_0	PRESSURE	
			DEG. C	DEG. F		IN. OF Hg	RATIO P/P_0
0	1.0000	1.0000	15.000	59.000	1.000	29.92	1.0000
1000	.9710	1.0148	13.019	55.434	.997	28.86	.9644
2000	.9428	1.0299	11.038	51.868	.993	27.82	.9298
3000	.9151	1.0454	9.056	48.301	.990	26.81	.8962
4000	.8881	1.0611	7.075	44.735	.986	25.84	.8636
5000	.8616	1.0773	5.094	41.169	.983	24.89	.8320
6000	.8358	1.0938	3.113	37.603	.979	23.98	.8013
7000	.8106	1.1107	1.132	34.037	.976	23.09	.7716
8000	.7859	1.1280	-0.850	30.471	.972	22.22	.7427
9000	.7619	1.1456	-2.831	26.904	.968	21.38	.7147
10,000	.7384	1.1637	-4.812	23.338	.965	20.58	.6876
11,000	.7154	1.1822	-6.793	19.772	.962	19.79	.6614
12,000	.6931	1.2012	-8.774	16.206	.958	19.03	.6359
13,000	.6712	1.2206	-10.756	12.640	.954	18.29	.6112
14,000	.6499	1.2404	-12.737	9.074	.950	17.57	.5873
15,000	.6291	1.2608	-14.718	5.507	.947	16.88	.5642
16,000	.6088	1.2816	-16.699	1.941	.943	16.21	.5418
17,000	.5891	1.3029	-18.680	-1.625	.940	15.56	.5202
18,000	.5698	1.3247	-20.662	-5.191	.936	14.94	.4992
19,000	.5509	1.3473	-22.643	-8.757	.932	14.33	.4790
20,000	.5327	1.3701	-24.624	-12.323	.929	13.75	.4594
21,000	.5148	1.3937	-26.605	-15.890	.925	13.18	.4405
22,000	.4974	1.4179	-28.586	-19.456	.922	12.63	.4222
23,000	.4805	1.4426	-30.568	-23.022	.917	12.10	.4045
24,000	.4640	1.4681	-32.549	-26.588	.914	11.59	.3874
25,000	.4480	1.4940	-34.530	-30.154	.910	11.10	.3709
26,000	.4323	1.5209	-36.511	-33.720	.906	10.62	.3550
27,000	.4171	1.5484	-38.493	-37.287	.903	10.16	.3397
28,000	.4023	1.5768	-40.474	-40.853	.899	9.720	.3248
29,000	.3879	1.6056	-42.455	-44.419	.895	9.293	.3106
30,000	.3740	1.6352	-44.436	-47.985	.891	8.880	.2968
31,000	.3603	1.6659	-46.417	-51.551	.887	8.483	.2834
32,000	.3472	1.6971	-48.399	-55.117	.883	8.101	.2707
33,000	.3343	1.7295	-50.379	-58.684	.879	7.732	.2583
34,000	.3218	1.7628	-52.361	-62.250	.875	7.377	.2465
35,000	.3098	1.7966	-54.342	-65.816	.871	7.036	.2352
36,000	.2962	1.8374	-55.000	-67.000	.870	6.708	.2242
37,000	.2824	1.8818	-55.000	-67.000	.870	6.395	.2137
38,000	.2692	1.9273	-55.000	-67.000	.870	6.096	.2037
39,000	.2566	1.9738	-55.000	-67.000	.870	5.812	.1943
40,000	.2447	2.0215	-55.000	-67.000	.870	5.541	.1852
41,000	.2332	2.0707	-55.000	-67.000	.870	5.283	.1765
42,000	.2224	2.1207	-55.000	-67.000	.870	5.036	.1683
43,000	.2120	2.1719	-55.000	-67.000	.870	4.802	.1605
44,000	.2021	2.2244	-55.000	-67.000	.870	4.578	.1530
45,000	.1926	2.2785	-55.000	-67.000	.870	4.364	.1458
46,000	.1837	2.3332	-55.000	-67.000	.870	4.160	.1391
47,000	.1751	2.3893	-55.000	-67.000	.870	3.966	.1325
48,000	.1669	2.4478	-55.000	-67.000	.870	3.781	.1264
49,000	.1591	2.5071	-55.000	-67.000	.870	3.604	.1205
50,000	.1517	2.5675	-55.000	-67.000	.870	3.436	.1149

FDB-1-(108)

Figure 11-13

WIND COMPONENTS

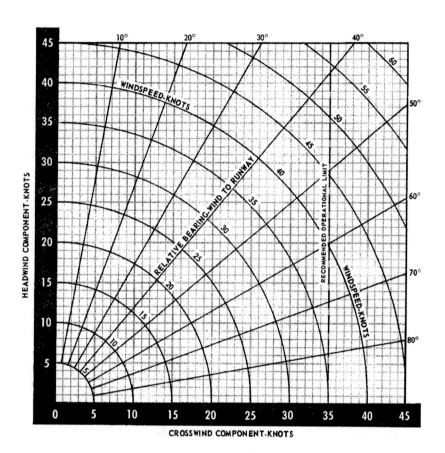

PART 2 TAKEOFF

CHARTS

DEFINITIONS OF TERMS USED

REFUSAL SPEED

Refusal speed is the maximum speed to which the aircraft can accelerate and then stop within the available runway length.

REFUSAL DISTANCE

Refusal distance is the distance required to accelerate to refusal speed under normal conditions.

CRITICAL ENGINE FAILURE SPEED

The critical engine failure speed is the speed at which the aircraft, after an engine failure, will accelerate to takeoff in the same distance required to decelerate to a complete stop. If engine failure occurs at a lower speed, a shorter distance is required to stop than to takeoff, while engine failure at a higher speed results in a shorter distance to takeoff than to stop.

CRITICAL FIELD LENGTH

The critical field length is the total runway length required to accelerate the aircraft, experience an engine failure, and then either take off with the remaining engine or decelerate the aircraft to a complete stop. The critical field length may be no greater than the length of the available runway.

TAKEOFF-ABORT CRITERIA

This chart (figure 11-15) is presented to provide the pilot with an integrated picture of the takeoff planning criteria.

CRITICAL ENGINE FAILURE SPEED OR CRITICAL FIELD LENGTH CHART

These charts (figures 11-16 thru 11-19) are used to determine the critical engine failure speed and corresponding critical field length under conditions of maximum or military thrust and with or without the drag chute deployed. Single-engine takeoff/climb-out limits for gross weights above 40,000 pounds are cross-plotted on the pressure altitude graph. If the combined temperature and pressure altitude point falls above the interpolated limit curve for a particular gross weight, a single-engine takeoff/climb-out cannot be effected.

USE

Enter the chart at the applicable temperature and project vertically to intersect the pressure altitude. (Note single-engine takeoff and climb-out limit.) Then proceed horizontally to the right and intersect

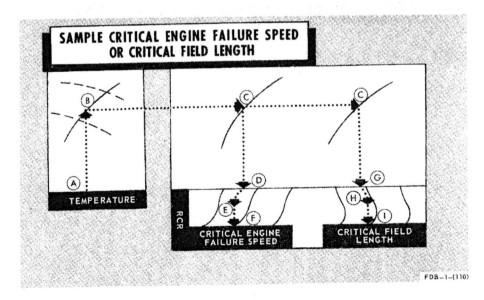

SAMPLE CRITICAL ENGINE FAILURE SPEED OR CRITICAL FIELD LENGTH

FDB-1-(110)

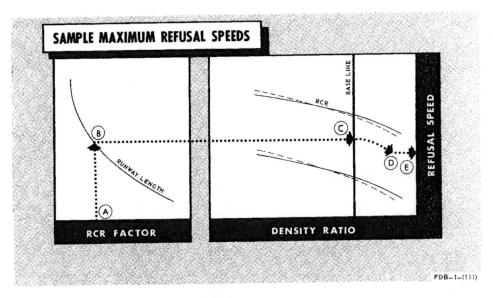

SAMPLE MAXIMUM REFUSAL SPEEDS

FDB-1-(111)

both series of gross weight curves. From the intersection of the gross weight curve in the first series,
project vertically downward to the base line. From
this point, parallel the closest guide line to the RCR
factor, then project vertically downward to read
critical engine failure speed. From the intersection
of the gross weight curve in the second series, project vertically downward to the base line. From this
point, again parallel the closest guide line to the RCR
factor and further downward to read critical field
length. Refer to the Wind Effects on Takeoff chart,
this part, to determine wind effects on critical field
length.

Sample Problem

Maximum Thrust, Without Drag Chute, With Drooped
Ailerons

A.	Temperature	20° C
B.	Pressure altitude	2000 Ft.
C.	Gross weight (intersect both series of curves)	50,000 Lbs.
D.	RCR base line	
E.	RCR factor	15
F.	Critical engine failure speed	102 Kts.
G.	RCR base line	
H.	RCR factor	15
I.	Critical field length	9000 Ft.

DENSITY RATIO CHART

This chart (figure 11-20) provides density ratio
values for various combinations of pressure altitude
and temperature. Density ratio is required for determining maximum refusal speed.

USE

Enter the chart with the pressure altitude and project
horizontally to the right to intersect the appropriate
temperature curve. From this intersection, project
vertically downward to read density ratio.

Sample Problem

A.	Pressure altitude	5000 Ft.
B.	Temperature	0° C
C.	Density ratio	0.88

MAXIMUM REFUSAL SPEED CHARTS

These charts (figures 11-21 thru 11-28) provide the
capability to determine maximum refusal speed under conditions of maximum or military thrust and
with or without drag chute deployment. Separate
plots are utilized to present the three takeoff gross
weights.

Note

These charts are based on a no-wind condition.

USE

Enter the chart at the applicable RCR factor and proceed vertically to intersect the available runway
length. From this intersection, proceed horizontally
to the right and intersect the base line. From this
point, parallel the applicable RCR guide line (right or
left) to the previously computed density ratio. Then
project horizontally to the right and read maximum
refusal speed.

Sample Problem

Maximum Thrust, Without Drag Chute, 40,000 Lbs.
Gross Weight, With Drooped Ailerons.

A.	RCR factor	23
B.	Available runway length	8000 Ft.
C.	RCR base line	
D.	Density ratio (pre-viously computed)	0.88
E.	Maximum refusal speed	105 Kts.

SAMPLE TAKEOFF DISTANCE

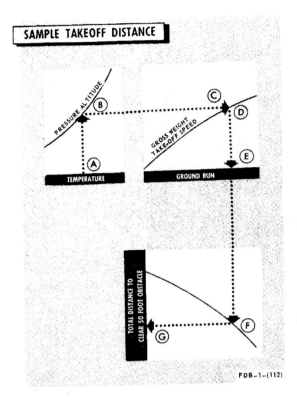

FDB-1-(112)

TAKEOFF DISTANCE CHARTS

These charts (figures 11-29 thru 11-32) provide the capability of determining the airplane takeoff speed, normal ground-run distance, and the total distance required to clear a 50-foot obstacle. Separate charts are provided for maximum and military thrust, with or without drooped ailerons.

USE

Enter the chart at the applicable temperature and proceed vertically to intersect the pressure altitude. From this point, proceed horizontally to the right and intersect the takeoff gross weight line (note airplane takeoff speed). Then descend vertically to read ground run distance. To find the total distance required to clear a 50-foot obstacle, continue downward to the reflector line and project horizontally to the left scale. Refer to the Wind Effects on Takeoff

chart, this part, to determine wind effects on these distances.

Sample Problem

Military Thrust, Without Drooped Ailerons.

A.	Temperature	20° C
B.	Pressure altitude	2000 Ft.
C.	Gross weight	40,000 Lbs.
D.	Takeoff speed	155 Kts.
E.	Ground run distance	4100 Ft.
F.	Intersect reflector line	
G.	Total distance required to clear 50-foot obstacle	5750 Ft.

Takeoff Ground Run - With Wind

A.	Effective wind (headwind)	25 Kts.
B.	Lift-off speed (previously computed)	155 Kts.
C.	Ground run distance (without wind)	4100 Ft.
D.	Ground run distance (with wind)	2900 Ft.

NOSEWHEEL LIFT-OFF SPEED CHART

These charts (figures 11-33 and 11-34) present nose-wheel lift-off speeds for various combinations of aircraft gross weight and center of gravity location. Under some extreme conditions (heavy gross weight with forward CG), the speeds required to rotate to takeoff angle of attack may approach or exceed the takeoff speeds shown on the Takeoff Distance charts.

USE

If the computed center of gravity location is forward of 33.0% MAC, enter the chart with takeoff gross weight and project horizontally to the computed CG location. From this point project vertically to the base scale to obtain nosewheel lift-off speed. Add 20 knots to nosewheel lift-off speed to obtain the takeoff speed.

Sample Problem

Configuration: 1/2 Flaps, Gear Down, With Drooped Ailerons

A.	Gross weight	47,000 Lbs.
B.	CG location	31% MAC
C.	Nosewheel lift-off speed	154 KCAS

SAMPLE WIND EFFECTS ON TAKEOFF

FDB-1-(113)

WIND EFFECTS ON TAKEOFF CHART

This chart (figure 11-35) provides the capability of adjusting the previously computed critical field length and takeoff ground run distance for wind effects.

USE

Enter the chart with the previously determined effective wind velocity (headwind or tailwind) and project horizontally to the right and intersect the previously computer aircraft velocity (critical engine failure speed or takeoff speed). From this point, descend vertically to intersect previously computed distance (critical field length or takeoff ground run). At this point of intersection, project horizontally to the left to read distance adjusted for wind effect.

Sample Problem

Critical Field Length - With Wind

A. Effective wind (headwind)   25 Kts.
B. Critical engine failure   102 Kts.
   speed (previously com-
   puted)
C. Critical field length   9000 Ft.
   (without wind)
D. Critical field length   5200 Ft.
   (with wind)

TAKEOFF ABORT CRITERIA

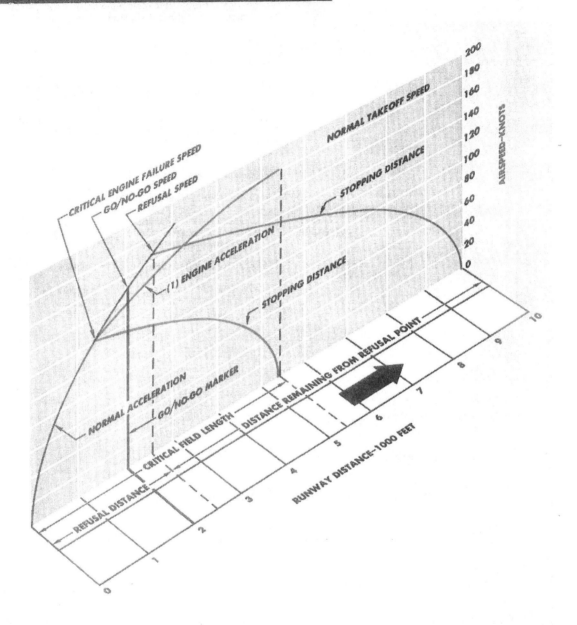

Figure 11-15

FDB-1-(114)

CRITICAL ENGINE FAILURE SPEED
OR CRITICAL FIELD LENGTH

MAXIMUM THRUST

AIRPLANE CONFIGURATION
ALL DRAG INDEXES
½ FLAPS

REMARKS
ENGINE(S): (2) J79-GE-8

AIRPLANES WITHOUT DROOPED AILERONS

GUIDE

NOTE

DATE: 1 FEBRUARY 1969
DATA BASIS: FLIGHT TEST

SINGLE-ENGINE TAKEOFF/CLIMB-OUT CAPABILITY IS CRITICAL WITH HIGH GROSS WEIGHT AT LOW DENSITY RATIOS.

FUEL GRADE: JP-5
FUEL DENSITY: 6.8 LB/GAL

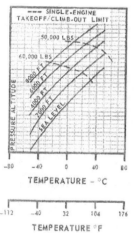

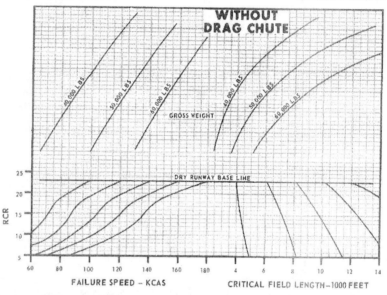

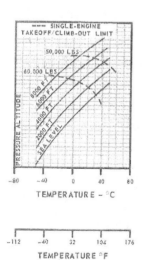

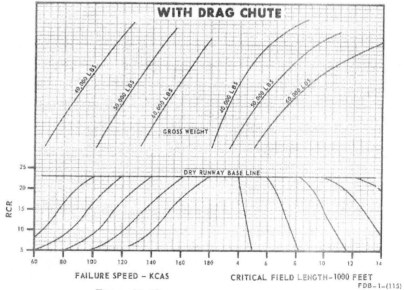

Figure 11-16

FDB-1-(115)

CRITICAL ENGINE FAILURE SPEED
OR CRITICAL FIELD LENGTH
MAXIMUM THRUST
REMARKS
ENGINE(S): (2) J79—GE—8
AIRPLANES WITH DROOPED AILERONS
NOTE

AIRPLANE CONFIGURATION

ALL DRAG INDEXES
1/2 FLAPS

GUIDE

SINGLE-ENGINE TAKEOFF/CLIMB-OUT CAPABILITY IS CRITICAL WITH HIGH GROSS WEIGHT AT LOW DENSITY RATIOS.

DATE: 15 FEBRUARY 1969
DATA BASIS: FLIGHT TEST

FUEL GRADE: JP-5
FUEL DENSITY: 6.8 LB/GAL

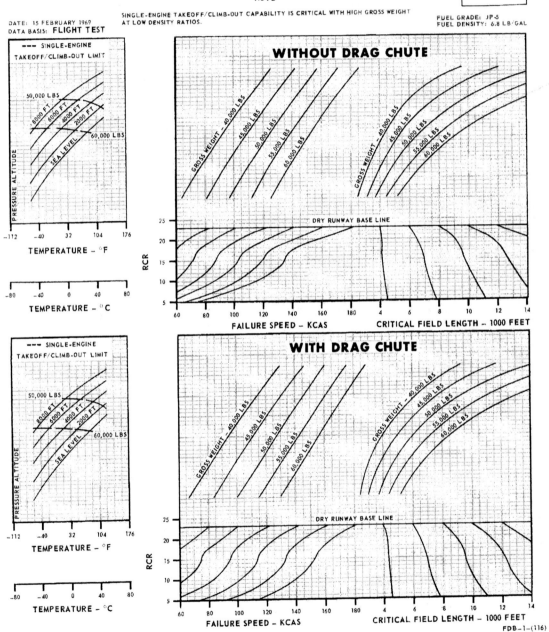

Figure 11-17

CRITICAL ENGINE FAILURE SPEED OR CRITICAL FIELD LENGTH

MILITARY THRUST

AIRPLANE CONFIGURATION
ALL DRAG INDEXES
½ FLAPS

REMARKS
ENGINE(S): (2) J79-GE-8

AIRPLANES WITHOUT DROOPED AILERONS

NOTE
- SINGLE ENGINE TAKEOFF, WITH AFTERBURNER IGNITED ON OPERATING ENGINE AFTER FAILURE.
- SINGLE-ENGINE TAKEOFF/CLIMB-OUT CAPABILITY IS CRITICAL WITH HIGH GROSS WEIGHT AT LOW DENSITY RATIOS.

FUEL GRADE: JP-5
FUEL DENSITY: 6.8 LB/GAL

GUIDE

DATE: 1 FEBRUARY 1969
DATA BASIS: **FLIGHT TEST**

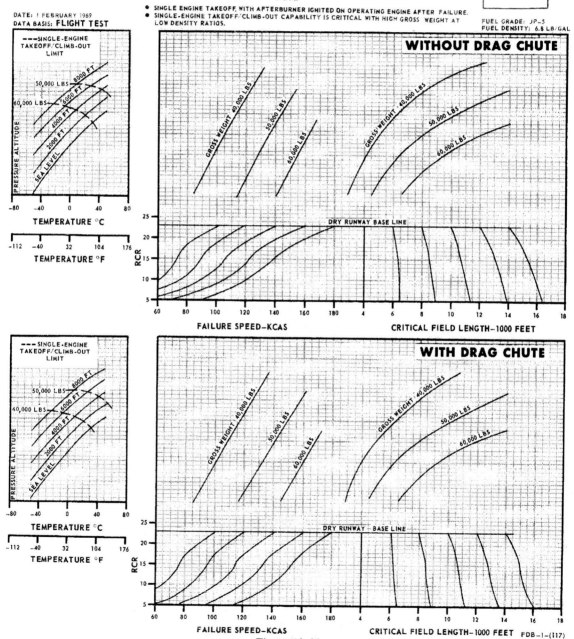

Figure 11-18

FDB-1-(117)

CRITICAL ENGINE FAILURE SPEED
OR CRITICAL FIELD LENGTH
MILITARY THRUST
REMARKS
ENGINE(S): (2) J79—GE—8

AIRPLANES WITH DROOPED AILERONS

AIRPLANE CONFIGURATION
ALL DRAG INDEXES
1/2 FLAPS

GUIDE

NOTES

- SINGLE ENGINE TAKEOFF WITH AFTERBURNER IGNITED ON OPERATING ENGINE AFTER FAILURE.
- SINGLE-ENGINE TAKEOFF/CLIMB-OUT CAPABILITY IS CRITICAL WITH HIGH GROSS WEIGHT AT LOW DENSITY RATIOS.

FUEL GRADE: JP-5
FUEL DENSITY: 6.8 LB/GAL

DATE: 15 FEBRUARY 1969
DATA BASIS: FLIGHT TEST

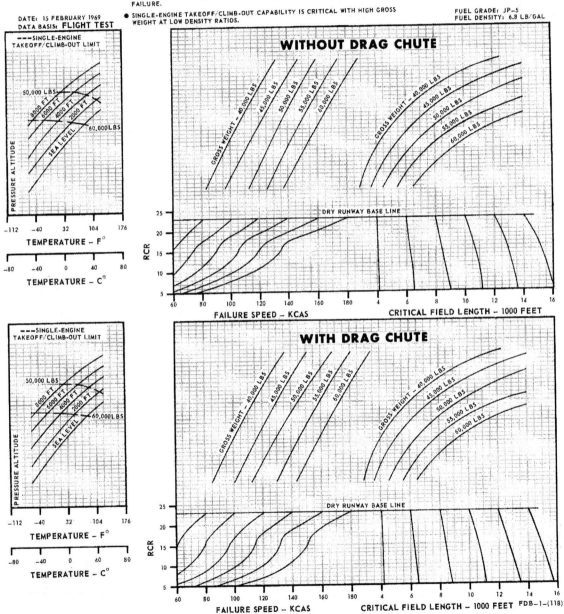

Figure 11-19

DENSITY RATIO

AIRPLANE CONFIGURATION

ALL DRAG INDEXES

GUIDE

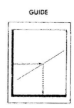

DATE: 1 FEBRUARY 1969
DATA BASIS: ESTIMATED (BASED ON FLIGHT TEST)

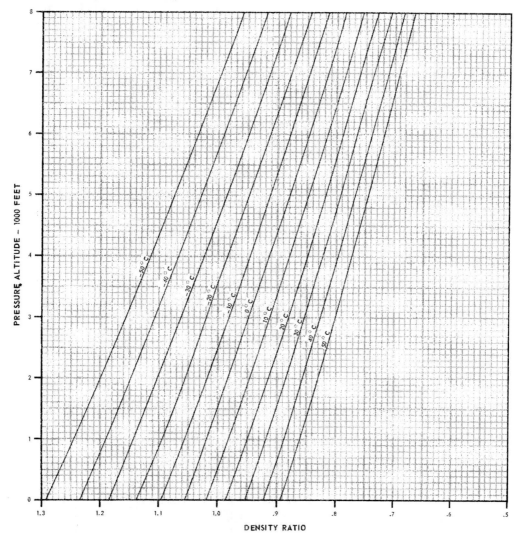

FDB-1-(119)

Figure 11-20

MAXIMUM REFUSAL SPEED
MAXIMUM THRUST-WITHOUT DRAG CHUTE

AIRPLANE CONFIGURATION
ALL DRAG INDEXES
1/2 FLAPS

REMARKS
ENGINE(S): (2) J79-GE-8

AIRPLANES WITHOUT DROOPED AILERONS

DATE: 1 FEBRUARY 1969
DATA BASIS: FLIGHT TEST

NOTE
DATA BASED ON NO-WIND CONDITION

FUEL GRADE: JP-5
FUEL DENSITY: 6.8 LB/GAL

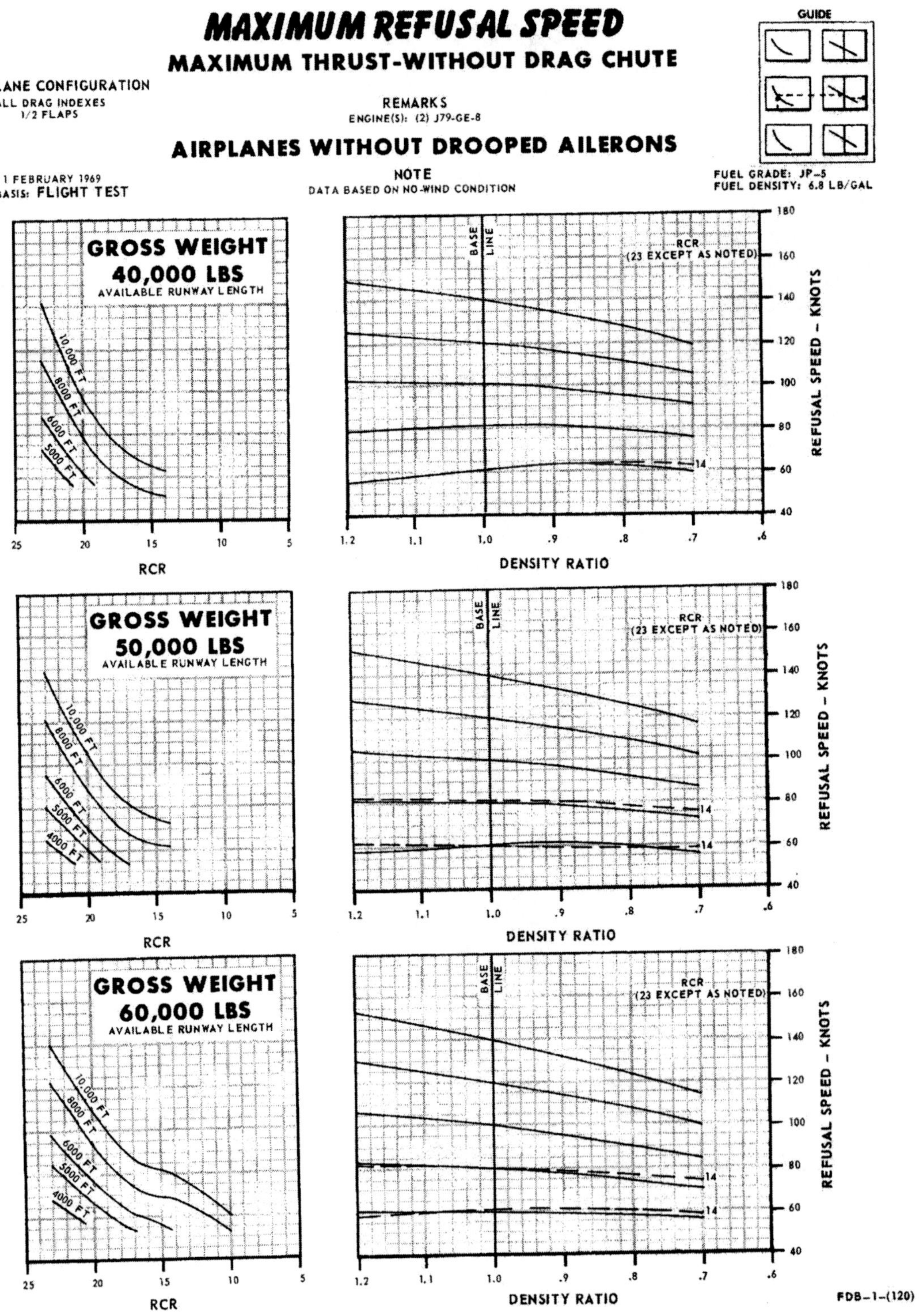

GUIDE

Figure 11-21

MAXIMUM REFUSAL SPEED
MAXIMUM THRUST-WITH DRAG CHUTE
REMARKS
ENGINE(S): (2) J79-GE-8

AIRPLANE CONFIGURATION

ALL DRAG INDEXES
1/2 FLAPS

AIRPLANES WITHOUT DROOPED AILERONS

DATE: 1 FEBRUARY 1969
DATA BASIS: FLIGHT TEST

NOTE
DATA BASED ON NO-WIND CONDITION

GUIDE

FUEL GRADE: JP-5
FUEL DENSITY: 6.8 LB/GAL

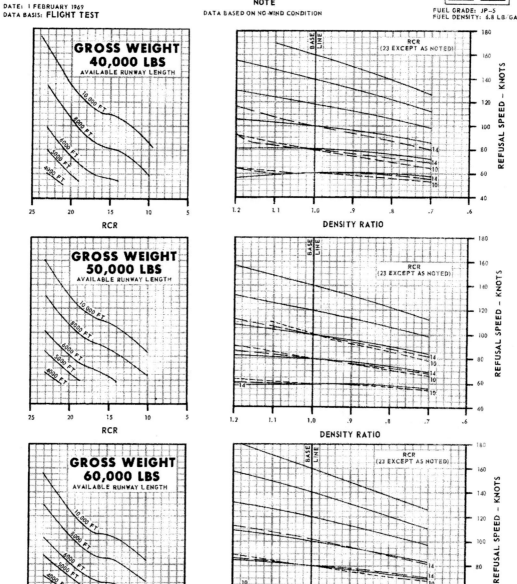

Figure 11-22

FDB-1-(121)

MAXIMUM REFUSAL SPEED
MAXIMUM THRUST-WITHOUT DRAG CHUTE
REMARKS

AIRPLANE CONFIGURATION

ALL DRAG INDEXES
1/2 FLAPS

ENGINE(S): (2) J79-GE-8

AIRPLANES WITH DROOPED AILERONS

GUIDE

NOTE

DATA BASED ON NO-WIND CONDITION

DATE: 1 APRIL 1969
DATA BASIS: ESTIMATED (BASED ON FLIGHT TEST)

FUEL GRADE: JP-5
FUEL DENSITY: 6.8 LB/GAL

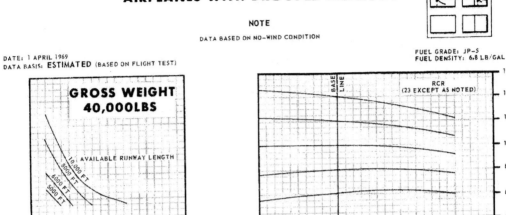

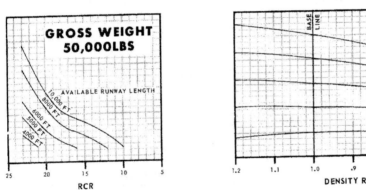

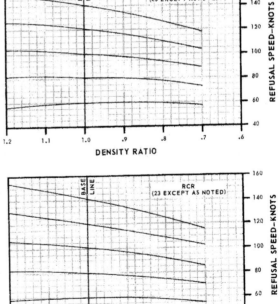

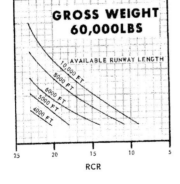

FDB-1-(122)

Figure 11-23

MAXIMUM REFUSAL SPEED
MAXIMUM THRUST - WITH DRAG CHUTE

AIRPLANE CONFIGURATION

ALL DRAG INDEXES
1/2 FLAPS

REMARKS

ENGINE(S): (2) J79-GE-8

GUIDE

AIRPLANES WITH DROOPED AILERONS

NOTE

DATA BASED ON NO-WIND CONDITION

DATE: 1 APRIL 1969
DATA BASIS: **ESTIMATED** (BASED ON FLIGHT TEST)

FUEL GRADE: JP-5
FUEL DENSITY: 6.8 LB/GAL

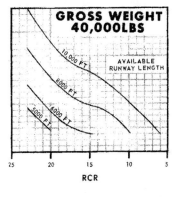

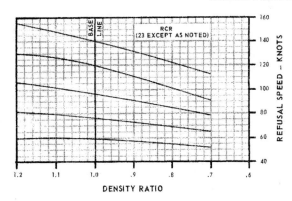

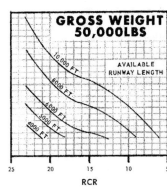

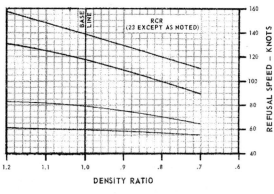

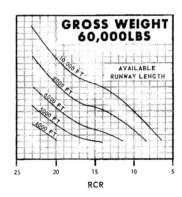

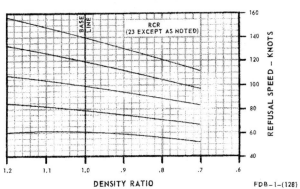

FDB-1-(128)

Figure 11-24

MAXIMUM REFUSAL SPEED
MILITARY THRUST-WITHOUT DRAG CHUTE

AIRPLANE CONFIGURATION
ALL DRAG INDEXES
1/2 FLAPS

REMARKS
ENGINE(S): (2) J79-GE-8

AIRPLANES WITHOUT DROOPED AILERONS
NOTE
DATA BASED ON NO-WIND CONDITION

DATE: 1 FEBRUARY 1969
DATA BASIS: FLIGHT TEST

GUIDE

FUEL GRADE: JP-5
FUEL DENSITY: 6.8 LB/GAL.

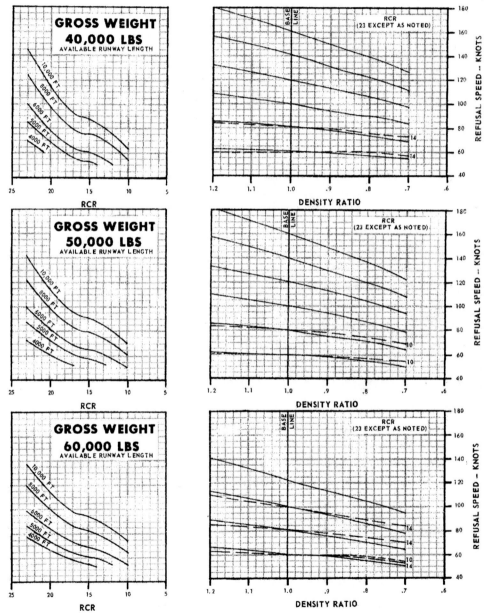

FDB—1—(129)

Figure 11-25

MAXIMUM REFUSAL SPEED
MILITARY THRUST-WITH DRAG CHUTE

AIRPLANE CONFIGURATION
ALL DRAG INDEXES
1/2 FLAPS

REMARKS
ENGINE(S): (2) J79-GE-8

AIRPLANES WITHOUT DROOPED AILERONS

DATE: 1 FEBRUARY 1969
DATA BASIS: FLIGHT TEST

NOTE
DATA BASED ON NO-WIND CONDITION

GUIDE

FUEL GRADE: JP-5
FUEL DENSITY: 6.8 LB/GAL

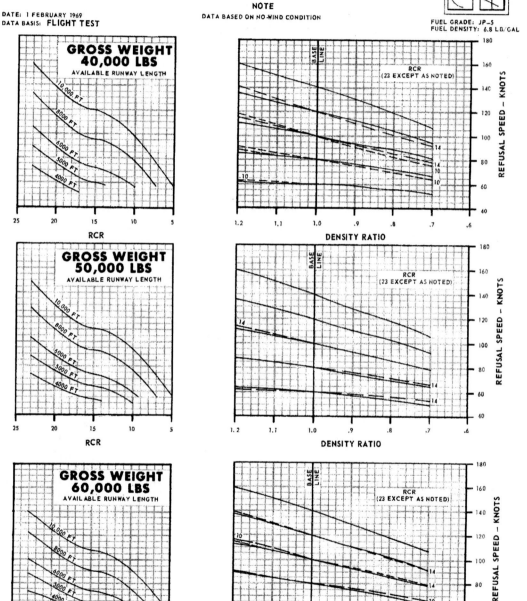

Figure 11-26

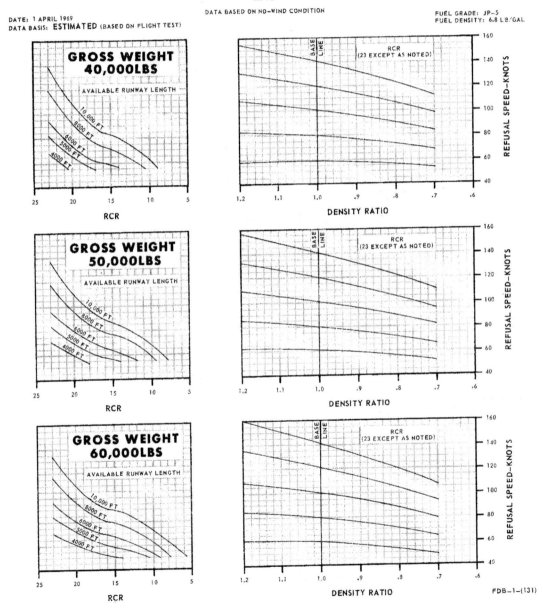

MAXIMUM REFUSAL SPEED
MILITARY THRUST - WITHOUT DRAG CHUTE

AIRPLANE CONFIGURATION

ALL DRAG INDEXES
1/2 FLAPS

REMARKS

ENGINE(S): (2) J79-GE-8

GUIDE

AIRPLANES WITH DROOPED AILERONS

NOTE

DATA BASED ON NO-WIND CONDITION

DATE: 1 APRIL 1969
DATA BASIS: ESTIMATED (BASED ON FLIGHT TEST)

FUEL GRADE: JP-5
FUEL DENSITY: 6.8 LB/GAL

FDB-1-(131)

Figure 11-27

MAXIMUM REFUSAL SPEED
MILITARY THRUST - WITH DRAG CHUTE

AIRPLANE CONFIGURATION

ALL DRAG INDEXES
1/2 FLAPS

REMARKS

ENGINE(S): (2) J79-GE-8

GUIDE

AIRPLANES WITH DROOPED AILERONS

NOTE

DATA BASED ON NO-WIND CONDITION

DATE: 1 APRIL 1969
DATA BASIS: ESTIMATED (BASED ON FLIGHT TEST)

FUEL GRADE: JP-5
FUEL DENSITY: 6.8 LB/GAL

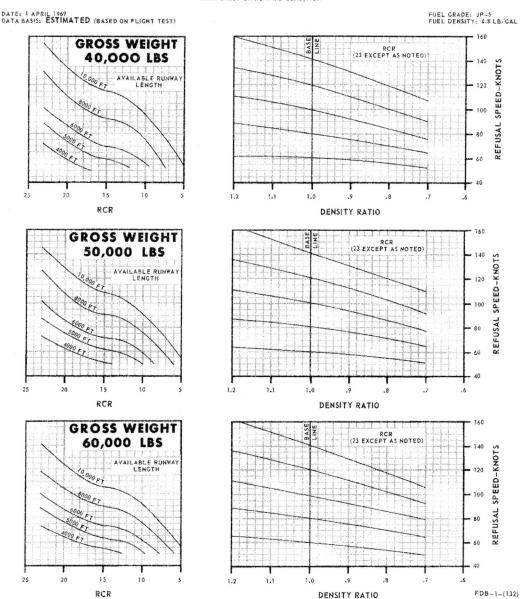

FDB-1-(132)

Figure 11-28

TAKEOFF DISTANCE
MAXIMUM THRUST
HARD DRY RUNWAY
REMARKS
ENGINE(S): (2) J79-GE-8

AIRPLANE CONFIGURATION
1/2 FLAPS, GEAR DOWN
ALL DRAG INDEXES

GUIDE

AIRPLANES WITHOUT DROOPED AILERONS

DATE: 15 JANUARY 1969
DATA BASIS: FLIGHT TEST

FUEL GRADE: JP-5
FUEL DENSITY: 6.8 LB/GAL

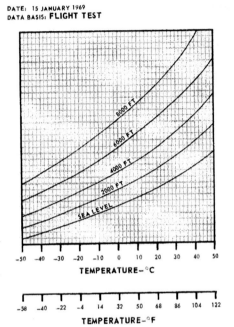

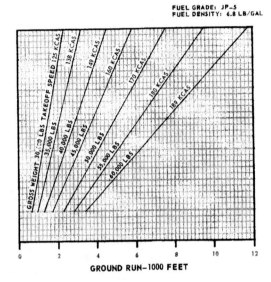

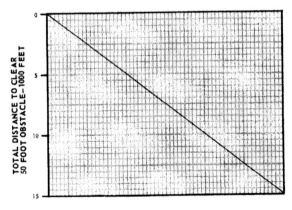

FDB-1-(133)

Figure 11-29

TAKEOFF DISTANCE
MAXIMUM THRUST
HARD DRY RUNWAY

AIRPLANE CONFIGURATION

ALL DRAG INDEXES
1/2 FLAPS

REMARKS
ENGINE(S):(2) J79-GE-8

GUIDE

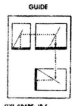

AIRPLANES WITH DROOPED AILERONS

DATE: 1 OCTOBER 1968
DATA BASIS: FLIGHT TEST

FUEL GRADE: JP-5
FUEL DENSITY: 6.8 LB/GAL

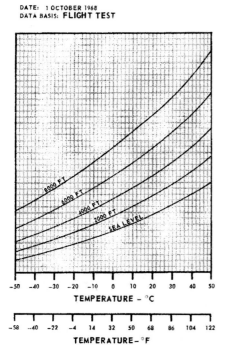

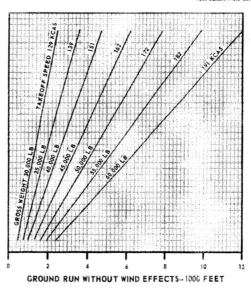

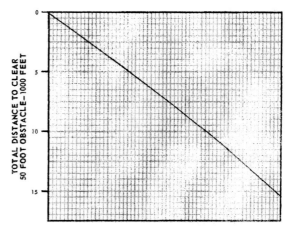

FDB-1-(123)

Figure 11-30

TAKEOFF DISTANCE
MILITARY THRUST
HARD DRY RUNWAY
REMARKS
ENGINE(S): (2) J79–GE–8

GUIDE

AIRPLANE CONFIGURATION
½ FLAPS, GEAR DOWN
ALL DRAG INDEXES

AIRPLANES WITHOUT DROOPED AILERONS

FUEL GRADE: JP–5
FUEL DENSITY: 6.8 LB/GAL

DATE: 1 AUGUST 1968
DATA BASIS: FLIGHT TEST

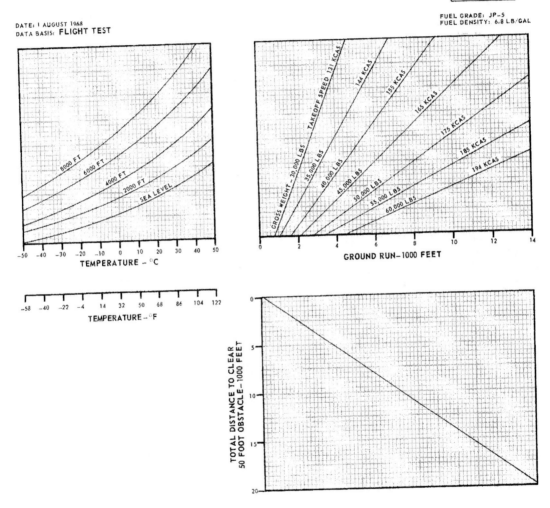

Figure 11-31

FDB–1–(124)

TAKEOFF DISTANCE
MILITARY THRUST
HARD DRY RUNWAY
REMARKS
ENGINE(S):(2) J79-GE-8

AIRPLANE CONFIGURATION

ALL DRAG INDEXES
1/2 FLAPS

GUIDE

AIRPLANES WITH DROOPED AILERONS

DATE: 1 OCTOBER 1968
DATA BASIS: **ESTIMATED** (BASED ON FLIGHT TEST)

FUEL GRADE: JP-5
FUEL DENSITY: 6.8 LB/GAL

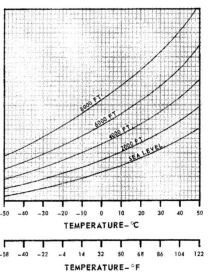

TEMPERATURE- °C

TEMPERATURE- °F

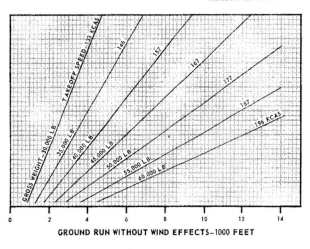

GROUND RUN WITHOUT WIND EFFECTS–1000 FEET

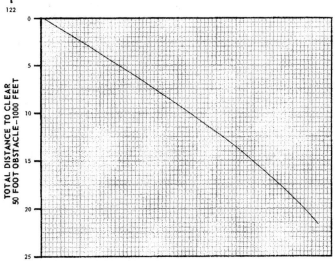

TOTAL DISTANCE TO CLEAR
50 FOOT OBSTACLE–1000 FEET

FDB–1–(125)

Figure 11-32

NOSEWHEEL LIFT-OFF SPEED

AIRPLANE CONFIGURATION
1/2 FLAP, GEAR DOWN
ALL DRAG INDEXES

REMARKS
ENGINE(S): (2) J79-GE-8

GUIDE

AIRPLANES WITHOUT DROOPED AILERONS

DATE: 15 JANUARY 1969
DATA BASIS: FLIGHT TEST

FUEL GRADE: JP-5
FUEL DENSITY: 6.8 LB/GAL

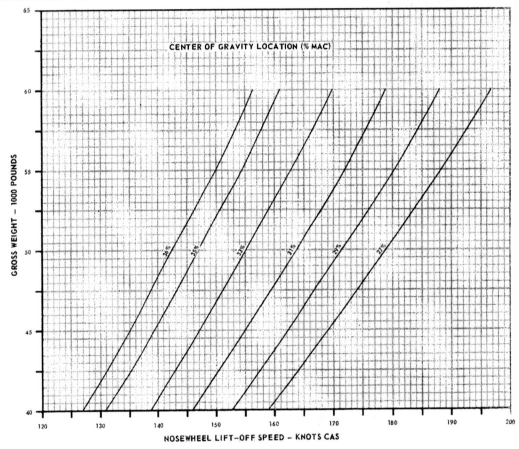

FDB-1-(127)

Figure 11-33

NOSE WHEEL LIFT-OFF SPEED

AIRPLANE CONFIGURATION
ALL DRAG INDEXES

REMARKS
ENGINE(S): (2) J79-GE-8

GUIDE

AIRPLANES WITH DROOPED AILERONS

DATE 15 JANUARY 1969
DATA BASIS: **FLIGHT TEST**

FUEL GRADE: JP-5
FUEL DENSITY: 6.8 LB./GAL

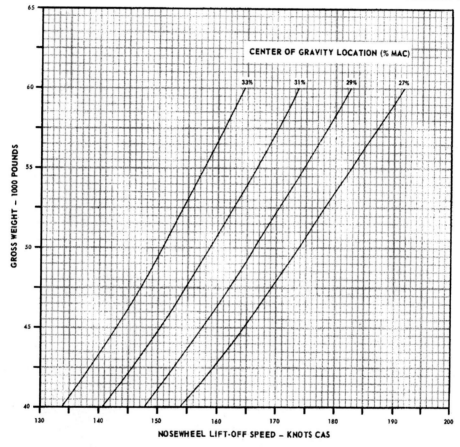

FDB-1-(285)

Figure 11-34

WIND EFFECTS ON TAKEOFF

AIRPLANE CONFIGURATION

ALL DRAG INDEXES
1/2 FLAPS

GUIDE

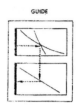

DATE: 1 FEBRUARY 1969
DATA BASIS: FLIGHT TEST

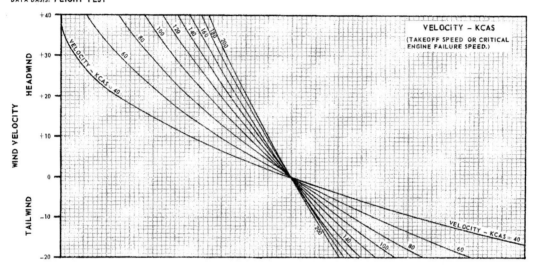

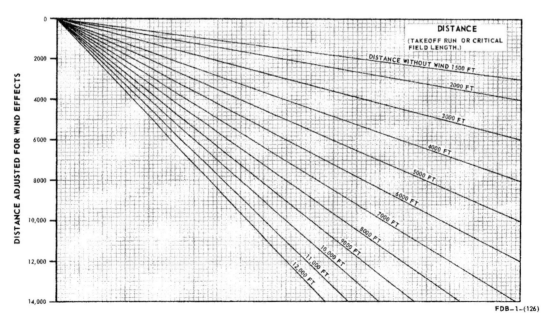

FDB-1-(126)

Figure 11-35

PART 3 CLIMB

CLIMB CHARTS

Subsonic climb data (figures 11-36 thru 11-45) are provided for both maximum and military thrust climb schedules. Separate charts are utilized to present speed, time, fuel, and distance data for the entire drag index range. The charts may be used to obtain climb data from brake-release to desired altitude or incrementally between altitudes.

USE

Tables

Select the climb speed schedule table corresponding to the desired climb thrust (MIL or MAX) setting. From the applicable drag index column, read the optimum climb speeds (calibrated airspeed with corresponding standard-day Mach number) for each 5000-foot increment of the climb. The listed pre-climb requirements (time, fuel, and distance required to intercept the climb schedule) should be noted if the takeoff/acceleration phase is to be considered in the climb planning.

CHARTS

The method of presenting data on the time, fuel, and distance charts is identical and the use of all three charts will be simultaneously undertaken in this example. Enter the charts with the initial climb gross weight and project horizontally to the right to intersect the desired cruise altitude. Project vertically downward to intersect the computed drag index, then horizontally to the left to intersect the temperature deviation base line (corresponds to ICAO Standard Day). If non-standard-day temperatures are forecast, project parallel to the applicable guide line (hotter or colder) to intersect a vertical grid line corresponding to the degree of temperature deviation. From the temperature intersect-point (standard day or deviation), continue horizontally to the left to read the planning data (time, fuel, and distance).

Sample Problem

Time to Climb - Military Thrust

A. Gross weight   50,000 Lbs.
B. Cruise altitude   30,000 Ft.
C. Drag index   50.0
D. Temperature base line
E. Temperature deviation +5°
F. Time to climb   10.6 Min.

Fuel Required to Climb - Military Thrust

A. Gross weight 50,000 Lbs.
B. Cruise altitude 30,000 Ft.
C. Computed drag index 50.0
D. Temperature base line
E. Temperature deviation +5°
F. Fuel required to climb 2075 Lbs.
G. Fuel required for MIL power takeoff and acceleration to climb speed (from climb speed schedule) 525 Lbs.
H. Fuel used from brake-release to cruise altitude 2600 Lbs.

Distance Required to Climb - Military Thrust

A. Gross weight 50,000 Lbs.
B. Cruise altitude 30,000 Ft.
C. Drag index 50.0
D. Temperature base line
E. Temperature deviation +5°
F. Distance required to climb 71 Miles

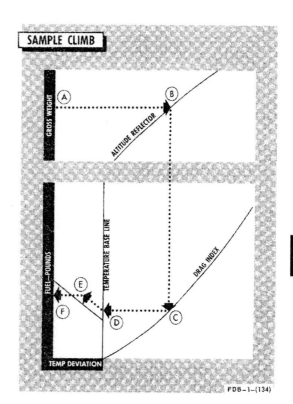

SAMPLE CLIMB

FDB-1-(134)

RATE OF CLIMB CHARTS

Rate of climb charts (figures 11-44 and 11-45) are presented for both maximum and military thrust, for all computed drag indexes. The charts provide the instantaneous rate of climb for any given altitude-gross weight condition.

USE

Enter the chart with the appropriate gross weight and then proceed horizontally to the right to intersect the desired altitude. From this point reflect downward to intercept the computed drag index, then horizontally to the left to read rate of climb.

Sample Problem

Maximum Thrust

A. Gross weight   40,000 Lbs.
B. Altitude   25,000 Ft.
C. Drag index   60
D. Rate of climb   15,000 Ft/Min

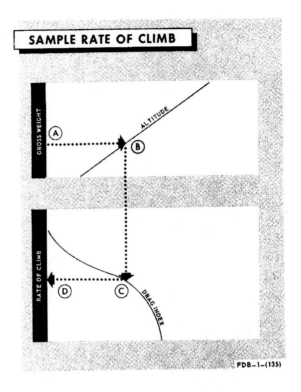

SAMPLE RATE OF CLIMB

FDB-1-(135)

CLIMB SPEED SCHEDULE

MAXIMUM THRUST

AIRPLANE CONFIGURATION

ALL DRAG INDEXES

REMARKS
ENGINE(S):(2) J79-GE-8
ICAO STANDARD DAY

DATE: 15 MAY 1968
DATA BASIS: FLIGHT TEST

FUEL GRADE: JP-5
FUEL DENSITY: 6.8 LB/GAL

ALTITUDE	DRAG INDEX													
	0		10		20		30		40		50		60	
	KCAS	MACH	KCAS	MACH	KCAS	MACH	KCAS	MACH	KCAS	MACH	KCAS	MACH	KCAS	MACH
S.L.	595	.90	594	.90	587	.89	581	.88	574	.87	567	.86	553	.84
5000	556	.91	556	.91	550	.90	544	.89	538	.88	521	.87	519	.85
10000	519	.92	514	.91	507	.90	501	.89	496	.88	490	.87	485	.86
15000	481	.93	475	.92	470	.91	465	.90	460	.89	453	.88	449	.87
20000	435	.93	435	.92	429	.91	429	.91	424	.90	419	.89	413	.88
25000	402	.94	398	.93	393	.92	389	.91	384	.90	380	.89	374	.88
30000	363	.94	360	.93	354	.92	355	.92	350	.91	346	.90	342	.89
35000	326	.94	326	.94	322	.93	319	.92	315	.91	310	.90	307	.89
40000	291	.94	291	.94	288	.93	284	.92	281	.91	276	.90	274	.89
45000	259	.94	259	.94	256	.93	252	.92	250	.91	246	.90	243	.89
50000	232	.94	231	.94	229	.93	226	.92	223	.91	219	.90	217	.89

ALTITUDE	DRAG INDEX													
	70		80		90		100		110		120		130		140	
	KCAS	MACH	KCAS	MACH	KCAS	MACH	KCAS	MACH	KCAS	MACH	KCAS	MACH	KCAS	MACH	KCAS	MACH
S.L.	547	.83	534	.81	520	.79	501	.76	489	.74	469	.71	448	.68	429	.65
5000	506	.83	500	.82	488	.80	475	.78	462	.76	450	.74	433	.71	413	.68
10000	473	.84	467	.83	460	.82	448	.80	436	.78	425	.76	415	.74	402	.72
15000	443	.86	432	.84	426	.83	421	.82	410	.80	400	.78	394	.77	384	.75
20000	403	.86	398	.85	393	.84	388	.83	384	.82	378	.81	374	.80	358	.77
25000	370	.87	365	.86	365	.86	360	.85	356	.84	347	.82	342	.81	338	.80
30000	338	.88	333	.87	334	.87	329	.86	325	.85	321	.84	316	.83	308	.81
35000	302	.88	300	.87	299	.87	300	.87	295	.86	288	.84	284	.83	280	.82
40000	270	.88	267	.87	266	.87	267	.87	263	.86	256	.84	251	.83	248	.82
45000	240	.88	237	.87	237	.87	237	.87	234	.86	228	.84	225	.83	222	.82
50000	214	.88	211	.87	211	.87	211	.87	208	.86	202	.84	200	.83	197	.82

TAKEOFF ALLOWANCES & ACCELERATION TO CLIMB SPEED

START – 65 LBS/ENG

TAXI – 21 LB/MIN/ENG

RUNUP 50 LB/ENG

BRAKE RELEASE TO CLIMB SPEED	
	MAX T.O. MAX ACCEL TO MAX CLIMB SPEED
FUEL – LBS	1225
DIST – NM	5.0
TIME – MIN	1.0

FDB-1-(136)

Figure 11-36

TIME TO CLIMB
MAXIMUM THRUST

AIRPLANE CONFIGURATION
ALL DRAG INDEXES

REMARKS
ENGINE(S): (2) J79-GE-8

NOTE
OPTIMUM CRUISE ALTITUDE AT END OF CLIMB MUST BE READ
ON THE OPTIMUM CRUISE ALTITUDE CHART.

GUIDE

DATE: 15 MAY 1968
DATA BASIS: FLIGHT TEST

FUEL GRADE: JP-5
FUEL DENSITY: 6.8 LB/GAL

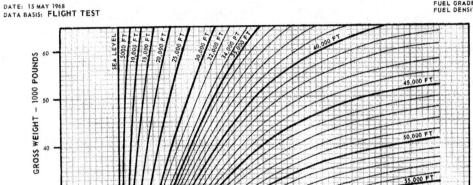

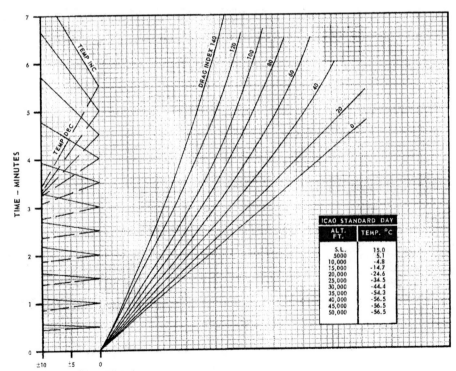

ICAO STANDARD DAY	
ALT. FT.	TEMP. °C
S.L.	15.0
5000	5.1
10,000	-4.8
15,000	-14.7
20,000	-24.6
25,000	-34.5
30,000	-44.4
35,000	-54.3
40,000	-56.5
45,000	-56.5
50,000	-56.5

TEMPERATURE DEVIATION FROM
ICAO STANDARD DAY – °C

FDB-1-(292)

Figure 11-37

FUEL REQUIRED TO CLIMB
MAXIMUM THRUST

AIRPLANE CONFIGURATION
ALL DRAG INDEXES

REMARKS

ENGINE(S): (2) J79-GE-8

NOTE

OPTIMUM CRUISE ALTITUDE AT END OF CLIMB MUST BE READ
ON THE OPTIMUM CRUISE ALTITUDE CHART.

GUIDE

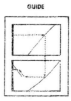

DATE: 15 MAY 1968
DATA BASIS: **FLIGHT TEST**

FUEL GRADE: JP-5
FUEL DENSITY: 6.8 LB/GAL

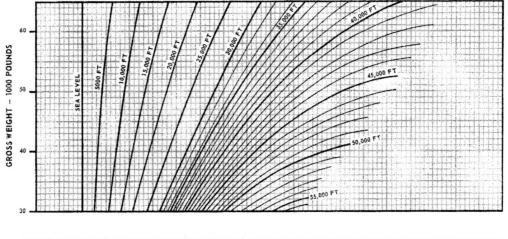

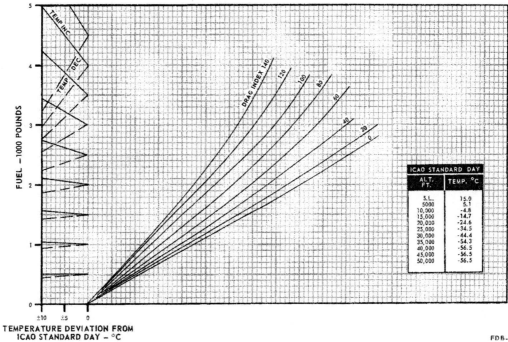

TEMPERATURE DEVIATION FROM
ICAO STANDARD DAY – °C

FDB-1-(293)

Figure 11-38

DISTANCE REQUIRED TO CLIMB
MAXIMUM THRUST

AIRCRAFT CONFIGURATION
ALL DRAG INDEXES

REMARKS
ENGINE(S): (2) J79-GE-8

GUIDE

NOTE
OPTIMUM CRUISE ALTITUDE AT END OF CLIMB MUST BE READ
ON THE OPTIMUM CRUISE ALTITUDE CHART.

DATE: 15 MAY 1968
DATA BASIS: FLIGHT TEST

FUEL GRADE: JP-5
FUEL DENSITY: 6.8 LB/GAL

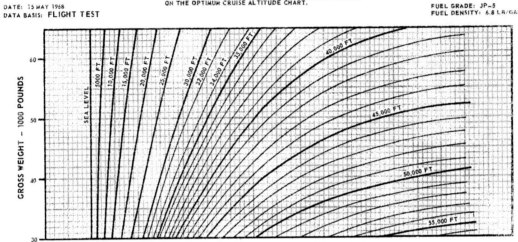

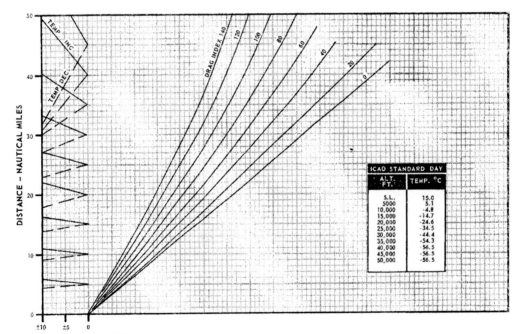

ICAO STANDARD DAY	
ALT. FT.	TEMP. °C
S.L.	15.0
5000	5.1
10,000	-4.8
15,000	-14.7
20,000	-24.6
25,000	-34.5
30,000	-44.4
35,000	-54.3
40,000	-56.5
45,000	-56.5
50,000	-56.5

TEMPERATURE DEVIATION FROM
ICAO STANDARD DAY – °C

FDB-1-(294)

Figure 11-39

CLIMB SPEED SCHEDULE

MILITARY THRUST

REMARKS
ENGINE(S):(2) J79-GE-8
ICAO STANDARD DAY

AIRPLANE CONFIGURATION
ALL DRAG INDEXES

DATE: 15 MAY 1968
DATA BASIS: FLIGHT TEST

FUEL GRADE: JP-5
FUEL DENSITY: 6.8 LB/GAL

ALTITUDE	DRAG INDEX													
	0		10		20		30		40		50		60	
	KCAS	MACH	KCAS	MACH	KCAS	MACH	KCAS	MACH	KCAS	MACH	KCAS	MACH	KCAS	MACH
S.L.	461	.70	441	.67	421	.64	410	.62	395	.60	383	.58	363	.55
5000	445	.73	426	.70	414	.68	401	.66	389	.64	370	.61	357	.59
10000	425	.76	415	.74	401	.72	390	.70	374	.67	361	.65	350	.63
15000	405	.79	394	.77	383	.75	373	.73	362	.71	351	.69	341	.67
20000	384	.82	374	.80	364	.78	354	.76	345	.74	334	.72	325	.70
25000	360	.85	351	.83	343	.81	334	.79	325	.77	315	.75	311	.74
30000	333	.87	325	.85	316	.83	313	.82	304	.80	295	.78	288	.76
35000	300	.88	295	.86	284	.84	284	.83	262	.82	276	.81	257	.79
40000	266	.88	263	.86	252	.84	251	.83	242	.82	245	.81	229	.79
45000	237	.88	234	.86	228	.84	225	.83	222	.82	219	.81	203	.79

ALTITUDE	DRAG INDEX													
	70		80		90		100		110		120		130		140	
	KCAS	MACH	KCAS	MACH	KCAS	MACH	KCAS	MACH	KCAS	MACH	KCAS	MACH	KCAS	MACH	KCAS	MACH
S.L.	356	.54	350	.53	343	.52	335	.51	330	.50	330	.50	324	.49	324	.49
5000	351	.58	345	.57	340	.56	326	.54	327	.54	320	.53	320	.53	315	.52
10000	345	.62	333	.60	327	.59	321	.58	316	.57	310	.56	305	.55	305	.55
15000	330	.65	320	.63	315	.62	309	.61	304	.60	298	.59	294	.58	289	.57
20000	319	.69	310	.67	304	.66	294	.64	290	.63	280	.61	275	.60	270	.59
25000	301	.72	292	.70	284	.68	275	.66	266	.64	261	.63	257	.62	256	.62
30000	279	.74	271	.72	262	.70	255	.68	250	.67	242	.65	239	.64	234	.63
35000	261	.77	243	.74	239	.71	228	.68	224	.67	217	.65	213	.64	210	.63
40000	232	.77	216	.74	212	.71	203	.68	200	.67	193	.65	190	.64	187	.63
45000	206	.77	192	.74	189	.71	180	.68	177	.67	172	.65	168	.64	165	.63

TAKEOFF ALLOWANCES & ACCELERATION TO CLIMB SPEED

START - 65 LBS /ENG
TAXI - 21 LB /MIN/ENG
RUNUP 50 LB /ENG

BRAKE RELEASE TO CLIMB SPEED	MIL T.O. MIL ACCEL TO MIL CLIMB SPEED	MAX T.O. MIL ACCEL TO MIL CLIMB SPEED	MAX T.O. MAX ACCEL TO MIL CLIMB SPEED
FUEL - LBS	525	725	925
DIST - N M	6.0	5.3	3.0
TIME - MIN	1.7	1.3	.8

FDB-1-(137)

Figure 11-40

TIME TO CLIMB
MILITARY THRUST

GUIDE

AIRPLANE CONFIGURATION
ALL DRAG INDEXES

REMARKS
ENGINE(S): (2) J79–GE–8

NOTE

OPTIMUM CRUISE ALTITUDE AT END OF CLIMB MUST BE READ
ON THE OPTIMUM CRUISE ALTITUDE CHART.

DATE: 15 MAY 1968
DATA BASIS: **FLIGHT TEST**

FUEL GRADE: JP–5
FUEL DENSITY: 6.8 LB/GAL

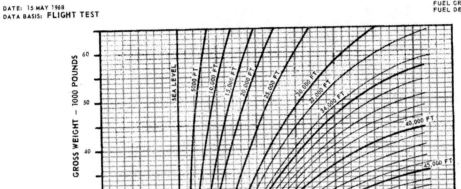

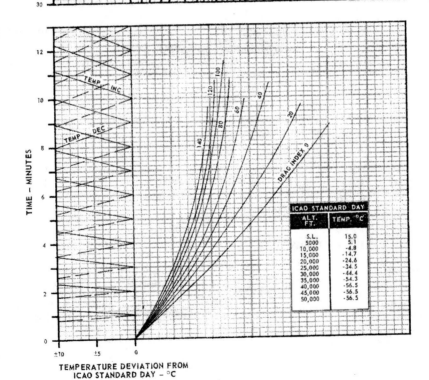

TEMPERATURE DEVIATION FROM
ICAO STANDARD DAY – °C

ICAO STANDARD DAY	
ALT. FT.	TEMP. °C
S.L.	15.0
5000	5.1
10,000	-4.8
15,000	-14.7
20,000	-24.6
25,000	-34.5
30,000	-44.4
35,000	-54.3
40,000	-56.5
45,000	-56.5
50,000	-56.5

FDB-1-(295)

Figure 11-41

FUEL REQUIRED TO CLIMB
MILITARY THRUST

AIRPLANE CONFIGURATION
ALL DRAG INDEXES

REMARKS

ENGINE(S): (2) J79-GE-8

GUIDE

DATE: 15 MAY 1968
DATA BASIS: **FLIGHT TEST**

NOTE

OPTIMUM CRUISE ALTITUDE AT END OF CLIMB MUST BE READ
ON THE OPTIMUM CRUISE ALTITUDE CHART

FUEL GRADE: JP-5
FUEL DENSITY: 6.8 LB/GAL

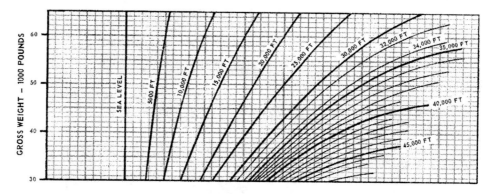

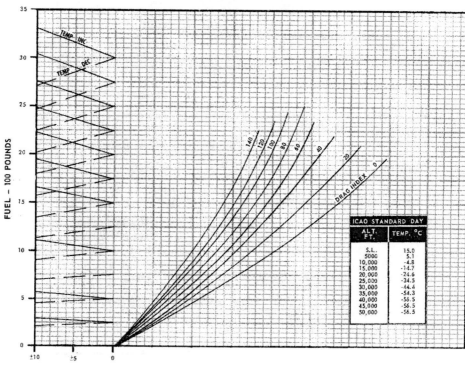

ICAO STANDARD DAY	
ALT. FT.	TEMP. °C
S.L.	15.0
5000	5.1
10,000	-4.8
15,000	-14.7
20,000	-24.6
25,000	-34.5
30,000	-44.4
35,000	-54.3
40,000	-56.5
45,000	-56.5
50,000	-56.5

TEMPERATURE DEVIATION FROM
ICAO STANDARD DAY °C

FDB-1-(296)

Figure 11-42

DISTANCE REQUIRED TO CLIMB
MILITARY THRUST
REMARKS

ENGINE(S): (2) J79-GE-8

AIRPLANE CONFIGURATION
ALL DRAG INDEXES

NOTE
OPTIMUM CRUISE ALTITUDE AT END OF CLIMB MUST BE READ ON THE OPTIMUM CRUISE ALTITUDE CHART.

DATE: 15 MAY 1968
DATA BASIS: FLIGHT TEST

GUIDE

FUEL GRADE: JP-5
FUEL DENSITY: 6.8 LB/GAL

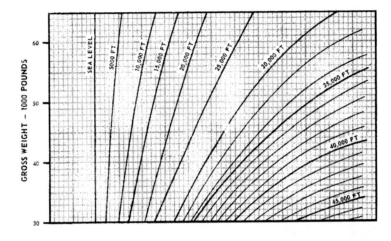

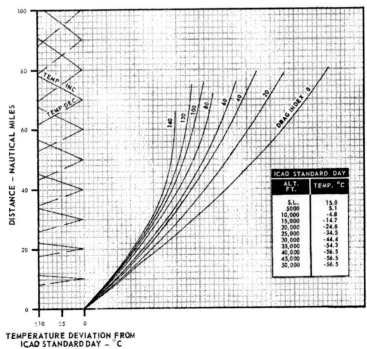

ICAO STANDARD DAY	
ALT. FT.	TEMP. °C
S.L.	15.0
5000	5.1
10,000	-4.8
15,000	-14.7
20,000	-24.6
25,000	-34.5
30,000	-44.4
35,000	-54.3
40,000	-56.5
45,000	-56.5
50,000	-56.5

TEMPERATURE DEVIATION FROM ICAO STANDARD DAY – °C

FDB–1–(297)

Figure 11-43

RATE OF CLIMB
MAXIMUM THRUST

AIRPLANE CONFIGURATION
ALL DRAG INDEXES

REMARKS
ENGINE(S): (2) J79–GE–8
ICAO STANDARD DAY

DATE: 15 MAY 1968
DATA BASIS: FLIGHT TEST

GUIDE

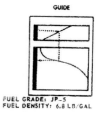

FUEL GRADE: JP-5
FUEL DENSITY: 6.8 LB/GAL

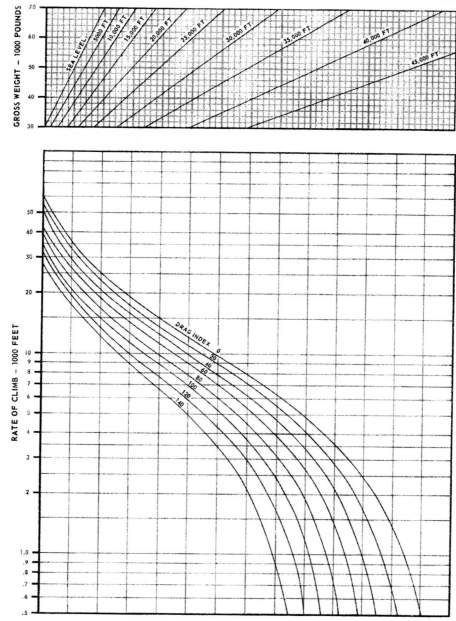

FDB–1–(138)

Figure 11-44

RATE OF CLIMB
MILITARY THRUST

AIRPLANE CONFIGURATION
ALL DRAG INDEXES

REMARKS

ENGINE(S): (2) J79-GE-8
ICAO STANDARD DAY

GUIDE

DATE: 15 MAY 1968
DATA BASIS: FLIGHT TEST

FUEL GRADE: JP-5
FUEL DENSITY: 6.8 LB/GAL

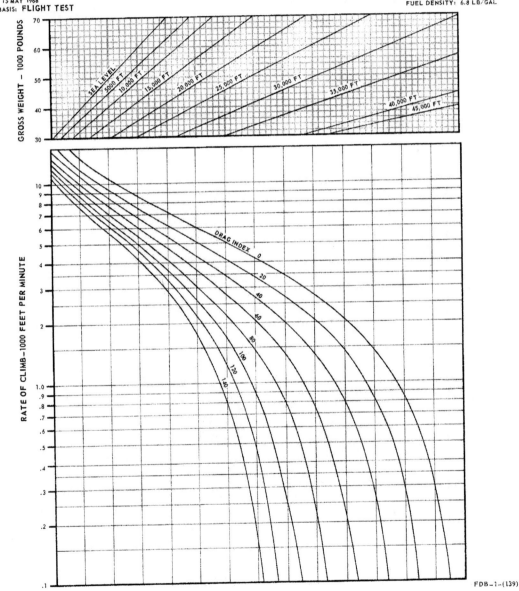

FDB-1-(139)

Figure 11-45

PART 4 RANGE

CHARTS

RANGEWIND CORRECTION CHART

This chart (figure 11-46) provides a means of correcting computed range (specific or total) for existing wind effects. The presented range factors consider wind speeds up to 150 knots (TAS) from any relative wind direction for airplane speeds of 200 to 1300 knots (TAS).

USE

Determine the relative wind direction by subtracting the aircraft heading from the forecast wind direction. If the aircraft heading is greater than the forecast wind direction, add 360° to the wind direction and then perform the subtraction. Enter the chart with relative wind direction and proceed vertically to the interpolated wind speed. From this point, project horizontally to intersect the airplane true airspeed and reflect to the lower scale to read the range factor. Multiply computed range by this range factor to find range as affected by wind.

Sample Problem

A.	Relative wind direction	150°
B.	Wind speed	125 Kts.
C.	Airplane speed (TAS)	400 Kts.
D.	Range factor	1.25

OPTIMUM CRUISE ALTITUDE CHARTS

These charts (figures 11-47 and 11-48) present the optimum cruising altitudes for both two-engine and single-engine operations and for various combinations of gross weight and drag index.

USE

Enter the chart with the estimated gross weight at end of climb. Project vertically upward to intersect applicable drag index, then horizontally to the left to read optimum cruise altitude.

LOW ALTITUDE CRUISE

These charts (figures 11-49 thru 11-54) present total fuel flow values for various combinations of airspeed and drag index at altitudes of sea level, 4000, 8000, and 12,000 feet. Separate charts are provided for several gross weights. Fuel flow values are tabulated for ICAO Standard Day; however, correction factors are given for non-standard temperatures.

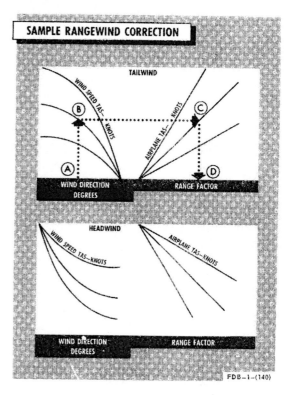

SAMPLE RANGEWIND CORRECTION

FDB-1-(140)

USE

After selecting the applicable chart for gross weight and altitudes, enter with the desired airspeed and project horizontally to the applicable drag index column. Read total fuel flow for a standard day.

CONSTANT MACH/ALTITUDE CRUISE

These charts (figures 11-55 thru 11-61) present nautical miles per pound and total fuel flow for various combinations of Mach number, gross weight, altitude, and drag index. This data is based on cruise at a constant Mach number and a constant altitude. Specifics are presented for 0°C; however, correction factors are provided for non-standard temperatures.

USE

After selecting the desired cruise Mach, enter the chart with the estimated gross weight at end of climb. Project horizontally to the right to intersect the desired cruise altitude, then vertically downward to intersect the applicable drag index. From this point, project horizontally to both sides of the graph and read nautical miles per pound and total fuel flow for 0°C temperature. If required, correct these values for the actual temperatures.

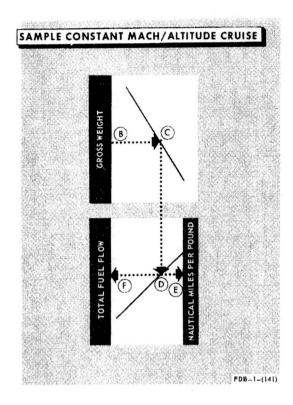

SAMPLE CONSTANT MACH/ALTITUDE CRUISE

FDB-1-(141)

Sample Problem

One Engine Operating

A.	Mach number	0.40
B.	Gross weight	40,000 Lbs.

C.	Altitude	Sea Level
D.	Drag index	20
E.	Nautical miles per pound	0.05
F.	Total fuel flow	5250 Lbs.

OPTIMUM CRUISE AT CONSTANT ALTITUDE

These charts (figures 11-62 thru 11-63) present the necessary planning data to set up optimum cruise schedules for a constant altitude. The recommended procedure is to use an average gross weight for a given leg of the mission. One way to find the average gross weight is to divide the mission into weight segments. With this method, readjust the cruise schedule each time a given amount of fuel is used. Subtract one-half of the fuel weight alloted for the first leg from the initial cruise gross weight. The remainder is the average gross weight for the leg. It is possible to obtain instantaneous data if desired.

USE

Enter the left side of sheet 1 with the average gross weight. Project horizontally to the right to intersect desired cruise altitude, vertically downward to the computed drag index, then horizontally to the right to obtain specific range (nautical miles per pound). Repeat these procedures on the right side of sheet 1 to obtain optimum cruise Mach number for the desired altitude. Enter sheet 2 with the optimum cruise Mach number. Project horizontally to the right to intersect predicted flight-level temperature, then vertically downward to obtain corresponding true airspeed. Continue this projection vertically downward to intersect the interpolated specific range (obtained from sheet 1), then horizontally to the left to obtain total fuel flow required.

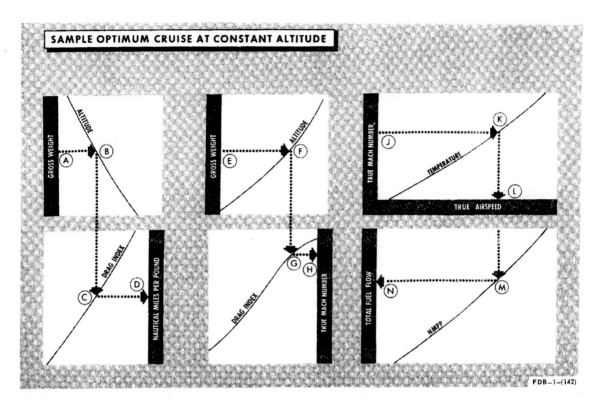

SAMPLE OPTIMUM CRUISE AT CONSTANT ALTITUDE

FDB-1-(142)

Sample Problem

Two-Engines

A.	Average gross weight for first leg	45,000 Lbs.
B.	Cruise altitude	15,000 Ft.
C.	Computed drag index	60.0
D.	Specific range	0.054
E.	Gross weight	45,000 Lbs.
F.	Altitude	15,000 Ft.
G.	Drag index	60.0
H.	True Mach number	0.59
J.	True Mach number	0.59
K.	Temperature at flight altitude	10°C
L.	True airspeed	380 KTAS
M.	Specific range	0.054
N.	Total fuel flow	7000 PPH

CHECKLIST CHARTS

BINGO

Tabulated Bingo specifics are contained in the checklist. This chart presents, fuel required, cruise altitude, cruise Mach, and descent distance for various Bingo distances, also included is fuel required for a 315-knot/sea level cruise, and descent distances to a 20,000-foot fix for these same Bingo distances.

RANGEWIND CORRECTION

AIRPLANE CONFIGURATION

ALL CONFIGURATIONS

NOTE: RELATIVE WIND DIRECTION = ANGULAR DIFFERENCE
MEASURED CLOCKWISE, BETWEEN AIRPLANE HEADING
AND TRUE WIND DIRECTION

GUIDE

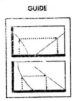

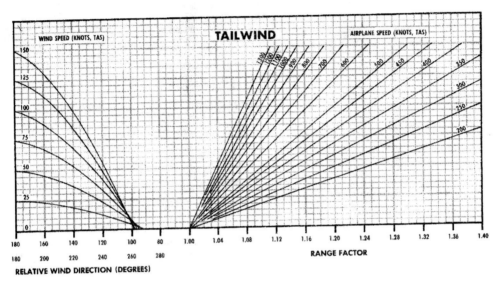

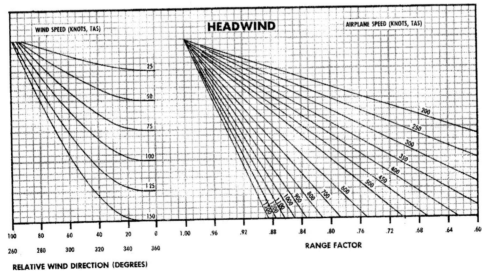

FDB-1-(143)

Figure 11-46

OPTIMUM CRUISE ALTITUDE

AIRPLANE CONFIGURATION
INDIVIDUAL DRAG INDEXES

REMARKS
ENGINE(S): (2) J79-GE-8
ICAO STANDARD DAY

GUIDE

DATE: 15 MAY 1968
DATA BASIS: **FLIGHT TEST**

FUEL GRADE: JP-5
FUEL DENSITY: 6.8 LB/GAL

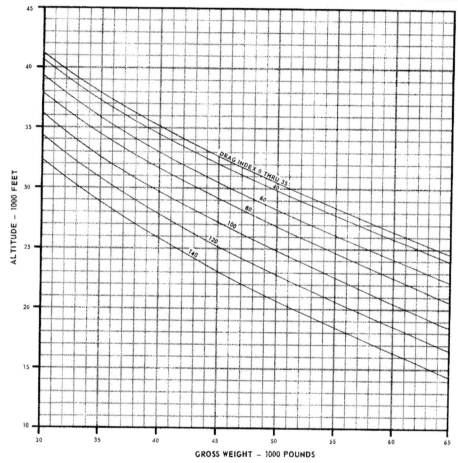

FDB-1-(144)

Figure 11-47

OPTIMUM CRUISE ALTITUDE
ONE ENGINE OPERATING

AIRPLANE CONFIGURATION
INDIVIDUAL DRAG INDEXES

REMARKS
ENGINE(S): (2) J79-GE-8
ICAO STANDARD DAY
INOPERATIVE ENGINE WINDMILLING

NOTE
OPTIMUM CRUISE ALTITUDE AT END OF CLIMB MUST BE READ
ON THE OPTIMUM CRUISE ALTITUDE CHART.

DATE: 15 MAY 1968
DATA BASIS: **FLIGHT TEST**

GUIDE

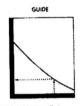

FUEL GRADE: JP-5
FUEL DENSITY: 6.8 LB/GAL

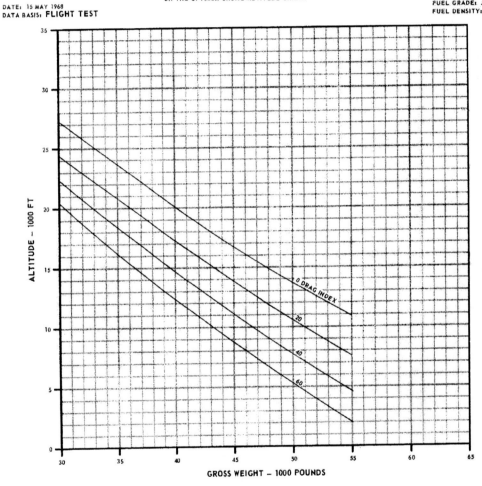

FDB-1-(145)

Figure 11-48

LOW ALTITUDE CRUISE

AIRPLANE CONFIGURATION
INDIVIDUAL DRAG INDEXES

GROSS WEIGHT – 35,000 POUNDS

REMARKS
ENGINES: (2) J79–GE–8

DATE: 15 MAY 1968
DATA BASIS: **FLIGHT TEST**

FUEL GRADE: JP–5
FUEL DENSITY: 6.8 LB./GAL

KTAS	DRAG INDEX	TOTAL FUEL FLOW-LB/HR							TEMP. EFFECTS	
		0	20	40	60	80	100	120	°C.	FACTOR
SEA LEVEL (15°C)										
360		6736	7524	8309	9092	9918	10738	11639		
400		7890	8893	9875	10855	11966	12980	14129	−40	.899
440		9261	10492	11751	13000	14348	15833	17461	−20	.937
480		10845	12387	13835	15460	17337	19364	21999	0	.973
520		12863	14565	16390	18568	21348			20	1.008
560		15147	17277	19581	23472				40	1.042
600		18452	21263							
MIL		26000	25680	25120	24440	23800	23240	22760		
V MAX		636.2	621.0	598.5	570.0	542.93	515.2	490.7		
4,000 FEET (7°C)										
360		5946	6640	7330	8002	8674	9370	10100		
400		6867	7760	8592	9411	10291	11345	12372	−40	.912
440		8019	9096	10128	11264	12528	13857	15328	−20	.949
480		9310	10589	11963	13419	15120	16912	19235	0	.987
520		10980	12594	14252	16246	18733			20	1.022
560		13066	15053	17154	20371				40	1.057
600		16087	18530							
MIL		23520	23280	22760	22140	21680	21200	20640		
V MAX		630.6	618.8	596.7	571.2	545.1	518.4	494.9		
8,000 FEET (-1°C)										
360		5252	5844	6421	7039	7615	8196	8762		
400		6012	6736	7526	8216	8896	9691	10611	−40	.925
440		6922	7859	8747	9617	10678	11878	13120	−20	.963
480		8020	9102	10185	11464	12911	14607	16255	0	1.001
520		9365	10666	12110	13891	15858	18416		20	1.037
560		11062	12752	14721	17254				40	1.072
600		13623	15900							
MIL		20840	20620	20240	19840	19440	18900	18600		
V MAX		624.9	613.3	595.3	571.5	547.8	522.0	498.2		
12,000 FEET (-9°C)										
360		4708	5198	5685	6177	6715	7214	7729		
400		5280	5902	6520	7197	7776	8375	9019	−40	.939
440		6015	6767	7549	8304	9070	9984	11067	−20	.978
480		6889	7805	8712	9681	10861	12194	13820	0	1.016
520		7995	9064	10181	11629	13334	15271		20	1.052
560		9365	10675	12246	14583				40	1.088
600		11406	13281							
MIL		19000	18760	18480	18100	17660	17200	16700		
V MAX		619.5	606.8	591.6	571.3	547.3	523.8	498.5		

FDB–1–(146)

Figure 11-49

LOW ALTITUDE CRUISE

GROSS WEIGHT – 40,000 POUNDS

AIRPLANE CONFIGURATION
INDIVIDUAL DRAG INDEXES

REMARKS
ENGINES: (2) J79-GE-8

DATE: 15 MAY 1968
DATA BASIS: FLIGHT TEST

FUEL GRADE: JP-5
FUEL DENSITY: 6.8 LB/GAL

SEA LEVEL (15°C)

KTAS	DRAG INDEX 0	20	40	60	80	100	120	°C	FACTOR
360	6935	7725	8492	9286	10104	10937	11814		
400	8020	9014	10000	10980	12094	13103	14264	-40	.899
440	9390	10623	11879	13118	14487	15988	17606	-20	.937
480	10924	12462	13910	15539	17419	19463	22127	0	.973
520	12943	14652	16480	18662	21477			20	1.008
560	15246	17377	19688	23629				40	1.042
600	18552	21393							
MIL	26000	25680	25110	24425	23785	23225	22745		
V$_{MAX}$	636.2	621.0	597.8	569.4	542.1	514.5	490.0		

4,000 FEET (7°C)

KTAS	DRAG INDEX 0	20	40	60	80	100	120	°C	FACTOR
360	6141	6818	7547	8190	8858	9558	10316		
400	7024	7931	8759	9574	10469	11552	12554	-40	.912
440	8165	9219	10252	11402	12660	14019	15491	-20	.949
480	9447	10716	12101	13561	15257	17080	19450	0	.987
520	11065	12686	14353	16344	18866			20	1.022
560	13172	15171	17268	20503				40	1.057
600	16193	18641							
MIL	23520	23280	22760	22100	21660	21180	20620		
V$_{MAX}$	630.6	618.8	596.1	570.6	544.5	517.7	493.6		

8,000 FEET (-1°C)

KTAS	DRAG INDEX 0	20	40	60	80	100	120	°C	FACTOR
360	5498	6080	6663	7298	7856	8417	9011		
400	6194	6929	7695	8405	9083	9909	10859	-40	.925
440	7057	7988	8873	9761	10841	12038	13316	-20	.963
480	8146	9223	10324	11621	13076	14756	16440	0	1.001
520	9469	10786	12246	14044	15998			20	1.037
560	11157	12851	14853	17383				40	1.072
600	13740	16020							
MIL	20840	20620	20220	19840	19420	18880	18580		
V$_{MAX}$	624.9	613.3	594.7	570.9	546.5	520.7	496.3		

12,000 FEET (-9°C)

KTAS	DRAG INDEX 0	20	40	60	80	100	120	°C	FACTOR
360	4973	5475	5961	6461	7007	7482	7972		
400	5512	6134	6761	7397	8006	8586	9276	-40	.939
440	6205	6962	7729	8474	9269	10219	11341	-20	.978
480	7018	7933	8840	9826	11030	12372	14048	0	1.016
520	8105	9179	10309	11783	13509	15424		20	1.052
560	9480	10798	12378	14714				40	1.088
600	11524	13408							
MIL	19000	18740	18460	18085	17640	17180	16680		
V$_{MAX}$	619.5	606.8	591.0	570.7	546.6	521.9	496.6		

TOTAL FUEL FLOW-LB/HR — TEMP. EFFECTS

FDB-1-(298)

Figure 11-50

LOW ALTITUDE CRUISE

GROSS WEIGHT — 45,000 POUNDS

AIRPLANE CONFIGURATION
INDIVIDUAL DRAG INDEXES

REMARKS
ENGINES: (2) J79-GE-8

DATE: 15 MAY 1968
DATA BASIS: FLIGHT TEST

FUEL GRADE: JP-5
FUEL DENSITY: 6.8 LB/GAL

| KTAS | DRAG INDEX | TOTAL FUEL FLOW-LB/HR | | | | | | | TEMP EFFECTS | |
		0	20	40	60	80	100	120	°C	FACTOR
SEA LEVEL (15°C)										
360	7121	7936	8683	9488	10298	11143	11990			
400	8186	9168	10150	11135	12226	13260	14434		−40	.899
440	9522	10741	12010	13238	14616	16145	17753		−20	.937
480	11049	12581	14029	15663	17546	19617	22326		0	.973
520	13024	14740	16570	18757	21608				20	1.008
560	15347	17479	19797	23788					40	1.042
600	18653	21524								
MIL	25995	25660	25100	24410	23770	23210	22730			
V_MAX	635.5	620.3	597.2	568.7	541.3	513.7	489.0			
4,000 FEET (7°C)										
360	6377	7059	7764	8440	9104	9808	10593			
400	7213	8103	8930	9765	10687	11789	12779		−40	.912
440	8293	9331	10379	11543	12795	14185	15657		−20	.949
480	9582	10854	12252	13715	15406	17260	19684		0	.987
520	11175	12806	14485	16471	19039				20	1.022
560	13263	15291	17383	20636					40	1.057
600	16301	18754								
MIL	23520	23260	22760	22100	21640	21160	20600			
V_MAX	630.1	618.2	595.4	570	543.8	516.7	492.3			
8,000 FEET (-1°C)										
360	5769	6344	6946	7537	8125	8669	9281			
400	6414	7161	7895	8594	9302	10169	11155		−40	.925
440	7252	8173	9052	9967	11074	12265	13594		−20	.963
480	8269	9347	10467	11783	13245	14908	16629		0	1.001
520	9582	10917	12381	14212	16150				20	1.037
560	11273	12972	14997	17539					40	1.072
600	13860	16141								
MIL	20820	20600	20200	19820	19400	18860	18560			
V_MAX	624.3	612.7	594.0	570.3	545.2	518.8	494.4			
12,000 FEET (-9°C)										
360	5284	5768	6262	6816	7295	7802	8254			
400	5758	6370	7039	7625	8213	8824	9568		−40	.939
440	6419	7179	7927	8660	9486	10465	11591		−20	.978
480	7206	8120	9024	10035	11273	12628			0	1.016
520	8217	9296	10440	11920	13689				20	1.052
560	9602	10927	12517	14852					40	1.088
600	11706	13605								
MIL	18980	18720	18840	18080	17620	17160	16660			
V_MAX	618.8	606.2	590.3	569.8	545.4	519.9	494.7			

FDB-1-(299)

Figure 11-51

LOW ALTITUDE CRUISE

GROSS WEIGHT – 50,000 POUNDS

AIRPLANE CONFIGURATION
INDIVIDUAL DRAG INDEXES

REMARKS
ENGINES: (2) J79–GE–8

DATE: 15 MAY 1968
DATA BASIS: FLIGHT TEST

FUEL GRADE: JP–5
FUEL DENSITY: 6.8 LB/GAL

SEA LEVEL (15°C)

KTAS	DRAG INDEX 0	20	40	60	80	100	120	TEMP. EFFECTS °C	FACTOR
	TOTAL FUEL FLOW-LB/HR								
360	7337	8137	8909	9741	10539	11401	12208		
400	8387	9349	10328	11342	12404	13469	14664	–40	.899
440	9658	10863	12144	13360	14748	16305	17903	–20	.937
480	11181	12718	14165	15806	17693	19795	22556	0	.973
520	13116	14840	16673	18866	21757			20	1.008
560	15449	17582	19906	23949				40	1.042
600	18755	21656							
MIL	25990	25640	25080	24390	23750	23190	22710		
V_{MAX}	634.9	619.6	596.5	567.9	540.3	512.3	487.4		

4,000 FEET (7°C)

KTAS	DRAG INDEX 0	20	40	60	80	100	120	TEMP. EFFECTS °C	FACTOR
360	6631	7320	7993	8665	9361	10074	10887		
400	7416	8287	9111	9962	10913	11992	13019	–40	.912
440	8474	9513	10585	11773	13014	14430	15926	–20	.949
480	9704	10996	12407	13873	15558	17443	19919	0	.987
520	11303	12932	14636	16616	19238			20	1.022
560	13362	15414	17510	20783				40	1.057
600	16410	18869							
MIL	23520	23240	22720	22060	21620	21140	20580		
V_{MAX}	629.6	617.5	594.7	569.2	542.8	515.3	491.0		

8,000 FEET (-1°C)

KTAS	DRAG INDEX 0	20	40	60	80	100	120	TEMP. EFFECTS °C	FACTOR
360	6052	6635	7274	7828	8392	8972	9608		
400	6659	7445	8135	8819	9562	10467	11489	–40	.925
440	7459	8366	9239	10181	11317	12501	13885	–20	.963
480	8442	9522	10668	12010	13482	15120	16895	0	1.001
520	9698	11052	12512	14385	16305			20	1.037
560	11402	13106	15126	17713				40	1.072
600	14015	16298							
MIL	20800	20580	20180	19800	19380	18840	18540		
V_{MAX}	623.6	612.0	593.4	569.4	543.9	516.9	492.5		

12,000 FEET (-9°C)

KTAS	DRAG INDEX 0	20	40	60	80	100	120	TEMP. EFFECTS °C	FACTOR
360	5691	6183	6722	7219	7725	8171	8667		
400	6060	6684	7334	7934	8489	9160	9959	–40	.939
440	6657	7447	8192	8908	9776	10793	11915	–20	.978
480	7405	8315	9216	10254	11528	12895	14558	0	1.016
520	8390	9476	10641	12128	13963			20	1.052
560	9728	11058	12660	14993				40	1.088
600	11912	13828							
MIL	18940	18680	18420	18060	17590	17140	16620		
V_{MAX}	618.2	605.5	589.1	568.5	543.5	517.5	492.2		

FDB-1-(300)

Figure 11-52

LOW ALTITUDE CRUISE

AIRPLANE CONFIGURATION
INDIVIDUAL DRAG INDEXES

GROSS WEIGHT – 55,000 POUNDS

REMARKS
ENGINES: (2) J79-GE-8

DATE: 15 MAY 1968
DATA BASIS: **FLIGHT TEST**

FUEL GRADE: JP-5
FUEL DENSITY: 6.8 LB/GAL

	KTAS	DRAG INDEX 0	20	40	60	80	100	120	TEMP. EFFECTS °C	FACTOR
SEA LEVEL (15°C)	360	7584	8364	9150	9973	10797	11681	12451		
	400	8562	9532	10512	11558	12588	13686	14900	−40	.899
	440	9814	11029	12327	13527	14926	16523	18106	−20	.937
	480	11315	12859	14303	15952	17842	19975		0	.973
	520	13236	14971	16806	19006	21950			20	1.008
	560	15553	17686	20019	24113				40	1.042
	600	18858	21791							
	MIL	25985	25620	25060	24350	23710	23150	22670		
	VMAX	634.3	619.0	595.8	566.9	539.0	510.5	485.6		
4,000 FEET (7°C)	360	6912	7634	8289	8954	9656	10410	11266		
	400	7689	8530	9350	10222	11212	12258	13332	−40	.912
	440	8664	9704	10799	12012	13240	14659	16205	−20	.949
	480	9845	11161	12574	14057	15734	17656	20137	0	.987
	520	11433	13052	14790	16765	19441			20	1.022
	560	13484	15534	17659	20963				40	1.057
	600	16520	18984							
	MIL	23520	23220	22700	22020	21600	21100	20540		
	VMAX	629.0	616.8	594.1	568.3	541.5	513.5	489.0		
8,000 FEET (-1°C)	360	6426	7045	7620	8201	8756	9362	10054		
	400	6929	7695	8405	9081	9865	10812	11804	−40	.925
	440	7728	8615	9479	10457	11629	12802	14242	−20	.963
	480	8636	9717	10892	12224	13747	15355	17214	0	1.001
	520	9831	11206	12661	14582	16483			20	1.037
	560	11530	13243	15257	17889				40	1.072
	600	14223	16508							
	MIL	20780	20560	20140	19760	19340	18800	18500		
	VMAX	623.0	611.4	592.6	568.1	542.0	514.6	489.9		
12,000 FEET (-9°C)	360	6201	6744	7236	7744	8188	8676	9233		
	400	6378	7049	7633	8218	8799	9541	10384	−40	.939
	440	6910	7681	8429	9169	10084	11142	12258	−20	.978
	480	7648	8556	9459	10526	11811	13238	14847	0	1.016
	520	8591	9683	10857	12369	14283			20	1.052
	560	9883	11219	12836	15166				40	1.088
	600	12126	14058							
	MIL	18940	18660	18400	18010	17550	17120	16580		
	VMAX	617.5	604.9	587.8	566.6	541.6	515.0	488.4		

TOTAL FUEL FLOW-LB/HR

FDB-1-(301)

Figure 11-53

LOW ALTITUDE CRUISE

GROSS WEIGHT – 60,000 POUNDS

AIRPLANE CONFIGURATION
INDIVIDUAL DRAG INDEXES

REMARKS

ENGINES: (2) J79-GE-8

DATE: 15 MAY 1968
DATA BASIS: **FLIGHT TEST**

FUEL GRADE: JP-5
FUEL DENSITY: 6.8 LB/GAL

KTAS	DRAG INDEX	TOTAL FUEL FLOW-LB/HR							TEMP. EFFECTS	
		0	20	40	60	80	100	120	°C	FACTOR
SEA LEVEL (15°C)										
360	7871	8624	9426	10238	11079	11921	12725			
400	8772	9750	10731	11816	12805	13940	15181		−40	.899
440	9998	11233	12551	13729	15143	16760	18353		−20	.937
480	11452	13002	14445	16100	17994	20160			0	.973
520	13358	15103	16941	19148	22147				20	1.000
560	15681	17815	20159						40	1.042
600	18963	21927								
MIL	25980	25600	25040	24300	23660	23100	22620			
VMAX	633.7	618.3	595.2	565.6	537.0	508.5	483.4			
4,000 FEET (7°C)										
360	7220	7906	8579	9266	9973	10759	11603			
400	7954	8782	9602	10495	11528	12536	13662		−40	.912
440	8862	9901	11023	12234	13475	14895	16494		−20	.949
480	10034	11382	12769	14301	15967	17939	20427		0	.987
520	11566	13175	14948	16916	19649				20	1.022
560	13608	15656	17803	21145					40	1.057
600	16695	19167								
MIL	23500	23200	22680	22040	21540	21060	20500			
VMAX	628.4	616.1	592.8	567.0	540.2	511.5	486.4			
8,000 FEET (-1°C)										
360	6861	7465	8051	8594	9188	9843	10596			
400	7279	7995	8687	9408	10249	11252	12200		−40	.925
440	7973	8858	9744	10758	11937	13147	14573		−20	.963
480	8839	9920	11105	12441	14022	15597	17545		0	1.001
520	10035	11415	12888	14839	16752				20	1.037
560	11657	13382	15390	18070					40	1.072
600	14438	16724								
MIL	20760	20540	20160	19740	19300	18760	18460			
VMAX	622.3	610.8	591.2	566.2	540.0	512.0	486.7			
12,000 FEET (-9°C)										
360	6860	7330	7833	8278	8776	9335	9984			
400	6844	7466	8067	8624	9290	10107	11033		−40	.939
440	7274	8013	8741	9529	10495	11586	12740		−20	.978
480	7905	8811	9745	10854	12156	13673	15209		0	1.016
520	8790	9875	11080	12619	14552				20	1.052
560	10083	11466	13106	15430					40	1.088
600	12318	14296								
MIL	18920	18640	18380	17960	17500	17040	16530			
VMAX	616.8	604.3	586.5	564.7	539.0	512.8	484.6			

FDB-1-(302)

Figure 11-54

CONSTANT MACH/ALTITUDE CRUISE

AIRPLANE CONFIGURATION
INDIVIDUAL DRAG INDEXES

DATE: 15 MAY 1968
DATA BASIS: FLIGHT TEST

REMARKS
ENGINE(S): (2) J79-GE-8

GUIDE

FUEL GRADE: JP-5
FUEL DENSITY: 6.8 LB/GAL

ICAO STANDARD DAY

ALT. FT.	TEMP. °C
S.L.	15.0
5000	5.1
10,000	-4.8
15,000	-14.7
20,000	-24.6
25,000	-34.5
30,000	-44.4
35,000	-54.3
40,000	-56.5
45,000	-56.5
50,000	-56.5

FUEL FLOW CORRECTION FACTORS						
TEMPERATURE °C	-60	-40	-20	0	20	40
FUEL FLOW FACTOR	0.88	0.92	0.96	1.00	1.04	1.07

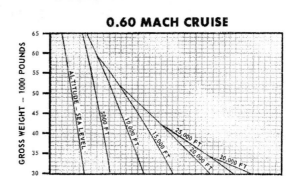

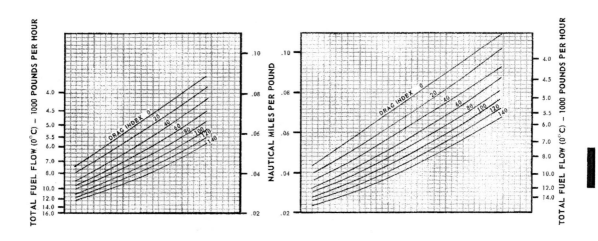

FDB-1-(147)

Figure 11-55

CONSTANT MACH/ALTITUDE CRUISE

AIRPLANE CONFIGURATION
INDIVIDUAL DRAG INDEXES

REMARKS
ENGINE(S): (2) J79-GE-8

DATE: 15 MAY 1968
DATA BASIS: FLIGHT TEST

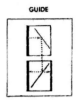

GUIDE

FUEL GRADE: JP-5
FUEL DENSITY: 6.8 LB/GAL

ICAO STANDARD DAY	
ALT. FT.	TEMP. °C
S.L.	15.0
5000	5.1
10,000	-4.8
15,000	-14.7
20,000	-24.6
25,000	-34.5
30,000	-44.4
35,000	-54.3
40,000	-56.5
45,000	-56.5
50,000	-56.5

FUEL FLOW CORRECTION FACTORS						
TEMPERATURE °C	-60	-40	-20	0	20	40
FUEL FLOW FACTOR	0.88	0.92	0.96	1.00	1.04	1.07

0.65 MACH CRUISE

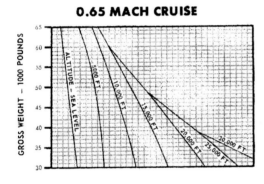

0.70 MACH CRUISE

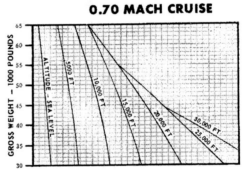

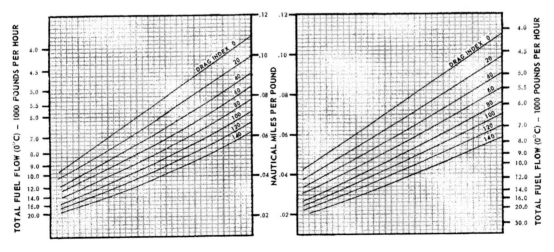

FDB-1-(148)

Figure 11-56

CONSTANT MACH/ALTITUDE CRUISE

AIRPLANE CONFIGURATION
INDIVIDUAL DRAG INDEXES

DATE: 15 MAY 1968
DATA BASIS: **FLIGHT TEST**

REMARKS
ENGINE(S): (2) J79-GE-8

GUIDE

FUEL GRADE: JP-5
FUEL DENSITY: 6.8 LB/GAL

ICAO STANDARD DAY	
ALT. FT.	TEMP. °C
S.L.	15.0
5000	5.1
10,000	-4.8
15,000	-14.7
20,000	-24.6
25,000	-34.5
30,000	-44.4
35,000	-54.3
40,000	-56.5
45,000	-56.5
50,000	-56.5

FUEL FLOW CORRECTION FACTORS						
TEMPERATURE °C	-60	-40	-20	0	20	40
FUEL FLOW FACTOR	0.88	0.92	0.96	1.00	1.04	1.07

0.75 MACH CRUISE

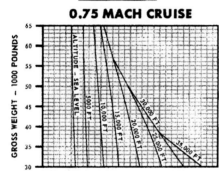

0.80 MACH CRUISE

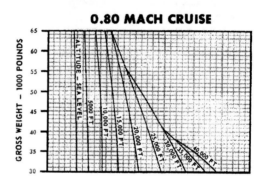

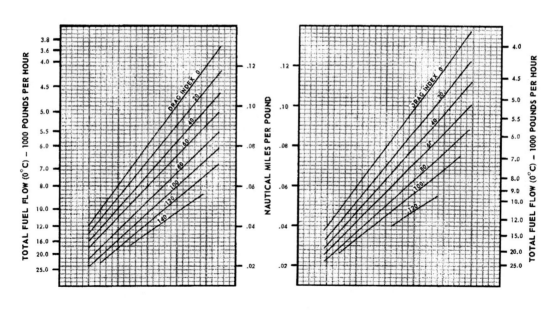

FDB-1-(149

Figure 11-57

CONSTANT MACH/ALTITUDE CRUISE

AIRPLANE CONFIGURATION

INDIVIDUAL DRAG INDEXES

REMARKS

ENGINE(S): (2) J79–GE–8

DATE: 15 MAY 1968
DATA BASIS: **FLIGHT TEST**

GUIDE

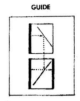

FUEL GRADE: JP–5
FUEL DENSITY: 6.8 LB./GAL

ICAO STANDARD DAY	
ALT. FT.	TEMP. °C
S.L.	15.0
5000	5.1
10,000	-4.8
15,000	-14.7
20,000	-24.6
25,000	-34.5
30,000	-44.4
35,000	-54.3
40,000	-56.5
45,000	-56.5
50,000	-56.5

FUEL FLOW CORRECTION FACTORS						
TEMPERATURE °C	-60	-40	-20	0	20	40
FUEL FLOW FACTOR	0.88	0.92	0.96	1.00	1.04	1.07

0.85 MACH CRUISE

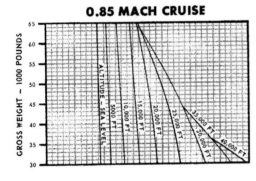

0.90 MACH CRUISE

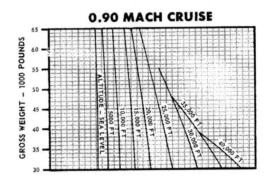

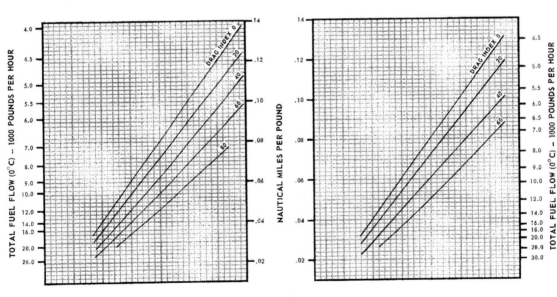

FDB–1–(150)

Figure 11-58

CONSTANT MACH/ALTITUDE CRUISE
ONE ENGINE OPERATING

AIRPLANE CONFIGURATION
INDIVIDUAL DRAG INDEXES

REMARKS
ENGINE(S): (2) J79-GE-8
INOPERATIVE ENGINE WINDMILLING

GUIDE

DATE: 15 MAY 1968
DATA BASIS: FLIGHT TEST

FUEL GRADE: JP-5
FUEL DENSITY: 6.8 LB/GAL

ICAO STANDARD DAY	
ALT. FT.	TEMP. °C
S.L.	15.0
5000	5.1
10,000	-4.8
15,000	-14.7
20,000	-24.6
25,000	-34.5
30,000	-44.4
35,000	-54.3
40,000	-56.5
45,000	-56.5
50,000	-56.5

FUEL FLOW CORRECTION FACTORS						
TEMPERATURE °C	-60	-40	-20	0	20	40
FUEL FLOW FACTOR	0.88	0.92	0.96	1.00	1.04	1.07

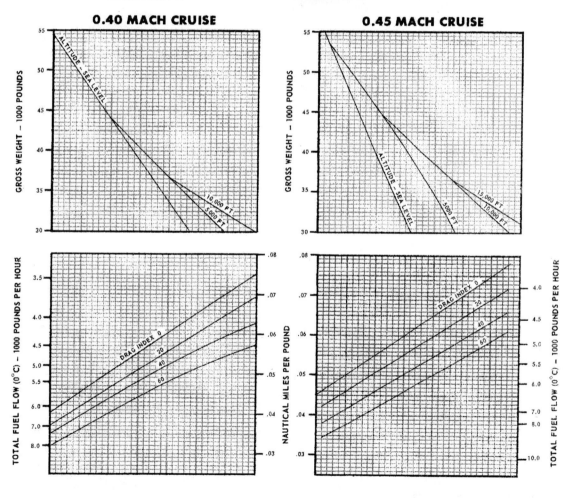

FDB-1-(151)

Figure 11-59

CONSTANT MACH/ALTITUDE CRUISE
ONE ENGINE OPERATING

AIRPLANE CONFIGURATION

INDIVIDUAL DRAG INDEXES

REMARKS

ENGINE(S): (2) J79-GE-8
INOPERATIVE ENGINE WINDMILLING

DATE: 15 MAY 1968
DATA BASIS: FLIGHT TEST

GUIDE

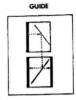

FUEL GRADE: JP-5
FUEL DENSITY: 6.8 LB/GAL

ICAO STANDARD DAY	
ALT. FT.	TEMP. °C
S.L.	15.0
5000	5.1
10,000	-4.8
15,000	-14.7
20,000	-24.6
25,000	-34.5
30,000	-44.4
35,000	-54.3
40,000	-56.5
45,000	-56.5
50,000	-56.5

FUEL FLOW CORRECTION FACTORS						
TEMPERATURE °C	-60	-40	-20	0	20	40
FUEL FLOW FACTOR	0.88	0.92	0.96	1.00	1.04	1.07

0.50 MACH CRUISE

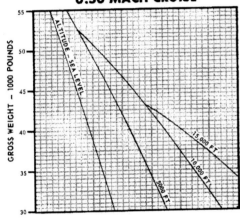

0.55 MACH CRUISE

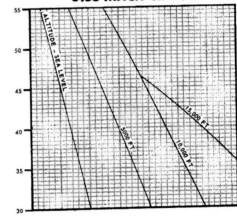

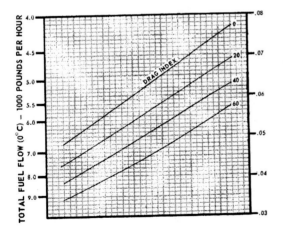

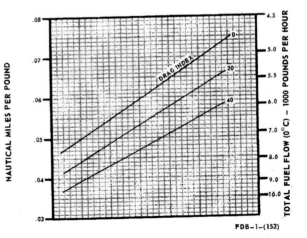

FDB-1-(152)

Figure 11-60

CONSTANT MACH/ALTITUDE CRUISE
ONE ENGINE OPERATING

AIRPLANE CONFIGURATION
INDIVIDUAL DRAG INDEXES

REMARKS
ENGINE(S): (2) J79-GE-8
INOPERATIVE ENGINE WINDMILLING

GUIDE

DATE: 15 MAY 1968
DATA BASIS: FLIGHT TEST

FUEL GRADE: JP-5
FUEL DENSITY: 6.8 LB/GAL

ICAO STANDARD DAY	
ALT. FT.	TEMP. °C
S.L.	15.0
5000	5.1
10,000	-4.8
15,000	-14.7
20,000	-24.6
25,000	-34.5
30,000	-44.4
35,000	-54.3
40,000	-56.5
45,000	-56.5
50,000	-56.5

FUEL FLOW CORRECTION FACTORS						
TEMPERATURE °C	-60	-40	-20	0	20	40
FUEL FLOW FACTOR	0.88	0.92	0.96	1.00	1.04	1.07

0.60 MACH CRUISE

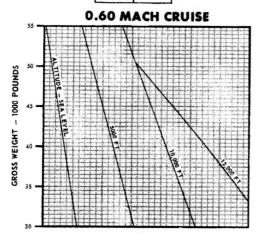

0.65 MACH CRUISE

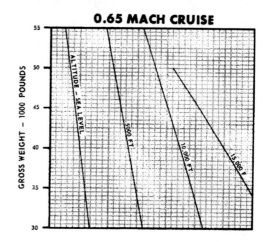

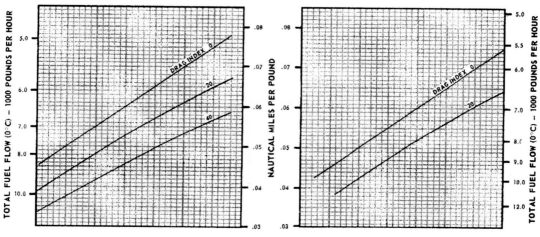

FDB-1-(153)

Figure 11-61

OPTIMUM CRUISE AT CONSTANT ALTITUDE
NAUTICAL MILES PER POUND AND MACH NUMBER

AIRPLANE CONFIGURATION
INDIVIDUAL DRAG INDEXES

REMARKS
ENGINE(S): (2) J79–GE–8

GUIDE

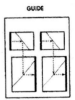

DATE: 1 APRIL 1969
DATA BASIS: **FLIGHT TEST**

FUEL GRADE: JP–5
FUEL DENSITY: 6.8 LB/GAL.

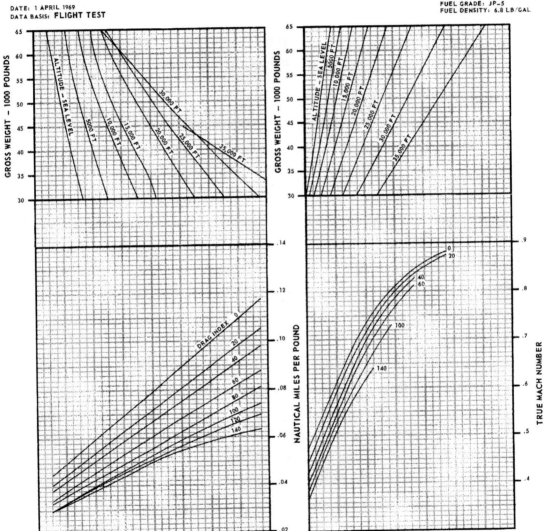

FDB–1–(154)

Figure 11-62 (Sheet 1 of 2)

OPTIMUM CRUISE AT CONSTANT ALTITUDE
TRUE AIRSPEED AND FUEL FLOW

AIRPLANE CONFIGURATION
INDIVIDUAL DRAG INDEXES

REMARKS
ENGINE(S): (2) J79-GE-8

GUIDE

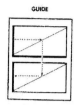

DATE: 15 MAY 1968
DATA BASIS: FLIGHT TEST

FUEL GRADE: JP-5
FUEL DENSITY: 6.8 LB/GAL

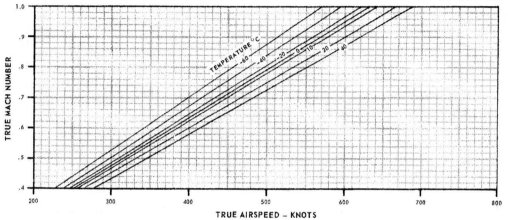

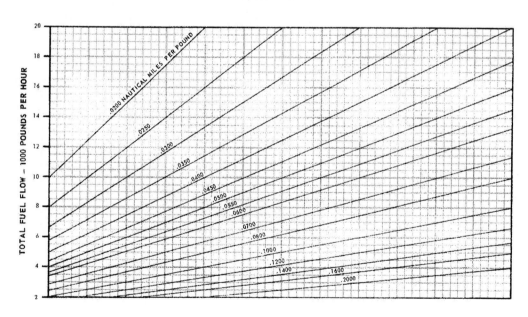

FDB-1-(303)

Figure 11-62 (Sheet 2 of 2)

OPTIMUM CRUISE AT CONSTANT ALTITUDE
NAUTICAL MILES PER POUND AND MACH NUMBER
ONE ENGINE OPERATING

AIRPLANE CONFIGURATION
INDIVIDUAL DRAG INDEXES

REMARKS
ENGINE(S): (2) J79-GE-8
INOPERATIVE ENGINE WINDMILLING

GUIDE

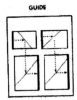

DATE: 15 MAY 1968
DATA BASIS: FLIGHT TEST

FUEL GRADE: JP-5
FUEL DENSITY: 6.8 LB/GAL

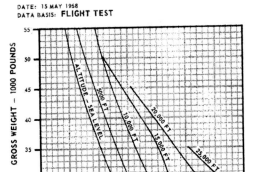

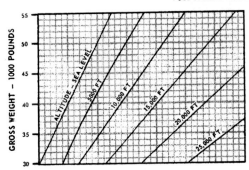

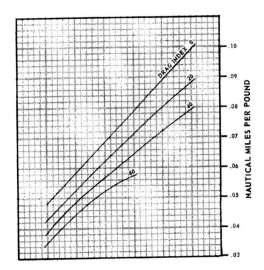

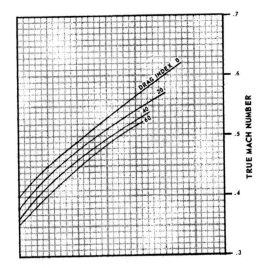

FDB-1-(155)

Figure 11-63 (Sheet 1 of 2)

OPTIMUM CRUISE AT CONSTANT ALTITUDE
TRUE AIRSPEED AND FUEL FLOW
ONE ENGINE OPERATING

AIRPLANE CONFIGURATION
INDIVIDUAL DRAG INDEXES

REMARKS
ENGINE(S): (2) J79-GE-8
INOPERATIVE ENGINE WINDMILLING

GUIDE

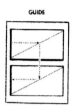

DATE: 15 MAY 1968
DATA BASIS: FLIGHT TEST

FUEL GRADE: JP-5
FUEL DENSITY: 6.8 LB/GAL

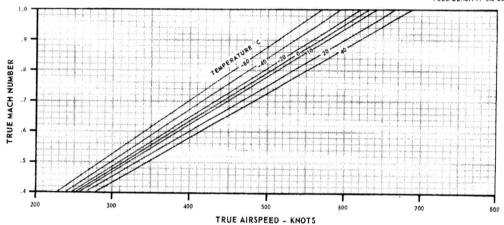

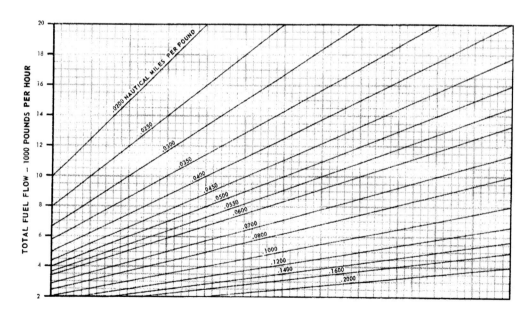

FDB-1-(304)

Figure 11-63 (Sheet 2 of 2)

MAXIMUM ENDURANCE CHARTS

These charts (figures 11-64 thru 11-68) present optimum endurance altitude and maximum endurance specifics (fuel flow and Mach number) for all combinations of effective gross weight and altitude.

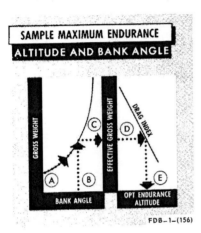

FDB-1-(156)

USE

Enter the Altitude and Bank Angle chart with the average gross weight. If bank angles are to be considered, follow the gross weight curve until it intersects the bank angle to be used; then horizontally to the right to obtain effective gross weight. (If bank angles are not to be considered, enter the chart at the effective gross weight scale.) From this point proceed horizontally to the right and intersect the computed drag index. Reflect downward and read the optimum endurance altitude. Enter the Mach number plots with the effective gross weight, and proceed horizontally to intersect the optimum endurance altitude. Then descend downward and intersect the computed drag index and horizontally to read true Mach number. A further plot to read calibrated airspeed is also available. Enter the Fuel Flow plots with the effective gross weight, proceed horizontally to intersect the optimum endurance altitude. Reflect downward to the computed drag index, and then horizontally to read total fuel flow.

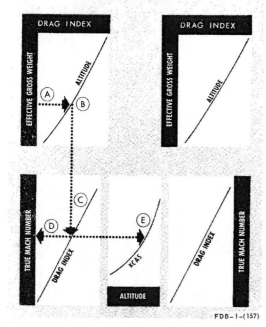

SAMPLE MAXIMUM ENDURANCE
MACH NUMBER

FDB-1-(157)

Mach Number

A. Effective gross weight	47,800 Lbs.
B. Endurance altitude	20,500 Ft.
C. Drag index	40
D. Mach number	0.62
E. Airspeed (CAS)	282 Kts.

Fuel Flow

A. Effective gross weight	47,800 Lbs.
B. Endurance altitude	20,500 Ft.
C. Drag index	40
D. Fuel flow	6000 PPH

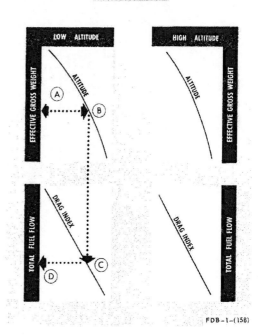

SAMPLE MAXIMUM ENDURANCE
FUEL FLOW

FDB-1-(158)

Sample Problem

Altitude and Bank Angle

A. Gross weight	45,000 Lbs.
B. Bank angle	20
C. Effective gross weight	47,800 Lbs.
D. Drag index	40
E. Optimum endurance altitude	20,500 Ft.

MAXIMUM ENDURANCE
ALTITUDE & BANK ANGLE

AIRPLANE CONFIGURATION
INDIVIDUAL DRAG INDEXES

REMARKS
ENGINE(S): (2) J79-GE-8
ICAO STANDARD DAY

GUIDE

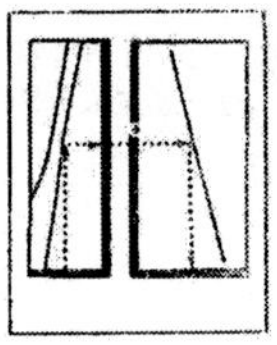

DATE: 15 MAY 1968
DATA BASIS: FLIGHT TEST

FUEL GRADE: JP-5
FUEL DENSITY: 6.8 LB/GAL

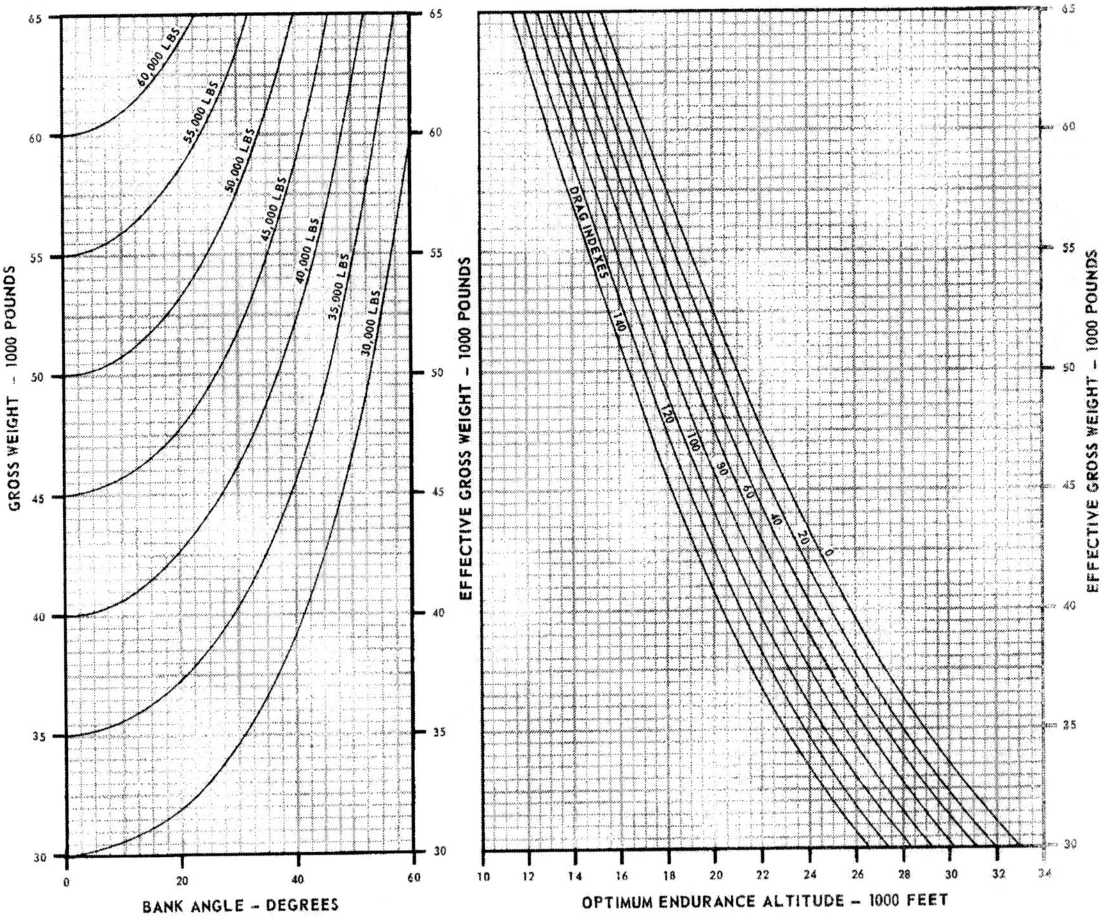

60,000 LBS
55,000 LBS
50,000 LBS
45,000 LBS
40,000 LBS
35,000 LBS
30,000 LBS
GROSS WEIGHT - 1000 POUNDS
BANK ANGLE - DEGREES
EFFECTIVE GROSS WEIGHT - 1000 POUNDS
DRAG INDEXES 140
120
100
80
60
40
20
0
OPTIMUM ENDURANCE ALTITUDE - 1000 FEET

FDB-1-(159)

Figure 11-64

MAXIMUM ENDURANCE
MACH NUMBER

AIRPLANE CONFIGURATION

INDIVIDUAL DRAG INDEXES
(0–140)

REMARKS

ENGINE(S): (2) J79–GE–8
ICAO STANDARD DAY

GUIDE

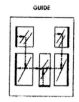

DATE: 15 OCTOBER 1968
DATA BASIS: **FLIGHT TEST**

FUEL GRADE: JP–5
FUEL DENSITY: 6.8 LB/GAL

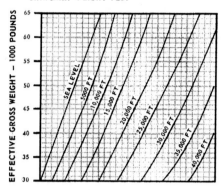

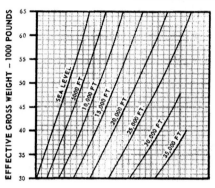

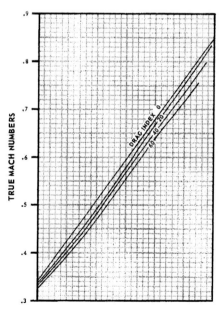

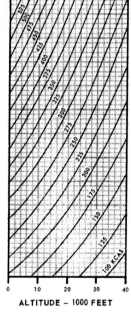

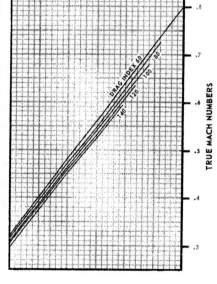

FDB–1–(160)

Figure 11-65

MAXIMUM ENDURANCE
FUEL FLOW

AIRPLANE CONFIGURATION

INDIVIDUAL DRAG INDEXES
(0—140)

REMARKS

ENGINE(S): (2) J79—GE—8
ICAO STANDARD DAY

GUIDE

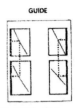

DATE: 15 OCTOBER 1968
DATA BASIS: **FLIGHT TEST**

FUEL GRADE: JP—5
FUEL DENSITY: 6.8 LB/GAL

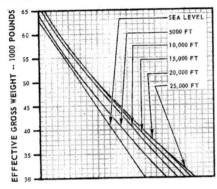

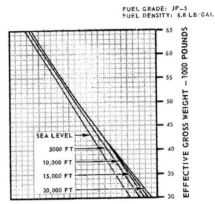

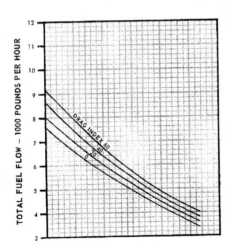

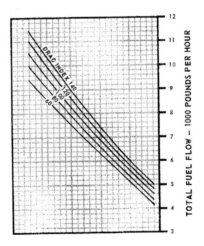

FDB—1—(161)

Figure 11-66

MAXIMUM ENDURANCE
ONE ENGINE OPERATING
ALTITUDE AND BANK ANGLE

AIRPLANE CONFIGURATION
INDIVIDUAL DRAG INDEXES

REMARKS
ENGINE(S): (2) J79-GE-8
ICAO STANDARD DAY
INOPERATIVE ENGINE WINDMILLING

GUIDE

FUEL GRADE: JP-5
FUEL DENSITY: 6.8 LB/GAL

DATE: 15 MAY 1968
DATA BASIS: FLIGHT TEST

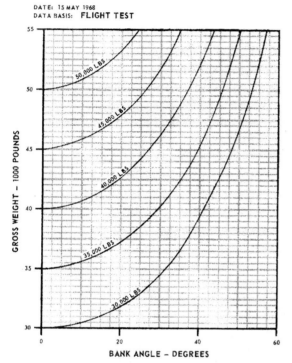

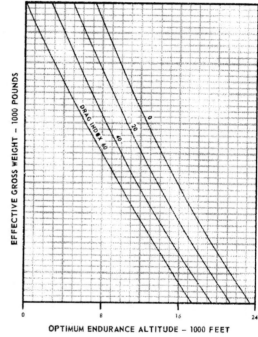

FDB-1-(162)

Figure 11-67

MAXIMUM ENDURANCE
FUEL FLOW

AIRPLANE CONFIGURATION
ALL DRAG INDEXES

ONE ENGINE OPERATING

REMARKS

ENGINE(S): (2) J79-GE-8
ICAO STANDARD DAY
INOPERATIVE ENGINE WINDMILLING

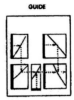

GUIDE

DATE: 15 MARCH 1968
DATA BASIS: **FLIGHT TEST**

FUEL GRADE: JP-5
FUEL DENSITY: 6.8 LB/GAL

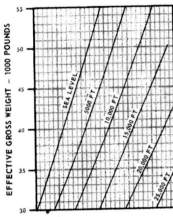

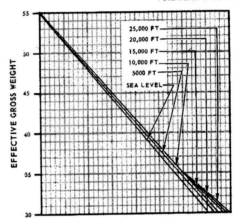

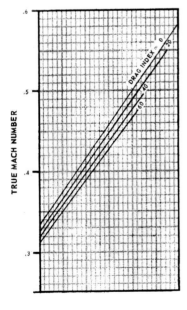

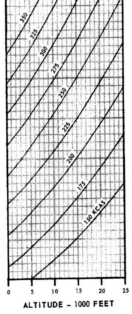

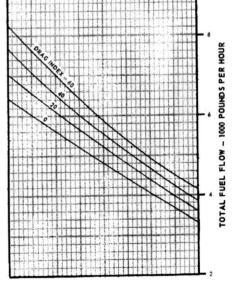

FDB-1-(163)

Figure 11-68

PART **6** *AIR REFUELING*

Note

Refer to NATOPS Air Refueling Manual.

AIR REFUELING TRANSFER TIME CHART

This chart (figure 11-69) provides the capability of determining the amount of time required to take on a certain amount of fuel at a specified rate. This time segment should then be added to the planning profile.

USE

Enter the chart with a specified amount of fuel to be received and project horizontally to the right and intersect the applicable rate of transfer. From this point descend vertically to read the amount of time required for the transfer.

Sample Problem

D704 Buddy Tank

A.	Total fuel transferred	12,000 Lbs.
B.	Transfer rate for D704 Buddy Tank	180 Gal/Min.
C.	Time of transfer	10 Min.

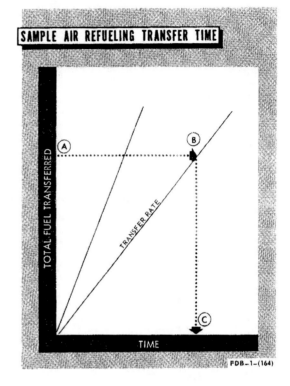

SAMPLE AIR REFUELING TRANSFER TIME

FDB-1-(164)

AIR REFUELING TRANSFER TIME
D-704 BUDDY TANK C-130 AND KA3B/EKA3B TANKER

AIRPLANE CONFIGURATION
ALL CONFIGURATIONS

GUIDE

DATE: 1 DECEMBER 1968
DATA BASIS: FLIGHT TEST

FUEL GRADE: JP-5
FUEL DENSITY: 6.8 LB/GAL

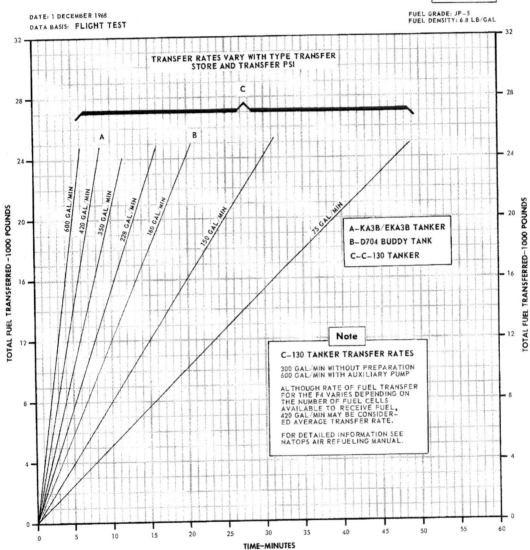

TRANSFER RATES VARY WITH TYPE TRANSFER
STORE AND TRANSFER PSI

600 GAL/MIN
420 GAL/MIN
350 GAL/MIN
228 GAL/MIN
180 GAL/MIN
150 GAL/MIN
75 GAL/MIN

A—KA3B/EKA3B TANKER
B—D704 BUDDY TANK
C—C-130 TANKER

Note

C-130 TANKER TRANSFER RATES

300 GAL/MIN WITHOUT PREPARATION
600 GAL/MIN WITH AUXILIARY PUMP

ALTHOUGH RATE OF FUEL TRANSFER
FOR THE F4 VARIES DEPENDING ON
THE NUMBER OF FUEL CELLS
AVAILABLE TO RECEIVE FUEL,
420 GAL/MIN MAY BE CONSIDER-
ED AVERAGE TRANSFER RATE.

FOR DETAILED INFORMATION SEE
NATOPS AIR REFUELING MANUAL.

TOTAL FUEL TRANSFERRED –1000 POUNDS

TOTAL FUEL TRANSFERRED–1000 POUNDS

TIME–MINUTES

FDB-1-(165)

Figure 11-69

DESCENT CHART

This chart (figure 11-70) provides distance, time, fuel used, and corresponding Mach number for an idle-power/250-knot descent. Incremental data may be obtained for distance, time, and fuel by subtracting data corresponding to level-off altitude from the data for the original cruising altitude.

USE

Enter the upper plot of the chart with the cruising flight-level and project horizontally across the graph to intersect both drag index reflectors at the applicable computed drag-index. From the first intersection, project vertically downward to intersect and read distance traveled. From the second intersection, project vertically downward to intersect and read time required. Enter the lower plot with the cruising altitude and project horizontally across the graph to intersect both drag index reflectors at the applicable computed drag index. From the first intersection, project vertically downward to intersect and read fuel required. From the second intersection, project vertically downward to intersect and read corresponding Mach number at start of descent.

Sample Problem

A.	Altitude	30,000 Ft.
B.	Computed drag index	20.0
C.	Distance traveled	46 Miles
D.	Computed drag index	20.0
E.	Time required	9.0 Mins.
F.	Altitude	30,000 Ft.
G.	Computed drag index	20.0
H.	Fuel used	190 lbs.
J.	Single drag reflector	
K.	Mach number at start of descent	0.665

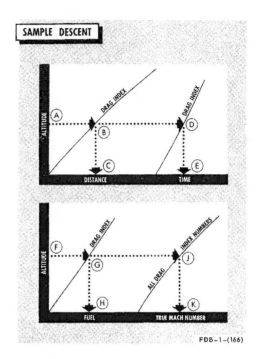

DESCENT
250 KCAS-IDLE THRUST
SPEED BRAKES RETRACTED

AIRPLANE CONFIGURATION
INDIVIDUAL DRAG INDEXES

REMARKS
ENGINE(S): (2) J79-GE-8
ALL GROSS WEIGHTS
ICAO STANDARD DAY

GUIDE

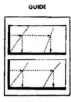

DATE: 15 MAY 1968
DATA BASIS: FLIGHT TEST

FUEL GRADE: JP-5
FUEL DENSITY: 6.8 LB/GAL

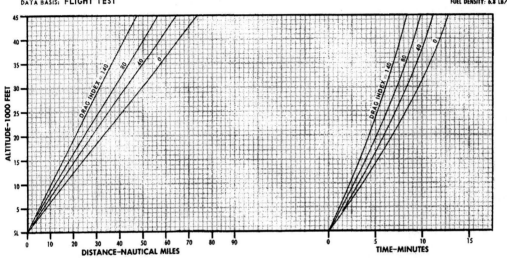

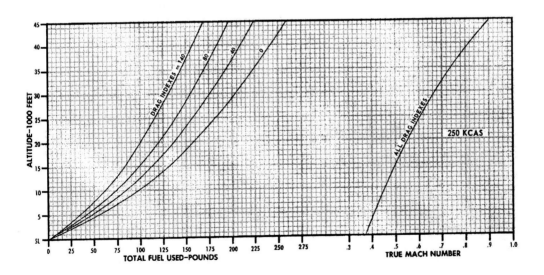

FDB-1-(167)

Figure 11-70

PART **8** LANDING

CHARTS

LANDING SPEEDS CHART

The Landing Speeds charts (figures 11-71 and 11-72) show recommended approach and stall warning (pedal shaker) speed curves for the various gross weights of the airplane.

USE

Enter the applicable chart at estimated landing gross weight. Proceed vertically to the reflector lines and project horizontally to the left to read recommended approach and stall warning speed.

Sample Problem

Aircraft Thru 152994y Before AFC 218

   A. Estimated landing gross weight   32,000 Lbs.
   B. Speed reflector line
   C. Recommended approach speed (CAS)   133 Kts.
   D. Stall warning speed   122 Kts.

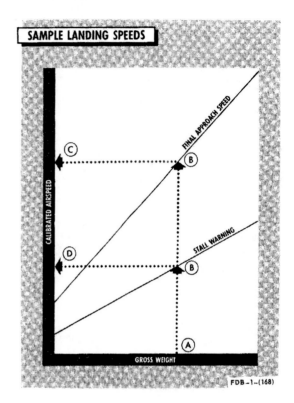

SAMPLE LANDING SPEEDS

FDB-1-(168)

LANDING DISTANCE CHARTS

These charts (figures 11-73 and 11-74) contain landing roll distance information. The variables of temperature, altitude, gross weight, wind, runway condition reading (RCR), and drag chute are taken into consideration.

USE

Enter the chart with the runway temperature and project vertically upward to the correct pressure altitude. From this point, proceed horizontally to the right to the landing gross weight. Project vertically downward to the wind plot and proceed parallel to the wind guide lines (headwind or tailwind) to the intersection of the guide line and the wind speed. From this point, descend further to the appropriate runway condition reading (RCR) and then horizontally to the left to read landing roll distance with drag chute. If the landing is to be made without the drag chute, continue further to the left to the appropriate RCR reflector and then proceed down to read the landing roll distance. If the landing is to be made over a 50-foot obstacle, add 1000 feet to the landing roll distance. If field RCR factors are not available, use RCR 23 for dry, RCR 14 for wet and RCR 5 for icy.

Sample Problem

Airplanes with Drooped Ailerons

A.	Temperature	15°C
B.	Pressure altitude	2000 Ft.
C.	Gross weight	30,000 Lbs.
D.	Wind base line	
E.	Effective headwind	20 Kts.
F.	RCR	14
G.	Landing roll distance	3700 Ft.

If operating without drag chute:

H.	RCR	14
J.	Landing roll distance	5000 Ft.

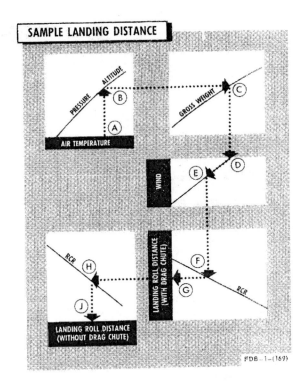

SAMPLE LANDING DISTANCE

FDB-1-(169)

LANDING SPEEDS

AIRPLANE CONFIGURATION
ALL DRAG INDEXES
FLAPS EXTENDED, GEAR DOWN

REMARKS
ENGINE(S): (2)J79—GE—8
ICAO STANDARD DAY

GUIDE

AIRCRAFT THRU 152994y BEFORE AFC 218

DATE: 15 FEBRUARY 1970
DATA BASIS: **FLIGHT TEST**

FUEL GRADE: JP—5
FUEL DENSITY: 6.8 LB/GAL

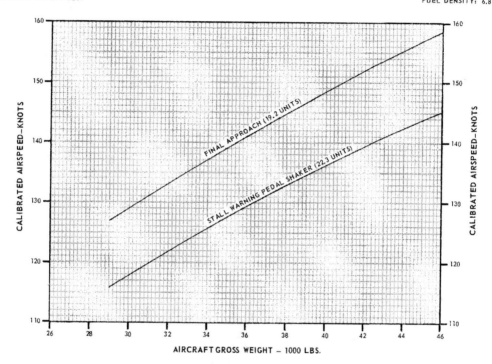

Note

Above speeds are on glide slope, not level flight. Because of thrust effects, airspeed position errors, and SPC cam tolerances, the indicated airspeeds corresponding to the above calibrated airspeeds may vary as follows (thrust and position error
effects are additive):

	SPC OFF	SPC ON
Thrust effect from glide slope to level flight	−2 KT	−2 KT
Position error altitude effect:		
Sea Level	+8 KT	+2 KT
5,000 feet	+8 KT	+4 KT
10,000 feet	+8 KT	+6 KT

FDB-1-(170)

Figure 11-71

LANDING SPEEDS

AIRPLANE CONFIGURATION
ALL DRAG INDEXES
FLAPS EXTENDED, GEAR DOWN

REMARKS
ENGINE(S): (2) J79-GE-8
ICAO STANDARD DAY

GUIDE

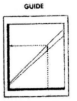

AIRCRAFT 152995z AND UP, AND ALL OTHERS AFTER AFC 218

DATE: 15 FEBRUARY 1970
DATA BASIS: **FLIGHT TEST**

FUEL GRADE: JP-5
FUEL DENSITY: 6.8 LB/GAL

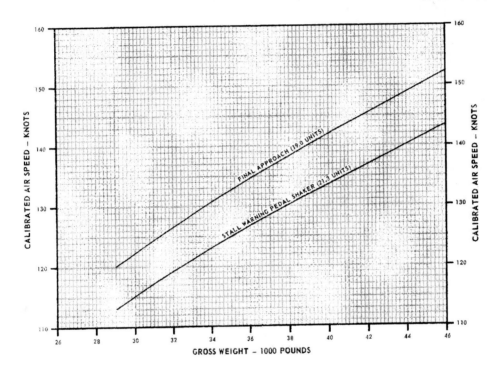

Note

Above speeds are on glide slope, not level flight. Because of thrust effects, airspeed position errors, and SPC cam tolerances, the indicated airspeeds corresponding to the above calibrated airspeeds may vary as follows (thrust and position error effects are additive):

	SPC OFF	SPC ON
Thrust effect from glide slope to level flight	−2 KT	−2 KT
Position error altitude effects:		
Sea Level	+8 KT	+2 KT
5,000 feet	+8 KT	+4 KT
10,000 feet	+8 KT	+6 KT

FDB-1-(171)

Figure 11-72

LANDING SPEEDS

AIRPLANE CONFIGURATION
ALL DRAG INDEXES
FLAPS EXTENDED, GEAR DOWN

REMARKS
ENGINE(S): (2)J79-GE-8
ICAO STANDARD DAY

GUIDE

AIRCRAFT THRU 152994y BEFORE AFC 218

DATE: 15 FEBRUARY 1970
DATA BASIS: **FLIGHT TEST**

FUEL GRADE: JP-5
FUEL DENSITY: 6.8 LB/GAL

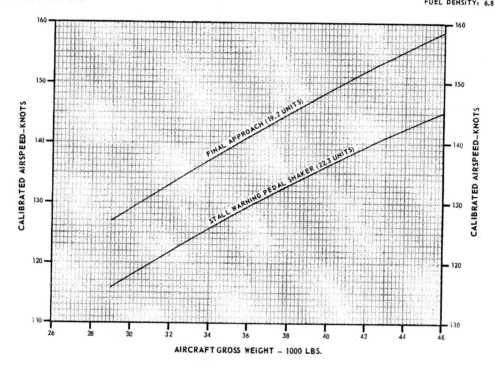

Note

Above speeds are on glide slope, not level flight. Because of thrust effects, air-speed position errors, and SPC cam tolerances, the indicated airspeeds correspond-ing to the above calibrated airspeeds may vary as follows (thrust and position error effects are additive):

	SPC OFF	SPC ON
Thrust effect from glide slope to level flight	-2 KT	-2 KT
Position error altitude effect:		
Sea Level	+8 KT	+2 KT
5,000 feet	+8 KT	+4 KT
10,000 feet	+8 KT	+6 KT

FDB-1-(170)

Figure 11-71

LANDING SPEEDS

AIRPLANE CONFIGURATION
ALL DRAG INDEXES
FLAPS EXTENDED, GEAR DOWN

REMARKS
ENGINE(S): (2) J79-GE-8
ICAO STANDARD DAY

GUIDE

AIRCRAFT 152995z AND UP, AND
ALL OTHERS AFTER AFC 218

DATE: 15 FEBRUARY 1970
DATA BASIS: **FLIGHT TEST**

FUEL GRADE: JP-5
FUEL DENSITY: 6.8 LB/GAL

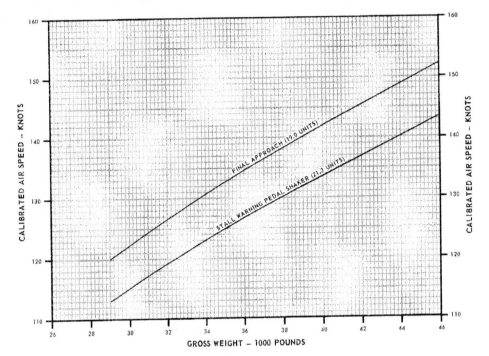

| Note |

Above speeds are on glide slope, not level flight. Because of thrust effects, airspeed position errors, and SPC cam tolerances, the indicated airspeeds corresponding to the above calibrated airspeeds may vary as follows (thrust and position
error effects are additive):

	SPC OFF	SPC ON
Thrust effect from glide slope to level flight	−2 KT	−2 KT
Position error altitude effects:		
Sea Level	+8 KT	+2 KT
5,000 feet	+8 KT	+4 KT
10,000 feet	+8 KT	+6 KT

FDB-1-(171)

Figure 11-72

LANDING DISTANCE
HARD DRY RUNWAY

AIRPLANE CONFIGURATION
ALL DRAG INDEXES
FULL FLAPS, GEAR DOWN
DRAG CHUTE DEPLOYED

REMARKS
ENGINE(S): (2) J79-GE-8

GUIDE

AIRPLANES WITHOUT DROOPED AILERONS

DATE: 1 APRIL 1969
DATA BASIS: FLIGHT TEST

FUEL GRADE: JP-5
FUEL DENSITY: 6.8 LB/GAL

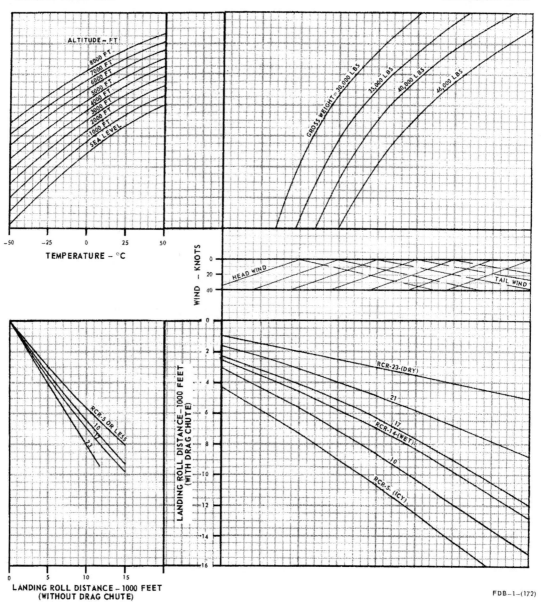

Figure 11-73

FDB-1-(172)

LANDING DISTANCE
IDLE THRUST
HARD DRY RUNWAY

AIRPLANE CONFIGURATION
ALL DRAG INDEXES
FLAPS EXTENDED, GEAR DOWN
DRAG CHUTE DEPLOYED

REMARKS
ENGINE(S): (2) J79-GE-8

GUIDE

AIRPLANES WITH DROOPED AILERONS

DATE: 1 MAY 1968
DATA BASIS: ESTIMATED (BASED ON FLIGHT TEST)

FUEL GRADE: JP-5
FUEL DENSITY: 6.8 LB/GAL

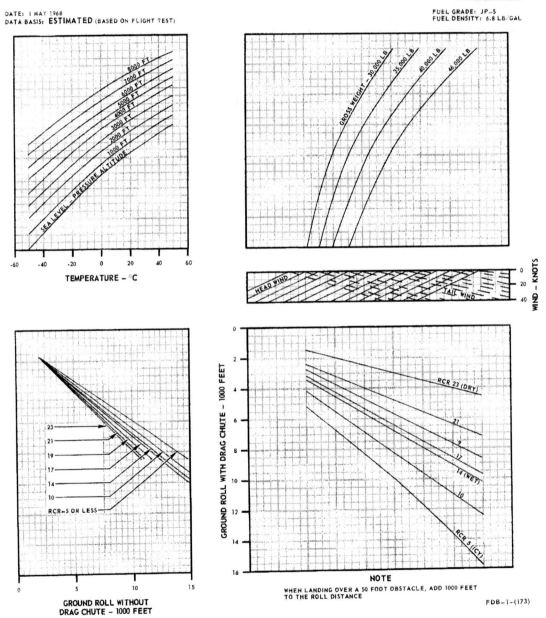

NOTE
WHEN LANDING OVER A 50 FOOT OBSTACLE, ADD 1000 FEET
TO THE ROLL DISTANCE

FDB-1-(173)

Figure 11-74

PART 9 COMBAT PERFORMANCE

CHARTS

COMBAT FUEL FLOW CHART

These charts (figures 11-75 thru 11-79) present the specific fuel flow and general power settings required to maintain a constant Mach number for ICAO standard day, ICAO standard day +10°C, and for all interpolated altitudes from Sea Level to 50,000 feet. The fuel flow values are based on a stabilized level flight condition, and do not represent the fuel flow required to accelerate to a given Mach number.

USE

Enter the chart with the Mach number desired for stabilized level flight. Proceed vertically to the interpolated altitude and temperature, and note the general power setting required. From this point, project to the left scale to read the corresponding fuel flow relationship.

Sample Problem

Configuration: (4) AIM-7 and (2) Wing tanks

A.	Desired mach number	1.3
B.	Altitude (ICAO standard day +10°C)	20,000 Ft.
C.	Power setting required	(Modulated Afterburners)
D.	Fuel flow (pounds per minute)	1000 PPM

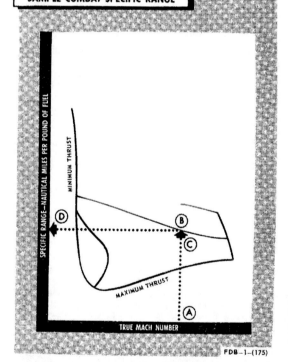

SAMPLE COMBAT SPECIFIC RANGE

FDB–1–(175)

COMBAT SPECIFIC RANGE

These charts (figures 11-80 thru 11-84) present the specific range in nautical miles per pound, and general power settings required to maintain a constant Mach number for ICAO standard day; ICAO standard day +10°C, and for all interpolated altitudes from Sea Level to 50,000 feet. The specific range values are based on a stabilized level flight condition, and do not represent the fuel flow required to accelerate to a given Mach number.

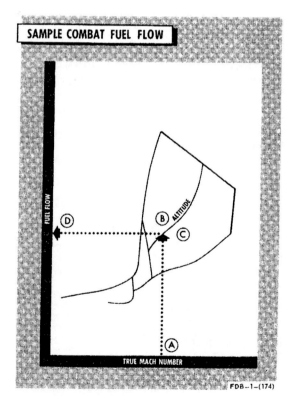

SAMPLE COMBAT FUEL FLOW

FDB–1–(174)

USE

Enter the chart with the Mach number desired for stabilized level flight. Proceed vertically to the interpolated altitude and temperature, and note the general power setting required. From this point, project to the left scale to read the corresponding specific range.

Sample Problem

Configuration: (4) AIM-7 and (2) Wing tanks

A. Desired Mach number	1.2
B. Altitude (ICAO standard day)	15,000 Ft.
C. Power setting required	(modulated afterburner)
D. Specific range (nautical miles per pound)	0.013 NMPP

SUPERSONIC MAXIMUM THRUST CLIMB CHARTS

These charts (figures 11-85 thru 11-89) are plotted for supersonic maximum thrust climb from 35,000 feet. Distance from 35,000 feet to combat ceiling is plotted vs. gross weight with guide lines to show the reduction in gross weight during climb as fuel is consumed. The time relationship to distance is superimposed on the graph. A portion of the chart, is devoted to acceleration at 35,000 feet and provides a capability of determining the time, fuel, and distance required for level flight acceleration from subsonic climb Mach number to supersonic climb Mach number at that altitude. If supersonic flight is contemplated, acceleration at 35,000 feet followed by supersonic climb is recommended since transonic accelerations at the higher altitudes are limited.

USE

To obtain acceleration and climb data from the climb charts, enter the proper climb chart at the initial gross weight. Proceed vertically to the initial Mach number and note time and distance. From the initial Mach number, parallel a guide curve until it intersects the supersonic climb Mach number. Note time and distance, and project vertically and note gross weight. Subtract time, distance, and gross weight values to determine time, distance, and fuel for acceleration. From the supersonic Mach number gross weight intersection, continue paralleling the guide curve until it intersects the desired altitude at end of climb. Read the time, distance, and gross weight. The difference between time at start of climb and completed time is the elapsed time (Δ time) required to climb. The difference between start of climb and end of climb values for distance and for gross weight gives, respectively, the distance traveled (Δ distance) and fuel used (Δ weight, change in gross weight = pounds of fuel used) to climb. To obtain total fuel, time, and distance (including acceleration to climb Mach number), add the noted acceleration requirements to climb values.

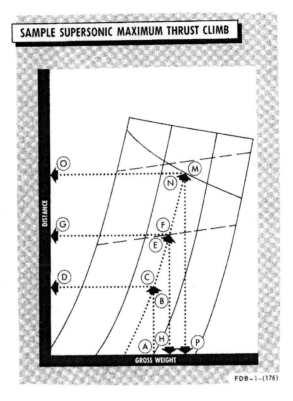

SAMPLE SUPERSONIC MAXIMUM THRUST CLIMB

FDB-1-(176)

Sample Problem

Configuration: (4) AIM-7, Missiles

A.	Initial gross weight	40,000 Lbs.
B.	Initial Mach number	1.2 Mach
C.	Time corresponding to initial Mach number	0.8 Min
D.	Distance corresponding to initial Mach number	8 Miles
E.	Supersonic Mach number at end of acceleration (start of climb)	1.8 Mach
F.	Time at end of acceleration (start of climb)	2.4 Min
G.	Distance at end of acceleration (start of climb)	32 Miles
H.	Gross weight at end of acceleration (start of climb)	38,600 Lbs.
J.	Time required for acceleration (F-C)	1.6 Min
K.	Distance required for acceleration (G-D)	24 Miles
L.	Fuel required for acceleration (A-H)	1400 Lbs.
M.	Altitude at end of climb	57,000 Ft.
N.	Time at end of climb	6.3 Min
O.	Distance at end of climb	94 Miles
P.	Gross weight at end of climb	36,600 Lbs.
Q.	Time required for climb (N-F)	3.9 Min
R.	Distance required for climb (O-G)	62 Miles
S.	Fuel used during climb (H-P)	2000 Lbs.

Note

To obtain total fuel, time, and distance (including acceleration to climb Mach number), apply the noted acceleration requirements to climb values.

T.	Time required from start of acceleration time to end of climb (N-C)	5.5 Min
U.	Distance traveled from start of acceleration to end of climb (O-D)	86 Miles
V.	Fuel used from start of acceleration to end of climb (A-P)	3400 Lbs.

LOW ALTITUDE ACCELERATIONS

These charts (figures 11-90 thru 11-99) present time and fuel required to accelerate from 0.5 to 0.9 Mach at altitudes of Sea Level, 2000, 4000, and 6000 feet. Separate charts are provided for several gross weights and for both maximum and military thrust. The time and fuel values are tabulated for ICAO Standard Day conditions; however, correction factors are given for non-standard temperatures.

USE

After selecting the applicable chart for thrust, gross weight, and altitude, enter with the Mach number desired at end of acceleration and project horizontally to the applicable drag index column. Read time/fuel required to accelerate from 0.5 Mach.

ACCELERATION CHARTS

These charts (figures 11-100 thru 11-144) show the relationship of time, distance, and fuel required for level flight maximum or military thrust accelerations. The data is presented for various altitudes and configurations.

USE

Enter the applicable chart with the aircraft gross weight. Proceed vertically upward to the initial Mach number and note the time. Project horizontally and note the distance. From the initial Mach number proceed parallel to the guide lines to the Mach number desired at the end of acceleration. At this point note the time, then project horizontally and vertically and note the distance and gross weight. From this data, subtract the time, distance, and weight corresponding to the initial Mach number to determine the time, distance, and fuel required for acceleration.

Sample Problem

Configuration: (4) AIM-7 and (4) AIM-9 Max. Thrust 45,000 Ft.

A.	Gross weight	40,000 Lbs.
B.	Initial Mach number	1.6 Mach
C.	Time corresponding to initial Mach number	2.0 Min
D.	Distance	29 Miles
E.	Parallel guide curve	
F.	Desired Mach number	1.8 Mach
G.	Time correspond to desired Mach number	4.0 Min
H.	Distance	62 Miles
I.	Gross weight	38,600 Lbs.
J.	Time required for acceleration (G-C)	2.0 Min
K.	Distance required for acceleration (H-D)	33 Miles
L.	Fuel required for acceleration (A-I)	1400 Lbs.

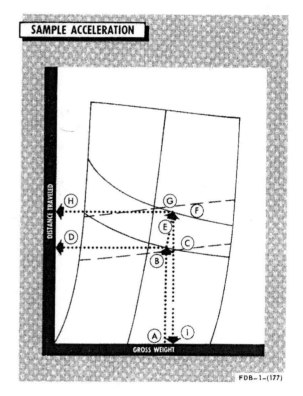

SAMPLE ACCELERATION

FDB-1-(177)

IDLE THRUST DECELERATION

These charts (figures 11-145 thru 11-148) show the relationship between time and distance at various altitudes and gross weights during a minimum time, idle thrust deceleration. Lines of constant Mach number from M_{max} to maximum endurance airspeeds provide a capability of determining the time and distance required for a minimum time idle thrust deceleration.

USE

To determine time and distance required for deceleration, select the applicable chart (35, 40, 45, or 50,000 ft.) and enter the chart with gross weight.

SAMPLE IDLE THRUST DECELERATION

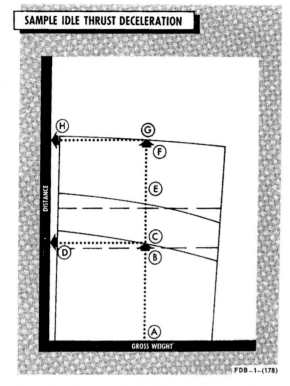

FDB-1-(178)

Proceed vertically to initial Mach number, note time, and project horizontally and note distance. From initial Mach number, parallel a gross weight line until it intersects the desired Mach number at the end of deceleration and note time. Project horizontally and note distance. Subtract time and distance values to determine time and distance required for deceleration.

Sample Problem

Configuration: All configurations, 35,000 Ft.

A.	Gross weight	40,000 Lbs.
B.	Initial Mach number	1.6 Mach
C.	Time corresponding to initial Mach number	0.27 Min
D.	Distance	4.45 Miles
E.	Parallel gross weight line	
F.	Desired Mach number	Max Endurance
G.	Time corresponding to Max endurance	1.18 Min
H.	Distance	14.6 Miles
I.	Time required for deceleration (G-C)	0.91 Min
J.	Distance required for deceleration (H-D)	10.15 Miles

LEVEL FLIGHT ENVELOPE

These charts (figures 11-149 and 11-150) present the airplane's level flight envelope for various configurations and an average combat gross weight.

Parameters of the envelopes extend from buffet limit to the airplane's M_{max} throughout the altitude range. Maximum Mach number curves for additional airplane configurations are plotted within the envelopes.

USE

Enter the appropriate graph at combat altitude, and project horizontally to intersect the desired configuration curve. From this point, descend to the base scale to read maximum attainable Mach number in level flight.

Sample Problem

Configuration: (4) AIM-7 Missiles

A.	Combat altitude	32,000 Ft.
B.	Complete configuration: (4) AIM-7 and (1) C_L Tank	
C.	Maximum attainable Mach number (M_{max})	1.85 Mach

SAMPLE LEVEL FLIGHT ENVELOPE

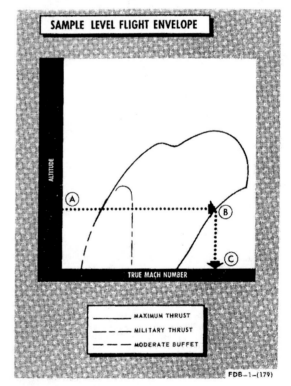

FDB-1-(179)

TEMPERATURE EFFECT ON MAXIMUM SPEED

This chart (figure 11-151) shows the effect of non-standard day temperatures on the maximum speed at maximum thrust. The speed variation is read out as the change in Mach number (Δ Mach) for a 10°C variation in temperature (hot or cold) from standard day.

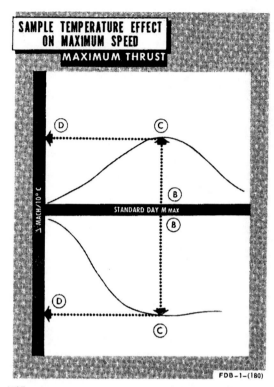

FDB-1-(180)

USE

Determine the temperature variation from standard day for the desired altitude. M_{max} may be obtained from the Maximum Thrust Acceleration charts. Enter the chart at the standard day M_{max} line. Proceed horizontally along this line to the desired Mach number. Proceed vertically into either the Hot or Cold Day plot depending on the temperature variation. Continue vertically to the selected altitude, then proceed horizontally to the left to read Δ Mach. When the temperature variation differs from 10°C simply divide the variation by 10 to reduce it to a decimal. Then multiply the Δ Mach by the decimal to obtain the Δ Mach for a specific situation.

Sample Problem

Find Δ Mach for a standard day M_{max} of 1.8 at 30,000 feet. Forecast flight level temperature is -46.8°C.

A. Temperature variation   -2.4°C
B. Standard day M_{max} 1.8 Mach
C. Altitude   30,000 Ft.
D. Mach/10°C variation   .135 Mach
E. Mach/2.4°C variation   .03 Mach
F. Mach number (B + E)   1.83 Mach

DIVE RECOVERY CHARTS

These charts (figures 11-152 thru 11-155) present the airplane's dive recovery capability for various Mach numbers, altitudes, dive angles, and constant G pull-outs.

USE

Enter the chart at the start of pull-out, and project horizontally to intersect the Mach number at start of pull-out. From this point, descend vertically to intersect dive angle at start of pull-out. Project a line horizontally to read altitude lost during pull-out.

Sample Problem

Configuration: Supersonic - 4 G dive recovery

A. Altitude at start of pull-out   40,000 Ft.
B. Mach number at start of pull-out   1.5 Mach
C. Dive angle at start of pull-out   70°
D. Altitude lost during constant 4 G pull-out   17,000 Ft.

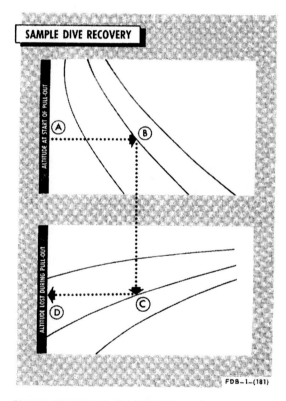

FDB-1-(181)

SYMMETRICAL FLIGHT V-N DIAGRAM

The Symmetrical Flight V-N diagrams (figures 11-156 thru 11-159) are a graphical presentation of airspeed Mach number versus acceleration with lines of indicated angle of attack superimposed. The data are supplied for two different gross weights at four altitudes. The charts may be used to determine the allowable maximum symmetrical maneuvering capability of the airplane as well as the indicated angle of attack for any desired G.

USE

To find the allowable maximum symmetrical performance capability, enter the chart with the calibrated airspeed and proceed vertically to the stall boundary (positive or negative G) or the maximum allowable acceleration (upper and lower) as applicable. From these intersections, project horizontally to the left to read the positive and negative G obtainable in the case of the stall boundaries, or the upper and lower maximum allowable G for the selected gross weight. To find the angle of attack for a given condition of G and airspeed, enter the appropriate chart with these parameters. Project horizontally to the right from the load factor and vertically upward from the airspeed. At the intersection of these two projections, read the indicated angle of attack.

Sample Problem

Altitude -20,000 feet, gross weight-37,500 pounds.

A. Speed (CAS)	500 kts.
B. Load factor	5 G
C. Angle of attack	11 Units

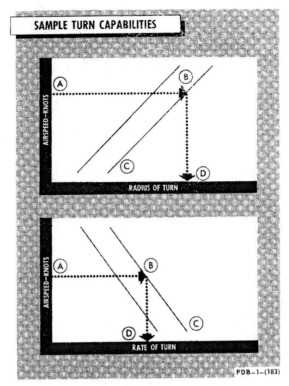

SAMPLE TURN CAPABILITIES

FDB-1-(183)

TURN CAPABILITIES

This chart (figure 11-160) presents the radius of turn and the rate of turn for a constant altitude, constant speed turn. Turn data is available for various speeds and bank angles. Load factor is also included for each bank angle.

USE

Enter the radius of turn plot with the true airspeed. Proceed horizontally to the right to the desired bank angle. Note the load factor, then proceed vertically downward and read the radius of turn. Enter the rate of turn plot with the true airspeed. Proceed horizontally to the right to the bank angle, note the load factor and then proceed vertically downward to read the rate of turn.

Sample Problem

Radius of Turn

A. True airspeed	400 Kts.
B. Bank angle	30°
C. Load factor	1.15 G
D. Radius of turn	25,000 Ft.

Rate of Turn

A. True airspeed	600 Kts.
B. Bank angle	40°
C. Load factor	1.3 G
D. Rate of turn	1.5°/sec.

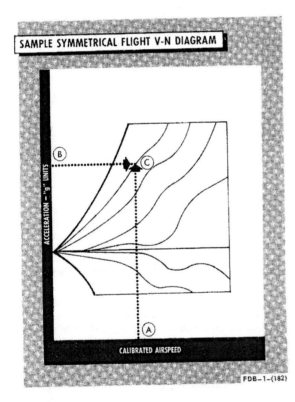

SAMPLE SYMMETRICAL FLIGHT V-N DIAGRAM

FDB-1-(182)

COMBAT FUEL FLOW
STABILIZED LEVEL FLIGHT

AIRPLANE CONFIGURATION

(4) AIM-7

REMARKS

ENGINE(S): (2) J79-GE-8

GUIDE

DATE: 15 MAY 1968
DATA BASIS: **FLIGHT TEST**

FUEL GRADE: JP-5
FUEL DENSITY: 6.8 LB/GAL

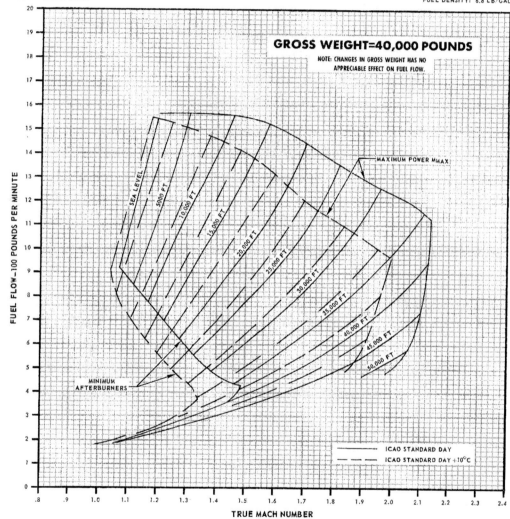

GROSS WEIGHT=40,000 POUNDS

NOTE: CHANGES IN GROSS WEIGHT HAS NO APPRECIABLE EFFECT ON FUEL FLOW.

MAXIMUM POWER MMAX

MINIMUM AFTERBURNERS

—— ICAO STANDARD DAY
– – – ICAO STANDARD DAY +10°C

FUEL FLOW-100 POUNDS PER MINUTE

TRUE MACH NUMBER

FDB-1-(184)

Figure 11-75

COMBAT FUEL FLOW
STABILIZED LEVEL FLIGHT

AIRPLANE CONFIGURATION
(4) AIM-7, (4) AIM-9
OR
(4) AIM-7, (1) ℄ TANK

REMARKS
ENGINE(S):(2) J79-GE-8

GUIDE

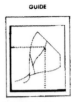

FUEL GRADE: JP-5
FUEL DENSITY: 6.8 LB/GAL

DATE: 15 MAY 1968
DATA BASIS: FLIGHT TEST

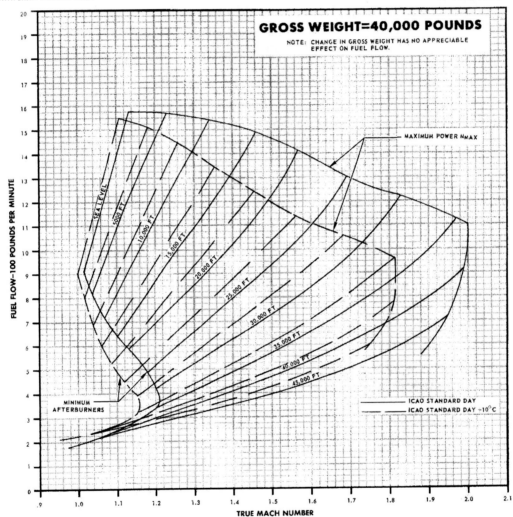

FDB-1-(185)

Figure 11-76

COMBAT FUEL FLOW
STABILIZED LEVEL FLIGHT

AIRPLANE CONFIGURATION
(4) AIM-7 AND (2) WING TANKS

REMARKS
ENGINE(S):(2) J79-GE-8

GUIDE

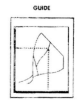

DATE: 15 MAY 1968
DATA BASIS: **FLIGHT TEST**

FUEL GRADE: JP-5
FUEL DENSITY: 6.8 LB/GAL

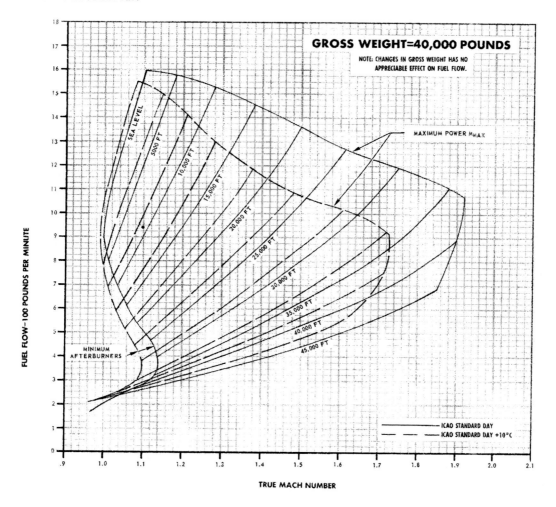

GROSS WEIGHT=40,000 POUNDS

NOTE: CHANGES IN GROSS WEIGHT HAS NO
APPRECIABLE EFFECT ON FUEL FLOW.

MAXIMUM POWER M$_{MAX}$

SEA LEVEL
5000 FT
10,000 FT
15,000 FT
20,000 FT
25,000 FT
30,000 FT
35,000 FT
40,000 FT
45,000 FT

MINIMUM
AFTERBURNERS

ICAO STANDARD DAY
ICAO STANDARD DAY +10°C

FUEL FLOW-100 POUNDS PER MINUTE

TRUE MACH NUMBER

FDB-1-(186)

Figure 11-77

COMBAT FUEL FLOW
STABILIZED LEVEL FLIGHT

AIRPLANE CONFIGURATION
(4) AIM-7, (4) AIM-9
AND (1) ⊄ TANK

REMARKS
ENGINE(S):(2) J79-GE-8

GUIDE

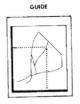

FUEL GRADE: JP-5
FUEL DENSITY: 6.8 LB/GAL.

DATE: 15 MAY 1968
DATA BASIS: FLIGHT TEST

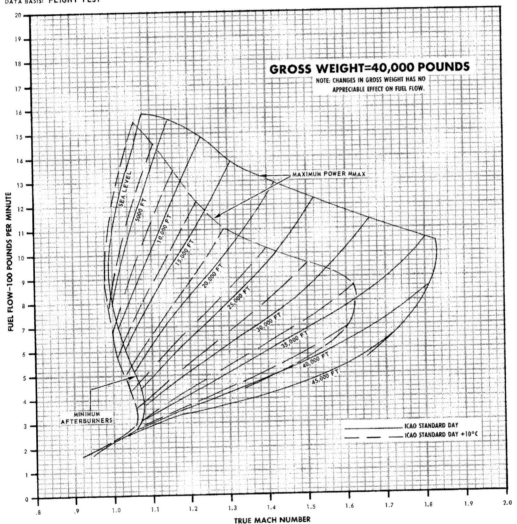

FDB-1-(187)

Figure 11-78

COMBAT FUEL FLOW
STABILIZED LEVEL FLIGHT
REMARKS

AIRPLANE CONFIGURATION
(4) AIM-7, (4) AIM-9
AND (2) WING TANKS

ENGINE(S): (2) J79-GE-8
ICAO STANDARD DAY

GUIDE

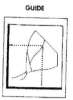

DATE: 15 MAY 1968
DATA BASIS: FLIGHT TEST

FUEL GRADE: JP-5
FUEL DENSITY: 6.8 LB/GAL

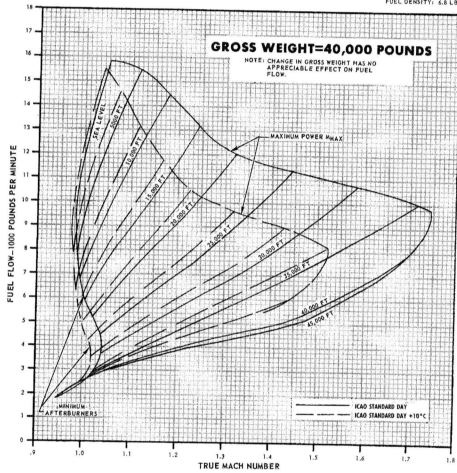

GROSS WEIGHT=40,000 POUNDS
NOTE: CHANGE IN GROSS WEIGHT HAS NO APPRECIABLE EFFECT ON FUEL FLOW.

MAXIMUM POWER M_MAX

SEA LEVEL
5000 FT
10,000 FT
15,000 FT
20,000 FT
25,000 FT
30,000 FT
35,000 FT
40,000 FT
45,000 FT

MINIMUM AFTERBURNERS

ICAO STANDARD DAY
ICAO STANDARD DAY +10°C

FUEL FLOW-1000 POUNDS PER MINUTE

TRUE MACH NUMBER

FDB-1-(188)

Figure 11-79

COMBAT SPECIFIC RANGE
STABILIZED LEVEL FLIGHT

AIRPLANE CONFIGURATION

(4) AIM-7

REMARKS

ENGINE(S):(2) J79-GE-8

GUIDE

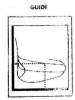

FUEL GRADE: JP-5
FUEL DENSITY: 6.8 LB/GAL

DATE: 15 MAY 1968
DATA BASIS: FLIGHT TEST

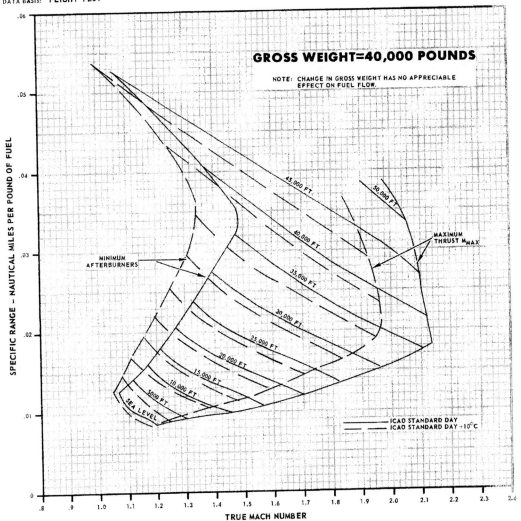

FDB-1-(189)

Figure 11-80

COMBAT SPECIFIC RANGE
STABILIZED LEVEL FLIGHT

AIRPLANE CONFIGURATION
(4) AIM-7 AND (2) WING TANKS

REMARKS
ENGINE(S):(2) J79-GE-8

GUIDE

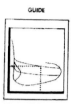

DATE: 15 MAY 1968
DATA BASIS: **FLIGHT TEST**

FUEL GRADE: JP-5
FUEL DENSITY: 6.8 LB/GAL

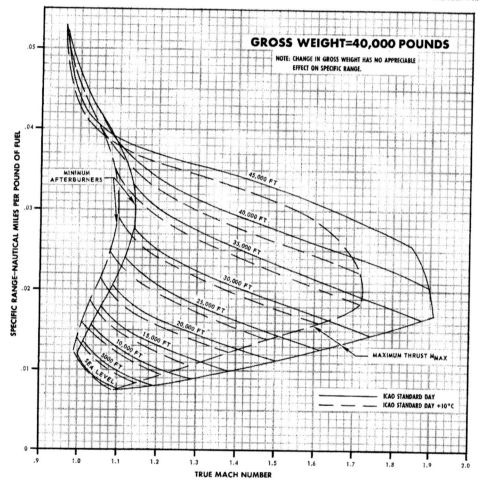

GROSS WEIGHT=40,000 POUNDS

NOTE: CHANGE IN GROSS WEIGHT HAS NO APPRECIABLE EFFECT ON SPECIFIC RANGE.

MINIMUM AFTERBURNERS

45,000 FT
40,000 FT
35,000 FT
30,000 FT
25,000 FT
20,000 FT
15,000 FT
10,000 FT
5000 FT
SEA LEVEL

MAXIMUM THRUST M_{MAX}

——— ICAO STANDARD DAY
— — — ICAO STANDARD DAY +10°C

SPECIFIC RANGE-NAUTICAL MILES PER POUND OF FUEL

TRUE MACH NUMBER

FDB-1-(190)

Figure 11-81

COMBAT SPECIFIC RANGE
STABILIZED LEVEL FLIGHT

AIRPLANE CONFIGURATION
(4) AIM-7, (4) AIM-9
AND (1) ℄ TANK

REMARKS

ENGINE(S): (2) J79-GE-8

GUIDE

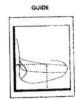

DATE: 15 MAY 1968
DATA BASIS: FLIGHT TEST

FUEL GRADE: JP-5
FUEL DENSITY: 6.8 LB/GAL

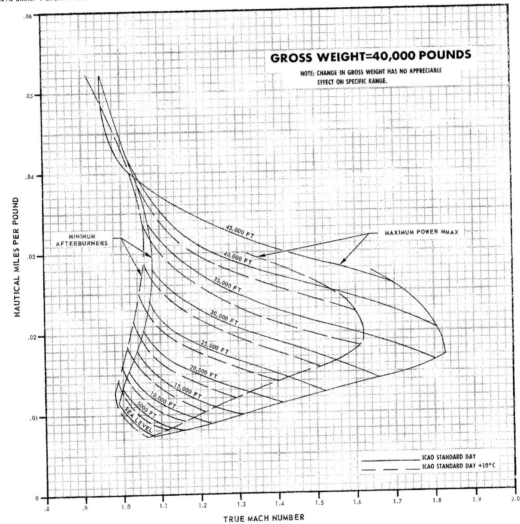

FDB-1-(191)

Figure 11-82

COMBAT SPECIFIC RANGE
STABILIZED LEVEL FLIGHT

AIRPLANE CONFIGURATION
(4) AIM-7, (4) AIM-9
AND (2) WING TANKS

REMARKS
ENGINE(S): (2) J79-GE-8

GUIDE

DATE: 15 MAY 1968
DATA BASIS: **FLIGHT TEST**

FUEL GRADE: JP-5
FUEL DENSITY: 6.8 LB/GAL

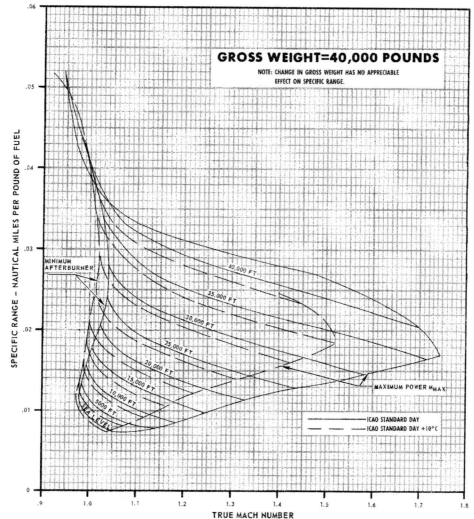

GROSS WEIGHT=40,000 POUNDS
NOTE: CHANGE IN GROSS WEIGHT HAS NO APPRECIABLE EFFECT ON SPECIFIC RANGE.

FDB-1-(192)

Figure 11-83

COMBAT SPECIFIC RANGE
STABILIZED LEVEL FLIGHT

AIRPLANE CONFIGURATION
(4) AIM-7, (4) AIM-9
OR
(4) AIM-7, (1) ₵ TANK

REMARKS
ENGINE(S):(2) J79-GE-8

GUIDE

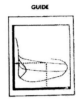

FUEL GRADE: JP-5
FUEL DENSITY: 6.8 LB/GAL

DATE: 15 MAY 1968
DATA BASIS: FLIGHT TEST

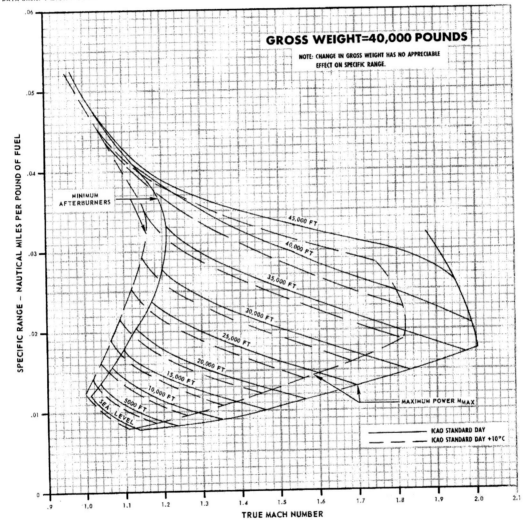

FDB-1-(193)

Figure 11-84

SUPERSONIC MAXIMUM THRUST CLIMB

AIRPLANE CONFIGURATION
(4) AIM-7

REMARKS

ENGINE(S): (2) J79-GE-8
ICAO STANDARD DAY

GUIDE

DATE: 15 MAY 1968
DATA BASIS: FLIGHT TEST

FUEL GRADE: JP-5
FUEL DENSITY: 6.8 LB/GAL

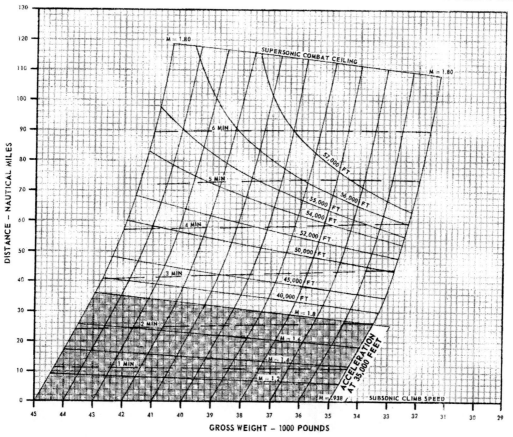

FDB-1-(194)

Figure 11-85

SUPERSONIC MAXIMUM THRUST CLIMB

AIRPLANE CONFIGURATION
(4) AIM-7 AND (4) AIM-9

REMARKS
ENGINE(S): (2) J79-GE-8
ICAO STANDARD DAY

GUIDE

DATE: 15 MAY 1968
DATA BASIS: FLIGHT TEST

FUEL GRADE: JP-5
FUEL DENSITY: 6.8 LB/GAL

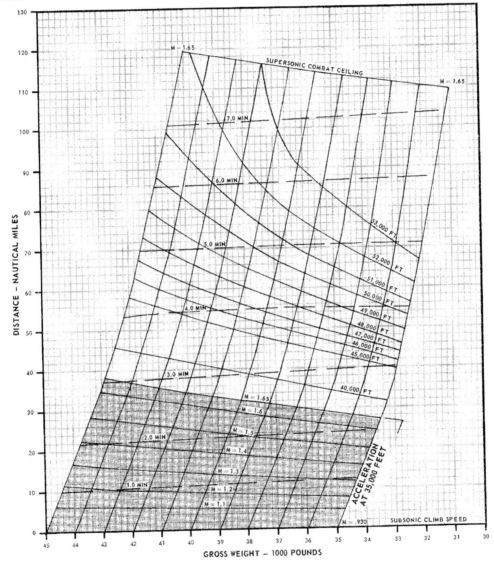

FDB-1-(195)

Figure 11-86

SUPERSONIC MAXIMUM THRUST CLIMB

AIRPLANE CONFIGURATION
(4) AIM-7 AND (1) ₵ TANK

REMARKS
ENGINE(S): J79-GE-8
ICAO STANDARD DAY

GUIDE

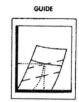

DATE: 15 MAY 1968
DATA BASIS: **FLIGHT TEST**

FUEL GRADE: JP-5
FUEL DENSITY: 6.8 LB/GAL

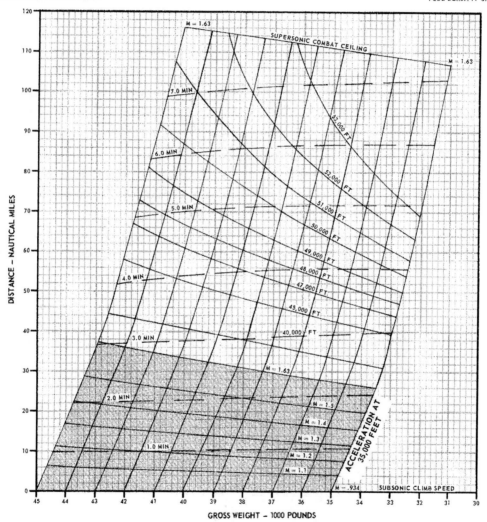

SUPERSONIC MAXIMUM THRUST CLIMB

AIRPLANE CONFIGURATION
(4) AIM–7 AND (2) WING TANKS

REMARKS
ENGINE(S): (2) J79–GE–8
ICAO STANDARD DAY

GUIDE

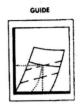

FUEL GRADE: JP–5
FUEL DENSITY: 6.8 LB/GAL

DATE: 15 MAY 1968
DATA BASIS: FLIGHT TEST

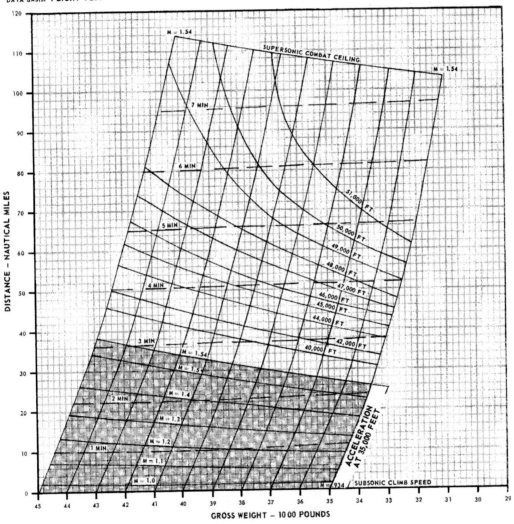

FDB–1–(197)

Figure 11-88

SUPERSONIC MAXIMUM THRUST CLIMB

AIRPLANE CONFIGURATION

(4) AIM-7, (4) AIM-9
AND (1) C_L TANK

REMARKS

ENGINE(S): (2) J79-GE-8
ICAO STANDARD DAY

GUIDE

DATE: 15 MAY 1968
DATA BASIS: **FLIGHT TEST**

FUEL GRADE: JP-5
FUEL DENSITY: 6.8 LB/GAL

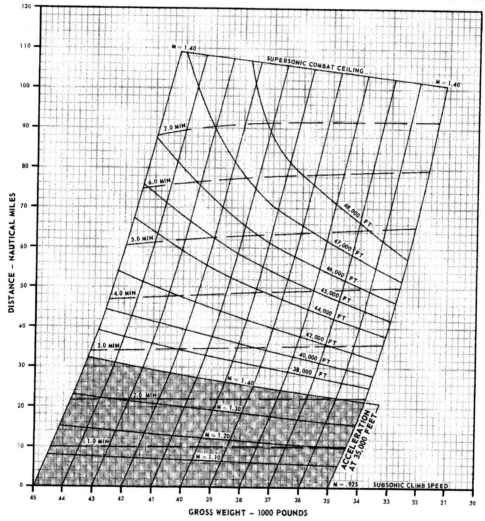

FDB-1-(198)

Figure 11-89

11-125

LOW ALTITUDE ACCELERATION
MAXIMUM THRUST

AIRPLANE CONFIGURATION
INDIVIDUAL DRAG INDEXES

GROSS WEIGHT – 35,000 POUNDS

REMARKS

ENGINES: (2) J79–GE–8

DATE: 15 MAY 1968
DATA BASIS: FLIGHT TEST

FUEL GRADE: JP-5
FUEL DENSITY: 6.8 LB/GAL

| MACH | DRAG INDEX | TIME TO ACCELERATE (MIN.)/FUEL TO ACCELERATE (LBS) | | | | | | | TEMP. EFFECTS FACTOR | |
		0	20	40	60	80	100	120	+10°C	−10°C
SEA LEVEL (15°C)									.0/.0	.0/.0
.5		.0/0	.0/0	.0/0	.0/0	.0/0	.0/0	.0/0	1.08/1.05	.93/.95
.55		.04/43	.04/44	.04/46	.04/47	.04/49	.04/50	.04/52	1.08/1.05	.93/.95
.6		.07/87	.07/90	.07/93	.08/96	.08/99	.08/103	.09/107	1.08/1.05	.93/.95
.65		.10/132	.11/136	.11/141	.12/147	.12/153	.13/159	.13/166	1.08/1.05	.93/.95
.7		.14/177	.14/184	.15/192	.16/200	.16/209	.17/219	.18/230	1.08/1.06	.93/.95
.75		.17/224	.18/233	.19/243	.20/255	.21/268	.22/283	.23/301	1.09/1.06	.93/.95
.8		.21/271	.22/284	.23/297	.24/313	.25/332	.27/354	.29/381	1.09/1.06	.93/.95
.85		.24/320	.25/336	.26/354	.28/375	.30/402	.32/434	.35/476	1.09/1.06	.93/.95
.9		.27/371	.29/391	.30/414	.32/445	.35/483	.39/532	.43/601	1.09/1.07	.93/.95
2000 FEET (11°C)									.0/.0	.0/.0
.5		.0/0	.0/0	.0/0	.0/0	.0/0	.04/50	.04/51	1.08/1.05	.93/.95
.55		.04/43	.04/44	.04/45	.04/47	.04/48	.09/102	.09/106	1.08/1.05	.93/.95
.6		.07/86	.08/89	.08/92	.08/95	.08/98	.13/157	.14/164	1.08/1.05	.93/.95
.65		.11/131	.11/135	.12/140	.12/145	.13/151	.18/215	.19/226	1.08/1.06	.93/.95
.7		.14/176	.15/182	.16/189	.16/197	.17/206	.23/278	.24/295	1.09/1.06	.93/.95
.75		.18/222	.19/231	.20/240	.20/251	.21/264	.28/347	.30/373	1.09/1.06	.93/.95
.8		.21/268	.22/280	.23/293	.25/309	.26/326	.33/425	.36/464	1.09/1.06	.93/.95
.85		.25/316	.26/332	.27/349	.29/369	.31/394	.40/519	.44/582	1.09/1.07	.93/.95
.9		.28/366	.30/385	.32/408	.34/437	.36/473				
4000 FEET (7°C)									.0/.0	.0/.0
.5		.0/0	.0/0	.0/0	.0/0	.0/0	.04/49	.05/51	1.08/1.05	.93/.95
.55		.04/43	.04/44	.04/45	.04/46	.04/48	.09/101	.09/104	1.08/1.05	.93/.95
.6		.08/86	.08/88	.08/91	.08/94	.09/97	.14/155	.14/161	1.08/1.05	.93/.95
.65		.11/129	.12/134	.12/138	.13/143	.13/149	.18/212	.19/223	1.08/1.06	.93/.95
.7		.15/174	.16/180	.16/187	.17/195	.18/203	.23/274	.25/290	1.09/1.06	.93/.95
.75		.19/219	.20/228	.20/238	.21/248	.22/260	.29/341	.31/365	1.09/1.06	.93/.95
.8		.22/265	.23/277	.25/290	.26/304	.27/321	.35/416	.37/453	1.09/1.06	.93/.95
.85		.26/313	.27/327	.29/344	.30/364	.32/388	.41/507	.46/566	1.09/1.07	.93/.95
.9		.30/362	.31/380	.33/402	.35/429	.38/463				
6000 FEET (3°C)									.0/.0	.0/.0
.5		.0/0	.0/0	.0/0	.0/0	.0/0	.05/49	.05/50	1.08/1.05	.93/.95
.55		.04/42	.04/43	.04/45	.04/46	.05/47	.09/100	.10/103	1.08/1.05	.93/.95
.6		.08/85	.08/88	.09/90	.09/93	.09/96	.14/153	.15/160	1.08/1.05	.93/.95
.65		.12/129	.12/133	.13/137	.13/142	.14/147	.19/210	.20/220	1.08/1.06	.93/.95
.7		.16/173	.17/179	.17/185	.18/193	.19/201	.25/270	.26/286	1.09/1.06	.93/.95
.75		.20/217	.21/226	.21/235	.22/245	.23/257	.30/336	.32/359	1.09/1.06	.93/.95
.8		.24/263	.25/274	.26/286	.27/300	.28/317	.36/409	.39/443	1.09/1.06	.93/.95
.85		.27/309	.29/324	.30/339	.32/358	.34/381	.43/495	.47/550	1.09/1.07	.93/.95
.9		.31/357	.33/375	.34/396	.37/423	.39/455				

FDB–1–(199)

Figure 11-90

LOW ALTITUDE ACCELERATION
MAXIMUM THRUST

AIRPLANE CONFIGURATION
INDIVIDUAL DRAG INDEXES

GROSS WEIGHT — 40,000 POUNDS

REMARKS

ENGINES: (2) J79-GE-8

DATE: 15 MAY 1968
DATA BASIS: FLIGHT TEST

FUEL GRADE: JP-5
FUEL DENSITY: 6.8 LB/GAL

	MACH	DRAG INDEX 0	20	40	60	80	100	120	TEMP. EFFECTS FACTOR +10°C	−10°C
SEA LEVEL (15°C)	.5	.0 / 0	.0 / 0	.0 / 0	.0 / 0	.0 / 0	.0 / 0	.0 / 0	.0 / .0	.0 /.0
	.55	.04/ 50	.04/ 51	.04/ 53	.04/ 54	.05/ 56	.05/ 58	.05/ 60	1.08/1.05	.93/.95
	.6	.08/100	.08/103	.09/107	.09/111	.09/114	.10/119	.10/123	1.08/1.05	.93/.95
	.65	.12/152	.12/157	.13/163	.13/169	.14/176	.14/183	.15/191	1.08/1.05	.93/.95
	.7	.16/204	.17/212	.17/220	.18/229	.19/240	.20/252	.21/265	1.08/1.06	.93/.95
	.75	.20/257	.21/268	.22/280	.23/293	.24/308	.25/325	.27/346	1.09/1.06	.93/.95
	.8	.24/312	.25/326	.26/341	.27/360	.29/381	.31/407	.33/438	1.09/1.06	.93/.95
	.85	.27/367	.29/386	.30/406	.32/431	.34/461	.37/499	.40/547	1.09/1.06	.93/.95
	.9	.31/425	.33/448	.35/476	.37/511	.40/554	.44/611	.50/691	1.09/1.07	.93/.95
2000 FEET (11°C)	.5	.0 / 0	.0 / 0	.0 / 0	.0 / 0	.0 / 0	.0 / 0	.0 / 0	.0 / .0	.0 /.0
	.55	.04/ 49	.04/ 51	.05/ 52	.05/ 54	.05/ 56	.05/ 57	.05/ 59	1.08/1.05	.93/.95
	.6	.08/ 99	.09/103	.09/106	.09/109	.10/113	.10/117	.10/122	1.08/1.05	.93/.95
	.65	.13/150	.13/155	.13/161	.14/167	.14/173	.15/181	.16/189	1.08/1.05	.93/.95
	.7	.17/202	.17/210	.18/218	.19/227	.19/237	.20/248	.21/261	1.08/1.06	.93/.95
	.75	.21/255	.22/265	.22/276	.23/289	.25/304	.26/320	.27/340	1.09/1.06	.93/.95
	.8	.25/308	.26/322	.27/337	.28/355	.30/375	.32/399	.34/429	1.09/1.06	.93/.95
	.85	.29/363	.30/381	.31/400	.33/424	.36/453	.38/488	.42/534	1.09/1.06	.93/.95
	.9	.33/420	.34/442	.36/468	.39/502	.42/543	.46/596	.51/670	1.09/1.07	.93/.95
4000 FEET (7°C)	.5	.0 / 0	.0 / 0	.0 / 0	.0 / 0	.0 / 0	.0 / 0	.0 / 0	.0 / .0	.0 /.0
	.55	.04/ 49	.05/ 50	.05/ 52	.05/ 53	.05/ 55	.05/ 57	.05/ 59	1.08/1.05	.93/.95
	.6	.09/ 99	.09/102	.09/105	.10/108	.10/112	.10/116	.11/121	1.08/1.05	.93/.95
	.65	.13/149	.14/154	.14/159	.15/165	.15/172	.16/179	.16/186	1.08/1.05	.93/.95
	.7	.17/200	.18/208	.19/216	.20/224	.20/234	.21/245	.22/257	1.08/1.06	.93/.95
	.75	.22/252	.23/262	.23/273	.25/286	.26/300	.27/316	.29/334	1.09/1.06	.93/.95
	.8	.26/305	.27/318	.28/333	.30/350	.31/370	.33/393	.35/421	1.09/1.06	.93/.95
	.85	.30/359	.31/376	.33/395	.35/418	.37/446	.40/479	.43/522	1.09/1.06	.93/.95
	.9	.34/415	.36/437	.38/462	.40/494	.43/533	.47/583	.53/652	1.09/1.07	.93/.95
6000 FEET (3°C)	.5	.0 / 0	.0 / 0	.0 / 0	.0 / 0	.0 / 0	.0 / 0	.0 / 0	.0 / .0	.0 /.0
	.55	.05/ 49	.05/ 50	.05/ 52	.05/ 53	.05/ 55	.05/ 57	.06/ 58	1.08/1.05	.93/.95
	.6	.09/ 98	.10/101	.10/104	.10/108	.11/111	.11/115	.11/120	1.08/1.05	.93/.95
	.65	.14/148	.14/153	.15/158	.15/164	.16/170	.17/177	.17/184	1.08/1.05	.93/.95
	.7	.18/199	.19/206	.20/214	.21/222	.21/232	.22/242	.23/254	1.08/1.06	.93/.95
	.75	.23/250	.24/260	.25/271	.26/283	.27/296	.28/312	.30/329	1.09/1.06	.93/.95
	.8	.27/302	.28/315	.30/329	.31/346	.33/365	.35/387	.37/413	1.09/1.06	.93/.95
	.85	.31/356	.33/372	.34/390	.36/413	.39/439	.41/471	.45/511	1.09/1.06	.93/.95
	.9	.36/411	.38/431	.40/456	.42/486	.45/523	.49/571	.54/634	1.09/1.07	.93/.95

FDB-1-(200)

Figure 11-91

LOW ALTITUDE ACCELERATION
MAXIMUM THRUST

AIRPLANE CONFIGURATION
INDIVIDUAL DRAG INDEXES

GROSS WEIGHT — 45,000 POUNDS

REMARKS

ENGINES: (2) J79-GE-8

DATE: 15 MAY 1968
DATA BASIS: FLIGHT TEST

FUEL GRADE: JP-5
FUEL DENSITY: 6.8 LB/GAL

	MACH	DRAG INDEX	TIME TO ACCELERATE (MIN.)/FUEL TO ACCELERATE (LBS).							TEMP. EFFECTS FACTOR	
			0	20	40	60	80	100	120	+10°C	−10°C
SEA LEVEL (15°C)	.5		.0 / 0	.0 / 0	.0 / 0	.0 / 0	.0 / 0	.0 / 0	.0 / 0	.0 / .0	.0 / .0
	.55		.05/ 56	.05/ 58	.05/ 60	.05/ 62	.05/ 64	.05/ 66	.06/ 68	1.08/1.05	.93/.95
	.6		.09/114	.09/117	.10/121	.10/125	.10/130	.11/135	.11/140	1.08/1.05	.93/.95
	.65		.14/172	.14/178	.15/184	.15/191	.16/199	.16/208	.17/217	1.08/1.05	.93/.95
	.7		.18/231	.19/240	.19/249	.20/260	.21/272	.22/285	.23/300	1.08/1.06	.93/.95
	.75		.22/291	.23/303	.24/317	.25/332	.27/349	.28/369	.30/392	1.09/1.06	.93/.95
	.8		.27/352	.28/368	.29/386	.31/407	.33/431	.35/460	.37/496	1.09/1.06	.93/.95
	.85		.31/415	.33/436	.34/459	.36/488	.39/522	.42/564	.46/619	1.09/1.06	.93/.95
	.9		.35/481	.37/507	.39/538	.42/578	.46/627	.50/692	.57/783	1.09/1.07	.93/.95
2000 FEET (11°C)	.5		.0 / 0	.0 / 0	.0 / 0	.0 / 0	.0 / 0	.0 / 0	.0 / 0	.0 / .0	.0 /.0
	.55		.05/ 56	.05/ 58	.05/ 59	.05/ 61	.05/ 63	.06/ 65	.06/ 67	1.08/1.05	.93/.95
	.6		.10/113	.10/116	.10/120	.11/124	.11/129	.11/133	.12/139	1.08/1.05	.93/.95
	.65		.14/170	.15/176	.15/183	.16/189	.16/197	.17/205	.18/214	1.08/1.05	.93/.95
	.7		.19/229	.20/237	.20/247	.21/257	.22/269	.23/281	.24/296	1.08/1.06	.93/.95
	.75		.23/288	.24/300	.25/313	.27/328	.28/344	.29/363	.31/385	1.09/1.06	.93/.95
	.8		.28/349	.29/365	.31/382	.32/402	.34/425	.36/453	.39/486	1.09/1.06	.93/.95
	.85		.32/411	.34/431	.36/453	.38/481	.40/513	.43/553	.47/605	1.09/1.06	.93/.95
	.9		.37/475	.39/500	.41/530	.44/568	.47/615	.52/676	.58/760	1.09/1.07	.93/.95
4000 FEET (7°C)	.5		.0 / 0	.0 / 0	.0 / 0	.0 / 0	.0 / 0	.0 / 0	.0 / 0	.0 / .0	.0 /.0
	.55		.05/ 56	.05/ 57	.05/ 59	.06/ 61	.06/ 63	.06/ 65	.06/ 67	1.08/1.05	.93/.95
	.6		.10/112	.10/116	.11/119	.11/123	.11/128	.12/132	.12/137	1.08/1.05	.93/.95
	.65		.15/169	.15/175	.16/181	.17/188	.17/195	.18/203	.19/212	1.08/1.05	.93/.95
	.7		.20/227	.21/236	.21/245	.22/255	.23/266	.24/278	.25/292	1.08/1.06	.93/.95
	.75		.25/286	.26/297	.27/310	.28/324	.29/340	.31/358	.33/380	1.09/1.06	.93/.95
	.8		.29/346	.31/361	.32/377	.34/397	.35/419	.38/446	.40/477	1.09/1.06	.93/.95
	.85		.34/407	.36/426	.37/448	.39/474	.42/505	.45/543	.49/592	1.09/1.06	.93/.95
	.9		.39/470	.41/494	.43/523	.46/559	.49/604	.54/661	.60/739	1.09/1.07	.93/.95
6000 FEET (3°C)	.5		.0 / 0	.0 / 0	.0 / 0	.0 / 0	.0 / 0	.0 / 0	.0 / 0	.0 / .0	.0 /.0
	.55		.05/ 56	.06/57	.06/ 59	.06/ 61	.06/ 63	.06/ 65	.07/ 67	1.08/1.05	.93/.95
	.6		.11/112	.11/115	.11/119	.12/123	.12/127	.12/131	.13/136	1.08/1.05	.93/.95
	.65		.16/168	.16/174	.17/180	.17/187	.18/194	.19/201	.20/210	1.08/1.05	.93/.95
	.7		.21/226	.22/234	.22/243	.23/253	.24/263	.25/275	.27/289	1.08/1.06	.93/.95
	.75		.26/284	.27/295	.28/307	.29/321	.31/337	.32/354	.34/375	1.09/1.06	.93/.95
	.8		.31/343	.32/358	.34/374	.35/392	.37/414	.39/439	.42/470	1.09/1.06	.93/.95
	.85		.36/403	.37/422	.39/443	.41/468	.44/498	.47/534	.51/580	1.09/1.06	.93/.95
	.9		.41/465	.42/489	.45/516	.48/551	.51/594	.56/648	.62/721	1.09/1.07	.93/.95

FDB-1-(201)

Figure 11-92

LOW ALTITUDE ACCELERATION
MAXIMUM THRUST

AIRPLANE CONFIGURATION
INDIVIDUAL DRAG INDEXES

GROSS WEIGHT – 50,000 POUNDS

REMARKS

ENGINES: (2) J79-GE-8

DATE: 15 MAY 1968
DATA BASIS: FLIGHT TEST

FUEL GRADE: JP-5
FUEL DENSITY: 6.8 LB/GAL

	MACH	DRAG INDEX	TIME TO ACCELERATE (MIN.)/FUEL TO ACCELERATE (LBS).							TEMP. EFFECTS FACTOR	
			0	20	40	60	80	100	120	+10°C	−10°C
SEA LEVEL (15°C)	.5	.0 / 0	.0 / 0	.0 / 0	.0 / 0	.0 / 0	.0 / 0	.0 / 0	.0 / .0	.0 /.0
	.55	.05/ 63	.05/ 65	.05/ 67	.06/ 69	.06/ 71	.06/ 74	.06/ 76	1.08/1.05	.93/.95
	.6	.10/127	.11/131	.11/136	.11/141	.12/146	.12/151	.13/157	1.08/1.05	.93/.95
	.65	.15/192	.16/199	.16/206	.17/214	.18/223	.18/233	.19/243	1.08/1.05	.93/.95
	.7	.20/258	.21/268	.22/279	.23/291	.24/304	.25/319	.26/337	1.08/1.06	.93/.95
	.75	.25/325	.26/339	.27/354	.29/371	.30/391	.32/413	.34/439	1.09/1.06	.93/.95
	.8	.30/394	.31/412	.33/432	.34/455	.36/483	.39/515	.42/555	1.09/1.06	.93/.95
	.85	.35/464	.36/487	.38/513	.41/545	.43/584	.47/631	.51/693	1.09/1.06	.93/.95
	.9	.40/537	.42/566	.44/601	.47/646	.51/701	.56/774	.63/877	1.09/1.07	.93/.95
2000 FEET (11°C)	.5	.0 / 0	.0 / 0	.0 / 0	.0 / 0	.0 / 0	.0 / 0	.0 / 0	.0 / .0	.0 /.0
	.55	.05/ 63	.06/ 65	.06/ 67	.06/ 69	.06/ 71	.06/ 73	.06/ 76	1.08/1.05	.93/.95
	.6	.11/127	.11/131	.11/135	.12/140	.12/145	.13/150	.13/156	1.08/1.05	.93/.95
	.65	.16/191	.16/198	.17/205	.18/213	.18/221	.19/230	.20/241	1.08/1.05	.93/.95
	.7	.21/256	.22/266	.23/277	.24/288	.25/301	.26/316	.27/332	1.08/1.06	.93/.95
	.75	.26/323	.27/336	.28/351	.30/367	.31/386	.33/407	.35/432	1.09/1.06	.93/.95
	.8	.31/390	.33/408	.34/427	.36/450	.38/476	.40/507	.43/545	1.09/1.06	.93/.95
	.85	.36/460	.38/482	.40/507	.42/538	.45/575	.49/620	.53/678	1.09/1.06	.93/.95
	.9	.41/531	.43/559	.46/593	.49/593	.49/636	.53/688	.58/756	1.09/1.07	.93/.95
4000 FEET (7°C)	.5	.0 / 0	.0 / 0	.0 / 0	.0 / 0	.0 / 0	.0 / 0	.0 / 0	.0 / .0	.0 /.0
	.55	.06/ 63	.06/ 65	.06/ 66	.06/ 68	.06/ 71	.07/ 73	.07/ 75	1.08/1.05	.93/.95
	.6	.11/126	.12/130	.12/134	.12/139	.13/144	.13/149	.14/155	1.08/1.05	.93/.95
	.65	.17/190	.17/196	.18/203	.19/211	.19/219	.20/228	.21/238	1.08/1.05	.93/.95
	.7	.22/255	.23/264	.24/274	.25/286	.26/298	.27/312	.29/328	1.08/1.06	.93/.95
	.75	.28/320	.29/333	.30/348	.31/363	.33/381	.34/402	.37/426	1.09/1.06	.93/.95
	.8	.33/387	.34/404	.36/423	.38/445	.40/470	.42/500	.45/536	1.09/1.06	.93/.95
	.85	.38/455	.40/477	.42/501	.44/531	.47/566	.50/609	.55/664	1.09/1.06	.93/.95
	.9	.43/526	.45/553	.48/585	.51/626	.55/676	.60/741	.67/829	1.09/1.07	.93/.95
6000 FEET (3°C)	.5	.0 / 0	.0 / 0	.0 / 0	.0 / 0	.0 / 0	.0 / 0	.0 / 0	.0 / .0	.0 /.0
	.55	.06/ 63	.06/ 65	.06/ 66	.07/ 69	.07/ 71	.07/ 73	.07/ 75	1.08/1.05	.93/.95
	.6	.12/126	.12/130	.13/134	.13/138	.14/143	.14/148	.15/154	1.08/1.05	.93/.95
	.65	.18/189	.18/196	.19/203	.20/210	.20/218	.21/227	.22/237	1.08/1.05	.93/.95
	.7	.23/254	.24/263	.25/273	.26/284	.27/296	.29/310	.30/326	1.08/1.06	.93/.95
	.75	.29/319	.30/331	.31/345	.33/361	.34/378	.36/398	.38/422	1.09/1.06	.93/.95
	.8	.35/385	.36/401	.38/419	.39/440	.42/465	.44/494	.47/528	1.09/1.06	.93/.95
	.85	.40/452	.42/473	.44/496	.46/525	.49/559	.53/600	.57/652	1.09/1.06	.93/.95
	.9	.45/521	.48/548	.50/579	.54/618	.58/666	.63/727	.69/809	1.09/1.07	.93/.95

FDB-1-(202)

Figure 11-93

LOW ALTITUDE ACCELERATION
MAXIMUM THRUST

AIRPLANE CONFIGURATION
INDIVIDUAL DRAG INDEXES

GROSS WEIGHT — 55,000 POUNDS

REMARKS

ENGINES: (2) J79–GE–8

DATE: 15 MAY 1968
DATA BASIS: **FLIGHT TEST**

FUEL GRADE: JP–5
FUEL DENSITY: 6.8 LB./GAL

	MACH	DRAG INDEX	\multicolumn{7}{c}{TIME TO ACCELERATE (MIN.)/FUEL TO ACCELERATE (LBS).}							\multicolumn{2}{c}{TEMP. EFFECTS FACTOR}	
			0	20	40	60	80	100	120	+10°C	−10°C
SEA LEVEL (15°C)	.5		.0 / 0	.0 / 0	.0 / 0	.0 / 0	.0 / 0	.0 / 0	.0 / 0	.0 / .0	.0 / .0
	.55		.06/ 70	.06/ 72	.06/ 75	.06/ 77	.06/ 80	.07/ 82	.07/ 85	1.08/1.05	.93/.95
	.6		.11/141	.12/146	.12/151	.13/156	.13/162	.13/168	.14/175	1.08/1.05	.93/.95
	.65		.17/213	.17/221	.18/229	.19/238	.20/248	.20/259	.21/271	1.08/1.05	.93/.95
	.7		.22/286	.23/297	.24/310	.25/323	.26/338	.28/355	.29/374	1.08/1.06	.93/.95
	.75		.28/360	.29/376	.30/393	.32/412	.33/433	.35/458	.37/488	1.09/1.06	.93/.95
	.8		.33/436	.35/456	.36/479	.38/505	.40/535	.43/572	.47/616	1.09/1.06	.93/.95
	.85		.38/514	.40/539	.42/568	.45/604	.48/647	.52/700	.57/769	1.09/1.06	.93/.95
	.9		.44/594	.46/627	.49/665	.52/715	.57/777	.62/858	.70/973	1.09/1.07	.93/.95
2000 FEET (11°C)	.5		.0 / 0	.0 / 0	.0 / 0	.0 / 0	.0 / 0	.0 / 0	.0 / 0	.0 / .0	.0 /.0
	.55		.06/ 70	.06/ 72	.06/ 74	.07/ 77	.07/ 79	.07/ 82	.07/ 85	1.08/1.05	.93/.95
	.6		.12/141	.12/145	.13/150	.13/155	.14/161	.14/167	.15/174	1.08/1.05	.93/.95
	.65		.18/212	.18/220	.19/228	.20/236	.20/246	.21/256	.22/268	1.08/1.05	.93/.95
	.7		.23/284	.24/295	.25/307	.26/320	.28/335	.29/351	.30/369	1.08/1.06	.93/.95
	.75		.29/358	.30/373	.32/389	.33/407	.35/438	.37/452	.39/481	1.09/1.06	.93/.95
	.8		.35/433	.36/452	.38/474	.40/499	.42/528	.45/563	.48/605	1.09/1.06	.93/.95
	.85		.40/509	.42/534	.44/562	.47/596	.50/637	.54/688	.59/753	1.09/1.06	.93/.95
	.9		.46/588	.48/620	.51/657	.54/704	.59/763	.64/839	.72/946	1.09/1.07	.93/.95
4000 FEET (7°C)	.5		.0 / 0	.0 / 0	.0 / 0	.0 / 0	.0 / 0	.0 / 0	.0 / 0	.0 / .0	.0 /.0
	.55		.06/. 70	.07/ 72	.07/ 74	.07/ 77	.07/ 79	.07/ 82	.08/ 85	1.08/1.05	.93/.95
	.6		.13/140	.13/145	.13/150	.14/155	.14/160	.15/166	.15/173	1.08/1.05	.93/.95
	.65		.19/211	.19/219	.20/227	.21/235	.22/244	.22/255	.23/266	1.08/1.05	.93/.95
	.7		.25/283	.26/294	.27/305	.28/318	.29/332	.30/348	.32/366	1.09/1.06	.93/.95
	.75		.31/356	.32/370	.33/386	.35/404	.36/425	.38/448	.41/475	1.09/1.06	.93/.95
	.8		.36/430	.38/449	.40/470	.42/494	.44/522	.47/556	.50/596	1.09/1.06	.93/.95
	.85		.42/505	.44/529	.46/556	.49/589	.52/629	.56/677	.61/738	1.09/1.06	.93/.95
	.9		.48/583	.50/613	.53/649	.57/695	.61/751	.67/823	.75/922	1.09/1.07	.93/.95
6000 FEET (3°C)	.5		.0 / 0	.0 / 0	.0 / 0	.0 / 0	.0 / 0	.0 / 0	.0 / 0	.0 / .0	.0 /.0
	.55		.07/ 70	.07/ 72	.07/ 74	.07/ 77	.08/ 79	.08/ 82	.08/ 85	1.08/1.05	.93/.95
	.6		.13/140	.14/145	.14/150	.15/155	.15/160	.16/166	.16/173	1.08/1.05	.93/.95
	.65		.20/211	.20/218	.21/226	.22/235	.23/244	.24/254	.25/265	1.08/1.05	.93/.95
	.7		.26/282	.27/293	.28/304	.29/317	.31/331	.32/346	.34/364	1.08/1.06	.93/.95
	.75		.32/354	.34/369	.35/384	.37/402	.38/422	.40/444	.43/470	1.09/1.06	.93/.95
	.8		.38/427	.40/446	.42/466	.44/490	.46/518	.49/550	.53/589	1.09/1.06	.93/.95
	.85		.44/502	.46/525	.49/551	.51/584	.55/622	.59/668	.64/726	1.09/1.06	.93/.95
	.9		.50/578	.53/608	.56/642	.60/687	.64/740	.70/808	.78/901	1.09/1.07	.93/.95

FDB–1–(203)

Figure 11-94

LOW ALTITUDE ACCELERATION
MILITARY THRUST

AIRPLANE CONFIGURATION
INDIVIDUAL DRAG INDEXES

GROSS WEIGHT — 35,000 POUNDS

REMARKS

ENGINES: (2) J79—GE—8

DATE: 15 MAY 1968
DATA BASIS: FLIGHT TEST

FUEL GRADE: JP-5
FUEL DENSITY: 6.8 LB/GAL

| | MACH | DRAG INDEX | TIME TO ACCELERATE (MIN.)/FUEL TO ACCELERATE (LBS). | | | | | | | TEMP. EFFECTS FACTOR | |
			0	20	40	60	80	100	120	+10°C	—10°C
SEA LEVEL (15°C)	.5	.0 / 0	.0 / 0	.0 / 0	.0 / 0	.0 / 0	.0 / 0	.0 / 0	.0 / .0	.0 /.0
	.55	.07/ 25	.08/ 27	.08/ 29	.09/ 31	.10/ 33	.11/ 36	.11/ 39	1.13/1.09	.91/.94
	.6	.15/ 52	.16/ 56	.17/ 60	.19/ 65	.21/ 71	.23/ 79	.25/ 88	1.14/1.09	.90/.93
	.65	.23/ 81	.25/ 87	.27/ 95	.30/105	.33/117	.38/132	.44/154	1.14/1.09	.89/.93
	.7	.32/112	.35/122	.38/135	.43/152	.49/175	.58/207	.74/263	1.15/1.10	.88/.92
	.75	.41/146	.45/162	.51/183	.59/211	.71/257	.94/341		1.16/1.10	.88/.92
	.8	.51/184	.57/209	.66/242	.81/297	1.13/417			1.16/1.11	.87/.91
	.85	.62/230	.72/267	.87/326	1.27/479				1.17/1.11	.86/.90
	.9	.76/287	.92/351	1.34/516					1.17/1.11	.85/.90
2000 FEET (11°C)	.5	.0 / 0	.0 / 0	.0 / 0	.0 / 0	.0 / 0	.0 / 0	.0 / 0	.0 / .0	.0 /.0
	.55	.08/ 25	.08/ 27	.09/ 28	.09/ 30	.10/ 33	.11/ 35	.12/ 38	1.13/1.09	.91/.94
	.6	.16/ 51	.17/ 55	.18/ 59	.19/ 64	.21/ 70	.23/ 77	.26/ 85	1.14/1.09	.90/.93
	.65	.24/ 80	.26/ 86	.28/ 93	.31/102	.34/114	.38/128	.44/148	1.14/1.09	.89/.93
	.7	.33/110	.36/120	.39/132	.44/148	.50/168	.58/198	.72/245	1.15/1.10	.88/.92
	.75	.42/143	.46/158	.52/178	.59/204	.71/244	.91/314		1.16/1.10	.88/.92
	.8	.52/180	.59/203	.67/234	.81/282	1.08/379			1.16/1.11	.87/.91
	.85	.64/224	.73/259	.88/311	1.21/432				1.17/1.11	.86/.90
	.9	.77/278	.93/335	1.26/466					1.17/1.11	.85/.90
4000 FEET (7°C)	.5	.0 / 0	.0 / 0	.0 / 0	.0 / 0	.0 / 0	.0 / 0	.0 / 0	.0 / .0	.0 /.0
	.55	.08/ 25	.09/ 26	.09/ 28	.10/ 30	.10/ 32	.11/ 35	.12/ 38	1.13/1.09	.91/.94
	.6	.16/ 51	.17/ 54	.19/ 58	.20/ 63	.22/ 68	.24/ 75	.27/ 83	1.14/1.09	.90/.93
	.65	.25/ 79	.27/ 85	.29/ 92	.32/100	.35/111	.39/124	.45/142	1.14/1.09	.89/.93
	.7	.34/108	.37/118	.41/130	.45/144	.51/163	.59/190	.72/231	1.15/1.10	.88/.92
	.75	.44/141	.48/155	.53/173	.61/197	.72/233	.90/293		1.16/1.10	.88/.92
	.8	.54/177	.60/198	.69/226	.82/270	1.05/350			1.16/1.11	.87/.91
	.85	.66/219	.75/251	.89/298	1.17/398				1.17/1.11	.86/.90
	.9	.79/270	.94/321	1.25/430					1.17/1.11	.85/.90
6000 FEET (3°C)	.5	.0 / 0	.0 / 0	.0 / 0	.0 / 0	.0 / 0	.0 / 0	.0 / 0	.0 / .0	.0 /.0
	.55	.09/ 25	.09/ 26	.10/ 28	.10/ 30	.11/ 34	.12/ 34	.13/ 37	1.13/1.09	.91/.94
	.6	.17/ 50	.18/ 54	.20/ 58	.21/ 62	.23/ 67	.25/ 74	.28/ 82	1.14/1.09	.90/.93
	.65	.26/ 78	.28/ 84	.30/ 91	.33/ 99	.36/109	.41/121	.46/138	1.14/1.09	.89/.93
	.7	.36/107	.39/116	.42/127	.47/141	.53/159	.60/183	.73/220	1.15/1.10	.88/.92
	.75	.45/139	.50/152	.55/169	.62/192	.73/225	.90/277		1.16/1.10	.88/.92
	.8	.56/174	.62/194	.71/220	.83/259	1.04/328			1.16/1.11	.87/.91
	.85	.68/214	.77/244	.90/286	1.16/371				1.17/1.11	.86/.90
	.9	.82/263	.96/310	1.23/401					1.17/1.11	.85/.90

FDB-1-(204)

Figure 11-95

LOW ALTITUDE ACCELERATION
MILITARY THRUST

AIRPLANE CONFIGURATION
INDIVIDUAL DRAG INDEXES

GROSS WEIGHT – 40,000 POUNDS

REMARKS

ENGINES: (2) J79–GE–8

DATE: 15 MAY 1968
DATA BASIS: **FLIGHT TEST**

FUEL GRADE: JP–5
FUEL DENSITY: 6.8 LB/GAL

SEA LEVEL (15°C)

MACH	DRAG INDEX 0	20	40	60	80	100	120	TEMP. EFFECTS FACTOR +10°C	−10°C
.5	.0 / 0	.0 / 0	.0 / 0	.0 / 0	.0 / 0	.0 / 0	.0 / 0	.0 / .0	.0 / .0
.55	.09/ 29	.09/ 31	.10/ 33	.10/ 36	.11/ 39	.12/ 42	.13/ 46	1.13/1.09	.91/.94
.6	.17/ 60	.19/ 65	.20/ 70	.22/ 76	.24/ 83	.26/ 92	.30/103	1.14/1.09	.90/.93
.65	.27/ 93	.29/101	.32/110	.35/122	.39/136	.44/154	.51/180	1.14/1.09	.89/.93
.7	.36/129	.40/142	.44/157	.50/176	.57/203	.68/242	.86/309	1.15/1.10	.88/.92
.75	.47/169	.52/187	.59/212	.68/245	.82/299	1.10/400		1.16/1.10	.88/.92
.8	.58/213	.66/241	.77/281	.94/345	1.35/501			1.16/1.11	.87/.91
.85	.72/265	.83/309	1.01/379	1.52/577				1.17/1.11	.86/.90
.9	.88/331	1.07/407	1.66/644					1.17/1.11	.85/.90

2000 FEET (11°C)

MACH	DRAG INDEX 0	20	40	60	80	100	120	+10°C	−10°C
.5	.0 / 0	.0 / 0	.0 / 0	.0 / 0	.0 / 0	.0 / 0	.0 / 0	.0 / .0	.0 / .0
.55	.09/ 29	.10/ 31	.10/ 33	.11/ 35	.12/ 38	.13/ 41	.14/ 45	1.13/1.09	.91/.94
.6	.18/ 60	.19/ 64	.21/ 69	.23/ 75	.25/ 81	.27/ 90	.30/100	1.14/1.09	.90/.93
.65	.28/ 92	.30/100	.33/109	.36/119	.40/132	.45/150	.52/173	1.14/1.09	.89/.93
.7	.38/127	.41/139	.46/154	.51/172	.58/196	.68/231	.85/288	1.15/1.10	.88/.92
.75	.49/166	.54/183	.60/206	.69/237	.83/284	1.07/368		1.16/1.10	.88/.92
.8	.60/209	.68/235	.78/271	.94/328	1.26/444			1.16/1.11	.87/.91
.85	.74/259	.85/299	1.02/361	1.43/512				1.17/1.11	.86/.90
.9	.90/321	1.08/389	1.49/546					1.17/1.11	.85/.90

4000 FEET (7°C)

MACH	DRAG INDEX 0	20	40	60	80	100	120	+10°C	−10°C
.5	.0 / 0	.0 / 0	.0 / 0	.0 / 0	.0 / 0	.0 / 0	.0 / 0	.0 / .0	.0 / .0
.55	.09/ 29	.10/ 31	.11/ 33	.11/ 35	.12/ 38	.13/ 41	.14/ 44	1.13/1.09	.91/.94
.6	.19/ 59	.20/ 63	.22/ 68	.24/ 73	.26/ 80	.28/ 88	.31/ 98	1.14/1.09	.90/.93
.65	.29/ 91	.31/ 98	.34/107	.37/117	.41/130	.46/146	.53/167	1.14/1.09	.89/.93
.7	.39/126	.43/137	.47/151	.52/168	.60/191	.69/222	.85/273	1.15/1.10	.88/.92
.75	.50/163	.56/180	.62/201	.71/230	.84/273	1.05/345		1.16/1.10	.88/.92
.8	.62/205	.70/230	.80/263	.95/314	1.24/411			1.16/1.11	.87/.91
.85	.76/253	.87/291	1.03/346	1.37/466				1.17/1.11	.86/.90
.9	.92/312	1.09/373	1.46/503					1.17/1.11	.85/.90

6000 FEET (3°C)

MACH	DRAG INDEX 0	20	40	60	80	100	120	+10°C	−10°C
.5	.0 / 0	.0 / 0	.0 / 0	.0 / 0	.0 / 0	.0 / 0	.0 / 0	.0 / .0	.0 / .0
.55	.10/ 29	.11/ 31	.11/ 32	.12/ 35	.13/ 37	.14/ 40	.15/ 44	1.13/1.09	.91/.94
.6	.20/ 59	.21/ 63	.23/ 68	.25/ 73	.27/ 79	.30/ 87	.33/ 96	1.14/1.09	.90/.93
.65	.30/ 91	.33/ 98	.36/106	.39/116	.43/128	.48/143	.55/163	1.15/1.09	.89/.93
.7	.41/125	.45/135	.49/149	.54/165	.62/186	.71/216	.86/261	1.15/1.10	.88/.92
.75	.53/161	.58/177	.64/198	.73/224	.86/264	1.06/327	1.57/491	1.16/1.10	.88/.92
.8	.65/202	.72/225	.82/256	.97/303	1.227/386	2.489/802		1.16/1.11	.87/.91
.85	.79/248	.90/283	1.05/373	1.36/435				1.17/1.11	.86/.90
.9	.95/305	1.12/360	1.44/469					1.17/1.11	.85/.90

FDB–1–(205)

Figure 11-96

LOW ALTITUDE ACCELERATION
MILITARY THRUST

AIRPLANE CONFIGURATION
INDIVIDUAL DRAG INDEXES

GROSS WEIGHT – 45,000 POUNDS

REMARKS

ENGINES: (2) J79-GE-8

DATE: 15 MAY 1968
DATA BASIS: FLIGHT TEST

FUEL GRADE: JP-5
FUEL DENSITY: 6.8 LB/GAL

	MACH	DRAG INDEX 0	20	40	60	80	100	120	+10°C	−10°C
SEA LEVEL (15°C)	.5	.0 / 0	.0 / 0	.0 / 0	.0 / 0	.0 / 0	.0 / 0	.0 / 0	.0 /.0	.0 /.0
	.55	.10/ 34	.10/ 36	.11/ 38	.12/ 41	.13/ 44	.14/ 48	.16/ 53	1.13/1.09	.91/.94
	.6	.20/ 69	.21/ 74	.23/ 80	.25/ 87	.28/95	.31/106	.34/119	1.14/1.09	.90/.93
	.65	.30/107	.33/116	.36/126	.40/140	.45/156	.51/178	.59/208	1.14/1.09	.89/.93
	.7	.42/147	.46/162	.51/179	.57/202	.66/233	.78/279	1.00/359	1.15/1.10	.88/.92
	.75	.53/192	.59/214	.67/242	.78/281	.95/343	1.30/472		1.16/1.10	.88/.92
	.8	.67/243	.75/275	.88/320	1.08/396	1.56/581			1.16/1.11	.87/.91
	.85	.82/302	.95/353	1.16/433	1.76/668				1.17/1.11	.86/.90
	.9	1.00/377	1.22/465	1.99/776					1.17/1.11	.85/.90
2000 FEET (11°C)	.5	.0 / 0	.0 / 0	.0 / 0	.0 / 0	.0 / 0	.0 / 0	.0 / 0	.0 /.0	.0 /.0
	.55	.10/ 33	.11/ 35	.12/ 38	.13/ 41	.14/ 44	.15/ 48	.16/ 52	1.13/1.09	.91/.94
	.6	.21/ 68	.22/ 73	.24/ 79	.26/ 86	.29/ 94	.31/104	.35/116	1.14/1.09	.90/.93
	.65	.32/106	.34/114	.37/125	.41/137	.46/153	.52/173	.60/201	1.14/1.09	.89/.93
	.7	.43/146	.47/159	.52/176	.58/197	.67/226	.79/267	.99/336	1.15/1.10	.88/.92
	.75	.55/189	.61/210	.69/236	.79/272	.95/328	1.25/433		1.16/1.10	.88/.92
	.8	.69/238	.77/269	.89/310	1.08/377	1.48/522			1.16/1.11	.87/.91
	.85	.84/295	.97/342	1.17/413	1.65/592				1.17/1.11	.86/.90
	.9	1.02/367	1.23/445	1.78/653					1.17/1.11	.85/.90
4000 FEET (7°C)	.5	.0 / 0	.0 / 0	.0 / 0	.0 / 0	.0 / 0	.0 / 0	.0 / 0	.0 /.0	.0 /.0
	.55	.11/ 33	.11/ 35	.12/ 38	.13/ 40	.14/ 44	.15/ 47	.17/ 52	1.13/1.09	.91/.94
	.6	.22/ 68	.23/ 73	.25/ 78	.27/ 85	.30/ 93	.33/102	.37/114	1.14/1.09	.90/.93
	.65	.33/105	.36/113	.39/123	.43/135	.47/150	.53/169	.62/195	1.14/1.09	.89/.93
	.7	.45/144	.49/157	.54/173	.60/193	.69/220	.80/258	.99/319	1.15/1.10	.88/.92
	.75	.58/187	.64/206	.71/231	.81/265	.97/315	1.24/405	2.22/736	1.16/1.10	.88/.92
	.8	.71/234	.80/263	.92/302	1.10/362	1.45/482			1.16/1.11	.87/.91
	.85	.87/289	.99/333	1.18/397	1.59/541				1.17/1.11	.86/.90
	.9	1.05/357	1.25/427	1.71/592					1.17/1.11	.85/.90
6000 FEET (3°C)	.5	.0 / 0	.0 / 0	.0 / 0	.0 / 0	.0 / 0	.0 / 0	.0 / 0	.0 /.0	.0 /.0
	.55	.11/ 33	.12/ 35	.13/ 38	.14/ 40	.15/ 43	.16/ 47	.18/ 51	1.13/1.09	.91/.94
	.6	.23/ 68	.25/ 73	.27/ 78	.29/ 85	.31/ 92	.34/101	.38/113	1.14/1.09	.90/.93
	.65	.35/104	.38/113	.41/122	.45/134	.50/148	.56/167	.64/191	1.14/1.09	.89/.93
	.7	.47/143	.52/156	.57/171	.63/191	.71/216	.83/251	1.01/306	1.15/1.10	.88/.92
	.75	.60/185	.67/204	.74/227	.84/259	.99/306	1.24/384	1.90/595	1.16/1.10	.88/.92
	.8	.74/231	.83/259	.95/295	1.12/350	1.44/452			1.16/1.11	.87/.91
	.85	.90/284	1.03/325	1.21/384	1.57/504				1.17/1.11	.86/.90
	.9	1.09/349	1.28/413	1.68/548					1.17/1.11	.85/.90

FDB-1-(206)

Figure 11-97

LOW ALTITUDE ACCELERATION
MILITARY THRUST

AIRPLANE CONFIGURATION
INDIVIDUAL DRAG INDEXES

GROSS WEIGHT — 50,000 POUNDS

REMARKS

ENGINES: (2) J79-GE-8

DATE: 15 MAY 1962
DATA BASIS: FLIGHT TEST

FUEL GRADE: JP-5
FUEL DENSITY: 6.8 LB/GAL

	MACH	DRAG INDEX	TIME TO ACCELERATE (MIN.)/FUEL TO ACCELERATE (LBS.)							TEMP. EFFECTS FACTOR	
			0	20	40	60	80	100	120	+10°C	−10°C
SEA LEVEL (15°C)	.5	.0 / 0	.0 / 0	.0 / 0	.0 / 0	.0 / 0	.0 / 0	.0 / 0	.0 /.0	.0 /.0
	.55	.11/ 38	.12/ 41	.13/ 43	.14/ 47	.15/ 51	.16/ 55	.18/ 61	1.13/1.09	.91/.94
	.6	.23/ 78	.24/ 84	.26/ 91	.29/ 99	.31/109	.35/121	.39/136	1.14/1.09	.90/.93
	.65	.34/121	.37/131	.41/143	.45/158	.51/178	.58/203	.68/239	1.14/1.09	.89/.93
	.7	.47/166	.52/183	.57/203	.65/229	.75/266	.90/319	1.17/419	1.15/1.10	.88/.92
	.75	.60/217	.67/242	.76/274	.88/319	1.08/392	1.50/546		1.16/1.10	.88/.92
	.8	.75/273	.85/311	.99/363	1.22/450	1.82/678			1.16/1.11	.87/.91
	.85	.92/340	1.07/398	1.31/490	2.06/782				1.17/1.11	.86/.90
	.9	1.13/425	1.38/525	2.32/907					1.17/1.11	.85/.90
2000 FEET (11°C)	.5	.0 / 0	.0 / .0	.0 / 0	.0 / 0	.0 / 0	.0 / 0	.0 / 0	.0 /.0	.0 /.0
	.55	.12/ 38	.12/ 40	.13/ 43	.14/ 46	.15/ 50	.17/ 55	.19/ 60	1.13/1.09	.91/.94
	.6	.24/ 78	.25/ 83	.27/ 90	.30/ 98	.33/107	.36/119	.41/134	1.14/1.09	.90/.93
	.65	.36/120	.39/130	.43/142	.47/156	.52/174	.59/198	.69/232	1.14/1.09	.89/.93
	.7	.49/165	.54/181	.59/200	.67/225	.76/258	.91/307	1.15/392	1.15/1.10	.88/.92
	.75	.63/214	.70/238	.78/268	.90/310	1.09/375	1.45/502		1.16/1.10	.88/.92
	.8	.78/269	.88/304	1.01/352	1.23/430	1.71/603			1.16/1.11	.87/.91
	.85	.95/333	1.10/387	1.32/469	1.88/677				1.17/1.11	.86/.90
	.9	1.15/414	1.39/503	2.06/759					1.17/1.11	.85/.90
4000 FEET (7°C)	.5	.0 / 0	.0 / 0	.0 / 0	.0 / 0	.0 / 0	.0 / 0	.0 / 0	.0 /.0	.0 /.0
	.55	.12/ 38	.13/ 40	.14/ 43	.15/ 46	.16/ 50	.18/ 54	.19/ 60	1.13/1.09	.91/.94
	.6	.25/ 77	.27/ 83	.29/ 89	.31/ 97	.34/106	.38/117	.42/132	1.14/1.09	.90/.93
	.65	.38/119	.41/129	.44/140	.49/154	.54/172	.62/194	.71/226	1.14/1.09	.89/.93
	.7	.51/163	.56/179	.62/197	.69/221	.79/252	.93/297	1.16/373	1.15/1.10	.88/.92
	.75	.65/211	.72/234	.81/263	.93/302	1.11/361	1.43/469		1.16/1.10	.88/.92
	.8	.81/265	.91/298	1.04/343	1.25/413	1.67/556			1.16/1.11	.87/.91
	.85	.98/327	1.13/377	1.34/451	1.83/621				1.17/1.11	.86/.90
	.9	1.19/403	1.42/484	1.96/677					1.17/1.11	.85/.90
6000 FEET (3°C)	.5	.0 / 0	.0 / 0	.0 / 0	.0 / 0	.0 / 0	.0 / 0	.0 / 0	.0 /.0	.0 /.0
	.55	.13/ 38	.14/ 41	.15/ 43	.16/ 47	.17/ 50	.19/ 55	.21/ 60	1.13/1.09	.91/.94
	.6	.26/ 78	.28/ 83	.31/ 90	.33/ 97	.36/106	.40/118	.45/131	1.14/1.09	.90/.93
	.65	.40/119	.43/129	.47/140	.52/154	.57/171	.65/193	.75/223	1.14/1.09	.89/.93
	.7	.54/163	.59/178	.65/196	.72/219	.82/249	.96/292	1.18/360	1.15/1.10	.88/.92
	.75	.69/210	.76/232	.85/260	.97/297	1.14/352	1.44/446	2.33/729	1.16/1.10	.88/.92
	.8	.85/262	.95/294	1.08/336	1.28/401	1.66/523			1.16/1.11	.87/.91
	.85	1.02/322	1.17/369	1.38/437	1.81/581				1.17/1.11	.86/.90
	.9	1.23/395	1.45/469	1.92/628					1.17/1.11	.85/.90

FDB-1-(207)

Figure 11-98

LOW ALTITUDE ACCELERATION
MILITARY THRUST

AIRPLANE CONFIGURATION
INDIVIDUAL DRAG INDEXES

GROSS WEIGHT – 55,000 POUNDS

REMARKS

ENGINES: (2) J79-GE-8

DATE: 1 MAY 1968
DATA BASIS: ESTIMATED (BASED ON FLIGHT TEST)

FUEL GRADE: JP-5
FUEL DENSITY: 6.8 LB/GAL

	MACH	DRAG INDEX	TIME TO ACCELERATE (MIN.)/FUEL TO ACCELERATE (LBS.)							TEMP. EFFECTS FACTOR	
			0	20	40	60	80	100	120	+10°C	−10°C
SEA LEVEL (15°C)	.5	.0/0	.0/0	.0/0	.0/0	.0/0	.0/0	.0/0	.0/.0	.0/.0
	.55	.13/43	.13/46	.14/49	.15/53	.17/58	.18/63	.20/70	1.13/1.09	.91/.94
	.6	.25/88	.27/94	.30/102	.32/112	.36/123	.40/137	.45/156	1.14/1.09	.90/.93
	.65	.39/135	.42/147	.46/161	.51/179	.57/201	.66/231	.78/274	1.14/1.09	.89/.93
	.7	.53/186	.58/205	.64/228	.73/259	.85/301	1.02/363	1.35/454	1.15/1.10	.88/.92
	.75	.67/242	.75/271	.85/308	1.00/360	1.23/446	1.74/633		1.16/1.10	.88/.92
	.8	.84/306	.95/348	1.11/407	1.38/508	2.11/784			1.16/1.11	.87/.91
	.85	1.02/380	1.20/446	1.47/551	1.36/897				1.17/1.11	.86/.90
	.9	1.26/475	1.55/589	2.88/1131					1.17/1.11	.85/.90
2000 FEET (11°C)	.5	.0/0	.0/0	.0/0	.0/0	.0/0	.0/0	.0/0	.0/.0	.0/.0
	.55	.13/43	.14/46	.15/49	.16/53	.18/57	.19/62	.21/69	1.13/1.09	.91/.94
	.6	.27/87	.29/94	.31/102	.34/111	.37/122	.41/136	.46/153	1.14/1.09	.90/.93
	.65	.40/135	.44/146	.48/160	.53/177	.59/198	.68/226	.80/266	1.14/1.09	.89/.93
	.7	.55/185	.60/203	.67/225	.75/254	.87/293	1.04/351	1.34/454	1.15/1.10	.88/.92
	.75	.70/240	.78/267	.88/302	1.02/350	1.24/427	1.67/577		1.16/1.10	.88/.92
	.8	.87/301	.98/341	1.14/396	1.39/486	1.98/697			1.16/1.11	.87/.91
	.85	1.06/373	1.23/434	1.49/528	2.18/783				1.17/1.11	.86/.90
	.9	1.29/463	1.57/565	2.36/868					1.17/1.11	.85/.90
4000 FEET (7°C)	.5	.0/0	.0/0	.0/0	.0/0	.0/0	.0/0	.0/0	.0/.0	.0/.0
	.55	.14/43	.15/46	.16/49	.17/53	.19/57	.20/63	.22/69	1.13/1.09	.91/.94
	.6	.28/88	.30/94	.33/102	.36/111	.39/122	.43/135	.49/152	1.14/1.09	.90/.93
	.65	.43/134	.46/146	.50/159	.56/176	.62/196	.71/223	.82/261	1.14/1.09	.89/.93
	.7	.58/184	.63/202	.70/223	.78/251	.90/288	1.06/342	1.35/434	1.15/1.10	.88/.92
	.75	.74/238	.82/264	.92/297	1.06/343	1.27/414	1.66/542		1.16/1.10	.88/.92
	.8	.91/298	1.02/336	1.18/387	1.42/469	1.92/642			1.16/1.11	.87/.91
	.85	1.10/367	1.27/424	1.52/510	2.11/715				1.17/1.11	.86/.90
	.9	1.33/452	1.60/545	2.24/777					1.17/1.11	.85/.90
6000 FEET (3°C)	.5	.0/0	.0/0	.0/0	.0/0	.0/0	.0/0	.0/0	.0/.0	.0/.0
	.55	.15/44	.16/47	.17/50	.19/54	.20/58	.22/64	.24/70	1.13/1.09	.91/.94
	.6	.30/88	.32/95	.35/103	.38/112	.42/122	.46/136	.52/153	1.14/1.09	.90/.93
	.65	.45/135	.49/146	.54/160	.59/176	.66/196	.75/223	.87/259	1.14/1.09	.89/.93
	.7	.61/184	.67/202	.74/223	.83/250	.94/286	1.11/337	1.38/421	1.15/1.10	.88/.92
	.75	.78/237	.86/263	.96/295	1.10/338	1.31/404	1.68/519	2.93/920	1.16/1.10	.88/.92
	.8	.95/296	1.07/332	1.22/381	1.46/456	1.91/602			1.16/1.11	.87/.91
	.85	1.15/362	1.32/416	1.56/495	2.08/666				1.17/1.11	.86/.90
	.9	1.38/444	1.64/529	2.20/719					1.17/1.11	.85/.90

FDB-1-(208)

Figure 11-99

MAXIMUM THRUST ACCELERATION
10,000 FEET

AIRPLANE CONFIGURATION

(4) AIM-7

REMARKS

ENGINE(S): (2) J79-GE-8
ICAO STANDARD DAY

GUIDE

FUEL GRADE: JP-5
FUEL DENSITY: 6.8 LB/GAL

DATE: 15 MAY 1968
DATA BASIS: FLIGHT TEST

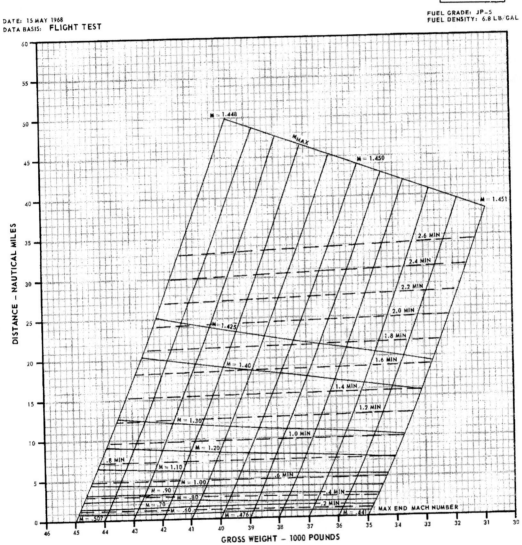

FDB-1-(209)

Figure 11-100

MAXIMUM THRUST ACCELERATION
ALTITUDE 30,000 FEET

AIRPLANE CONFIGURATION

(4) AIM-7

REMARKS

ENGINE(S): (2) J79-GE-8
ICAO STANDARD DAY

GUIDE

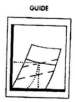

DATE: 15 MAY 1968
DATA BASIS: FLIGHT TEST

FUEL GRADE: JP-5
FUEL DENSITY: 6.8 LB/GAL

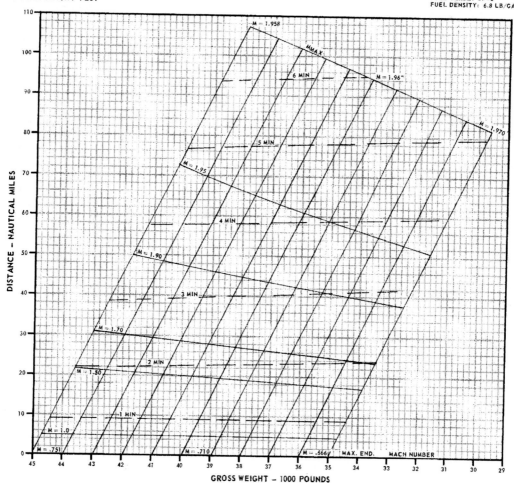

FDB-1-(210)

Figure 11-101

MAXIMUM THRUST ACCELERATION
ALTITUDE 25,000 FEET

AIRPLANE CONFIGURATION

(4) AIM-7

REMARKS

ENGINE(S): (2) J79-GE-8
ICAO STANDARD DAY

GUIDE

FUEL GRADE: JP-5
FUEL DENSITY: 6.8 LB/GAL

DATE: 15 MAY 1968
DATA BASIS: FLIGHT TEST

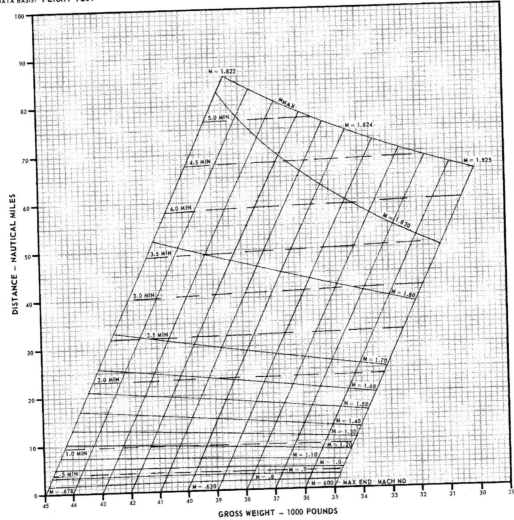

FDB-1-(211)

Figure 11-102

MAXIMUM THRUST ACCELERATION
35,000 FEET

AIRPLANE CONFIGURATION

(4) AIM-7

REMARKS
ENGINE(S):(2) J79-GE-8
ICAO STANDARD DAY

GUIDE

FUEL GRADE: JP-5
FUEL DENSITY: 6.8 LB/GAL

DATE: 15 MAY 1968
DATA BASIS: FLIGHT TEST

Figure 11-103

FDB-1-(212)

MAXIMUM THRUST ACCELERATION
40,000 FEET

AIRPLANE CONFIGURATION

(4) AIM-7

REMARKS

ENGINE(5): (2) J79-GE-8
ICAO STANDARD DAY

GUIDE

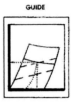

DATE: 15 MAY 1968
DATA BASIS: FLIGHT TEST

FUEL GRADE: JP-5
FUEL DENSITY: 6.8 LB/GAL

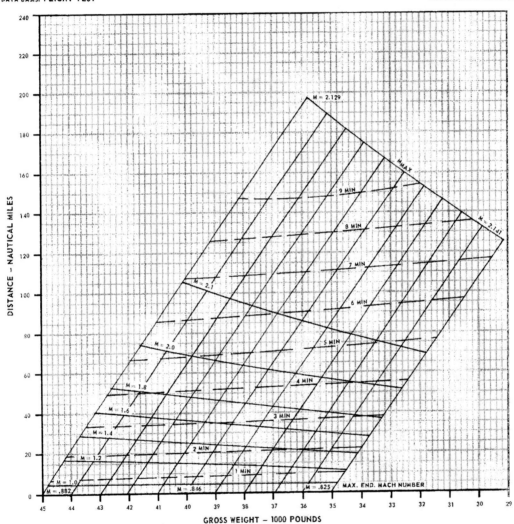

FDB-1-(213)

Figure 11-104

MAXIMUM THRUST ACCELERATION
45,000 FEET

AIRPLANE CONFIGURATION

(4) AIM-7

REMARKS

ENGINE(S): (2) J79-GE-8
ICAO STANDARD DAY

GUIDE

DATE: 15 MAY 1968
DATA BASIS: **FLIGHT TEST**

FUEL GRADE: JP-5
FUEL DENSITY: 6.8 LB/GAL

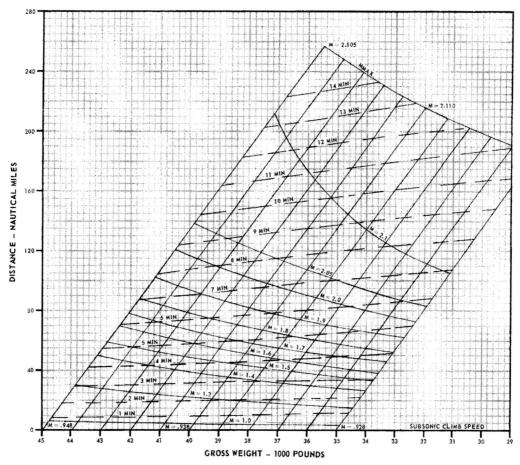

FDB-1-(214)

Figure 11-105

MAXIMUM THRUST ACCELERATION
50,000 FEET

AIRPLANE CONFIGURATION

(4) AIM-7

REMARKS

ENGINE(S): (2) J79-GE-8
ICAO STANDARD DAY

GUIDE

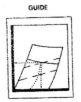

FUEL GRADE: JP-5
FUEL DENSITY: 6.8 LB/GAL

DATE: 15 MAY 1968
DATA BASIS: FLIGHT TEST

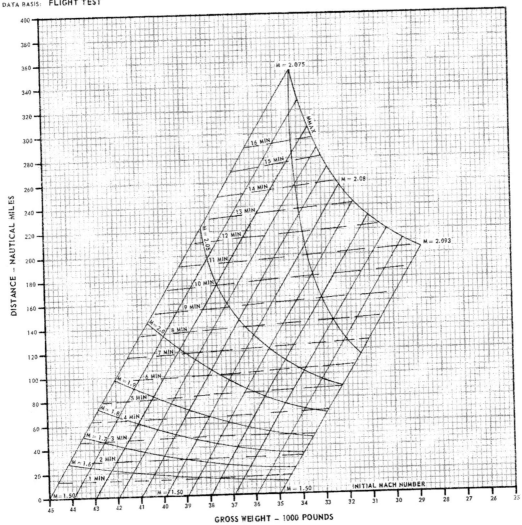

FDB-1-(215)

Figure 11-106

MAXIMUM THRUST ACCELERATION
ALTITUDE 25,000 FEET

AIRPLANE CONFIGURATION
(4) AIM-7 AND (1) ₵ TANK

REMARKS
ENGINE(S): (2) J79-GE-8
ICAO STANDARD DAY

GUIDE

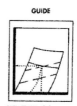

FUEL GRADE: JP-5
FUEL DENSITY: 6.8 LB/GAL

DATE: 15 MAY 1968
DATA BASIS: FLIGHT TEST

M = 1.674

M = 1.682

7.0 MIN

HMAX

M = 1.684

6.0 MIN

M = 1.686

5.0 MIN

M = 1.67

4.0 MIN

M = 1.65

3.0 MIN

M = 1.6

M = 1.5

2.0 MIN

M = 1.4

M = 1.3

M = 1.2

1.0 MIN

M = 1.1

.5 MIN

M = 1.0

M = .80

M = .70

M = .688

M = .625

M = .590   MAX. END. MACH NUMBER

DISTANCE-NAUTICAL MILES (120, 110, 100, 90, 80, 70, 60, 50, 40, 30, 20, 10, 0)

GROSS WEIGHT-1000 POUNDS (52, 50, 48, 46, 44, 42, 40, 38, 36, 34, 32, 30, 28)

FDB-1-(216)

Figure 11-107

MAXIMUM THRUST ACCELERATION
ALTITUDE 30,000 FEET

AIRPLANE CONFIGURATION

(4) AIM-7 AND (1) C TANK

REMARKS

ENGINE(S): (2) J79-GE-8
ICAO STANDARD DAY

GUIDE

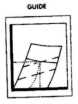

FUEL GRADE: JP-5
FUEL DENSITY: 6.8 LB/GAL

DATE: 15 MAY 1968
DATA BASIS: FLIGHT TEST

DISTANCE – NAUTICAL MILES

GROSS WEIGHT – 1000 POUNDS

M = 1.812
M = 1.814
8.0 MIN
MMAX
7.0 MIN
M = 1.818
6.0 MIN
M = 1.82
5.0 MIN
M = 1.80
4.0 MIN
M = 1.70
3.0 MIN
M = 1.60
M = 1.50
M = 1.40
2.0 MIN
M = 1.30
M = 1.20
M = 1.10
1.0 MIN
M = 1.00
.50 MIN
M = .779
M = .745
M = .704
M = .659 MAX. END. MACH NUMBER

FDB-1-(217)

Figure 11-108

MAXIMUM THRUST ACCELERATION
35,000 FEET

AIRPLANE CONFIGURATION

(4) AIM–7 AND (1) ℂ TANK

REMARKS

ENGINE(S): (2) J79–GE–8
ICAO STANDARD DAY

GUIDE

DATE: 15 MAY 1968
DATA BASIS: FLIGHT TEST

FUEL GRADE: JP–5
FUEL DENSITY: 6.8 LB/GAL

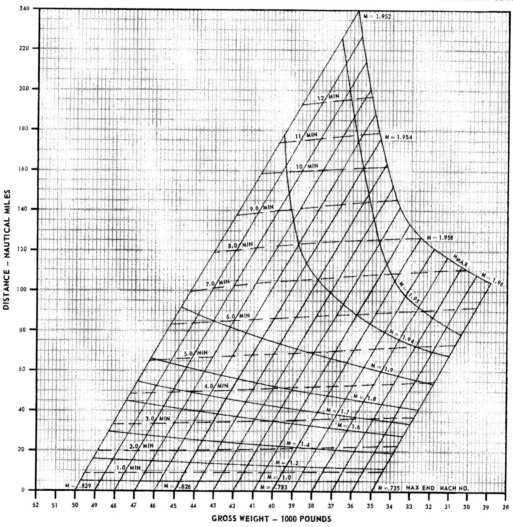

FDB–1–(218)

Figure 11-109

MAXIMUM THRUST ACCELERATION
40,000 FEET

AIRPLANE CONFIGURATION

(4) AIM-7 AND (1) ⊄ TANK

REMARKS
ENGINE(S): (2) J79-GE-8
ICAO STANDARD DAY

GUIDE

FUEL GRADE: JP-5
FUEL DENSITY: 6.8 LB/GAL

DATE: 15 MAY 1968
DATA BASIS: FLIGHT TEST

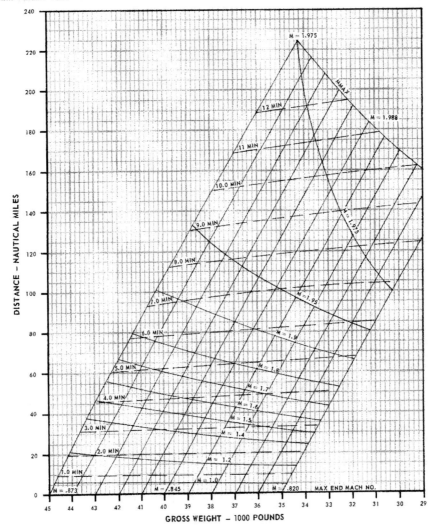

FDB-1-(219)

Figure 11-110

MAXIMUM THRUST ACCELERATION
45,000 FEET

AIRPLANE CONFIGURATION
(4) AIM-7 AND (1) ℄ TANK

REMARKS
ENGINE(S):(2) J79-GE-8
ICAO STANDARD DAY

GUIDE

FUEL GRADE: JP-5
FUEL DENSITY: 6.8 LB/GAL

DATE: 15 MAY 1968
DATA BASIS: FLIGHT TEST

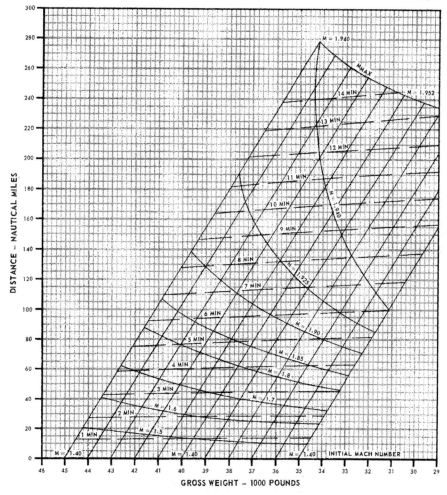

FDB-1-(220)

Figure 11-111

11-147

MAXIMUM THRUST ACCELERATION
50,000 FEET

AIRPLANE CONFIGURATION
(4) AIM-7 AND (1) ¢ TANK

REMARKS
ENGINE(S): (2) J79-GE-8
ICAO STANDARD DAY

GUIDE

FUEL GRADE: JP-5
FUEL DENSITY: 6.8 LB/GAL

DATE: 15 MAY 1968
DATA BASIS: FLIGHT TEST

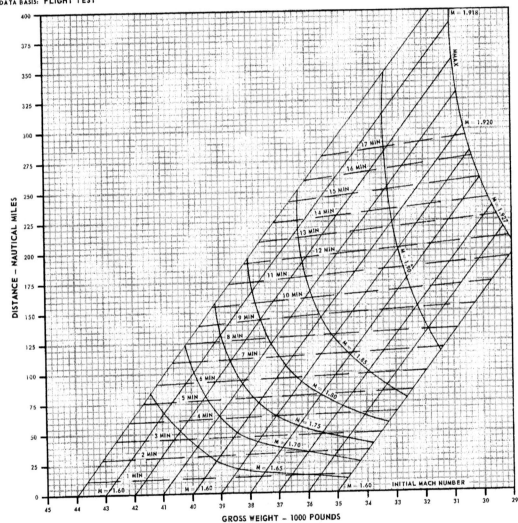

FDB-1-(221)

Figure 11-112

MAXIMUM THRUST ACCELERATION
ALTITUDE 25,000 FEET

AIRPLANE CONFIGURATION
(4) AIM-7 AND (2) WING TANKS

REMARKS
ENGINE(S):(2) J79-GE-8
ICAO STANDARD DAY

GUIDE

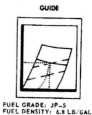

DATE: 15 MAY 1968
DATA BASIS: FLIGHT TEST

FUEL GRADE: JP-5
FUEL DENSITY: 6.8 LB/GAL

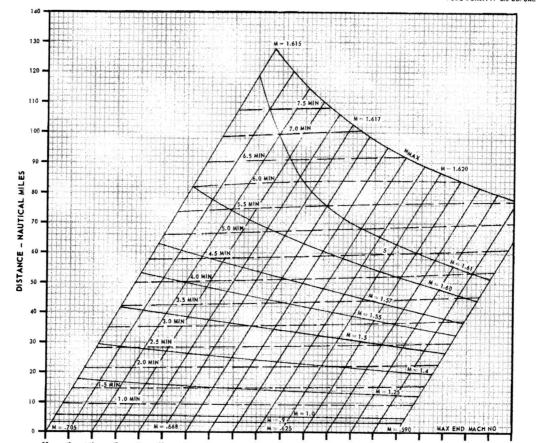

FDB-1-(222)

Figure 11-113

MAXIMUM THRUST ACCELERATION
ALTITUDE 30,000 FEET

AIRPLANE CONFIGURATION
(4) AIM-7 AND (2) WING TANKS

REMARKS
ENGINE(S): (2) J79-GE- 8
ICAO STANDARD DAY

GUIDE

FUEL GRADE: JP-5
FUEL DENSITY: 6.8 LB/GAL

DATE: 15 MAY 1968
DATA BASIS: FLIGHT TEST

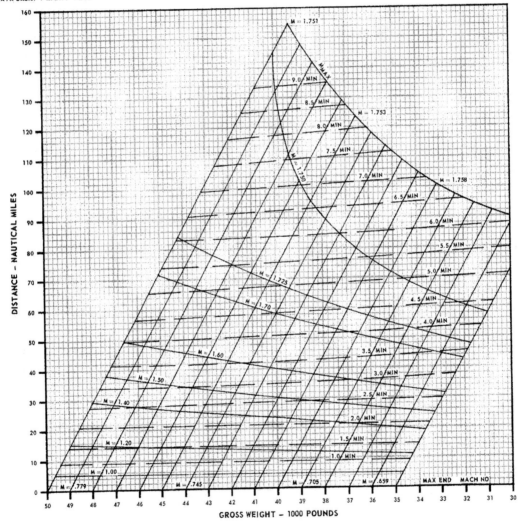

FDB-1-(223)

Figure 11-114

MAXIMUM THRUST ACCELERATION
35,000 FEET

AIRPLANE CONFIGURATION

(4) AIM-7   AND   (2) WING TANKS

REMARKS

ENGINE(S): (2) J79-GE-8
ICAO STANDARD DAY

GUIDE

DATE: 15 MAY 1968
DATA BASIS: **FLIGHT TEST**

FUEL GRADE: JP-5
FUEL DENSITY: 6.8 LB/GAL

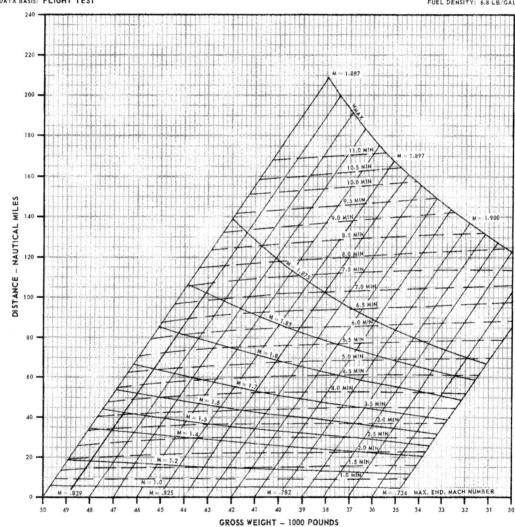

FDB-1-(224)

Figure 11-115

MAXIMUM THRUST ACCELERATION
40,000 FEET

AIRPLANE CONFIGURATION
(4) AIM-7 AND (2) WING TANKS

REMARKS
ENGINE(S): (2) J79-GE-8
ICAO STANDARD DAY

GUIDE

FUEL GRADE: JP-5
FUEL DENSITY: 6.8 LB/GAL

DATE: 15 MAY 1968
DATA BASIS: FLIGHT TEST

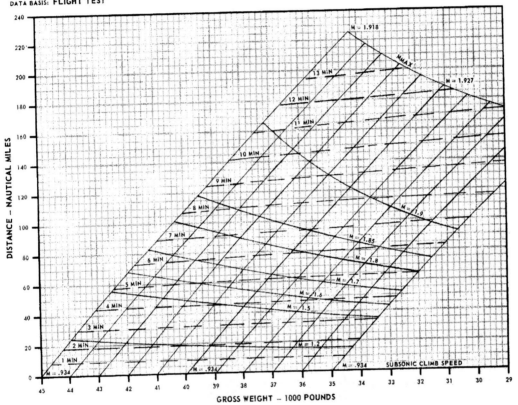

FDB-1-(225)

Figure 11-116

MAXIMUM THRUST ACCELERATION
45,000 FEET

AIRPLANE CONFIGURATION

(4) AIM-7 AND (2) WING TANKS

REMARKS

ENGINE(S): (2) J79-GE-8
ICAO STANDARD DAY

GUIDE

DATE: 15 MAY 1968
DATA BASIS: **FLIGHT TEST**

FUEL GRADE: JP-5
FUEL DENSITY: 6.8 LB./GAL.

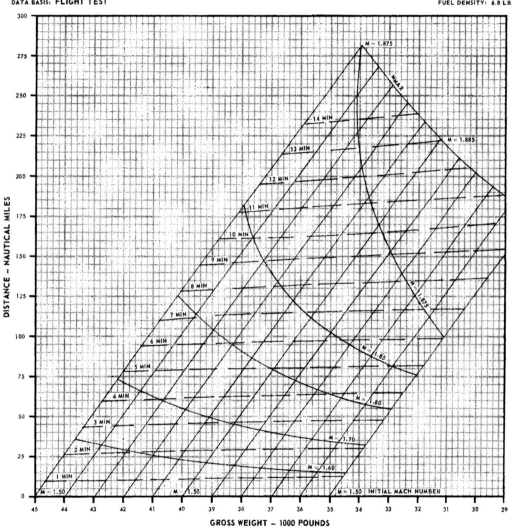

FDB-1-(226)

Figure 11-117

11-153

MAXIMUM THRUST ACCELERATION
ALTITUDE 25,000 FEET
REMARKS

AIRPLANE CONFIGURATION
(4) AIM-7 AND (4) AIM-9

ENGINE(S): (2) J79-GE-8
ICAO STANDARD DAY

GUIDE

FUEL GRADE: JP-5
FUEL DENSITY: 6.8 LB./GAL

DATE: 15 MAY 1968
DATA BASIS: FLIGHT TEST

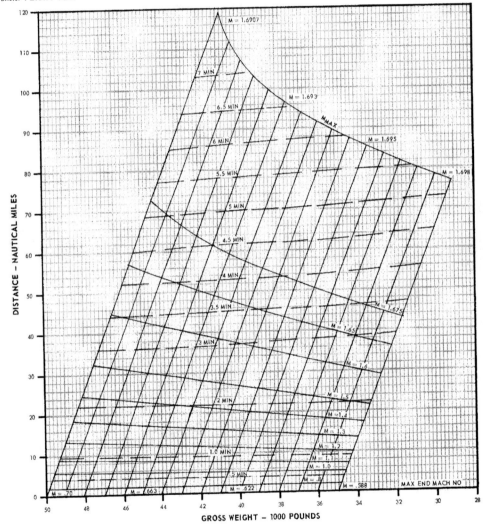

FDB-1-(227)

Figure 11-118

MAXIMUM THRUST ACCELERATION
ALTITUDE 30,000 FEET

AIRPLANE CONFIGURATION

(4) AIM–7 AND (4) AIM–9

REMARKS

ENGINE(S): (2) J79–GE–8
ICAO STANDARD DAY

GUIDE

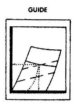

DATE: 15 MAY 1968
DATA BASIS: **FLIGHT TEST**

FUEL GRADE: JP–5
FUEL DENSITY: 6.8 LB/GAL

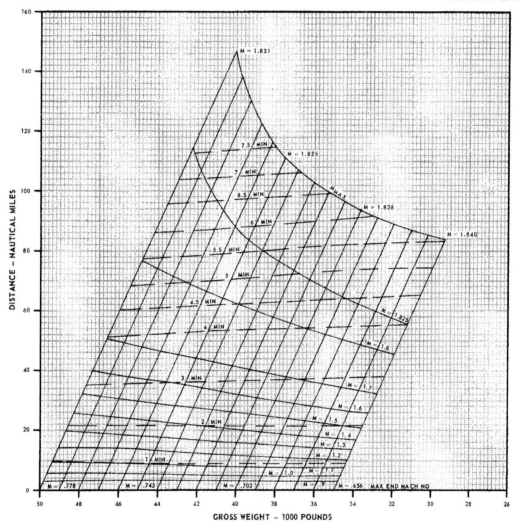

FDB–1–(228)

Figure 11-119

11-155

MAXIMUM THRUST ACCELERATION
35,000 FEET

AIRPLANE CONFIGURATION

(4) AIM-7 AND (4) AIM-9

REMARKS
ENGINE(S):(2) J79-GE-8
ICAO STANDARD DAY

GUIDE

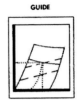

FUEL GRADE: JP-5
FUEL DENSITY: 6.8 LB/GAL

DATE: 15 MAY 1968
DATA BASIS: **FLIGHT TEST**

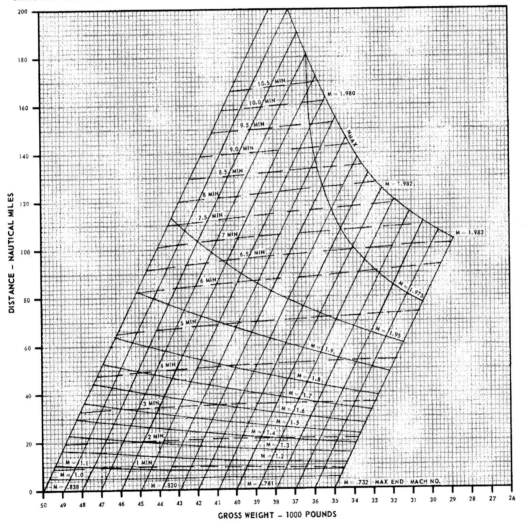

FDB-1-(229)

Figure 11-120

MAXIMUM THRUST ACCELERATION
40,000 FEET

AIRPLANE CONFIGURATION

(4) AIM-7 AND AIM-9

REMARKS

ENGINE(S): (2) J79-GE-8
ICAO STANDARD DAY

GUIDE

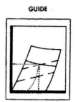

DATE: 15 MAY 1968
DATA BASIS: **FLIGHT TEST**

FUEL GRADE: JP-5
FUEL DENSITY: 6.8 LB/GAL

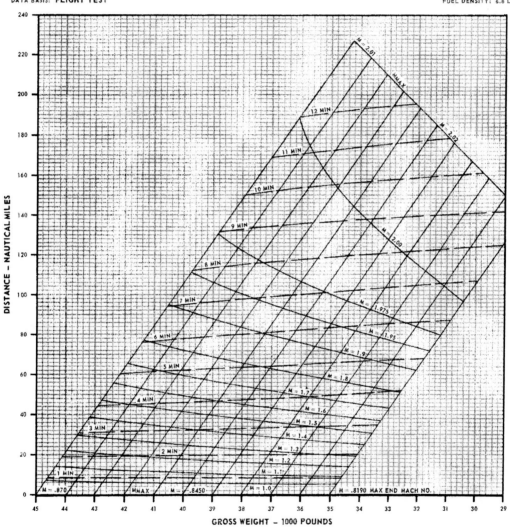

FDB-1-(230)

Figure 11-121

MAXIMUM THRUST ACCELERATION
45,000 FEET

AIRPLANE CONFIGURATION

(4) AIM-7   AND (4) AIM-9

REMARKS

ENGINE(S): (2) J79-GE-8
ICAO STANDARD DAY

GUIDE

DATE: 15 MAY 1968
DATA BASIS: FLIGHT TEST

FUEL GRADE: JP-5
FUEL DENSITY: 6.8 LB/GAL

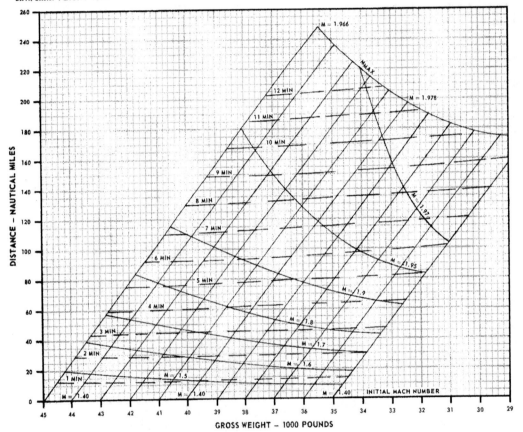

FDB-1-(231)

Figure 11-122

MAXIMUM THRUST ACCELERATION
50,000 FEET

AIRPLANE CONFIGURATION
(4) AIM-7   AND (4) AIM-9

REMARKS
ENGINE(S): (2) J79-GE-8
ICAO STANDARD DAY

GUIDE

DATE: 15 MAY 1968
DATA BASIS: FLIGHT TEST

FUEL GRADE: JP-5
FUEL DENSITY: 6.8 LB/GAL

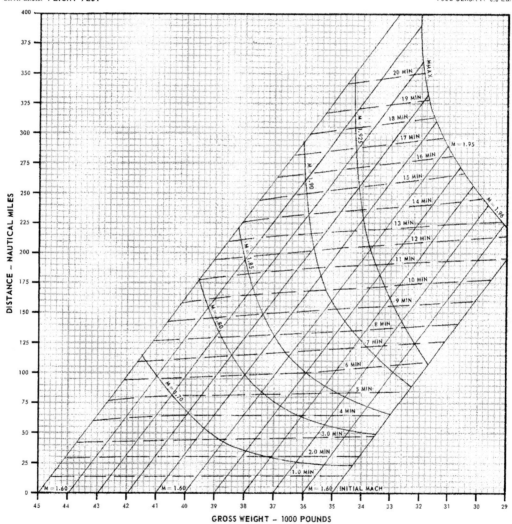

FDB-1-(232)

Figure 11-123

MAXIMUM THRUST ACCELERATION
ALTITUDE 25,000 FEET

AIRPLANE CONFIGURATION

(4) AIM-7, (4) AIM-9
AND (1) C_L TANK

REMARKS

ENGINE(S):(2) J79-GE-8
ICAO STANDARD DAY

GUIDE

FUEL GRADE: JP-5
FUEL DENSITY: 6.8 LB/GAL

DATE: 15 MAY 1968
DATA BASIS: FLIGHT TEST

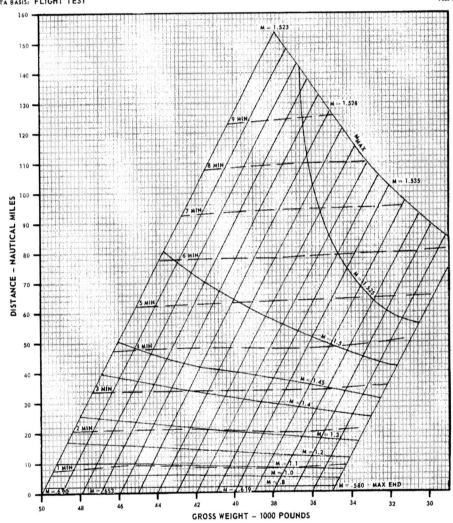

FDB-1-(233)

Figure 11-124

MAXIMUM THRUST ACCELERATION
ALTITUDE 30,000 FEET

AIRPLANE CONFIGURATION
(4) AIM-7, (4) AIM-9
AND (1) C TANK

REMARKS
ENGINE(S): (2) J79-GE-8
ICAO STANDARD DAY

GUIDE

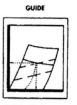

DATE: 15 MAY 1968
DATA BASIS: FLIGHT TEST

FUEL GRADE: JP-5
FUEL DENSITY: 6.8 LB/GAL

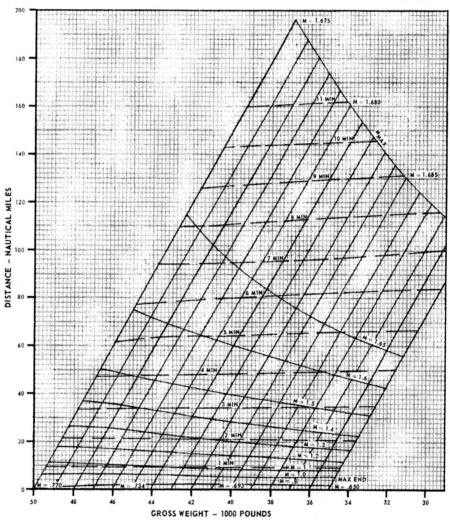

FDB-1-(234)

Figure 11-125

11-161

MAXIMUM THRUST ACCELERATION
35,000 FEET

AIRPLANE CONFIGURATION

(4) AIM-7 , (4) AIM-9.
AND (1) Cₗ TANK

REMARKS

ENGINE(S): (2) J79-GE-8
ICAO STANDARD DAY

GUIDE

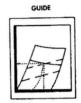

FUEL GRADE: JP-5
FUEL DENSITY: 6.8 LB/GAL

DATE: 15 MAY 1968
DATA BASIS: FLIGHT TEST

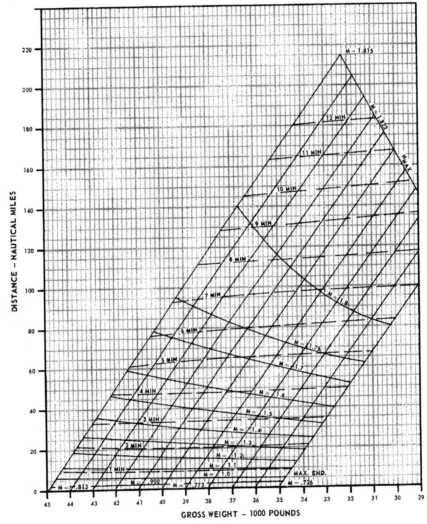

FDB-1-(235)

Figure 11-126

MAXIMUM THRUST ACCELERATION
40,000 FEET

AIRPLANE CONFIGURATION
(4) AIM-7, (4) AIM-9,
AND (1) C_L TANK

REMARKS

ENGINE(S): (2) J79-GE-8
ICAO STANDARD DAY

GUIDE

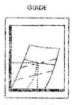

DATE: 15 MAY 1968
DATA BASIS: FLIGHT TEST

FUEL GRADE: JP-5
FUEL DENSITY: 6.8 LB/GAL

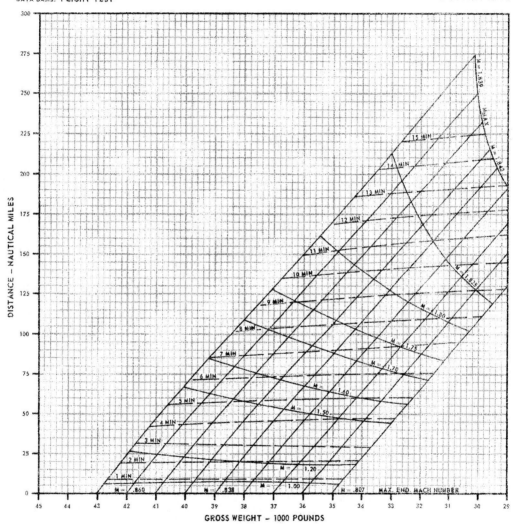

FDB-1-(236)

Figure 11-127

MAXIMUM THRUST ACCELERATION
45,000 FEET

AIRPLANE CONFIGURATION
(4) AIM-7, (4) AIM-9
AND (1) ⊄ TANK

REMARKS
ENGINE(S): (2) J79-GE-8
ICAO STANDARD DAY

GUIDE

DATE: 15 MAY 1968
DATA BASIS: FLIGHT TEST

FUEL GRADE: JP-5
FUEL DENSITY: 6.8 LBS/GAL

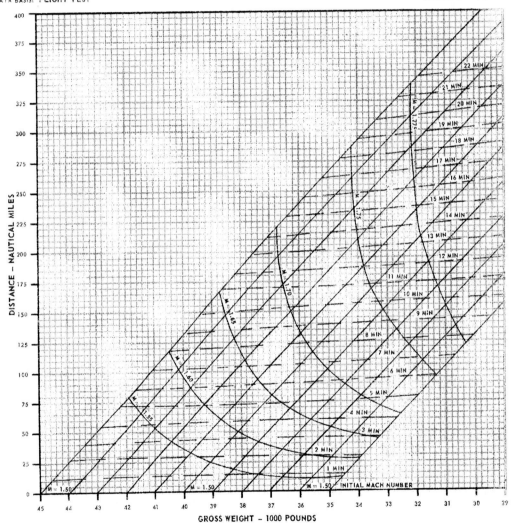

FDB-1-(237)

Figure 11-128

MAXIMUM THRUST ACCELERATION
ALTITUDE 25,000 FEET

AIRPLANE CONFIGURATION
(4) AIM-7, (4) AIM-9
AND (2) WING TANKS

REMARKS

ENGINE(S): (2) J79-GE-8
ICAO STANDARD DAY

GUIDE

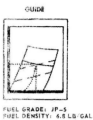

DATE: 15 MAY 1968
DATA BASIS: FLIGHT TEST

FUEL GRADE: JP-5
FUEL DENSITY: 6.8 LB/GAL

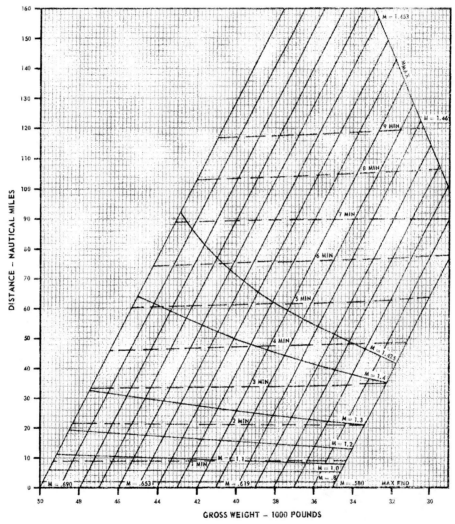

FDB-1-(238)

Figure 11-129

MAXIMUM THRUST ACCELERATION
ALTITUDE 30,000 FEET
REMARKS

AIRPLANE CONFIGURATION
(4) AIM-7,   (4) AIM-9
AND (2) WING TANKS

ENGINE(S): (2) J79-GE-8
ICAO STANDARD DAY

GUIDE

FUEL GRADE: JP-5
FUEL DENSITY: 6.8 LB/GAL

DATE: 15 MAY 1968
DATA BASIS: FLIGHT TEST

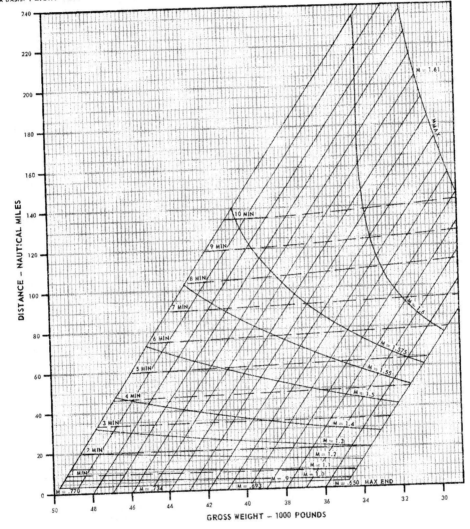

GROSS WEIGHT - 1000 POUNDS

FDB-1-(239)

Figure 11-130

MAXIMUM THRUST ACCELERATION
35,000 FEET

AIRPLANE CONFIGURATION
(4) AIM-7, (4) AIM-7
AND (2) WING TANKS

REMARKS
ENGINE(S): (2) J79-GE-8
ICAO STANDARD DAY

GUIDE

DATE: 15 MAY 1968
DATA BASIS: **FLIGHT TEST**

FUEL GRADE: JP-5
FUEL DENSITY: 6.8 LB/GAL

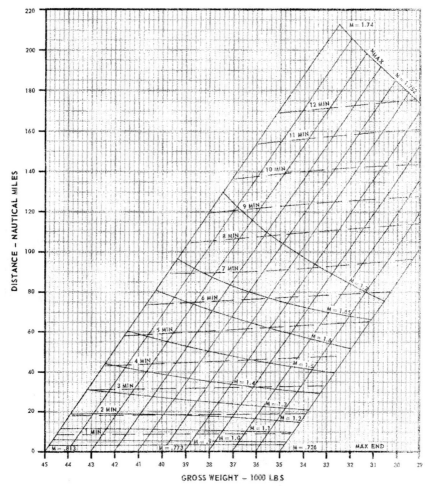

DISTANCE – NAUTICAL MILES

GROSS WEIGHT – 1000 LBS

FDB-1-(240)

Figure 11-131

MAXIMUM THRUST ACCELERATION
40,000 FEET
REMARKS

AIRPLANE CONFIGURATION
(4) AIM-7, (4) AIM-9
AND (2) WING TANKS

ENGINE(S): (2) J79-GE-8
ICAO STANDARD DAY

GUIDE

FUEL GRADE: JP-5
FUEL DENSITY: 6.8 LB/GAL

DATE: 15 MAY 1968
DATA BASIS: FLIGHT TEST

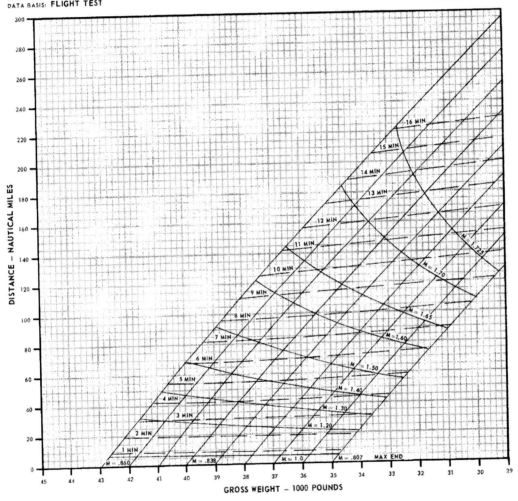

FDB-1-(241)

Figure 11-132

MILITARY THRUST ACCELERATION
15,000 FEET

AIRPLANE CONFIGURATION
(4) AIM-7

REMARKS

ENGINE(S): (2) J79-GE-8
ICAO STANDARD DAY

GUIDE

DATE: 15 MAY 1968
DATA BASIS: FLIGHT TEST

FUEL GRADE: JP-5
FUEL DENSITY: 6.8 LB/GAL

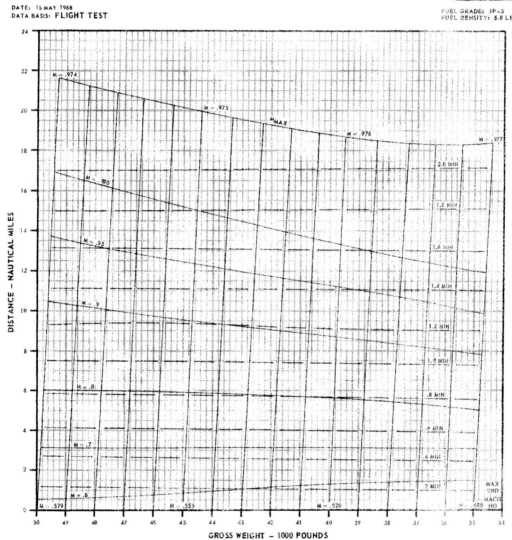

FDB-1-(242)

Figure 11-133

MILITARY THRUST ACCELERATION
25,000 FEET
REMARKS

AIRPLANE CONFIGURATION
(4) AIM-7

ENGINE(S): (2) J79-GE-8
ICAO STANDARD DAY

GUIDE

FUEL GRADE: JP-5
FUEL DENSITY: 6.8 LB/GAL

DATE: 15 MAY 1968
DATA BASIS: FLIGHT TEST

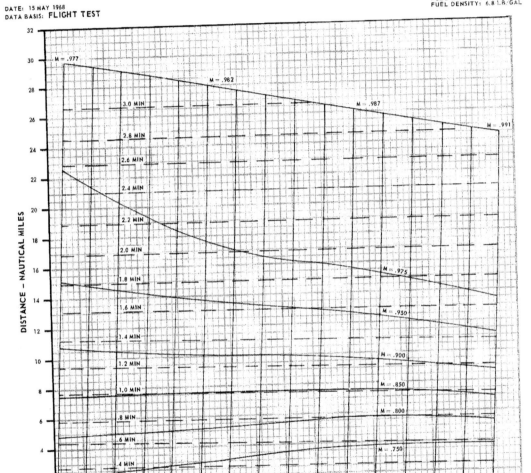

FD8-1-(243)

Figure 11-134

MILITARY THRUST ACCELERATION
35,000 FEET
REMARKS

AIRPLANE CONFIGURATION
(4) AIM--7

ENGINE(S): (2) J79--GE--8
ICAO STANDARD DAY

GUIDE

DATE: 15 MAY 1968
DATA BASIS: FLIGHT TEST

FUEL GRADE: JP--5
FUEL DENSITY: 6.8 LB/GAL

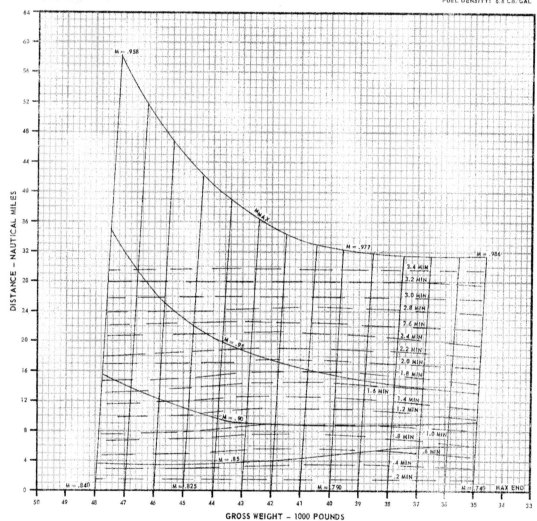

Figure 11-135

FDB--1--(244)

MILITARY THRUST ACCELERATION
15,000 FEET

AIRPLANE CONFIGURATION
(4) AIM-7, (4) AIM-9, (1) C TANK
AND (2) WING TANKS

REMARKS
ENGINE(S): (2) J79-GE-8
ICAO STANDARD DAY

GUIDE

DATE: 15 MAY 1968
DATA BASIS: FLIGHT TEST

FUEL GRADE: JP-5
FUEL DENSITY: 6.8 LB/GAL

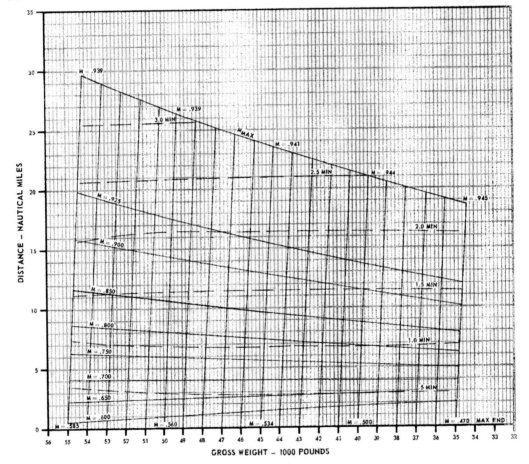

FDB-1-(245)

Figure 11-136

MILITARY THRUST ACCELERATION
25,000 FEET

AIRPLANE CONFIGURATION
(4) AIM-7, (4) AIM-9, (1) ℄ TANK
AND (2) WING TANKS

REMARKS

ENGINE(S): (2) J79-GE-8
ICAO STANDARD DAY

GUIDE

DATE: 15 MAY 1968
DATA BASIS: FLIGHT TEST

FUEL GRADE: JP-5
FUEL DENSITY: 6.8 LB/GAL

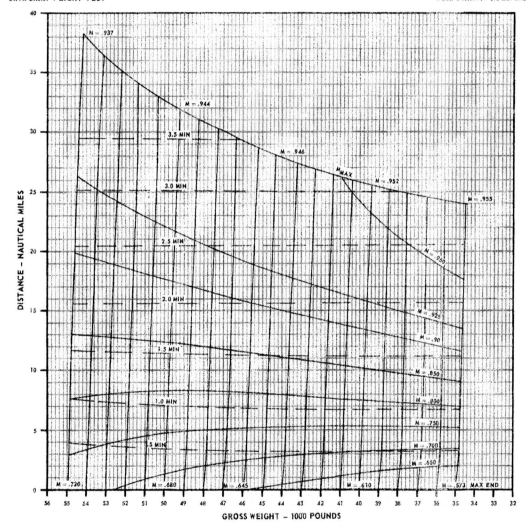

FDB-1-(246)

Figure 11-137

MILITARY THRUST ACCELERATION
35,000 FEET

AIRPLANE CONFIGURATION
(4) AIM–7, (4) AIM–9, (1) ₵ TANK
AND (2) WING TANKS

REMARKS

ENGINE(S): (2) J79–GE–8
ICAO STANDARD DAY

GUIDE

FUEL GRADE: JP–5
FUEL DENSITY: 6.8 LB/GAL

DATE: 15 MAY 1968
DATA BASIS: FLIGHT TEST

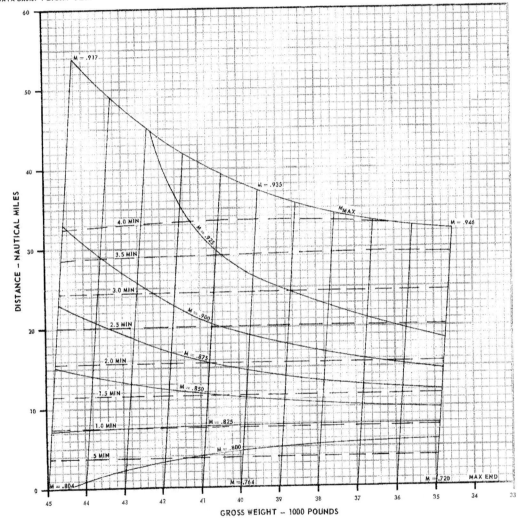

FDB–1–(247)

Figure 11-138

MILITARY THRUST ACCELERATION
15,000 FEET
REMARKS

AIRPLANE CONFIGURATION
(4) AIM-7 AND (1) ₵ TANK
OR
(4) AIM-7 AND (2) WING TANKS
OR
(4) AIM-7 AND (4) AIM-9

ENGINE(S): (2) J79-GE-8
ICAO STANDARD DAY

GUIDE

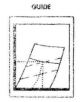

DATE: 15 MAY 1968
DATA BASIS: **FLIGHT TEST**

FUEL GRADE: JP-5
FUEL DENSITY: 6.8 LB/GAL

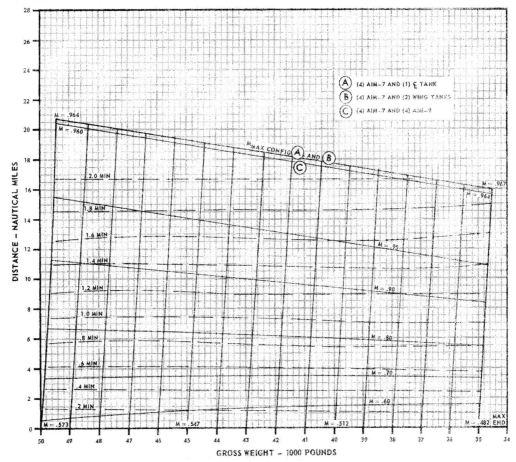

Ⓐ (4) AIM-7 AND (1) ₵ TANK
Ⓑ (4) AIM-7 AND (2) WING TANKS
Ⓒ (4) AIM-7 AND (4) AIM-9

FDB-1-(248)

Figure 11-139

MILITARY THRUST ACCELERATION
25,000 FEET

AIRPLANE CONFIGURATION
(4) AIM–7 AND (1) ₵ TANK
OR
(4) AIM–7 AND (2) WING TANKS
OR
(4) AIM–7 AND (4) AIM–9

REMARKS
ENGINE(S): (2) J79–GE–8
ICAO STANDARD DAY

GUIDE

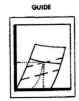

FUEL GRADE: JP–5
FUEL DENSITY: 6.8 LB/GAL

DATE: 15 MAY 1968
DATA BASIS: FLIGHT TEST

Ⓐ (4) AIM–7 AND (1) ₵ TANK
Ⓑ (4) AIM–7 AND (2) WING TANKS
Ⓒ (4) AIM–7 AND (4) AIM–9

DISTANCE – NAUTICAL MILES

GROSS WEIGHT – 1000 POUNDS

FDB–1–(249)

Figure 11-140

MILITARY THRUST ACCELERATION
35,000 FEET

AIRPLANE CONFIGURATION
(4) AIM-7 AND (1) ℄ TANK
OR
(4) AIM-7 AND (2) WING TANKS
OR
(4) AIM-7 AND (4) AIM 9

REMARKS
ENGINE(S): (2) J79-GE-8
ICAO STANDARD DAY

GUIDE

DATE: 15 MAY 1968
DATA BASIS: FLIGHT TEST

FUEL GRADE: JP-5
FUEL DENSITY: 6.8 LB/GAL

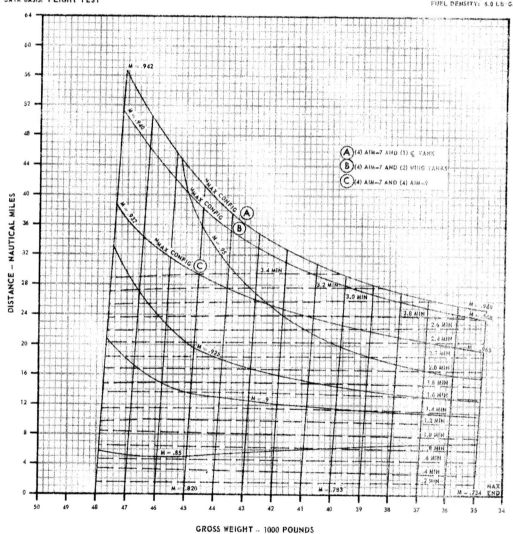

Figure 11-141

FDB-1-(250)

11-177

MILITARY THRUST ACCELERATION
15,000 FEET
REMARKS

AIRPLANE CONFIGURATION
(4) AIM-7, (4) AIM-9 AND (1) ₵ TANK
OR
(4) AIM-7, (4) AIM-9 AND (2) WING TANKS
OR
(4) AIM-7, (1) ₵ TANK AND (2) WING TANKS

ENGINE(S): (2) J79-GE-8
ICAO STANDARD DAY

GUIDE

FUEL GRADE: JP-5
FUEL DENSITY: 6.8 LB/GAL

DATE: 15 MAY 1968
DATA BASIS: **FLIGHT TEST**

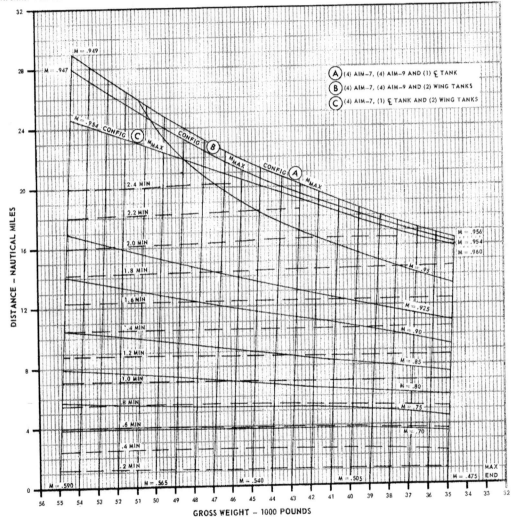

Ⓐ (4) AIM-7, (4) AIM-9 AND (1) ₵ TANK
Ⓑ (4) AIM-7, (4) AIM-9 AND (2) WING TANKS
Ⓒ (4) AIM-7, (1) ₵ TANK AND (2) WING TANKS

GROSS WEIGHT – 1000 POUNDS

DISTANCE – NAUTICAL MILES

FDB–1–(251)

Figure 11-142

MILITARY THRUST ACCELERATION
25,000 FEET
REMARKS

AIRPLANE CONFIGURATION
(4) AIM-7, (4) AIM-9 AND (1) ℄ TANK
OR
(4) AIM-7, (4) AIM-9 AND (2) WING TANKS
OR
(4) AIM-7, (1) ℄ TANK AND (2) WING TANKS

ENGINE(S): (2) J79-GE-8
ICAO STANDARD DAY

GUIDE

FUEL GRADE: JP-5
FUEL DENSITY: 6.8 LB/GAL.

DATE: 15 MAY 1968
DATA BASIS: FLIGHT TEST

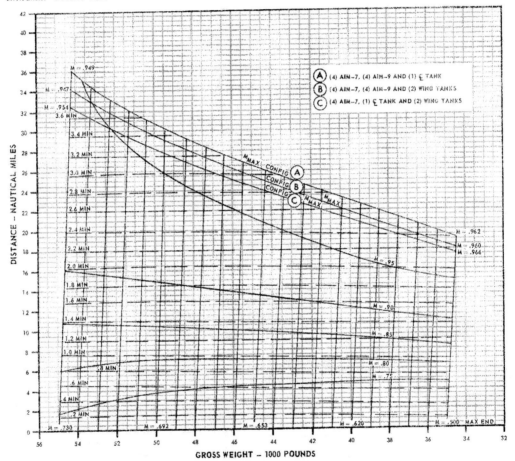

(A) (4) AIM-7, (4) AIM-9 AND (1) ℄ TANK
(B) (4) AIM-7, (4) AIM-9 AND (2) WING TANKS
(C) (4) AIM-7, (1) ℄ TANK AND (2) WING TANKS

FDB-1-(252)

Figure 11-143

MILITARY THRUST ACCELERATION
35,000 FEET

AIRPLANE CONFIGURATION
(4) AIM-7, (4) AIM-9 AND (1) ₡ TANK
OR
(4) AIM-7, (4) AIM-9 AND (2) WING TANKS
OR
(4) AIM-7, (1) ₡ TANK AND (2) WING TANKS

REMARKS
ENGINE(S): (2) J79-GE-8
ICAO STANDARD DAY

GUIDE

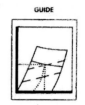

DATE: 15 MAY 1968
DATA BASIS: FLIGHT TEST

FUEL GRADE: JP-5
FUEL DENSITY: 6.8 LB/GAL

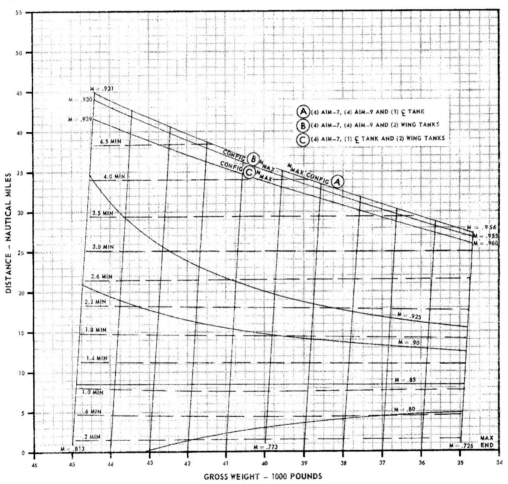

(A) (4) AIM-7, (4) AIM-9 AND (1) ₡ TANK
(B) (4) AIM-7, (4) AIM-9 AND (2) WING TANKS
(C) (4) AIM-7, (1) ₡ TANK AND (2) WING TANKS

GROSS WEIGHT - 1000 POUNDS

DISTANCE - NAUTICAL MILES

FDB-1-(253)

Figure 11-144

IDLE THRUST DECELERATION
MINIMUM TIME
35,000 FEET

AIRPLANE CONFIGURATION
(4) AIM-7,
SPEED BRAKES EXTENDED

REMARKS
ENGINE(S): (2) J79-GE-8
ICAO STANDARD DAY

GUIDE

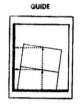

DATE: 15 MAY 1968
DATA BASIS: FLIGHT TEST

FUEL GRADE: JP-5
FUEL DENSITY: 6.8 LB/GAL

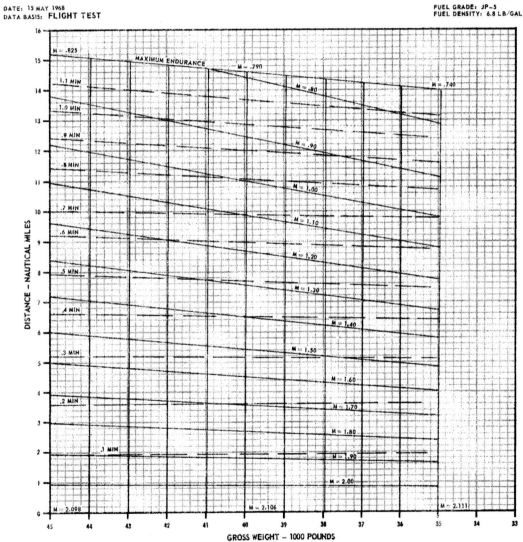

FDB-1-(254)

Figure 11-145

IDLE THRUST DECELERATION
MINIMUM TIME
40,000 FEET

AIRPLANE CONFIGURATION
(4) AIM-7,
SPEED BRAKES EXTENDED

REMARKS
ENGINE(S)-(2) J79-GE-8
ICAO STANDARD DAY

GUIDE

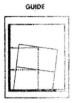

DATE: 15 MAY 1968
DATA BASIS: FLIGHT TEST

FUEL GRADE: JP-5
FUEL DENSITY: 6.8 LB/GAL

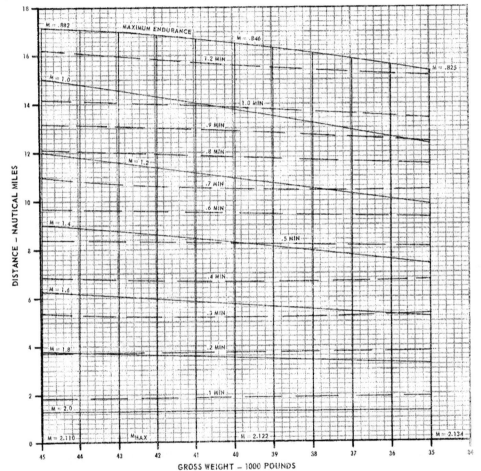

FDB--1--(255)

Figure 11-146

IDLE THRUST DECELERATION
MINIMUM TIME
45,000 FEET

AIRPLANE CONFIGURATION
(4) AIM-7
SPEED BRAKES EXTENDED

REMARKS
ENGINE(S): (2) J79-GE-8
ICAO STANDARD DAY

GUIDE

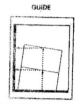

DATE: 15 MAY 1968
DATA BASIS: FLIGHT TEST

FUEL GRADE: JP-5
FUEL DENSITY: 6.8 LB/GAL

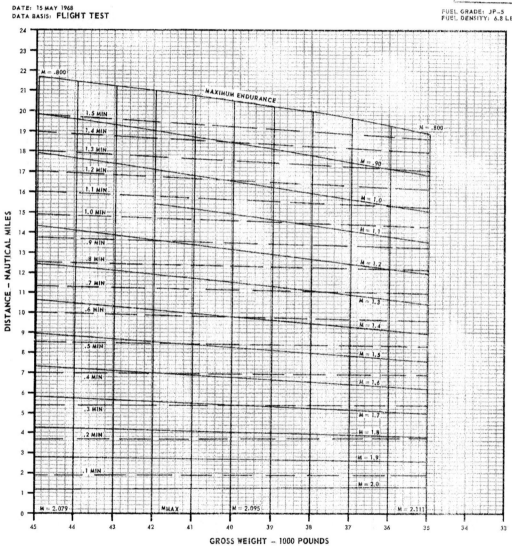

GROSS WEIGHT – 1000 POUNDS

FDB-1-(256)

Figure 11-147

IDLE THRUST DECELERATION
MINIMUM TIME
50,000 FEET

AIRPLANE CONFIGURATION
(4) AIM-7
SPEED BRAKES EXTENDED

REMARKS
ENGINES (S) : (2) J79-GE-8
ICAO STANDARD DAY

GUIDE

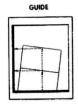

FUEL GRADE: JP-5
FUEL DENSITY: 6.8 LB/GAL

DATE: 15 MAY 1968
DATA BASIS: FLIGHT TEST

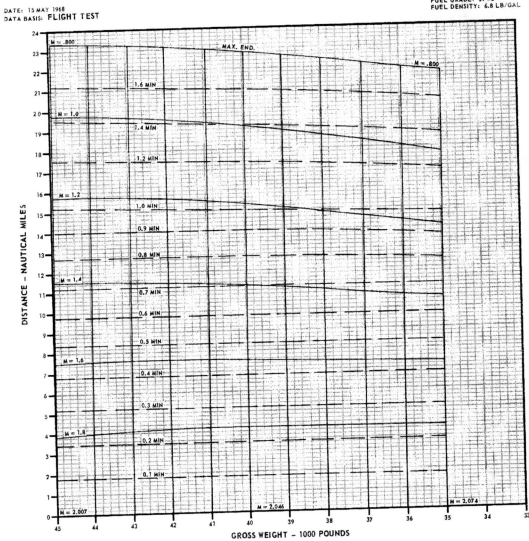

FDB-1-(257)

Figure 11-148

LEVEL FLIGHT ENVELOPE

CONFIGURATION: (4) AIM-7

ENGINE(S): (2) J79-GE-8
ICAO STANDARD DAY

DATE: 15 MAY 1968
DATA BASIS: FLIGHT TEST

FUEL GRADE: JP-5
FUEL DENSITY: 6.8 LB/GAL

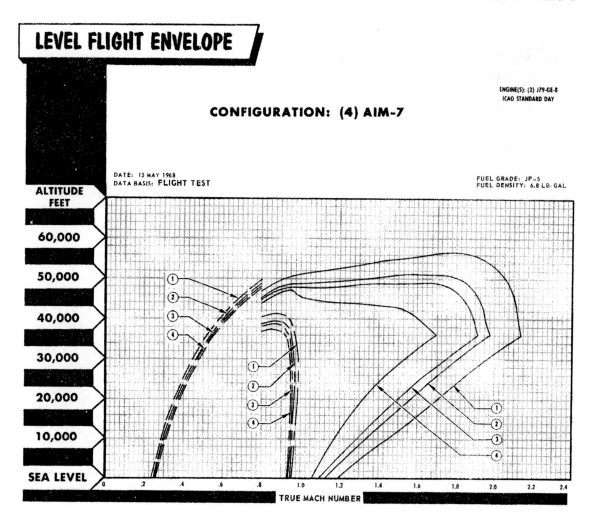

CURVE NO.	CONFIGURATION	GROSS WEIGHT
1	(4) AIM-7	38,942 LBS
2	(4) AIM-7, AND (1) ₵ TANK	41,690 LBS
3	(4) AIM-7, AND (2) WING TANKS	42,641 LBS
4	(4) AIM-7, (1) ₵ TANK, AND (2) WING TANK	45,324 LBS

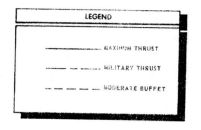

LEGEND
———————— MAXIMUM THRUST
— — — — MILITARY THRUST
— — — — MODERATE BUFFET

FDB-1-(258)

Figure 11-149

LEVEL FLIGHT ENVELOPE

ENGINE(S): (2) J79-GE-8
ICAO STANDARD DAY

CONFIGURATION: (4) AIM-7 AND (4) AIM-9

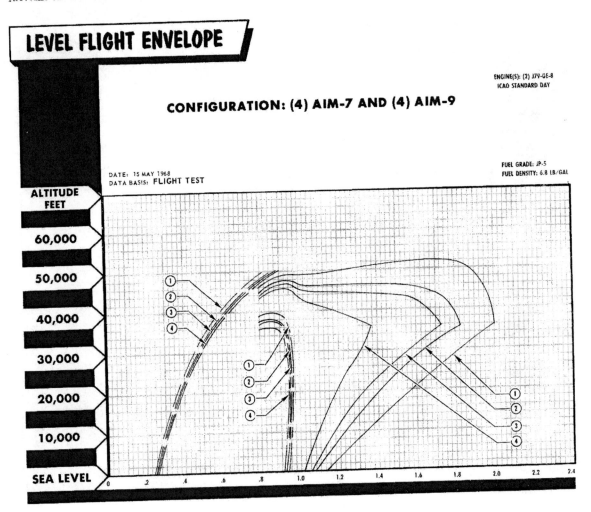

DATE: 15 MAY 1968
DATA BASIS: FLIGHT TEST

FUEL GRADE: JP-5
FUEL DENSITY: 6.8 LB/GAL

CURVE NO.	CONFIGURATION	GROSS WEIGHT
1	(4) AIM-7 AND (4) AIM-9	40,350 LBS
2	(4) AIM-7, (4) AIM-9 AND (1) ₵ TANK	43,098 LBS
3	(4) AIM-7, (4) AIM-9 AND (2) ₵ TANKS	44,049 LBS
4	(4) AIM-7, (4) AIM-9, (1) ₵ TANK AND (2) WING TANKS	46,732 LBS

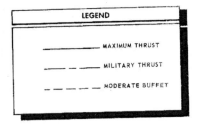

LEGEND	
————————	MAXIMUM THRUST
— — — —	MILITARY THRUST
– – – –	MODERATE BUFFET

FDB-1-(259)

Figure 11-150

TEMPERATURE EFFECT ON MAXIMUM SPEED
MAXIMUM THRUST

AIRPLANE CONFIGURATION
ALL DRAG INDEXES

REMARKS
ENGINE(S):(2) J79-GE-8

GUIDE

DATE: 15 OCTOBER 1967
DATA BASIS: FLIGHT TEST

FUEL GRADE: JP-5
FUEL DENSITY: 6.8 LB/GAL

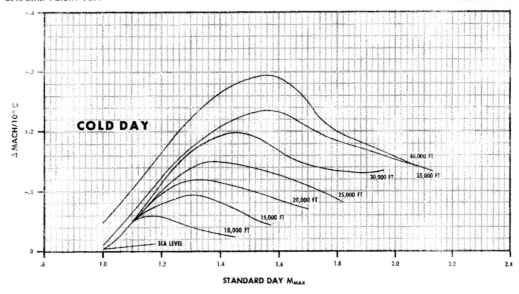

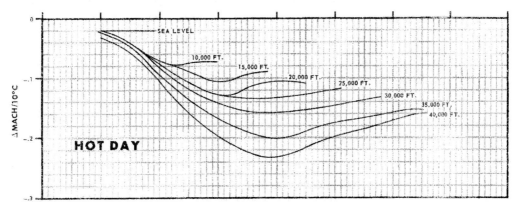

FDB-1-(260)

Figure 11-151

11-187

DIVE RECOVERY-4G
SUBSONIC-SPEED BRAKES RETRACTED
GROSS WEIGHT 40,000 POUNDS

AIRPLANE CONFIGURATION

CLEAN

REMARKS

ENGINE(S): (2) J79-GE—8

ICAO STANDARD DAY

NOTES

1. ALTITUDE LOSS WITH MAXIMUM THRUST IS ESSENTIALLY THE SAME AS WITH MILITARY THRUST.
2. MILITARY THRUST PULL-OUT BASED ON 1.0 "G" PER SECOND ACCELERATION BUILD-UP TO 4.0 "G's" OR MODERATE BUFFET WHICHEVER OCCURS FIRST.

GUIDE

DATE: 1 MAY 1968
DATA BASIS: FLIGHT TEST

FUEL GRADE: JP-5
FUEL DENSITY: 6.8 LB/GAL

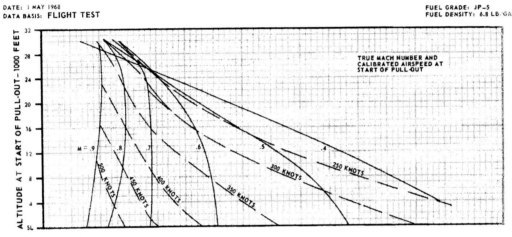

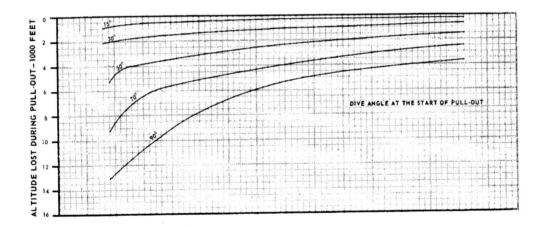

FDB-1-(261)

Figure 11-152

DIVE RECOVERY-6G
SUBSONIC-SPEED BRAKES RETRACTED
GROSS WEIGHT 40,000 POUNDS

AIRPLANE CONFIGURATION

CLEAN

REMARKS

ENGINE(S): (2) J79-GE-8
ICAO STANDARD DAY

NOTES

1. ALTITUDE LOSS WITH MAXIMUM THRUST IS ESSENTIALLY THE SAME AS WITH MILITARY THRUST.
2. MILITARY THRUST PULL-OUT BASED ON 1.0 "G" PER SECOND ACCELERATION BUILD-UP TO MODERATE BUFFET OR 6.0 "G" WHICHEVER OCCURS FIRST.

DATE: 1 MAY 1968
DATA BASIS: FLIGHT TEST

GUIDE

FUEL GRADE: JP-5
FUEL DENSITY: 6.8 LB/GAL

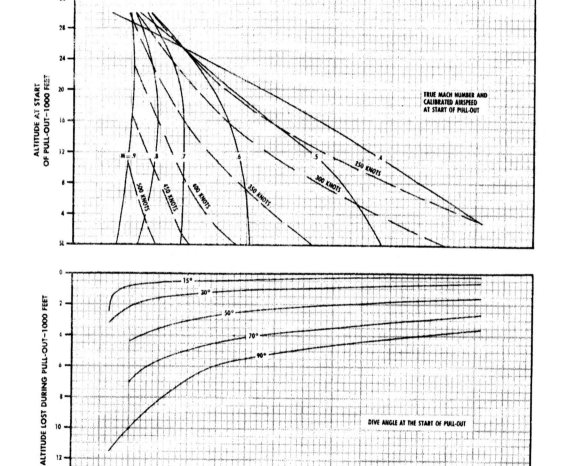

Figure 11-153

FDB-1-(262)

DIVE RECOVERY-4 G
SUPERSONIC-SPEED BRAKES RETRACTED

AIRPLANE CONFIGURATION
(4) AIM-7

GROSS WEIGHT 40,000 POUNDS

REMARKS
ENGINE(S): (2) J79-GE-10
ICAO STANDARD DAY

GUIDE

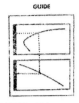

NOTES

1. ALTITUDE LOSS WITH MAXIMUM THRUST IS ESSENTIALLY THE SAME AS WITH MILITARY THRUST.
2. MILITARY THRUST PULL-OUT BASED ON 1.0 "G" PER SECOND ACCELERATION BUILD-UP TO 4.0 "G's" OR MODERATE BUFFET WHICHEVER OCCURS FIRST.

DATE: 1 MAY 1968
DATA BASIS: ESTIMATED (BASED ON FLIGHT TEST)

FUEL GRADE: JP-5
FUEL DENSITY: 6.8 LB/GAL

AIRPLANES 153088aa AND UP

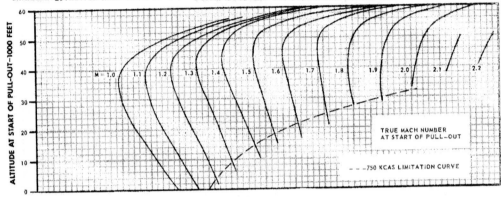

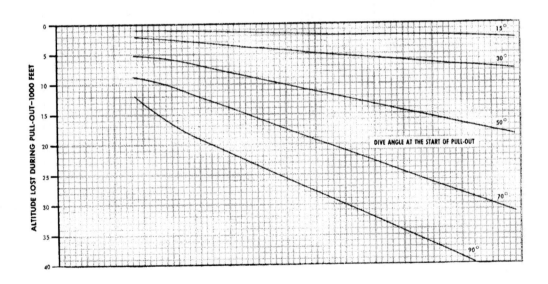

FDB-1-(263)

Figure 11-154

DIVE RECOVERY-6 G
SUPERSONIC-SPEED BRAKES RETRACTED

AIRPLANE CONFIGURATION

CLEAN

GROSS WEIGHT 40,000 POUNDS

REMARKS

ENGINE(S): (2) J79-GE-10
ICAO STANDARD DAY

NOTES

1. ALTITUDE LOSS WITH MAXIMUM THRUST IS ESSENTIALLY THE SAME AS WITH MILITARY THRUST.
2. MILITARY THRUST PULL-OUT BASED ON 1.0 "G" PER SECOND ACCELERATION BUILD-UP TO MODERATE BUFFET OR 6.0 "G's" WHICHEVER OCCURS FIRST.

DATE: 1 MAY 1968
DATA BASIS: **FLIGHT TEST**

GUIDE

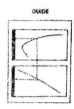

FUEL GRADE: JP-5
FUEL DENSITY: 6.8 LB/GAL

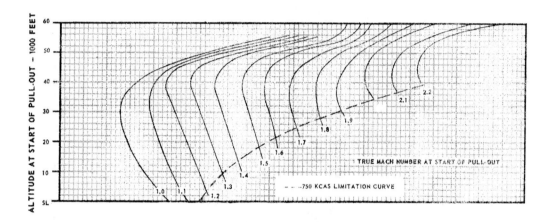

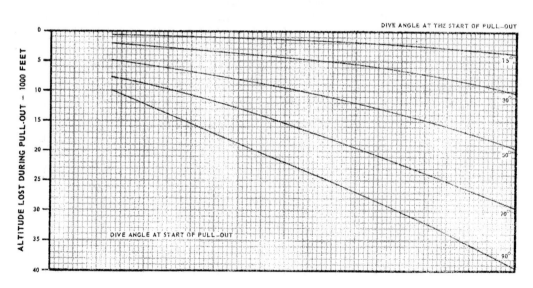

FDB-1-(264)

Figure 11-155

SYMMETRICAL FLIGHT V-N DIAGRAM
ALTITUDE SEA LEVEL
GROSS WEIGHT 37,500 POUNDS
REMARKS

AIRPLANE CONFIGURATION

CLEAN

ENGINE(S): (2) J79-GE-8
ICAO STANDARD DAY

GUIDE

DATE: 1 MAY 1968
DATA BASIS: ESTIMATED (BASED ON FLIGHT TEST)

FUEL GRADE: JP-5
FUEL DENSITY: 6.8 LB/GAL

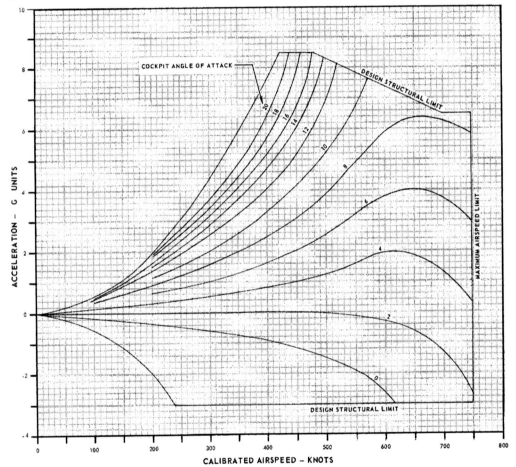

FDB-1-(265)

Figure 11-156

SYMMETRICAL FLIGHT V-N DIAGRAM
ALTITUDE 20,000 FEET
GROSS WEIGHT 37,500 POUNDS

AIRPLANE CONFIGURATION

CLEAN

REMARKS
ENGINE(S): (2) J79-GE-8
ICAO STANDARD DAY

GUIDE

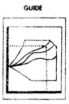

DATE: 1 MAY 1968
DATA BASIS: FLIGHT TEST

FUEL GRADE: JP-5
FUEL DENSITY: 6.8 LB/GAL

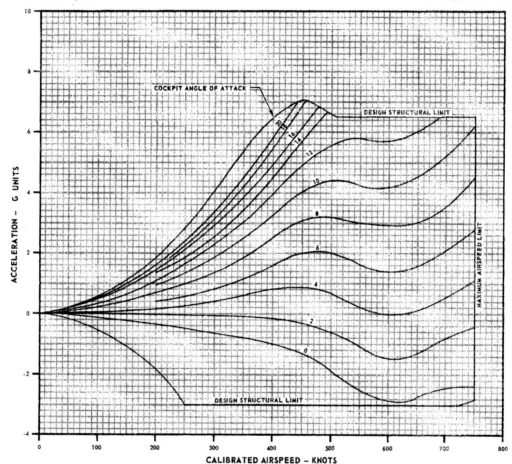

FDB-1-(266)

Figure 11-157

SYMMETRICAL FLIGHT V-N DIAGRAM
ALTITUDE 30,000 FEET
GROSS WEIGHT 37,500 POUNDS

AIRPLANE CONFIGURATION

CLEAN

REMARKS

ENGINE(S): (2) J79-GE-8
ICAO STANDARD DAY

GUIDE

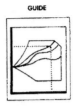

DATE: 1 MAY 1968
DATA BASIS: FLIGHT TEST

FUEL GRADE: JP-5
FUEL DENSITY: 6.8 LB./GAL.

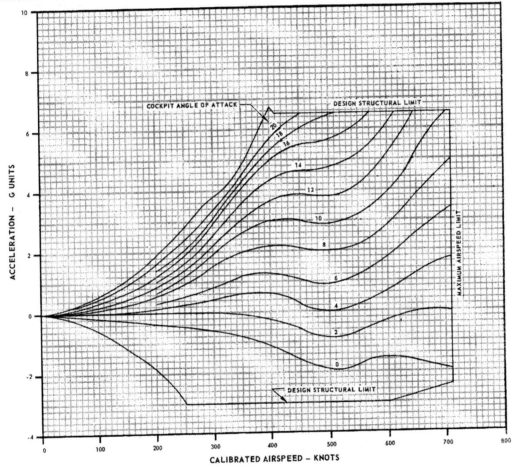

FDB-1-(267)

Figure 11-158

SYMMETRICAL FLIGHT V-N DIAGRAM
ALTITUDE 40,000 FEET
GROSS WEIGHT 37,500 POUNDS

AIRPLANE CONFIGURATION

CLEAN

REMARKS
ENGINE(S): (2) J79-GE-8
ICAO STANDARD DAY

GUIDE

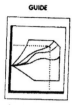

DATE: 1 MAY 1968
DATA BASIS: FLIGHT TEST

FUEL GRADE: JP-5
FUEL DENSITY: 6.8 LB/GAL

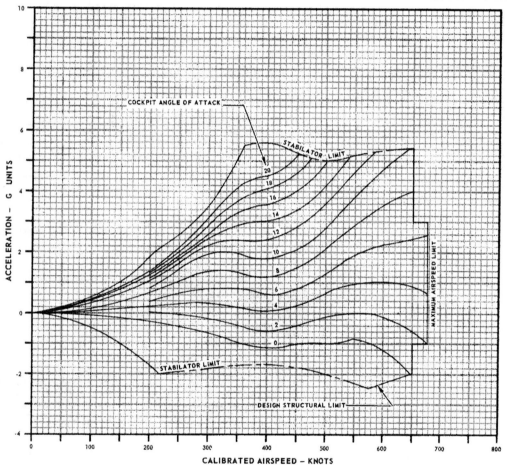

FDB-1-(268)

Figure 11-159

TURN CAPABILITIES
CONSTANT SPEED AND ALTITUDE

GUIDE

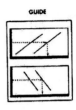

RADIUS OF TURN

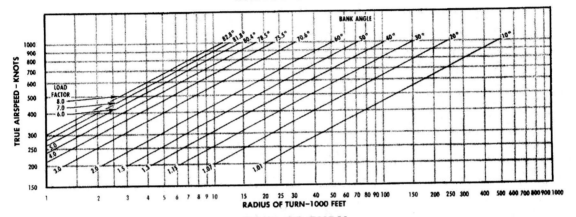

RATE OF TURN

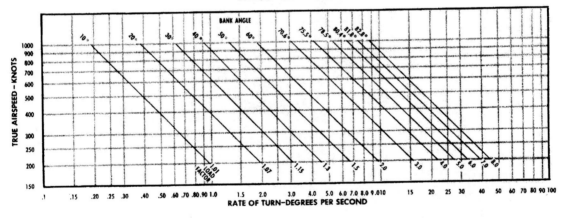

FDB-1-(269)

Figure 11-160

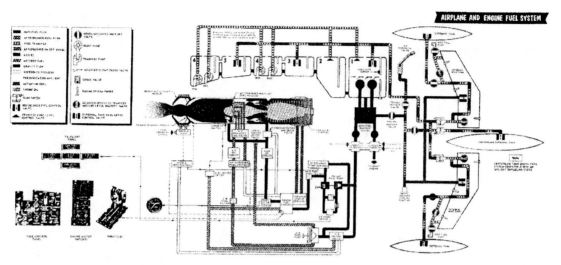

AIRPLANE AND ENGINE FUEL SYSTEM

FDB-1-(270)

APPENDIX A
FOLDOUT ILLUSTRATIONS

TABLE OF CONTENTS

GENERAL

The illustrations listed in the table of contents have been removed from section I, parts 1 and 2, redesigned, and reinserted into this newly created section. These illustrations in some cases have been combined and in all cases have been made into foldout pages.

The purpose behind this change in Flight Manual Format is to make the subject illustrations always available for quick and ready reference while reading the associated text. The subject illustrations are referenced from several sections throughout the manual and are referred to, within the text, as (figure A- , appendix A).

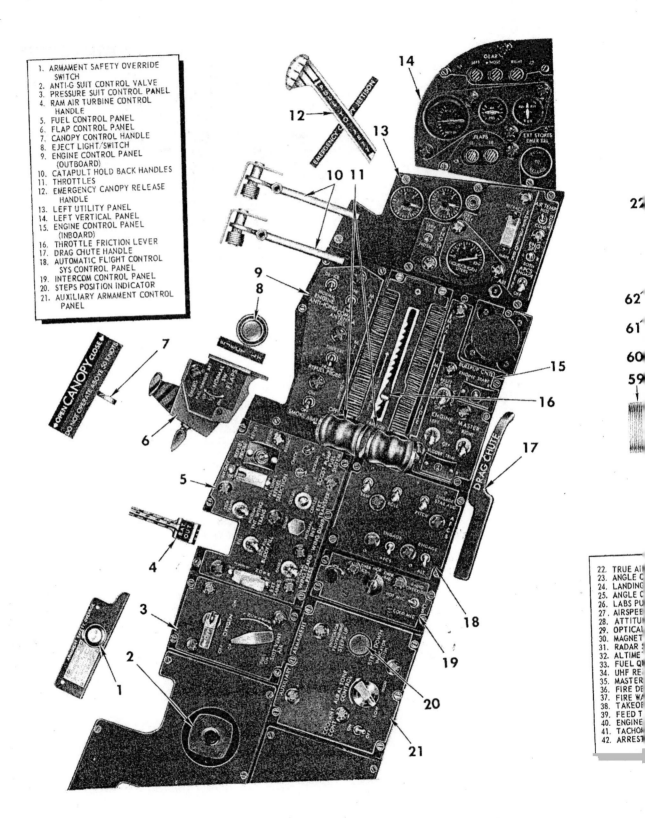

1. ARMAMENT SAFETY OVERRIDE SWITCH
2. ANTI-G SUIT CONTROL VALVE
3. PRESSURE SUIT CONTROL PANEL
4. RAM AIR TURBINE CONTROL HANDLE
5. FUEL CONTROL PANEL
6. FLAP CONTROL PANEL
7. CANOPY CONTROL HANDLE
8. EJECT LIGHT/SWITCH
9. ENGINE CONTROL PANEL (OUTBOARD)
10. CATAPULT HOLD BACK HANDLES
11. THROTTLES
12. EMERGENCY CANOPY RELEASE HANDLE
13. LEFT UTILITY PANEL
14. LEFT VERTICAL PANEL
15. ENGINE CONTROL PANEL (INBOARD)
16. THROTTLE FRICTION LEVER
17. DRAG CHUTE HANDLE
18. AUTOMATIC FLIGHT CONTROL SYS CONTROL PANEL
19. INTERCOM CONTROL PANEL
20. STEPS POSITION INDICATOR
21. AUXILIARY ARMAMENT CONTROL PANEL

22. TRUE AI
23. ANGLE C
24. LANDING
25. ANGLE C
26. LABS PU
27. AIRSPEE
28. ATTITU
29. OPTICAL
30. MAGNET
31. RADAR
32. ALTIME
33. FUEL QU
34. UHF RE
35. MASTER
36. FIRE DE
37. FIRE WA
38. TAKEOF
39. FEED T
40. ENGINE
41. TACHO
42. ARREST

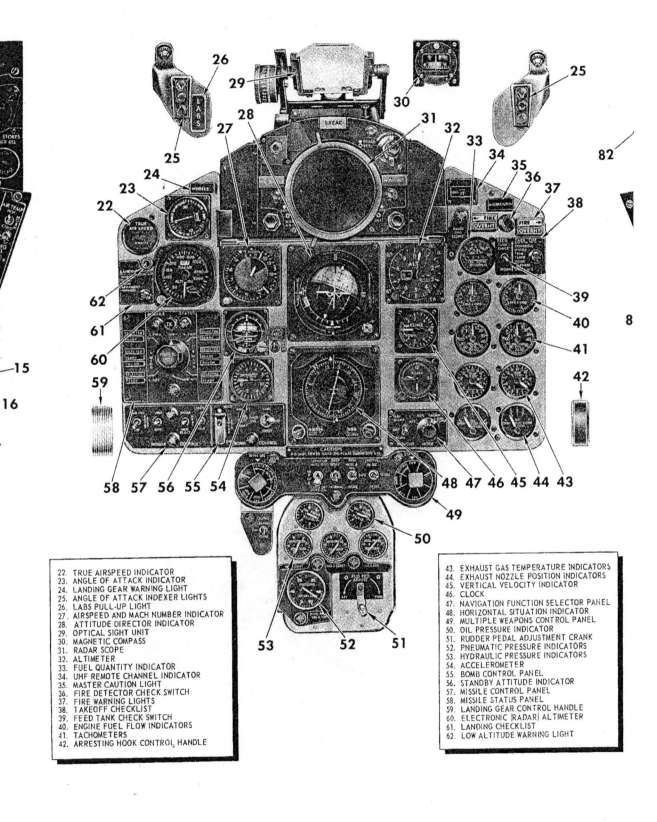

22. TRUE AIRSPEED INDICATOR
23. ANGLE OF ATTACK INDICATOR
24. LANDING GEAR WARNING LIGHT
25. ANGLE OF ATTACK INDEXER LIGHTS
26. LABS PULL-UP LIGHT
27. AIRSPEED AND MACH NUMBER INDICATOR
28. ATTITUDE DIRECTOR INDICATOR
29. OPTICAL SIGHT UNIT
30. MAGNETIC COMPASS
31. RADAR SCOPE
32. ALTIMETER
33. FUEL QUANTITY INDICATOR
34. UHF REMOTE CHANNEL INDICATOR
35. MASTER CAUTION LIGHT
36. FIRE DETECTOR CHECK SWITCH
37. FIRE WARNING LIGHTS
38. TAKEOFF CHECKLIST
39. FEED TANK CHECK SWITCH
40. ENGINE FUEL FLOW INDICATORS
41. TACHOMETERS
42. ARRESTING HOOK CONTROL HANDLE

43. EXHAUST GAS TEMPERATURE INDICATORS
44. EXHAUST NOZZLE POSITION INDICATORS
45. VERTICAL VELOCITY INDICATOR
46. CLOCK
47. NAVIGATION FUNCTION SELECTOR PANEL
48. HORIZONTAL SITUATION INDICATOR
49. MULTIPLE WEAPONS CONTROL PANEL
50. OIL PRESSURE INDICATOR
51. RUDDER PEDAL ADJUSTMENT CRANK
52. PNEUMATIC PRESSURE INDICATORS
53. HYDRAULIC PRESSURE INDICATORS
54. ACCELEROMETER
55. BOMB CONTROL PANEL
56. STANDBY ATTITUDE INDICATOR
57. MISSILE CONTROL PANEL
58. MISSILE STATUS PANEL
59. LANDING GEAR CONTROL HANDLE
60. ELECTRONIC (RADAR) ALTIMETER
61. LANDING CHECKLIST
62. LOW ALTITUDE WARNING LIGHT

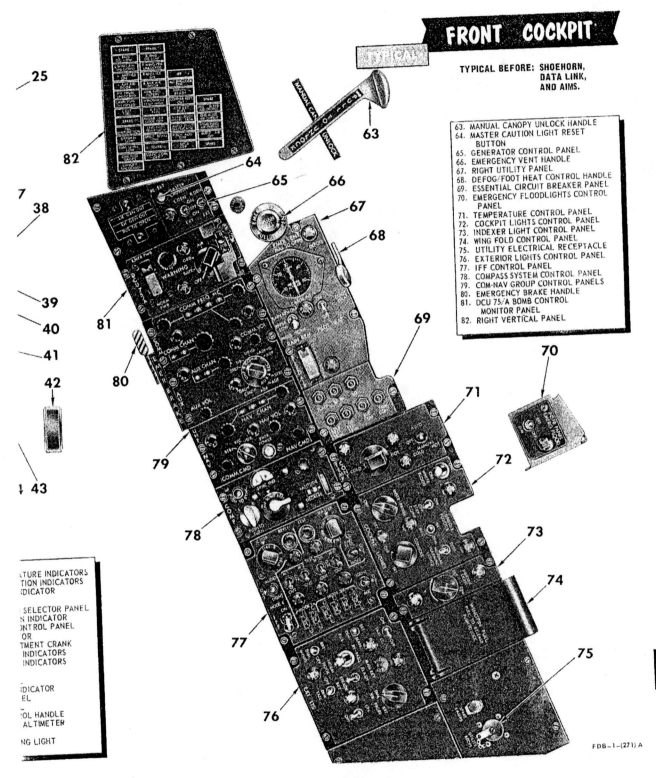

FRONT COCKPIT

TYPICAL BEFORE: SHOEHORN,
DATA LINK,
AND AIMS.

63. MANUAL CANOPY UNLOCK HANDLE
64. MASTER CAUTION LIGHT RESET
    BUTTON
65. GENERATOR CONTROL PANEL
66. EMERGENCY VENT HANDLE
67. RIGHT UTILITY PANEL
68. DEFOG/FOOT HEAT CONTROL HANDLE
69. ESSENTIAL CIRCUIT BREAKER PANEL
70. EMERGENCY FLOODLIGHTS CONTROL
    PANEL
71. TEMPERATURE CONTROL PANEL
72. COCKPIT LIGHTS CONTROL PANEL
73. INDEXER LIGHT CONTROL PANEL
74. WING FOLD CONTROL PANEL
75. UTILITY ELECTRICAL RECEPTACLE
76. EXTERIOR LIGHTS CONTROL PANEL
77. IFF CONTROL PANEL
78. COMPASS SYSTEM CONTROL PANEL
79. COM-NAV GROUP CONTROL PANELS
80. EMERGENCY BRAKE HANDLE
81. DCU 75/A BOMB CONTROL
    MONITOR PANEL
82. RIGHT VERTICAL PANEL

FDB-1-(271)A

Figure A-1

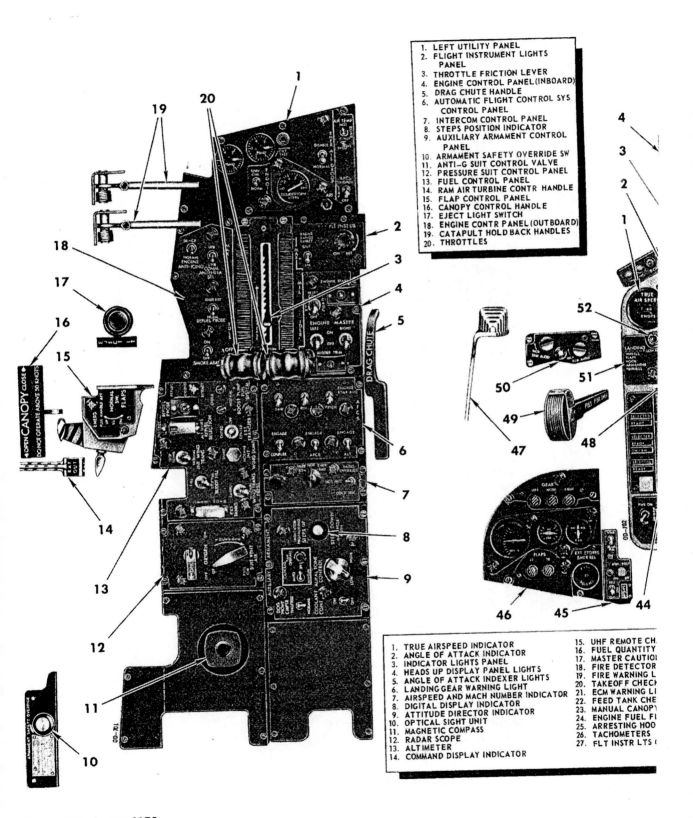

1. LEFT UTILITY PANEL
2. FLIGHT INSTRUMENT LIGHTS PANEL
3. THROTTLE FRICTION LEVER
4. ENGINE CONTROL PANEL (INBOARD)
5. DRAG CHUTE HANDLE
6. AUTOMATIC FLIGHT CONTROL SYS CONTROL PANEL
7. INTERCOM CONTROL PANEL
8. STEPS POSITION INDICATOR
9. AUXILIARY ARMAMENT CONTROL PANEL
10. ARMAMENT SAFETY OVERRIDE SW
11. ANTI-G SUIT CONTROL VALVE
12. PRESSURE SUIT CONTROL PANEL
13. FUEL CONTROL PANEL
14. RAM AIR TURBINE CONTR HANDLE
15. FLAP CONTROL PANEL
16. CANOPY CONTROL HANDLE
17. EJECT LIGHT SWITCH
18. ENGINE CONTR PANEL (OUTBOARD)
19. CATAPULT HOLD BACK HANDLES
20. THROTTLES

1. TRUE AIRSPEED INDICATOR
2. ANGLE OF ATTACK INDICATOR
3. INDICATOR LIGHTS PANEL
4. HEADS UP DISPLAY PANEL LIGHTS
5. ANGLE OF ATTACK INDEXER LIGHTS
6. LANDING GEAR WARNING LIGHT
7. AIRSPEED AND MACH NUMBER INDICATOR
8. DIGITAL DISPLAY INDICATOR
9. ATTITUDE DIRECTOR INDICATOR
10. OPTICAL SIGHT UNIT
11. MAGNETIC COMPASS
12. RADAR SCOPE
13. ALTIMETER
14. COMMAND DISPLAY INDICATOR
15. UHF REMOTE CH.
16. FUEL QUANTITY
17. MASTER CAUTION
18. FIRE DETECTOR
19. FIRE WARNING L
20. TAKEOFF CHECK
21. ECM WARNING LI
22. FEED TANK CHE
23. MANUAL CANOPY
24. ENGINE FUEL FI
25. ARRESTING HOO
26. TACHOMETERS
27. FLT INSTR LTS (

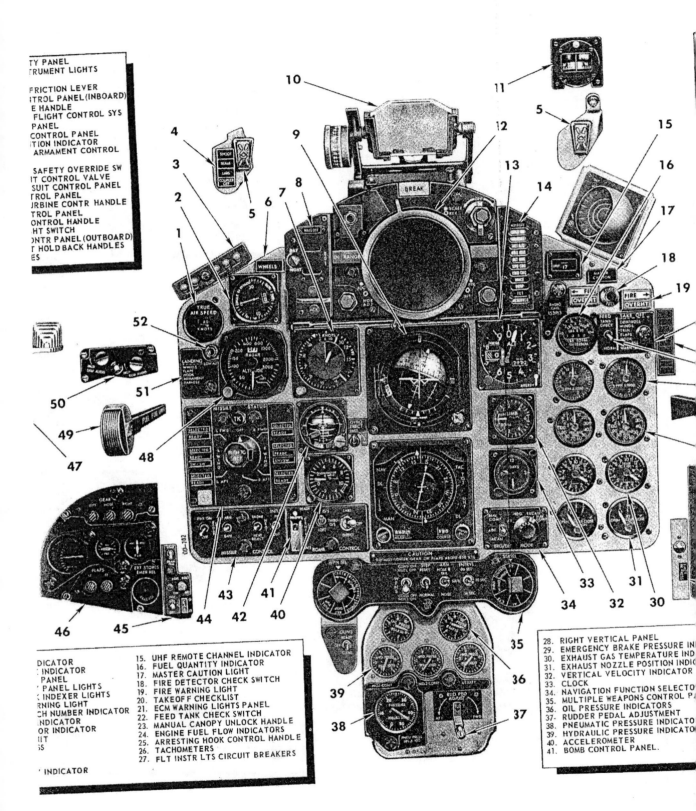

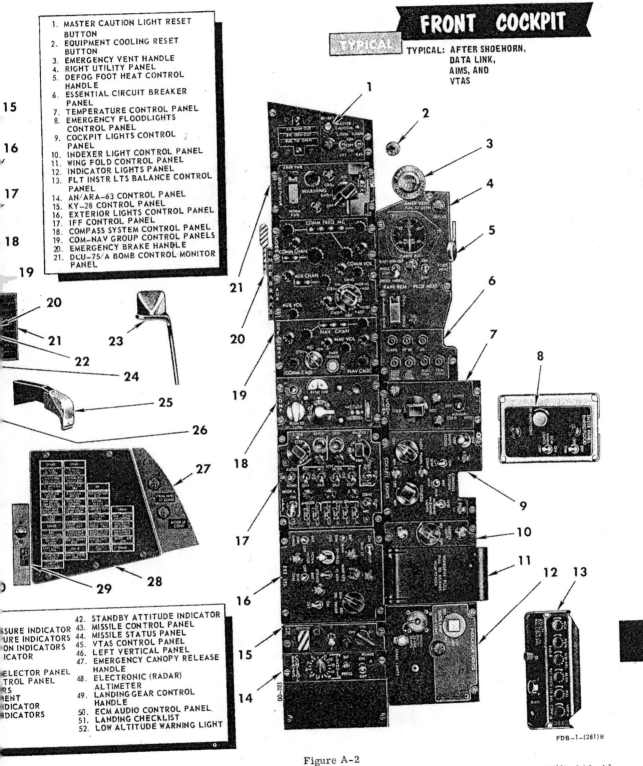

FRONT COCKPIT

TYPICAL

TYPICAL: AFTER SHOEHORN,
DATA LINK,
AIMS, AND
VTAS

1. MASTER CAUTION LIGHT RESET BUTTON
2. EQUIPMENT COOLING RESET BUTTON
3. EMERGENCY VENT HANDLE
4. RIGHT UTILITY PANEL
5. DEFOG FOOT HEAT CONTROL HANDLE
6. ESSENTIAL CIRCUIT BREAKER PANEL
7. TEMPERATURE CONTROL PANEL
8. EMERGENCY FLOODLIGHTS CONTROL PANEL
9. COCKPIT LIGHTS CONTROL PANEL
10. INDEXER LIGHT CONTROL PANEL
11. WING FOLD CONTROL PANEL
12. INDICATOR LIGHTS PANEL
13. FLT INSTR LTS BALANCE CONTROL PANEL
14. AN/ARA-63 CONTROL PANEL
15. KY-28 CONTROL PANEL
16. EXTERIOR LIGHTS CONTROL PANEL
17. IFF CONTROL PANEL
18. COMPASS SYSTEM CONTROL PANEL
19. COM-NAV GROUP CONTROL PANELS
20. EMERGENCY BRAKE HANDLE
21. DCU-75/A BOMB CONTROL MONITOR PANEL

42. STANDBY ATTITUDE INDICATOR
43. MISSILE CONTROL PANEL
44. MISSILE STATUS PANEL
45. VTAS CONTROL PANEL
46. LEFT VERTICAL PANEL
47. EMERGENCY CANOPY RELEASE HANDLE
48. ELECTRONIC (RADAR) ALTIMETER
49. LANDING GEAR CONTROL HANDLE
50. ECM AUDIO CONTROL PANEL
51. LANDING CHECKLIST
52. LOW ALTITUDE WARNING LIGHT

Figure A-2

FDB-1-(281)B

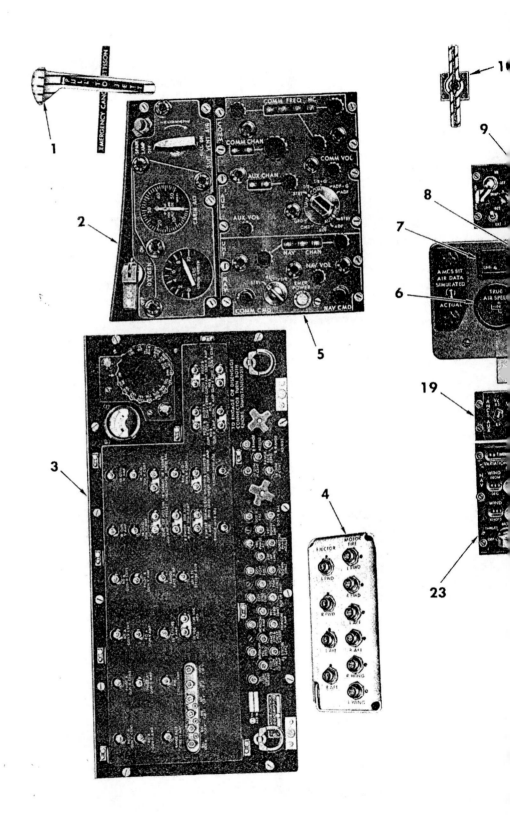

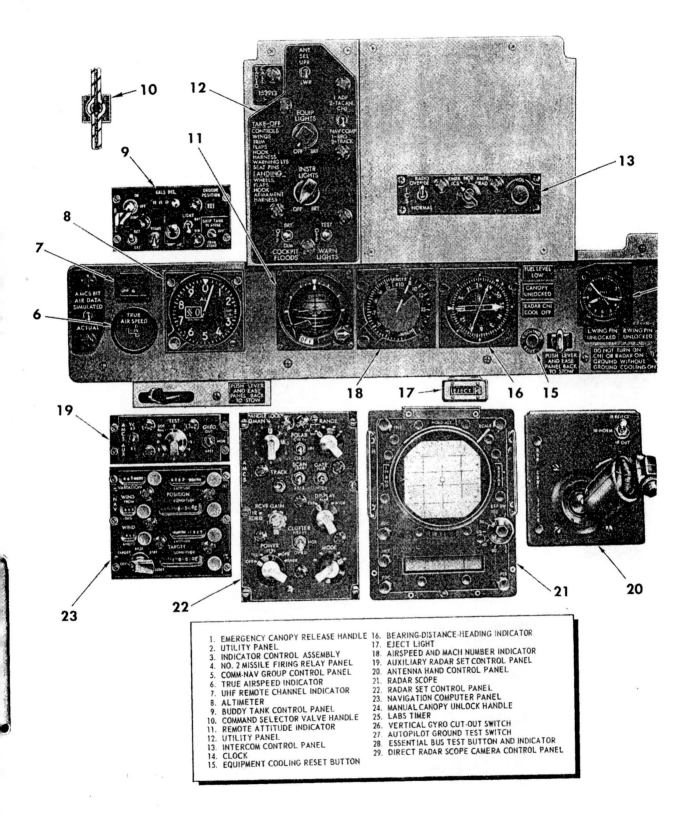

1. EMERGENCY CANOPY RELEASE HANDLE
2. UTILITY PANEL
3. INDICATOR CONTROL ASSEMBLY
4. NO. 2 MISSILE FIRING RELAY PANEL
5. COMM-NAV GROUP CONTROL PANEL
6. TRUE AIRSPEED INDICATOR
7. UHF REMOTE CHANNEL INDICATOR
8. ALTIMETER
9. BUDDY TANK CONTROL PANEL
10. COMMAND SELECTOR VALVE HANDLE
11. REMOTE ATTITUDE INDICATOR
12. UTILITY PANEL
13. INTERCOM CONTROL PANEL
14. CLOCK
15. EQUIPMENT COOLING RESET BUTTON
16. BEARING-DISTANCE-HEADING INDICATOR
17. EJECT LIGHT
18. AIRSPEED AND MACH NUMBER INDICATOR
19. AUXILIARY RADAR SET CONTROL PANEL
20. ANTENNA HAND CONTROL PANEL
21. RADAR SCOPE
22. RADAR SET CONTROL PANEL
23. NAVIGATION COMPUTER PANEL
24. MANUAL CANOPY UNLOCK HANDLE
25. LABS TIMER
26. VERTICAL GYRO CUT-OUT SWITCH
27. AUTOPILOT GROUND TEST SWITCH
28. ESSENTIAL BUS TEST BUTTON AND INDICATOR
29. DIRECT RADAR SCOPE CAMERA CONTROL PANEL

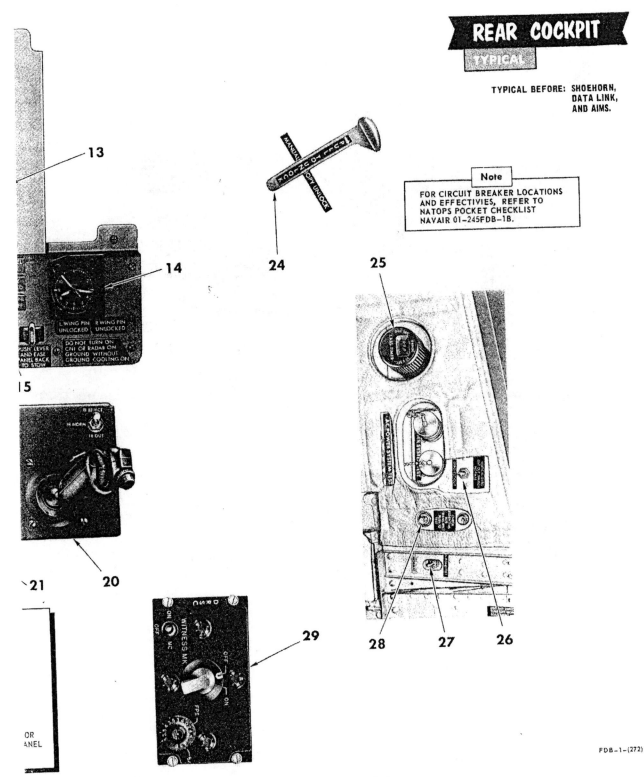

REAR COCKPIT

TYPICAL

TYPICAL BEFORE: SHOEHORN,
DATA LINK,
AND AIMS.

Note

FOR CIRCUIT BREAKER LOCATIONS
AND EFFECTIVES, REFER TO
NATOPS POCKET CHECKLIST
NAVAIR 01-245FDB-1B.

Figure A-3

FDB-1-(272)

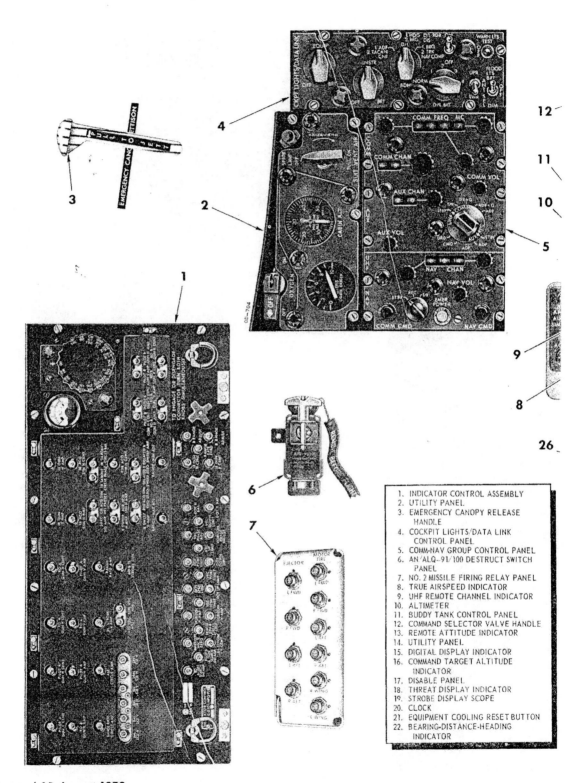

1. INDICATOR CONTROL ASSEMBLY
2. UTILITY PANEL
3. EMERGENCY CANOPY RELEASE HANDLE
4. COCKPIT LIGHTS/DATA LINK CONTROL PANEL
5. COMM-NAV GROUP CONTROL PANEL
6. AN/ALQ-91/100 DESTRUCT SWITCH PANEL
7. NO. 2 MISSILE FIRING RELAY PANEL
8. TRUE AIRSPEED INDICATOR
9. UHF REMOTE CHANNEL INDICATOR
10. ALTIMETER
11. BUDDY TANK CONTROL PANEL
12. COMMAND SELECTOR VALVE HANDLE
13. REMOTE ATTITUDE INDICATOR
14. UTILITY PANEL
15. DIGITAL DISPLAY INDICATOR
16. COMMAND TARGET ALTITUDE INDICATOR
17. DISABLE PANEL
18. THREAT DISPLAY INDICATOR
19. STROBE DISPLAY SCOPE
20. CLOCK
21. EQUIPMENT COOLING RESET BUTTON
22. BEARING-DISTANCE-HEADING INDICATOR

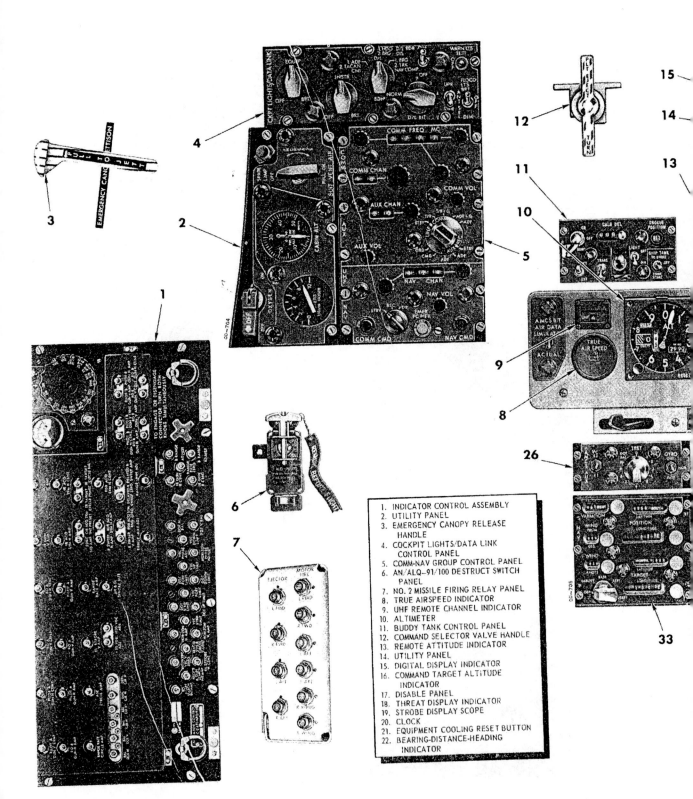

3. EMERGENCY CANOPY RELEASE

1. INDICATOR CONTROL ASSEMBLY
2. UTILITY PANEL
3. EMERGENCY CANOPY RELEASE
   HANDLE
4. COCKPIT LIGHTS/DATA LINK
   CONTROL PANEL
5. COMM-NAV GROUP CONTROL PANEL
6. AN/ALQ-91/100 DESTRUCT SWITCH
   PANEL
7. NO. 2 MISSILE FIRING RELAY PANEL
8. TRUE AIRSPEED INDICATOR
9. UHF REMOTE CHANNEL INDICATOR
10. ALTIMETER
11. BUDDY TANK CONTROL PANEL
12. COMMAND SELECTOR VALVE HANDLE
13. REMOTE ATTITUDE INDICATOR
14. UTILITY PANEL
15. DIGITAL DISPLAY INDICATOR
16. COMMAND TARGET ALTITUDE
    INDICATOR
17. DISABLE PANEL
18. THREAT DISPLAY INDICATOR
19. STROBE DISPLAY SCOPE
20. CLOCK
21. EQUIPMENT COOLING RESET BUTTON
22. BEARING-DISTANCE-HEADING
    INDICATOR

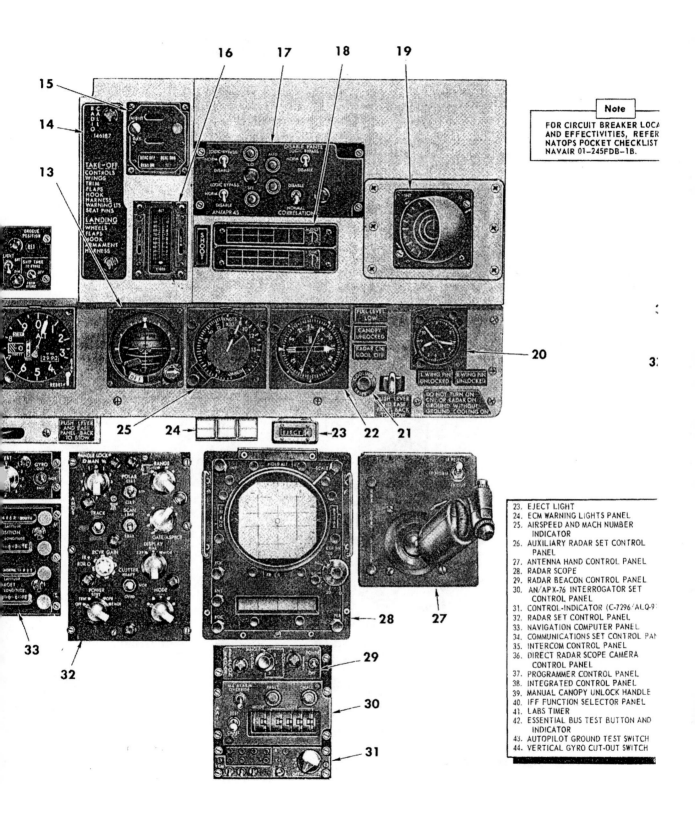

Note

FOR CIRCUIT BREAKER LOCA
AND EFFECTIVITIES, REFER
NATOPS POCKET CHECKLIST
NAVAIR 01-245FDB-1B.

23. EJECT LIGHT
24. ECM WARNING LIGHTS PANEL
25. AIRSPEED AND MACH NUMBER
    INDICATOR
26. AUXILIARY RADAR SET CONTROL
    PANEL
27. ANTENNA HAND CONTROL PANEL
28. RADAR SCOPE
29. RADAR BEACON CONTROL PANEL
30. AN/APX-76 INTERROGATOR SET
    CONTROL PANEL
31. CONTROL-INDICATOR (C-7296/ALQ-9
32. RADAR SET CONTROL PANEL
33. NAVIGATION COMPUTER PANEL
34. COMMUNICATIONS SET CONTROL PAN
35. INTERCOM CONTROL PANEL
36. DIRECT RADAR SCOPE CAMERA
    CONTROL PANEL
37. PROGRAMMER CONTROL PANEL
38. INTEGRATED CONTROL PANEL
39. MANUAL CANOPY UNLOCK HANDLE
40. IFF FUNCTION SELECTOR PANEL
41. LABS TIMER
42. ESSENTIAL BUS TEST BUTTON AND
    INDICATOR
43. AUTOPILOT GROUND TEST SWITCH
44. VERTICAL GYRO CUT-OUT SWITCH

REAR COCKPIT

TYPICAL AFTER: SHOEHORN, DATA LINK, AIMS, AND VTAS

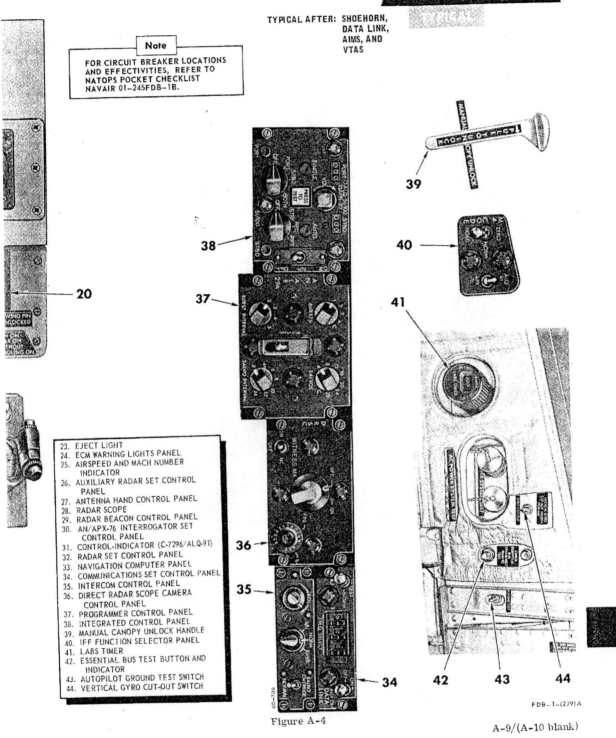

Note

FOR CIRCUIT BREAKER LOCATIONS AND EFFECTIVITIES, REFER TO NATOPS POCKET CHECKLIST NAVAIR 01-245FDB-1B.

20

38

37

39

40

41

23. EJECT LIGHT
24. ECM WARNING LIGHTS PANEL
25. AIRSPEED AND MACH NUMBER INDICATOR
26. AUXILIARY RADAR SET CONTROL PANEL
27. ANTENNA HAND CONTROL PANEL
28. RADAR SCOPE
29. RADAR BEACON CONTROL PANEL
30. AN/APX-76 INTERROGATOR SET CONTROL PANEL
31. CONTROL-INDICATOR (C-7296/ALQ-91)
32. RADAR SET CONTROL PANEL
33. NAVIGATION COMPUTER PANEL
34. COMMUNICATIONS SET CONTROL PANEL
35. INTERCOM CONTROL PANEL
36. DIRECT RADAR SCOPE CAMERA CONTROL PANEL
37. PROGRAMMER CONTROL PANEL
38. INTEGRATED CONTROL PANEL
39. MANUAL CANOPY UNLOCK HANDLE
40. IFF FUNCTION SELECTOR PANEL
41. LABS TIMER
42. ESSENTIAL BUS TEST BUTTON AND INDICATOR
43. AUTOPILOT GROUND TEST SWITCH
44. VERTICAL GYRO CUT-OUT SWITCH

36

35

34

42   43   44

Figure A-4

FDB-1-(279)A

A-9/(A-10 blank)

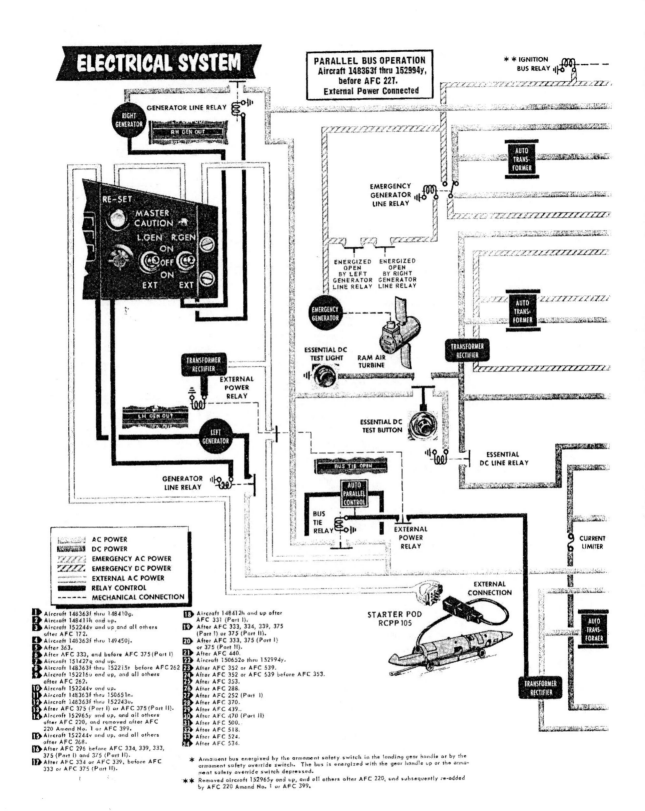

ELECTRICAL SYSTEM

PARALLEL BUS OPERATION
Aircraft 148363f thru 152994y, before AFC 227. External Power Connected

** IGNITION BUS RELAY

RIGHT GENERATOR

GENERATOR LINE RELAY

RH GEN OUT

RE-SET

MASTER CAUTION

L.GEN R.GEN

ON

OFF

ON

EXT EXT

EMERGENCY GENERATOR LINE RELAY

AUTO TRANSFORMER

ENERGIZED OPEN BY LEFT GENERATOR LINE RELAY

ENERGIZED OPEN BY RIGHT GENERATOR LINE RELAY

EMERGENCY GENERATOR

AUTO TRANSFORMER

ESSENTIAL DC TEST LIGHT

RAM AIR TURBINE

TRANSFORMER RECTIFIER

TRANSFORMER RECTIFIER

EXTERNAL POWER RELAY

LH GEN OUT

ESSENTIAL DC TEST BUTTON

LEFT GENERATOR

BUS TIE OPEN

ESSENTIAL DC LINE RELAY

GENERATOR LINE RELAY

AUTO PARALLEL CONTROL

BUS TIE RELAY

EXTERNAL POWER RELAY

CURRENT LIMITER

Legend:

- AC POWER
- DC POWER
- EMERGENCY AC POWER
- EMERGENCY DC POWER
- EXTERNAL AC POWER
- RELAY CONTROL
- MECHANICAL CONNECTION

EXTERNAL CONNECTION

STARTER POD RCPP 105

AUTO TRANSFORMER

TRANSFORMER RECTIFIER

1 Aircraft 148363f thru 148410g.
2 Aircraft 148411h and up.
3 Aircraft 152244v and up and all others after AFC 172.
4 Aircraft 148363f thru 149450j.
5 After 363.
6 After AFC 333, and before AFC 375 (Part I)
7 Aircraft 151427q and up.
8 Aircraft 148363f thru 152215t before AFC 262
9 Aircraft 152216u and up, and all others after AFC 262.
10 Aircraft 152244v and up.
11 Aircraft 148363f thru 150651n.
12 Aircraft 148363f thru 152243u.
13 After AFC 375 (Part I) or AFC 375 (Part II).
14 Aircraft 152965y and up, and all others after AFC 220, and removed after AFC 220 Amend No. 1 or AFC 399.
15 Aircraft 152244v and up, and all others after AFC 268.
16 After AFC 296 before AFC 334, 339, 333, 375 (Part I) and 375 (Part II).
17 After AFC 334 or AFC 339, before AFC 333 or AFC 375 (Part II).

18 Aircraft 148412h and up after AFC 331 (Part I).
19 After AFC 333, 334, 339, 375 (Part I) or 375 (Part II).
20 After AFC 333, 375 (Part I) or 375 (Part II).
21 After AFC 440.
22 Aircraft 150652o thru 152994y.
23 After AFC 352 or AFC 539.
24 After AFC 352 or AFC 539 before AFC 353.
25 After AFC 353.
26 After AFC 286.
27 After AFC 252 (Part I)
28 After AFC 370.
29 After AFC 439.
30 After AFC 470 (Part II)
31 After AFC 500.
32 After AFC 518.
33 After AFC 524.
34 After AFC 534.

* Armament bus energized by the armament safety switch in the landing gear handle or by the armament safety override switch. The bus is energized with the gear handle up or the armament safety override switch depressed.

** Removed aircraft 152965y and up, and all others after AFC 220, and subsequently re-added by AFC 220 Amend No. 1 or AFC 399.

Changed 1 March 1972

NAVAIR 01-245FDB-1

ELECTRICAL SYSTEM

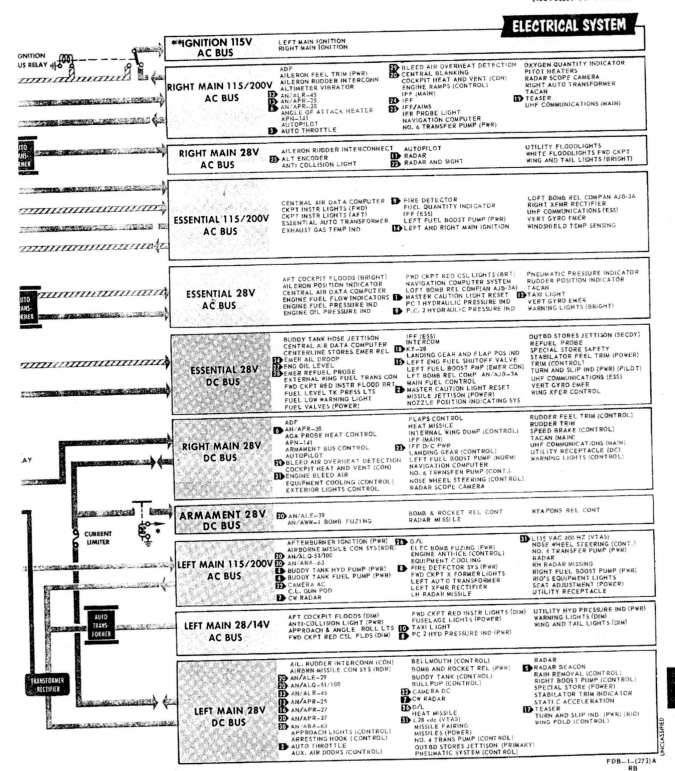

Figure A-5

A-11/(A-12 blank)

ELECTRICAL SYSTEM

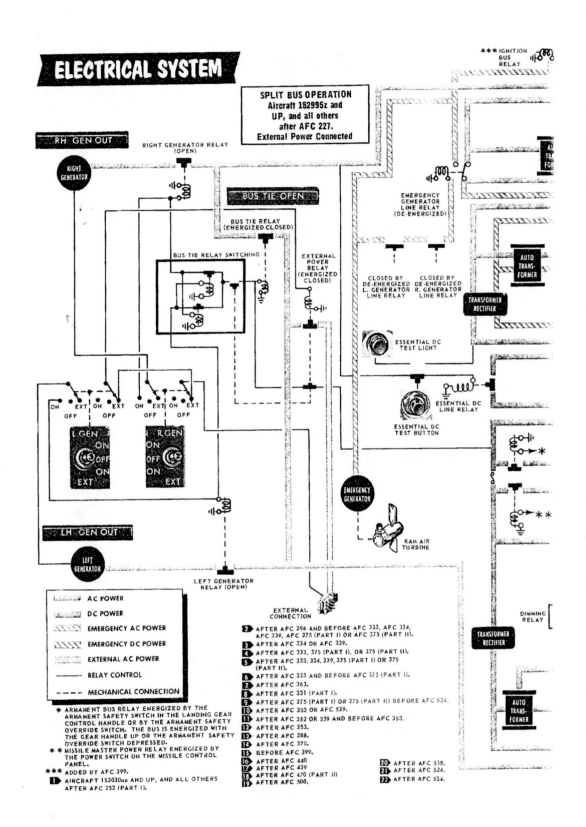

SPLIT BUS OPERATION
Aircraft 152995z and UP, and all others after AFC 227. External Power Connected

RH GEN OUT

RIGHT GENERATOR RELAY (OPEN)

RIGHT GENERATOR

BUS TIE OPEN

BUS TIE RELAY (ENERGIZED CLOSED)

BUS TIE RELAY SWITCHING

EXTERNAL POWER RELAY (ENERGIZED CLOSED)

*** IGNITION BUS RELAY

EMERGENCY GENERATOR LINE RELAY (DE-ENERGIZED)

CLOSED BY DE-ENERGIZED L. GENERATOR LINE RELAY

CLOSED BY DE-ENERGIZED R. GENERATOR LINE RELAY

AUTO TRANSFORMER

TRANSFORMER RECTIFIER

ESSENTIAL DC TEST LIGHT

ESSENTIAL DC LINE RELAY

ESSENTIAL DC TEST BUTTON

ON EXT ON EXT ON EXT ON EXT
OFF OFF OFF OFF

L. GEN ON OFF ON EXT

R. GEN ON OFF ON EXT

EMERGENCY GENERATOR

RAM AIR TURBINE

LH GEN OUT

LEFT GENERATOR

LEFT GENERATOR RELAY (OPEN)

EXTERNAL CONNECTION

DIMMING RELAY

TRANSFORMER RECTIFIER

AUTO TRANSFORMER

Legend:
- AC POWER
- DC POWER
- EMERGENCY AC POWER
- EMERGENCY DC POWER
- EXTERNAL AC POWER
- —— RELAY CONTROL
- - - - MECHANICAL CONNECTION

* ARMAMENT BUS RELAY ENERGIZED BY THE ARMAMENT SAFETY SWITCH IN THE LANDING GEAR CONTROL HANDLE OR BY THE ARMAMENT SAFETY OVERRIDE SWITCH. THE BUS IS ENERGIZED WITH THE GEAR HANDLE UP OR THE ARMAMENT SAFETY OVERRIDE SWITCH DEPRESSED.

** MISSILE MASTER POWER RELAY ENERGIZED BY THE POWER SWITCH ON THE MISSILE CONTROL PANEL.

*** ADDED BY AFC 399.

1 AIRCRAFT 153030ᴅᴅ AND UP, AND ALL OTHERS AFTER AFC 252 (PART I).

2 AFTER AFC 296 AND BEFORE AFC 333, AFC 334, AFC 339, AFC 375 (PART I) OR AFC 375 (PART II).

3 AFTER AFC 334 OR AFC 339.

4 AFTER AFC 333, 375 (PART I), OR 375 (PART II).

5 AFTER AFC 333, 334, 339, 375 (PART I) OR 375 (PART II).

6 AFTER AFC 333 AND BEFORE AFC 375 (PART I).

7 AFTER AFC 263.

8 AFTER AFC 331 (PART I).

9 AFTER AFC 375 (PART I) OR 375 (PART II) BEFORE AFC 524.

10 AFTER AFC 352 OR AFC 539.

11 AFTER AFC 352 OR 539 AND BEFORE AFC 353.

12 AFTER AFC 353.

13 AFTER AFC 288.

14 AFTER AFC 370.

15 BEFORE AFC 399.

16 AFTER AFC 440.

17 AFTER AFC 439.

18 AFTER AFC 470 (PART II).

19 AFTER AFC 500.

20 AFTER AFC 518.

21 AFTER AFC 524.

22 AFTER AFC 534.

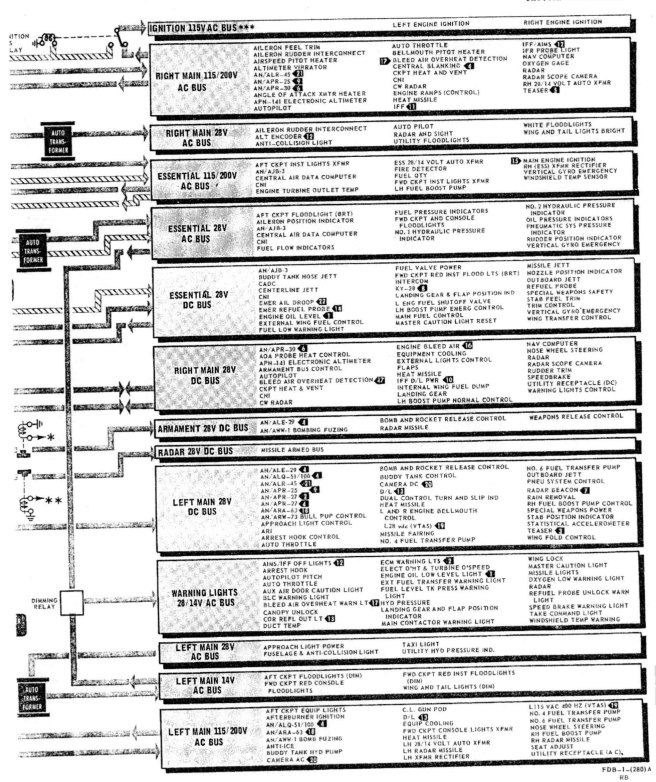

Figure A-6

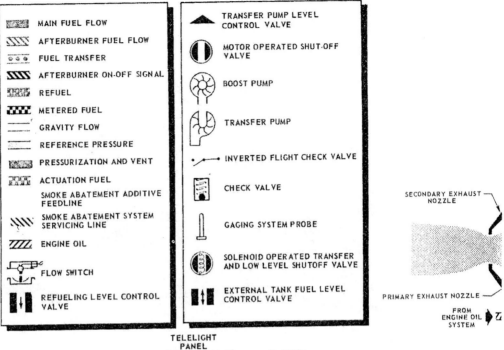

MAIN FUEL FLOW

AFTERBURNER FUEL FLOW

FUEL TRANSFER

AFTERBURNER ON-OFF SIGNAL

REFUEL

METERED FUEL

GRAVITY FLOW

REFERENCE PRESSURE

PRESSURIZATION AND VENT

ACTUATION FUEL

SMOKE ABATEMENT ADDITIVE FEEDLINE

SMOKE ABATEMENT SYSTEM SERVICING LINE

ENGINE OIL

FLOW SWITCH

REFUELING LEVEL CONTROL VALVE

TRANSFER PUMP LEVEL CONTROL VALVE

MOTOR OPERATED SHUT-OFF VALVE

BOOST PUMP

TRANSFER PUMP

INVERTED FLIGHT CHECK VALVE

CHECK VALVE

GAGING SYSTEM PROBE

SOLENOID OPERATED TRANSFER AND LOW LEVEL SHUTOFF VALVE

EXTERNAL TANK FUEL LEVEL CONTROL VALVE

TELELIGHT PANEL

SECONDARY EXHAUST NOZZLE

PRIMARY EXHAUST NOZZLE

FROM ENGINE OIL SYSTEM

CHK FUEL FILTERS

L EXT FUEL   R EXT FUEL   CTR EXT FUEL

FUEL LEVEL LOW

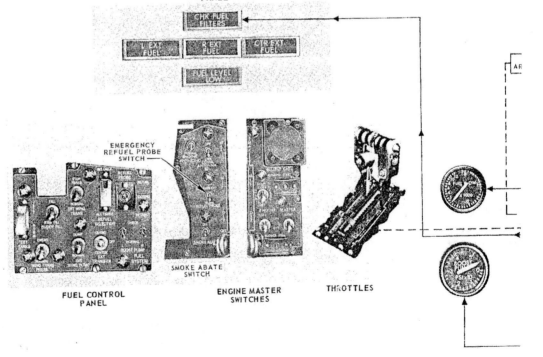

EMERGENCY REFUEL PROBE SWITCH

SMOKE ABATE SWITCH

FUEL CONTROL PANEL

ENGINE MASTER SWITCHES

THROTTLES

AR

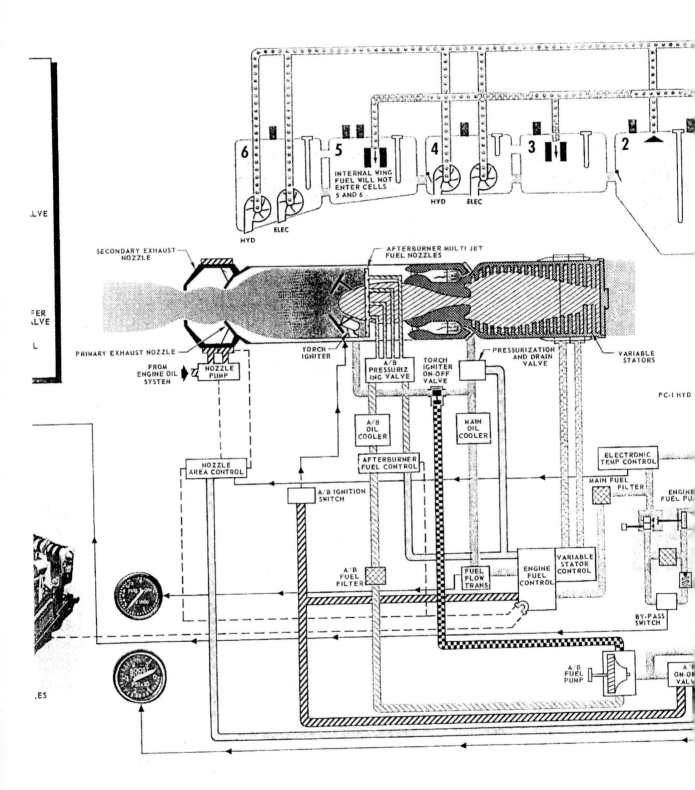

SECONDARY EXHAUST NOZZLE

AFTERBURNER MULTI JET FUEL NOZZLES

6

5

INTERNAL WING FUEL WILL NOT ENTER CELLS 5 AND 6

4

HYD   ELEC

3

2

ELEC

HYD

PRIMARY EXHAUST NOZZLE

TORCH IGNITER

PRESSURIZATION AND DRAIN VALVE

VARIABLE STATORS

FROM ENGINE OIL SYSTEM

NOZZLE PUMP

A/B PRESSURIZING VALVE

TORCH IGNITER ON-OFF VALVE

PC-1 HYD

A/B OIL COOLER

MAIN OIL COOLER

ELECTRONIC TEMP CONTROL

NOZZLE AREA CONTROL

AFTERBURNER FUEL CONTROL

MAIN FUEL FILTER

ENGINE FUEL PU

A/B IGNITION SWITCH

A/B FUEL FILTER

FUEL FLOW TRANS

ENGINE FUEL CONTROL

VARIABLE STATOR CONTROL

BY-PASS SWITCH

A/B FUEL PUMP

A/B ON-O VAL

ES

LVE

ER VLVE

L

AIRPLANE AND ENGINE FUEL SYSTEM

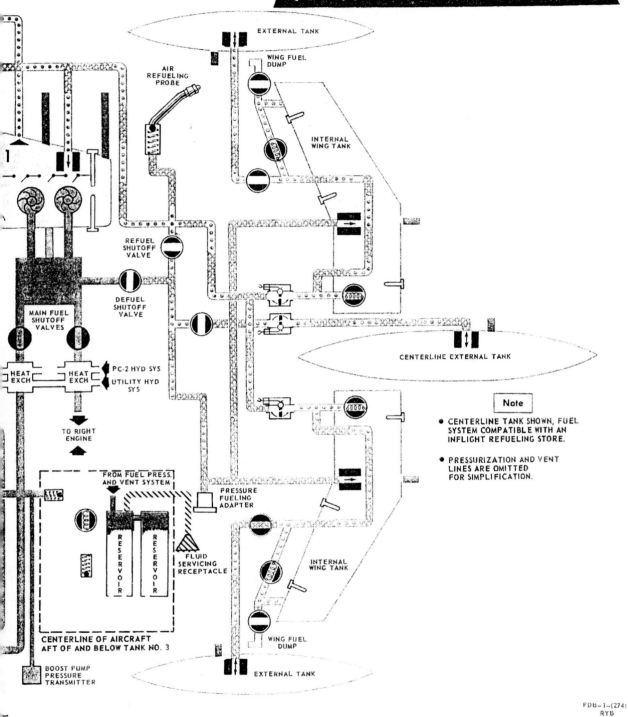

Figure A-7

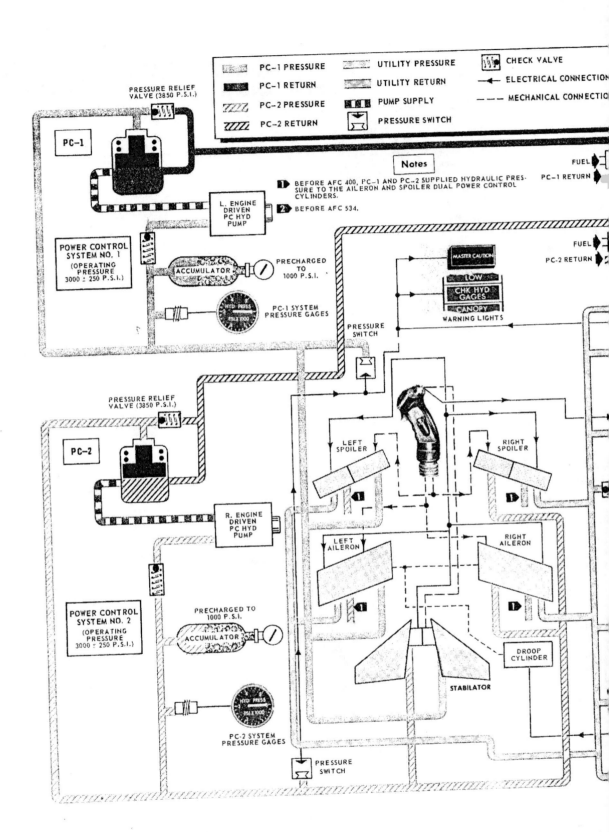

PRESSURE RELIEF
VALVE (3850 P.S.I.)

PC-1 PRESSURE   UTILITY PRESSURE   CHECK VALVE
PC-1 RETURN   UTILITY RETURN   ELECTRICAL CONNECTION
PC-2 PRESSURE   PUMP SUPPLY   MECHANICAL CONNECTION
PC-2 RETURN   PRESSURE SWITCH

PC-1

Notes

▶1 BEFORE AFC 400, PC-1 AND PC-2 SUPPLIED HYDRAULIC PRES-
SURE TO THE AILERON AND SPOILER DUAL POWER CONTROL
CYLINDERS.

▶2 BEFORE AFC 534.

FUEL
PC-1 RETURN

L. ENGINE
DRIVEN
PC HYD
PUMP

FUEL
PC-2 RETURN

POWER CONTROL
SYSTEM NO. 1
(OPERATING
PRESSURE
3000 ± 250 P.S.I.)

ACCUMULATOR

PRECHARGED
TO
1000 P.S.I.

MASTER CAUTION

LOW

CHK. HYD
GAGES

CANOPY

WARNING LIGHTS

PC-1 SYSTEM
PRESSURE GAGES

PRESSURE
SWITCH

PRESSURE RELIEF
VALVE (3850 P.S.I.)

LEFT
SPOILER

RIGHT
SPOILER

PC-2

R. ENGINE
DRIVEN
PC HYD
PUMP

LEFT
AILERON

RIGHT
AILERON

POWER CONTROL
SYSTEM NO. 2
(OPERATING
PRESSURE
3000 ± 250 P.S.I.)

PRECHARGED TO
1000 P.S.I.

ACCUMULATOR

DROOP
CYLINDER

STABILATOR

PC-2 SYSTEM
PRESSURE GAGES

PRESSURE
SWITCH

Changed 1 March 1972

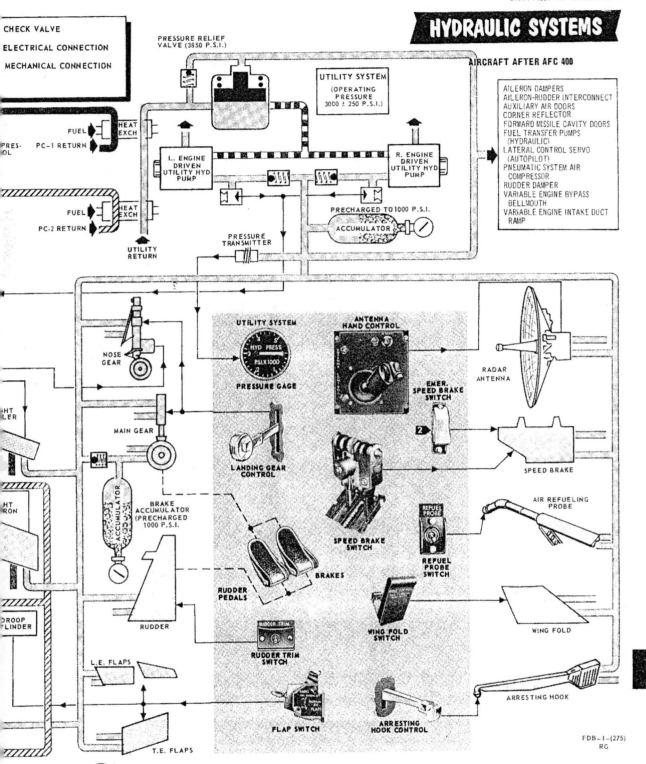

Figure A-8

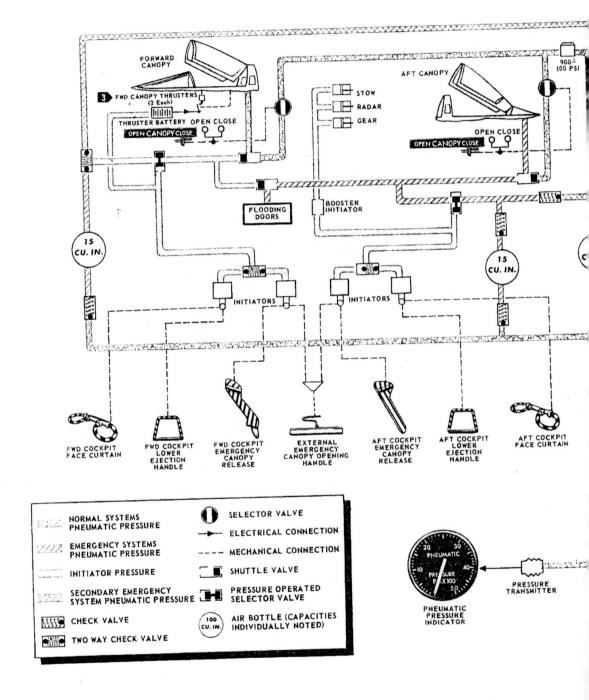

FORWARD CANOPY

AFT CANOPY

900 ± 100 PSI

3 FWD CANOPY THRUSTERS (2 Each)

THRUSTER BATTERY OPEN CLOSE

OPEN CANOPY CLOSE

STOW

RADAR

GEAR

OPEN CANOPY CLOSE

OPEN CLOSE

FLOODING DOORS

BOOSTER INITIATOR

15 CU. IN.

15 CU. IN.

INITIATORS

INITIATORS

FWD COCKPIT FACE CURTAIN

FWD COCKPIT LOWER EJECTION HANDLE

FWD COCKPIT EMERGENCY CANOPY RELEASE

EXTERNAL EMERGENCY CANOPY OPENING HANDLE

AFT COCKPIT EMERGENCY CANOPY RELEASE

AFT COCKPIT LOWER EJECTION HANDLE

AFT COCKPIT FACE CURTAIN

NORMAL SYSTEMS PNEUMATIC PRESSURE

EMERGENCY SYSTEMS PNEUMATIC PRESSURE

INITIATOR PRESSURE

SECONDARY EMERGENCY SYSTEM PNEUMATIC PRESSURE

CHECK VALVE

TWO WAY CHECK VALVE

SELECTOR VALVE

ELECTRICAL CONNECTION

MECHANICAL CONNECTION

SHUTTLE VALVE

PRESSURE OPERATED SELECTOR VALVE

100 CU. IN. AIR BOTTLE (CAPACITIES INDIVIDUALLY NOTED)

PNEUMATIC

PRESSURE PSI X 100

PNEUMATIC PRESSURE INDICATOR

PRESSURE TRANSMITTER

Changed 1 March 1972

PNEUMATIC SYSTEM

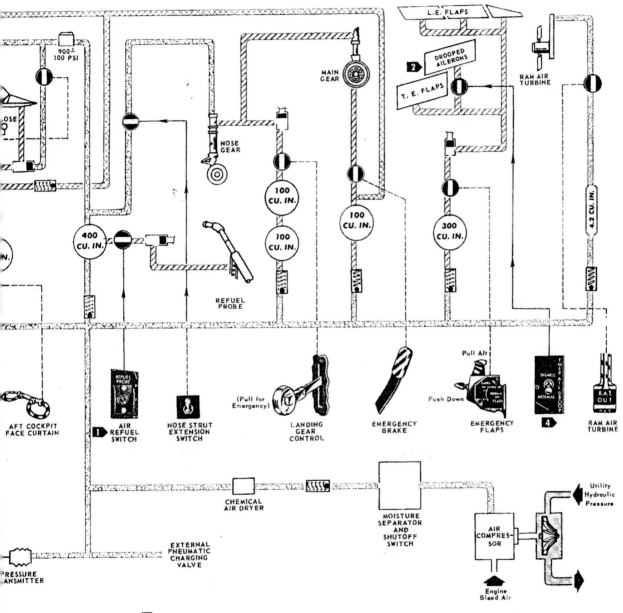

1 ON ALL AIRCRAFT AFTER AFC 370.

2 ON AIRCRAFT AFTER AFC 400 AND BEFORE AFC 534, THE
AILERONS WILL NOT DROOP DURING EMERGENCY FLAP OPERATIONS.

3 ON AIRCRAFT AFTER AFC 497.

4 ON ALL AIRCRAFT AFTER AFC 534.

Figure A-9

FDB-1-(276)A
B

ALPHABETICAL INDEX

☆ U.S. GOVERNMENT PRINTING OFFICE: 1972— 769-105/4120

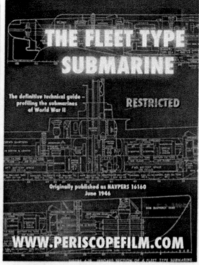

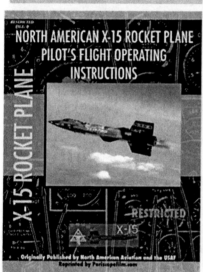
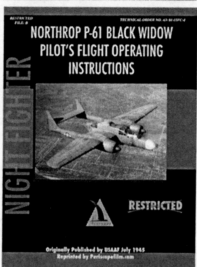

F-4 PHANTOM
PILOT'S FLIGHT OPERATING MANUAL
©2007-2010 PERISCOPE FILM LLC

WWW.PERISCOPEFILM.COM
ISBN: 978-1-935700-41-8

CPSIA information can be obtained
at www.ICGtesting.com
Printed in the USA
FFOW01n0324171016
28515FF

9 781935 70041